PassKey EA Review

Complete: Individuals, Businesses and Representation:

IRS Enrolled Agent Exam Study Guide 2011-2012 Edition

Author: Christy Pinheiro, EA ABA®
Author: Collette Szymborski, CPA
Editor: Cynthia Sherwood, MSJ

Do you want to test yourself?
Then get the PassKey EA Exam Workbook!

PassKey EA Review Workbook
Three Complete Enrolled Agent Practice Exams 2011-2012 Edition

ISBN-13: 978-1935664123, $49.00

This workbook features three complete Enrolled Agent practice exams, with detailed answers, to accompany the PassKey EA Review course books. Take three full, 100-question exams on Individuals, Businesses, and Representation. All of the answers are clearly explained in the back of the book.

Test yourself, time yourself, and learn!

Available anywhere fine books are sold.

ISBN-13: 978-1935664086

PassKey EA Review Complete: Individuals, Businesses and Representation: IRS Enrolled Agent Exam Study Guide 2011-2012 Edition

First Printing. PassKey EA Review
PassKey EA Review® is a U.S. Registered Trademark

PassKey Publications, PO Box 580465, Elk Grove, CA 95758

www.PassKeyPublications.com

Praise for the PassKey EA Review Series

Chris Davidson (Orange County, CA)

I wanted to purchase a book with an easy writing style, so I could enjoy the process of preparing myself for the test. Text is bolded and bulleted to break the monotony. The examples (a big learning boost for me!) are completely enclosed in a box, so they clearly stand out. Each [unit] is followed by questions, complete with an explanation as to why the answer is correct. I showed the book to a CPA friend last night, and he went online immediately and ordered it! I HIGHLY recommend this book!

Cynthia Adcock (Manchester, TN)

After using both the book and the audio book, I had no problems passing all three parts of the exam. It's a wonderful tool for anyone studying to become an Enrolled Agent.

J. Lancaon (San Francisco, CA)

I passed all three parts of the EA exam! I have passed all parts of the EA exam using your book (thank you), and have recommended other coworkers to use your book for their studying. The content of the tax material is right on point so that there were no surprises on the exams.

M. Avila (Las Vegas, NV)

This is a great low cost study guide; I used it along with the IRS Pubs to pass. There are not many books available for this program at an affordable price.

A. Engbretsen (Jacksonville, FL)

I purchased this item to use alongside of classroom training that I am receiving. It has been so helpful, especially since I found out that the teacher uses the book to find his teaching material! Definitely recommend!

Table of Contents

Introduction

Congratulations on taking the first step toward becoming an Enrolled Agent, the most widely respected professional tax designation. Enrolled Agents are licensed to practice by the Internal Revenue Service. You are taking the first step to an exciting and rewarding career as a tax professional!

This study guide is designed to help you study for the IRS Enrolled Agent's Exam. Although designed to be a comprehensive guide, we still recommend that you study IRS publications, and also try to learn as much as you can about tax law in general so that you are well-equipped to take the exam.

Enrolled Agents have passed all three parts of the exam, which is formally called the *Special Enrollment Examination* or *SEE*. The exam covers all aspects of federal tax law, including the taxation of individuals, corporations, partnerships, exempt entities, ethics, and IRS collections and audit procedures.

This book is designed for the 2011 to 2012 testing season. Prometric will begin testing candidates on May 1, 2011. The testing window closes on February 29, 2012. Any candidate taking the Enrolled Agent Exam during this time period will be tested on 2010 tax law.

These are the average pass rates for the IRS Enrolled Agent's Exam, according to Prometric:

Pass Rate: Part I: 42%
Pass Rate: Part II: 45%
Pass Rate: Part III: 70%

The IRS Enrolled Agent's Exam is exclusively administered by Prometric, and exam candidates can find lots of valuable information on Prometric's IRS/EA Exam website at:

http://www.prometric.com/IRS

Candidates can easily sign up for the exam online and schedule convenient exam dates to accommodate their schedules.

Prometric has designed the exam with content derived from input by experts from the Enrolled Agent community. Each exam section is formatted with multiple choice questions. There are no essay questions or questions requiring written answers. At the time of this book's publication, the EA Exam has 100 questions per part.

Computerized EA Exam Format
Part 1 - Individual Taxation-100 Questions
Part 2 - Business Taxation-100 Questions
Part 3 - Representation, Practice, and Procedures-100 Questions

An exam-taker is given 3.5 hours to complete each part. The actual seat time is four hours to allow for a tutorial and survey at the end. There are multiple versions of each exam. Each year, the exam is updated, and new questions are added. If you fail an exam section, do not expect the questions to be identical the next time you take the exam.

Each exam question is equally weighted. A panel of subject matter experts comprised of Enrolled Agents and IRS representatives developed the definition of the minimally qualified candidate. The IRS has set the scaled passing score at 105, which corresponds to the minimum level of knowledge deemed acceptable by those persons who will be practicing before the IRS.

Failing candidates are provided a scaled score value so that they may see how close they are to being successful. Candidates with a score of 104 are very close to passing. Candidates with a score of 45 are far from being successful. Candidates receive their exam results before leaving the test site.

The test has been designed to identify those who passed, NOT to rank the scores of exam-takers. Scaled scores are determined by calculating the number of questions answered correctly from the total number of questions in the examination and converting that sum to a scale ranging from 40 to 130. Scores are scaled because there are "sample" questions that the IRS adds to each candidate's exam. These "sample" questions do not count toward the score.

The IRS has typically thrown out questions or allowed multiple answers for about five questions per exam, per part. This is no longer the case. When a candidate takes the exam, scores are given immediately after completion of the section. Prometric will not tell the candidates the questions that they got correct or missed—exam-takers will only receive a score report reflecting whether or not they passed.

Old EA exam questions will no longer be released or published by the IRS. Therefore, you will not be able to anticipate exactly what will be on the exam. Be prepared to be tested on anything that is in the IRS publications.

In addition to this study guide, we highly recommend that all exam candidates read:

- **Publication 17, *Your Federal Income Tax*** (for Part 1 of the exam), and
- **Circular 230, *Regulations Governing the Practice of Attorneys, Certified Public Accountants, Enrolled Agents, Enrolled Actuaries, and Appraisers before the Internal Revenue Service*** (for Part 3 of the exam).

Anyone can download these publications for free from the IRS website or can call the IRS directly and receive a copy in the mail.

If an exam-taker requires special accommodations for a disability, he or she must contact a Prometric test center in advance. For example, a blind or deaf candidate could have a special proctor administer the exam upon request. However, no accommodations will be made for EA candidates with limited English skills. According to the official IRS bulletin, "difficulty understanding English" is **not** considered a disability for the purposes of the EA examination.

Prometric's policy is to prohibit candidates from bringing in anything, including bottles of water, to the test center to minimize the opportunities for cheating. A second reason for prohibiting water is to avoid the possibility for computers to be inadvertently damaged.

The examination is offered throughout the year, providing candidates the opportunity to find a time that fits their schedules. The test will be offered at approximately 290 Prometric Testing Center sites throughout North America, in a highly secure, professional testing environment.

If necessary, candidates are able to re-take each part of the examination several times each year, and there is no longer a deadline for registering. Candidates now apply online throughout the year and pay with a credit card.

It is beneficial for candidates to register and schedule as far in advance as possible. Allowing a longer lead time between scheduling and testing will enable candidates to choose a test date and time that is convenient. If space permits, a candidate may register and schedule up to two days prior to a test date. Candidates are no longer required to take the entire exam in one sitting.

Once the EA Exam candidate passes the test, he or she must undergo a background check and complete an application prior to enrollment. This includes a review of the candidate's tax transcript. Failure to timely file or pay personal income taxes can be grounds for denial of enrollment. A person may not practice as an Enrolled Agent until the application process is complete, and the IRS approves the EA's application and issues the candidate a Treasury Card.

Just like CPAs and tax attorneys, EAs can handle any type of tax matter and represent their clients' interests before the IRS. Unlike CPAs and tax attorneys, Enrolled Agents are tested directly by the IRS and Enrolled Agents focus exclusively on tax accounting.

Successfully passing the EA Exam can launch you into a fulfilling and lucrative new career. The exam requires intense preparation and diligence, but with the help of PassKey's comprehensive EA Review, you will have the tools you need to learn how to become an Enrolled Agent. As the authors of the PassKey EA Review, we wish you much success.

Christy Pinheiro, EA, ABA
Collette Szymborski, CPA

Nine Steps for the IRS EA Exam

STEP 1-Learn

Learn about the Enrolled Agent program. An Enrolled Agent has passed a three-part test covering all aspects of federal taxation and has passed an IRS background check. As a result, an Enrolled Agent (EA) can represent people before the Internal Revenue Service, just like attorneys and CPAs.

STEP 2-Gather information

Gather information about the Special Enrollment Examination. The IRS publishes basic information about becoming an Enrolled Agent on the Enrollment Overview page of its website. Additionally, candidates will find important information about registering, scheduling, fees, and the format of the EA Exam from the Prometric/IRS website. Prometric administers the Special Enrollment Exam on behalf of the IRS. Candidates will want to download the *"Enrolled Agent Candidate Information Bulletin"* from the Prometric site.

STEP 3-Sign up with PROMETRIC

Sign up to take the Special Enrollment Examination. The easiest way is to sign up online. Candidates sign up for the test using IRS Form 2587 or by using the online Form 2587 found on the Prometric / IRS Web site. The online form is easier and more secure. The fee to take the exam is $101 for each part of the exam.

STEP 4-Choose a test site

Choose a test site and test date with Prometric. There are test sites throughout the United States and all over the world. Choose a site that's convenient for you.

STEP 5-Adopt a study plan

Adopt a study plan that covers all the tax topics on the Special Enrollment Examination. Approach each study unit at a pace of three to four hours each. A good rule of thumb is to study at least 60 hours for each of the three exam sections, committing at least 15 hours per week. Start well in advance of the exam date. There's absolutely no point in cramming at the last minute, especially for a test covering something as hard as taxation. Take your time. Try focusing on the "big picture," especially in areas of taxation that might be new to you.

STEP 6-Get plenty of rest, exercise, and good nutrition

Get plenty of rest, exercise, and good nutrition in the two weeks before the EA Exam. Don't focus on studying. Instead, review your notes to get an overall feel for the main points of the test. Don't cram in the last two weeks. It will prove counterproductive.

STEP 7-Test day has arrived!

On test day, don't forget your driver's license, ID, or passport! Arrive early to the test site, sign in, and get situated. Have breakfast or lunch, and go to the bathroom before entering to take the exam, because any breaks you take will cut into your exam time. Although you will be able to leave the test center to go to the restroom or take a quick break, the clock does not stop on the exam. You won't be able to bring anything into the test room except glasses and an ID, so make sure you eat and go to the bathroom BEFORE the test. If you need accommodations for a medical condition or a disability, call the test site in advance. The testing site will give each candidate scratch paper, pencils, and a calculator. A candidate cannot bring his or her own paper or calculator.

STEP 8-During the Exam

During the test, do not speak with other students or you may be asked to leave the testing center. Also, with the computer-based test format, the exam questions may differ slightly from what other test-takers have seen. Don't fuss over one question. If you are unsure, just guess and move on! You can always go back at the end if you have time. The exam will allow you to review all your answers if you have time left over. Your scores will be available immediately after the exam. Candidates are not penalized additional points for wrong answers, so it is better to answer every question rather than leave one blank.

Step 9-Congratulations! You passed!

Now you must begin the process of applying for your EA designation through the IRS. You must submit your application fee and IRS Form 23 to the IRS in order to become an Enrolled Agent. Each application is examined by the IRS and each applicant is investigated for suitability. This process takes about three months, although some candidates have reported that the process goes faster if they submit copies of their exam scores along with the application.

Exam candidates can download IRS **Form 23** at *www.IRS.gov*. Incomplete applications will not be processed. The most common delays are due to:
- Lack of an original signature on IRS Form 23 (NO PHOTOCOPIES)
- Unsigned check for the application fee
- Missing application fee
- Incomplete or unfinished applications

*Note: Although it is not required, it is easier for the IRS to process your Enrolled Agent application (**Form 23**) if you include copies of your Prometric score reports. Candidates who include photocopies of their score reports tend to get their applications processed much faster.

After the application is processed, the IRS will issue you a Treasury Card. Once you have your Treasury Card and your enrollment number, you are officially an Enrolled Agent!

Essential Tax Figures for 2010

On December 17, 2010, the President signed the *Tax Relief, Unemployment Reauthorization, and Job Creation Act of 2010*. This last-minute legislation extended the Bush era tax cuts, as well as added a number of new tax breaks.

These are the most common figures you will see on the IRS Enrolled Agent Exam. Although you do not have to memorize exact figures most of the time, the following basic figures are necessary and you should know them. Here's a quick summary of all the essential tax figures for the year 2010:

Income Tax Return Filing Deadline: April 18, 2011 (due date for tax returns and extensions)[1]

The Personal Exemption: $3,650 (remained unchanged)
*Note: in 2010, the personal exemption does NOT phase-out as in prior years!

2010 Social Security Taxable Wage Base: $106,800

Social Security Tax Rate for Self-Employed Individuals: $15.30% (SE Tax)

The annual gift tax exclusion: $13,000

2010 Standard Deduction Amounts
- Married Filing Jointly $11,400
- Head of Household $8,400
- Single $5,700
- Married Filing Separately $5,700
- Dependents $950
- Blind taxpayers and senior citizens (over 65) qualify for an increased standard deduction. The amount is $1,100 (per taxpayer) for married filers and $1,400 for Single and Head of Household.

2010 Self-Employed Health Insurance Deduction: 100% (offsets SE tax in 2010)
Section 179 Expense: $500,000 of qualified expenditures/phase-out at $2 million

Mileage Rates 2010
- 50 cents per mile for business miles
- 16.5 cents per mile driven for medical or moving purposes
- 14 cents per mile for charitable purposes

---

[1] Note that the normal filing date is April 15. However, the IRS has announced April 18, 2011 as the tax filing deadline for 2010 tax returns and extension requests in observation of Emancipation Day, which is a federal holiday in the District of Columbia (Washington, D.C.)

2010 Retirement Plan Rules and Limits

- 401(k), 403(b) and 457 plan elective deferral limit: $16,500 (Over 50: an additional $5,500)
- SIMPLE IRA elective deferral limit: $11,500 (Over 50: an additional $2,500)
- Maximum annual contribution for defined contribution plans: $49,000
- Maximum annual benefit for defined benefit plans: $195,000
- Traditional and Roth IRA contribution limit: $5,000 (Over 50: $6,000)

Roth IRA Phase-Out AGI limits
- Married Filing Jointly: $167,000 to $177,000
- Single or Head of Household: $105,000 to $120,000
- Married Filing Separately: $0 to $10,000

Tax Year 2010 Earned Income Tax Credit (EITC) Income Thresholds
Earned income and Adjusted Gross Income (AGI) must each be less than:
- $43,352 ($48,362 Married Filing Jointly) with three or more qualifying children
- $40,363 ($45,373 Married Filing Jointly) with two qualifying children
- $35,535 ($40,545 Married Filing Jointly) with one qualifying child
- $13,460 ($18,470 Married Filing Jointly) with no children

The **Adoption Credit** is refundable in 2010: $13,170 (maximum credit)

Education Credits and Deductions

- The Hope credit is not available for 2010.
- The American opportunity credit is a maximum annual credit of $2,500 per student.
- The Lifetime Learning Credit is a maximum of $2,000 per return
- The Tuition and Fees deduction is a maximum of $4,000 in 2010
- The Student Loan Interest deduction is $2,500 of qualified loan interest paid in 2010.

New Rules for Businesses/2010 Tax Year

Temporary exclusion of 100% of gain on certain small business stock

Investors in qualified small business stock can exclude up to 100% of the capital gain upon sale of the stock. Under current law, the earliest tax year for which this 100% capital gain exclusion can be claimed is 2015.

General business credits of eligible small businesses for 2010 carried back 5 years

The new law allows an eligible small business to carry back general business credits five years. Previously, the credits could only be carried back one year.

General business credits not subject to alternative minimum tax

The new law allows general business credits to offset both regular income tax and alternative minimum tax of eligible small businesses. The provision also applies to any business credit carrybacks. This is only applicable to 2010.

Increased Section 179 expensing

In 2010, the Section 179 expense deduction was increased and expanded. The Section 179 limit was increased to $500,000. For the first time, Section 179 includes the following types of real property: qualified leasehold improvement property, qualified restaurant property and qualified retail improvement property.

Increased deduction for start-up expenditures in 2010

In 2010, taxpayers are allowed to deduct up to $10,000 as a deduction for start-up expenditures, but requires a dollar-for-dollar reduction of the $10,000 deduction if startup expenditures exceed $60,000.

Health insurance deduction offsets self-employment taxes in 2010

Previously, small business owners could use the cost of health insurance to calculate self-employment tax. In 2010, business owners can deduct the cost of health insurance for themselves and their family in the calculation of their 2010 self-employment tax. This also includes health insurance for children under 27, even if the child is not a dependent.

Part 1: Individuals

Thou art still required to pay taxes even though ye traveled through time.

Tammy the Tax Lady ®
Tammy the Tax Lady is a registered trademark of Passkey Publications

Unit 1.1: Preliminary Work and Individual Taxpayer Data

More Reading:
Publication 17, *Your Federal Income Tax*
Publication 519, *U.S. Tax Guide for Aliens*

Use of Prior Years' Returns for Comparison

Enrolled Agents are required to perform due diligence. Due diligence is covered in Part 3 of the EA Exam; however, the use of prior year tax returns is tested in Part 1. When a professional preparer sits down to prepare a tax return for a client, he or she is expected to perform due diligence in collecting, verifying, and gathering taxpayer data. EAs are also expected to review prior year tax returns for compliance, accuracy, and completeness.

A tax professional is required by law to notify a taxpayer of an error on his or her tax return. A tax professional is also required by law to notify the taxpayer of the consequences of *not* correcting the error. However, a tax professional is not required to actually correct the error.

> **Example:** Terrence Jones is a taxpayer who goes to Janice Smith, EA in order to prepare his tax returns. Terrence is a new client who has always prepared his own tax returns. When Terrence makes his tax interview appointment, Janice tells him to bring his prior year return. When Terrence arrives for his appointment, Janice notices that Terrence made a large error on his prior-year, self-prepared tax return when calculating his Mortgage Interest Deduction. Janice is required to notify Terrence of the error, as well as the consequences of not correcting the error. She encourages Terrence to file an amended tax return in order to correct the mistake. Terrence declines because he does not want to pay for an amended tax return for the prior year. Janice notes in her work papers that Terrence has declined to amend his return, even though she has warned him of the consequences. Janice has therefore fulfilled her professional obligation to notify the taxpayer of the prior year error. [2]

Most tax practitioners use professional tax software to prepare their clients' tax returns. Tax professionals must be knowledgeable about tax law as well as the application of the law as it relates to their particular software program. Tax software is NOT a substitute for competency and understanding of tax law. In other words, you, as a tax professional, must understand how tax law applies to each individual client.

Tax returns are now primarily filed electronically; tax practitioners have led the way toward a future of completely electronic returns. E-filed returns are also called paperless tax returns. Taxpayers who agree to e-file their returns save the IRS an enormous amount of money in processing and human labor hours. E-filed returns also reduce human error. E-file regulations are tested on **Part 3** of the Enrolled Agent Exam. For **Part 1** of the exam, you will probably not see any questions about the IRS e-file program.

---

[2] In recognition that taxpayers and exam-takers are both genders, we'll alternate using "he" and "she" and "his" and "her" throughout this book.

Taxpayer Biographical Information

Tax preparers are expected to collect biographical information. Examples of necessary biographical information include date of birth, marital status, dependents, a client's legal name, and address. All of this information is required in order to prepare an accurate tax return. Taxpayer biographical information is considered highly sensitive and confidential. Severe preparer penalties exist for preparers who do not protect taxpayer biographical information. Wrongful disclosure of taxpayer information is a criminal offense.

Important Tip: The U.S. Internal Revenue Code makes it a federal crime for tax professionals who "knowingly or recklessly" disclose confidential taxpayer information to third parties or who use such information for any non-preparation purpose. This is a federal misdemeanor punishable by a fine of $1,000 and prison of up to one year. Exceptions apply for disclosures mandated by law or a court or for disclosure for use in preparing state or local tax returns. Generally, in order for the criminal penalties to apply, criminal intent must be proven. Ordinary preparer negligence does not qualify as "criminal intent." This law became effective in 1997. You will be tested more on client privacy and disclosure rules on Part 3 of the exam (U.S. Code Title 26, section 6103).

A tax preparer is also required to determine a taxpayer's residency. In other words, the preparer must determine whether or not the taxpayer is considered a *resident* or *non-resident*. The rules for determining residency for tax purposes are completely different than what is established under current immigration law. A person who has a "green card" or a "student visa" may still be considered a resident of the United States for tax purposes, even if he or she does not have a Social Security Number.

There are numerous examples of when this may occur. A common example is when a soldier marries a foreign spouse and brings him or her to the United States. Usually, the spouse must wait to be assigned a Social Security Number. However, the couple may still file a joint tax return by requesting an Individual Tax Identification Number (ITIN) for the foreign spouse from the IRS. ITINs are also requested for parents adopting a foreign child while they wait for the adoption to become final.

The Importance of a Taxpayer Identification Number (TIN)

IRS regulations require that each individual listed on a U.S. federal income tax return have a valid Taxpayer Identification Number (TIN). The types of TINs are:

- Social Security Number (SSN)
- Individual Taxpayer Identification Number (ITIN)
- Adoption Taxpayer Identification Number (ATIN)

An Employer Identification Number (EIN) is also a type of identifying number, but it is used for entities and businesses. The Employer Identification Number will be covered and discussed at length in Part 2, Businesses.

One of the first things you should do when preparing an individual's tax return is to ask for a Social Security card for each individual who will be listed on the return. Then, verify the accuracy of the Social Security Number and the spelling of the individual's name by ensuring that the information on the tax return matches the Social Security card.

A Social Security Number is required for the taxpayer, the taxpayer's spouse (if married), and any dependent listed on the tax return. A nonresident alien who is not eligible for a Social Security Number must request an Individual Taxpayer Identification Number. The issuance of an ITIN does not:

- Entitle the recipient to Social Security benefits or the Earned Income Tax Credit[3] (EITC)
- Create a presumption regarding the individual's immigration status
- Give the individual the right to work in the United States

Taxpayers who cannot obtain an SSN must apply for an ITIN if they file a U.S. tax return or are listed on a tax return as a spouse or dependent. These taxpayers must file **Form W-7,** *Application for Individual Taxpayer Identification Number*, and supply documentation that will establish foreign status and true identity. A federal tax return must generally be filed along with **Form W-7**.

Example: Kamala is a U.S. citizen and has a Social Security Number. In January 2010, Kamala marries José Martinez, a citizen of Mexico. José has one child from a prior marriage named Graciela. Kamala decides to file jointly with Jose in 2010, and also claim her stepdaughter Graciela as a dependent. In order to file jointly and claim the child, they must request ITINs for José and Graciela. They must file **Form W-7**, *Application for Individual Taxpayer Identification Number*, and supply the required documentation.

Adopted children may be claimed as dependents even if they do not have a Social Security Number yet. If the taxpayer is unable to secure a Social Security Number for a child until the adoption is final, he may request an Adoption Taxpayer Identification Number (ATIN). The ATIN may not be used in order to claim the Earned Income Credit. A taxpayer should apply for an ATIN only if he or she is adopting a child *and* meets all of the following qualifications:

- The child is legally placed in the taxpayer's home for legal adoption.
- The adoption is a domestic adoption OR the adoption is a legal foreign adoption and the child has a Permanent Resident Alien Card or Certificate of Citizenship.
- The taxpayer cannot obtain the child's existing SSN even though she has made a reasonable attempt to obtain it from the birth parents, the placement agency, and other persons.
- The taxpayer cannot obtain an SSN for the child from the Social Security Administration for any reason (for example, the adoption is not final).

An ATIN can be requested for an adopted child using IRS **Form W-7A,** *Application for Taxpayer Identification Number for Pending U.S. Adoptions.* The dependent must meet the dependency qualifications (covered next) in order to be claimed as a dependent on the taxpayer's tax return.

The Preparer Tax Identification Number (PTIN) is also an identifying number, but it is used exclusively by tax preparers to identify themselves on a taxpayer's return. It is not an identifying number for taxpayer use.

---

[3] The IRS uses both the terms "EIC" and "EITC." "EIC" stands for "Earned Income Credit" and "EITC" stands for "Earned Income Tax Credit." They mean essentially the same thing.

Generally, anyone who files a tax return or claims a dependent must have a Taxpayer Identification Number: either an ITIN, ATIN, or an SSN.

*Exception: A Child Who Is Born and Dies in the Same Tax Year

There is *one* exception to the rule that requires all dependents to have either a Social Security Number, ATIN, or an ITIN. If a child is born *and* dies within the same tax year and is not granted a Social Security Number, the taxpayer may still claim that child as a dependent. The tax return must be filed on paper and the birth and death certificate attached to the return. The birth certificate must show that the child was born alive. The taxpayer would enter "DIED" in the space for the dependent's Social Security Number on the tax return. A stillborn child does not qualify. The child must have been born alive, even if he only lived for a short time. This might seem like an obscure rule, but this question has showed up on prior exams, so try to remember it.

Tax Home and Work Location

A taxpayer's "tax home" is his principal place of work, *regardless of where he actually lives.* A taxpayer's tax home is used for tax purposes, including determining if travel expenses are deductible. Travel and meal expenses are considered deductible if the taxpayer is traveling away from her *tax home*. These rules are also used in determining if the taxpayer qualifies for the foreign earned income exclusion.

Multiple work locations: If a taxpayer has *more than one* place of business or work, the tax home must be determined using several factors. The following facts should be used to determine which one is the main place of business or work:

- The total time ordinarily spent in each place
- The level of business activity in each place
- Whether income from each place is significant

In determining which is the "main place of business," the most important consideration is the length of time spent at each location.

Example: Gary is a marketing consultant who lives with his family in Chicago, but works regularly (full-time) in Milwaukee where he stays in a hotel and eats in restaurants. Gary returns to Chicago every weekend. Gary may not deduct any of his travel, meals, or lodging expenses in Milwaukee because that is his tax home. Gary's travel on weekends to his family home in Chicago is not for work, so these expenses are also not deductible.

If a taxpayer regularly works in more than one place, her tax home is the general area where the main place of business or work is located. If a taxpayer has *more than one* place of business, then her tax home is her *main* place of business. If a person does not have a regular place of business because of the nature of her work, then her tax home can be the place where she lives.

> **Example:** Seville is a truck driver. He and his family live in Tucson. Seville is employed by a trucking firm that has its main terminal in Phoenix. At the end of his long trucking runs, Seville returns to his home terminal in Phoenix and spends one night there before returning home. Seville cannot deduct any expenses he has for meals and lodging in Phoenix or the cost of traveling from Phoenix to Tucson. This is because Phoenix is Seville's "tax home" (example in Publication 463).

There are special rules for temporary work assignments. When a taxpayer is working away from his main place of business and the job assignment is temporary, his *tax home* does not change. The taxpayer can also deduct his travel expenses because the job assignment is of a temporary nature, and therefore, the travel is considered business-related.

*Important Tip: A temporary work assignment is any work assignment that is expected to last for *one year or less*. Travel expenses paid or incurred in connection with a temporary work assignment away from home are deductible. However, travel expenses paid in connection with an *indefinite* work assignment are *not deductible*. Any work assignment over one year in duration is considered *indefinite*. A taxpayer cannot deduct travel expenses at a work location if it is realistically expected that he will work there for more than one year.

There is an exception for federal crime investigations or prosecutions. If a taxpayer is a federal employee participating in a federal crime investigation or prosecution, he or she is not subject to the one year rule and may deduct travel expenses as long as the investigation takes place.

There is also a special rule for military personnel. Members of the armed forces on a permanent duty assignment overseas are not considered to be "traveling away from home." Therefore, members of the military cannot deduct their travel expenses for meals and lodging while on permanent duty assignment. However, military personnel that are permanently transferred from one duty station to another may be able to deduct their *moving expenses* as an adjustment to income (which will be explained in a later unit under Moving Expenses).

> **Example:** Terry is a construction worker who lives and works primarily in Los Angeles. Terry is also a member of a trade union in Los Angeles that helps him get work in the Los Angeles area. Because of a shortage of work, Terry agrees to take a job on a construction site in Fresno. The Fresno job lasts ten months. Since the job lasts less than one year, the Fresno job is considered *temporary* and Terry's tax home is still in Los Angeles. Therefore, Terry's travel expenses are deductible since he was traveling away from his "tax home" for business or work. Terry can deduct travel expenses, *including* meals and lodging, while traveling between his temporary place of work and his tax home in Los Angeles (example in Publication 463).

Once a taxpayer has determined that she is traveling away from her *tax home*, she can deduct "ordinary and necessary" expenses incurred while traveling on business. Lodging, airline tickets, and meals are all examples of deductible travel expenses.

Office in the Home

If a taxpayer has an office in her home that qualifies as a principal place of business, she can deduct daily transportation costs between the home office and another work location in the same trade or business. Commuting expenses are never deductible. However, the travel between a home office to a business location would be considered deductible travel. The rules regarding home office expenses are covered more extensively in Part 2.

Example: Vince is a self-employed bookkeeper who works exclusively out of a home office. Vince has many clients. Vince travels from his home office directly to the client's business and performs his bookkeeping services on-site. Vince does not have any other office. In this case, the travel from his home office to the client's location is deductible as business mileage.

Filing Requirements

Not every person is required to file a tax return. A taxpayer is required to file a tax return if his or her 2010 income exceeds the *combined total* of the standard deduction and personal exemption.[4] There are different rules for taxpayers who are self-employed. In order to determine whether someone must file a tax return, a tax professional must also determine if:

- The person can be claimed as a dependent on another's tax return
- The person received Advance Earned Income Credit (AEIC) payments
- Special taxes might be owed on different types of income
- Some of the taxpayer's income is excludable (or exempt)

Generally, a taxpayer is required to file a tax return if he or she has self-employment earnings of $400 or more. However, the filing requirements listed below apply mainly to wage earners. There will be numerous examples at the end of the section in order to demonstrate different filing scenarios. In the case of an individual taxpayer, filing requirements vary based on gross income, age, and filing status.

2010 Filing Requirements for Most Taxpayers

Sometimes, a taxpayer is required to file even though none of his income is taxable. To determine whether a person should file a return, a tax preparer must check the taxpayer's **Form W-2**, and/or **Form(s) 1099.** Here are the 2010 filing requirement thresholds:

- Single: $9,350
- Single, 65 or over: $10,750
- Head of Household (HOH): $12,050
- Head of Household, 65 or over: $13,450
- Married Filing Jointly (MFJ): $18,700
  - *Over 65, (MFJ): $19,800 (65 or over, one spouse)
  - *Over 65, (MFJ): $20,900 (65 or over, both spouses)

---

[4] See the tables at the beginning of the book for the standard deduction and personal exemption amounts.

- Married Filing Separately (MFS): $3,650 (any age)
- Qualifying Widow/Widower: $15,050 ($16,150 if age 65 and older)

> **Example**: Fredericka is 36 years old, single, and her gross income was $20,000. She does not have any children. She must file a tax return and will use the Single filing status since her income was over $9,350.

> **Example**: Frances and Javier are married and plan to file a joint return. Frances is 65 and had a gross income of $11,000 for the tax year. Javier is 66 and his gross income was $5,000 for the year. Since their combined gross income was $16,000 (which is under $20,900), they are not required to file a tax return.

> **Example**: Bob is single and 27 years old. No one can claim him as a dependent. His gross income was $9,550 during the tax year. Based only on this information, Bob is required to file a return because his gross income was over the filing threshold for single taxpayers.

There are special rules for dependents with taxable income, self-employed persons, and nonresident aliens. A dependent is required to file when he or she has *any* of the following:

- Unearned income of *more than* $950 (such as interest income)
- Earned income of *more than* $5,700 (such as wages)
- Gross income of *more than* the larger of:
  - $950 or
  - Earned income (up to $5,400) plus $300

Generally, if a dependent child who must file an income tax return cannot file it for any reason, such as age, then the parent (or other legally responsible person) must file it on the child's behalf. If a child cannot sign his or her own tax return, the guardian must sign the child's name followed by the words "By (signature), parent for minor child."

> **Example:** Danny is a 16-year-old high school student who is claimed as a dependent on his parents' tax return. He works as a pizza delivery boy ten hours a week and in 2010 earned $3,200 in wages. He also had $1,100 of interest income from a Certificate of Deposit his grandmother gave him last year. Danny is required to file a tax return because his unearned income exceeds $950.

Not all income is taxable. There are many types of income that are *reportable*, but not taxable, to the recipient. Even if a taxpayer is not legally required to file a tax return, she should—if eligible to receive a refund. Taxpayers should still file tax returns if any of the following are true:

- They had income tax withheld from their pay.
- They made estimated tax payments or had a prior year overpayment.
- They qualify for the Earned Income Tax Credit (EITC).
- They qualify for the additional child tax credit (which is a refundable credit).

Example: Rita is 65 years old, married, and has $9,500 of wage income in 2010. Her husband Roger has $11,000 in wage income. They have no dependents. Normally, Roger and Rita would not have a filing requirement. However, Rita has decided that she wants to file separately from her husband in 2010. Rita is therefore required to file a tax return because the filing threshold for MFS is $3,650. In this case, it is Rita's filing status that forces her to file a return. Roger must also file a tax return, because his filing status is also MFS by default. Roger cannot choose to file jointly with his wife unless she agrees, since both spouses are required to sign a joint return.

Example: Holly is single with a dependent four-year-old child and qualifies for Head of Household filing status. Holly earns $8,500 in wages during 2010. She also earns $700 in self-employment income from cleaning houses on the side. Even though Holly makes less than the filing threshold for Head of Household filing status, Holly is required to file a tax return because her self-employment earnings exceed $400. Even if Holly did not have self-employment earnings, she should still file a tax return, because she likely qualifies for the Earned Income Credit, which is a refundable credit for low income wage earners. The Earned Income Credit will give her a nice refund in 2010.

Other Odd Filing Requirement Situations

Sometimes, the taxpayer is required to file a tax return in situations where the gross income threshold is not met. Here are examples where the taxpayer is required to file a tax return, even when gross income is below the regular filing requirement thresholds:

- If the taxpayer has self-employment earnings of $400 or more
- **Church employees:** If a taxpayer is a church employee who is exempt from employers' Social Security and Medicare taxes and has wages of $108.28 or more (***Note:** this seems like an odd exception, however, it has shown up on prior exams. Remember this special rule for church employees only.)
- If the taxpayer received Advance Earned Income Tax Credit (AEITC)[5] in 2010 (**Important Note:** *The Education Jobs and Medicaid Assistance Act of 2010* signed into law August 10, 2010 repealed the Advance EITC. After December 31, 2010, workers will not receive Advance EITC in their paychecks. However, there will still be cases where employees received AEITC during 2010.)
- If the taxpayer owes Social Security tax or Medicare tax on unreported tips
- If the taxpayer owes tax on an IRA, qualified retirement plan, Health Savings Account, Coverdell Education Savings Account, or Alternative Minimum Tax
- If the taxpayer owes household employment taxes for a household worker such as a nanny
- If the taxpayer is a nonresident alien with a U.S. business or tax liability not covered by tax withholding

---

[5] The Advance Earned Income Tax Credit or the AEITC is a refundable federal income tax credit for low income working individuals. The AEITC allows qualifying taxpayers to receive part of the credit in each paycheck during the year. The credit was repealed in December 2010.

- If the taxpayer must *recapture* an education credit, investment credit or other credit
- If a nonresident alien has income from a trade or business in the U.S., or has passive income from a U.S. investment, and not all the required U.S. tax was withheld from that income

Nonresident Aliens and Form 1040NR

Taxpayers who are not citizens or legal residents (green card holders) are generally considered nonresidents for income tax purposes. Legal resident aliens (green card holders) are taxed in the same way as U.S. citizens. "Residency" for tax purposes is not the same as legal residency for green card status. It is an important concept to understand. An individual may still be considered a "U.S. resident" for tax purposes, based on the physical time he or she spends in the United States.

A nonresident can be someone who lives outside the U.S. and simply invests in U.S. property or stocks, and is therefore required to file a tax return in order to correctly report his or her earnings.

Each year, thousands of nonresident aliens are also gainfully employed in the United States. Thousands more own rental property or earn interest or dividends from U.S. investments, and are therefore required to file U.S. tax returns.

How to Determine Alien Tax Status

If the taxpayer is an alien (not a U.S. citizen), she is considered a *nonresident* for tax purposes *unless* she meets one of two tests:

1. The Green Card Test: A taxpayer is considered a U.S. resident if she is a Lawful Permanent Resident of the United States (if the taxpayer has a "green card"). Green card holders are taxed just like U.S. citizens, regardless of where they live.
OR

2. The "Substantial Presence" Test: The "Substantial Presence" test is based on a calendar year (January 1 – December 31). A taxpayer will also be considered a U.S. resident for tax purposes only if she meets the "substantial presence" test for the calendar year. To meet this test, the taxpayer must be physically present in the United States on at least:
- 31 days during the current year, and
- 183 days during the previous three years. When counting days of physical presence, count:
    - All the days she was present in the current year, and
    - One-third of the days she was present in the first year before the current year, and
    - One-sixth of the days she was present in the second year before the current year.

Taxpayers that qualify as U.S. residents (including all U.S. citizens and green card holders) must file a U.S. tax return (unless they are exempt, such as taxpayers who are below the income requirements), and ALL their worldwide income is subject to U.S. tax and must be reported on their U.S. tax return (**Form 1040**, *U.S. Individual Income Tax Return*). If the taxpayer does *not* meet either the Green Card Test or the Substantial Presence Test, then the taxpayer is considered a nonresident for tax purposes.

Nonresident aliens are subject to U.S. income tax *only* on their U.S. source income.

Example: Grace is a German citizen who was physically present in the United States for 120 days in each of the years 2008, 2009, and 2010. She earned $18,000 in 2010 as a translator. To determine if she meets the *Substantial Presence Test* for 2010, count the full 120 days of presence in 2010, 40 days in 2009 (1/3 of 120), and 20 days in 2008 (1/6 of 120). Since the total for the three-year period is 180 days, she is not considered a resident for tax purposes under the *Substantial Presence Test* for 2010. Therefore, her earnings are taxed as a nonresident. Grace is required to file a nonresident tax return in 2010 (**Form 1040NR**, *U.S. Nonresident Alien Income Tax Return*).

Nonresidents are subject to *two different tax rates*, one for Effectively Connected Income (ECI), and one for Fixed, Determinable, Annual, or Periodic income (FDAP).

- **Effectively Connected Income (ECI)** is earned from the operation of a business in the U.S. or from personal service income earned in the U.S. (such as wages or self-employment income). It is taxed for a nonresident at the same rates as for a U.S. citizen.
- **FDAP income** is passive income (such as interest, dividends, rents, or royalties). This income is taxed at a flat 30% rate, unless a tax treaty specifies a lower rate.

Example: Gérard is an Australian citizen living in Australia. In 2010, Gérard earned $150,000 in royalty income from his U.S. investments. This income is FDAP income and is taxed at a flat 30% rate (unless a tax treaty applies). He is required to file a Form 1040NR.

Example: Benita Silva is a Brazilian citizen. Benita earned $45,000 of wage income in 2010 working as a translator for the Brazilian consulate. She worked in the United States for 70 days and then returned home to Brazil. She does not meet the Substantial Presence Test or the Green Card Test; therefore, she is a nonresident for tax purposes. Her income is ECI income and is taxed at the same rate as a U.S. citizen. Benita is required to file a Form 1040NR.

---

*Special rule for nonresident spouses: Nonresident alien individuals who are *married* to U.S. citizens or green card holders (legal residents) may choose to be treated as resident aliens for income tax purposes.

> **Example:** Lola and Bruno D'Souza are married and both are nonresident aliens at the beginning of the year. In June, Bruno became a legal U.S. resident alien and obtained a green card and a Social Security Number. Lola and Bruno may both choose to be treated as resident aliens by attaching a statement to their joint return. Lola is not eligible for a Social Security Number, so she must apply for an ITIN (an Individual Tax Identification Number). Lola and Bruno must file a joint return for the year they make the election, but they can file either joint or separate returns for later years.

Tax Treaties

The United States has income tax treaties with a number of foreign countries. For nonresident aliens, these treaties can often reduce or even eliminate U.S. tax on various types of personal services and other income, such as pensions, interest, dividends, royalties, and capital gains. Each individual treaty must be reviewed to determine whether specific types of income are exempt from U.S. tax or taxed at a reduced rate. More details about tax treaties can be found in **Publication 901**, *U.S. Tax Treaties*. Tax treaties are generally not tested on the Enrolled Agent Exam; however, you must know that they exist.

Due Dates for Nonresident Aliens

Nonresident aliens who have income that is not subject to U.S. withholding are required to file an income tax return by June 15, two months *after* the regular filing deadline for individuals. However, Nonresident Employees (such as a nonresident alien that earns wages while living or visiting the U.S.) who received wages that are subject to U.S. income tax withholding must file Form 1040NR by April 15.

*Basic Rule: Due Dates for Nonresident Tax Returns: If the alien is an employee who receives wages or nonemployee compensation that IS SUBJECT to U.S. income tax withholding, or if he has a place of business in the United States, he must generally file by April 15.

If the alien is an employee or self-employed person whose income is NOT SUBJECT to U.S. income tax withholding, AND if she DOES NOT have a place of business in the United States, she must file by June 15.

Basic Tax Forms for Individuals

Form 1040EZ: Of the tax return forms, Form 1040EZ is the simplest. The one-page form is designed for single and joint filers with *no dependents*. It shows the taxpayer's filing status, income, adjusted gross income, standard deduction, taxable income, tax, Earned Income Credit (EIC), amount owed or refund, and signature. A taxpayer may use the 1040EZ under the following conditions (this list is not exhaustive):

- Taxable income is below $100,000
- The filing status is Single or Married Filing Jointly
- The taxpayer(s) are under age 65 and not blind
- The taxpayer is not claiming any dependents
- Interest income is $1,500 or less

29

Form 1040A is a two-page form. Page one shows the filing status, exemptions, income, and adjusted gross income. Page two shows standard deduction, exemption amount, taxable income, tax, credits, payments, amount owed or refund, and signature. A taxpayer may use the 1040A under the following conditions:

- Taxable income is below $100,000
- The taxpayer has capital gain distributions
- The taxpayer is entitled to claim only the following tax credits:
    - The credit for child and dependent care expenses
    - The credit for the elderly or the disabled
    - The child tax credit
    - The additional child tax credit
    - The education credits
    - The retirement savings contributions credit (The Savings Credit).
    - The Earned Income Credit
    - The Making Work Pay credit
- The taxpayer claims an adjustment to income for IRA contributions and student loan interest

Form 1040 is also called the "long form." It is a two-page form that contains all specialized entries for additional types of income, itemized deductions, and other taxes. If a taxpayer cannot use Form 1040EZ or Form 1040A, he or she must use Form 1040. Form 1040 is designed to report all types of income, deductions, and credits. Taxpayers who plan to itemize their deductions are required to use Form 1040. Among the most common reasons why taxpayers must use Form 1040 are:

- Their taxable income exceeds $100,000 or more
- They want to itemize their deductions
- They are reporting self-employment income
- They are reporting income from the sale of property (such as the sale of stock or rental property)

Form 1040NR: This is the form used by nonresident aliens to report their U.S. source income.

Recordkeeping for Individuals

Taxpayers should keep copies of tax returns and records until the statute of limitations runs out for their return. Usually, this is three years from the date the return was filed, or two years from the date the tax was paid, whichever is later.

For example, if a taxpayer files his return one year late, then he should retain the records pertaining to that tax year at least three years after the date he filed the return.

Unit 1.1: Questions

1. Generally, every taxpayer that files a tax return must use an identifying number. Which of the following is NOT a Taxpayer Identification Number for IRS purposes?

A. Social Security Number (SSN)
B. Adoption Taxpayer Identification Number (ATIN)
C. Individual Tax Identification Number (ITIN)
D. Preparer Tax Identification Number (PTIN)

The answer is D. A Preparer Tax Identification Number (PTIN) is used by preparers to identify themselves on a taxpayer's return. It is not an identifying number for taxpayer use. The three types of tax ID numbers are the Social Security Number (SSN), the Adoption Taxpayer Identification Number (ATIN), and the Individual Tax Identification Number (ITIN). ###

2. Which IRS form is used to request an ATIN for an adopted child where the adoption is not yet final?

A. IRS Form W-7A
B. IRS Form W-2
C. IRS Form SSA
D. IRS Form 1099

The answer is A. An ATIN can be requested for an adopted child by using IRS Form W-7A. ###

3. A person who is not required to file a tax return should still file a return for any of the following reasons except to _____.

A. Report self-employment net earnings of $400 or more
B. Claim a refund of withheld taxes
C. Claim the Earned Income Credit
D. Claim the additional child tax credit

The answer is A. Even if the thresholds indicate that a return does not have to be filed, individuals who want to claim tax refunds, EIC, or additional child tax credits should still file a return. A taxpayer with self-employment earnings of $400 or more is *required* to file a tax return.

4. Helen and Edward were married in 2010. They have no dependents. Edward wants to file jointly, but Helen does not want to file jointly with her husband. Helen is 65 and had a gross income of $2,000 for the tax year. Edward is 72. His gross income was $28,000 for the year. Which of the following statements is true?

A. Edward is required to file a tax return, and he must file MFS. Helen is not required to file a return.
B. Edward may still file jointly with Helen and sign on her behalf.
C. Edward and Helen are both required to file tax returns, and they must both file MFS.
D. Edward and Helen may both file SINGLE.

The answer is A. Since Edward and Helen are married, they must either file jointly or separately. Since Helen does not agree to file jointly with Edward, Edward is forced to file MFS. Helen is not required to file a tax return because her gross income in 2010 was $2,000. The filing requirement threshold for Married Filing Separately (MFS) is $3,650. ###

5. Janet and Harry are married and usually file jointly. During the tax year, Janet turned 67 and Harry turned 66. Janet's gross income was $19,400, and Harry's gross income from self-employment was $420. Based on this information, which of the following statements is true?

A. Janet and Harry are not required to file because their combined gross income was less than $19,800.
B. Janet and Harry are required to file a tax return because their combined gross income exceeds $18,700.
C. Janet and Harry are required to file a tax return because Harry's income from self-employment exceeds $400.
D. Only Harry is required to file a tax return.

The answer is C. Normally, Janet and Harry would not be required to file because their combined gross income was less than $20,900, and they are both over 65 (this threshold applies to taxpayers who are 65 or over, both spouses). However, they are required to file a tax return because Harry's self-employment income exceeds $400. ###

6. A taxpayer who claims a dependent can use any form EXCEPT _____.

A. Form 1040
B. Form 1040A
C. Form 1040EZ
D. Form 1040A or 1040EZ

The answer is C. A taxpayer who is claiming a dependent cannot use Form 1040EZ. ###

7. Horace and Dorothy, who are married and file jointly, are 68 and 62, respectively. Their gross combined income for the year was $19,980. Although they receive some assistance from friends and relatives, they cannot be claimed as dependents by anyone. Are Horace and Dorothy required to file a tax return?

A. Yes, they are required to file a tax return.
B. No, they are not required to file a tax return.
C. They are required to file a tax return only if either spouse chooses to file MFS.
D. None of the above.

The answer is A. Horace and Dorothy are required to file a tax return, whether they file jointly or separately. If a married couple files jointly and only one spouse is over 65, when the combined gross income exceeds $19,800, then the couple must file a return.###

8. Cynthia is divorced and will file as Head of Household. She has two children she will claim as dependents. She works as a secretary and earned $35,000 in wages for the tax year. She plans to itemize her deductions. Which tax form should Cynthia use?

A. Form 1040
B. Form 1040A
C. Form 1040EZ
D. Form 1040NR

The answer is A. Since Cynthia plans to itemize her deductions, she must file Form 1040. ###

9. Trinity is a single, 22-year-old, full-time college student and is claimed as a dependent on her mother's tax return. Last year Trinity earned $6,800 in wages from her part-time job as an administrative assistant. Is she required to file a tax return?

A. No, Trinity is not required to file a tax return.
B. Yes, Trinity is required to file a tax return.
C. Trinity is only required to file a tax return if she is a full-time student.
D. None of the above.

The answer is B. A single dependent who earns more than $5,700 in gross income must file a return. ###

10. Clark and Christy are filing jointly. They have no dependents. Their combined income was $31,000, which included $35 in taxable interest and two months of unemployment income for Christy. The remainder of the income was from wages. They want to take the standard deduction. Which is the simplest form that Clark and Christy can use for their tax return?

A. Form 1040
B. Form 1040A
C. Form 1040EZ
D. Form 1040NR

The answer is C. Clark and Christy can use Form 1040EZ to file their tax return. ###

11. Which taxpayer is required to have an Individual Taxpayer Identification Number (ITIN)?

A. All nonresident aliens
B. All nonresident and resident aliens
C. Anyone who doesn't have a Social Security Number
D. All nonresident and resident aliens who must file a return or who are claimed on someone else's return and are not eligible for a valid SSN

The answer is D. If a taxpayer must file a U.S. tax return or is listed on a tax return as a spouse or dependent and is not eligible for an SSN, he or she must apply for an ITIN. ###

12. Steven and Rochelle had a child on December 2, 2010. The child only lived for an hour and died before midnight. What is the true statement regarding the child?

A. Steven and Rochelle may NOT claim the child as a dependent on their tax return for 2010, because the child did not live with them for the entire tax year.
B. Steven and Rochelle may NOT claim the child as a dependent on their tax return for 2010, unless they get a Social Security Number for the child.
C. Steven and Rochelle MAY claim the child as a dependent on their tax return for 2010, even if they are unable to get a Social Security Number.
D. Steven and Rochelle may not claim the child as a dependent on their tax return for 2010, but they may claim the child for tax year 2011.

The answer is C. If a child is born and died in the same tax year, an SSN is not required in order to take the dependency exemption. The tax return must be filed on paper, and the child's death certificate or other medical records must be attached. The taxpayer would enter "DIED" in the space normally reserved for the SSN. ###

13. Larry and Zelda are married but will not file jointly. Larry is 42 and Zelda is 36. Larry's gross income from wages was $30,150, and Zelda's was $5,000. Which of the following is true?

A. Only Larry is required to file.
B. Only Zelda is required to file.
C. Both Larry and Zelda are required to file.
D. Neither Larry nor Zelda are required to file.

The answer is C. Taxpayers under 65 who use the Married Filing Separately status and earn more than $3,650 must file a return. ###

14. Ray is married, but he and his wife are filing separately. Their combined income was $105,000. Ray's income was $64,000, half of which was self-employment income. Ray is claiming only one exemption for himself, and he wants to itemize his deductions. Which is the simplest form that Ray can use for his tax return?

A. Form 1040
B. Form 1040A
C. Form 1040EZ
D. Form 1040A or 1040EZ

The answer is A. Ray will need to file Form 1040 for two reasons: he had self-employment income, and he is itemizing deductions.

15. Generally, how long should taxpayers keep the supporting documents for their tax returns?

A. Five years from the due date
B. Three years from the due date
C. Two years from the due date
D. One year from the due date

The answer is B. Taxpayers should keep the supporting documentation for their tax returns for at least three years from the date the return was filed, or two years from the date the tax was paid, whichever is later. This includes applicable worksheets and forms. ###

16. Stella, 65, is single and has a dependent son, William, 18, who lives with her. William is still in high school. Stella provides all of William's support. She had $12,900 in gross income from wages in 2010. Is she required to file a return?

A. Yes
B. No
C. Depends on her net income
D. None of the above

The answer is B. Stella qualifies for Head of Household filing status because her dependent son lives with her. A taxpayer who qualifies for Head of Household and who is also 65 or older does not have to file unless she had at least $13,450 in gross income. ###

17. Alfred lives in Cincinnati where he has a seasonal job for eight months each year and earns $25,000. He works the other four months in Miami, also at a seasonal job, and earns $9,000. Where is Alfred's tax home?

A. Miami.
B. Cincinnati.
C. Alfred is a transient for tax purposes.
D. Alfred has no tax home.

The answer is B. Cincinnati is Alfred's main place of work because he spends most of his time there and earns most of his income there. Therefore, Cincinnati is Alfred's tax home for IRS purposes. ###

18. Brad is working on a temporary work assignment in another city. He's not sure how long the assignment will last. He travels overnight every week. So far, the work assignment has lasted 11 months in 2010, and Brad has incurred $800 in travel expenses and $300 in meal expenses. What is his deductible expense for this activity in 2010?

A. $0
B. $800
C. $950
D. $1,100

The answer is A. Brad cannot deduct any of the expenses, because, travel expenses paid in connection with an indefinite work assignment are not deductible. Any work assignment over one year in duration is considered indefinite, but it the taxpayer cannot determine the end date of the assignment, (or even estimate the end date) then the travel expenses cannot be deducted. ###

19. Felicity is a self-employed bookkeeper and has a home office. Felicity's principal place of business is in her home, although she does not meet clients in her home. Instead, she goes out to her clients' offices and performs their bookkeeping on-site. Which of the following statements is true?

A. Felicity can deduct the cost of round-trip transportation between her home office and her clients' place of business.
B. Felicity can NOT deduct the cost of round-trip transportation between her home office and her clients' or customers' place of business.
C. Felicity does not have a qualified home office, because she does not meet clients in her home.
D. None of the above.

The answer is A. Felicity does not have to meet with clients in her home, in order for her home office to qualify as her principal place of business. Felicity can deduct daily transportation costs between the home office and a client's location. The transportation costs between two work locations are considered a deductible travel expense (Publication 17). ###

20. Megan, an engineer, maintains a residence for herself in Phoenix, Arizona where her employer has a permanent satellite office. In 2010, Megan's employer enrolls her in an eleven-month executive training program at their corporate offices in Santa Clara, California.

Megan will attend classroom training in Santa Clara and temporary work assignments throughout the United States, but she does expect to return to work in Phoenix after she completes her training. Every Monday she takes a commuter flight to Santa Clara. She maintains a small, one-bedroom apartment in Santa Clara and incurs all the ordinary and necessary expenses in the upkeep of a home.

Her grandparents live in a separate residence in Phoenix, so she returns to Arizona on weekends to spend time with them and also attend to her personal affairs from her Phoenix residence. Where can Megan consider her "tax home" to be for the year 2010?

A. Santa Clara, California
B. Phoenix, Arizona
C. Neither, because Megan is a transient for tax purposes
D. Both, because Megan spends time in both places

The answer is B. Her tax home is still in Phoenix, because her work assignment is temporary. For IRS purposes, a "temporary work assignment" is any work assignment that is expected to last for one year or less. Since Megan is going to be away for only eleven months, her tax home remains in Arizona.

Travel expenses paid or incurred in connection with a temporary work assignment away from home are deductible. However, travel expenses paid in connection with an indefinite work assignment are not deductible. Any work assignment in excess of one year is considered indefinite. Also, a taxpayer may not deduct travel expenses at a work location if it is realistically expected that work will continue for more than one year, whether or not she actually works there that long. ###

Unit 1.2: Filing Status

More Reading:
Publication 17, *Your Federal Income Tax*
Publication 501, *Exemptions, Standard Deduction, and Filing Information*

In order to file a tax return, a tax preparer must identify the taxpayer's filing status. There are five filing statuses, and you must clearly understand the rules governing each status. There are also special rules that you must know regarding annulled marriages and widows/widowers.

1. Single and "Considered Unmarried"

A taxpayer is considered SINGLE if, on the last day of the tax year, the taxpayer was:

- Unmarried
- Legally separated or divorced, or
- Widowed (and not remarried during the year)

Although a taxpayer is considered SINGLE, the taxpayer may qualify for another filing status that gives her a lower tax, such as Head of Household or Qualifying Widow(er).

A taxpayer who is single (or legally divorced) on the *last* day of the year is considered "single" for the *entire tax year*. A taxpayer is also "considered unmarried" if, on the last day of the tax year, she is legally separated from her spouse under a divorce decree or separate maintenance decree.

> **Example:** Jim and Jennifer legally divorced on December 31, 2010. Jim and Jennifer do not have any dependents. They each must file SINGLE for tax year 2010. They may NOT file a joint return for 2010.

State law governs whether a person is considered *married* or *legally separated*. If a taxpayer is legally divorced on the last day of the year, she is considered single for the whole year. Divorced taxpayers CANNOT choose "Married Filing Jointly" as their filing status.

*Special Note: Annulled Marriages (Single): If a marriage is annulled, then the marriage is considered *never to have existed*. Annulment is a legal procedure for declaring a marriage null and void. Unlike divorce, an annulment is *retroactive*. If a taxpayer obtains a court decree of annulment that holds that no valid marriage ever existed, the couple is considered unmarried even if they filed joint returns for earlier years.

Taxpayers who have annulled their marriage must file amended returns (**Form 1040X**) claiming Single (or Head of Household status, if applicable) for all the tax years affected by the annulment that are not closed by the statute of limitations. The statute of limitations for filing generally does not expire until *three years* after an original return was filed.

> **Example:** Sarah and Robert were granted an annulment on October 31, 2010. They were married for two years. They do not have any dependents. They each must file SINGLE for 2010, and the prior two years tax returns must be amended to reflect "Single" as their filing status.

2. Married Filing Jointly (MFJ)

Married taxpayers may file jointly even if one spouse did not earn any income. Taxpayers MAY use the Married Filing Jointly (MFJ) status if they are married and:

- Live together as husband and wife, or
- Live apart but are not legally separated or divorced
- They are separated under an interlocutory (not final) divorce decree
- The taxpayer's spouse died during the year and the taxpayer has not remarried

For federal tax purposes, a "marriage" only qualifies for joint filing status if the marriage is between a man and a woman. Although many states now offer same-sex unions, they are not recognized for federal tax purposes. The IRS will recognize a common law marriage if it is recognized by the state where the taxpayers now live or where the common law marriage began.[6]

On a joint return, spouses report combined income and deduct combined allowable expenses. Spouses can file a joint return even if only one spouse had income. Both spouses must include all of their income, exemptions, and deductions on their joint return. Both husband and wife must agree to sign the return, and are responsible for any tax owed. Both spouses may be held responsible for all the tax due, even if all the income was earned by only one spouse. A subsequent divorce usually does not relieve either spouse of the liability associated with the original joint return.

If a taxpayer files a separate return, he may elect to amend the filing status to "Married Filing Jointly" at any time within three years of the due date of the original return. This does not include any extensions. A "separate return" includes a return filed claiming "Married Filing Separately," "Single," or "Head of Household" filing status.

Once a taxpayer files a joint return, he cannot choose to file a separate return (MFS) for the year *after* the due date of the return. So, for example, if a married couple filed their joint tax 2010 return on March 25, 2011, and one of the spouses decides to file MFS, then they only have until April 18,[7] 2011, to elect MFS filing status.

If a spouse dies during the year, the couple is still considered married for the whole year and can choose Married Filing Jointly as their filing status. In this case, the surviving spouse signs the joint return as the "surviving spouse" on the signature line of Form 1040.

---

[6] Only nine U.S. states recognize common-law marriage (Alabama, Colorado, Kansas, Rhode Island, South Carolina, Iowa, Montana, Oklahoma, Texas, and the District of Columbia). You will not be required to memorize the states for the exam. Just realize and understand that common-law marriage exists and is a valid basis for the MFJ filing status.

[7] Don't forget that the due date for tax returns in 2010 is April 18, not April 15!

*Exception: A personal representative for a decedent (deceased taxpayer) can change from a joint return elected by the surviving spouse to a separate return for the decedent, up to a year *after* the filing deadline.

> **Example:** John and his wife Susan have always filed jointly. Susan dies suddenly in 2010, and her will names Harriet, her daughter from a previous marriage, as the executor for her estate and all her legal affairs. John files a joint return with Susan in 2010, but Harriet, as the executor, decides that it would be better for Susan's estate if her tax return was filed MFS. Harriet has the right to change Susan's filing status on her 2010 tax return to MFS. Harriet files an amended return for 2010 claiming MFS status for Susan, and signs the return as the executor.

3. Married Filing Separately (MFS)

The Married Filing Separately (MFS) status is for taxpayers who are married and either:

- Choose to file separate returns, or
- Do not agree to file a joint return

Taxpayers who are married may choose the Married Filing Separately status, which means the husband and wife report their own incomes and deductions on separate returns, even if one spouse had no income. A married taxpayer who files separately must write the spouse's name and Social Security Number (or ITIN) on the front of the Form 1040 (see image).

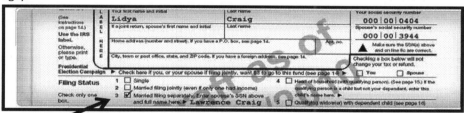

If a taxpayer files a separate return, he generally reports only his own income, exemptions, credits, and deductions (although there are special rules in community property states). Special rules apply to Married Filing Separately taxpayers, which usually results in the taxpayer paying a higher tax. For example, when filing separately:

- The tax rate is generally higher than on a joint return, and
- Taxpayers cannot take credits for child and dependent care expenses, earned income, and certain adoption and education expenses.

There are some rare instances when MFS might be a more beneficial filing status. There is a potential advantage of using MFS status whenever:

- Both spouses have taxable income, and
- At least one (usually the person with the lower income) has high itemized deductions that are limited by Adjusted Gross Income (AGI). For example, it may happen that one spouse has very high medical expenses and the MFS filing status will give him a lower taxable income, because the medical expenses would have been "phased out" on a joint return.

One common reason taxpayers file as Married Filing Separately is to avoid an offset of their refund against their current spouse's outstanding prior debt. This includes past due child support, past due student loans, or a tax liability a spouse incurred before the marriage.

> **Example:** Jerry and Danielle usually file jointly. However, Danielle has chosen to separate her finances from her husband. Jerry wishes to file jointly with Danielle, but she has refused. Danielle files using "Married Filing Separately" as her filing status; therefore, Jerry is forced to file MFS as well.

> **Example:** Frederick and Molly were married in 2010. Frederic owes past due taxes from a prior year. Molly chooses to file separately from Frederick, so her refund will not be offset by Frederick's overdue tax debt. If they were to file jointly, their refund would be retained in order to pay the debt.

There are special rules on MFS returns regarding itemized deductions. If a married couple files separately and one spouse itemizes deductions, the other spouse must either:

- Also itemize deductions, or
- Claim "0" (zero) as the standard deduction

In other words, a taxpayer whose spouse itemizes deductions cannot take the standard deduction. The question of who is itemizing only becomes a consideration when *both* taxpayers are filing MFS. If one spouse qualifies for Head of Household, the fact that the other one is filing MFS and is itemizing doesn't apply.

> **Example:** Tom and Judith always keep their finances separate. They want to file Married Filing Separately. Tom plans to itemize his casualty losses, so then Judith is forced to either itemize her deductions or claim a zero standard deduction.

The Basic Rules on an MFS Tax Return

1. The tax rate will generally be higher than it would be on a joint return.
2. The exemption amount for the Alternative Minimum Tax will be half that allowed to a joint return filer.
3. Neither spouse can take the credit for child and dependent care expenses.
4. Neither spouse can take the Earned Income Credit.
5. Taxpayers cannot take the exclusion or credit for adoption expenses in most cases.
6. Neither spouse can take education credits.
7. Neither spouse can exclude any interest from qualified U.S. savings bonds used for higher education expenses.
8. If one spouse itemizes deductions, the other spouse cannot claim the standard deduction, even if he does not have qualified expenses to itemize. If the taxpayers choose to claim the standard deduction, the basic standard deduction is half the amount allowed on a joint return.
9. A taxpayer's capital loss deduction for MFS is $1,500 instead of $3,000 when filing a joint return.
10. A taxpayer cannot roll over amounts from a traditional IRA into a Roth IRA on an MFS return.

11. For calculating the taxable portion of Social Security, the "provisional income amount" is zero (not $25,000 for Single or $32,000 for Married Filing Jointly).

4. Head of Household

Taxpayers may use the Head of Household (HOH) status if they meet three criteria:

- The taxpayer must be "considered unmarried" (single, divorced, or legally separated) on the last day of the year, or meet the tests for married persons living apart with dependent children.
- The taxpayer must have also paid more than half the cost of maintaining a main home.
- The taxpayer must have had a qualifying person living in her home *more* than half the year (an exception exists for qualifying parent).

In general, the Head of Household status is for unmarried taxpayers who paid *more* than half the cost of keeping up a home for a qualified dependent relative who lived with them in the home more than half the tax year. Valid household expenses include:

- Rent, mortgage interest, real estate taxes
- Home insurance, repairs, utilities
- Domestic help, such as in-home cleaning services and lawn care
- Food eaten in the home

Welfare payments are not considered amounts that the taxpayer provides to maintain a home.

*Special Rule for Dependent Parents: If a taxpayer's qualifying person is a dependent *parent*, the taxpayer may still file Head of Household even if the parent *does not live* with the taxpayer. The taxpayer must pay more than half the cost of keeping up a home that was the parent's main home for the entire year. A taxpayer also is considered "keeping up a main home" if he pays more than half the cost of keeping his parent in a rest home (Publication 17).

> **Example:** Sharon is 54 years old and single. She pays the monthly bill for Shady Pines Nursing Home, where her 75-year-old mother lives. Sharon's mother has lived at Shady Pines for two years and has no income. Since Sharon pays more than half of the cost of her mother's living expenses, Sharon qualifies to use the Head of Household filing status.

This rule also applies to parents, step-parents, grandparents, etc. who are related to the taxpayer by blood, marriage, or adoption (other examples include a step-mother or father-in-law).

*Special Rule for a Death or Birth during the Year: A taxpayer may still file as Head of Household if the qualifying individual is born (or dies) during the year. The taxpayer must have provided more than half of the cost of keeping up a home that was the individual's main home while the person was alive.

> **Example:** Tina is single and financially supports her mother Rue, who lives in her own apartment. Rue dies suddenly on September 15, 2010. Tina may still claim her mother as a dependent and file Head of Household in 2010.

> **Example:** Tony and Velma have a child in 2010. The child only lives for one month. Tony and Velma may still claim the child on their tax return as a qualifying child. That is because a dependent can still be claimed, even though the child only lived for a short while.

For the purposes of the Head of Household filing status, a "qualifying person" is defined as:

- A qualifying child,
- A married child who can be claimed as a dependent, or
- A dependent parent.

The taxpayer's qualifying child includes the taxpayer's child or stepchild (whether by blood or adoption); foster child, sibling, or stepsibling; or a descendant of any of these. For example, a niece or nephew, stepbrother, foster child, or a grandchild may all be eligible as "qualifying persons" for the purpose of the Head of Household filing status.

> **Example:** Lewis's unmarried son Lincoln lived with him all year. Lincoln turned 18 at the end of the year. Lincoln does not have a job and did not provide any of his own support. Lincoln is not a dependent of anyone else. As a result, Lincoln is Lewis's qualifying child. Lewis may claim Head of Household filing status (Publication 501).

The "qualifying person" for Head of Household filing status must always be related to the taxpayer either by blood or marriage (with the exception of a foster child, who also qualifies if the child was legally placed in the home by a government agency or entity).

> **Example:** Jeffrey has lived with his girlfriend Patricia and her son Thomas for five years. Jeffrey pays all of the costs of keeping up their home. Patricia is unemployed and does not contribute to the household costs. Jeffrey is not related to Thomas and cannot claim him as a dependent. No one else lives in the household. Jeffrey cannot file as Head of Household because neither Patricia nor Thomas is a "qualifying person" for Jeffrey.

An unrelated individual may still be considered a "qualifying relative" for a dependency exemption, but will NOT be a qualifying person for the Head of Household filing status. In the example below, the taxpayer lives with an unrelated person (a friend), who qualifies as his dependent, but since they are unrelated (either by blood or marriage), then the taxpayer cannot claim Head of Household filing status.

> **Example:** Since her husband died five years ago, Joan has lived with her friend Wilson. Joan is a U.S. citizen, is single, and lived with Wilson all year. Joan had no income and received all of her financial support from Wilson. Joan falls under the definition of a Qualifying Relative, and Wilson can claim Joan as a dependent on his return. However, Joan would not qualify Wilson to file as Head of Household.

In order for a taxpayer to file as Head of Household, a qualifying child does not have to be a dependent of the taxpayer (unless the qualifying person is married). So, to explain further, a taxpayer may still file as Head of Household and NOT claim the qualifying person as his dependent. This happens most often with divorced parents. The example below illustrates a common scenario.

Example: George and Elizabeth have been divorced for five years. They have one child, a 12-year-old daughter named Rebecca. Rebecca lives with her mother Elizabeth and only sees her father on weekends. Therefore, Elizabeth is the custodial parent. Elizabeth and George have an agreement with each other that allows George to claim the dependency exemption for Rebecca on his tax return. In 2010, George correctly files SINGLE and claims Rebecca as his dependent. Elizabeth may still file as Head of Household. There is an area on Form 1040 that allows Elizabeth to indicate Head of Household status and supply Rebecca's name and Social Security Number (see sample image below).

Taxpayers must always specify the qualifying person who makes them eligible for Head of Household filing status. If the qualifying person is also the taxpayer's dependent, then the dependent's name is entered on the Form 1040 Exemptions section, (line 6c). If the qualifying person is the taxpayer's child and is NOT a dependent, then the taxpayer must enter the child's name on the return's Filing Status section, (Form 1040, line 4).

Special Rules for HOH: Married and Living Apart with Dependent Child

Some married taxpayers who live apart from their spouses and provide for dependent children may be considered "unmarried" for Head of Household purposes. These taxpayers are permitted to file as Head of Household if they meet all the following criteria:

- The married taxpayer chooses to not file a joint return with his or her spouse.
- The taxpayer paid more than half the cost of keeping up the qualifying child's home for the year.
- The taxpayer's spouse *did not live in the home* during the last six months of the year.

Example: Luke and Laura separated in February 2010 and lived apart for the rest of the year. They do not have a written separation agreement and are not divorced yet. Their six-year-old daughter Pauline lived with Luke all year. Luke and Laura will not file a joint tax return. Luke paid more than half the cost of keeping up his home. Luke claims Pauline's exemption because he is the custodial parent. Luke can also claim Head of Household status for 2010. Although Luke is still legally married, he can file as Head of Household because he meets all the requirements to be "considered unmarried."

The taxpayer's home must be the *main home* of the taxpayer's qualifying child, stepchild, or eligible foster child for more than half the year in order to qualify under this special rule for married spouses who are living apart.

Example: Janine and Richard separated on July 10, but were not divorced at the end of the year. They have one minor child Madeline, who is 10 years old. Even though Janine lived with Madeline and supported her for the remainder of the year, Janine does not qualify for Head of Household filing status because she and Richard **did not live apart** for the last six months of the year.

*Special Rule for Nonresident Alien Spouses: A taxpayer who is married to a *nonresident alien* spouse may elect to file as Head of Household even if both spouses lived together throughout the year.

Example: In 2009, Tim Jones met and married Maria Consuela, a nonresident alien. Maria is a citizen and resident of Spain. They lived together in Spain while Tim was on a sabbatical from his university teaching position. Tim and Maria have a child named Taylor, who is born in 2010. Tim may still file as Head of Household, even though Tim and Maria lived together all year, because Maria is a nonresident alien.

5. Qualifying Widow/Widower (With a Dependent Child)

This filing status yields a tax rate *equal to* Married Filing Jointly. Surviving spouses receive the same standard deduction and tax rates as taxpayers who are Married Filing Jointly. In the year of the spouse's death, a taxpayer can file a joint return. For the following two years after death, the surviving spouse can use the "Qualifying Widow(er)" filing status as long as he or she has a qualifying dependent.

After two years, the filing status converts to Single or Head of Household, whichever applies.

For example, if the taxpayer's spouse died in 2008 and the surviving spouse did not remarry, he or she can use the "Qualifying Widow(er)" filing status for 2009 and 2010.

Example: Barbara and Kenneth are married. Kenneth dies on December 3, 2008. Barbara has one dependent child, a 15-year-old daughter named Hannah. Barbara does not remarry. Therefore, Barbara's filing status for 2008 is MFJ. Barbara can file as a Qualifying Widow in 2009 and 2010, which is a more favorable filing status than Single or Head of Household. In 2011, Barbara would qualify for Head of Household filing status.

To qualify for the Qualifying Widow(er) filing status, the taxpayer must:

- Not have remarried before the end of the tax year
- Have been eligible to file a joint return for the year the spouse died; it does not matter if a joint return was actually filed
- Have a child, stepchild, or adopted child who qualifies as the taxpayer's qualifying child for the year
- Have furnished over half the cost of keeping up the child's home for the entire year.

Example: Janelle's husband Randy died on July 20, 2008. Janelle has a dependent son who is three. Janelle files a joint return with Randy in 2008. In 2009, Janelle correctly files as a Qualifying Widow with Dependent Child. In 2010, however, Janelle remarries, so she no longer qualifies for the Qualifying Widow filing status. She must now file jointly with her new husband, or MFS.

Filing Status Summary

Take a moment to review what you have covered in this lesson.

The five filing statuses are:

- Single
- Married Filing Jointly
- Married Filing Separately
- Head of Household
- Qualifying Widow(er) With Dependent Child

Filing status is used to determine a taxpayer's filing requirements, standard deduction, eligibility for certain credits and deductions, and the correct tax. If a taxpayer qualifies for more than one filing status, he or she may choose the one that produces a lower tax. If married taxpayers choose to file separately, they must show their spouse's name and Social Security Number on the return.

1. A person's marital status on the *last day of the year* determines the marital status for the entire year.
2. SINGLE filing status generally applies to anyone who is unmarried, divorced (or legally separated according to state law).
3. A married couple may elect file a joint return together. Both spouses must agree to file a joint return.
4. If one spouse died during the year, the taxpayer may file a joint return in the year of death.
5. Head of Household usually applies to taxpayers who are unmarried. A taxpayer must have paid more than half the cost of maintaining a home for a qualifying person in order to qualify for HOH.
6. A widow or widower with one or more dependent children may be able to use the Qualifying Widow(er) with Dependent Child filing status, which is only available for two years following the year of the spouse's death.

After a Spouse's Death

The chart shows which filing status to use for a widowed taxpayer who does not remarry and has a qualifying dependent.

Tax Year	Filing Status	Exemption for Deceased Spouse?
The year of death	Married Filing Jointly or Married Filing Separately	Yes
First year after death	Qualifying Widow(er)	No
Second year after death	Qualifying Widow(er)	No
After second year of death	Head of Household	No

Unit 1.2: Questions

1. Carol and Raul were married three years ago and have no children. Although they lived apart during the entire tax year, they are neither divorced nor legally separated. Which of the following filing statuses can they use?

A. Single or Married Filing Separately
B. Married Filing Jointly or Married Filing Separately
C. Married Filing Separately or Head of Household
D. Single or Qualifying Widow(er)

The answer is B. As long as they are married and are neither divorced nor legally separated, Carol and Raul can file a joint return, or they can choose to file separately. They cannot file Single. ###

2. Kathy, divorced with no children, lived with her unemployed roommate Sandra for the entire year. Kathy had to pay more than half of the cost of keeping up their apartment. Which filing status can Kathy use?

A. Head of Household
B. Married Filing Separately
C. Single
D. Qualifying Widow(er)

The answer is C. The person who qualifies a taxpayer as Head of Household must be the taxpayer's qualifying child or a qualifying relative. However, a taxpayer cannot use Head of Household filing status simply because a qualifying relative lived with the taxpayer for the whole tax year. ###

3. The two filing statuses that generally result in the lowest tax amounts are Married Filing Jointly and _____.

A. Married Filing Separately
B. Head of Household
C. Qualifying Widow(er) with Dependent Child
D. Single

The answer is C. The Qualifying Widow(er) with Dependent Child filing status yields as low a tax amount as Married Filing Jointly. ###

4. Samantha is divorced and provided over half the cost of keeping up a home. Her five-year-old daughter Pamela lived with her for seven months last year. Samantha allows her ex-husband Jim to claim their child Pamela as a dependent. Which of the following statements is true?

A. Jim may take Pamela as his dependent and also file as Head of Household.
B. Jim may take Pamela as his dependent, and Samantha may still file as Head of Household.
C. Neither parent qualifies for Head of Household filing status because Pamela did not live with either parent for the entire year.
D. Samantha cannot release the dependency exemption to Jim, because their daughter did not live with Jim for over six months.

The answer is B. Samantha may use Head of Household status because she is not married and she provided over half the cost of keeping up the main home of her dependent child for more than six months. However, because Samantha's ex-husband claims Pam as his dependent, the preparer must write Pamela's name on line 4 of the filing status section of Form 1040 or 1040A. ###

5. To determine if a widowed taxpayer can use the Qualifying Widow(er) with Dependent Child status, a preparer needs to know all the following information EXCEPT _____.

A. The year the spouse died
B. If the taxpayer filed a joint return for the year the spouse died
C. Whether the taxpayer furnished more than half the cost for keeping up the main home of a qualified child
D. Whether the taxpayer remarried before the end of the tax year

The answer is B. The taxpayer must have been eligible to file a joint return; it does not matter if a joint return was actually filed. ###

49

6. Which dependent relative may qualify a taxpayer for Head of Household filing status?

A. An adult stepdaughter whom the taxpayer supports, but who lives across town
B. A family friend who lives with the taxpayer all year
C. A father who lives in his own home and not with the taxpayer
D. A child who lived with the taxpayer for three months of the tax year

The answer is C. A parent is the only dependent relative who does not have to live with the taxpayer in order for the taxpayer to claim Head of Household status. ###

7. Jane White and Todd Thompson have a 5-year-old daughter, Amanda, but they are not married. Jane and her daughter lived together all year. Todd lived alone in his own apartment. Jane earned $13,000 working as a clerk in a clothing store. Todd earned $48,000 as an assistant manager of a hardware store. He paid over half the cost of Jane's apartment for rent and utilities. He also gave Jane extra money for groceries. Todd does not pay any expenses or support for any other family member. All are U.S. citizens and have valid SSNs. Which of the following is true?

A. Todd may file Head of Household.
B. Jane may file Head of Household.
C. Todd and Jane may file jointly.
D. Neither may claim Head of Household filing status.

The answer is D. Todd provided over half the cost of providing a home for Jane and Amanda, but he cannot file Head of Household since Amanda (his child) did not live with him for over half the year. Jane cannot file HOH either, because she does not provide more than one-half the cost of keeping up the home for her daughter, Amanda. However, either Todd or Jane may still claim Amanda as their dependent. ###

8. Debbie has a 10-year-old child. She separated from her husband during the tax year. Which of the following would prevent Debbie from filing as Head of Household?

A. Debbie has maintained a separate residence from her husband since April of the tax year.
B. The qualifying child's principal home is now with Debbie.
C. Debbie's parents assisted with 25% of the household costs.
D. The child lived with Debbie beginning in mid-July of the tax year.

The answer is D. For Debbie to file as Head of Household, Debbie's home must have been the main home of her qualifying child for more than half the tax year. ###

9. Alexandra's younger brother Sebastian is seventeen years old. Sebastian lived with friends from January through February of 2010. From March through July of 2010, he lived with Alexandra. On August 1, Sebastian moved back in with his friends, with whom he stayed for the rest of the year. Since Sebastian did not have a job, Alexandra gave him money every month. Alexandra had no other dependents. Which of the following statements is true?

A. Alexandra may file as Head of Household for 2010.
B. Alexandra may file jointly with Sebastian in 2010.
C. Alexandra cannot file as Head of Household in 2010.
D. Sebastian may file as Head of Household in 2010.

The answer is C. Alexandra cannot claim Head of Household status because Sebastian lived with her for only five months, which is less than half the year. ###

10. The person who qualifies a taxpayer as Head of Household must be _____.

A. A minor child
B. A blood relative
C. The taxpayer's dependent OR the taxpayer's qualifying child
D. Someone who lives away from the taxpayer's main home

The answer is C. The taxpayer must claim the person as a dependent unless the non-custodial parent claims the child as a dependent. Answer A is incorrect, because a qualifying dependent does not have to be a minor in many cases. Answer B is incorrect because a qualifying dependent may be related by blood, marriage, or adoption. ###

11. Gerald takes care of his grandson Kyle, who is 10 years old. How long must Kyle live in the taxpayer's home in order for Gerald to qualify for Head of Household status?

A. At least three months
B. More than half the year
C. The entire year
D. More than 12 months

The answer is B. The relative must have lived with the taxpayer *more than half the year* (over six months) and have been the taxpayer's dependent. The exception is that a taxpayer's *dependent parent* does not have to live with the taxpayer. ###

12. Dana's husband died in 2010. She has one dependent son who is four years old. What is the best filing status in 2010 for Dana?
A. Married Filing Jointly
B. Single
C. Qualifying Widow
D. Head of Household

The answer is A. If a taxpayer's spouse died during the year, the taxpayer is considered married for the whole year for filing status purposes, and may file as "MFJ." So Debbie may file a joint return with her husband in 2010, which is the year he died. (Publication 17) ###

13. Victor is 39 years old. He has been legally separated from his wife Janet since February 1, 2010. Their divorce was not yet final at the end of the year. They have two minor children. One child lives with Victor and the other child lives with Janet. The children have been with their respective parents from February through December of the tax year. Victor provides all of the support for the minor child living with him. Janet refuses to file jointly with Victor this year. Therefore, the most beneficial filing status that Victor qualifies for is:

A. Married Filing Separately
B. Single
C. Head of Household
D. Qualifying Widower with a Dependent Child

The answer is C. Victor qualifies for Head of Household filing status. His child lived with him for more than six months. Victor may file as Head of Household because he is "considered unmarried" on the last day of the year and he paid more than half the cost of keeping up a home for the year for a qualifying child. Victor cannot file jointly with Janet, if she does not agree. ###

14. Sean is single. His mother Clara lives in an assisted living facility. Sean provides all of Clara's support. Clara died on June 1, 2010. She had no income. Which of the following is true?

A. Sean may file as Head of Household and may also claim his mother as a dependent on his 2010 tax return.
B. Sean must file Single in 2010, and he cannot claim his mother as a dependent on his tax return.
C. Sean may claim his mother as a dependent on his tax return, but he cannot claim Head of Household status for 2010.
D. None of the above.

The answer is A. Because Sean paid more than half the cost of his mother's care in a care facility from the beginning of the year until her death, then he is entitled to claim an exemption for her, and he can also file as Head of Household (Publication 501). ###

15. Regina's marriage was annulled in December 2010. She was married to her husband in 2008 and filed jointly with him in 2008 and 2009. Regina has no dependents. Which of the following statements is true?

A. Regina must file amended returns, claiming Single filing status for all open years affected by the annulment.
B. Regina is not required to file amended returns, and she must file Single on her 2010 tax return.
C. Regina is not required to file amended returns, and she must file Married Filing Separately on her 2010 tax return.
D. Regina is not required to file amended returns, and she must file Married Filing Jointly on her 2010 tax return.

The answer is A. Regina must file amended tax returns for 2008 and 2009. She cannot file jointly with her husband in 2010. If a couple obtains a court decree of annulment, which holds that no valid marriage ever existed, they are considered unmarried *even if* the couple filed joint returns for earlier years. A taxpayer must file amended returns **(Form 1040X)** claiming Single or Head of Household status for all tax years affected by the annulment that are not closed by the statute of limitations for filing a tax return. The statute of limitations generally does not expire until three years after an original return is filed (Publication 501). ###

16. A taxpayer may NEVER amend a joint tax return from "Married Filing Jointly" to "Married Filing Separately" after the filing deadline.

A. True
B. False

The answer is B, False. There is only one exception: The personal representative for a decedent (a deceased taxpayer) can change from a joint return elected by the surviving spouse to a separate return for the decedent. ###

17. Lisa married Harry in 2005, and they have two dependent children. Harry died in 2008. Lisa has never remarried. Which filing status should Lisa use for her 2010 tax return?

A. Single
B. Married Filing Jointly
C. Head of Household
D. Qualifying Widow with Dependent Child

The answer is D. In 2010, Lisa qualifies for "Qualifying Widow with Dependent Child" filing status. Lisa and Harry qualified to file jointly in 2008, and Lisa signed the tax return as a surviving spouse. The year of death is the last year for which a taxpayer can file jointly with a deceased spouse. Then, in 2009, Lisa was eligible to file as a Qualifying Widow with Dependent Child. She would be eligible for the same filing status in 2010. This filing status yields as low a tax amount as Married Filing Jointly and is available for only two years following the year of the spouse's death. After two years, the filing status then converts to Single or Head of Household, whichever applies. ###

18. Mary and Troy are married and live together. Mary earned $7,000 in 2010, and Troy earned $42,000. Mary wants to file a joint return, but Troy refuses to file with Mary and instead files a separate return. Which of the following statements is true?

A. Mary may still file a Married Filing Joint tax return and sign Troy's name as an "absentee" spouse.
B. Mary and Troy must both file separate returns.
C. Mary may file as Single because Troy refuses to sign a joint return.
D. Mary does not have a filing requirement.

The answer is B. In this case, both spouses are required to file a tax return. Married couples must agree to file jointly. If one spouse does not agree to file jointly, they must file separately. ###

19. Dwight and Angela are married, but they choose to file separate tax returns for tax year 2010, because Dwight is being investigated by the IRS for an older tax year. Dwight and Angela file their separate tax returns on time. A few months later, after the investigation is over and Dwight is cleared of all wrongdoing, Dwight wishes to file amended returns and file jointly with his wife in order to claim the Earned Income Credit. Which of the following is TRUE?

A. Dwight is prohibited from changing his filing status in order to claim this credit.
B. Dwight and Angela may amend their separate tax returns to Married Filing Jointly in order to claim the credit.
C. Dwight may amend his tax return to joint filing status, but he may not claim the credit.
D. Angela may not file jointly with Dwight after she has already filed a separate tax return.

The answer is B. If a taxpayer files a separate return, the taxpayer may elect to amend the filing status to "Married Filing Jointly" at any time within three years from the due date of the original return. This does not include any extensions. However, the same does not hold true in reverse. Once a taxpayer files a *joint return*, the taxpayer cannot choose to file a separate return for that year after the due date of the return (with a rare exception for deceased taxpayers). ###

20. Cecily is in the process of adopting an infant boy. She qualifies to take the child as a dependent, but she cannot obtain a Social Security Number for the child yet. What can you advise Cecily to do in order to claim the child?

A: Cecily may file a tax return on paper and put "adopted" in the line for the SSN.
B: Cecily must wait until a valid Social Security Number is issued in order to claim the child.
C. Cecily may apply for an ATIN in order to claim the baby.
D: Cecily may not claim the child until the adoption is final.

The answer is C. Cecily may request an ATIN and claim the child. An ATIN is an Adoption Taxpayer Identification Number issued by the IRS as a temporary taxpayer identification number for the child in a domestic adoption where the taxpayers are unable to obtain the child's Social Security Number. The ATIN is to be used by the adopting taxpayers on their federal income tax return to identify the child while final domestic adoption is pending. ###

21. Which of the following statements is TRUE regarding the Head of Household filing status?

A. The taxpayer is considered unmarried on the first day of the year.
B. The taxpayer's spouse must live in the home during the tax year.
C. The taxpayer's dependent parent does not have to live with the taxpayer in order to qualify for Head of Household.
D. The taxpayer paid less than half of the cost of keeping up the house for the entire year.

The answer is C. Parents do not have to live with a taxpayer in order to take the dependency exemption. This is a special rule only for dependent parents. This rule also applies to parents or grandparents who are related to the taxpayer by blood, marriage, or adoption (examples include a stepmother or father-in-law). A taxpayer must pay over half of the household costs in order to qualify for this filing status. ###

Unit 1.3: Personal Exemptions and Dependents

More Reading:
Publication 501, *Exemptions, Standard Deduction, and Filing Information*

Taxpayers are allowed to take an exemption for themselves and also for their dependents. The 2010 exemption amount is $3,650 per person. The personal exemption is just like a tax deduction. It can reduce a person's taxable income to zero. In prior years, the exemption was phased out for high income taxpayers. Not so in 2010—the personal exemption phase-out was eliminated; even the highest income taxpayers are still allowed to claim their personal exemptions.

A *dependency* exemption is not the same thing as a *personal* exemption. Taxpayers may qualify to claim two kinds of exemptions:

- Personal exemptions, which taxpayers can generally claim for themselves (and their spouses)
- Dependency exemptions, which taxpayers claim for their dependents

On a joint tax return, a married couple is allowed *two* personal exemptions, one for each spouse. A spouse is never considered the "dependent" of the other spouse. However, taxpayers may claim a personal exemption for their spouse simply because they are married. This is true even if only one person has income during the year. Only one exemption is allowed per person. So, for example, a married couple with one child would claim three exemptions on a jointly filed return.

Example: Jenny married Rick in April of the tax year. Neither can be claimed as a dependent on another taxpayer's return. Both worked full-time and earned wage income for the tax year. Jenny and Rick may claim two personal exemptions on their jointly filed return.

Rules for Dependents

A taxpayer can claim one exemption for each dependent, thereby reducing their taxable income. Some examples of dependents include a child, stepchild, brother, sister, or parent. If a taxpayer can claim another person as a dependent—even if the taxpayer does not actually do so—the dependent cannot take a personal exemption on their own tax return.

Again, a dependent claimed on another taxpayer's return *cannot* claim a personal exemption on his own return. The dependent is only entitled to one personal exemption, whether he files his own return, or is listed as a dependent on someone else's return.

Example: Stacy is 20 and a full-time college student. Her parents provide all her support. She has a small part-time job where she earns $7,200 in 2010. Stacy cannot file a tax return and claim a dependency exemption for herself because her parents have claimed her on their own return. Stacy may file a tax return in order to obtain a refund of federal income tax withheld (if applicable). She may do so without claiming a personal exemption for herself.

A dependent may still be required to file a tax return. This happens most often with teenagers who also have jobs. They are usually claimed as dependents on their parents' tax return, but they also file their own return to report their wage income.

Example: Stevie is a 15-year-old high school student who also works part-time at a video rental store. In 2010, Stevie earned $5,210 from his part-time job. Stevie still lives with his parents, who file jointly and claim him as a dependent on their return. Stevie also files his own tax return in 2010, in order to obtain a refund of the income taxes that were withheld at his job. He does not claim a personal exemption for himself (because his parents already claimed Stevie's exemption on their joint return). However, Stevie is still entitled to the standard deduction for single taxpayers. This wipes out all of his taxable income, and he receives a refund of the income tax withheld on his **Form W-2.**

Whether or not a dependent is required to file is determined by the amount of the dependent's earned income, unearned income, and gross income. Even though a dependent child may lose a personal exemption, most dependent children usually owe little or no tax on their individual returns because they can still offset a small amount of income with the standard deduction. In actual practice, it is rare to see a dependent who owes a large amount of tax.

Taxpayers may not claim a dependency exemption for an individual if they are themselves dependents of another taxpayer. (This is true even if the taxpayer has a qualifying child or relative).

Example: Dora is unmarried, 17, and lives at home with her mother Rose. Dora has a six-month-old baby named Vinnie. Debbie has $2,100 in wage income from a part-time job in 2010. Rose provides all of the financial support for her daughter Dora and her grandson Vinnie. Dora allows her mother Rose to claim her as a dependent. Dora cannot file a tax return claiming Vinnie as her dependent, because Dora has already been claimed as a dependent on Rose's tax return.

There are certain rules that must be followed in order to claim a dependent on a tax return. The following sections discuss these rules in detail.

The Tests for Dependency

In order to determine if a taxpayer may claim a dependency exemption for another person, you must first determine if the dependent can legally be claimed on the taxpayer's return.

1. Citizenship or Residency Test: In order for a taxpayer to claim a dependency exemption for someone, a residency test must be met. To meet the *"citizen, national, or resident test,"* an individual must be a citizen of the United States, a resident of the United States, or a citizen or resident of Canada or Mexico. There is an exception for foreign-born adopted children.

Example: Horatio is an American citizen. He provides all of the financial support for his mother, who is a resident of Canada. Horatio may claim his mother as a dependent (she does not have to live with him, since she is a parent). Horatio may need to request an ITIN number for his mother if she does not have a valid Social Security Number (Publication 501).

2. Joint Return Test: A dependent must not file a joint return with his or her spouse. Generally, once an individual files a joint return, that person can no longer be taken as a dependent.

> **Example:** Ellen is 18 years old and had no income in 2010. She got married on November 1, 2010. Ellen's new husband had $16,700 income and they file jointly, claiming two personal exemptions on their tax return. Ellen's father Joseph supported her throughout the year and even paid for their wedding. However, Ellen's father cannot claim Ellen as his dependent because she filed a joint return with her new husband.

However, the **Joint Return Test** does *not apply* if the joint return is filed by the dependent only to claim a refund and no tax liability exists for either spouse, even if they filed separate returns.

> **Example:** Greg and Sandy are both 18 and married. They live with Sandy's mother Michelle. In 2010, Greg had $800 of wage income from a part-time job and no other income. Neither Greg nor Sandy is required to file a tax return. Taxes were taken out of Greg's wages due to backup withholding so they file a joint return only to get a refund of the withheld taxes. The exception to the Joint Return Test applies, so Michelle may claim exemptions for both Greg and Sandy on her tax return, as long as all the other tests to do so are met.

3. Qualifying Child of More Than One Person Test: Sometimes a child meets the rules to be a qualifying child of more than one person. However, only one person can claim that dependent on his or her tax return.

> **Example:** Dan and Linda live together with their daughter Savannah. They are not married. Savannah is a qualifying child for both Dan and Linda, but only one of them can claim her as a dependent on their tax return.

4. Dependent Taxpayer Test: If a person can be claimed as a dependent by another taxpayer, that person cannot claim *anyone else* as a dependent. A person who is claimed as a dependent on *someone else's* return cannot claim a dependency exemption on *his own* return.

> **Example:** Eva is a 17-year-old single mother who has an infant son. Eva is claimed as a dependent by her parents. Therefore, Eva is prohibited from claiming her son as a dependent on her own tax return.

The Definition of a Dependent

There are two types of dependents, a ***qualifying child*** and a ***qualifying relative***. Taxpayers may claim a dependency exemption for a *qualifying child* or a *qualifying relative*. There are specific tests for identifying the difference between a qualifying child and a qualifying relative. For the Enrolled Agent Exam, you must understand the differences between these two terms.

Tests for a Qualifying Child

The tests for a qualifying child are more stringent than the tests for a qualifying relative. A qualifying child entitles a taxpayer to numerous tax credits, including the Earned Income Tax Credit and the Child Tax Credit. A qualifying relative does not qualify a taxpayer for EITC. To determine if a taxpayer may claim a dependency exemption for another person, begin with the four tests for a qualifying child:

1. Relationship test: The qualifying child must be related to the taxpayer by blood, marriage, or legal adoption. Qualifying children include:

a. A child or stepchild

b. An adopted child with a valid Social Security Number

c. A sibling or stepsibling

d. A descendant of one of the above (such as a grandchild or a niece or nephew)

2. Age test: In order to be a qualifying child, the dependent must be:

- Under the age of 19 at the end of the tax year, OR
- Under the age of 24 *and* a full-time student, OR
- Permanently and totally disabled at any time during the year (of any age)

A child is considered a full-time student if she attends a qualified educational institution full-time at least five months out of the year.

> **Example:** Andrew is 45 years old and permanently disabled. Karen, his 27-year-old sister, pro-vides all of Andrew's support and cares for him in her home, where he lives with her full-time. Although Andrew does not meet the age test, since he is **completely disabled,** he is still con-sidered a *qualifying child* for tax purposes. Karen may claim Andrew as her qualifying child, and also file as Head of Household (*Note: watch out for "trick" questions with disabled depend-ents!).

Also, a child who is claimed as a dependent must be *younger than* the taxpayer who is claiming him. There is an exception for dependents who are disabled. For taxpayers filing joint-ly, the child must be *younger* than *one spouse* listed on the return, but does not have to be younger than both spouses.

> **Example #1:** Owen and Sydney are both 22 years old and file jointly. Sydney's 23-year-old brother; Parker, is a full-time student, unmarried, and lives with Owen and Sydney. Parker is not disabled. Owen and Sydney are both younger than Parker. Therefore, Parker is not their qualifying child, even though he is a full-time student.

> **Example #2:** Lucius, age 34, and Paige, age 20, are married and file jointly. Paige's 23-year-old nephew Jason is a full-time student, unmarried, and lives with Lucius and Paige. Lucius and Paige provide all of Jason's support. In this case, Lucius and Paige may claim Jason as a qualify-ing child on their joint tax return because he is *younger than* Lucius. Jason is a full-time student, so he is a qualifying child for tax purposes.

3. Support test: A qualifying child cannot provide more than one-half of his own sup-port.

> **Example #1:** Samuel has a 17-year-old daughter named Tiffany. Samuel provided $4,000 to-ward his teenage daughter's support for the year. Tiffany has a part-time job and provided $12,000 of her own support. Therefore, Tiffany provided over half of *her own support* for the year. Tiffany does not pass the support test, and consequently, she is not Samuel's qualifying child. Tiffany can file a tax return as "Single" and claim her own exemption (Publication 501).

> **Example #2:** Penelope is 15 years old and had a small role in a television series. She earned $40,000 as a child actor, but her parents put all the money in a trust fund to pay for college. She lived at home all year. Penelope meets the support test since her earnings were not used for her own support. Since she meets the tests for a qualifying child, Penelope can be claimed as a dependent by her parents.

Multiple Support Agreements: There are special rules for *multiple support* agreements. A *multiple support agreement* is when two or more people agree to join together to provide a person's support. This happens commonly with adult children who are taking care of their parents. There are special rules for claiming a dependency exemption when a taxpayer has a multiple support agreement. IRS **Form 2120** is used to declare a *multiple support agreement.*

Example: Benjamin and Matthew are two brothers who support their disabled mother Abigail. Abigail is 83 and lives with Benjamin. In 2010, Abigail receives 20% of her financial support from Social Security, 40% from Benjamin, and 60% from Matthew. Under the IRS rules for multiple support agreements, either Matthew or Benjamin can take the exemption for their mother if the other signs a statement agreeing not to do so. The one who takes the exemption must attach a **Form 2120** (or a similar declaration) to his tax return (Publication 17).

In order for a *multiple support agreement* to be valid, the taxpayer who claims the dependent must provide over 10% of the person's support, at a minimum.

Example: Olivia, Sophia, and Emily are sisters who help support their 72-year-old father Logan. Olivia provides 80% percent support, Sophia provides 15%, and Emily provides 5%. Under a multiple support agreement, either Olivia or Sophia can claim an exemption for their father. Emily did not provide over 10% of her father's support, so she is not eligible to claim him as a dependent. The one who claims the exemption must attach a **Form 2120** to her return. Emily does not have to sign the form (Publication 17).

---

4. Residence (or Abode) Test: In general, a *qualifying child* must live with the taxpayer for more than half the tax year (over six months). Exceptions apply for children of divorced parents, kidnapped children, temporary absences, and for children who were born or died during the year. [8]

A *temporary absence* includes illness, college, vacation, military service, and incarceration in a juvenile facility. It must be reasonable to assume that the absent child will return to the home after the temporary absence. The taxpayer must continue to maintain the home during the absence.

Example: Scott is unmarried and lives with his 10-year-old son Elijah. Scott provides all of Elijah's support. In 2010, Elijah became very ill and was hospitalized for seven months. Elijah is still considered Scott's qualifying child, because the illness and hospitalization count as a temporary absence from home. Scott may claim Elijah as his qualifying child and also file for Head of Household status.

Example: Gary and Andrea file jointly. They have one daughter named Isabella who is 32 years old. In March of 2009, Isabella moved back in with her parents. Isabella earned $13,000 at the beginning of 2009 before she was laid off. Gary and Andrea therefore provided the majority of Isabella's support for the rest of the year. Isabella got a new job in December and moved out. Isabella is not a qualifying child for federal tax purposes. Although Isabella meets the relationship, residence, and support test, she *does not* meet the age test.

---

[8] A taxpayer cannot claim an exemption for a stillborn child.

61

*Special rules: Kidnapped child: A taxpayer can treat a kidnapped child as meeting the residency test; but both of the following must be true:

- The child is presumed to have been kidnapped by someone who is not a family member.
- In the year the kidnapping occurred, the child lived with the taxpayer for more than half of the year before the kidnapping.

This special tax treatment applies for all years until the child is returned. However, the last year this treatment can apply is the earlier of:

- The year there is a determination that the child is dead, or
- The year the child would have reached age 18.

Tests for "Qualifying Relatives"

A person who is not a "qualifying child" may still qualify as a dependent under the rules for a qualifying relative. There is a five-part test for *qualifying relatives*. Under these tests, even an individual who is *not a family member* can still be a "qualifying relative." Unlike a qualifying child, a *qualifying relative* can be any age. There is no age test for a qualifying relative.

In order to be claimed as a "qualifying relative," the dependent must meet all of the following criteria:

1. Relationship Test (or Member of Household):

The dependent must be related to the taxpayer in certain ways. A family member who is related to the taxpayer in any of the following ways **does not** have to live with the taxpayer to meet this test:

- A child, stepchild, foster child, or a descendant of any of them (for example, a grandchild).
- A sibling, stepsibling, or a half sibling
- A parent, grandparent, stepparent, or other direct ancestor (but this does not include foster parents)
- A niece or nephew, a son-in-law, daughter-in-law, father-in-law, mother-in-law, brother-in-law, or sister-in-law[9]

- ***OR** the dependent **must have lived with** the taxpayer the ENTIRE tax year, and the individual cannot have earned more than the personal exemption amount (in 2010, the amount is $3,650).

---

[9] ***Note:** The listing of family members for the "relationship test" does NOT include COUSINS. A cousin must live with the taxpayer for the entire year and also meet the *gross income test* in order to qualify as a dependent. In that respect, they are treated by the IRS just like an unrelated person.

Example: Isaac's 12-year-old grandson Josh lived with him for three months in 2010. For the rest of the year, Josh lived with his mother Natalie in another state. Natalie is Isaac's 21-year-old daughter. Even though Josh and Natalie lived in another state, Isaac still provided all of their financial support. Josh is not Isaac's *qualifying child* because he does not meet the residency test (Josh did not live with Isaac for more than half the year). However, Josh is Isaac's *qualifying relative*. Natalie can also be Isaac's qualifying relative if the *gross income test* is met.

*Note: Any of these relationships that are established by marriage are *not ended* by death or divorce. So, for example, if a taxpayer supports a mother-in-law, he can continue to claim her as a dependent even if he and his ex-spouse are divorced or if he becomes widowed.

Example #1: Mia and Caleb have always financially supported Mia's elderly mother Gertrude and claim her as their dependent on their jointly filed returns. However, in 2009, Mia dies. Caleb remarries in 2010, but continues to support his former mother-in-law Gertrude. Caleb can continue to claim Gertrude on his tax returns, even though he has remarried. This is because of the special rule that dependency relationships established by marriage do not end by death or divorce.

Example #2: Bella and Dean are married. Together they support Dean's 18-year-old daughter Sarah. Sarah is Dean's daughter from a previous marriage. Dean dies in 2008, and Bella becomes a widow. In 2010, Bella remarries, but she continues to support Dean's daughter Sarah, her stepdaughter. Bella may continue to claim Sarah as her dependent since dependency relationships established by marriage do not end with death or divorce.

2. Dependency Test: The dependent cannot be claimed as a dependent of another taxpayer.

3. Gross Income Test: The dependent cannot earn more than the personal exemption amount. In 2010, the personal exemption amount is $3,650.

4. Support Test: A taxpayer must provide over half of the dependent's support during the year. "Support" includes amounts from Social Security and welfare payments, even if that support is nontaxable. "Support" does not include amounts received from nontaxable scholarships. Support can include the Fair Market Value of lodging.

Example #1: Ella is 78 and lives in her own apartment. She received $7,000 in Social Security benefits in 2010. Ella's daughter Rosalie provided $6,200 in support to her mother in 2010 by paying her utility bills and buying her groceries. Even though Ella's Social Security benefits are not taxable and she does not have a filing requirement, Rosalie cannot claim her mother as a dependent because Ella provided more than one-half of her own support.

Example #2: Nicholas lives with Gavin, who is an old army buddy of his. Nicholas provided all of the support for Gavin, who lived with Nicholas all year in his home. Gavin has no income and does not file a 2010 tax return. Nicholas can claim Gavin as his qualifying relative if all of the other tests are met.

Example #3: Ben lives with his brother Steven. Ben received $3,200 in wages in 2010. Steven provided $2,200 in monetary support to Ben in 2010 by paying his medical bills and groceries. However, Steven also provided a home for Ben, of which the Fair Rental Value was approximately $500 per month. Steven can claim his brother Ben as a dependent because Steven provided more than one-half of Ben's support.

5. Joint Return Test: If the dependent is married, the dependent cannot file a joint return with his or her spouse (the same exceptions apply for a qualifying relative as for qualifying children).

Child in Canada or Mexico

A child who lives in Canada or Mexico may be a qualifying relative of a US taxpayer. Even If the child does not live with the taxpayer, the child may still be eligible to be claimed as a *qualifying relative*. The example below is from IRS Publication 501.

Example: Manuel provides all the financial support of his children, ages 6 and 12, who live in Mexico with Manuel's mother. Manuel is unmarried and lives in the United States. He is a legal U.S. resident alien (green card holder) and has a valid Social Security Number. However, Manuel's children are citizens of Mexico. Regardless, both his children are still "qualifying relatives" for tax purposes. Manuel may claim them as dependents if all the tests are met. Manuel may also be able to claim his mother as a dependent if all the tests are met. He will have to request ITINs for his children and his mother using **Form W-7** (Publication 501).

The Exception for Divorced or Separated Parents

Generally, to claim a child as a dependent, the child must live with the taxpayer for over half the year (over six months). If the child did not live with the taxpayer, the custodial parent may still allow the noncustodial parent to claim the dependency exemption.

A noncustodial parent may still qualify to take the dependency exemption for a child if the custodial parent agrees in writing. The noncustodial parent must attach IRS **Form 8332** in order to claim the dependency exemption. A copy of a divorce decree is not sufficient.[10] Regardless of the language of a divorce agreement, without Form 8332 signed and attached to the return, the IRS will not recognize the deduction by a noncustodial parent.

If a divorce decree does not specify which parent is the custodial parent or which parent receives the dependency exemption, the exemption will automatically go to the parent who has physical custody for the majority of the year.

Example #1: Alexis and Nathan are divorced. They have one child named Dylan. In 2010, Dylan lived with Alexis for 210 nights and with Nathan for 155 nights. Therefore, Alexis is the custodial parent. Alexis has the right to claim Dylan on her tax return as her qualifying child. Alexis may release the exemption to Nathan by signing **Form 8332.**

*Note: Even if the custodial parent releases the dependency exemption, the custodial parent still has the right to claim Head of Household status, the Earned Income Credit, and

---

[10] A noncustodial parent claiming an exemption for a child can no longer attach pages from a divorce decree or separation agreement instead of Form 8332 if the decree or agreement was executed after 2008.

Dependent Care Credit. However, if the custodial parent waives the dependency exemption, the noncustodial parent may claim the child tax credit along with the dependency exemption.

A child will be treated as the qualifying child (or qualifying relative) of the noncustodial parent if ALL of the following apply:

- The parents are divorced or legally separated
- The parents are separated under a written separation agreement
- The parents lived apart at all times during the last six months of the year
- The child received over half of her support from the parents
- The child is in the custody of either of the parents for more than half of the year

A taxpayer *may not* claim a dependency exemption for a household employee (such as a housekeeper), even if the employee lived with the taxpayer.

The Kiddie Tax

The "kiddie tax" deals with the taxation of unearned income of children (such as interest income). Years ago, wealthy families would transfer investments to their minor children and save thousands of dollars in investment income because the money would be taxed at a lower rate. This was completely legal until Congress closed this tax loophole, and now, investment income earned by dependent children is taxed at the parents' marginal rate. This new law became known as the "kiddie tax." Originally, it only applied to children under age 14. In 2006, the age limit was increased to 18. In 2008, the kiddie tax was extended to apply to dependent students until they reach age 24.

The kiddie tax does not "kick in" until the dependent has a certain amount of investment income. In 2010, the threshold is $1,900 in investment income. The kiddie tax does not apply to wages or self-employment income—it applies to *investment income* only. Examples of unearned income include bank interest, dividends, and capital gains distributions.

A child may still owe income tax, even with less than $1,900 in income. But this is rare. The $1,900 threshold only applies to investment income. Until the child turns 18, (or a full-time student up to age 24) the kiddie tax is applied automatically if investment income is above $1,900.

The kiddie tax rules allow children under 19 (24 if a student) to have unearned income (interest, rental, capital gain, dividends, etc.) up to $950 in 2010 and to use their standard deduction to shelter it from tax. The next $950 in 2010 of income is taxed at the child's tax rate. Any additional unearned income to the child will be taxed at the marginal tax rate of his parents. If the parents are divorced or single, the rate taxed to the child (above $1,900) will be the higher of the two parents'.

Any additional investment income would then be taxed at the parents' rate (*remember, the Kiddie Tax rules apply to passive income, not to wages!). For 2010, a person who is claimed as a dependent is entitled to a standard deduction amount of the **larger** of:

   o Earned income (such as wages) + $300, or
   o $950 (unearned income)

Example: Bill and Donna have one 14-year-old son named Jack. In 2010, Jack has $2,900 of interest income. He does not have any other income. The first $950 of investment income is not taxable, because the standard deduction for dependents is $950. The next $950 will be taxed at the 10% income tax rate. The remainder, $1,000, will be taxed at the parents' tax rate.

After the child turns 18, the kiddie tax applies *unless* her earned income is more than half her overall support. In this case, "earned income" could be income from wages or self-employment. For dependents who are 19 to 23 years old, the kiddie tax applies to a dependent child who is a full-time student *unless* the child's earned income is more than half her overall support.

The kiddie tax does not apply if the child is Married Filing Jointly.

There are two ways to report investment income for a child and the resulting kiddie tax. First, the parents may choose to report the child's income on their own return. A parent can do so by attaching **Form 8814,** *Parents' Election to Report Child's Interest and Dividends,* to the return.

In order to use Form 8814 to report a dependent's income, the child's investment income must be *more than* $950 and less than $9,500.

If the parent chooses instead to report his child's investment income on a separate return, the child must report the income on **Form 1040** and include **Form 8615,** *Tax for Certain Children Who Have Investment Income of More Than $1,900.* **Form 8615** figures the tax computation using the parent's highest marginal tax rate.

Summary of Dependency and Exemption Rules

1. You cannot claim any dependents if you, or your spouse if filing jointly, could be claimed as a dependent by another taxpayer.

2. You cannot claim a married person who files a joint return as a dependent unless the joint return is only a claim for refund and there would be no tax liability for either spouse on separate returns.

3. You cannot claim a person as a dependent unless that person is a U.S. citizen, U.S. resident alien, U.S. national, or a resident of Canada or Mexico, for some part of the year (Publication 501).

Tests for a **Qualifying Relative**

The person cannot be the qualifying child of anyone else.
The person either (a) must be related to the taxpayer in certain ways OR (b) must live with the taxpayer all year as a member of the household. There is no age test for a qualifying relative.
The person's gross income for the year must be less than $3,650.
The taxpayer must provide more than half of the person's total support for the year.

Tests for a **Qualifying Child**

The child must be a son, daughter, stepchild, foster child, brother, sister, half-brother, half-sister, stepbrother, stepsister, or a descendant of any of these.
The child must be (a) Under age 19 at the end of the year and younger than you (or your spouse, if filing jointly), (b) Under age 24 at the end of the year, a full-time student, and younger than you (or your spouse, if filing jointly), or (c) Any age if disabled.
The child must have lived with the taxpayer for more than half of the year (over six months). Exceptions exist for temporary absences, kidnapped children, and dependents that died/were born during the year.
The child must not have provided more than half of his own support for the year.
The child cannot file a joint return for the year (unless that joint return is filed only as a claim for refund).
If the child meets the rules to be a qualifying child of more than one person, only one taxpayer can claim the child.

Unit 1.3: Questions

1. Ray is a client who tells you that his wife died in September 2010. Based on this information, Ray can claim _____.

A. Only the personal exemption for himself
B. Only the personal exemption for his wife
C. Personal exemptions for both himself and for his wife
D. A personal exemption for himself and a partial exemption for his wife

The answer is C. In 2010, Ray can claim a personal exemption for his deceased wife, along with a personal exemption for himself. A taxpayer whose spouse dies during the year may file jointly in the year of death. ###

2. Alyssa is 18 years old and a full-time student. She comes into your office with some questions about her tax return. She says that she is claimed as a dependent on her parents' tax return. Over the summer, she worked in a clothing boutique and earned $17,000. Alyssa wants to file Form 1040EZ to report her wage income and get a refund. How many exemptions may she claim on her tax return?

A. Zero
B. One
C. Two
D. Three

The answer is A. Since Alyssa is claimed as a dependent on her parents' tax return, she cannot claim an exemption for herself. Therefore, her total number of exemptions is zero. She can still file a tax return in order to claim a refund of taxes withheld. ###

3. John is the sole support of his mother. To claim her as a dependent on his Form 1040, John's mother must be a resident of which of the following countries?

A. United States
B. Mexico
C. Canada
D. Any of the above

The answer is D. To qualify as a dependent, the dependent must be a citizen or resident alien of the United States, Canada, or Mexico (Publication 17). ###

4. Avery, 52, is a single father with one adopted son named Wyatt who has Down syndrome. Wyatt is 32 years old and permanently disabled. He lives with Avery, who supports him. Wyatt had $800 in interest income and $2,000 in wages from a part-time job in 2010. Which of the following statements is true?

A. Avery can file as Head of Household, with Wyatt as his qualifying child.
B. Avery does not qualify for Head of Household, but he could still claim Wyatt as his qualifying child.
C. Avery can file as Head of Household, with Wyatt as his qualifying relative, since Wyatt does not pass the Age Test for a qualifying child.
D. Avery must file Single and he can claim Wyatt only as his qualifying relative.

The answer is A. Even though Wyatt is over the normal age threshold for a qualifying child, he is still considered a qualifying child for tax purposes. This is because Wyatt is disabled and Avery provides his financial support and care. ###

5. Clifford and Lily divorced in 2009 and they have one child together. Clifford's child lived with him for ten months of the year in 2010. The child lived with Lily for the other two months. The divorce decree states that Lily is supposed to be the custodial parent, not Clifford. Who is considered the custodial parent for IRS purposes?

A. Clifford
B. Lily
C. Neither
D. Both

The answer is A. For IRS purposes, the "custodial parent" is the parent with whom the child lived for the greater part of the year. The other parent is the non-custodial parent. If the parents divorced or separated during the year and the child lived with both parents before the separation, the custodial parent is the one with whom the child lived for the greater part of the rest of the year (Publication 501). ###

6. Haley is 23 and a full-time college student. During the year, Haley lived at home with her parents for four months and lived in the dorm for the remainder of the year. During the tax year, Haley worked part-time and earned $6,000, but that income did not amount to half of her total support. Can Haley's parents still claim her as a dependent?

A. No, because Haley earned more than the personal exemption amount.
B. No, because Haley does not meet the age test.
C. Yes, Haley's parents can claim her as a qualifying child.
D. Yes, Haley's parents can claim her as a dependent, but only as a qualifying relative, not as a qualifying child.

The answer is C. Haley meets all the qualifying child tests: the relationship test; the age test (because she is under 24 and was a full-time student for at least five months of the year); the residence test (because the time spent at college is a legitimate temporary absence); and the support test (because she did not provide over half of her own support).

7. Carson has a 12-year-old daughter named Emma. In 2010, Emma had $900 in interest income from a bank account. Which of the following statements regarding Emma's unearned income is correct?

A. Tax will be assessed to Carson and is calculated using Emma's tax rate.
B. Emma is not required to file a return, and Carson is not required to report his daughter's income on his own tax return.
C. Emma is required to file a tax return, and income tax will be assessed at a flat rate of 10%.
D. Carson may elect to report Emily's interest income on his own tax return. Her income will be taxed at the parents' highest marginal rate.

The answer is B. Emma is not required to file a tax return, because her unearned income is less than the standard deduction amount for dependents. The first $950 of investment income (which is equal to the dependent's standard deduction) escapes income tax. Emma has no filing requirement, and her father is not required to report the income on his own return. The next $950 is taxable at the minor's minimum tax rate. Tax on the unearned income only in excess of $1,900 for a minor under the age of 19 (under 24 if a student) is calculated using the parents' marginal tax rate. ###

8. Chloe's nephew Bradley lived with her all year and was 18 years old at the end of the year. Bradley did not provide more than half of his own support. He had $4,200 in income from wages and $1,000 in investment income. Which of the following is true?

A. Bradley qualifies as Chloe's "qualifying child" for tax purposes.
B. Bradley is not a qualifying child; however, he can be claimed by Chloe as a qualifying relative.
C. Bradley is not a qualifying child or qualifying relative, because he had income that exceeded the personal exemption amount.
D. Chloe can claim Bradley only if he is a full-time student, since he is no longer a minor child.

The answer is A. Bradley is Chloe's qualifying child because he meets the age test, support test, and relationship test. Also, because Bradley is single, he is a qualifying person for Chloe to claim Head of Household filing status. Bradley is not required to be a full-time student, because the IRS says that any child under the age of 19 at the end of the tax year will be treated as a qualifying child if all the other tests are met. Bradley is only 18 years old, and therefore, he passes the age test (Publication 501). ###

9. Jon and Suzanna have two children: Wendy, age 13, and Rachel, age 16. Wendy received $948 in dividends on XYZ stock that she legally owns. Rachel worked part-time at the mall during the Christmas holiday and earned $5,600. Rachel also held stocks in an account in her name but no dividends were paid. Which statement is TRUE with regard to filing tax returns for Jon and Suzanna's two children?

Wendy: $0 Wages, $948 interest income
Rachel: $5,500 Wages, $10 interest income
A. Both children are required to file a tax return.
B. Rachel needs to file, but Wendy does not.
C. Wendy needs to file, but Rachel does not.
D. Neither needs to file a tax return.

The answer is D. For dependent children, a return must be filed only if there is any unearned income that exceeds $950 (Wendy's unearned income was less than $950; therefore, she has no filing requirement). If there is only earned income and it does not exceed the standard deduction amount for a single taxpayer, the dependent is not required to file (Rachel had only $10 in unearned income and her earned income was less than the standard deduction amount of $5,700 for 2010). Rachel may still choose to file an income tax return in order to obtain a refund for any income tax that was withheld by her employer. ###

10. Donnie's daughter Violet, age 16, lived with him for six months of the year. Donnie also paid for Violet to go to summer camp for two months. Violet then lived with Donnie's ex-wife for the rest of the year. Who is considered the custodial parent for tax purposes?

A. Donnie
B. Donnie's ex-wife
C. Neither
D. The summer camp director

The answer is A. The time at summer camp would be considered a temporary absence. The custodial parent is the parent with whom the child lived for the greater part of the year. Therefore, Donnie is allowed to claim Violet as his qualifying child. Under the special rules for divorced parents, Donnie may release the exemption for Violet to his ex-wife using IRS Form 8332 (Publication 504). ###

11. Tony and Isabelle are the sole support of the following individuals (All are U.S. citizens but none lives with them, files a tax return, or has any income):

1. Jennie, Tony's grandmother
2. Julie, Isabelle's stepmother
3. Jonathan, father of Tony's first wife
4. Timothy, Isabelle's cousin
How many exemptions may Tony and Isabelle claim on their joint return?

A. 3
B. 2
C. 4
D. 5
E. 6

The answer is D. They may take three dependency exemptions on their tax return, and two personal exemptions for themselves. The taxpayers may take dependency exemptions for all the dependents listed, except for Timothy. Timothy would have to live with Tony and Isabelle all year in order for them to claim him as their dependent. Parents (or grandparents, in-laws, stepparents, etc.) do not have to live with a taxpayer in order to qualify as dependents. Tony can claim Jonathan, because Jonathan was once his father-in-law. Relationships established by marriage do not end in death or divorce for tax purposes (Publication 17). ###

12. In a multiple support agreement, what is the minimum amount of support that a taxpayer can provide and still claim the dependent?

A. 10% support
B. 15% support
C. 50% support
D. 75% support

The answer is A. The law provides for multiple-support agreements. These multiple-support agreements usually exist when family members collectively support a relative, oftentimes a parent. The taxpayer can claim the dependent if he paid more than 10% of the support. ###

13. Ted and Sharon (husband and wife) are the sole support of their 23-year-old son Ashton, who lives with them. Ashton is not a student. Ashton was unable to find steady work in 2010, but received $4,900 from a charitable foundation for a speaking engagement. Which of the following statements is true?

A. Ted and Sharon may claim Ashton as a qualifying child on their 2010 federal income tax return.
B. Ted and Sharon may claim Ashton as a qualifying relative on their 2010 federal income tax return.
C. Ted and Sharon may not claim Ashton as a dependent in 2010.
D. None of the above.

The answer is C. Ashton is not a minor, and does not pass the "Gross Income Test." The person must have gross income of less than $3,650 for the tax year 2010. A dependent must either (a) be a child who is under the age of 19, or under the age of 24 and a full-time student, OR (b) have gross income that is less than the amount of the dependency exemption for the year. Since Ashton earned $4,900 in 2010, he cannot be claimed as a dependent. ###

14. If a child being adopted is eligible to be claimed as a dependent by the adoptive parents, what must occur in order for the child to be taken as a dependent on the adoptive parents' tax return?

A. An identifying number must be obtained for the child (an ATIN, ITIN, or Social Security Number).
B. The adoption must become final first.
C. The child must always be related to the taxpayer by blood.
D. Only domestic adoptions qualify; a taxpayer cannot claim a dependency exemption for a foreign-born child.

The answer is A. A Tax Identification Number must be obtained for the child. The adoption does not have to be final. Parents in the process of a U.S. adoption who are unable to obtain the child's Social Security Number should request an Adoption Taxpayer Identification Number (ATIN) in order to claim the child as a dependent. The term "adopted child" includes a child who was lawfully placed with the taxpayer for legal adoption (The adoption does not have to be final for the parents to take a dependency exemption if the child has been lawfully placed by a government authority or U.S. court). ###

15. There are many tests which must be met for a taxpayer to claim an exemption for a dependent as a qualifying relative. Which of the following is NOT a requirement?

A. Citizen or Resident Test
B. Member of Household or Relationship Test
C. Disability Test
D. Joint Return Test

The answer is C. There is no such thing as a "disability test." To be claimed as a qualifying relative, the person (dependent) must meet all of the following criteria:
1. Dependent of another taxpayer – the dependent cannot be a qualifying child of another taxpayer.
2. Gross Income – The dependent must earn less than the personal exemption amount during the year.
3. Support Test – The dependent cannot provide more than half of his total support during the year.
4. Relationship – The taxpayer must be "related" to the dependent in certain ways (see a complete listing in the study unit).
5. Joint Return – The dependent cannot file a joint return with his/her spouse. ###

16. Peter filed for divorce in 2010. He and his wife moved into separate residences on April 20, 2010. Peter's 10-year-old daughter lived with him for the entire year in 2010. Peter owns the home and pays all the costs of upkeep for it. His ex-wife did not live in the home at any time during the year. Which of the following is true?

A. Peter must file jointly with his wife in 2010, since they are still legally married. They may claim their daughter as a dependent on their jointly filed return.
B. Peter must file Single in 2010.
C. Peter must file MFS in 2010.
D. Peter qualifies for HOH filing status.

The answer is D. Peter qualifies for Head of Household filing status. Since Peter and his wife lived in separate residences for the last six months of the year and Peter had a qualifying child, he may file as Head of Household (Publication 17). ###

17. Tyler is single and 17 years old. He works a part-time job at night and is going to school full-time. His total income for 2010 was $10,500. Tyler lives with his parents, who provided the majority of Tyler's support. Tyler's parents are claiming him as a dependent on their 2010 tax return. Which of the following statements is true?

A. Tyler is required file his own return, and he may also take an exemption for himself.
B. Tyler is not required to file his own return.
C. Tyler's parents may not claim him as a dependent because Tyler earned more than the standard deduction amount for 2010.
D. His parents may claim Tyler as their qualifying child. Tyler is required to file a tax return, but he cannot claim a personal exemption for himself. He is still entitled to the standard deduction for SINGLE filers.

The answer is D. Tyler's parents may claim him as their qualifying child because he is a minor child under the age of 19 and does not provide more than half of his own support. Since his earned income was more than $5,700 in 2010, Tyler is required to file a tax return but cannot claim an exemption for himself (Publication 501). ###

Unit 1.4: Due Dates, Estimated Payments, and Extensions

More Reading:
Publication 505, *Tax Withholding and Estimated Tax*
Publication 594, *Understanding the Collection Process*
Publication3, *Armed Forces' Tax Guide*

Due Dates and Extensions for Individual Tax Returns

The regular due date for individual tax returns is *usually* April 15. If April 15 falls on a Saturday, Sunday, or legal holiday, the due date will be delayed until the next business day. In 2011, there is a legal holiday in Washington, D.C. on April 15. Therefore, the IRS has extended the due date for 2010 individual tax returns to **April 18, 2011.** Extended individual tax returns are due by **October 17, 2011** (the normal IRS deadline is October 15).

If the taxpayer cannot file his tax return by the due date, he may request an extension by filing IRS **Form 4868**, *Application for Automatic Extension of Time to File*. An extension will grant a taxpayer an additional six months to file his individual tax return. **Form 4868** may be filed electronically. An extension will give a taxpayer extra time to file his return, but it does not extend the time to pay any tax due.

A taxpayer will owe interest on any unpaid amount that is not paid by the filing deadline, plus a late payment penalty if she has not paid at least 90 percent of her total tax due by that date. Taxpayers are expected to estimate and pay the amount of tax due by the filing deadline.

The IRS will accept a postmark as proof of a timely-filed return. For example, if the tax return is postmarked on April 10 but does not arrive at the IRS Service Center until April 30, the IRS will accept the tax return as having been filed on time. You will need to memorize the due dates for tax returns and extensions for the EA Exam.

Penalties and Interest

An extension only grants a taxpayer additional time to file, not additional time to pay. Interest and penalties will continue to accrue on any unpaid balance until the taxpayer finally files his tax return and pays any amounts that are owed. There are three separate penalties:

- Failure-to-file penalty (the failure to file on time)
- Failure-to-pay penalty (the failure to pay on time)
- Interest on the delinquent amount due

An extension request allows a taxpayer to avoid the "failure to file" penalty. The *failure to file* penalty can be up to a maximum of 25% of the additional tax due on the return. The *failure to file* penalty is calculated based on the time from the deadline of the tax return to the date the taxpayer actually files her tax return. The penalty is 5% for each month the tax return is late, up to a total maximum of 25%.

77

If the taxpayer has filed an extension on time and files his tax return on or before October 15, the IRS will not assess a "failure to file" penalty; however, the taxpayer will still be responsible for interest and a penalty for *failure to pay*.

Estimated Tax Payments

The federal income tax is a "pay-as-you-go tax." A taxpayer must pay taxes as she earns or receives income throughout the year. If a taxpayer earns income that is not subject to withholding (such as self-employment income, rents, alimony, etc.), she will often be required to make estimated tax payments each quarter of the tax year.

Taxes are generally not withheld from payments that are made to independent contractors (1099 income). Taxes are withheld from wages, salaries, and pensions. Taxpayers can avoid making estimated tax payments by ensuring they have enough tax withheld from their income.

A taxpayer must make estimated tax payments if:

- He expects to owe at least $1,000 in tax (after subtracting withholding and tax credits)
- He expects the total amount of withholding and tax credits to be less than the smaller of:
    - 100% of the tax shown on the taxpayer's prior year return
    - 90% of the tax shown on the taxpayer's current year return

A U.S. citizen or U.S. resident is not required to make estimated tax payments if he had zero tax liability in the prior year.[11]

> **Example**: Cassius, who is single and 25 years old, was unemployed for most of 2009. He earned $2,700 in wages before he was laid off, and he received $1,500 in unemployment compensation afterward. He had no other income. Even though he had gross income of $4,200, he did not have to pay income tax because his gross income was less than the filing requirement. In 2010, Cassius began working as a self-employed independent contractor. He made no estimated tax payments in 2010. Even though he owed $5,000 in tax at the end of the year, Cassius does not owe the underpayment penalty for 2010 because he had no tax liability in the prior year.

Generally, a taxpayer will not have an underpayment penalty if either:

- Total estimated tax is less than $1,000, or
- The taxpayer had no tax liability for the prior year.

Safe Harbor Rule for Estimated Payments

The majority of taxpayers who pay estimated tax rely on the "Safe Harbor Rule" in order to avoid any potential penalties.

Regardless of the taxpayer's income level, there will be no underpayment penalty if the taxpayer pays at least 90% of whatever the current year's tax bill turns out to be.

---

[11] This rule only applies to U.S. citizens or residents; it does not apply to nonresident aliens.

Since it is often difficult to guess what a person or business will earn during the year, most taxpayers find it easier to use the Safe Harbor Rule.

The first "safe harbor" applies to taxpayers whose adjusted gross income is $150,000 or less.[12] The taxpayer will not be assessed penalties in 2011 if the taxpayer pays *at least* the amount of the tax liability on her 2010 tax return (the amount on line 60 of Form 1040 reduced by any tax credits).

> **Example:** Gerald earned $95,000 in 2010. His overall tax liability for the tax year was $8,200 (after taking into account his deductions and credits). Although Gerald expects his income to increase in 2011, he will not be assessed a penalty for underpayment of estimated taxes as long as he pays at least $8,200 in estimated tax during the year.

*Note: For high income taxpayers with an Adjusted Gross Income of over $150,000 ($75,000 if MFS), the safe harbor amount is 110% of the previous year's tax liability.

Less Than $1,000 Due

A taxpayer will not face an underpayment penalty if the total tax shown on her return (minus the amount paid through withholding) is less than $1,000.

> **Example:** Dominique has a full-time job as a secretary. She also earns money as a self-employed manicurist part-time. In 2010, she did not make estimated payments. However, Dominique made sure to increase her withholding at her job in order to cover any amounts that she would have to pay on her self-employment earnings. When she files her 2010 tax return, she discovers that she owes $750. She will not owe an underpayment penalty, because the total tax shown on her return was less than $1,000.

Estimated Payment Due Dates (Quarterly Payments)

For estimated tax purposes, the year is divided into four payment periods. Each period has a specific payment due date. Taxpayers generally must have made their first estimated tax payment for the year by April 15.[13] If the due date falls on a Saturday, Sunday, or legal holiday, the due date is the next business day. If a payment is mailed, the date of the U.S. postmark is considered the date of payment.

> First Payment Due: April 15
> Second Payment Due: June 15
> Third Payment Due: September 15
> Fourth Payment Due: January 15 (of the following year)

Special Exception for Farmers and Fishermen

Estimated tax requirements are different for farmers and fishermen. Farmers and fishermen are not required to pay estimated taxes throughout the year. Farmers and fish-

---

[12]No underpayment penalty will apply if the balance on the 2010 tax return is $1,000 or less.

[13] Don't forget that April 15 is a holiday in Washington, D.C. in 2011, so the due date has been extended to April 18.

ermen that receive at least *two-thirds of their gross income* from farming or fishing activities may pay all their estimated tax in one installment.

Qualified farmers and fishermen only have one due date for estimated taxes (if they choose). The farmers and fishermen have two choices:

- They may pay all of their 2010 estimated taxes by January 15, 2011, OR
- If they are able to file their 2010 tax return by March 1, 2011 and pay all the tax they owe, they do not need to make an estimated tax payment.

Example #1: Jay is the self-employed owner of a commercial fishing vessel. One hundred percent of his income is from commercial fishing. Therefore, Jay is not required to pay quarterly estimated taxes. Jay's records are incomplete, so he asks his tax accountant to file an extension on his behalf. Since Jay is unable to file his tax return by March 1, 2011, his Enrolled Agent notifies Jay that he is required to pay his estimated taxes in a lump sum by January 15, 2011.

Example #2: Karla owns a farm, and 100 percent of her income is from farming. She is not required to pay quarterly estimated taxes. Karla filed her tax return on February 20, 2011 and enclosed a check for her entire balance due, which was $4,900. Since Karla filed before the March 1 deadline, she will not be subject to any penalty.

*NOTE: Income from **wages** received as an employee (on a farm or a fishing vessel) is not considered "farm income" for the purpose of this rule.

Backup Withholding

Sometimes, individuals will be subject to "backup withholding." This is when an entity is required to "withhold" certain amounts from a payment, and remit the amounts to the IRS. Most US taxpayers are exempt from back-up withholding. However, the IRS requires backup withholding if a taxpayer's name and Social Security Number on **Form W-9,** *Request for Taxpayer Identification Number and Certification* does not match their records.

Example: Heath owns a number of investments through the Big Corp Investment Company. In 2010, the IRS notifies Big Corp that Heath's Social Security Number is incorrect. Big Corp notifies Heath by mail that they need his correct Social Security Number, or they will have to start automatic backup withholding on his investment income. Heath ignores the notice. Big Corp is forced to begin backup withholding on Heath's investment income.

The IRS will often require mandatory backup withholding if a taxpayer has a delinquent tax debt, or if a taxpayer fails to report all their interest, dividends and other income.

Payments that may be subject to "backup withholding" include interest, dividends, rents, and royalties, payments to independent contractors for services, and broker payments. The current backup withholding rate is 28%. Under the backup withholding rules, the business or bank must withhold on a payment if:

- The individual did not provide the payer with a valid Taxpayer Identification Number or Social Security Number.
- The IRS notified the payer that the Taxpayer Identification Number (or SSN) is incorrect.

- The IRS has notified the payer to start withholding on interest and dividends because the payee failed to report income in prior years; or
- The payee failed to certify that it was not subject to backup withholding for underreporting of interest and dividends.

If a taxpayer wishes to change his withholding amounts, **Form W4,** *Employee's Withholding Allowance Certificate,* is used to change withholding from wages. The employee must submit this form to his employer, NOT to the IRS.

Oddball Situations

There are special rules that are favorable for taxpayers who live outside the United States. A taxpayer will be granted an automatic two-month extension to file **and pay any tax due** if the taxpayer is a U.S. citizen or legal U.S. resident AND

- The taxpayer is living outside the United States and her main place of business is outside the United States; OR
- The taxpayer is on military service duty outside the U.S.

Special Deadlines Exist for Taxpayers Serving in a Combat Zone

Additionally, the deadline for filing a tax return, claim for refund, AND deadline for tax owed will be automatically extended for any service member, Red Cross personnel, accredited correspondents, or contracted civilians serving in a combat zone. In fact, taxpayers serving in a combat zone have all of their tax deadlines suspended until they leave the combat zone.

> **Example:** Philip is a member of the U.S. Armed Forces who has been serving in a combat zone since March 1. Philip is entitled to an extension of time for filing and paying his federal income taxes. In addition, IRS deadlines for filing, collections, etc., are suspended while Philip is serving in the combat zone, **plus** another 180 days after his last day in the combat zone. During this period, assessment and collection deadlines are extended, and Philip will not be charged interest or penalties attributable to the extension period.

The deadline extension provisions apply not only to members serving in the U.S. Armed Forces in combat zones, but to their spouses as well.

Statute of Limitations for Claiming a Refund

Generally, the taxpayer must file a claim for a credit or refund within three years from the date of the original return was filed or two years from the date the taxpayer paid the tax, whichever is later.[14]

There is no penalty for failure to file if the taxpayer is due a refund. However, the taxpayer may have many legal deductions that the IRS doesn't know about. In order to claim a refund and avoid possible collection action, a tax return must be filed. If the taxpayer does not file a claim for a refund within this three-year period, he usually won't be entitled to a credit or a refund.

---

[14] Section 6511 (3-year refund statute)

> **Example:** Juan wants to file six years of delinquent tax returns: 2004 through 2009. He files the returns and realizes that he had refunds for each year. If Juan files all the back tax returns by April 18, 2010, Juan will receive the refunds for his 2006, 2007, 2008, and 2009 tax returns. His refunds for 2004 and 2005, however, have expired.

> **Example:** David made estimated tax payments of $1,000 and filed an extension to file his 2006 income tax return. When David filed his return on August 15, 2007, he paid an additional $200 tax due. Three years later, on August 15, 2010, David files an amended return and claims a refund of $700.

The same statute of limitations applies on refunds being claimed on amended returns. In general, if a refund is expected on an amended return, taxpayers must file the return within three years from the due date of the original return, or within two years after the date they paid the tax, whichever is later.

> **Example:** Luciano's 2007 tax return was due April 15, 2008. He filed it on March 20, 2008. In 2010, Luciano discovered that he missed a big deduction on his 2007 return. Now he wants to amend his 2007 return, expecting the correction to result in a large refund. If he gets it postmarked on or before April 18, 2011, it will be within the three-year limit and the return will be accepted. But if the amended 2007 return is received by the IRS after April 18, 2011, it will fall outside the three-year period and Luciano will not receive the refund.

Special Cases (Extended Statute for Claiming Refunds)

In some cases, a request for a tax refund will be honored past the normal three-year deadline. These special cases are:

- A bad debt from a worthless security (up to seven years prior)
- A payment or accrual of foreign tax
- A net operating loss carryback
- A carryback of certain tax credits
- An injured spouse claim (may be filed for up to seven prior years)
- Exceptions for military personnel

Time periods for claiming a refund are also extended when a taxpayer is "financially disabled." This usually requires that the taxpayer be mentally or physically disabled to the point that he is unable to manage his financial affairs. If the taxpayer qualifies, he may file a refund after the three year period of limitations.

Statute of Limitations for IRS Audit

The IRS is required to assess tax or audit a taxpayer's return within three years after the return is filed.[15] If a taxpayer files his tax return late, then the IRS has the later of three years from:

- The due date of the return or
- The date the return was actually filed.

---

[15] Internal Revenue Code, Section 6501 (3-year audit statute)

If a taxpayer never files a return, the statute will remain open. If a taxpayer files her return prior to the April 15 deadline, the time is measured from the April 15 deadline. If a taxpayer omitted 25% of her income or more, the IRS has up to six years to assess a deficiency.

There is an exception for outright fraud; if the taxpayer files a fraudulent tax return, the statute for IRS audit never expires. However, the burden of proof switches to the IRS in cases where the statute has expired.

> **Example:** Caroline filed her 2007 tax return on February 27, 2008. The three-year statute period for an audit began April 15, 2008 (the filing deadline) and will stop on April 15, 2011. After that date, the IRS must be able to prove fraud or a substantial understatement of income (25% or more) in order to audit the tax return.

Statute of Limitations for IRS Collections

The statute of limitations for IRS collection is ten years.[16] However, the clock only starts ticking when the return is filed. The statute of limitations on a tax assessment begins on the day after the taxpayer files his tax return. If a taxpayer never files a return, the IRS can attempt to collect indefinitely. In other words, there is no statute of limitations for assessing and collecting tax if no return has been filed.

The ten-year period begins on the day after the date of assessment; that is, the date of assessment is excluded from the computation of the ten-year period.

Statute of Limitations: Snapshot	
Claims for a refund	Three years from the time the original return was filed, or two years from the time the tax was paid, (whichever is later)
IRS assessment	Three years after return is considered filed. Exceptions apply in cases of fraud, failure to file, and substantial omission.
Collections	The statute of limitations for IRS collections is 10 years from the date of assessment.

---

[16] Section 6502 (10-year debt collection statute)

Unit 1.4: Questions

1. Rory filed his 2010 Form 1040 on February 20, 2011. Later, he finds an error that would result in a larger refund. What is the last day that Rory can amend his 2010 tax return and still receive a refund?

A. April 15, 2010
B. February 20, 2011
C. April 15, 2014
D. April 15, 2013

The answer is C. Rory has until April 15, 2014 to file an amended return. After that date, his refund "expires." The tax code says that a taxpayer has three years from the original filing deadline to claim a refund. ###

2. Which statement pertaining to estimated tax payments is NOT correct?

A. An individual whose only income is from self-employment will have to pay estimated payments.
B. If insufficient tax is paid through withholding, estimated payments may still be necessary.
C. Estimated tax payments are required when the withholding taxes are greater than the overall tax liability.
D. Estimated tax is used to pay not only income tax, but self-employment tax and Alternative Minimum Tax as well.

The answer is C. If a taxpayer's withholding *exceeds* his tax liability, no estimated payments would be required. The taxpayer would get a refund of the overpaid tax when he files his tax return. ###

3. Which of the following is NOT an acceptable reason for extending the statute of limitations for a refund (past the normal deadline)?

A. A bad debt from a worthless security
B. Living outside the country for three years
C. Exceptions for military personnel
D. An injured spouse claim

The answer is A. Living outside the country is not a valid excuse for extending the statute of limitations for claiming a refund. In some cases, a request for a tax refund will be honored past the normal three-year deadline. ###

4. Dottie is a U.S. resident who paid estimated tax in 2009 totaling $2,500. In 2010, Dottie quit her business as a self-employed contractor and is now unemployed. She expects to have zero tax liability in 2010. Which of the following statements is true?

A. Dottie is still required to make estimated tax payments in 2010.
B. Dottie is not required to make estimated tax payments in 2010.
C. Dottie must pay a minimum of $2,500 in estimated tax in 2010, or she will be subject to a penalty.
D. Dottie must make a minimum of $2,250 (90% X $2,500) in estimated tax payments in 2010, or she will be subject to a penalty.

The answer is B. A taxpayer is not required to pay estimated tax if she expects to have zero tax liability. ###

5. Charles had a $4,500 tax liability in 2009. In 2010, Charles expects to owe approximately $3,200 in federal taxes. In 2010 he has $1,200 in income tax withheld from his paycheck. Which of the following statements is true?

A. Charles does not need to pay estimated taxes in 2010.
B. Charles is required to make estimated tax payments in 2010.
C. Charles is required to adjust his withholding. He cannot make estimated tax payments because he is an employee.
D. None of the above.

The answer is B. Charles is required to make estimated tax payments because his expected tax liability for 2010 exceeds $1,000. His withholding is insufficient to cover his tax liability. If Charles does not adjust his withholding, he will be required to make estimated tax payments. Charles could elect to adjust his withholding with his employer so the taxes are taken out of his pay automatically. ###

6. Audrey is self-employed and expects to owe $2,500 in taxes for 2010. Her tax liability for her prior tax year was zero, because her business had a loss. Which of the following is true?

A. Audrey is required to pay estimated tax in 2010.
B. Audrey is NOT required to pay estimated tax for 2010.
C. Audrey must pay at least $1,500 in estimated tax for 2010.
D. None of the above.

The answer is B. Since Audrey had no tax due on her prior year return, she is not required to pay estimated tax. The taxpayer must pay estimated tax *only if both* of the following apply:
1. The taxpayer expects to owe at least $1,000 in tax after subtracting withholding and credits.
2. The taxpayer expects withholding and credits to be less than the smaller of (1) 90% of the tax to be shown on a current year tax return, or (2) 100% of the tax shown on the prior year tax return. ###

7. Which of the following statements is TRUE regarding the filing of **Form 4868**, *Application for an Automatic Extension of Time to File?*

A. Interest is not assessed on any income tax due if Form 4868 is filed.
B. Form 4868 provides the taxpayer with an automatic six-month extension to file and pay.
C. Even though a taxpayer files Form 4868, she will owe interest and may be charged a late payment penalty on the amount owed if the tax is not paid by the due date.
D. A U.S. citizen, who is out of the country on vacation on April 18, 2011, will be allowed an additional twelve months to file as long as "Out of the Country" is written across the top of Form 1040.

The answer is C. If a taxpayer is not able to file her income tax return by the due date, she can get an automatic six-month extension of time to file. To do so, she must file an extension by the due date. Even though a taxpayer files Form 4868, she will owe interest and may be charged a late payment penalty on the amount owed if she does not pay the tax due by the regular due date. ###

Unit 1.5: Types of Taxable and Nontaxable Income

> **More Reading:**
> Publication 504, *Divorced or Separated Individuals*
> Publication 4681, *Canceled Debts, Foreclosures, Repossessions, and Abandonments*
> Publication 514, *Foreign Tax Credit for Individuals*
> Publication 550, *Investment Income and Expenses*
> Publication 529, *Miscellaneous Deductions*
> Publication 525, *Taxable and Nontaxable Income*

Gross income includes all money, goods, property, and services that are not exempt from tax. In addition to wages, salaries, commissions, fees, and tips, this includes other forms of compensation such as fringe benefits and stock options.

Basically, all income is taxable unless otherwise exempt. The IRS's position is that all income is taxable unless it is specifically excluded.

Do not confuse an *exclusion* with a *tax deduction*. "Exclusions" are sources of income that are completely nontaxable. A "deduction" is an expense that is deductible from a taxpayer's gross income. It is important to understand the difference, because many deductions are phased out as the taxpayer's gross income increases. However, excluded income generally retains its character as excluded income, no matter what the taxpayer's actual gross income is.

Most of the time, excluded income does not have to be reported. There are some instances where excluded income must be reported on a tax return, but it is still not taxable to the recipient. An example of this is nontaxable combat pay. Combat pay must be reported on a taxpayer's return, but it is not subject to income tax.

> **Example:** Brock is a popular recording artist and makes over $600,000 in wages per year. Because of his high income, Brock is phased out for most deductions. However, in 2010 Brock is involved in an auto accident where he sustained major injuries. Brock sues the other driver and receives a settlement of $80,000 from the insurance company. The insurance settlement is excluded income, because compensation for physical injuries is not taxable to the recipient.

Sources of All Income

When taxpayers prepare a federal income tax return such as IRS Form 1040, they must calculate three levels of income:

Gross Income: To calculate a taxpayer's liability, the IRS requires that she first calculate "total income" or "gross income." This is the sum of all sources of taxable income that the taxpayer receives during the year.

Adjusted Gross Income (AGI): AGI is total income minus certain allowable deductions. These deductions include, but are not limited to, IRA contributions, qualified student loan interest, some expenses if self-employed, alimony payments, and moving expenses.

Taxable Income: This is the amount of income on which a taxpayer owes income taxes (calculated by subtracting any deductions and exemptions from Adjusted Gross Income).

How to Calculate Gross Individual Income (Tax Formula)
Start with GROSS INCOME
MINUS- Adjustments to Income ("Above the Line" Deductions)
= ADJUSTED GROSS INCOME
MINUS- Greater of Itemized Deductions (or Standard Deduction)
MINUS- Personal Exemptions
= TAXABLE INCOME
X Tax Rate
= GROSS TAX Liability
MINUS- Credits
= NET TAX Liability or Refund Receivable

The Internal Revenue Code (IRC) describes types of income that are taxable. There are many types of income that are nontaxable. Some common examples of nontaxable income are welfare benefits, nontaxable combat pay, child support, inheritances, and municipal bond interest.

Earned Income vs. Unearned Income

Earned income is received for services performed, such as wages, salaries, tips, or professional fees. *Unearned* income is also called passive income, or investment income. Earned income (such as wages) is treated differently from passive income (such as dividends).

Earned income is generally subject to Social Security tax and Medicare tax (also called the FICA tax). Some income is considered variable, which means it is considered earned income for some taxpayers and unearned income for others.

The Doctrine of Constructive Receipt

The doctrine of constructive receipt is very important. This concept is often tested on the Enrolled Agent Exam. It means that the IRS believes that taxpayers should be taxed on their income when it becomes available, regardless of whether it is actually in their physical possession.

For example, a check that a taxpayer receives before the end of the tax year is considered income constructively received in that year, even if the taxpayer does not deposit the check into her account until the next year. Therefore, a cash basis taxpayer must include in income any amounts that are constructively received during the tax year.

Example: Gerardo is on vacation in Las Vegas. The postal service tries to deliver a check to Gerardo on December 31, but he is not at home to receive it, so it's left in his mailbox. Even though he did not have the check in his physical possession, it is still considered to have been constructively received by the taxpayer. Gerardo must still include the amount in gross income for that tax year.

If a taxpayer refuses income, such as a prize or an award, then the income is not considered to have been "constructively received." Also, if there are significant restrictions on the income, or if the income is not accessible to the taxpayer, then it is also not considered to have been "constructively received."

> **Example:** Owen won a big prize for concert tickets from a local radio station. The front-row concert tickets were valued at $1,200. This was a taxable award for Owen, and he is required to pay taxes on the Fair Market Value (FMV) of the tickets. However, on the day of the concert, the radio station does not receive the tickets in time from the promoter. Owen is not able to attend the concert. Since Owen never actually received the proceeds, the prize is not taxable to Owen. He never had "constructive receipt" of his prize.

"Claim of Right" Doctrine

Under the claim of right doctrine, income received without restriction—(income the taxpayer has complete control over)—must be reported in the year received, even if there's a possibility it may have to be repaid in a later year. If it is repaid, the repayment is deductible in the year paid. However, this does not include income that has substantial restrictions applied to it. The issue usually lies with control over the income.

Assignment of Income to a Third Party

Income received by an agent for a taxpayer is income constructively received in the year the agent received it. If a taxpayer agrees by contract that a third party is to receive income for him, he must include the amount in his own income when the third party receives it.

> **Example:** Holden's wages are being garnished for back child support. Holden's employer garnishes part of Holden's salary. Since the amount would have normally been included in Holden's paycheck, he must still recognize the income as if he had received it himself. Holden must include that amount in his gross income, even though he never actually received it.

Prizes and Awards

Prizes and awards are usually taxable. If the prize or award is in a form other than money, the FMV of the property is treated as the taxable amount. The winner may avoid taxation of the award by rejecting the prize, or if the prize is transferred to a charity or other nonprofit.

> **Example:** Jerry is a college instructor. He is chosen as *teacher of the year* by a national education association. He is awarded $1,000, but Jerry does not accept the prize. Instead, Jerry directs the association to transfer his winnings to a college scholarship fund. The award is not taxable to Jerry (Publication 535).

Some prizes and awards are excludable from income. An award recipient may exclude the FMV of the prize from gross income if:

- The amount received is in recognition of religious, scientific, charitable, or similar meritorious achievement (Example: a charity awards a Christmas gift to a needy individual);
- The recipient is selected without action on her part;
- The receipt of the award is not conditioned on substantial future services; and the amount is paid by the organization making the award to a tax-exempt organization (including a governmental unit) designated by the recipient.

Employee Awards (Exclusion)

There is also an exclusion for awards given to employees. Certain employee achievement awards may qualify for exclusion from the employee's gross income as a *non-taxable* fringe benefit. A prize may also qualify for exclusion from income if it is a scholarship.

Amounts paid for employee awards are still deductible to the employer and not taxable to the employee if certain rules are followed. A cash award is always taxable to the employee. An achievement award in the form of property, if given to the employee for length of service or as a safety achievement, would not be taxable to the employee and would still be deductible by the employer.

Employers can exclude from wages the value of achievement awards given to an employee from the employee's wages if the cost is not more than the amount the employer can deduct as a business expense for the year. The excludable annual amount is $1,600 for qualified plan awards.

The limit is $400 for awards that are not "qualified plan awards." A "qualified plan award" is an award that does not favor Highly Compensated Employees (HCE). Basically, a nonqualified award is an award that is given to highly compensated executives, but not to rank-and-file employees.

> **Example:** Space Corporation awards a set of golf clubs to an employee as a nonqualified plan employee achievement award. The Fair Market Value of the golf clubs is $750. The amount included in taxable wages to the employee is $350 ($750 – $400). If the award had been a *qualified plan award*, the employee would not have been taxed on the FMV of the award.

HCEs are defined as owning more than 5% of the company or employees whose compensation exceeds $110,000 and are among the 20% highest paid.

> **Example:** Rowan received three employee achievement awards during the year: a watch valued at $250, a stereo valued at $1,000, and a set of golf clubs valued at $500. She received each of the awards for length of service and exceptional safety achievement. They are all qualified plan awards and would normally be excluded from her income, assuming that the other requirements for qualified plan awards are satisfied. However, because the $1,750 total value of the awards is more than $1,600, Rowan must include $150 ($1,750 – $1,600) in her income.

The employer must make the award as part of a meaningful presentation, and it should not simply be disguised pay.

Forgiven Debt or Canceled Debt

In general, taxpayers must include "discharge of indebtedness" in their gross income. Forgiven debt can result in taxable income. When an entity cancels a debt of $600 or more, the taxpayer will receive a **Form 1099-C**, *Cancellation of Debt*.

Generally, if a taxpayer's debt is canceled or forgiven, the taxpayer must include the canceled debt in his gross income. Canceled debt should be reported on Schedule C if the debt was incurred in a business. If the debt is a non-business debt, the canceled debt amount should be reported as "other income" on **Form 1040.**

If a financial institution offers a discount for the early payment of a mortgage loan, the amount of the discount is canceled debt.

> **Example:** Phoebe borrows $10,000 to take a vacation and defaults on the loan after paying back only $2,000. She spends all the money and is unwilling to make payments on the loan. The lender is unable to collect the remaining amount of the loan. Phoebe is not insolvent. Therefore, there is a cancellation of debt of $8,000, which is taxable income to Phoebe. She must include it on her tax return as "other income."

There are some exceptions to this rule, most notably the exception in 2009-2010 for the debt forgiveness from the foreclosure or sale of a primary residence (covered in detail next). There is also an exception for taxpayers who are insolvent. If a debt is forgiven as a gift or bequest, then the canceled debt does not have to be included in income.

Nontaxable Canceled Debt
There are examples where canceled debt is not included in income (not taxable), but may still have to be reported on the taxpayer's return. The most common situations when cancellation of debt income is not taxable involve the following:

Qualified Principal Residence Indebtedness (QPRI)
This is the exception created by the *Mortgage Debt Relief Act of 2007* and applies to most homeowners. The provisions in the act were extended by Congress and apply to mortgage debt forgiven in 2007 through 2012. The IRS generally allows taxpayers to exclude income from the discharge of debt on their principal residence. Debt reduced through mortgage restructuring, as well as mortgage debt forgiven in foreclosure, qualifies for exclusion.

When a bank forecloses on a home and then sells the home for *less than* the borrower's outstanding mortgage and forgives the unpaid mortgage debt, the canceled debt previously would have been taxable income to the homeowner. The basis of the principal residence must be reduced (but not below zero) by the amount excluded from gross income. Debt reduced through mortgage restructuring (as well as mortgage debt forgiven in connection with a foreclosure) qualifies for this relief.

The amount excluded reduces the taxpayer's basis in the home. To claim the exclusion, the taxpayer must file **Form 982,** *Reduction of Tax Attributes Due to Discharge of Indebtedness*, with his individual income tax return.

Up to $2 million of forgiven debt is eligible for this exclusion ($1 million if Married Filing Separately). The exclusion doesn't apply if the discharge is due to services performed for the lender or any other reason not directly related to a decline in the home's value or the taxpayer's financial condition. A taxpayer can exclude canceled debt if it is qualified principal residence indebtedness.

Qualified Principal Residence Indebtedness is debt incurred in:
- Acquiring,
- Constructing, or
- Substantially improving the taxpayer's principal residence.

The qualified debt also includes debt secured by the residence from refinancing, as long as the refinancing was incurred to acquire, construct, or substantially improve the home.

A *qualified* "principal residence" does NOT include rentals or vacation homes.

> **Example:** Adam's home is subject to a $320,000 mortgage debt. Adam's creditor forecloses in April 2010. Due to declining real estate values, the residence is sold for $280,000 in December 2010. Adam has $40,000 of income from discharge of indebtedness. Before the new law, the $40,000 would have been includable in Adam's gross income. However, Adam may claim the exclusion by filing **Form 982** with his 2010 tax return.

"Ordering Rule" for Principal Residence Indebtedness

If only a *part* of a loan is qualified principal residence indebtedness, the exclusion from income for QPRI applies only to the extent the amount canceled exceeds the amount of the loan that is NOT qualified principal residence indebtedness. However, the remaining part of the loan may qualify for another exclusion.

> **Example:** Ken incurred debt of $800,000 when he purchased his home for $880,000. Ken made a down payment of $80,000 and financed the rest. When the FMV of the property was $1 million, Ken refinanced the debt for $850,000. At the time of the refinancing, the balance of the original loan was $740,000. Ken used the $110,000 he obtained from the refinancing ($850,000 minus $740,000) to buy a luxury car and take a vacation to the Bahamas. About two years after the refinancing, Ken lost his job. Ken's residence declined in value to $750,000. Based on Ken's circumstances, the lender agreed to a short sale of the property for $735,000 and to cancel the remaining $115,000 of the $850,000 debt. Under the "ordering rule," Ken can exclude only $5,000 of the canceled debt from his income using the exclusion for canceled qualified principal residence indebtedness ($115,000 canceled debt minus the $110,000 amount of the debt that was not qualified principal residence indebtedness—basically the money he spent on personal purchases, such as a car). Ken must include the remaining $110,000 of canceled debt in income (unless another exception or exclusion applies).

Canceled Debt that is Otherwise Deductible

If a taxpayer uses the cash method of accounting, he should NOT recognize canceled debt income if payment of the debt would have been a deductible expense.

> **Example:** Warren is a cash-basis self-employed farmer. Warren gets $2,200 in accounting services for his farm on credit. Later, Warren has trouble paying his farm debts and his accountant forgives the amount Warren owes. Warren does not include the canceled debt in his gross income because payment of the debt would have been deductible as a business expense anyway.

Bankruptcy

Debts discharged through bankruptcy court in a Title 11 bankruptcy case are not considered taxable income. The taxpayer must attach **Form 982** to his federal income tax return to report debt that is cancelled in bankruptcy.

Insolvency

If a taxpayer is insolvent when the debt is canceled, the canceled debt is not taxable. A taxpayer is "insolvent" when total debts are more than the Fair Market Value of her total assets. For purposes of determining insolvency, assets include the value of everything the taxpayer owns (*including* the value of pensions and retirement accounts).

Example: In 2010, Darnell had $5,000 in credit card debt, which he did not pay. Darnell received a Form 1099-C from his credit card company showing canceled debt of $5,000. Darnell's total liabilities immediately before the cancellation were $15,000, and the FMV of his total assets immediately before the cancellation was $7,000. This means that at the time the debt was canceled, Darnell was insolvent to the extent of $8,000 ($15,000 total liabilities minus $7,000 FMV of his total assets). Therefore, Darnell can exclude the entire $5,000 canceled debt from income.

Qualifying Farm Debts

If a taxpayer incurred the canceled debt in farming, the canceled debt is generally not considered taxable income.

Nonrecourse Loans

A nonrecourse loan is a loan for which the lender's only remedy in case of default is to repossess the property being financed or used as collateral. That is, the lender cannot pursue the taxpayer personally in case of default. Forgiveness of a nonrecourse loan resulting from a foreclosure does not result in cancellation of debt income.

Certain Canceled Student Loans are Not Taxable

Some student loans contain a provision that the debt will be canceled if the student eventually works for a certain period of time in certain professions. A taxpayer does not have to recognize income if the student loan is canceled after he performs the agreed-upon required services. To qualify, the loan must have been made by:

- The federal government,
- A state or local government, or government agency,
- A tax-exempt public benefit corporation that has assumed control of a state, county, or municipal hospital, and whose employees are considered public employees under state law, or
- An educational institution, as part of a program of the institution designed to encourage students to serve in occupations or areas with unmet needs and under which the services provided are for or under the direction of a governmental unit or a tax-exempt section 501(c)(3) organization.

Example: Tatum is a medical student completing her residency. She agrees to work as a doctor in a state program in Minnesota serving rural and poor communities. Tatum agreed to take a job as a pediatrician in the state's rural towns for four years in return for the forgiveness of her student loans. The canceled debt qualifies for non-recognition treatment, and the canceled debt does not have to be recognized as income.

All of these exceptions are discussed in detail in IRS **Publication 4681**, *Canceled Debts, Foreclosures, Repossessions, and Abandonments.*

Canceled Debt: Summary
*Canceled Debt that is Excludable from Gross Income
These amounts are not reported on the tax return:

- Gifts or bequests
- Cancellation of qualified student loans
- Canceled debt that if paid by a cash basis taxpayer is otherwise deductible
- A purchase price reduction given by a seller (such as a discount on a car purchase from a car dealer)

*Canceled Debt that Qualifies for Exclusion from Gross Income
These amounts must be reported on the tax return, but are excludable from gross income:

- Cancellation of qualified principal residence indebtedness
- Debt canceled in a Title 11 bankruptcy case
- Debt canceled due to insolvency
- Cancellation of qualified farm indebtedness
- Cancellation of qualified real property business indebtedness

The exclusion for *"qualified principal residence indebtedness"* provides debt tax relief for many homeowners involved in the mortgage foreclosure crisis currently affecting much of the country. The exclusion allows taxpayers to exclude up to $2 million ($1 million if Married Filing Separately) of "qualified principal residence indebtedness." On the Enrolled Agent Exam, the principal residence exclusion is the exclusion most commonly tested on the subject of canceled debt.

Gambling Winnings
Gambling winnings are fully taxable and must be reported on the tax return. Gambling winnings are reported to the taxpayer on IRS **Form W-2G**. A taxpayer will receive a **Form W-2G** if he wins:

- $600 or more in winnings from gambling
- $1,200 or more in winnings from bingo or slot machines;
- $1,500 or more in proceeds from keno; or
- Any gambling winnings subject to federal income tax withholding.

A taxpayer must report and pay tax on all gambling winnings, even if she does not receive a **Form W-2G** for the winnings. Gambling income includes winnings from lotteries, raffles, horse races, and casinos. It includes cash winnings and also the Fair Market Value of prizes such as cars and trips.

Gambling losses are deductible, but only on **Schedule A** as an itemized deduction. The amount of the deduction is limited to the amount of gambling winnings. So, for example, if a taxpayer wins $11,000 in 2010 but has $12,000 in gambling losses, the taxpayer can only deduct $11,000 (the amount of his gambling winnings) on **Schedule A**. Taxpayers may only deduct gambling losses if they itemize.

Example: Yolanda had $1,000 in gambling winnings for the year. She had $3,000 in gambling losses. Her deduction for gambling losses cannot exceed $1,000, the amount of her gambling winnings. Yolanda must itemize and list her gambling losses on Schedule A, Form 1040. Yolanda's gambling winnings are reported to her on IRS Form W-2G.

An accurate diary or similar record of gambling winnings and losses must be kept along with tickets, receipts, canceled checks, and other documentation. These supporting records need not be sent in with the tax return, but should be retained in case of an audit.

Self-Employment Income

- Taxpayers must include income from self-employment on their tax returns. Self-employment tax is reported on IRS **Schedule SE**. If a taxpayer operates more than one business, she may combine the net incomes together and use only one Schedule SE. If a taxpayer's self-employment net earnings are $400 or more in a year, she must file a tax return and report the earnings from self-employment to the IRS. Self-employment income includes:
- Self-employment income reported on Schedule C;
- Farming income reported on Schedule F;
- Income of ministers, priests, and rabbis for the performance of services such as baptisms and marriages;
- The distributive share of partnership income allocated to general partners or managers of a Limited Liability Company (the income is reported to the partner on IRS **Form K-1**).

Estimated Taxes and Self-Employed Taxpayers

Federal income tax is a pay-as-you-go tax. Taxpayers are required to pay their income tax liabilities as they earn or receive income during the year. A taxpayer generally must make estimated tax payments if he expects to owe tax, including SE tax, of $1,000 or more when he files his return. Self-employed individuals must generally make estimated tax payments.

Self-Employment Taxes

The self-employment tax is a very confusing concept for most exam candidates. The Social Security tax rate for 2010 is 15.3% on self-employment income up to $106,800. If net earnings exceed $106,800, the taxpayer will continue to pay only the Medicare portion of the Social Security tax, which is 2.9%, on the rest of their earnings.

A person who is self-employed must pay his own Social Security and Medicare taxes. If an employee is working for an employer, the employer pays half of these taxes and the employee pays the other half. But self-employed people are responsible for paying the entire amount. This rate consists of 12.4% for Social Security and 2.9% for Medicare.

The part that may be confusing is the fact that there is a "cap" on Social Security tax, but there is NO "cap" on Medicare tax. The Social Security tax rate is 15.3% on self-employment income up to $106,800. If your net earnings exceed $106,800, you continue to pay only the Medicare portion of the Social Security tax, which is 2.9%, on the rest of your earnings. Incidentally, this cap also applies to people who are regular wage earners.

If a taxpayer has wages in addition to self-employment earnings, then the tax on the wages is paid first.

Example: Kendall has a job where she earns a salary in 2010. She also earns extra money as a self-employed web designer. She will pay the appropriate Social Security taxes on both her wages and her business earnings. In 2010, Kendall earns $77,500 in wages and $30,000 in net earnings from her web design business. Kendall's employer will withhold 7.65% in Social Security and Medicare taxes on her $77,500 in wages. Kendall must pay 15.3% in Social Security and Medicare taxes on her first $29,300 in self-employment earnings and 2.9% in Medicare tax on the remaining $700 in earnings. She does not pay Social Security taxes on her earnings over $106,800 (example from SSA.gov).

Remember, taxpayers are required to pay Social Security tax on their wages ONLY up to $106,800—but they must continue to pay Medicare taxes on any additional amount they make, even if they earn a million dollars.

There are two income tax deductions related to the self-employment tax that reduce overall taxes on a taxpayer with self-employment income.

- First, net earnings from self-employment are reduced by half of the total Social Security tax. This is similar to the way employees are treated under the tax laws, because the employer's share of the Social Security tax is not considered wages to the employee.
- Second, the taxpayer can deduct half of the Social Security tax on IRS Form 1040 as an adjustment to gross income. The amount is not an itemized deduction and must not be listed on Schedule A or Schedule C.

More than One Business

If a taxpayer runs more than one business, then he will "net" the profit (or loss) from each to determine the *total earnings* subject to SE tax.

Taxpayers cannot combine a spouse's income or loss to determine their individual earnings subject to SE tax. However, a single person with two sole proprietorships may combine income and losses from both businesses to figure self-employment tax.

Example: Tanner is a sole proprietor who owns a barbershop. Tanner has $19,000 in net income for 2010. His wife Erin has a candle-making business, and she has a business LOSS of ($12,000) for 2010. Tanner must pay self-employment tax on $19,000, regardless of how he and Erin choose to file. That is because married couples cannot "offset" each other's self-employment tax. The income of each business is allocated to the individual—not the gross amount shown on a joint tax return.

Example: Darren is a single taxpayer and has two small sole-proprietorships. He owns a computer repair shop and he also runs a car wash. The computer repair business has net income of $45,000 in 2010. The car wash, however, is doing poorly. It has a net LOSS of ($23,000) in 2010. Darren only has to pay self-employment tax on $22,000 ($45,000-$23,000) of income, because he may "net" the income and losses from both his businesses.

Fringe Benefits (Taxable and Nontaxable)

Most employers offer fringe benefits to their employees. These include health benefits, vacation pay, and parking passes. Most employee fringe benefits are nontaxable. However, there are some benefits that must be included in an employee's taxable income. *Taxable* fringe benefits include:

- OFF-SITE athletic facilities and health club memberships
- The value of employer-provided life insurance over $50,000
- Any cash benefit or benefit in the form of a credit card or gift card
- Season tickets to sporting events, although single tickets can be excluded in certain cases
- Transportation benefits, if the value of a benefit for any month is more than the nontaxable limit. Employers cannot exclude the excess from the employee's wages as a de minimis transportation benefit
- Employer-provided vehicles, if they are used for personal purposes

Example: Tanning Town Inc. owns a tropical resort employees can use free of charge. Sam decides to visit the resort with his family. The Fair Market Value of the stay is $5,000. Sam must include the FMV of the accommodations in his taxable income. The employer usually figures the taxable amount. If the FMV is $5,000 for Sam's two-week stay, then $5,000 will be included in his taxable wages.

Nontaxable Employee Fringe Benefits

Fringe benefits are offered to employees by employers as a condition of their employment. Some fringe benefits are taxable and some are not. This next section will cover taxable and non-taxable fringe benefits, which are frequently tested on the EA exam.

Cafeteria Plans

A *cafeteria plan* provides employees an opportunity to receive certain benefits on a pre-tax basis. The plan may make benefits available to employees, their spouses, and dependents. The most common type of cafeteria plan offers health benefits to an employee and his or her family. Some cafeteria plans may also offer coverage to former employees. Generally, qualified benefits under a cafeteria plan are not subject to FICA, FUTA, Medicare tax, or income tax withholding.

Employer contributions to the cafeteria plan are usually made via salary reduction agreements (taken directly out of the employee's paycheck). The employee usually agrees to contribute a portion of his or her salary on a pre-tax basis to pay for the qualified benefits.

Participants in a cafeteria plan must be permitted to choose among at least one taxable benefit (such as cash) and one *qualified* benefit. A *qualified* benefit is a benefit that is non-taxable. Qualified benefits include:

- Accident, dental, vision, and medical benefits (but NOT Archer medical savings accounts or long-term care insurance)
- Adoption assistance
- Dependent care assistance

97

- Group-term life insurance coverage (up to $50,000 of life insurance coverage may be provided as a nontaxable benefit to an employee, covered in more detail later)
- Health Savings Accounts

*Note: If an employer pays the cost of an accident insurance plan for an employee, then the amounts received under the plan are taxable to the employee. If a taxpayer pays the cost of an accident insurance plan *for himself*, then the benefits received under the plan are not taxable.

FSA: A Flexible Spending Arrangement

An FSA is a form of cafeteria plan benefit, funded by salary reduction, which reimburses employees for expenses incurred for certain qualified benefits. An FSA may be offered for dependent care assistance, adoption assistance, and medical care reimbursements. The benefits are subject to an annual maximum and an annual "use-or-lose" rule. An FSA cannot provide a cumulative benefit to the employee beyond the plan year. The employee must substantiate his expenses, and then the distributions to the employee are tax-free.

Dependent Care Assistance

An employee can generally exclude from gross income up to $5,000 ($2,500 if MFS) of benefits received under a dependent care assistance program each year. Amounts paid directly to the taxpayer or to a daycare provider qualify for exclusion. IRS **Form 2441,** *Child and Dependent Care Expenses,* must be filed in order to claim the exclusion. The amount that qualifies for exclusion is limited to:

- The total amount of the dependent care benefits received
- The employee's earned income
- The spouse's earned income
- $5,000 ($2,500 if Married Filing Separately)

> **Example:** John's employer offers a cafeteria plan that allows for dependent care assistance. John files jointly with his wife Cindy. Cindy works part-time as a bookkeeper. John makes $50,000 in 2010. Cindy earns $4,500 as a part-time bookkeeper. They have $5,500 in day-care costs for 2010. The maximum amount that can be excluded in 2010 is $4,500, the amount of Cindy's earned income.

De Minimis Employee Benefits

Some employee benefits are so small that it would be impractical for the employer to account for them. The exclusion applies, for example, to the following items:

- Coffee, doughnuts, or soft drinks provided to employees
- Occasional meals while employees work overtime (100% of the cost)
- Occasional company picnics for employees
- Occasional use of the employer's copy machine
- Holiday gifts, other than cash, such as a gift basket or holiday ham

De Minimis meals: An exclusion for 100% of the cost of meals provided to employees on the employer's premises *for the employer's convenience* are not taxable to the employee and *not subject* to the 50% limit.[17] Meals employers furnish to a restaurant employee during, immediately before, or after, the employee's working hours are considered furnished for the employer's convenience.

> **Example:** Ellen is a registered nurse who is not allowed to leave the hospital premises during her long shifts. She works in the emergency room, and she must always be available to help patients immediately. So the hospital provides meals and a place for Ellen to sleep during her shift. Ellen does not have to recognize the value of the meals as income. The hospital does not have to add the value of Ellen's meals to her wages. In addition, the meals are 100% deductible by the employer and not subject to the 50% limit.

    *NOTE: Most *cash* benefits or their equivalent (such as gift cards or credit cards) cannot be excluded as *de minimis* fringe benefits under any circumstances. Season tickets to sporting events, commuting use of an employer-provided car more than once a month, and membership to a private country club or athletic facility are never excludable as *de minimis* fringe benefits. There is a rare exception for unusual or emergency circumstances (explained next).

> **Example:** A commuter ferry breaks down unexpectedly, and the engineers are required to work overtime to make repairs. After working eight hours, the engineers break for dinner because they will be working overtime until the engine is repaired. The supervisor gives each employee $10 for a meal. The meal is not taxable to the engineers because it was provided to permit them to work overtime in a situation that is not routine.

No-Additional-Cost Services

    Nontaxable fringe benefits include services provided to employees that do not impose any substantial additional cost. They may be excludable as a no-additional-cost fringe benefit. A "no-additional-cost service" is a service offered by the employer to its customers in the ordinary course of the line of business of the employer in which the employee performs substantial services, and the employer incurs no substantial additional cost (including foregone revenue) in providing the service to the employee; IRC 132(b).

    An employer can offer discounts, as well as on-site benefits, such as an on-site gym.[18] Example: Troy works for a local fitness club. He is allowed to work out for free as a condition of his employment. This is because this fringe benefit is a "no-additional cost" service. It doesn't cost the employer anything to allow this employee benefit. Troy is also

---

[17] Meals are generally 50% deductible. This means when a business pays for a meal, only 50% of its cost is deductible by the employer. There are some exceptions for employer-provided meals during company parties and picnics, and if the meal is given to the employee for the convenience of the employer.

[18] If the employer provides employees with the free or low cost use of an employer-operated gym or other athletic club on the employer's premises, the value is not included in the employee's compensation. The gym must be used primarily by employees, their spouses, and their dependent children. If the employer pays for a fitness program provided to the employee at an off-site resort hotel, country club, or athletic club, the value of the program is included in the employee's compensation (*frequently tested).

allowed a 10% discount on vitamins that the gym sells to patrons, as long as the vitamins are for his own use.

Other examples include transportation tickets, free flights, hotel rooms, entertainment facilities, etc.; however, these services may occur in connection with governmental facilities as well (for example, the use of a municipal golf course or recreation center).

Transportation fringe benefits also include the FMV of flights that are offered to airline employees.

> **Example:** Henrietta is a flight attendant with Jet Way Airlines. She is allowed to fly for free on stand-by flights when there is an extra seat. This is an example of a fringe benefit that is allowed for no additional cost to the employer and is therefore nontaxable to the employee (Publication 15-B).

Employer-Provided Educational Assistance

An employer-provided educational assistance program can be excluded up to a certain amount. (The amounts must be for tuition, books, required fees, and supplies). Room and board do not qualify as educational expenses for the purposes of an employer-sponsored educational assistance plan. The maximum excluded educational benefit is $5,250.

Transportation Fringe Benefits

Employers may provide transportation benefits to their employees up to certain amounts without having to include the benefit in the employee's income. Qualified transportation benefits include transit passes, paid parking, and transportation in a commuter highway vehicle (shuttle). The employer may also offer cash reimbursement under a qualified reimbursement arrangement (also called an "accountable plan," which is explained later).

In 2010, employees may exclude $230 per month in transit benefits and $230 per month in parking benefits: up to a maximum of $460 per month. Employees may receive transit passes and benefits for parking during the same month; they are not mutually exclusive.

Commuting expenses are not deductible. So if an employer allows an employee to use a company vehicle for commuting, then the value of the vehicle's use is taxable to the employee. Personal use of an employer's vehicle is considered "taxable wages" to the employee.

> **Example:** Joe, an employee of Blue-Blood Corp., uses an employer-provided car. In 2010, Joe drives the car 20,000 miles, of which 4,000 were personal miles or 20% (4,000/20,000 = 20%). The car has an annual lease value of $4,100. Personal use is therefore valued at $820 and is included in Joe's wages.

Accountable Plans

An *accountable plan* is a plan where an employer reimburses employees for business-related expenses such as mileage, meals, and travel expenses. For expenses to qualify under an accountable plan, the employee must follow certain rules in order to have the expenses reimbursed. An accountable plan requires employees to meet all of the following requirements. Employees must:

- Have incurred the expenses while performing services as employees
- Adequately account for the expenses within a reasonable period of time
- Adequately account for their travel, meals, and entertainment expenses
- Provide evidence of their employee business expenses, such as receipts or other records
- Return any excess reimbursement or allowance within a reasonable period of time

Under an accountable plan, a business may advance money to employees; however, certain conditions must be met. The cash advance must be reasonably calculated to equal the anticipated expenses. The business owner must make the advance within a reasonable period of time. If any expenses reimbursed under this arrangement are not substantiated, a business is not allowed to deduct them under an accountable plan. Instead, the reimbursed expenses are considered a non-accountable plan and become taxable to the employee.

Example: Donna is an Enrolled Agent who runs a tax preparation business. She advances $250 to her employee Ayden so that he can become a Notary. Ayden spends $90 on a Notary course and then another $100 to take the Notary exam, which he passes. Ayden returns the unused funds ($60) as well as copies of his receipts to Donna, his boss. The expenses are qualified expenses under an accountable plan. Donna may deduct the $190 ($90 + $100) as a business expense, and the amounts are not taxable to Ayden.

Cash reimbursements are excludable if an employer establishes a bona fide reimbursement plan. This means there must be reasonable procedures to verify reimbursements and the employees must substantiate the expenses using receipts or other substantiation.

Example: Mai Ling buys a transit pass for $120 each month in 2011. At the end of each month, she presents her used transit pass to her employer and certifies that she purchased and used it during the month. The employer reimburses her $120 in cash. The employer has established a bona fide reimbursement arrangement for purposes of excluding the $120 reimbursement from the employee's gross income in 2011. The reimbursement is not taxable to Mai Ling, and it is deductible by the employer.

Travel Expenses and Travel Reimbursements

Qualifying expenses for travel are excludable if they are incurred for temporary travel on business away from the general area of the employee's tax home. Travel expense reimbursements include:

- Costs to travel to and from the business destination (flights, mileage reimbursements)
- Transportation costs while at the business destination (taxi fare, shuttles)

101

- Lodging, meals, and incidental expenses
- Cleaning, laundry, and other miscellaneous expenses

Example: Woody works for a travel agency in Detroit. He flies to Denver to conduct business for an entire week. His employer pays the cost of transportation to and from Denver, as well as lodging and meals while there. The reimbursements for substantiated travel expenses are excludable from Woody's income, and the reimbursements are deductible by his employer.

Employer-Provided Life Insurance as a Fringe Benefit

Employers may deduct the cost of life insurance premiums provided to employees. Employer-provided life insurance is a nontaxable fringe benefit only up to $50,000. Coverage amounts over $50,000 are taxable to the employee. The employer must calculate the taxable portion of the premiums for coverage that exceeds $50,000.

Example: Carol, a 47-year-old employee, receives $40,000 of life insurance coverage per year under a policy carried by her employer. Her employer agrees to pay the premiums on the first $40,000 of coverage as part of Carol's cafeteria plan. She is also entitled to $100,000 of additional insurance at her own expense. This additional, optional coverage is also carried by her employer. The cost of $10,000 of this additional amount is excludable; the cost of the remaining $90,000 of coverage is included in income. Since only $50,000 of life insurance coverage can be nontaxable to the employee, Carol will be taxed on the difference between the premiums.

Employer-Provided Retirement Plan Contributions

Many employers contribute to their employees' retirement plans. When employers contribute to employee retirement plans, the contribution is not taxable to the employee when it is made. The contribution only becomes taxable when the employee finally withdraws the funds from his or her retirement account.

This rule also applies to elected deferrals. Employees may elect to have part of their pretax compensation contributed to a retirement fund. An elective deferral is excluded from wages, but is still subject to Social Security and Medicare tax. Elective deferrals include contributions into the following retirement plans:

- 401(k) plans, 403(B) plans, Section 457 plans
- SIMPLE plans
- Thrift Savings Plans for federal employees

Elective deferrals to a **Roth** retirement plan are taxable to the employee. That is because a Roth plan is always funded with post-tax income.

Special Rules for Highly Compensated Employees (HCEs)

Highly Compensated Employees cannot exclude the value of employer-provided benefits from income unless certain specific requirements are met. This is to discourage companies from offering spectacular tax-free benefits to their highly compensated execu-

102

tives, while ignoring the needs of lower-paid employees. A Highly Compensated Employee (HCE) is anyone who:

- Is an officer, OR
- Was at least a "5% shareholder" at any time during 2009 or 2010, OR
- Received over $110,000 in compensation during 2009 or 2010 and is in the top twenty percent of employees based upon compensation, OR
- Is a spouse or dependent of any of the individuals listed above.

The law for Highly Compensated Employees includes a "look-back provision," so employees who earned more than $110,000 in 2009 are generally still considered HCEs for 2010 plan year testing, and employees who earned more than $110,000 in 2010 are generally considered HCEs for 2011 plan year testing (Publication 15-B).

Example: Fengrew Inc. is a C Corporation. Fengrew has 300 employees, 45 of which are considered "Highly Compensated Employees." Fengrew's cafeteria plan is available to all the employees; therefore, the discrimination rules do not apply, and the benefits are not taxable.

If a plan favors key (HCE) employees, the employer is required to include the value of the benefits they could have selected in their wages. A plan is considered to have "favored" HCEs if over 25% of all the benefits are given to HCEs.

A plan that covers union employees under a collective bargaining agreement is not included in this rule.

Interest Income

Interest is a passive form of income. Taxable interest includes interest received from bank accounts and other sources. Certain distributions commonly called "dividends" are actually interest. Credit unions, for instance, commonly call their distributions "dividends." The IRS considers these credit union distributions to be interest income, rather than dividends.

Interest income is reported to the taxpayer on IRS **Form 1099-INT**. If interest income exceeds $1,500 in 2010, the taxpayer must report the interest on **Schedule B, Form 1040**. A taxpayer cannot file **Form 1040EZ** if his interest income exceeds $1,500.

Tax-exempt interest is reported on page one (the front) of IRS **Form 1040.**

Dividends that are Actually Interest

Taxpayers must report these so-called "dividends" on deposits as interest income. The following are some other sources of taxable interest:

- Credit unions
- Domestic building and loan associations
- Domestic savings and loan associations
- Federal savings and loan associations
- Mutual savings banks
- Certificates of Deposits (CDs) and other deferred interest accounts

Taxpayers should report these earnings as interest on their **Form 1040.**

Gift for Opening a Bank Account

If a taxpayer receives noncash gifts or services for making deposits or for opening an account in a savings institution, the value of the gift may have to be reported as interest. For deposits of less than $5,000, gifts or services valued at more than $10 must be reported as interest. For deposits of $5,000 or more, gifts or services valued at more than $20 must be reported as interest. The value of the gift is determined by the financial institution.

Interest on Insurance Dividends

Interest on insurance dividends left on deposit with an insurance company that can be withdrawn annually is taxable in the year it is credited to the taxpayer's account. However, if the taxpayer cannot withdraw the income except on a certain date (the anniversary date of the policy or other specified date), the income is considered restricted and not taxable when it is earned. The interest is taxable in the year that the withdrawal is allowed.

U.S. Treasury Bills, Notes, & Bonds

Interest on U.S. obligations, such as U.S. Treasury bills, notes, and bonds issued by any agency of the United States, is taxable for federal income tax purposes.

*Special NOTE: Money borrowed to invest in Certificate of Deposits: The interest a taxpayer pays on loans borrowed from a bank to meet the minimum deposit required for a Certificate of Deposit (investment CD) from the institution and the interest a taxpayer earns on the certificate are *two separate things*.[19] The taxpayer must include the total interest earned on the certificate in income. If the taxpayer itemizes deductions, he can deduct the interest paid as investment interest paid, up to the amount of net investment income. (This is a concept frequently tested on the EA Exam.)

Example: Sienna wanted to invest in a $10,000 six-month CD. So she deposited $5,000 in a CD with a credit union and borrowed $5,000 from another bank to make up the $10,000 minimum deposit required to buy the six-month CD. The certificate earned $575 at maturity in 2010, but Sienna actually received NET $265 in interest income that year. This represented the $575 Sienna earned on the CD, minus $310 interest charged on the $5,000 loan. The credit union gives Sienna a **Form 1099-INT** for 2010 showing the $575 interest Sienna earned. The bank also gives Sienna a statement showing that Sienna paid $310 interest for 2010. Sienna must include the total interest amount earned, $575, in her interest income for 2010. Only if Sienna itemizes can she deduct the interest expense of $310. The investment interest paid is a deduction on Schedule A (Form 1040). Sienna can deduct $310 as investment interest.

Original Issue Discount (OID)

Original Issue Discount (OID) is a form of imputed income interest. OID income occurs when a debtor issues a debt instrument, such as a zero coupon bond, for less than the "issue price" of the debt instrument. If there is OID of at least $10 for the calendar year, the interest income must be reported to the taxpayer on **Form 1099-OID**. Generally, OID interest must be reported on the taxpayer's tax return as interest income.

---

[19] This concept has been tested on multiple prior exams.

Nontaxable Interest Income (Excluded Interest)

There are numerous examples of interest income that are not taxable to the recipient.

I. Muni Bonds

A taxpayer may exclude interest income on municipal or "muni" bonds, which are debt obligations by state and local governments. Taxpayers must still report the interest on their income tax returns, but it is not taxable. Although a muni bond is generally exempt from federal income tax, it is often still taxable at the state level.

II. Frozen Deposits

A taxpayer may EXCLUDE interest income on Frozen Deposits. A deposit is considered frozen if, at the end of the year, the taxpayer cannot withdraw any part of the deposit because:

- The financial institution is bankrupt or insolvent, or
- The state where the institution is located has placed limits on withdrawals because other financial institutions in the state are bankrupt or insolvent.

Example: Creed earned $2,500 in interest at Belly-Up Bank in 2010. The bank became insolvent at the end of 2010 and all of Creed's money was frozen. He was unable to access any of his accounts until the following year. Creed does not have to recognize the income as taxable in 2010, because the interest qualified as a frozen deposit. Creed would recognize the income in 2011 when the funds finally became available for him to withdraw and use. Creed must still report the income on his 2010 tax return, but he may mark it as a "frozen deposit" and therefore not subject to income tax in the 2010 tax year.

III. Mutual Funds Investing in Tax-Exempt Securities

Distributions from a fund investing in tax-exempt securities will be tax-exempt interest.

IV. Series EE Savings Bond Exclusion

Taxpayers may choose to purchase and then eventually redeem Series EE bonds on a tax-free basis to pay college expenses. The expenses must be for the taxpayer, the taxpayer's spouse, or the taxpayer's dependents. The exclusion is calculated and reported on IRS **Form 8815**, *Exclusion of Interest from Series EE and I U.S. Savings Bonds*. There are certain rules that must be followed in order for the educational exclusion to qualify:

- The bonds must be purchased by the owner. The bonds cannot be a gift.
- The money received on redemption must be used for tuition and fees. The taxpayer cannot use tax-exempt bond proceeds for tuition and also attempt to take educational credits (such as the Lifetime Learning Credit) for the same amount. No "double dipping" is allowed.
- Couples who file "Married Filing Separately" tax returns do not qualify for the educational savings bond exclusion.

- The total interest received may *only* be excluded if the combined amounts of the principal and the interest received *do not exceed* the taxpayer's qualified educational expenses.

Example #1: In 2010, Denise redeems her Series EE Bonds and receives a total of $4,000. Of that amount, $1,000 is interest income and the remainder is the return of principal ($3,000). Denise's qualified educational expenses (tuition and fees) are $5,800. Therefore, all of the interest earned on her Series EE Bonds qualifies for tax-exempt treatment.

Example #2: In February 2010, Daniel and Delilah, a married couple, cash a qualified Series EE savings bond they bought in April 1996. They receive proceeds of $8,124, representing principal of $5,000 and interest of $3,124. In 2010, they paid $4,000 of their daughter's college tuition. They are not claiming an education credit for that amount, and their daughter does not have any tax-free educational assistance (scholarships or grants). Daniel and Delilah can exclude $1,538 ($3,124 × ($4,000 ÷ $8,124)) of interest in 2010. They must pay tax on the remaining $1,586 ($3,124 − $1,538) interest.

Wages and Employee Compensation

Wages are the most common type of employee compensation. All income from wages, salaries, and tips is taxable to the employee and deductible by the employer. Wages, salaries, bonuses, and commissions are compensation received by employees for services performed.

Wages paid by an employer are reported on IRS **Form W-2.** Employers are generally required to issue a **Form W-2** to their employees by January 31 of each year. Wages are reported as taxable income on **Form 1040.**

Employers are required by law to withhold Social Security and Medicare taxes. If the employer fails to withhold Social Security and Medicare, the employee is required to file IRS **Form 8919,** *Uncollected Social Security and Medicare Tax on Wages.*

Advance commissions and other advance earnings are all taxable in the year they are received. It doesn't matter whether or not the employee has earned the income. If the employee receives wages in advance, she recognizes the income in the year it is constructively received. This is true even if the employee is forced to pay back some of the money at a later date. If the employee later pays back a portion of the earnings, that sum would be deducted from wages at that time.

Example: Maddox requests a salary advance of $1,000 on December 18, 2010 in order to go on a two-week vacation. Maddox must recognize the income on his 2010 tax return, even though he will not actually earn the money until 2011 when he returns from his vacation.

Severance pay is taxable as ordinary income, just like wages. Even though severance pay is usually issued to employees who are being terminated and is not actually for work performed, it is still taxable as wages and still subject to Social Security and Medicare tax.

Tip Income

Tips are taxable as ordinary income. Individuals who receive $20 or more per month in tips must report their tip income to their employer. Tips are received by food servers, baggage handlers, hairdressers, and others for performing services.

Taxpayers who do not report all of their tips to their employer must report the Social Security and Medicare taxes on their Form 1040. Employees use **Form 4137**, *Social Security and Medicare Tax on Unreported Tip Income,* to compute and report the additional tax.

Taxpayers who are *self-employed* and receive tips must include their tips in gross receipts on **Schedule C.** Examples of this type of taxpayer include self-employed hair stylists and manicurists.

Example: Mandy works two jobs. She is a quality inspector during the week and a bartender on the weekends. She reports all of her tip income ($3,000) to her employer. Her Forms W-2 show wage income of $21,000 (quality inspector) and $8,250 (bartender). Mandy must report $29,250 on her Form 1040. Mandy reported the tip income to her employer, so her bartending tips are *already included* on her W-2 for that job, so the amount she reports is $21,000 + $8,250.

Individuals who receive **less than** $20 per month in tips while working one job do not have to report their tip income to their employer. They do not have to report noncash tips either (for example, tickets or passes). Tips of less than $20 per month are:

- Exempt from Social Security and Medicare taxes
- Subject to federal income tax and must be reported on Form 1040

Noncash tips (for example, tickets or passes) do not have to be reported to the employer, but must be included in the taxpayer's income at their Fair Market Value.

Garnished Wages

An employee may have his wages garnished for many different reasons. Sometimes the employee owes child support, back taxes due, or other debts. It doesn't matter how much is actually garnished from the employee's paycheck. The full amount (the gross wages) is taxable to the employee and must be included in the employee's wages at year end.

Disability Retirement Benefits

Disability retirement benefits are taxable as wages if a taxpayer retired on disability before reaching the minimum retirement age. These benefits are taxable as wages on the taxpayer's Form 1040. Once the taxpayer reaches retirement age, the payments are no longer taxable as wages. They are then taxable as pension income.

Disability Payments from an Insurance Policy

For payments made pursuant to an individual disability income insurance policy, benefits normally are free of income tax. Disability income benefits are excluded from income if the taxpayer pays the premiums for the policy. For health insurance paid for by the employer, the employer deducts the cost and the employee pays no tax on the premiums paid by the employer. The employee also does not pay any tax on the benefits received.

Sick pay is not the same thing as "disability pay." Sick pay is always taxable as wages, just like vacation pay.

Property In Lieu Of Wages

An employee who receives property instead of wages for services performed must generally recognize the Fair Market Value of the property when it is received. However, if an employee receives stock or other property that is restricted, the property is not included in income until it is available without restriction to the employee.

> **Example:** Barry receives stock from his company as part of his promotion. He receives $5,000 worth of stock, a total of 500 shares. However, Barry cannot sell or exercise the shares for five years. If Barry quits his job, he forfeits the shares. He does not have to recognize this restricted stock as income in the year he received it. This is because the stock is subject to multiple restrictions. This stock will be taxable when Barry chooses to sell it or otherwise gains complete control over it.

Supplemental Wages

"Supplemental wages" is compensation that is paid to an employee in addition to her regular pay. These amounts are listed on the employee's Form W-2 and are taxable just like regular wages, even if the pay is not actually for work performed. Vacation pay is an example of supplemental wages that is taxable just like any other wage income, even though the employee has not technically "worked" for the income. Supplemental wages include:

- Bonuses, commissions, prizes
- Severance pay, back pay, and holiday pay
- Accumulated vacation pay and sick leave
- Payment for nondeductible moving expenses

Military Pay Exclusion-Combat Zone Wages

Wages earned by military personnel are generally taxable. However, there are special rules for military personnel regarding taxable income, including many exclusions for those on active duty. Combat zone wages and hazardous duty pay are excludable for certain military personnel. Enlisted persons who serve in a combat zone (including commissioned warrant officers) for any part of a month may exclude their pay from tax. For officers, pay is excluded up to a certain amount, depending on the branch of service.

> **Example:** Lee is a Marine. He served in a combat zone from January 1, 2010 to November 3, 2010. He will only be required to report his income for December 2010, because all of the other income is excluded from taxation as combat zone pay. Even though Lee only served three days in November in a combat zone, his income for the entire month of November is excluded.

Special Deadlines for Military Personnel

Military personnel serving in a combat zone also have an automatic extension for most tax matters. Military personnel, unlike civilian taxpayers, are granted extensions for filing and also paying their income tax due. While a taxpayer is serving in a combat zone, he is granted extensions for requesting innocent spouse relief and collection due process hearing. A 90-day limit for filing a Tax Court petition also does not apply while the taxpayer is serving in a combat zone.

Substitute W-2 Form

If for some reason an employee does not receive his **Form W-2** (perhaps the employer went out of business), the employee may file his tax return on paper using IRS **Form 4852,** *Substitute for Form W-2, Wage and Tax Statement.* **Form 4852** is a substitute wage and tax statement that taxpayers may use when it is impossible to get a W-2 from the employer.

Taxpayers should only use IRS **Form 4852** as a last resort. IRS **Form 4852** is used to essentially re-create the W-2 form that the employee would have received. Usually, an earnings statement or similar document is used as a basis to re-create the data required in order to complete and file the taxpayer's return.

Example: Manny was working for a plumbing company in 2010. In December 2010, the owner died, and final information returns were never filed. The business was closed and Manny never got a **Form W-2** for the wages he earned in 2010. Manny may file a **Form 4852** as a substitute for the **Form W-2,** explaining the circumstances why he could not obtain a **Form W-2.** Then Manny may use his earnings statement or other records to attempt a re-creation on his taxable income and withholding.

Barter Exchanges and Barter Income

Bartering is an exchange of property or services. Usually there is no exchange of cash. Barter may take place on an informal, one-on-one basis between individuals and businesses, or it can take place on a third party basis through a barter exchange company.

While our ancestors may have exchanged eggs for corn, today a person can barter computer services for auto repair. Another example of a one-on-one exchange transaction is a plumber doing repair work for a dentist in exchange for dental services. The Fair Market Value of the goods and services exchanged must be reported as income by both parties. Income from bartering is taxable in the year it is performed.

If a taxpayer agrees to exchange services with another person and both have agreed ahead of time as to the value of the services, the agreed-upon value will be accepted as Fair Market Value.

Alimony (as Income to the Recipient)

Alimony is taxable income to the recipient and deductible by the payor. If the divorce agreement specifies payments of both alimony and child support and only partial payments are made by the payor, then the partial payments are considered to be child support until this obligation is fully paid, and any excess is then treated as alimony. Child support is not taxable income to the receiver and not deductible by the payor.

If the payment amount is to be reduced based on a contingency *relating to a child* (e.g., attaining a certain age, marrying), the amount of the reduction will be treated as child support. Any "alimony" payments that continue after the receiving spouse has died will automatically be considered child support, not alimony.

Property Settlements Pursuant to Divorce are Not Alimony!

Property settlements, which are simply a division of property, are not treated as alimony. Property transferred to a former spouse incident to a divorce is treated as a gift. "Incident to a divorce" means a transfer of property within one year after the date of the divorce, or a transfer of property related to the cessation of the marriage, as determined by the courts. Alimony payments made under a divorce agreement are deductible by the PAYOR if all of the following requirements are met:

- The spouses may not file joint returns with each other.
- Payments are made in cash or a cash equivalent (such as checks or money orders). Payments made to a third party can be considered alimony. For example, if one spouse pays the medical bills of his ex-wife, the cash payment to the hospital can count as alimony.

Example: Ben is required to pay $1,000 per month in alimony to Karen, his former spouse. Karen has medical bills of $1,500, and Ben agrees to pay the medical bills in lieu of the regular alimony payment. The $1,500 would qualify as alimony payment to a third party, since it was made on Karen's behalf to her creditor.

In order for a payment to qualify as alimony,

- The divorce agreement may not include a clause indicating that the payment is something else (such as child support or repayment of a loan, etc.).
- If the spouses are legally separated, the spouses cannot live together when the payments are made.
- The payor must have no liability to make any payment (in cash or property) after the death of the former spouse.
- The alimony payment must not be treated as child support.

Child Support is Not Alimony!

The IRS treats alimony very differently from child support in the United States. Alimony is treated as income to the receiving spouse and deducted from the income of the paying spouse. Child support, however, is never deductible because it is viewed as a payment that a parent is making simply for the support of his child.

Example: Under Cary's divorce decree, he must pay his ex-wife Jennifer $30,000 per year. The payments will stop after 15 years (or upon Jennifer's death). Jennifer dies ten years later. The divorce decree provided that if Jennifer dies before the end of the 15-year period, Cary must still pay Jennifer's estate the difference between $450,000 ($30,000 annually × 15 years) and the total amount paid up to that time. Since Jennifer dies at the end of the tenth year, Cary must pay Jennifer's estate $150,000 ($450,000–$300,000). Since the payment is required even after Jennifer's death, none of the annual payments are considered alimony for tax purposes. The payments are actually "disguised child support," and cannot be deducted by Cary as alimony.

Alimony "Paid" is an Adjustment to Income

Spouses do not have to itemize in order to deduct their alimony payments. The alimony paid is listed on the first page of **Form 1040** as an adjustment to income. Taxpayers must claim the deduction on **Form 1040**. They cannot use **Form 1040A** or **Form 1040EZ**. Taxpayers must provide the Social Security Number of the former spouse receiving the alimony payments. Alimony paid is an adjustment to income for the payor, and is taxable to the receiving spouse.

Qualifying Alimony (General Rules)

The following rules apply to alimony regardless of when the divorce or separation instrument was executed. Alimony does NOT include:

- Child support
- Noncash property settlements
- Payments that are community income
- Payments to keep up the payor's property
- Free use of the payor's property

An Amended Divorce Decree

An amendment to a divorce decree may change the nature of the payments. Amendments are not ordinarily retroactive for federal tax purposes. However, a retroactive amendment to a divorce decree correcting a clerical error to reflect the original intent of the court will generally be effective retroactively for federal tax purposes (Publication 504).

> **Example:** A court order retroactively corrected a mathematical error on Pat's divorce decree to express the original intent to spread the alimony payments over more than ten years. This change also is effective retroactively for federal tax purposes, since it is a correction of an error by the courts.

Legal Fees and the Cost of Divorce

A taxpayer cannot deduct legal fees and court costs for getting a divorce. But she may deduct legal fees paid for tax advice in connection with a divorce and legal fees to obtain alimony. In order to be deductible, the tax advice fees must be separately stated on the attorney's bill. In addition, a taxpayer may deduct fees paid to appraisers, actuaries, and accountants for services in determining the correct tax or in helping to get alimony.

A taxpayer can deduct fees for legal advice on federal, state, and local taxes of all types, including income, estate, gift, inheritance, and property taxes, even if the advice is related to a divorce. If an attorney's legal fee includes amounts for tax advice and other tax services, the taxpayer must be able to prove the expense was incurred for tax advice and not for some other legal issue.

> **Example:** The lawyer handling Jenna's divorce consults another law firm, which handles only tax matters, to get information on how the divorce will affect her taxes. Since Jenna consulted with the second law firm specifically to discuss tax matters, Jenna can deduct the part of the fee paid to the second firm and separately stated on her bill, as an itemized deduction on Schedule A, subject to a 2% limit (Publication 504).

> **Example:** The lawyer handling Mack's divorce uses the firm's tax department for tax matters related to his divorce. Mack's statement from the firm shows the part of the total fee for tax matters. This is based on the time required, the difficulty of the tax questions, and the amount of tax involved. Mack can deduct this part of his bill as an itemized deduction on **Schedule A**, subject to a 2% limit.

Because a taxpayer must include alimony received in gross income, a taxpayer may deduct fees paid to an attorney to collect alimony.

The taxpayer can claim deductible legal fees only by itemizing deductions on Schedule A (Form 1040). The fees must be claimed as miscellaneous itemized deductions subject to the 2%-of-adjusted-gross-income limit. (For more information on this issue, see IRS Publication 529, *Miscellaneous Deductions*.)

> **Example #1:** The lawyer handling Paul's divorce also works on the tax matters. The fee for tax advice and the fee for other services are shown separately on the lawyer's statement. They are based on the time spent on each service and the fees charged for similar services. Paul can deduct the fee charged for tax advice only, subject to a 2% limit.

> **Example #2:** Betty pays an attorney $4,500 for handling her divorce. Betty also pays an additional $1,500 fee for services in collecting alimony that her former husband refuses to pay. Betty can deduct the fee for collecting alimony ($1,500), subject to a 2% limit, if it is separately stated on the attorney's bill.

Income from Securities (Dividends from Stocks & Bonds)

Investors typically buy and sell securities and then report income from dividends, interest, or capital appreciation. The sales of these securities result in capital gains and losses that must be reported on Form 1040, Schedule D, Capital Gains and Losses.

Investors can deduct the expenses related to investment income. These include expenses for investment counseling and advice, legal and accounting fees, and investment newsletters. These expenses are deductible on Form 1040, Schedule A, Itemized Deductions, as miscellaneous deductions to the extent that they exceed 2% of adjusted gross income.

A. Dividends

A "dividend" is a distribution of income made by a corporation to its shareholders, out of net earnings and profits. Ordinary dividends are corporate distributions in cash (as opposed to property or stock shares). Amounts received as dividends are taxed as ordinary income. Dividends are passive income, so they are not subject to self-employment tax.

Any distribution *in excess* of earnings and profits (both current and accumulated) is considered a recovery of capital and is therefore not taxable.

Capital gains and losses from the sale of securities (stock sales and trades) are covered in a later unit. Distributions in excess of earnings and profits reduce the taxpayer's basis. Once basis is reduced to zero, any additional distributions are capital gain and are taxed as such.

Ordinary dividends are reported on **Schedule B**. If the total dividend income is $1,500 or less, all of the income can be reported directly on page one of IRS **Form 1040**. Qualified dividends are reported on Schedule B. *Qualified dividends* are dividends that are eligible for a lower tax rate than other ordinary income. Ordinary and qualified dividends are reported on Form 1099-DIV.

Capital gain distributions are also reported on Form 1099-DIV, are always reported as long-term capital gain on **Schedule B**.

B. Qualified Dividends

Qualified dividends are given preferred tax treatment. Qualified dividends are ordinary dividends that meet specific criteria in order to receive the lower 0% or 15% maximum tax rate that applies to capital gains. Qualified dividends are reported to the taxpayer on **Form 1099-DIV.**

Qualified dividends are subject to a 15% tax rate if the taxpayer's regular tax rate is 25% or higher. If the taxpayer's regular tax rate is under 25%, the qualified dividends are subject to a zero percent rate (they are essentially nontaxable). In order for the dividends to qualify for the lower rate, all of the following requirements must be met:

- The dividends must have been paid by a U.S. corporation or a qualified foreign corporation.
- The taxpayer must meet the holding period. The taxpayer must have held the stock for more than 60 days during the 121-day period that begins 60 days before the ex-dividend date. The ex-dividend date is the date *following* the declaration of a dividend.

When trying to figure the holding period for qualified dividends, the taxpayer may count the number of days she held the stock AND include the day she disposed of the stock. The date the taxpayer *acquires* the stock is not included in the holding period.

> **Example:** Tim bought 10,000 shares of GREENWAY Mutual Fund stock on July 9, 2010. GREENWAY Mutual Fund paid a cash dividend of 10 cents a share. The ex-dividend date was July 17, 2010. The GREENWAY Mutual Fund advises Tim that the portion of the dividend eligible to be treated as qualified dividends equals 2 cents per share. Tim's Form 1099-DIV from GREENWAY Mutual Fund shows total ordinary dividends of $1,000 and qualified dividends of $200. However, Tim sold the 10,000 shares on August 12, 2010. Tim has no qualified dividends from GREENWAY Mutual Fund because Tim held the GREENWAY Mutual Fund stock for less than 61 days.

Rules for IRS Schedule B

A taxpayer must file Schedule B, *Interest and Ordinary Dividends*, when any of the following apply:

- The taxpayer had over $1,500 of taxable interest or ordinary dividends.
- The taxpayer is claiming the education exclusion of interest from series EE savings bonds.
- The taxpayer received ordinary dividends as a nominee. "Nominee interest" occurs when a taxpayer receives a 1099-INT form, but the interest really be-

longs to another party. This is very common when taxpayers set up accounts for family members and minor children.

- The taxpayer had foreign accounts or received a distribution from a foreign trust.
- The taxpayer received interest as part of a seller-financed mortgage.

C. Mutual Fund Distributions/Capital Gain Distributions

Taxpayers who receive mutual fund distributions during the year will also receive IRS Form 1099-DIV identifying the type of distribution received. A distribution may be an ordinary dividend, a qualified dividend, a capital gain distribution, an exempt-interest dividend, or a non-dividend distribution. Mutual fund distributions can be reported on Form 1040 or Form 1040A. Taxpayers cannot use Form 1040EZ to report mutual fund distributions.

Mutual fund distributions are reported depending upon the character of the income source. Capital gain distributions from a mutual fund are *always* treated as long-term *regardless* of the actual period the mutual fund investment is held.

Distributions from a mutual fund investing in tax-exempt securities will be tax-exempt interest. In some cases, a mutual fund may pay tax-exempt interest dividends, paid from tax-exempt interest earned by the fund. Since the exempt-interest dividends keep their tax-exempt character, they are not taxable. Even so, the taxpayer must report them on his tax return. This is an information reporting requirement only, and does not convert tax-exempt interest to taxable interest. However, this income is generally a "tax preference item" and may be subject to the Alternative Minimum Tax.

The mutual fund will supply the taxpayer with a Form 1099-INT showing the tax-exempt interest dividends.

If a mutual fund or Real Estate Investment Trust (REIT) declares a dividend in October, November, or December payable to shareholders but actually pays the dividend during January of the following year, the shareholder is still considered to have received the dividend on December 31 of the prior tax year. The taxpayer must report the dividend in the year it was declared.

D. Stock Dividends

A stock dividend is simply a distribution of stock by a corporation to its own shareholders. This happens when a corporation chooses to distribute stock rather than money. A stock dividend is also called a "stock grant" or a "stock distribution."

Generally, a stock dividend is not a taxable event. This is because the receiver of the stock (a shareholder) is not actually receiving any money. A nontaxable stock dividend does not affect a taxpayer's income in the year of distribution. A stock dividend will affect a shareholder's basis in her existing stock. The basis of the stockholder's existing shares is divided to include the new stock. So a stock dividend will essentially reduce basis.

Example: Razor Ball Corporation agrees to a year-end stock dividend. Scarlett is a shareholder in Razor Ball. She currently owns 100 shares, and her basis in the shares is $50 each, for a total of $5,000. Scarlett is granted a stock dividend of 100 shares. After the dividend, Scarlett owns 200 shares. Her new basis in each individual share is $25 per share. However, her overall basis in the shares does not change (it is still $5,000). Scarlett would recognize income when she decided to sell the shares.

*Exception: If the taxpayer (shareholder) has the option to receive cash instead of stock, then the stock dividend becomes taxable. The recipient of the stock must then include the Fair Market Value of the stock in his gross income. That amount then becomes the basis of the new shares received.

Example: Fun Time Corporation agrees to issue a year-end stock dividend. Dale owns 1,000 shares in Fun Time, and his current basis in the shares is $10 each, for a total of $10,000. In 2010, Dale is granted a stock dividend of 100 shares, but Fun Time gives all the shareholders the option of receiving cash instead of stock. Therefore, the stock dividend becomes a taxable event. Dale decides to take the stock instead of the cash. The Fair Market Value of the stock at the time of the distribution is $15 per share. Dale must recognize $1,500 in income ($15 FMV X 100 shares=$1,500). After the dividend, Dale owns 1,100 shares. Dale's basis in the new shares is $15 per share. Dale's basis in the old shares remains the same.

Social Security and Equivalent Railroad Retirement Benefits

Generally, if the taxpayer *only* has Social Security income, the income is not taxable and a taxpayer is not required to file a tax return. Social Security benefits *become* taxable once the taxpayer starts to receive other types of income, such as wages or interest income. This usually happens when a retired person who is receiving Social Security benefits also has a job. The taxable portion of Social Security benefits is never more than 85%. In most cases, the taxable portion is less than 50%.[20]

To better understand the thresholds, if a taxpayer is filing Single or HOH and combined income* is

- Between $25,000 and $34,000 the taxpayer may have to pay income tax on up to 50% of Social Security benefits.
- More than $34,000, up to 85% of Social Security benefits may be taxable.

If a taxpayer filed jointly and combined income* is

- Between $32,000 and $44,000, the taxpayer has to pay income tax on up to 50% of Social Security benefits.
- More than $44,000, up to 85% of Social Security benefits may be taxable.

If a taxpayer is filing MFS, he will probably pay taxes on his Social Security benefits.

> *Formula: The T/P Adjusted Gross Income
> \+ Nontaxable interest
> \+ ½ of Social Security benefits
> = "Combined income"

---

[20] Social Security income is NOT THE SAME thing as SSI (Supplemental Security Income). SSI is a federal income supplement program for the poor and the disabled. SSI is not taxable.

If the taxpayer also received other income in addition to Social Security, such as income from a job, the benefits will not be taxed unless Modified Adjusted Gross Income (MAGI) is more than the base amount for the taxpayer's filing status. If a taxpayer has any income *in addition* to Social Security, he may be required to file a tax return *even if* none of the Social Security benefits are taxable. Social Security benefits are reported to the taxpayer on Form SSA-1099. Benefits (income) from Railroad Retirement are reported on Form RRB-1099.

Figuring the taxable portion of Social Security benefits is a little tricky. To find out the taxable portion of Social Security, first compare the BASE AMOUNT (shown below) for the taxpayer's filing status with the total of:

- One-half of the Social Security benefits, plus
- All other income, including tax-exempt interest.

When making this comparison, do not reduce other income by any exclusions for:

- Interest from qualified U.S. savings bonds,
- Employer-provided adoption benefits,
- Foreign earned income or foreign housing, or
- Income earned by bona fide residents of American Samoa or Puerto Rico.

BASE AMOUNTS: SOCIAL SECURITY

A taxpayer's BASE AMOUNT for figuring the taxability of Social Security is:

$25,000 for Single, Head of Household, or Qualifying Widow(er),

$32,000 for Married Filing Jointly, or

$25,000 for Married Filing Separately (and lived *apart* from his spouse all year)

$-0- if the taxpayer is MFS (if lived with spouse at any time during the tax year)

How to Figure the Taxability of Social Security

To figure out what percentages of a taxpayer's Social Security benefits are taxable, the taxpayer must first determine the sum of Modified AGI (MAGI) and add one-half of the Social Security benefits. After doing this calculation on a worksheet, if the amount is less than the "base amount," then none of the Social Security is taxable.

Example: Bo and Marie are both over 65. They file jointly and they both received Social Security benefits during the year. In January 2011, Bo received a Form SSA-1099 showing net benefits of $7,500. Marie received a Form SSA-1099 showing net benefits of $3,500. Bo also received wages of $20,000 and interest income of $500. Bo did not have any tax-exempt interest.

1. Total Social Security Benefits:	$11,000
2. Enter one-half of SS	$5,500
3. Enter taxable interest and wages	$20,500
4. Add ($5,500 + $20,500)	$26,000

Bo and Marie's benefits are not taxable for 2010 because their income is not more than the base amount ($32,000) for Married Filing Jointly.

Taxable State Income Tax Refunds

State income tax refunds are reportable as taxable income in the year received only if the taxpayer itemized deductions in the prior year. The state should send Form 1099-G, *Certain Government Payments*, by January 31. The IRS also will receive a copy of the Form 1099-G.

Example: Wally claimed the standard deduction on last year's tax return and received a state tax refund of $600. The state tax refund is not taxable. Only taxpayers who itemize deductions and receive a state or local refund in the prior year are required to include the state tax refund in their taxable income.

Rents and Royalties

Income from rents and royalties must be included in gross income. Rental income is income from the use (or occupation) of property (such as income from a rental home). Income from royalties includes income from copyrights, trademarks, and franchises. Rental and royalty income is reported on **Schedule E**. Rental and royalty income will be covered at length in a later unit.

Nontaxable Income

Some types of income are nontaxable. You need to understand the most common types of nontaxable income for the Enrolled Agent Exam. Some nontaxable income must be reported to the IRS, and some does not.

Veterans' Benefits

Veterans' benefits are nontaxable. Amounts paid by the Department of Veterans Affairs to a veteran or his family are nontaxable if they are for education, training, disability compensation, work therapy, dependent care assistance, or other benefits or pension payments given to the veteran because of disability.

Workers' Compensation

Workers' compensation is not taxable income if it is received because of an occupational injury. However, disability benefits paid by an employer (also called "sick pay") are taxable to the employee. Long-term disability income payments are included in gross income and are taxable to the employee.

Foreign Earned Income Exclusion

Generally, the income of U.S. citizens is taxed even if the income is earned outside the United States. Foreign earned income is income received for services performed in a foreign country while the taxpayer's tax home is ALSO in a foreign country. The taxpayer must pass one of two tests in order to claim the foreign earned income exclusion.

- **Test #1: "Bona Fide Residence Test" OR**
- **Test #2: The "Physical Presence" Test**

Bona Fide Residence Test: A U.S. citizen (or U.S. resident alien) who is a bona fide resident of a foreign country for an uninterrupted period that includes an entire tax year.

The Physical Presence Test: A U.S. citizen (or U.S. resident alien) who is physically present in a foreign country or countries for at least 330 full days during 12 consecutive months. A taxpayer may qualify under the physical presence test, and the income may span over a period of multiple tax years. If so, the taxpayer must prorate the foreign earned income exclusion based on the number of days spent in the foreign country.

For 2010, the maximum foreign earned income exclusion is $91,500. If the taxpayer is Married Filing Jointly and both individuals live and work abroad, both taxpayers can choose to claim the foreign earned income exclusion. Together, married taxpayers can exclude as much as $183,000.

> **Example:** Brenda earned $80,000 while employed overseas, and she qualifies for the foreign earned income exclusion. Brenda also has $6,000 in work-related expenses. Brenda cannot deduct any of her expenses, because she is already excluding all of her income from taxation by taking the foreign earned income exclusion.

> **Example:** Leila was a bona fide resident of China for all of 2010. In 2010, Leila was paid $92,400 for her work in China. She can exclude $91,500 of the $92,400 she was paid.

It does not matter whether the income is paid by a U.S. employer or a foreign employer.

The foreign earned income exclusion is figured using **Form 2555**, *Foreign Earned Income,* which must be attached to Form 1040. Once the choice is made to exclude foreign earned income, that choice remains in effect for the year the election is made and all later years, unless revoked.

Nonresident aliens do not qualify for the foreign earned income exclusion. A taxpayer must be either a U.S. citizen or a legal resident alien of the United States who lives and works abroad, and meets certain other qualifications to exclude a specific amount of his foreign earned income.

Foreign Tax Credit

Foreign tax credits allow U.S. taxpayers to avoid or reduce double taxation. The "foreign tax credit" is not the same as the foreign earned income exclusion. A taxpayer may claim either the foreign tax credit OR a deduction for foreign taxes paid each year. A taxpayer cannot take the foreign tax credit on income that has already been excluded from taxation by the foreign earned income exclusion.

Generally, the following four tests must be met for any foreign tax to qualify for the credit:

- The tax must be imposed on the taxpayer.
- The taxpayer must have paid or accrued the tax.
- The tax must be the legal and actual foreign tax liability.
- The tax must be an income tax.

A taxpayer can choose to alternate years, choosing to take a credit in one year and a deduction in the next year. The taxpayer can even change her credit to a deduction and vice versa by amending her tax return. To take the foreign tax credit, complete **Form 1116**, *Foreign Tax Credit.*

Example: Greer is a 3% shareholder of a German corporation. She received a $1,000 refund of the tax paid to Germany by the corporation on the earnings distributed to her as a dividend. The German government imposes a 15% withholding tax ($150) on the refund she received. Greer received a net check for $850. She includes $1,000 in her income, and the $150 of tax withheld is a qualified foreign tax and may be claimed as a credit.

The foreign tax credit cannot be more than the taxpayer's total U.S. tax liability multiplied by a fraction. This limit on this credit is figured by calculating the total tax liability multiplied by a fraction made up of total foreign income divided by total income from foreign and U.S. sources (see example below).

Example: Harold's total tax liability is $1,000. In 2010, he made $20,000 from foreign-based investments, along with another $60,000 from U.S. sources. To figure the limit on the foreign tax credit, Harold must take his total foreign income ($20,000) and divide it by the total income from all sources ($20,000 + $60,000). This gives Harold a fraction of .25. Multiply this by his total tax liability ($1,000 x .25= $250). This is the limit on his foreign tax credit.

(Foreign Source Taxable Income ÷ Worldwide Taxable Income) X
(U.S. Income Tax before Credit = FTC Limitation.)

Life Insurance Proceeds

Proceeds from life insurance are not taxable to the recipient. Consequently, life insurance premiums are not deductible by the payor, but an employer may choose to provide employees with life insurance as a fringe benefit and deduct the cost. However, a private individual, such as a sole proprietor purchasing life insurance for herself, may not deduct the premiums.

Life Insurance Proceeds Received in Installments

Sometimes, a taxpayer will choose to receive life insurance in installments, rather than a lump sum. In this case, part of the installment usually includes interest income. If a taxpayer receives life insurance proceeds in installments, he can exclude part of each installment from his income. To determine the excluded part, divide the amount held by the insurance company (generally the total lump sum payable at the death of the insured person) by the number of installments to be paid. Include anything over this excluded part as interest income (Publication 525).

Example: Rose's brother died in 2010, and she is the beneficiary of his life insurance. The face amount of the policy is $75,000 and, as beneficiary, Rose chooses to receive 120 monthly installments of $1,000 each. The excluded part of each installment is $625 ($75,000 ÷ 120), or $7,500 for an entire year. The rest of each payment, $375 a month (or $4,500 for an entire year), is interest income to Rose.

Clergy: Special Rules

There are special rules regarding the taxation of clergy members. "Ministers" or "clergy" are individuals who are ordained, commissioned, or licensed by a religious body or church denomination. They are given the authority to conduct religious worship, perform religious functions, and administer ordinances or sacraments according to the prescribed tenets and practices of that church.

Clergy members must include offerings and fees received for marriages, baptisms, and funerals as part of their income. Generally a clergy member's salary is reported on IRS Form W-2. Additional payments for services are reported on the clergy member's Schedule C.

Minister's Housing Allowance

A minister's housing allowance (sometimes called a "parsonage" allowance or a rental allowance) is excludable from gross income for income tax purposes, but not for self-employment tax purposes. A minister who receives a housing allowance may exclude the allowance from gross income to the extent it is used to pay expenses in providing a home. The exclusion for minister's housing is limited to:

- The lesser of the Fair Market Rental value (including utilities, etc.), or
- The actual amount used to provide a home.

The housing allowance cannot exceed reasonable pay. The payments must be used for housing in the year they are received by the minister.

> **Example:** William is an ordained minister. He received $32,000 in salary in 2010. He also received an additional $4,000 for performing marriages and baptisms. His housing allowance was $500 per month, for a total of $6,000 per year. William must report the $32,000 as wages, $4,000 as self-employment income, and $6,000 as the housing allowance subject only to self-employment tax, not income tax. Report this "SE taxable income" on Schedule SE.

Both salary and housing allowances must be included in income for the purpose of determining self-employment tax.

> **Example:** Jacob is a full-time ordained minister at Waterfront Presbyterian Church. The church allows him to use a cottage that has a rental value of $5,000. The church also pays Jacob a salary of $12,000. His income for self-employment tax purposes is $17,000 ($5,000 + $12,000 salary). Ministers must include the FMV of a home on Schedule SE.

> **Example:** Father Mark is an ordained priest at the local Catholic Church. His annual salary is $26,000 and he also receives a $10,000 housing allowance. His housing costs for the year are $14,000. Therefore, Mark's self-employment income is $36,000 ($26,000 salary + $10,000 housing allowance). But only his base salary ($26,000) is subject to income tax, because his actual housing expenses are more than his housing allowance.

Vow of Poverty

If a minister or other individual (nun, monk, etc.) is a member of a religious order who has taken a vow of poverty, the individual is exempt from paying SE tax on his earnings for qualified services. For income tax purposes, the earnings are tax-free, because the earnings are considered the income of the religious order, rather than of the individual.

Exemption from Social Security

A minister can request an exemption from self–employment tax for religious reasons. To request the exemption, ministers must file Form 4361, *Application for Exemption from Self-Employment Tax for Use by Ministers, Members of Religious Orders, and Christian Science Practitioners*, with the IRS.

Compensatory Damages and Court Settlements

Compensatory damages for personal physical injury or physical sickness are not taxable income, whether they are from a settlement or from an actual court award.

> **Example:** Felix was injured in a car accident in 2010. His legs were broken and he suffered other serious physical injuries. He received a settlement from the insurance company for his injuries totaling $950,000. This would be nontaxable income, because it is payment for a physical injury.

Compensatory damages for "emotional distress" are usually taxable. Emotional distress itself is not a physical injury. If the emotional distress is due to unlawful discrimination or injury to reputation, the taxpayer must include the damages in taxable income, except for any damages received for medical care due to that emotional distress.

> **Example:** Kristina recently won a court award for emotional distress due to unlawful discrimination. Kristina was hospitalized for nervous breakdown due to the emotional distress. She received damages of $100,000, including $20,000 to refund the cost of her medical care due to the nervous breakdown. In this case, $80,000 ($100,000 - $20,000) would be considered a taxable court award. The $20,000 of damages for her medical care would be nontaxable.

Punitive damages are taxable income. It does not matter if they relate to a physical injury or physical sickness. Court awards for lost wages are always taxable as ordinary income.

Unit 1.5: Questions

1. Hank received Social Security in 2010 totaling $11,724. Also in 2010, Hank sold all of his stock and moved into senior housing. He received $31,896 of taxable income from the sale of the stock. What is the maximum taxable amount of Hank's Social Security benefits?

A. $31,896
B. $20,172
C. $11,724
D. $9,965

The answer is D. The maximum amount that can ever be taxable on the net benefits is 85% or $9,965. ###

2. Bruce and Ann have three Forms 1099-INT:
- Epping National Bank, $62
- Epping Credit Union, $178
- Breton Savings and Loan, $760

How much interest income should they report on Schedule B (Form 1040)?

A. None
B. $760
C. $240
D. $1,000

The answer is A. Schedule B is not used to report regular interest totaling $1,500 or less. ###

3. Which of the following types of income are exempt from federal taxes?

A. Interest income
B. IRA distributions
C. Tips
D. Inheritances

The answer is D. Of the types of income listed here, only inheritances are exempt from federal taxes. ###

4. Ryan received a capital gain distribution in the amount of $75 and dividend income in the amount of $150 from his mutual fund. Which of the following is correct?

A. Ryan may report the capital gain distribution and the dividend on Form 1040.
B. Ryan must report the dividend on Schedule B and the capital gain distribution on Schedule D.
C. Ryan can report a capital gain distribution and the dividend on Schedule B.
D. Ryan can use Form 1040EZ to report both amounts.

The answer is A. Ryan may report both of these amounts on his Form 1040. Dividend income of $1,500 or less may be reported on page 1 of Form 1040 (or 1040A). He does not need to use Schedule B to report the dividend income. Ryan also meets the requirements for reporting the capital gain distribution directly on Form 1040 (or Form 1040A). He is not required to use Schedule D to report the capital gain distribution.

5. Toni owns a Series I savings bond, which she purchased as an investment to help pay for her daughter's education. Toni redeems the bond in 2010 and immediately uses all the funds to pay for her daughter Ruth's college tuition. The bond's interest is reported on _____.

A. It must be reported on Toni's tax return and is 100% taxable.
B. It must be reported on Ruth's tax return and is 100% taxable.
C. It must be reported on Toni's tax return and is 100% exempt from taxes.
D. It is not required to be reported.

The answer is C. As the buyer and owner of the bond, Toni reports the interest on her tax return, but excludes the interest from her income because she paid for qualified higher education expenses the same year.###

6. Joyce and Craig, a married couple, received $200 in interest from bonds issued by the State of Illinois. How should they report this on their Form 1040?

A. It must be reported as interest income, and it is 100% taxable.
B. It must be reported, but it is not taxable income.
C. They do not have to report it.
D. None of the above.

The answer is B. The interest is tax-exempt municipal bond interest. It must be reported on the taxpayer's return. ###

7. Which of the following types of income are taxable?

A. Credit union dividends
B. Veterans' life insurance dividends
C. Workers' compensation
D. Child support

The answer is A. Credit union dividends are subject to federal income tax. ###

8. Under what circumstances must a person report taxable income?

A. Always
B. Always, unless the income is only from interest
C. Always, unless the income is so small that reporting it is not required by law
D. Always, unless the person is identified as a dependent on someone else's tax return

The answer is C. All taxable income must be reported on a tax return, unless the amount is so small that the individual is not required to file a return. Filing thresholds depend on a taxpayer's marital status, age, and dependency status. ###

9. Which of the following tip income is exempt from federal income tax?

A. Tips of less than $20 per month
B. Tips not reported to the employer
C. Noncash tips
D. None of the above

The answer is D. All tip income is subject to federal income tax, whether it is cash or noncash. ###

10. Leona received the following income: wages, interest, child support, alimony, inheritance, workers' compensation, and lottery winnings. Determine what amount of Leona's income is taxable.

The answer is C. The wages, interest, alimony, and lottery winnings are taxable income and will appear on Leona's tax return ($13,000 + $15 + $2,000 + $5,000 = $20,015). Child support, inheritances, and workers' compensation are nontaxable income and will not appear on Leona's tax return. ###

Leona's Income:

SOURCE	TAXABLE?
Wages	$13,000
Interest	$15
Child support	$6,000
Alimony	$2,000
Inheritance	$10,000
Workers' compensation	$1,000
Lottery winnings	$5,000

A. S13,015
B. $16,015
C. $20,015
D. $30,015

11. Which of the following statements is TRUE?

A. Food servers do not need to report tips as taxable income.
B. Food servers are required to report tips on their tax return, even if the amounts have not been reported to the employer.
C. Tips received that total less than $20 a month are nontaxable.
D. Tips are nontaxable because they are considered gifts.

The answer is B. Tips are taxable income and must be reported on the tax return, even if they have not been reported to the employer. ###

12. Tom has worked for Parkway Construction for over two years. In November 2009, the owner of Parkway files for bankruptcy and leaves the country abruptly. Tom never received his Form W-2. What form may Tom use in order to file his 2010 tax return?

A: Form 1040X
B: Form 1099-MISC
C: Form 4852
D: Form W-3

The answer is C. Tom may use IRS Form 4852 in order to estimate the amounts on the W-2. Even if a taxpayer has not received a W-2, he must still file a tax return. The taxpayer may use a substitute W-2 form, Form 4852, to file with the IRS. ###

13. Seville is a member of the armed forces and served in a combat zone from January 1 to September 2 of the current tax year. He returned to the United States and received his regular duty pay for the remainder of the year. How many months of income are taxable?

A. Zero. All the income is tax-free.
B. Three months are subject to tax.
C. Four months are subject to tax.
D. Twelve months are taxable.

The answer is B. Since Seville served for a few days in September, all the income in September is excluded as combat pay. If a taxpayer serves in a combat zone as an enlisted person for *any part* of a month, all of his military pay received for military service that month is excluded from gross income. ###

14. Which form must banks use to report mutual fund distributions to a taxpayer?

A. Form 1099-DIV
B. Schedule B
C. Form 1099-Misc
D. Form W-4

The answer is A. Taxpayers who receive mutual fund distributions during the year will also receive a Form 1099-DIV identifying the type of distribution received. A mutual fund distribution may be an ordinary dividend, a qualified dividend, a capital gain distribution, an exempt-interest dividend, or a non-dividend distribution. ###

15. Sven and Samantha file jointly in 2010. They received the following income for 2010. How much income should be reported on their 2010 joint tax return?

1. W-2 income for Samantha for wages of $40,000.
2. W-2 for Samantha for $2,000, the value of a trip she won to the Bahamas. She never went on the trip. But she is planning to take the trip in 2011.
3. Court settlement of $10,000 paid to Sven from a car accident for serious injuries he suffered.
4. $4,000 child support for Samantha's son from a previous marriage.

A. $40,000
B. $42,000
C. $46,000
D. $52,000

The answer is B. The wages earned and prize won by Samantha should be included on the joint return, and the accident settlement should be excluded from income. Samantha must recognize the prize, because even though she did not take the trip, she had constructive receipt of the winnings. Child support is never taxable. The answer is $42,000 ($40,000 wages + $2,000 prize). ###

16. Which of the following is true?

A. Tips can be received in the form of money or goods.
B. Tips are only taxable if they are received in cash.
C. Only tips received as an employee are taxable.
D. None of the above.

The answer is A. Tips and wages can be received in the form of money or goods. For example, a customer at a casino may choose to leave a $10 poker chip as a tip. Although this is not actual money, it is still taxable at its Fair Market Value, which would be $10. ###

17. Sandy received the following income in 2010:

1. Wages: $70,000
2. Gambling winnings: $500
3. Dependent care benefits through her employer: $5,000
4. Employer-provided parking pass: $220 per month

Sandy had only $4,000 in qualified daycare expenses. How much gross income must she report on her tax return?

A. $70,000
B. $70,500
C. $71,500
D. $73,300

The answer is C. Dependent care assistance programs are not taxable up to the amount of qualified expenses. Since Sandy received $5,000, but only had $4,000 in actual daycare expenses, $1,000 is taxable to Sandy. The parking pass is also an excluded benefit. Both the wages and gambling winnings must be included in the gross income total of $71,500 ($70,000 + $500 + $1,000). ###

18. Ginny had the following in 2010:

- Social Security Income: $14,000
- Interest income: $125
- Gambling winnings: $1,000
- Gambling losses: $2,000
- Accident settlement for a bodily injury: $20,000
- Child support payments: $13,000
- Food stamp benefits: $5,000

How much income must Ginny include on her 2010 tax return?

A. $14,000
B. $14,125
C. $15,125
D. $30,000
E. $48,000

The answer is C. The Social Security income, gambling income, and interest income must all be reported. The accident settlement and the child support are not taxable. Food stamps and welfare payments also are not taxable income. The gambling losses do not affect the reporting of the gambling income. Gambling losses are a deduction on Schedule A, should Ginny choose to itemize. If Ginny does not itemize, the gambling losses are not deductible. ###

19. Brandi, a flight attendant, received wages of $30,000 in 2010. The airline provided transportation on a standby basis, at no charge, from her home in Detroit to the airline's hub in Chicago. The Fair Market Value of the commuting flights was $5,000. Also in 2010, Brandi received reimbursements under an accountable plan of $10,000 for overnight travel, but only spent $6,000. The excess was returned to Brandi's employer. Brandi became injured on the job in November of the current year and received workers' compensation of $4,000. What amount must Brandi include in gross income on her current year tax return?

A. $30,000
B. $34,000
C. $35,000
D. $37,000

The answer is A. Brandi only has to include her wages in her current year return. The free flights offered on standby to airline personnel are considered a nontaxable fringe benefit. Reimbursements under an accountable plan and amounts paid for workers' compensation are nontaxable. Since Brandi returned the unspent amounts to her employer, the travel reimbursements qualify under an accountable plan and the amounts spent are not taxable to her. ###

20. Debby broke her leg in a car accident in 2010 and was unable to work for three months. She received an accident settlement of $13,000 from the car insurance company. During this time she also received $2,500 in sick pay from her employer. In addition, she received $5,000 from her personally purchased accident policy. How much of this income is taxable income to Debby?

A. $2,500
B. $5,000
C. $5,500
D. $18,000

The answer is A. Only Debby's sick pay is taxable as wages. Sick pay from an employer is taxable like wages (similar to vacation pay), and is therefore includable in Debby's gross income. If a taxpayer pays the full cost of an accident insurance plan, the benefits for personal injury or illness are not includable in income. If the employer pays the cost of an accident insurance plan, then the amounts are taxable to an employee. ###

21. Income was "constructively received" in 2010 in each of the following situations EXCEPT:

A. Wages were deposited in the taxpayer's bank account on December 26, 2010, but was not withdrawn by the taxpayer until January 3, 2011.
B. A taxpayer was informed his check for services rendered was available on December 15, 2010. The taxpayer did not pick up the check until January 30, 2011.
C. A taxpayer received a check by mail on December 31, 2010, but could not deposit the check until January 5, 2011.
D. A taxpayer's home was sold on December 28, 2010. The payment was not received by the taxpayer until January 2, 2011 when the escrow company completed the transaction and released the funds.

The answer is D. Constructive receipt does not require physical possession of the income. However, income is not considered constructively received if the taxpayer cannot access the funds because of restrictions. Since the taxpayer's control of the receipt of the funds in the escrow account was substantially limited until the transaction had closed, the taxpayer did not constructively receive the income until the closing of the transaction in the following year. ###

22. Rob owns a business that has a $10,000 profit in 2010. His wife Cecilia has a business loss of $12,000 for 2010. Which of the following statements are true?

A. On their joint return, they will not have to pay self-employment tax because the losses from Cecilia's business offset Rob's income.
B. The spouses cannot file MFS because Cecilia will lose her right to carry forward her losses.
C. Rob must pay self-employment tax on $10,000, regardless of his wife's losses.
D. If they choose to file separate returns, they may split the profits and losses equally between their two businesses.

The answer is C. Rob must pay self-employment tax on $10,000, regardless of how he and Cecilia choose to file. Taxpayers cannot combine a spouse's income or loss to determine their individual earnings subject to SE tax. However, if a taxpayer has more than one business, then he must combine the net profit or loss from each to determine the total earnings subject to SE tax. ###

23. James is a self-employed attorney who performs legal services for a client, a small corporation. The corporation gives James 100 shares of its stock as payment for his services. Which of the following statements is true?

A. James does not have to include this transaction on his tax return.
B. James should report the income when he sells the stock.
C. The stock is taxable to James at its Fair Market Value.
D. None of the above.

The answer is C. James must include the Fair Market Value (FMV) of the shares in his gross income on **Schedule C (Form 1040)** in the year he receives them. The income would be considered payment for services he provided to his client, the corporation (Publication 17). ###

24. Brent, a plastic surgeon, agreed to exchange services with a handyman. Brent removed a mole and the handyman fixed Brent's running toilet in his medical office. Mole removal is generally charged at $200, and the handyman generally charges $150 to fix a toilet. They agreed in advance that the fee would be $150. Neither exchanged actual cash. How much income must Brent recognize for this barter transaction?

A. $50
B. $150
C. $200
D. $250

The answer is B. Brent must include $150 in income. He may also deduct the cost of the repair ($150) if it qualifies as a business expense. If the taxpayer exchanges services with another person and both have agreed ahead of time on the value of those services, that value will be accepted as Fair Market Value unless the value can be shown to be otherwise. ###

25. Ed received $32,000 in wages from his employer in 2010. He also won a prize from his employer because he helped develop a handbook for new employees. The prize was free lawn care service for a month, valued at $600. Ed also received $7,000 in child support and $2,000 in alimony from his ex-wife. Ed has full custody of his children. What is Ed's taxable income (before deductions and adjustments) for tax year 2010?
A. $32,000
B. $32,600
C. $34,600
D. $39,600

The answer is C. The wages and prize are both taxable income. Child support is not taxable to the receiver, nor deductible by the payor. The alimony is taxable to Ed and deductible by his ex-wife. The answer is figured as follows: ($32,000 + $600 + $2,000) = $34,600 ###

26. Fran won $5,000 playing slot machines in Reno, Nevada. How will these winnings be reported to Fran?

A. Form 1099-G
B. Form 1099-MISC
C. Form W-2
D. Form W-2G

The answer is D. Form W-2G is used to report a taxpayer's income and withholding related to gambling. ###

27. Which form is used by state taxing agencies to report state income tax refunds paid to a taxpayer?

A. Form 1099-MISC
B. Form 1099-G
C. Form 1098
D. Form W-3

The answer is B. State income tax refunds are reported to the taxpayer on **Form 1099-G**, *Certain Government Payments.* ###

28. Jan owns and operates a store in the downtown shopping mall. She reports her income and expenses as a sole proprietor on Schedule C. Jan is having financial difficulties and cannot pay all of her debts. In 2010, one of the banks that she borrowed money from in order to start her business cancels her debt. Jan is not insolvent. She had a balance due of $5,000 when the debt was canceled. Which of the following statements is true?

A. Jan does not have to report the forgiveness of the debt as income.
B. Jan must report the $5,000 debt cancellation on Schedule A.
C. Jan must report the $5,000 debt cancellation as income on her Schedule C.
D. Jan must report the $5,000 of cancelled debt as a long-term gain on Schedule D.

The answer is C. Canceled debt that is related to business income must be included on a taxpayer's Schedule C as business income. Generally, if a taxpayer's debt is canceled or forgiven other than as a gift or bequest, the taxpayer must include the canceled amount in gross income for tax purposes. Jan must report the canceled amount on Schedule C if the debt was incurred in a business. ###

29. Scott opened a savings account at his local bank and deposited $800. The account earns $20 interest in 2010. Scott also received a $15 calculator as a gift for opening the account. How much interest income must Scott report on his IRS Form 1040?

A. $15
B. $20
C. $35
D. $800

The answer is C. If no other interest is credited to Scott during the year, the Form 1099-INT he receives will show $35 interest for the year. Scott must report the Fair Market Value of the calculator on his return as interest income. A gift for opening a bank account is taxed as interest income. ###

30. During the current year, Andrew received interest income of $300 from municipal bonds and $200 in interest from a Certificate of Deposit (a CD). Which of the following statements is TRUE?

A. Andrew is required to report the $500 in interest income on his income tax return, but none of the interest is taxable.
B. Andrew is NOT required to any report any of the income on his tax return.
C. Andrew is required to report the total interest ($500) on his income tax return. The CD interest is taxable, but the muni bond interest is not.
D. Andrew is required to report only $200 of interest on his income tax return.

The answer is C. Under present federal income tax law, the interest income received from investing in municipal bonds is free from federal income taxes. However, the taxpayer is required to show any tax-exempt interest received on his tax return. This is an informational reporting requirement only. It does not change tax-exempt interest to taxable interest. The interest from the Certificate of Deposit ($200) is taxable and must be reported as interest income (Publication 17). ###

31. Kent invested in a mutual fund in 2010. The fund declared a dividend, and Kent earned $19. He did not get a Form 1099-DIV for the amount, and he did not withdraw the money from his mutual fund. Kent pulled the money out of his mutual fund on January 2, 2011. Which of the following statements is TRUE?

A. This dividend is not reportable in 2010 because Kent didn't receive the money yet.
B. This dividend is not reportable in 2010 because Kent didn't receive a 1099-DIV.
C. This dividend must be reported in 2010.
D. This dividend is reportable in 2011.

The answer is C. Kent earned the money in 2010, and whether or not he received a 1099 for the income is irrelevant. Mutual fund dividends are taxable in the year declared regardless of whether the taxpayer withdraws the money or reinvests it. The money was constructively earned and available for withdrawal in 2010, so therefore, Kent must report the earnings in 2010. ###

32. Harold owns shares in a Real Estate Investment Trust (REIT). The trust declares a dividend on October 25, 2010. However, the dividend is not actually paid to shareholders until January 3, 2011. How should Harold report his earnings?

A. Harold is not required to report this income, because income from a REIT is always nontaxable.
B. Harold must report this income in 2010.
C. Harold must report this income in 2011.
D. Harold is required to report this income as a capital gain from the sale of securities.

The answer is B. Harold must report the dividend in the year it was declared, 2010. If a mutual fund or Real Estate Investment Trust (REIT) declares a dividend in October, November, or December but actually pays the dividend during January of the next calendar year, the shareholder is still considered to have received the dividend on December 31 of the prior tax year. ###

33. Willy's bank became insolvent in 2010. One hundred dollars in interest was credited to Willy's frozen bank account during the year. Willy withdrew $80, but could not withdraw any more as of the end of the year. Willy's 1099-INT showed $100 in interest income. Which of the following is true?

A. Willy's tax return must reflect the full amount of the interest.
B. Willy must include the $20 in his income for the year he is able to withdraw it.
C. None of the interest is taxable on a frozen deposit.
D. There is no such thing as a "frozen deposit."

The answer is B. Willy must include $80 in his income for 2010 but may exclude $20. He must include the $20 in his income in the year he is able to withdraw it. A deposit is considered frozen if, at the end of the year, the taxpayer cannot withdraw the deposit because the financial institution is bankrupt or insolvent. ###

34. Lenore wanted to start investing. She deposited $4,000 of her own funds with a bank and also borrowed another $12,000 from the bank to make up the $16,000 minimum deposit required to buy a six-month Certificate of Deposit. The certificate earned $375 at maturity in 2010, but Lenore only received $175 in interest income, which represented the $375 she earned MINUS $200 in interest charged on the $12,000 loan. The bank gives Lenore a Form 1099-INT showing the $375 interest she earned. The bank also gives Lenore a statement showing that she paid $200 in interest. How should Lenore report all the interest amounts on her tax return?

A. Lenore can choose to report only $175 of income.
B. Lenore must report the $375 interest income. The $200 interest she paid to the bank is not deductible.
C. Lenore must include the $375 in her income. Lenore may deduct $200 on her Schedule A, subject to the net investment income limit.
D. Lenore does not have to report any income from this transaction.

The answer is C. Lenore must include the total amount of interest—$375—in her income. If she itemizes deductions on Schedule A (Form 1040), she can deduct $200 in interest expense, subject to the net investment income limit. To deduct investment expenses, the taxpayer must itemize. She may not "net" the investment income and expenses (Publication 17). ###

35. Luke and Barbie filed a joint return for 2010. Luke received $10,000 in Social Security benefits and Barbie received $16,000. No other income was received. What part of their Social Security benefits will be taxable for 2010?
A. $0
B. $6,000
C. $24,000
D. $12,000

The answer is A. If the only income received by the taxpayer is Social Security, the benefits generally are not taxable and the taxpayer probably does not have to file a return. If the taxpayer has additional income, he or she may have to file a return even if none of the Social Security benefits are taxable (Publication 17). ###

36. If a taxpayer's Social Security benefits are taxable, what is the *maximum* percent of taxable Social Security benefits?

A. 0%
B. 50%
C. 85%
D. 100%

The answer is C. Up to 85% of Social Security benefits may be taxable. ###

37. Sheila and Ralph are married and both have life insurance. In December 2009, Ralph dies and Sheila, as the beneficiary, is awarded the life insurance. The face amount of the policy is $270,000. Instead of a lump sum, Sheila chooses to receive 180 monthly installments of $1,800 each over 15 years, starting January 1, 2010. How should Sheila treat these installments on her 2010 tax return?

A. All of the payments are excluded from income.
B. $18,000 is excluded from income per year, and $3,600 must be recognized as interest income.
C. $21,600 must be included in Sheila's income.
D. $18,000 will be excluded from income, and the remainder is taxed as a capital gain.

The answer is B. The face amount of the policy is $270,000. The excluded part of each installment is $1,500 ($270,000 ÷ 180 months), or $18,000 for an entire year. The rest of each payment, $300 a month (or $3,600 for an entire year), is interest income to Sheila (Publication 525). ###

38. Alexander, age 64, is single and retired. He earned the following income in 2010. To determine if any of his Social Security is taxable, Alexander should compare how much of his income to the $25,000 base amount?

Part-time job	$8,000
Bank interest	$5,000
Social Security	$11,000
Taxable pension	$6,000
Total	**$30,000**

A. $30,000
B. $11,000
C. $24,500
D. $25,000

The answer is C. In order to figure out the taxable portion of Social Security, the taxpayer's Modified Adjusted Gross Income must be compared to the base amount.

Modified Adjusted Gross Income EQUALS adjusted gross income PLUS tax-exempt interest. To figure the amount of income that should be compared to the $25,000 BASE AMOUNT:

Part-time job	$8,000
Interest	$5,000
1/2 of Social Security	$5,500
Taxable pension	$6,000
Total	$24,500

Alexander does not have to pay tax on his Social Security. His provisional income plus Social Security is less than the base amount ($25,000). However, he is still required to file a tax return, because his overall income exceeds the minimum filing requirement. ###

39. Randall is an ordained minister in the Evangelical Church of Chicago. Randall owns his own home and his monthly house payment is $900. His monthly utilities total $150. Fair rental value in his neighborhood is $1,000. Randall receives a housing allowance from his church in the amount of $950 per month. How much income must Randall include from his housing allowance amount?

A. $0
B. $50 per month
C. $150 per month
D. $950 per month

The answer is A. Ministers may exclude from gross income the rental value of a home or a rental allowance to the extent the allowance is used to provide a home, even if deductions are taken for home expenses paid with the allowance. A minister's housing allowance (sometimes called a "parsonage" allowance or a rental allowance) is excludable from gross income for income tax purposes, but not for self-employment tax purposes. ###

40. Paul is an ordained minister of a church. Which of the following statements is false?

A. Paul is required to report all of the income he receives from performing baptisms.
B. Paul is not required to report any income if he has taken a vow of poverty.
C. All of the income received by Paul must be reported on Schedule C, even amounts received as an employee.
D. Ministers may request a religious exemption from Social Security tax and Medicare tax.

The answer is C. Paul must report self-employment income on Schedule C. However, amounts received as an employee should be reported as wages on IRS Form 1040. Ministers are allowed to request an exemption from Social Security and Medicare for religious reasons. Ministers who have taken a vow of poverty are not required to report income; generally they remit all their earnings back to the church and therefore have no taxable income. ###

41. Joe is a priest at a Catholic church. He receives an annual salary of $18,000. Joe also receives a housing allowance of $2,000 to pay for utilities. Joe lives rent-free in a small studio owned by the church. The fair rental value of the studio is $300 per month. Only the $18,000 salary was reported on the W-2. How much of Joe's income is subject to income tax?

A. $0
B. $18,000
C. $20,000
D. $21,600

The answer is B. Only $18,000, Joe's wages, is subject to income tax. The other amounts for the housing allowance and use of the studio are not subject to income tax, but they are subject to self-employment tax. ###

42. Polly receives the following income and fringe benefits in 2010:

- $30,000 in wages
- $2,000 Christmas bonus
- Parking pass at $90 per month
- Employer contributions to Polly's 401K plan in the amount of $900 for the year
- Free use of an indoor gym on the employer's premises, FMV valued at $500.

How much income must Polly report on her 2010 tax return?
A. $30,000
B. $32,000
C. $32,900
D. $33,980

The answer is B. Only the wages and the bonus are taxable. The parking pass is considered a non-taxable transportation benefit, and the employer contributions are not taxable until Polly withdraws the money from the retirement account. Polly does not have to report the use of the gym, because it is on the employer's premises and therefore not taxable. ###

43. Which of the following fringe benefits are taxable (or partially taxable) to the employee?

A. Health insurance, covered 100% by the employer
B. Employer-provided parking at $275 per month
C. Group-term life insurance coverage of $50,000
D. Employer contributions to an employee's 401K plan

The answer is B. Employer-provided parking is an excludable benefit, but only up to $230 per month for qualified parking. Therefore, the amount above $230 ($275 - $230 = $45) becomes taxable to the employee. ###

44. Supplemental wages and a holiday bonus are paid to Robert in 2010. Which items listed below are not considered taxable to Robert?

A. Holiday bonus
B. Overtime pay
C. Vacation pay
D. Travel reimbursements

The answer is D. Travel reimbursements are considered part of an accountable plan and are not included in an employee's wages. "Supplemental wages" is compensation that is paid to an employee in addition to his regular pay. These amounts are listed on the employee's Form W-2 and are taxable just like regular wages. ###

45. Max owns a restaurant. He furnishes his employee Caroline, a waitress, two meals during each workday. Max encourages (but does not require) Caroline to have her breakfast on the business premises before starting work so she can help him answer phones. She is required to have her lunch on the premises. How should Max treat this fringe benefit to Caroline?

A. Caroline's meals are not taxable.
B. Caroline's meals are ALL taxable.
C. Caroline's breakfast is not taxable, but her lunch is taxable.
D. Caroline's meals are taxed at a flat rate of 15%.

The answer is A. Meals furnished to Caroline are not taxable because they are for the convenience of the employer. Meals that employers furnish to a restaurant employee during, immediately before or after the employee's working hours are considered furnished for the employer's convenience. For example, if a waitress works through the breakfast and lunch periods, employers can exclude from her wages the value of the breakfast and lunch they furnish in the restaurant for each day she works. Since Caroline is a waitress who works during the normal breakfast and lunch periods, Max can exclude from her wages the value of her breakfast and lunch. If Max were to allow Caroline to have meals without charge on her days off, those meals must be included in her wages (Publication 15-B). ###

46. Elaine is a cash-basis taxpayer and sells cosmetics on commission. She sells $200,000 in 2010, and her commission is 5% of sales. Elaine receives $10,000 in income from commissions, plus an advance of $1,000 in December 2010 for future commissions in 2011. She also receives $200 in expense reimbursements from her employer after turning in her receipts as part of an accountable plan. How much income should Elaine report on her 2010 tax return?

A. $0
B. $11,000
C. $11,200
D. $10,200

The answer is B. Commissions must be included in gross income, as well as advance payments in anticipation of future services, if the taxpayer is on a cash basis. The expense reimbursements from her employer would not be included in gross income. ###

47. Antonio is employed as an accountant by the Giant Accounting Firm. When Antonio travels for his audit work, he submits his travel receipts for reimbursement by the Giant Accounting Firm, which has an accountable plan for its employees. Which of the following statements is TRUE?

A. Under an accountable plan, the reimbursed amounts are not taxable to Antonio.
B. Under an accountable plan, Antonio may still deduct his travel expenses on his tax return.
C. Under an accountable plan, Antonio's employer, Giant Accounting, may not deduct the travel expenses, even though Antonio was reimbursed in full.
D. Under an accountable plan, reimbursed expenses are taxable to the employee, and the employer may also deduct the expenses as they would any other current expense.

The answer is A. Under an accountable plan, employee reimbursements are not included in the employee's income. The employer can deduct the expenses as current expenses on their tax return. The employee is not required to be taxed on any amounts received under a qualified accountable plan. ###

48. Sam spends two years working overseas in Australia as a computer programmer for a private company. He has qualified foreign earned income. He makes $120,000 in 2010. What is the maximum Sam can exclude from his income?

A. $0
B. $82,400
C. $91,500
D. $94,200

The answer is C. For 2010, the maximum exclusion for the foreign earned income exclusion is $91,500. ###

49. Gary and Bernice have both worked in France for a foreign employer for the last three years. Assuming they meet all the tests and file jointly, what is the maximum they can exclude from their gross income using the foreign earned income exclusion in 2010?

A. $0
B. $91,500
C. $137,600
D. $183,000

The answer is D. If the taxpayers are married and both individuals work abroad and both meet either the bona fide residence test or the physical presence test, each one can choose the foreign earned income exclusion. Together, they can exclude up to $183,000 for the 2010 tax year. ###

50. Which IRS form is used to claim the foreign earned income exclusion?
A. Form 8228
B. Form 2555
C. Form 1040-NR
D. Form 2848

The answer is B. Form 2555 is used to claim the foreign earned income exclusion. The form must be attached to the taxpayer's Form 1040. ###

51. Brad had a $15,000 loan from his local credit union. He lost his job and was unable to make the payments on this loan. The credit union determined that the legal fees to collect might be higher than the amount Brad owed, so it canceled the $5,000 remaining amount due on the loan. Brad did not file bankruptcy nor is he insolvent. How much must Brad include in his income as a result of this occurrence?

A. $0
B. $5,000
C. $10,000
D. $15,000

The answer is B. Since Brad's inability to pay his debt is not a result of bankruptcy nor insolvency, the amount of the canceled debt ($5,000) should be included in gross income. ###

52. Which of the following fringe benefits provided by the employer will result in taxable income to the employee?

A. $220 monthly parking permit
B. Reimbursements paid by the employers for qualified business travel expenses
C. Use of a company van for moving personal items
D. Occasional coffee, doughnuts, and soft drinks

The answer is C. Use of a company vehicle for personal tasks is not a qualified fringe benefit. Commuting expenses are not deductible. Use of a company van after normal working hours is a personal use and not a business use. This would result in taxable income to the employee. The parking permit, reimbursements for business travel, and the occasional coffee and doughnuts are considered noncash fringe benefits that are not taxable. ###

Unit 1.6: Rental and Royalty Income

More Reading:
Publication 527, *Residential Rental Property*
Publication 550, *Investment Income and Expenses*
Publication 946, *How to Depreciate Property*

Rental Income

Rental income is income from the use or occupation of property. Most people think of residential rental property when they think of rental income, but rental income can be earned from the rental of all types of property. Generally, rental and royalty activities are considered "passive activities" and subject to the passive activity rules.

Passive Activities

Passive activity is any rental activity OR any business in which the taxpayer does not materially participate. A passive activity is an activity from which the taxpayer has the potential to profit, but in which the taxpayer does not materially participate. Rental income is generally considered passive income. "Non-passive" activities are businesses or activities in which the taxpayer works on a regular, continuous, and substantial basis.

Non-passive income includes wages and income from a sole proprietorship. It's important to understand the distinction, because losses from passive activities generally cannot offset "non-passive" income.

Example: Zach has a full-time job as a janitor making $32,000 a year. He also owns three rental homes and had $23,000 in rental income. Zach fixes up the homes himself and collects the rents personally. Zach's wages are ACTIVE income, and his rental income is PASSIVE INCOME (passive activity). Passive income is not subject to self-employment tax (Social Security and Medicare). The IRS sets strict limits on the amount of losses that can be claimed on passive activity.

Two Kinds of Passive Activities

There are two types of passive activities:

- Rentals, including equipment and rental real estate, regardless of the level of participation (a special exception exists for real estate brokers and dealers.)
- Businesses in which the taxpayer does not materially participate (such as a passive partnership interest).

Passive Activity Rules

The "Passive Activity Rule" states that passive activity losses may only be deducted against passive activity income and gains. The key regarding the passive activity loss rules is material participation. If the taxpayer does not "materially participate" in the activity, then the losses are disallowed against passive income. If there is no passive income, then no loss can be deducted. Passive activity losses can only be carried forward; they cannot be carried back.

> **Example:** Kate, a single taxpayer, has $90,000 in wages, $15,000 income from a limited partnership, and an $18,000 passive loss from an investment in an LLC. Kate can use $15,000 of her $18,000 loss to offset her $15,000 passive income from the partnership. The unused passive losses ($3,000) must be carried over to the following year.

The following entities are subject to the *passive activity loss* rules:

- Individuals
- Trusts and estates
- Personal Service Corporations
- Privately held corporations

The passive activity rules do not apply to S-Corporations, grantor trusts, or partnerships. But the passive activity rules *do apply* to the owners of these pass-through entities. If a taxpayer is a cash basis taxpayer, as are most individual taxpayers, she must report rental income when it is "constructively received." Income is constructively received when it is available without restrictions to the taxpayer.

Examples of Passive Activities

Income and losses from the following activities would generally be passive:

- Equipment leasing
- Rental real estate (with some exceptions for real estate professionals)
- A farm in which the taxpayer does not materially participate (rare)
- Limited partnerships
- Partnerships, S-Corporations, and Limited Liability Companies in which the taxpayer does not materially participate

Examples of Non-Passive Income

Non-passive income includes active income, such as wages, business income, and investment income. Income and losses from the following activities would generally be considered non-passive:

- Salaries, wages, and 1099-MISC income (independent contractors, sole proprietors, etc.)
- Guaranteed payments to partners
- Royalties derived from the ordinary course of business
- Businesses in which the taxpayer materially participates
- Partnerships, S-Corporations, and Limited Liability Companies in which the taxpayer materially participates
- Trusts in which the fiduciary materially participates

Losses from Rental Real Estate Activities: *Special Rule*

Usually, taxpayers cannot deduct losses from passive activities from their active income. There is an exception in the IRC for losses relating to real estate activities.

If a taxpayer *actively participates* in a rental real estate activity, she can deduct up to $25,000 of losses against non-passive income. This special allowance for rental activity is *an exception* to the general rule disallowing losses in excess of income from passive activities.

> **Example:** Philip and Susanne have wages of $98,000 and a rental loss of $26,800 in 2010. They manage the rental property themselves. Because they meet both the active participation and the gross income tests, they are allowed to deduct $25,000 of the rental loss. The loss offsets their active income (wages). The remaining amount over the $25,000 limit ($1,800) that cannot be deducted is carried over to the next year.

The maximum amount of the "special allowance" is reduced if the taxpayer's Modified Adjusted Gross Income exceeds $100,000 ($50,000 if Married Filing Separately). The amount of the deduction is reduced by one dollar for every two dollars over $100,000. Once MAGI exceeds $150,000, the $25,000 allowance is reduced to zero.

So basically, if a married couple has $150,000 in wages, and they have $10,000 in rental losses in the current year, they cannot use the rental losses to offset their wage income. The rental losses are suspended and carried over to the next year.

Suspended losses can be carried forward indefinitely and used in subsequent years against passive activity income. They are allowed in full upon the disposition of the activity (when the property is sold).

> **Example:** Hal and Sally file MFJ and have Adjusted Gross Income (AGI) of $140,000. They have accumulated $25,000 in expenses from their home rental that they actively manage. Because they actively manage the rental property, they qualify for the deduction of up to $25,000 in losses against non-passive income. Therefore, Hal and Sally's deduction is reduced by $20,000 (.5 x ($140,000-$100,000). They will be able to deduct $5,000 ($25,000-$20,000) against non-passive income. The additional $20,000 in expenses is carried forward to the following year.

If a taxpayer is married and filing a separate return, but lived apart from his spouse for the entire tax year, the taxpayer's special allowance for rental losses cannot exceed $12,500. If the taxpayer *lived with* his spouse at any time during the year and is filing MFS, the taxpayer cannot offset any active income with passive rental losses.

> **Example:** In March of 2010, Campbell and Michelle legally separate and plan to divorce. They jointly own a residential rental. Campbell earned $40,000 in wages in 2010, and Michelle earned $33,000. Their jointly-owned rental generated a loss of $6,000 for the year. Michelle and Campbell both filed MFS and reported $3,000 ($6,000 ÷ 2) of rental loss on their returns. Although Campbell and Michelle meet the active participation rules and the gross income test, neither is allowed to deduct any of the rental losses because they did not live apart for the entire year. So the loss is considered a "suspended passive activity loss" and must be carried over for use in a future year.

The Definition of Active Participation

To "actively participate" a taxpayer must own at least 10% of the rental property and make management decisions in a significant and bona fide way, such as approving new tenants and improvements, and establishing the lease and rental terms. Only individuals can actively participate in rental real estate activities (not entities).

However, a decedent's estate is treated as "actively participating" for its tax years ending less than 2 years after the decedent's death, if the decedent would have satisfied the active participation requirement for the activity for the tax year in which the taxpayer died.

The concept of "active participation" is frequently litigated by the IRS. [21] The IRS expects taxpayers to be able to prove that they actively participated in the management of the rental. If the taxpayer is deemed to not have "actively participated," then rental losses are disallowed, and the taxpayer is not eligible for the special $25,000 loss allowance that is allowed to most residential rental activity.

Reporting Rental Income and Losses

If a property is strictly a rental property, the income and loss should be reported on IRS Form Schedule E, *Supplemental Income and Loss*. Schedule E is filed along with the IRS Form 1040. Taxpayers use Schedule E to report income or loss from rental real estate, royalties, partnerships, S Corporations, estates, trusts, and residual interests in REMICs.

If a rental property is divided as personal use and rental use, the taxpayer must figure the income and losses differently (more on personal use property later).

Treatment of Advance Rent

"Advance rent" is any amount received before the period that it covers. Include advance rent in income in the year it is received, regardless of the period covered.

> **Example:** Earl signs a ten-year lease to rent his commercial office building. In 2010, the first year of the lease, Earl receives $5,000 for the first year's rent in a lump sum (in advance) and $5,000 as rent for the last year of the lease. It doesn't matter that the advance rent covers the last year of the rental agreement. Earl cannot postpone recognition of the payment. He must recognize the full $10,000 on his 2010 tax return (Publication 527).

Payment for Canceling a Lease

If a tenant pays the taxpayer to cancel a lease, the amount received for the cancellation is rental income. Also include the payment in income in the year received regardless of the taxpayer's accounting method or the period for which the rental income is covered.

Security Deposits

Security deposits are not considered taxable income, if the deposit is refundable to the tenant at the end of the lease. If the taxpayer (landlord) keeps the security deposit because the tenant does not live up to the terms of the lease or damages property, then recognize the retained deposit amount the year the deposit is retained. If the security deposit is to be used as a final payment of rent, it is advance rent, not a security deposit.

Property or Services In Lieu Of Rent

Sometimes, tenants and landlords will barter services for rent. If a taxpayer (landlord) receives property or services instead of cash rents, the Fair Market Value of the

---

[21] Rules regarding active participation: Ref. IRC § 469(i), Reg. § 1.469-1T(e)(3).

property or services must be recognized as rental income. Just like other barter exchanges, if the tenant and landlord agree in advance to a price, the agreed upon price is the Fair Market Value unless there is evidence to the contrary.

> **Example:** Beth's tenant Chris is a professional chimneysweep. Chris offers to clean all Beth's chimneys in her apartment building instead of paying three months' rent. Beth accepts Chris's offer. Beth must recognize income for the amount Chris would have paid for three months' rent. Then Beth may include that same amount as a business expense for repairing the rental property. This is the correct procedure for recognizing rental income from exchange of services.

Expenses Paid by Tenant

If a tenant pays any expenses, those payments are rental income and the landlord (taxpayer) must recognize them as such. Consequently, the landlord can then deduct the expenses as deductible rental expenses.

> **Example:** Rosetta owns an apartment building. While she is out of town, the furnace in the apartment building stops working. Kerry, Rosetta's tenant, pays for the emergency repairs out-of-pocket. Kerry then deducts the furnace repair bill from his rent payment. Rosetta must recognize both the rent income and the amount Kerry paid for the repairs. Rosetta can then deduct the cost of the furnace repair as a rental expense.

Partial Rental Use

The concepts for "partial rental use" are heavily tested on the EA Exam, so you must be clear about them. Different rules apply to a property that is partial rental use and partial personal use. The concept of "minimal rental use" is a situation where a taxpayer rents his actual home as a rental unit for a limited time.

The reason why the concept is so important is because if a property is deemed "personal use," then rental deductions are limited. If the taxpayer has a net profit from rental activity, she generally may deduct all of her rental expenses, including depreciation. However, if the taxpayer has a net loss and the property is considered "personal use," the deduction for rental expenses is limited, which means that the taxpayer cannot take a loss.

Taxpayers who use a property for personal and rental use must learn how to divide their expenses properly. If an expense is applied to both rental use and personal use, such as the heating bill for the entire house, the taxpayer must divide the expense between the two. The taxpayer is allowed to use any reasonable method for dividing the expense, as long as it is consistent. It may be reasonable to divide the cost of some items (for example, the water bill) based on the number of people using the unit. The two most common methods for dividing an expense are:

- The number of rooms in the home, and
- The square footage of the home.

Another common situation is a "duplex" where the landlord (taxpayer) lives in one unit and rents out the other side. Certain expenses apply to the entire property, such as mortgage interest and real estate taxes, and must be split to determine rental and personal expenses.

145

> **Example #1:** Pablo rents a granny cottage attached to his house. The granny cottage is 12 × 15 feet, or 180 square feet. Pablo's entire house, including the attachment, is 1,800 square feet. Pablo can deduct as a rental expense 10% of any expense that must be divided between rental use and personal use. Pablo's 2010 heating bill for the entire house was $600, and therefore, $60 ($600 × .10) is considered a rental expense. The balance, $540, is a personal expense that Pablo cannot deduct.

> **Example #2:** Gillian owns a duplex and lives in one half of it. She rents the other half. Both units are the same size. Last year, Gillian paid a total of $10,000 mortgage interest and $2,000 real estate taxes for the entire property. Gillian can deduct $5,000 mortgage interest and $1,000 real estate taxes on Schedule E. Then, Gillian can deduct the other $5,000 mortgage interest and $1,000 real estate taxes on Schedule A as a deductible personal expense.

Limit on Deductions for Personal-Use Property

When a taxpayer uses a dwelling unit both as a home AND a rental unit, expenses must be divided between rental use and personal use, and the taxpayer may not deduct rental expenses that exceed the rental income for that dwelling unit.

On personal-use property, if rental expenses exceed rental income, the taxpayer cannot use the excess expenses to offset income from other sources. The excess deductions can be carried forward to the next year and treated as rental expenses for the same property. Any expenses carried forward to the next year will be subject to any limits that apply for that year.

> **Example:** Jack owns a vacation condo on Miami Beach. He uses it as a personal residence four months out of the year, and rents it out the rest of the year. Since Jack uses the condo more than 15 days for his own personal use, the condo is considered a personal use dwelling. Jack's rental income is $5,000 in 2010. However, he had a bad tenant who damaged the property and was eventually evicted. Therefore, Jack's rental expenses were $7,000. Jack cannot deduct the full amount of rental expenses on his 2010 tax return, because the condo is still considered primarily a personal-use property for tax purposes. Jack must carry over the unused portion and deduct it from future rental income.

Personal Use of a Home (Definition)

The rules for personal use are as follows: the taxpayer is considered to have used his unit "as a personal home" during the tax year if he uses the home for personal purposes greater than:

- Fourteen days, or
- 10% of the total days it is rented at a fair rental price.

How to Figure Days of Personal Use: A day of personal use is any day that the unit/home is used by any of the following persons:

- The taxpayer or any person who has ownership interest in the property.

- A member of the taxpayer's family (unless the family member pays a fair rental price and uses the property as a "main home."[22]
- Anyone under an arrangement that allows for the use of some other dwelling unit (like a housing swap).
- Anyone at less than a fair rental price.

Days Used for Repairs and Maintenance

Any days that are designated for repair or maintenance of a property do not count as personal use days. Any day that the taxpayer or other owners spend working on repairs and maintaining the property is not counted as a day of personal use. The main purpose of the stay must be to complete the repairs or maintenance. Do not count such a day as a day of personal use even if family members use the property for recreational purposes on the same day.

> **Example:** Corey owns a cabin in the mountains that he normally rents out to tenants. He spends a week at the cabin with his family. Corey works on maintenance of the cabin each day during the week. Corey's family members, however, spend the rest of the time fishing and swimming. The main purpose of being at the cabin that week is to do maintenance work. Therefore, the use of the cabin during the week by Corey and his family will not be considered personal use by Corey.

> **Example:** Steve owns a rental condo in Hawaii. In March, Steve visits the unit to re-paint, replace the carpet, and repair damage done by the former tenant. Steve has records to prove all of the purchases and repairs. He is at the condo performing repairs for three weeks and stays at the condo during that time. None of his time at the condo is considered "personal use" time.

Donated Rental Property

A taxpayer also "personally uses" a dwelling unit for personal purposes if:

- He donates the use of the unit to a charitable organization,
- The organization sells the use of the unit at a fundraising event, and the "purchaser" of the unit uses the unit.

Exception: Minimal Rental Use, or the "15 Day Rule"

If a taxpayer rents her main home for FEWER than 15 days (14 days or less), then she does not have to recognize any of the income as taxable. This is called the "15 Day Rule." If the taxpayer rents her home for fewer than 15 days during the year, she does not have to include any of the rent income. She also cannot deduct any rental expenses.

---

[22] For this rental rule, "family" includes only brothers and sisters, half-brothers and half-sisters, spouses, and ancestors, meaning parents, grandparents, etc., and lineal descendants, meaning children, grandchildren, etc.

Example: Janice owns a condo in a resort area. It is her main home. She rented her condo for 14 days during the summer and stayed with her mother during that time. Janice charged $100 per day, for a total of $1,400. She also had $320 in expenses during that time. Janice does not report any of the income or expenses, since the rental qualifies under the exception for minimal rental use.

Example: April's main home is in Miami Gardens, Florida. In February 2010, April decided to rent her home during the Super Bowl. She rented her house for eight days, charging $100 a day. She stayed with her brother during that time. Since the rental period fell under the 15 day rule, the $800 that she earned is not taxable and not reported on her tax return.

An activity is also not considered a rental activity if any customer use of the property is seven days or less (this "7-day" rule applies to all other types of property, not just residential rentals).

Rental Expenses and the "Placed in Service" Date

Rental property is "placed in service" when it is ready and available for rent. A taxpayer can begin to depreciate property and deduct expenses as soon as he places the property in service for the production of income.

If a taxpayer just holds property for rental purposes, he may still be able to deduct ordinary and necessary expenses (including depreciation) for managing, conserving, or maintaining the property while it is vacant.

However, a taxpayer cannot deduct any loss of rental income for the period the property is vacant. But if a taxpayer is actively trying to rent the property, she can deduct ordinary and necessary expenses for managing, conserving, or maintaining a rental property as soon as the property is made available for rent.

Expenses for Rental Property Sold

If a taxpayer sells property originally held for rental purposes, he can deduct the ordinary and necessary expenses for managing, conserving, or maintaining the property until it is sold.

Example: Gerry owns a rental property and wants to sell it. It is currently vacant, and Gerry still must pay the utility bills and landscaping costs. Gerry can deduct these expenses from his rental income.

Converting a Primary Residence to Rental Use

If a taxpayer changes a primary residence to rental use at any time other than the beginning of a tax year, she must divide yearly expenses, such as taxes and insurance, between rental use and personal use. A taxpayer can deduct as rental expenses only the portion that is for the part of the year the property was used or held for rental purposes. For depreciation purposes, treat the property as being "placed in service" on the conversion date.

The taxpayer cannot deduct depreciation or insurance for the part of the year the property was held for personal use. However, the taxpayer can include the home mortgage interest, qualified mortgage insurance premiums, and real estate tax expenses for the part of the year the property was held for personal use as an itemized deduction on Schedule A (Form 1040).

Basis of a Primary Residence Converted to Rental Use

When a taxpayer changes property from personal use to rental use (for example, a taxpayer rents his former main home), the tax practitioner must figure the basis for depreciation using the lesser of:

- Fair Market Value (this is the price at which the property would sell on the open market) OR
- The home's adjusted basis on the date of the conversion.

Example: Several years ago, Lance built his home for $140,000 on a lot that cost him $14,000. Before changing the property to rental use this year, he spent $28,000 adding an extra bathroom to the house and claimed a $3,500 casualty loss deduction for fire damage to the house. Part of the improvements qualified for a $500 residential energy credit, which he claimed on his 2006 tax return. Because land is not depreciable, he can only include the actual costs of the house when figuring the basis for depreciation. The adjusted basis of the house at the time of the change in its use was $164,000 ($140,000 + $28,000 − $3,500 − $500). On the date of the change (the conversion date to a rental), the house had a Fair Market Value of $168,000, of which $21,000 was allocated to the land and $147,000 was for the house. The basis for depreciation on the house is the Fair Market Value on the date of the change ($147,000), because it is less than Lance's adjusted basis ($164,000).

Depreciation Rules for Rental Property

A taxpayer cannot claim the Section 179 Deduction for property held to produce rental income. The Section 179 Deduction allows taxpayers to deduct the full cost of a business asset in the year it is purchased, rather than depreciate the asset over its useful life. Individuals report the income and loss for rental properties on Schedule E. The depreciation of rentals is reported on **Form 4562,** *Depreciation and Amortization.*

Taxpayers must depreciate rental property; that is, they may deduct only a portion of the cost on their tax returns each year. Three basic factors determine how much depreciation a taxpayer can deduct:

- Basis
- Recovery period for the property
- Depreciation method used

*NOTE! Raw Land is NEVER DEPRECIATED!

A taxpayer can never depreciate the cost of land because land does not wear out, become obsolete, or get used up. The costs of clearing, grading, planting, and landscaping are usually all part of the cost of land and cannot be depreciated.

> **Example:** Diane owns an empty lot she purchased for $50,000, and she wishes to build an apartment complex. Diane pays an additional $15,000 to clear the property of trees and debris so she can begin construction. Diane's basis in the land is therefore $65,000 ($50,000 + $15,000). The cost of clearing the brush must be added to the basis of the land, and is not deductible.

Repairs and Improvements to Rental Property

A taxpayer can deduct the cost of repairs to rental property. A taxpayer cannot deduct the cost of "improvements." In order to pass the EA Exam, you must understand the difference between a "repair" and an "improvement."

A taxpayer recovers the cost of improvements by taking depreciation. The taxpayer must separate the costs of repairs and improvements, and keep accurate records. The taxpayer will need to know the cost of improvements when the property is later sold, because improvements increase a property's basis.

Repairs to Rental Property

A repair keeps a property in operating condition. It does not materially add to the value of a property or substantially prolong its life. Re-painting a property inside or out, fixing gutters or floors, fixing leaks, plastering, and replacing broken windows are examples of repairs.

> **Example:** Keith owns a rental home. A neighborhood kid broke a window with a baseball last month, and Keith replaced the window with an upgraded model—an insulated double-pane window that helps control heating and cooling costs. Even though this window is a substantial upgrade from the previous one, it is still considered a repair, because the old window was broken and needed to be replaced. If Keith had decided to replace ALL the windows, the upgrade would have been considered an "improvement," and Keith would have been required to depreciate the window upgrades.

However, if a taxpayer makes repairs as part of an extensive remodeling or restoration of the property, the whole job may be considered an improvement.

> **Example:** Keith's rental property also has a bad roof leak. Rather than repairing the roof for a third time, Keith replaces the entire roof at a cost of $7,000. This would be considered a substantial improvement and must be depreciated, usually 15 years for tax purposes. Keith cannot expense the cost of the roof against current income.

Examples of Improvements

An *improvement* adds to the value of property, prolongs its useful life, or adapts it to new uses. Improvements include the following items:

- Putting a recreation room in an unfinished basement
- Paneling a den, putting in a fireplace, or other major construction
- Adding another bathroom or bedroom
- Putting decorative grillwork on a balcony
- Putting up a fence

150

- Installing new plumbing or wiring
- Putting in new cabinets
- Putting on a new roof
- Paving a driveway or adding a garage

If a taxpayer makes an improvement to her property, the cost of the improvement must be capitalized and depreciated. It cannot be deducted on the tax return as an expense. Remember, rental property purchases are not eligible for Section 179. The capitalized cost is usually depreciated as if the improvement were separate property from the dwelling unit.

> **Example:** Griselda owns a rental home. In 2010, she spent $7,000 replacing the carpet, $2,540 to pay the driveway, and $350 to repair a cracked window. Only the window repair ($350) can be expensed on her 2010 tax return. The cost of the new carpet and the new driveway must be capitalized and depreciated.

Rental Property Depreciation

The depreciation periods for business and rental property vary from 3 years to 20 years. Land improvements must be depreciated over 15 or 20 years. Land improvements include things like fences, bridges, and shrubbery.

For property used in rental activities, a taxpayer must use the Modified Accelerated Cost Recovery System (MACRS). MACRS is the current method of accelerated asset depreciation required by the United States income tax code. Under MACRS, all assets are divided into classes that dictate the number of years over which an asset's cost will be recovered. Residential rentals are depreciated over 27.5 years.

Buildings are always depreciated using the straight-line method. Residential real estate is always recovered over 27.5 years, and commercial buildings are depreciated over 39 years. Residential realty is any structure that at least 80% of the gross rental income of the building is derived from dwelling units (such as an apartment complex), or a common residential rental home.

MACRS Recovery Periods for Depreciable Property Used in Rental Activities

Class of Property	Items Included
3-year property	Most computer software, tractor units, some manufacturing tools, and some livestock.
5-year property	Automobiles, computers and peripheral equipment, office machinery (faxes, copiers, calculators, etc.), appliances, stoves, refrigerators.
7-year property	Office furniture and fixtures, and any property that has not been designated as belonging to another class.
15-year property	Depreciable improvements to land such as shrubbery, fences, roads, and bridges.
20-year property	Farm buildings that are not agricultural or horticultural structures.
27.5-year property	Residential rental property (residential rental homes, condos, etc.)
39-year property	Nonresidential real estate, such as factory buildings. (Remember that the value of land is not depreciated.)

All other real property is classified as "commercial nonresidential property" and must be depreciated over 39 years. An example of commercial property that would be depreciated over 39 years would be a factory building.

> **Example:** A residential rental building with a cost basis of $137,500 would generate depreciation of $5,000 per year ($137,500 / 27.5 years).

Other Rental Property Expenses

Examples of other expenses a taxpayer can deduct from rental income include advertising, cleaning, maintenance, utilities, fire and liability insurance, taxes, interest, commissions for the collection of rent, and ordinary and necessary travel and transportation. If a taxpayer buys a leasehold for rental purposes, he can deduct an equal part of the cost each year over the term of the lease.

Travel Expenses Related to Rental Property

A taxpayer can deduct the ordinary and necessary expenses of traveling away from home if the primary purpose of the trip was to collect rental income or to manage, conserve, or maintain her rental property.

> **Example:** Walt owns a rental property 200 miles away from his home. Part of the rental home was damaged by fire. Walt travels to the property to inspect the damage and hire someone to do the repairs. His travel expenses are deductible as ordinary and necessary costs.

Cannot Deduct Prepaid Insurance Premiums: If a taxpayer pays an insurance premium on rental property for more than one year in advance, each year he can deduct the part of the premium payment that applies to that year. He cannot deduct the total premium in the year paid.

> **Example:** Holly owns a rental home. She gets a substantial discount from her insurance agent if she agrees to pay her hazard insurance two years in advance. Holly cannot deduct the full payment of the insurance in the year that she pays. She must prorate the insurance expense, even though she is a cash-basis taxpayer.

Cannot Deduct Local Benefit Taxes: Generally, a taxpayer cannot deduct charges for local benefits that increase the value of a property, such as charges for putting in streets, sidewalks, or water and sewer systems. These charges are non-depreciable capital expenditures. A taxpayer must add them to the basis of a property. He can deduct local benefit taxes if they are for maintaining, repairing, or paying interest charges for the benefits.

Exception for Real Estate Professionals

Real estate professionals are *exempt* from the passive activity rules if certain conditions are met. Rental activities in which real estate professionals materially participated during the year are not passive activities. A real estate professional may elect to treat his or her rental income as non-passive income. If the real estate professional elects this treatment, then the rental income is subject to self-employment tax. The taxpayer must file a Schedule C, rather than a Schedule E.

Real estate "dealers" are defined as those who are engaged in the business of selling real estate to customers with the purpose of making a profit from those sales. The benefit of being classified as a "real estate professional" is that the taxpayer is treated like a Schedule C business and there is no limit on the amount of losses the taxpayer can claim on the activity. A taxpayer will qualify as a real estate professional for the tax year if he or she meets BOTH of the following requirements:

- More than half of the services performed during the tax year are performed in real estate or real property businesses in which the taxpayer materially participates.
- The taxpayer performs more than 750 hours of services during the tax year in real property trades or businesses in which he or she materially participates.

Rental income received from the use of or occupancy of hotels, boarding houses, or apartment houses is included in self-employment income IF the real estate professional provided services to the occupants.

Services are considered "provided to the occupants" if they are for the convenience of the occupants and not normally provided with the rental of rooms or space for occupancy only. Daily maid service, for example, is a service provided for the convenience of occupants, while heat and light, cleaning of stairways, and the collection of trash are not.

Royalty Income

Royalties from copyrights, patents, and oil, gas, and mineral properties are taxable as ordinary income. Royalty income is generally considered passive income and subject to the passive activity rules.

"Royalties" are payments that are received for the use of property. The most common types of royalties are for the use of copyrights, trademarks, and patents. Royalties are also paid by companies that extract minerals and other substances from the earth. Examples are royalties from the extraction of oil, gas, or minerals. Mineral property includes oil and gas wells, mines, and other natural deposits including geothermal deposits.

Many different types of royalties exist. Royalties can be paid to a taxpayer for the use of his name or image. Royalty income and expenses are reported on **Schedule E,** *Supplemental Income and Loss*. Many special rules apply to the ownership and taxation of mineral property, and most of these complex concepts will not show up on the EA Exam. But exam-takers should still have a basic understanding of royalties and how they should be reported.

*Exception: There are special rules for taxpayers who are self-employed writers, artists, photographers, or inventors. In this case, the royalties are generated by a self-created copyright, trademark, or patent. Therefore, the royalties would be reported as business income on **Schedule C** and be subject to self-employment tax.

Copyrights and Patents

Royalties from copyrights on literary, musical, or artistic works, and similar property, or from patents on inventions, are amounts paid for the right to use the property over a specified period of time. Royalties generally are based on the number of units sold, such as the number of books, tickets to a performance, or machines sold.

> **Example:** Don inherited a copyright from his brother, who was an author. It was the copyright to an instruction manual for woodworking. Don then leased the copyrighted material to schools and colleges for their use in the classroom. Don would report the income from this copyright on Schedule E.

Unit 1.6: Questions

1. Thomas, who is single, owns a rental apartment building property. This is the only rental property that he owns. He "actively participates" in this rental activity as he collects the rents and performs ordinary and necessary repairs. In 2010, Thomas had an overall loss of $29,000 on this rental activity and had no other passive income. His total income from wages is $60,000. How much of the rental loss may Thomas deduct on his 2010 return?

A. $0
B. $6,000
C. $25,000
D. $29,000

The answer is C. Thomas may deduct $25,000 in rental losses. The remaining amount, $4,000 ($29,000 - $25,000), must be carried over to the following year. ####

2. In 2010, Jane is single and has $40,000 in wages, $2,000 of passive income from a limited partnership, and $3,500 of passive losses from a rental real estate activity in which she actively participated. Which of the following statements is TRUE?

A. $2,000 of Jane's $3,500 loss offsets her passive income. Jane may deduct the remaining $1,500 loss from her $40,000 wages.
B. Jane may not deduct the passive losses from her $40,000 in wages.
C. Jane may deduct any other losses.
D. Jane must carry over her losses to the subsequent tax year.

The answer is A. Jane may deduct the remaining $1,500 loss from her $40,000 wages. A taxpayer may deduct up to $25,000 per year of losses for rental real estate activities. This special allowance is an exception to the general rule disallowing losses in excess of income from passive activities. ###

3. Which of the following costs incurred on rental property should be classified as a capital improvement and must be depreciated rather than expensed?

A. Replacing an entire roof
B. Repairing a broken toilet
C. Refinishing the existing wood floors
D. Replacing a broken window pane

The answer is A. The replacement of the roof would be considered a depreciable improvement. The other choices are repairs (Publication 527). ###

155

4. Mike, a single taxpayer, had the following income and loss during the tax year:

- Salary $52,300
- Dividends $300
- Interest $1,400
- Rental losses ($4,000)

The rental loss came from a rental property that Mike owned. He advertised and rented the house to the current tenant himself. He also collected the rents and did the repairs or hired someone to do them. Which of the following statements is true?

A. Mike can claim the entire rental loss against his active income.
B. Mike cannot claim the rental loss because his income exceeds $50,000.
C. Mike cannot claim the rental loss because he is not a real estate professional.
D. Mike can claim $1,700 in rental losses and the remaining amount ($2,300) will be carried over to the following year.

The answer is A. Even though the rental loss is a loss from a passive activity, Mike can use the entire $4,000 loss to offset his other income because he actively participated. ###

5. Gene signs a three-year lease to rent his business property. In December 2010, he receives $12,000 for the first year's rent and $12,000 as rent for the last year of the lease. He also receives $500 in 2010 as a refundable security deposit. How much of this income must Gene include in his 2010 tax return?

A. $1,000
B. $12,000
C. $12,500
D. $24,000

The answer is D. Gene must include $24,000 in his income in the first year. He must recognize the advance rent as income immediately. The security deposit does not have to be recognized as income as it is refundable (Publication 17). ###

6. Rosemary's home is used exclusively as her residence all year except for 13 days. During this time, Rosemary rents out her home to alumni while the local college has its homecoming celebration. She made $3,000 in rental income and had $500 in rental expenses. Which of the following statements is TRUE?

A. All of the rental income may be excluded.
B. Rosemary may exclude only $2,500 of the rental income.
C. Rosemary may deduct her rental expenses when she reports her rental income on Schedule E.
D. Rosemary must recognize $3,000 in rental income.

The answer is A. All the rental income may be excluded. This is called the "15 Day Rule." This home is primarily personal use, and the rental period is "disregarded," which means the IRS does not consider it a rental. The rental income is not taxable, and any of the rental expenses (such as utilities or maintenance costs) are considered nondeductible personal expenses. ###

7. Eric incurred the following expenditures in connection with his rental property. Which of them should be capitalized and depreciated?

A. New roof
B. New cabinets
C. Paving of driveway
D. All of the above

The answer is D. All of the property listed must be capitalized and depreciated. A taxpayer can deduct only the cost of repairs to his rental property. He cannot "deduct" the cost of improvements, but can recover the cost of improvements by taking depreciation over the life of the asset. ###

8. Terry purchased a heating, ventilating, and air conditioning (HVAC) unit for her rental property on December 15, 2010. It was delivered on December 28, 2010, and was installed and ready for use on January 2, 2011. When should the HVAC unit be considered "placed in service" for depreciation purposes?

A. December 15, 2010
B. December 28, 2010
C. December 31, 2010
D. January 2, 2011

The answer is D. Placed-in-service date is the day on which an asset becomes available for use by a business. In most cases, the placed-in-service date and the purchase date are the same, but that is not necessarily the case. Depreciation begins on the placed-in-service date. ####

9. Passive rental income and losses are reported on which IRS form?

A. Schedule E
B. Schedule A
C. Schedule C
D. Schedule D

The answer is A. Rental income and loss is reported on Schedule E, which is then attached to the taxpayer's Form 1040. Rental income is any payment received for the use or occupation of property, and is generally passive income. An exception exists for real estate professionals, who may report rental income on Schedule C, subject to self-employment tax. ###

10. In January 2010, Kimberly purchased a commercial office building and used office furnishings. She intends to rent the building to tenants. The used office furnishings consisted of chairs, desks, and file cabinets. Nine hundred thousand dollars of the purchase price was allocated to the office building and $50,000 of the purchase price was allocated to the used office furnishings. According to the guidelines for MACRS depreciation, what recovery period must she use for the purchased items?

A. 27.5 years for the entire asset, building and furnishings
B. 39 years for the building and 5 years for the used office furnishings
C. 15 years for the building and 5 years for the used office furnishings
D. 39 years for the building and 7 years for the used office furnishings

The answer is D. Commercial real estate is depreciated as 39-year property. The recovery period under MACRS for furniture is seven years. ###

11. Brian has a house in Arizona that is rented out for eight months each year. How many days can he use the house without losing income tax deductions?

A. As many days as he wants
B. 14 days
C. Zero days
D. 24 days

The answer is D. Brian can personally use his rental home the *longer of* 14 days or 10% of the time the rental was in use. The rental home was used for 240 days (30 x 8). Brian can use his rental home for 24 days (240 x 10%) with no impact in deducting expenses from his rental property.###

12. Nick decides to convert his residence into rental property. His tax year is the calendar year. Nick moved out of his home in May and started renting it out on June 1. He had $12,000 in mortgage interest on the home. How should Nick report his mortgage interest expense?

A. Nick can report $7,000 on Schedule E as interest expense and $5,000 on Schedule A as mortgage interest.
B. Nick should report the entire $12,000 on Schedule A.
C. Nick should report the entire $12,000 on Schedule E.
D. Nick can report $8,000 on Schedule E as interest expense and $4,000 on Schedule A as mortgage interest.

The answer is A. Nick must allocate his expenses between personal use and rental use. He can deduct as rental expenses seven-twelfths (7/12) of his yearly expenses, such as taxes and insurance. Starting with June, he can deduct as rental expenses the amounts he paid for items generally billed monthly, such as utilities. When figuring depreciation, treat the property as placed in service on June 1 (Publication 527). ###

13. In 2010 Jacqueline has Modified Adjusted Gross Income of $120,000. She owns a rental house that has losses of $22,000 for the year. How much of the rental loss may she deduct on her tax return?

A. $0
B. $11,000
C. $15,000
D. $22,000

The answer is C. Jacqueline may only deduct $15,000 of the loss. The rental loss allowance is phased out when a taxpayer's MAGI is over $100,000. For every two dollars of income over $100,000, the rental loss allowance is reduced one dollar. The answer is figured as follows:

Jacqueline's income- MAGI threshold: ($120,000 - $100,000 = $20,000)

$20,000 X 50% = $10,000

$25,000 (normal rental loss allowance) - $10,000 = $15,000

$15,000 is the maximum in rental losses that Jacqueline can claim in 2010. The remaining unused losses ($7,000) must be carried over to the following year. ###

14. Aaron converted his basement level into a separate apartment with a bedroom, a bathroom, and a small kitchen. Aaron rented the basement apartment at a fair rental price to college students during the regular school year. He rented to them on a 9-month lease (273 days). He figured that 10% of the total days rented at a fair rental price is 27 days (273 days X 10%). In June Aaron's brothers stayed with him and lived in the basement apartment *rent-free* for 30 days. Which is the TRUE statement?

A. Aaron may deduct all of his expenses for the converted basement apartment, as it is 100% rental use.
B. Aaron may not deduct any of his rental losses because the converted basement apartment is considered personal use.
C. Aaron must recognize imputed rental income from his brothers' use of the property, even if he did not actually receive it.
D. Aaron must divide his expenses from personal use and rental use, but he is still allowed to deduct losses from the property.

The answer is B. Since Aaron's family members use the basement apartment for free, this usage counts as personal use. Therefore, the basement apartment is no longer considered a 100% rental unit. Aaron's personal use (the 30 days his family used it for free) *exceeds* the greater of 14 days or 10% of the total days it was rented (27 days). When a taxpayer uses a dwelling unit both as a home AND a rental unit, expenses must be divided between rental use and personal use, and the taxpayer may not deduct rental expenses that exceed the rental income for that dwelling unit. Aaron's losses, if he has any, are not deductible. ###

15. Jake is a full-time freelance writer. He earns $23,000 in royalty income from one of his copyrighted books in 2010. He also has $4,000 in travel expenses related to the promotion of the book. How should this income be reported?

A. Jake must report $23,000 in taxable income on Schedule C.
B. Jake must report $23,000 in taxable income on Schedule E.
C. Jake must report $19,000 in taxable income on Schedule E.
D. Jake must report $19,000 in taxable income on Schedule C.

The answer is D. As a full-time writer, his royalty income is not considered passive income and therefore is subject to self-employment tax. Jake must report $19,000 in taxable income on Schedule C ($23,000-$4,000 in expenses). ###

Unit 1.7: Adjustments to Gross Income

> **More Reading:**
> Publication 590, *Individual Retirement Arrangements*
> Publication 504, *Divorced or Separated Individuals*
> Publication 521, *Moving Expenses*
> Publication 970, *Tax Benefits for Education*

The "line" is the taxpayer's Adjusted Gross Income (AGI). Adjustments are taken before arriving at final AGI and appear as direct subtractions from gross income.

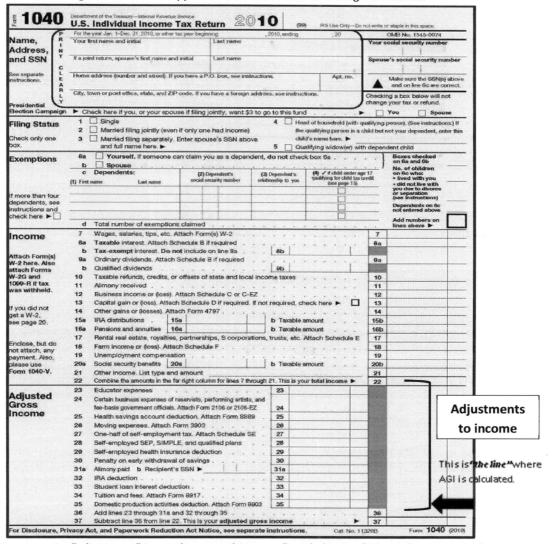

Adjustments to income

This is "the line" where AGI is calculated.

An "adjustment" is not the same thing as a "tax deduction." That is because an adjustment is the best type of deduction—it happens "above-the-line." Adjustments are referred to as "above-the-line deductions" because they are subtracted on Page 1 of Form

1040. Therefore, an adjustment is an expense that may be deducted even if the taxpayer does not itemize.

Adjustments are subtracted from gross income to arrive at Adjusted Gross Income. This is a difficult concept to understand, but you can visualize it much better if you look at the front of IRS Form 1040.

Adjustments to Gross Income

There are many types of adjustments to gross income. Some of them are obscure, and some of them are very common. We will cover the most common ones in this unit. These are also the most common adjustments tested on the IRS Enrolled Agent Exam:

1. Self-employment tax deduction
2. Adjustments for penalty for early withdrawal of savings
3. Alimony paid
4. Contributions to a traditional IRA
5. Student loan interest
6. Tuition and Fees Deduction
7. Income from jury duty that was turned over to an employer
8. Educator expenses (also called the "Teacher Credit")
9. Health Savings Account or HSA deduction (Form 8889)
10. Moving expense deduction

There are some other adjustments to income on Form 1040, such as SEP, SIMPLE, and qualified plans, and the Domestic Product Activities Deduction. The Domestic Production Activities Deduction and retirement plans are covered extensively in Part 2 (Businesses) of the EA Exam coursework.

One-Half of Self-Employment Tax

Self-employed taxpayers can subtract half of their self-employment tax from their income. This is equal to the amount of Social Security tax and Medicare tax that an employer normally pays for an employee, which is excluded from an employee's income. Self-employment tax is calculated on **Schedule SE**, *Self-Employment Tax.*

Penalty for Early Withdrawal

If a taxpayer withdraws money from a Certificate of Deposit (CD) prior to the certificate maturing, she usually incurs a penalty for early withdrawal. This penalty is charged by the bank and withheld directly from a taxpayer's proceeds from the certificate.

Taxpayers can take an adjustment to income for early withdrawal penalties. Early withdrawal penalties are reported on a taxpayer's Form 1099-INT, *Interest Income*, or Form 1099-OID, *Original Issue Discount*. These forms will list the interest income, as well as the penalty amount.

The reason why this adjustment is tested often on the EA Exam is because of a special rule that allows taxpayers to claim a penalty for early withdrawal, even if the penalty exceeds their interest income for the year.

This is very different from the normal rule that governs regular investment expenses. A penalty for early withdrawal is treated as an adjustment to income, rather than a deduction on Schedule A.

> **Example:** Earlier in 2010, Gloria invested in a Certificate of Deposit. However, in November, she had an unexpected medical expense and had to withdraw the money early. Gloria made an early withdrawal of $15,000 from a one-year, deferred-interest CD in the current tax year. She had to pay a penalty of three months' interest, which totaled $150. Gloria can claim the penalty ($150) as an adjustment to income.

The penalty for early withdrawal of an IRA is not tax-deductible.

Alimony PAID is an Adjustment to Income

Earlier in the book, we covered alimony as taxable income. Alimony is also a deductible expense by the individual who PAYS the alimony. By definition, alimony is a payment to a former spouse under a divorce or separation instrument.

The payments do not have to be made directly to the ex-spouse. For example, payments made on behalf of the ex-spouse for expenses such as medical bills, housing costs, and other expenses can also qualify as alimony.

> **Example:** Victoria divorced two years ago. Her settlement agreement states that she must pay her ex-husband $16,000 a year. She is also required per the divorce agreement to pay his ongoing medical expenses. In 2010, the medical expenses were $9,500. She can deduct the full amount ($25,500) because it is all required by her divorce agreement.

Alimony does NOT include child support. Child support is never deductible. Child support payments are not deductible by the payer and are not taxable to the recipient. Alimony will be disallowed and reclassified as child support if the divorce decree states that the "alimony" will discontinue based on a contingency relating to the child.

> **Example:** Neil pays child support and alimony to his ex-wife. They have one child together. The divorce decree states that he must pay $400 per month in child support and $500 per month in alimony. However, Neil's divorce agreement states that all payments will discontinue if the child gets married. This means that for tax purposes, ALL the payments must be treated as child support.

Payments after Death and Voluntary Payments are NOT Alimony

If any alimony payments must continue after the ex-spouse's death, those payments are not considered alimony for tax purposes, even if they are made before death. These payments would normally be reclassified as child support, and therefore, not taxable to the recipient and nondeductible to the payor. Voluntary payments *outside* the divorce agreement do not count as alimony.

> **Example:** Anthony has been divorced for three years. Under his divorce instrument, he paid his ex-wife $12,600 in 2010. As a favor, he also made $2,400 in payments to cover part of her vehicle lease so she could keep steady employment. Anthony can take the $12,600 as an adjustment to income. He cannot count the lease payments because they were not required by the divorce agreement.

The person paying alimony can subtract it as an adjustment to income; the person RECEIVING alimony claims it as taxable income. If a taxpayer's decree of divorce or separate maintenance provides for alimony and child support, and the payor *pays less* than the total

163

amount required, the payments apply first to child support. Any remaining amount is considered alimony.

> **Example:** Jeff must pay alimony and child support to his ex-wife Liz. His monthly payment for alimony is $200, and his monthly payment for child support is $800. Jeff falls behind on his payments and is only able to pay $500 per month in 2010. Since he is behind on his payments, none of his payments qualify as alimony. All of his payments must be allocated to child support first. The amount is calculated as follows: $200 x 12 = $2,400 (alimony due), $800 x 12 = $9,600 (child support due). Jeff can only pay $500 x 12 = $6,000; therefore he is short by $6,000 ($2,400 + $9,600 = $12,000 − $6,000). Since the $6,000 he can pay falls short of the required child support payment by itself, all of his $6,000 will be reclassified as child support. Therefore, Jeff can deduct NONE of his payments as alimony. Also, Jeff's ex-wife does not have to claim any of the payments as alimony income. Child support is not taxable and not deductible by either party.

Requirements for Payments to Qualify as Alimony

Noncash property settlements, whether in a lump sum or installments, are not considered alimony. Voluntary payments (i.e., payments not required by a divorce decree or separation instrument) do not qualify as alimony. To qualify as alimony, all of these requirements must be met:

- The payments must be in cash or cash equivalents (checks or money orders).
- Payments must be required by the divorce decree.
- Spouses may not live in the same household (if only legally separated).
- The payment may not be child support.
- The payor's liability for the alimony payments must stop upon the death of the recipient spouse.
- The parties may not file jointly.

A taxpayer does not have to itemize deductions in order to deduct alimony payments. Taxpayers may claim the deduction for "alimony paid" on Page 1 of Form 1040. They cannot use Form 1040A or Form 1040EZ. The PAYOR must provide the Social Security Number of the ex-spouse receiving the alimony payments.

IRA Contributions

An IRA (Individual Retirement Arrangement) is a personal savings plan that offers tax advantages for setting aside money for retirement. There are two basic types of IRAs that will be discussed in this chapter: a traditional IRA and a Roth IRA. Each IRA has different eligibility requirements.

Some contributions to IRAs may be deducted from income. There are several types of IRA accounts, but in Part 1, we will only discuss traditional IRAs and Roth IRAs.[23]

---

[23] For more detailed information on all types of IRAs, refer to the Individual Retirement Arrangements (IRAs) chapter in Publication 17 and Publication 590, *Individual Retirement Arrangements*.

Traditional IRA: A traditional IRA is the most common type of retirement savings plan. In most cases, taxpayers can deduct their traditional IRA contributions as an adjustment to income. Generally, amounts in a traditional IRA, including earnings and gains, are not taxed until distributed. Contributions to a traditional IRA may also be eligible for the Saver's Credit (formally known as the Retirement Savings Contributions Credit). If a taxpayer's income is too high, then the taxpayer's contributions to his traditional IRA might not be deductible.

Roth IRA: Only contributions to a traditional IRA are deductible as an adjustment to gross income. A Roth IRA is a retirement account that features nondeductible contributions and tax-free growth. In other words, a taxpayer funds her Roth IRA with after-tax income, and the income then grows tax-free. Not everyone can participate in a Roth IRA. There are strict income limits, and higher wage earners may be prohibited from participating in a Roth IRA account because of the income threshold.

Example: In 2010, Fred contributes $2,200 to a traditional IRA and $1,000 to a Roth IRA. The most Fred will be able to deduct as an adjustment to income is the $2,200 contribution to his traditional IRA. Roth IRA contributions are never deductible.

Traditional IRA Rules

To contribute to a traditional IRA, a taxpayer must follow a number of different rules:

1. The taxpayer must be under age 70½ at the end of the year.
2. The taxpayer must have qualifying compensation, such as wages, self-employed income, and alimony income. Investment income does not count.
3. If a taxpayer's income is too high, then he will not be allowed to deduct the contribution (if covered by an employer plan).
4. Contributions can be made to a traditional IRA at any time on or before the due date of the return (not including extensions).
5. IRAs cannot be owned jointly.
6. A taxpayer may withdraw funds from an IRA account at any time. However, early withdrawals from a traditional IRA before age 59½ will generally be subject to a 10% penalty.

*Note:** The contribution rules are very strict. Only certain types of compensation qualify as contributions to an IRA. For purposes of making an IRA contribution, taxable alimony (and nontaxable combat pay) count as qualifying income. This rule allows taxpayers to build retirement savings in IRAs even if they rely on alimony income for support. The rule applies only to taxable alimony income and does not include child support payments.

Example: Stan is an Army medic serving in a combat zone for all of 2010. None of his pay is taxable, but it is still qualifying compensation for the purposes of an IRA contribution.

For the 2010 tax year, a person may make an IRA contribution all the way up until April 18, 2011. This makes an IRA contribution a rare opportunity for after-tax planning, because it can occur after the tax year has already ended. A taxpayer can even file his return claiming a traditional IRA contribution *before* the contribution is actually made. The contribution must be made by the **due date of the tax return** (not including extensions).

Example: Paul files his 2010 tax return on March 5, 2011. He claims a $4,000 IRA contribution on his tax return. Paul may wait as late as April 18, 2011 (the due date of the return) to finally make the IRA contribution for tax year 2010.

In order to contribute to an IRA, the taxpayer must have "non-passive" income, such as wages, salaries, commissions, tips, bonuses, or self-employment income. Taxable alimony and nontaxable combat pay are treated as "non-passive" compensation for IRA purposes.

However, if a taxpayer has wages *in addition* to self-employment income, do not subtract the *loss* from self-employment from the taxpayer's wages when figuring total compensation.

Example: Finnegan is 45 and works as an employee for a local library. He earns $10,000 in wages during 2010. He also works part of the year as a self-employed photographer, and his business has a loss of $5,400. Even though the taxpayer's *net income* for 2010 is only $4,600 ($10,000 wages - $5,400 loss from self-employment), his qualifying income for the purposes of an IRA contribution is still $10,000 (the amount of his wages). This means that Finnegan can make a full IRA contribution of $5,000 in 2010.

Example: Larry is 54 and wants to contribute to his traditional IRA. He has $10,000 in passive income from rental properties (he is not a real estate professional). He also received $8,000 in interest income and has $3,000 in wages from a part-time job. The maximum Larry can contribute to his traditional IRA is $3,000. The rental and interest income is passive income and not considered "compensation" for IRA purposes, so cannot be used to fund his retirement account.

"Compensation" for the purposes of contributing to an IRA does NOT include passive income such as:
- Rental income
- Interest income
- Dividend and portfolio income
- Pension or annuity income
- Deferred compensation
- Income from a limited partnership
- Prize winnings or gambling income
- Any other income that is excluded from income, such as foreign earned income and housing costs (other than nontaxable combat pay)

Taxpayers cannot make IRA contributions that are greater than their qualifying compensation for the year. This means that if a taxpayer only has passive income for the year, she cannot contribute to an IRA at all. A taxpayer may choose to split her retirement plan contributions between a traditional IRA and a Roth IRA; however, the maximum contribution limits still apply.

Example: Alan is 32. He has a traditional IRA at his regular bank and a Roth IRA through his stockbroker. Alan can contribute to both of his retirement accounts this year, but the combined contributions for 2010 cannot exceed $5,000. Alan decides to contribute $3,000 to his Roth IRA and $2,000 to his traditional IRA.

2010 IRA Contribution Limits
Under 50 years of age:
- 2010 Contribution Limit: $5,000 per taxpayer
- Filing Jointly: $10,000

50 years and up:
- 2010 Contribution Limit: $6,000 per taxpayer
- Filing Jointly (Both 50 or older): $12,000

Example: Lucas, an unmarried college student working part-time, earns $3,500 in 2010. He also receives $500 in interest income and some tuition help from his parents. His IRA contributions for 2010 are limited to $3,500, the total amount of his wages.

There is an exception for taxpayers who file jointly. A married taxpayer may choose to make an IRA contribution on behalf of his or her spouse, even if only one spouse had compensation during the year.

Example: Joaquin, 48, and Meg, 52, are married and file jointly. Joaquin works as a paramedic and makes $46,000 per year. Meg has no income. Even though Meg has no taxable compensation, Joaquin may still contribute to her IRA account. Their combined maximum contribution for 2010 is $11,000. Joaquin may deposit $5,000, and Meg may deposit $6,000 because she is over 50 years of age.

Example: Naomi, 25, had only $3,000 in interest income in 2010. Naomi marries Carl during the year. For the year, Carl has taxable compensation of $34,000. He plans to contribute (and deduct) $5,000 to his traditional IRA. If he and Naomi file a joint return, each can contribute $5,000 to a traditional IRA. This is because Naomi, who has no "qualifying" compensation, can include Carl's compensation, reduced by the amount of his IRA contribution, ($34,000 − $5,000 = $29,000) to her own compensation ($0) to figure her maximum contribution to a traditional IRA. Since they are filing a joint return, she can substitute Carl's qualifying compensation in order to contribute to her own traditional IRA.

However, even if they file a joint return, married taxpayers' combined IRA contributions cannot exceed their combined compensation, and neither spouse can contribute more than $5,000 (or $6,000 for 50 and older) to his or her own IRA.

Once again, a married couple cannot set up a "joint" IRA account. Each individual must have his or her own IRA, but married spouses may choose to make contributions to a spouse's IRA, up to the legal limit, if they file jointly.

Example: Greg is 35, works full-time, and made $65,000 in 2010. His wife Laverne is 34, has a part-time job, and made $3,600 in 2010. They choose to file separately. Since they file MFS and Laverne only has $3,600 in compensation, Laverne is limited to a $3,600 IRA contribution. Greg may contribute a full $5,000 to his own IRA account.

A taxpayer cannot claim the deduction for an IRA contribution on Form 1040EZ; the taxpayer must use either Form 1040A or Form 1040.

Rules for Deductibility of a Traditional IRA

A *contribution* to an IRA and *the deductibility* of the contribution are two different things. Not everyone can deduct IRA contributions. Even if a taxpayer exceeds the income limits for making a tax-deductible contribution to a traditional IRA, he may always make an after-tax contribution to a traditional IRA. In either case, earnings will grow on a tax-deferred basis.

The deduction for contributions made to a traditional IRA depends on whether the taxpayer is covered by an employer retirement plan. The deduction is also affected by income and by filing status. If the taxpayer is covered by an employer retirement plan, he or she may be entitled to only a partial deduction or no deduction at all.

If a taxpayer makes **nondeductible** contributions to a traditional IRA, he must attach **Form 8606,** *Nondeductible IRAs.* **Form 8606** reflects a taxpayer's cumulative nondeductible contributions, which is his tax basis in the IRA. If a taxpayer does not report nondeductible contributions properly, then all future withdrawals from the IRA will be taxed unless the taxpayer can prove, with satisfactory evidence, that nondeductible contributions were made.

Phase-Out Ranges for Deductibility

A taxpayer can take a deduction for IRA contributions of:
- $5,000 ($6,000 if you are age 50 or older), or
- 100% of qualifying compensation (whichever is smaller).

If the taxpayer (or spouse) is not covered by an employer plan, then the traditional IRA contribution is deductible. However, the contribution will be phased-out (reduced) if either the taxpayer or his spouse (or both) are covered by a retirement plan at work. The rules get more complicated at this point.

Phase-Outs When Covered by an Employer Plan

If a taxpayer is covered by an employer retirement plan, then the tax-deductible contribution to a traditional IRA is phased out at the following income limits:
- For Single or Head of Household: $55,000 to $66,000
- For joint filers: $89,000 to $109,000
- For married couples filing separately: $0 to $10,000 (living together)

If the taxpayer's income for the year is below the phase-out limits, the IRA contribution is fully tax-deductible. If the income falls within the phase-out range, the IRA contribution will be partially deductible. If the income falls above the phase-out range, none of the IRA contribution will be deductible.

Example: Tamara is single and earned $95,000 in 2010. She is covered by a retirement plan at work, but she still wants to contribute to a traditional IRA. She is phased out for the deduction because her income exceeds the threshold for single filers. If she contributes to an IRA in 2010, she must file Form 8606 to report her nondeductible contribution.

Married taxpayers who are filing separately (MFS) have a much lower phase-out range than any other filing status. However, if a taxpayer files a separate return and **did not live** with his or her spouse at any time during the year, the taxpayer is not treated as married for the purpose of these limits, and the applicable dollar limit is that of a single taxpayer.

> **Example:** Don is separated from his wife. They have lived in separate residences since 2009. In 2010, Don earned $40,000 and files MFS. He is allowed to deduct his full IRA contribution. This is because he did not live with his spouse at any time during the year, and therefore he is not subject to the normal IRA phase-out limits that apply to separate filers.

> **Example:** For 2010, Edward and Samantha file a joint return. They are both 42 years old. Edward is covered by his employer's retirement plan. His salary is $45,000. Samantha is a housewife and had no compensation. Edward contributed $5,000 to his traditional IRA and $5,000 to a traditional IRA for Samantha (a spousal IRA). Their combined modified AGI includes $2,000 in interest income and $70,000 in gambling winnings. Because their combined modified AGI is $109,000 or more, Edward cannot deduct any of the contribution to HIS traditional IRA. He can either leave the $5,000 of nondeductible contributions in his IRA or he can choose to withdraw them by April 18, 2011.

Roth IRA Income Limits in 2010

Not everyone can *participate* in a Roth IRA account. There are income limits to who can participate and contribute to a Roth IRA. In contrast, there are no income limits to who can participate in a traditional IRA. In 2010, the following income limit rules apply to Roth IRAs:

2010 Roth IRA Participation Limits

Filing Status	Full Contribution	Phase-Out Range	No Roth IRA Allowed
Single filers	Less than $105,000	$105,000 -$120,000	$120,000 or more
Joint filers	Less than $167,000	$167,000 -$177,000	$177,000 or more

Anyone who earns income above the Roth threshold amount is not allowed to participate, contribute, or rollover into a Roth IRA.

New Rule: Roth IRA Conversions in 2010

In 2010, Congress eliminated the AGI and filing status requirements for converting a Traditional IRA to a Roth IRA. Before 2010, high income taxpayers could not participate or contribute funds to a Roth IRA.

The conversion is treated as a rollover. If a taxpayer wants to convert a Traditional IRA to a Roth IRA, he is required to pay federal income taxes on any pre-tax contributions, as well as any growth in the investment's value. Once the funds are converted to a Roth, all of the investment grows tax free, and funds could be withdrawn on a tax-free basis.

Although there are still income limits to who can *participate* in a Roth IRA, in 2010, the new rules allow anyone to convert an existing Traditional IRA to a Roth IRA. This new Roth conversion rule applies to all years beyond 2010, and the income taxes due on the initial conversion can be spread over two years. The 2010 conversion amount may be split and added back as taxable income in 2011 and 2012, helping to lessen the tax burden upon

169

conversion. The default option is for taxpayers to report 50% of the conversion income on 2011 and 2012.

The taxpayer may also choose to report the entire amount and pay all the tax due on their 2010 return. If the taxpayer elects to report all the income in 2010, he must make this election on Form 8606. Once made, the election cannot be changed after the due date (including extensions) for the 2010 tax return.

> **Example:** Cecily converted her Traditional IRA to a Roth IRA in 2010. The traditional IRA had a balance of $50,000. Under the default option, Cecily will report $25,000 on her 2011 return and $25,000 on her 2012 return.

Any Roth conversions in subsequent years are included in income during the tax year in which the conversion is made. A Roth conversion is reported on Form 8606.

In the case of an inherited IRA, only an IRA inherited from a spouse may be converted to a Roth.[24] As a general rule, a taxpayer is allowed to treat an inherited IRA from their deceased spouse as their own IRA, which also includes the choice to do a Roth conversion. This rule only applies to spouses. Non-spousal inheritors (for example, a child who inherits an IRA from a deceased parent) are not allowed to rollover or convert the IRA.

Retirement Plan Rollovers

Generally, a "rollover" is a tax-free transfer from one retirement plan to *another* retirement plan. The contribution to the second retirement plan is called a "rollover contribution." *Most* rollovers are nontaxable events. However, sometimes taxpayers will choose to roll a traditional IRA into a Roth IRA (explained previously). In this case, the conversion will result in taxation of any untaxed amounts in the traditional IRA. A conversion is reported to the IRS on **Form 8606,** *Nondeductible IRAs.*

A taxpayer can receive a distribution of cash or property from an IRA. The most common property in an IRA is stock or other securities. If a taxpayer sells the distributed property (such as stocks distributed from an IRA) and rolls over *all the proceeds* into another traditional IRA, no gain or loss is recognized. The sale proceeds (including any increase in value) are treated as part of the distribution and are not included in the taxpayer's gross income.

> **Example:** On September 4, 2010, Mike began a new job. He decided to transfer his retirement account to his new employer's plan. Mike received a total distribution from his employer's retirement plan of $50,000 in cash and $50,000 in stock. The stock was not stock of his employer. On September 24, he sold the stock for $60,000. On October 4, he rolled over the entire amount totaling $110,000 ($50,000 from the original distribution and $60,000 from the sale of stock). Mike is not taxed on the $10,000 gain from the sale of stock as part of his income because he rolled over the entire amount into a traditional IRA.

A taxpayer must make the rollover contribution by the 60th day after the day the taxpayer receives the distribution from a traditional IRA account (or an employer's plan).

---

[24] If a Roth IRA owner who has converted dies before including all of the amounts in income, any remaining amounts not included must generally be reported on the IRA owner's tax return in the year of death. However, if the owner's surviving spouse receives the deceased owner's Roth IRA, the spouse can elect to continue to ratably include the amounts in income in 2011 and 2012.

The IRS may waive the 60-day requirement where the failure to do so would be inequitable, such as in the event of a casualty, disaster, or other event beyond the taxpayer's reasonable control.

Death of an IRA Owner

After the death of an IRA owner, a surviving spouse can elect to treat the IRA as being his or her own. Surviving spouses may "rollover" their deceased spouse's IRA into their own. Only spouses are allowed this beneficial treatment.

An IRA may not be "rolled over" into the account of any other family member or beneficiary after death. However, any amounts remaining in an IRA upon a taxpayer's death can be paid to beneficiaries without penalty (although the amounts will still be subject to tax). After the IRA owner dies, the beneficiary can generally take distributions over his or her remaining life expectancy. The beneficiary's "life expectancy" is calculated by using the age of the beneficiary in the year following the year of the IRA owner's death. The IRS has tables for making these calculations.

> **Example:** Allison, 42, and Lorenzo, 53, are married. Allison dies in 2010, and, at the time of her death, she has $50,000 in her traditional IRA account. Lorenzo chooses to rollover the entire $50,000 into his own IRA account, thereby avoiding taxation on the income until he retires and starts taking distributions.

Tax on Excess Contributions

If a taxpayer *accidentally* contributes more to his IRA than he is legally entitled to, the excess contribution is subject to a 6% excise tax. The IRS will allow a taxpayer to *correct* an excess contribution if certain rules are followed. If he makes an excess contribution that exceeds his yearly maximum or his qualifying compensation, the excess contributions (and all related earnings) must be withdrawn from the IRA before the due date.

The excess contributions must be withdrawn by the due date of the tax return, *including* extensions. If a taxpayer corrects the excess contribution in time, the 6% penalty will apply only to the interest earned on the excess contribution. Contributions made in the year a taxpayer reaches 70½ are also considered excess contributions.

Each year that the excess amounts remain in the traditional IRA the taxpayer must pay a 6% tax. The tax can never exceed more than 6% of the combined value of all the taxpayer's IRAs at the end of the tax year. In order to correct an improper contribution to an IRA, the taxpayer must withdraw the improper contribution and any earnings on that amount. Relief from the 6% excise penalty is available only if the following are true:

The taxpayer must withdraw the full amount of the excess contribution on or before the due date (including extensions) for filing the tax return for the year of the contribution.

The withdrawal must include any income earned that is attributable to the excess contribution.

Taxpayers must include the earnings on the excess contribution as taxable income, and that income is reported on the return for the year in which the withdrawal was made.

Example: Betty is 66, self-employed, and also owns rental properties. Betty contributes the maximum amount of $6,000 to her traditional IRA in December 2010. She is very busy and her records are poor, so she files for an extension to prepare her tax return. When Betty finally gives her records to her accountant, he discovers that her taxable income from self-employment is only $3,000. Her rental income is $18,000. Only the self-employment income counts as "compensation" for the purposes of contributing to a traditional IRA, so Betty has inadvertently made an excess contribution of $3,000. She must withdraw the excess contribution (and any interest earned on the excess contribution) by the due date of her return or face an excise tax of 6% on the $3,000.

Quick Reference: Differences Between a Traditional IRA and a Roth IRA		
Issue	**Traditional IRA**	**Roth IRA**
Age Limit	A person over 70½ cannot contribute.	No age limit.
Contribution Limits	$5,000, or $6,000 if age 50 or older by the end of 2010.	$5,000, or $6,000 if age 50 or older by the end of 2010.
Are contributions deductible?	Usually, yes. Deductibity depends on AGI, filing status, and whether the person is covered by a retirement plan at work.	No. You can never deduct contributions to a Roth IRA.
Filing requirements	No filing requirement unless nondeductible contributions are made.	No filing requirement.
Mandatory distributions	A person must begin receiving required minimum distributions by April 1 of the year following the year he or she reaches age 70½.	No. If a taxpayer is the original owner of a Roth IRA, there are no required distributions. The rules are different for inherited IRAs.
How distributions are taxed	Distributions from a traditional IRA are taxed as ordinary income.	Distributions from a Roth IRA are not taxed.
Filing requirement for distributions	None, unless the taxpayer ever made a nondeductible contribution. If so, the taxpayer must file Form 8606.	Yes. The taxpayer must file Form 8606 if the taxpayer received distributions from a Roth IRA.[25]

Educator Expense Deduction: the "Teacher Credit"

Teachers are allowed to deduct up to $250 of unreimbursed expenses that they pay for books, supplies, computer equipment (including related software and services), other equipment, and supplementary materials used in the classroom. This is also mistakenly called the "Teacher Credit." In reality, it is not a credit; rather, it is an adjustment to income.

For courses in health and physical education, expenses are deductible if they are related to athletics. Teachers can deduct these expenses even if they do not itemize deduc-

---

[25] Unless the distribution is a rollover, qualified charitable distribution, one-time distribution to fund an HSA, recharacterization, or certain qualified distributions.

tions. Previously, educator expenses were deductible only as a miscellaneous itemized deduction (subject to the 2% of Adjusted Gross Income limit).

Only certain teachers qualify. An eligible educator must work at least 900 hours a school year in a school that provides elementary or secondary education (K-12). College instructors do not qualify. The term "educator" includes:

- Teacher
- Instructor
- Counselor
- Principal
- Teacher's aide

On a joint tax return, if both taxpayers are teachers, they both may take the credit, up to a maximum of $500. Any expenses that exceed the adjustment to income may still be deducted as "unreimbursed employee expenses" on Schedule A, subject to the 2% AGI limit (more on unreimbursed employee expenses later).

Student Loan Interest Deduction

Generally, personal interest (other than mortgage interest) is not deductible on a tax return. However, there is a special deduction for interest paid on a student loan (also known as an education loan) used for higher education. Only student loan interest paid to an accredited college or university is eligible for this deduction. A "qualified student loan" is used solely to pay qualified education expenses for the taxpayer (or the taxpayer's spouse and/or dependents).

The maximum deduction for student loan interest in 2010 is $2,500. Modified Adjusted Gross Income (MAGI) must be less than $75,000 ($150,000 if filing a joint return).

> **Example:** Veronica and her husband file jointly. Their MAGI is $162,000. She completed her doctoral degree in 2010 and paid $3,400 in student loan interest in 2010. Due to their high MAGI, they may not deduct their student loan interest as an adjustment to income.

Loans from "related persons" do not qualify for this deduction. A taxpayer cannot deduct interest on an educational loan from a related person. Related persons include:

- A spouse, brothers and sisters, half-brothers, and half-sisters
- Direct ancestors (parents, grandparents, etc.)
- Lineal descendants (children, grandchildren, etc.)

Loans from an employer plan also do not qualify for the deduction.

In order for the student loan interest to qualify, the student must be enrolled at least half-time in a higher education program leading to a degree, certificate, or other recognized educational credential. A student who is taking classes "just for fun" does not qualify.

> **Example:** Natalie is going to her local community college and attends part-time to take a typing course. She is not attempting to earn a degree. Therefore, Natalie cannot take the Student Loan Interest Deduction.

> **Example:** Peter attends a local technical college where he is enrolled full-time in a certificate program for automotive repair. Peter may take the Student Loan Interest Deduction.

For purposes of the Student Loan Interest Deduction, these expenses are the total costs of attending an eligible educational institution, including graduate school. They include amounts paid for the following items:

- Tuition and fees
- Room and board
- Books, supplies, and equipment
- Other necessary school-related expenses, such as transportation

The cost of room and board qualifies *only* to the extent that it is not more than the greater of:

- The allowance for room and board, as determined by the eligible educational institution, that was included in the cost of attendance (for federal financial aid purposes) for a particular academic period and living arrangement of the student, or
- The actual amount charged if the student is residing in housing owned or operated by the eligible educational institution.

Before calculating "qualified expenses" on a tax return, the following tax-free income amounts must be subtracted:

1. Employer-provided educational assistance benefits
2. Tax-free withdrawals from a Coverdell Education Savings Account
3. U.S. savings bond interest already excluded from income
4. Tax-free scholarships and fellowships
5. Veterans' educational assistance benefits
6. Any other nontaxable payments (EXCEPT gifts, bequests, or inheritances) received for educational expenses

> **Example**: In 2010, Patty's educational expenses are $7,200. She also receives a gift of $1,000 from her aunt and $1,000 in veterans' educational assistance. Therefore, in 2010 Patty's qualified higher education expenses for the purpose of the Student Loan Interest Deduction are $6,200. This is because veterans' assistance benefits must be subtracted from the taxpayer's educational expenses. The gift from her aunt does not have to be subtracted.

Qualified Student Loan Interest

In addition to simple interest on the loan, certain loan origination fees, capitalized interest, interest on revolving lines of credit, and interest on refinanced student loans can be deducted as "qualified student loan interest."

In order to qualify for this deduction, the loan must be a bona fide student loan. Simply paying tuition on a credit card does not make the credit card interest "qualified student loan interest."

A taxpayer cannot deduct student loan interest paid on a loan that the taxpayer is not legally obligated to pay. Generally, the taxpayer can claim the Student Loan Interest Deduction if all FOUR of these requirements are met:

- The taxpayer's filing status cannot be "Married Filing Separately."
- No other taxpayer is claiming the student on another tax return.

174

- The taxpayer is legally obligated to pay the interest on the loan.
- The taxpayer must actually PAY interest on the loan (not just accrue it).

Example: Trish's daughter Marla is 23 years old and a full-time student at Brown University. Trish pays for all of Marla's living expenses, including her dorm and her tuition. Trish took out an educational loan and pays $1,200 in interest on it in 2010. Marla also worked a part-time job in 2010 and made $6,000. Marla decides to file her own tax return as SINGLE and take a personal exemption for herself. Therefore, Trish can no longer take Marla as a dependent. Since Trish cannot take the exemption for Marla, Trish cannot deduct the interest that she paid on Marla's behalf.

Student Loan Interest Deduction Thresholds

The Student Loan Interest Deduction for 2010 is the smaller of:
- $2,500, or
- The interest actually paid in 2010.

A taxpayer can deduct a maximum of $2,500 per tax year, no matter *how many* qualifying students there are. The Student Loan Interest Deduction is "per return" not "per student." So, for example, if a taxpayer has three children in college and pays over $2,000 in student loan interest for each of them, the maximum deduction is still only $2,500. If a taxpayer pays over $600 of interest on a qualified student loan during the year, the taxpayer will receive Form 1098-E, *Student Loan Interest Statement*, from the lender.

Tuition and Fees Deduction

The *Tuition and Fees Deduction* is another education-related adjustment. A taxpayer may deduct qualified tuition and related expenses as an adjustment to income. The deduction is allowed for qualified higher education expenses paid for academic periods beginning in 2010 and the **first three months** of 2011. In 2010, the maximum deduction is either $2,000 or $4,000, depending on MAGI. A "qualified student" is:
- The taxpayer
- The taxpayer's spouse (if filing jointly)
- The taxpayer's dependent

A taxpayer cannot take the Tuition and Fees Deduction if his filing status is "Married Filing Separately." Nonresident aliens do not qualify for this deduction. The deduction is eliminated once a taxpayer's MAGI exceeds $80,000 ($160,000 if filing jointly).

The Tuition and Fees Deduction isn't affected by the phase-out rule for itemized deductions, and a taxpayer does not have to itemize in order to take this deduction. This deduction is claimed on IRS Form 8917.

A taxpayer cannot claim the Tuition and Fees Deduction and an education credit for the same student. A taxpayer who is eligible to claim the American Opportunity Credit or Lifetime Learning Credit is allowed to figure her return both ways and choose the deduction that results in the lowest tax.

Qualified Educational Expenses

The expenses that qualify for the Tuition and Fees Deduction are much different than the expenses that qualify for the Student Loan Deduction. Generally, qualified education expenses are amounts paid in 2010 for tuition and fees at an eligible college or vocational institution. It does not matter whether the expenses were paid in cash, by check, by credit card, or with loans.

Qualified education expenses do **NOT** include amounts paid for:

- Room and board, medical expenses (including student health fees), transportation, or other personal expenses
- Course-related books, supplies, equipment, and nonacademic activities, UNLESS they are required as a condition of enrollment
- Any course or other education involving sports, games, or hobbies, or any noncredit course

A taxpayer cannot claim the Tuition and Fees Deduction based on expenses that have already been paid with a tax-free scholarship, fellowship, grant, or education savings account funds such as a Coverdell Education Savings Account, tax-free savings bond interest, or employer-provided education assistance.

Tuition Received as a Gift

Another individual may make a payment directly to an eligible educational institution to pay for a student's education expenses. In this case, the student is treated as receiving the payment as a gift from the other person and, in turn, paying the institution. In order for the taxpayer to claim the deduction for tuition received as a gift, the taxpayer may not be claimed on anyone else's tax return. If someone else can claim an exemption for the student, no one will be allowed a deduction for the tuition payment (Publication 970). In this case, there is also a special exemption in the law; the giver does not have to file a gift tax return.

Specifically, any tuition payments made by a grandparent (or anyone else) directly to a college to cover a student's tuition expenses are exempt from federal gift tax. The money will not qualify for a gift tax exemption if it is first given to the student, with instructions to pay the college.

Refunded Tuition

If, after a tax return, a student receives a refund of an expense used to figure the Tuition and Fees Deduction on the original return, the taxpayer must report the refund as income in the following year. Add the recapture amount to income by entering it on the "Other Income" line of Form 1040 in the following year—the year the refund of tuition is received. The taxpayer's current year tax return does not need to be amended (Publication 970).

> **Example:** Keith has one daughter named Robin. Keith paid $8,000 in tuition and fees for Robin's college education in December 2010, and Robin began college in January 2011. Keith filed his 2010 tax return on March 1, 2011, and claimed a Tuition and Fees Deduction of $4,000. After Keith filed his return, Robin dropped three classes and Keith received a refund of $5,600. Keith must refigure his Tuition and Fees Deduction using $2,400 of qualified expenses instead of $8,000 ($8,000 - $5,600). He must include the difference of $1,600 ($4,000 - $2,400) on his 2011 Form 1040 (the following year).

*Study Tip: On the EA Exam, be prepared to understand the difference between the Tuition and Fees Deduction and the Student Loan Interest Deduction; qualifying expenses, AGI limits, and deduction amounts are all different. A common "trick question" will be to verify a type of qualifying expense. Remember that in the case of the Student Loan Interest Deduction, qualifying expenses include housing. For the Tuition and Fees Deduction, housing expenses are not considered a "qualified expense."

Moving Expenses Deduction

If a taxpayer moves due to a change in job or business location, he may deduct moving expenses. A taxpayer who starts his first job or returns to full-time work after a long absence can also qualify for the deduction. If a taxpayer starts a job for the first time, the place of work must be at least 50 miles from his former home to meet the distance test.

Moving expenses incurred within one year from the date the taxpayer first reported to work at the new location can generally be deducted. If a taxpayer does not move within one year of the date she begins the new job, the moving expenses are not deductible unless she can prove that circumstances existed that prevented the move within that time. Simply failing to sell one's former home would not be an adequate excuse.

Qualifying Moving Expenses

Only certain expenses qualify for the moving expense deduction. Deductible moving expenses are:

- The cost of moving household goods, pets, and family members.
- Storage costs (only while in transit and up to 30 days after the day of the move).
- Travel expenses (including lodging but NOT meals) for one trip. However, family members are not required to travel together. The taxpayer may choose to deduct actual costs, or mileage.
- Any costs of connecting or disconnecting utilities required because a taxpayer is moving his household goods, appliances, or personal effects.
- The cost of shipping a car, pet, or belongings to a new home.

Actual car expenses such as gas and oil are tax deductible if accurate records are kept, or a taxpayer can take 16.5 cents a mile (in 2010) instead. Parking fees and tolls are also tax deductible, but general car repairs, maintenance, insurance, or depreciation of a taxpayer's car are not tax deductible.

Example: In February 2010, Ethan and Riley moved from Minnesota to Washington, D.C. where Ethan was starting a new job. He drove the family car to Washington, D.C., a trip of 1,100 miles. His actual expenses were $181.50 for gas, plus $40 for tolls and $150 for lodging, for a total of $371.50. One week later, Riley flew from Minnesota to Washington, DC. Her only expense was a $400 plane ticket. The couple's moving expense deduction is $771.50 (Ethan's $371.50 + Riley's $400).

For the purpose of this rule, a taxpayer's home means a taxpayer's main residence. It can be a house, apartment, condominium, houseboat, house trailer, or similar dwelling. It does not include other homes owned by the taxpayer, such as vacation homes. Moving expenses are figured on **Form 3903;** the amount is then transferred to **Form 1040** as an adjustment to income. To qualify for the moving expense deduction, the taxpayer must satisfy these tests:

1. The move must be related to work or business, and
2. The taxpayer must meet the "distance test" and the "time test."

The Time Test

The *Time Test* is different for employees than for people who are self-employed. For employees, moving costs are deductible only if the taxpayer works full-time at the new work location for at least 39 weeks (in the first 12 months). For joint filers, only one spouse has to qualify for the Time Test in order to deduct moving expenses.

Self-employed taxpayers must work full-time 39 weeks in the first 12 months at the new location, and then at least 78 weeks within the first 24 months (two years) at the new location. For this test, any combination of full-time work as an employee or as a self-employed person qualifies.

If the taxpayer fails to meet the Time Test, the taxpayer must report the moving expenses as "other income" on a later tax year, or amend the tax return on which the moving expense was claimed.

Example: Randy quit his job and moved from Texas to California to begin a full-time job as a mechanic for Motorcycle Customs, Inc. Randy worked at the motorcycle shop 40 hours each week. Shortly after his move, Randy also began operating a motorcycle repair business from his home garage for several hours each afternoon and on weekends. Because Randy's principal place of business is Motorcycle Customs, he can satisfy the time test by meeting the 39-week test. However, if Randy is unable to satisfy the requirements of the 39-week test during the 12-month period, he can satisfy the 78-week test because he also works as a self-employed person.

Seasonal Work and Temporary Absences

For the purpose of the moving expense deduction, if a taxpayer's trade or business is seasonal, the off-season weeks when no work is required or available may be counted as weeks during which he worked full time. The off-season must be less than six months and the taxpayer must work full-time before and after the off-season.

Temporary absences from work are allowed. A taxpayer is still considered to be employed on a full-time basis during any week she is temporarily absent from work because of illness, strikes, natural disasters, or similar causes. There are some exceptions to the time test in case of death, disability, and involuntary separation, among other things.

> **Example:** Harriet moved to Florida from California to take a job with a new employer. After working 25 weeks, her union voted to go on strike. She was off work for five weeks until the issue was resolved. Those five weeks count as a temporary absence and still may be counted as full-time work for the purpose of satisfying the time test.

> **Example:** Marcus moves from Colorado to Lake Tahoe, California to take a job as a manager of a ski resort. He works full-time during the ski season, and he is off for five months during the summer. Marcus may still count this time as full-time work, since his regular employment is expected to be seasonal.

Exceptions to the Time Test

There are exceptions to the time test. These are also frequently tested on the EA Exam, especially the exception for armed services personnel. A taxpayer does NOT have to meet the time test if any of the following applies:

- The taxpayer is in the armed forces and moved because of a permanent change of station.
- The taxpayer's main job location was outside the United States and she moved to the United States because she retired.
- A taxpayer is the surviving widow(er) of a person whose main job location at the time of death was outside the United States.
- The taxpayer's job at the new location ends because of death or disability.
- The taxpayer is transferred or laid off for a reason other than willful misconduct.

> **Example:** Darrell moves to Florida from New York because he is transferred by his employer. Darrell correctly deducts his moving expenses. Darrell expects to continue his full-time employment in Florida for many years and does not expect it to be a temporary move. A few months later, Darrell's employer is forced into bankruptcy and closes the entire Florida division. Darrell is laid off. He does not have to satisfy the time test.

The Distance Test

The "distance test" says that the new job must be at least 50 miles farther from the taxpayer's old home than the old job location was from the taxpayer's old home. If the taxpayer had no previous workplace, the new job must be at least 50 miles from the old home (see the diagram for clarification).

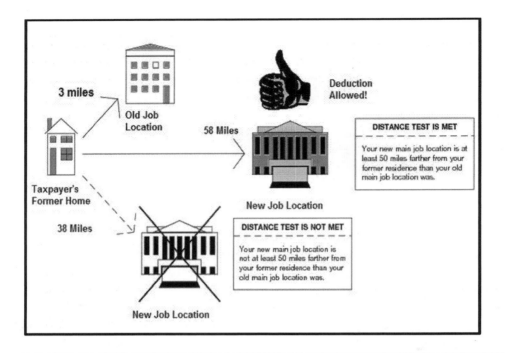

Example: Abe took a job as a plumber in another city. His old job was three miles from his former home. Therefore, in order to deduct his moving expenses, his new job location must be at least 53 miles from that former home. The distance test considers only the location of the former home, not the location of the former job.

Members of the armed forces moving because of a permanent change of station are NOT required to meet the distance test or the time test.

Example: Matt is enlisted in the Air Force, and has been transferred to another base 32 miles from his former home. Matt may still deduct his moving expenses without meeting the distance test, since he is a member of the armed forces.

Employer-Reimbursed Moving Expenses

Sometimes employers will reimburse a taxpayer for her moving expenses. If so, reimbursed moving expenses are excluded from taxable income and unreimbursed moving expenses are tax deductions in computing AGI rather than as an itemized tax deduction.

However, if an employer reimburses an employee for nondeductible expenses (such as the expense incurred from breaking a lease), this reimbursement is taxable as wages. It must be treated as paid under a non-accountable plan and be included as income on the employee's Form W-2. Expenses of buying or selling a home or breaking a lease (including closing costs, mortgage fees, and points) are never deductible as moving expenses.

> **Example:** Xavier is an engineer who has been offered a job at GenCorp Engineering. Xavier only agrees to accept the offer if GenCorp pays all his moving expenses. In order to entice Xavier to move out of state, GenCorp reimburses Xavier for a $7,500 loss on the sale of his home. Because this is a reimbursement of a nondeductible expense, it is treated as taxable to the employee and must be included in Xavier's **Form W-2.**

Nondeductible Moving Expenses

Only certain moving expenses are deductible. Moving expenses that cannot be deducted for income tax purposes include pre-move "house hunting" expenses, temporary living expenses, meals, expenses of buying or selling a home, home improvements to help sell a home, loss on a home sale, real estate taxes, car tags, driver's license fees, and storage charges except those paid in-transit and for foreign moves.

> **Extended Example: Nondeductible expenses**
>
> Todd and Peggy Smith are married and have two children. They owned a home in Detroit where Todd worked. On February 8, 2010, Todd's employer told him that he would be transferred to San Diego as of April 10, 2010. Peggy flew to San Diego on March 1 to look for a new home. She put a down payment of $25,000 on a house being built and returned to Detroit on March 4, 2010. The Smiths sold their Detroit home for $1,500 less than they paid for it. They contracted to have their personal belongings moved to San Diego on April 3, 2010. The family drove to San Diego where they found that their new home was not finished. They stayed in a nearby motel until the house was ready on May 1. On April 10, 2010, Todd went to work at his new job in San Diego.
>
> > They had $43,282 in total expenses:
> > Pre-move house hunting expenses of $524
> > Down payment on the San Diego home of $25,000
> > Real estate commission of $3,500 paid on the sale of the Detroit home
> > Loss of $1,500 on the sale of the Detroit home
> > Meal expenses of $320 for the drive to San Diego
> > Motel expenses of $3,730 while waiting for their home to be finished
> > Moving truck expense of $8,000
> > Gas and hotel expenses of $708 while driving to San Diego
>
> Out of all the expenses that Todd and Peggy incurred, only the cost of the moving truck and the actual trip to San Diego can be deducted ($8,000 + $708 = $8,708). The rest of the expenses totaling $34,574 ($43,282 − $8,708) cannot be deducted. Meals are not deductible as moving expenses. Losses on the sale of a primary residence are not deductible.

Health Savings Accounts

An HSA is a Health Savings Account. It is an account that is set up exclusively for paying medical expenses for the taxpayer, his spouse, and his dependents. To qualify, the taxpayer (or other eligible individuals):

- Must NOT be enrolled in Medicare
- May NOT be claimed as a dependent on anyone else's tax return

In 2010, Health Savings Accounts allow a taxpayer to avoid federal income tax on up to $3,050 for singles or $6,150 for joint filers. HSA owners who are 55 and over may save an extra $1,000, which means $4,050 for an individual and $7,150 for a family.

Health Savings Accounts (HSA)

Taxpayer	Minimum Deductible	Maximum Out-of-Pocket	Contribution Limit	55 and Over
Single	$1,200	$5,950	$3,050	+$1,000
Family	$2,400	$11,900	$6,150	+$1,000

HSA contributions are 100% tax deductible from gross income. The amounts deposited in an HSA become an "above the line" deduction on **Form 1040**. A taxpayer does not have to itemize in order to take this deduction.

If an employer makes a Health Savings Account contribution on behalf of employee, it is "excluded" from the employee's income, and not subject to income tax or Social Security tax.

A High Deductible Health Plan (HDHP) must be used in conjunction with HSAs. A *"High Deductible Health Plan"* has an annual deductible of at least $1,200 for self-only coverage or $2,400 for family coverage and annual out-of-pocket expenses up to $5,950 for self-only coverage or $11,900 for family coverage.

Withdrawals for nonmedical expenses from an HSA are allowed, but nonmedical distributions are subject to a 10 percent penalty tax, except in the following instances:

- When a taxpayer turns age 65 or older
- When a taxpayer becomes disabled
- When a taxpayer dies

A 6% penalty applies to excess contributions to an HSA.

The deduction for an HSA is reported on **Form 8889**, *Health Savings Accounts*. Taxpayers will receive Form 5498-SA from the HSA trustee showing the amount of their contributions for the year.

HSA accounts are usually set up with a bank, an insurance company, or by an employer. For an employee's HSA, the employee AND the employer may contribute to the employee's HSA in the same year. Contributions made by the employer are pretax and not subject to employment taxes (Social Security and Medicare). Similarly, any contributions made by a self-employed individual are deductible from AGI.

Contributions to an HSA must be made in cash. Contributions of stock or property are not allowed. To claim the HSA deduction for a particular year, the HSA contributions must be made on or before that year's tax filing date. For example, 2010 HSA contributions must be made on or before the filing deadline.

Deduction for One-Half of Self-Employment Tax

Self-employed taxpayers may take a deduction for one-half of self-employment tax paid. This is equal to the amount of Social Security and Medicare tax that an employer pays for an employee, which is normally excluded from an employee's income.

Self-employment (SE) tax is Social Security and Medicare tax collected primarily from individuals who work for themselves. SE tax must be paid if either of the following applies:

- The taxpayer had income as a church employee of $108.28 or more, or
- The taxpayer had self-employment income of $400 or more.

This deduction only affects *income tax*. It does not affect either net earnings from self-employment or SE tax. This deduction is reported as an adjustment to income and is claimed on Form 1040. It is available whether or not the taxpayer itemizes deductions.

Adjusted Gross Income				
	23	RESERVED (see page 28)	23	
	24	Certain business expenses of reservists, performing artists, and fee-basis government officials. Attach Form 2106 or 2106-EZ	24	
	25	Health savings account deduction. Attach Form 8889	25	
	26	Moving expenses. Attach Form 3903	26	
	27	One-half of self-employment tax. Attach Schedule SE	27	
	28	Self-employed SEP, SIMPLE, and qualified plans	28	
	29	Self-employed health insurance deduction (see page 30)	29	
	30	Penalty on early withdrawal of savings	30	

Self-Employed Health Insurance Deduction

A self-employed taxpayer may also deduct 100% of his health insurance premiums as an adjustment to income. Premiums paid by the taxpayer for his spouse and dependents are also deductible as an adjustment to income. For the first time, health insurance premiums paid for coverage of an adult child under age 27 at the end of the year, for the time period beginning on or after March 30, 2010, also qualify for this deduction, even if the child is NOT the taxpayer's dependent.

In addition, long-term care insurance is considered "health insurance" for the purpose of this deduction. The policy can be in the name of the business or in the name of the business owner.

Starting in 2010, the health insurance deduction reduces self-employment tax. This means that self-employed individuals may use the self-employed health insurance deduction to reduce their Social Security self-employment tax liability in addition to their income tax liability. As in the past, eligible taxpayers claim this deduction on Form 1040 Line 29. But in 2010, eligible taxpayers may also enter this amount on Schedule SE Line 3, thus reducing net earnings from self-employment, subject to the 15.3% Social Security self-employment tax.

In order to take the deduction, the taxpayer cannot be eligible to participate in an employer-sponsored health plan (neither spouse can be eligible to participate in an employer-sponsored health plan). Details, including a worksheet, are in the instructions to Form 1040.

183

Adjustment for Jury Duty Pay Given to an Employer

Jury duty pay is reported as taxable income on Form 1040. However, some employees continue to receive their regular wages when they serve on jury duty even though they are not at work, and their jury pay is turned over to their employers.

Employees who turn over jury duty pay to their employers can claim the deduction on Form 1040 as an adjustment to income. The amount is reported as a write-in adjustment. The taxpayer can report the entire amount as an adjustment to income, which is then subtracted from gross income. Therefore, the taxpayer's AGI will not include the jury duty pay.

Unit 1.7: Questions

1. Which of the following taxpayers, all of whom are covered by employer retirement plans, are entitled to a partial deduction for their traditional IRA contribution?

A. Evan, who is Single and has a modified AGI of $86,000
B. Connie, who is Married Filing Jointly and has a modified AGI of $111,000
C. Gabe, who is Married Filing Separately and has a modified AGI of $8,500
D. Calvin, a qualifying widower, who has a modified AGI of $110,500

The answer is C. According to the IRA deduction phase-out ranges, Gabe's allowable traditional IRA deduction is reduced because his modified AGI is less than $10,000. All of the other taxpayers listed have AGI limits that exceed the threshold. ###

2. Hubert and Felicity have a MAGI of $45,000. They are married and file a joint return. Two years ago, they took out a loan so Hubert's mother Miranda could earn her degree. They do not claim Hubert's mother as a dependent on their return. In 2010, they paid $3,000 in student loan interest. Miranda also earned a scholarship of $2,000. How much student loan interest can Hubert and Felicity deduct on their tax return?

A. $0
B. $1,000
C. $2,500
D. $3,000

The answer is A. Because his mother is not their dependent, they cannot deduct any part of the loan from their income. ###

3. Which IRS form is used to report nondeductible retirement plan contributions?

A. Form 8606
B. Form 1040
C. Form 8886
D. Form 8889

The answer is A. To designate IRA contributions as nondeductible, a taxpayer must file **Form 8606.** ###

4. Miguel is 47. In 2010, he contributed $1,000 to a Roth IRA. What is the maximum he can contribute to a traditional IRA in 2010?

A. $0
B. $3,000
C. $4,000
D. $5,000

The answer is C. The answer is $4,000; the 2010 maximum for contributions to all types of IRAs is $5,000. ###

5. Annette, age 40, and Gill, age 48, are married and file jointly. Annette is covered by a retirement plan at work, but Gill is not. Annette contributed $2,000 to her traditional IRA and $3,000 to a traditional IRA for Gill. Annette has a modified AGI of $90,000; Gill has a modified AGI of $88,000. What is their allowable traditional IRA deduction?

A. $5,000
B. $3,000
C. $2,000
D. Zero

The answer is D. Annette and Gill's allowable traditional IRA deduction is zero because their modified AGI is over the limit of $177,000. They are still allowed to make a nondeductible IRA contribution. Nondeductible IRA contributions are reported on Form 8606. ###

6. Elizabeth and Landon are 62 years old, married, and lived together all year. They both work and each has a traditional IRA. In 2010, Landon earned $4,000 and Elizabeth earned $52,000. If they file separate returns, what is the maximum that Landon can contribute to his IRA?

A. $1,000
B. $4,000
C. $5,000
D. $6,000

The answer is B. If Married Filing Separately, Landon can contribute no more than his $4,000 compensation. Taxpayers cannot make IRA contributions that are greater than their qualifying compensation for the year. ###

7. Colton, 49, and Molly, 52, are married and file jointly. They both work and each has a traditional IRA. In 2010, Molly earned $2,000 and Colton earned $50,000. If they file jointly, what is the maximum they can contribute to Molly's IRA?

A. $2,000
B. $5,000
C. $6,000
D. $12,000

The answer is C. They can agree to contribute up to $6,000 to Molly's IRA account. Colton can contribute $5,000 to his own IRA because he is under 50 years old. A married taxpayer may choose to make an IRA contribution on behalf of his or her spouse, even if only one spouse had compensation during the year. ###

8. Preston and Ruby are 50 years old and married. They both work and each has a traditional IRA. In 2010, Preston earned $5,000 and Ruby earned $32,000. If they file jointly, what is the maximum they can contribute to all their IRAs?

A. $2,000
B. $5,000
C. $6,000
D. $12,000

The answer is D. If Married Filing Jointly, they can contribute up to $12,000 to all their IRAs. This is because they are over 50. The maximum contribution for taxpayers who are 50 and above is $6,000 per person. ###

9. Frank, 72, and Sue, 61, are married and file jointly. In 2010, Frank earned $30,000 and Sue earned $7,500. If Frank and Sue file jointly, how much can they contribute to their traditional IRAs?

A. $5,000
B. $6,000
C. $11,000
D. $12,000

The answer is B. Only Sue can contribute to an IRA. Frank cannot contribute because he is over 70½ years old. Sue can contribute up to $6,000 to her IRA because she is over 50. ###

10. Contributions to a traditional IRA can be made:

A. Any time during the year or by the due date of the return, NOT including extensions.
B. Any time during the year or by the due date of the return, including extensions.
C. By December 31 (the end of the tax year).
D. Any time during the year, but only while the taxpayer is gainfully employed.

The answer is A. IRA contributions for tax year 2010 must be made by April 18, 2011. A taxpayer cannot make a contribution to an IRA after the due date of his tax return, even if he files for an extension. ###

11. Derek, age 62, is retired with $11,000 in interest income. He has no other compensation in 2010. Derek marries Virginia, age 46, on March 15. In 2010, Virginia has taxable compensation of $50,000. She plans to contribute $5,000 to a traditional IRA. How much can Derek contribute to an IRA in 2010?

A. $0
B. $4,000
C. $6,000
D. $8,000

The answer is C. Since Derek is over 50, he can choose to contribute $6,000 to an IRA. If spouses file a joint return, each can contribute to a traditional IRA, even if only one spouse has compensation. ###

12. An "excess contribution" to an IRA is subject to a tax. Which of the following is TRUE?

A. The taxpayer will not have to pay the 6% tax if she withdraws the excess contribution and any income earned on the excess contribution before the due date of her tax return for the year it is due, including extensions.
B. The 6% tax is due on both the excess contributions and any income earned on the excess contribution, even if the taxpayer withdraws the excess from the account.
C. A taxpayer will not have to pay the 6% tax if he withdraws the excess contribution and any income earned on the excess contribution before the due date of her tax return for the year it is due, NOT including extensions.
D. A taxpayer will not have to pay the 6% on interest earned on the excess contributions as long as the taxpayer is disabled.

The answer is A. The taxpayer will not have to pay the 6% tax if the excess contribution is withdrawn by the due date of her return, including extensions. The taxpayer must also withdraw interest or other income earned on the excess contribution. She must complete the withdrawal by the due date of the tax return, including extensions, in order to avoid the tax (Publication 17). ###

13. Which of the following statements is TRUE?

A. A school janitor may qualify for the teacher's credit.
B. A part-time teacher working only 905 hours a year qualifies for the teacher's credit.
C. A school counselor may not take the teacher's credit.
D. A college professor qualifies for the teacher's credit.

The answer is B. An eligible educator must work at least 900 hours a school year in a school that provides elementary or secondary education (K-12). College instructors do not qualify. The term "educator" includes teachers, instructors, counselors, principals, and aides. ###

14. Kristin, 42, is a full-time student with $1,200 in wages. She marries Omar, 50, during the year. Omar has taxable compensation of $46,000 in 2010. What is the maximum they can contribute to their traditional IRA accounts in 2010 if they file jointly?

A. $1,200
B. $6,200
C. $10,000
D. $11,000
E. $12,000

The answer is D. They can contribute $11,000 ($5,000 for Kristin and $6,000 for Omar). If they file jointly, Kristin can contribute $5,000 to a traditional IRA, and Omar can contribute $6,000 (because he is 50—the increased contribution starts at 50 years of age). Even though Kristin only has $1,200 in compensation, she can add Omar's compensation to her own compensation to figure her maximum contribution to a traditional IRA. ###

15. Polly is single, 51, and has the following compensation in 2010:

- $1,600 in annuity income
- $3,000 in wages
- $2,300 in alimony
- $3,000 in interest income
- $6,000 in rental income

What is the maximum amount that she can contribute to her traditional IRA in 2010?
A. $3,000
B. $5,000
C. $5,300
D. $6,600

The answer is C. Only Polly's wage income of $3,000 and the $2,300 in alimony qualify as "compensation" for the purposes of an IRA. The annuity income and the interest income do not qualify. ###

16. What is the maximum teacher's credit for two teachers who are married and file jointly?

A. $100
B. $250
C. $500
D. $750

The answer is C. On a joint tax return, if both taxpayers are teachers, they both may take the credit, up to a maximum of $500 ($250 each). ###

17. Vic, age 36 and single, is in the Marines. Vic has the following income in 2010 totaling $35,100:
- $30,500 of nontaxable combat pay
- $2,100 of regular wages
- $4,600 of interest income

What is the maximum amount of money that Vic can contribute to a traditional IRA?

A. $2,100
B. $4,600
C. $5,000
D. $6,000

The answer is C. Vic may contribute $5,000 (the maximum contribution allowed for his age). That is because a taxpayer may elect to treat nontaxable combat pay as taxable compensation for IRA purposes. The interest income would not be considered "compensation" for IRA purposes. ###

18. Rafael, 40, earns $26,000 in 2010. Although he is allowed to contribute up to $5,000 for 2010, he only has enough cash to contribute $2,000. On August 15, 2011, Rafael expects to get a big bonus, and he wishes to make a "catch-up" contribution for 2010. Which of the following statements is TRUE?

A. Rafael can contribute an additional $3,000 in August 2011 for his 2010 tax year as long as he amends his 2010 tax return.
B. Rafael cannot contribute an additional $3,000 after April 15, 2011.
C. Rafael can contribute an additional $3,000 in August 2011 for his 2010 tax year only if he files a timely extension.
D. Rafael cannot make a contribution to his IRA after December 31, 2010.

The answer is B. If contributions to a traditional IRA for the year were less than the limit, a taxpayer cannot contribute more after the due date of the tax return to make up the difference (Publication 590).###

19. Celeste, who is 50 and single, worked recently for a telephone company in France and earned $48,500 for which she claimed the foreign earned income exclusion. In addition to that she earned $3,200 as an employee of an answering service while she was in the U.S. She also received alimony of $400 for the year. What is her maximum amount of allowable contribution to a traditional IRA for year 2010?

A. $3,200
B. $3,600
C. $5,000
D. $6,000

The answer is B. Foreign earned income that is excluded from income is also excluded for IRA purposes. Alimony and wages earned in the U.S. are both earned income for IRA purposes. Therefore, only the $400 alimony and the $3,200 earned in the U.S. would be considered "compensation" for the purposes of an IRA contribution. ###

20. Which of the following statements is TRUE?

A. Credit card interest can be deductible as student loan interest if qualifying educational expenses are paid.
B. On a Married Filing Jointly return, a taxpayer may deduct student loan interest paid on behalf of her spouse.
C. The maximum deduction for student loan interest is $2,500 per student, up to $5,000 per return.
D. Taxpayers may deduct student loan interest even if they are not liable for the loan.

The answer is B. On a MFJ return, a taxpayer may deduct student loan interest paid on behalf of her spouse or dependents. This deduction is a maximum of $2,500 in 2010. ###

21. Jacob borrowed $15,000 from his half-sister to pay for college. He signed a notarized contract and is paying regular payments of $500 per month at 10% interest. In 2010, he paid $3,200 in student loan interest. Which of the following is TRUE?

A. Jacob can deduct all the interest as qualified student loan interest.
B. Jacob can deduct $2,500 of the interest as qualified student loan interest.
C. Jacob cannot deduct the interest.
D. Jacob can deduct $6,000 ($500 X 12 months).

The answer is C. Interest paid to a related person is not "qualified" interest for the purposes of the Student Loan Interest Deduction. Related persons include a spouse, brothers and sisters, half-brothers and half-sisters, ancestors (parents, grandparents, etc.), and lineal descendants (children, grandchildren, etc.). ###

22. Years ago, Sammy took out a student loan for $90,000 to help pay the tuition at Ivy League University. He graduated and began making payments on his student loan in 2010. Sammy made twelve payments in 2010, and he paid $1,600 in required interest on the loan. He also paid an additional $1,000 in principal payment voluntarily, attempting to get the debt paid off faster. How much is Sammy's Student Loan Interest Deduction?

A. $1,600
B. $2,500
C. $2,600
D. $90,000

The answer is A. Only the interest is deductible. A payment toward the principal on the loan is not a deductible expense. Student loan interest is interest a taxpayer paid during the year on a qualified student loan. It includes both required and voluntary interest payments. ###

23. Which of the following expenses does NOT qualify for the Student Loan Interest Deduction?

A. Tuition
B. Required books
C. Required equipment
D. Room and board
E. Tuition for a non-degree candidate

The answer is E. The student must be enrolled at least half-time in a program leading to a degree, certificate, or other recognized educational credential in order to qualify for the Student Loan Interest Deduction. ###

24. On which form are student loan interest payments reported to the taxpayer?

A. Form 1098
B. Form 1099-Misc
C. Form 1099-R
D. Form 1098-E

The answer is D. Taxpayers who pay student loan interest will receive Form 1098-E, *Student Loan Interest Statement*, from the lender. A lender (or bank) that receives interest payments of $600 or more must report the interest to the taxpayer. ###

25. In the case of the Tuition and Fees Deduction, qualified education expenses do NOT include amounts paid for:

A. Insurance
B. Medical expenses (including student health fees)
C. Room and board
D. Transportation
E. All of the above

The answer is E. None of the above expenses qualifies for the Tuition and Fees Deduction. This is true even if the amount must be paid to the institution as a condition of enrollment or attendance. Student activity fees, course-related books, supplies, and equipment may be deductible only if they are required by the institution as a condition of enrollment. ###

26. Which form is used to figure and report the Tuition and Fees Deduction?

A. Form 8917
B. Form 8883
C. Form 1099-INT
D. Form 1098-T

The answer is A. The deduction is figured on Form 8917, *Tuition and Fees Deduction*, which is attached to the taxpayer's Form 1040. ###

27. Tyler is a sophomore at Iowa State University's degree program in Anthropology. This year, he paid $3,000 in tuition and $10,000 to live in optional on-campus housing. In addition to tuition, he is required to pay a fee to the university for the rental of the equipment he will use in this program. The fee to rent the equipment is $300 per year. How much of these expenses qualify for the Tuition and Fees Deduction?

A. $3,000
B. $3,300
C. $13,000
D. $13,300

The answer is B. The rental fee and the tuition costs qualify for the Tuition and Fees Deduction, and Tyler may deduct the cost on his tax return. Because the equipment rental fee must be paid to the university and is a requirement for enrollment and attendance, Tyler's equipment rental fee is a qualified expense. Student activity fees and expenses for course-related books, supplies, and equipment can be included in qualified educational expenses if the fees and expenses paid to the institution are required. The housing is not a qualified educational expense. ###

28. Addie paid $2,000 tuition and fees in December 2010, and she began college in January 2011. Addie filed her 2010 tax return on February 1, 2011, and correctly claimed a Tuition and Fees Deduction of $2,000. But after Addie filed her return, she became ill and dropped two courses. She received a refund of tuition in the amount of $1,100 in March. How must Addie report the refund of fees?

A. Addie may use the refund to pay qualified tuition in 2010 and not report the refund.
B. Addie may report the refund on her next year's tax return as "Other Income."
C. Addie is not required to report the refund.
D. Addie may use the refund to go on vacation.

The answer is B. Addie may include the difference of $1,100 on the "Other Income" line of her Form 1040 in the following year. The 2010 return does not have to be amended (Publication 970). ###

29. On which form must taxpayers report deductible moving expenses?

A. Form 3903
B. Form 1041
C. Form 8821
D. Schedule A

The answer is A. Report deductible moving expenses on IRS Form 3903, *Moving Expenses*. The form must be attached to the taxpayer's Form 1040. ###

30. Patricia had the following moving expenses:

$1,200 for transporting her household goods
$550 in lodging for travel between her old home and her new home
$250 in meals during the trip
$250 to break the lease on her old home

Patricia moved to start a new job and met the distance and time tests. What are the total moving expenses that can be deducted on her tax return?

A. $2,150
B. $1,900
C. $1,750
D. $2,000

The answer is C. The answer is figured as follows:

Cost of transporting goods	$1,200
Lodging	$550
Deductible expenses	**$1,750**

A taxpayer cannot deduct any moving expenses for meals. The cost of breaking a lease to move to a new location is also not a deductible expense. ###

31. Dave and Bea file jointly. In March 2010, they moved from Texas to Connecticut, where Dave was starting a new job. Dave drove the car to Hartford. His expenses were $400 for gas, $40 for tolls, $150 for lodging, and $70 for meals. One week later, Bea drove to Hartford. Her expenses were $500 for gas, $40 for tolls, $35 for parking, $100 for lodging, and $25 for meals. A week later, they paid $600 to ship their pet, a miniature horse, to Connecticut. How much is their deduction for moving expenses?

A. $590
B. $1,265
C. $1,300
D. $1,360
E. $1,865

The answer is E. The cost of meals is not deductible. The costs of travel, transportation, and lodging are all deductible. The costs of moving personal items and pets are deductible. The answer is figured as follows:

Dave's expenses $400 + $40 + $150 = $590
Bea's expenses $500 + $40 + $35 + $100 = $675
Cost of shipping horse = $600
Total deductible expenses:
$590 + $675 + $600 = $1,865

If a married couple files jointly, either spouse can qualify for the full-time work test, and both are not required to travel together (Publication 521). ###

32. Chase is moving for a new job. He has the following expenses:
- $500 cost of moving truck rental
- $300 cost of moving family and pets
- $200 cost for a storage unit while moving
- $400 cost of breaking his existing apartment lease
- $500 pre-move house-hunting

Assuming that Chase passes all the required tests, what is his Moving Expense Deduction?

A. $500
B. $800
C. $1,000
D. $1,900

The answer is C. The cost of breaking a lease is not a deductible moving expense. House-hunting before a move is also not deductible. Therefore, Chase may only deduct the following:
($500 + $300 + $200 = $1,000). ###

33. Lynn was offered a position in another city. Her new employer reimburses her for the $9,500 loss on the sale of her home because of the move. How should this reimbursement be treated?

A. The employer can reimburse Lynn and make the payment nontaxable through an accountable plan, if properly documented.
B. Because this is a reimbursement of a nondeductible expense, it is treated as wages and must be included as pay on Lynn's Form W-2.
C. The reimbursement is tax-exempt because it is a qualified moving expense.
D. The expense is nontaxable as long as Lynn's employer makes the payment directly to her mortgage lender.

The answer is B. Because this is a reimbursement of a nondeductible expense, it is treated as paid under a non-accountable plan and must be included as pay on Lynn's Form W-2. Expenses of buying or selling a home (including closing costs, mortgage fees, and points) are never deductible as moving expenses. ###

34. Alimony does NOT include:

A. Noncash property settlements
B. Payments to a third-party on behalf of an ex-spouse
C. Medical expenses paid on behalf of an ex-spouse
D. Cash payments

The answer is A. Alimony does not include child support, noncash property settlements, payments to keep up the payor's property, or use of the payor's property. Payments made to a third party or medical expenses paid on behalf of a former spouse may qualify as alimony. ###

35. Ian and Pam are divorced. Pam has an auto accident and dies. Under their divorce decree, Ian must continue to pay his former spouse's estate $30,000 annually. The divorce decree states that upon Pam's death, the continued payments will be put into trust for their daughter, who is 12 years old. What is true about the $30,000 annual payment?

A. For tax purposes, it is alimony.
B. For tax purposes, it is child support.
C. For tax purposes, it is a gift.
D. Once Pam dies, the payments are taxable to the daughter.

The answer is B. The trust is to be used for the child's benefit and must continue after Pam's death. Therefore, the $30,000 annual payment is not alimony and is instead classified as child support for tax purposes. Any payment that is specifically designated as child support or treated as specifically designated as child support under a divorce agreement is not alimony. ###

36. Under his divorce decree, Rick must pay the medical expenses of his former spouse Linda. In January 2010, Rick sends a check totaling $4,000 directly to General Medical Hospital in order to pay for Linda's emergency surgery. Which of the following statements is TRUE?

A. This payment qualifies as alimony, and Linda must include the $4,000 as income on her return.
B. This payment does not qualify as alimony, but Rick can claim a deduction for the medical expenses on his return.
C. Linda must include the $4,000 as income on her return, but Rick cannot deduct the expense as alimony because it was paid to a third party.
D. None of the above.

The answer is A. The payment may be treated as alimony for tax purposes. Payments to a third party on behalf of an ex-spouse under the terms of a divorce instrument can be alimony, if they qualify. These include payments for a spouse's medical expenses, housing costs (rent and utilities), taxes, and tuition. The payments are treated as received by the ex-spouse and included as income (Publication 504).###

37. George paid $14,000 in alimony to his wife during the year. Which of the following is TRUE?

A. George can only deduct alimony he itemizes on his tax return.
B. The deduction for alimony is entered on Schedule A as an itemized deduction.
C. George can deduct alimony paid, even if he does not itemize.
D. George can deduct alimony paid on Form 1040EZ.

The answer is C. George can deduct alimony paid, even if he does not itemize. He must file Form 1040 and enter the amount of alimony paid as an adjustment to income. An adjustment for alimony cannot be claimed on Form 1040EZ (Publication 504). ###

38. Under the terms of a divorce decree, Blake transfers appreciated property to his ex-wife Ming. The property has a fair market value of $75,000 and an adjusted basis of $50,000 to Blake. This transaction creates taxable alimony of _____ for Ming.

A. $0
B. $25,000
C. $75,000
D. $50,000

The answer is A. Transfers of property in the fulfillment of a divorce decree are not taxable events. Property settlements due to a divorce decree are NOT alimony; they are simply a division of assets and are treated as such. ###

39. Which form is used to report HSA contributions to the IRS?

A. Form 8889
B. Form 5498
C. Schedule A
D. Form 2848

The answer is A. HSA contributions are reported to the IRS on Form 8889, *Health Savings Accounts*. Taxpayers will receive Form 5498-SA from the HSA trustee showing the amount of their contributions for the year. ###

40. Kyle has an HSA, and he becomes permanently disabled in 2010. Which of the following statements is true?

A. Kyle may withdraw money from his HSA for nonmedical expenses, but the withdrawals will be subject to income tax and also an additional 10% penalty.
B. Kyle may withdraw money from his HSA for nonmedical expenses. The withdrawals will be subject to income tax, but will not be subject to penalty.
C. Kyle may not take nonmedical distributions from his account.
D. Kyle must be at least 65 to take nonmedical distributions from an HSA.

The answer is B. Kyle is disabled, so his withdrawals are not subject to penalty. Withdrawals for nonmedical expenses from an HSA are allowed, but nonmedical distributions are subject to a 10% additional penalty tax, except when the taxpayer turns 65, becomes disabled, or dies. ###

41. Seth accidentally makes an excess contribution to his HSA. What is the penalty on excess contributions if Seth does not correct the problem?

A. No penalty
B. 6% penalty
C. 10% penalty
D. 15% penalty

The answer is B. The 6% penalty applies to excess contributions. Excess contributions made by an employer must be included in gross income. Excess contributions are not deductible. ###

42. During 2010, Deborah was self-employed. She had the following income and deductions:
- Net self-employment income of $32,000
- Self-employment tax of $4,896

Which of the following statements is true?

A. Deborah may deduct 100% of the self-employment tax she paid on Schedule C.
B. Deborah may deduct 50% of the self-employment tax she paid on Schedule C.
C. Deborah may deduct 50% of the self-employment tax she paid as an adjustment to income on Form 1040.
D. Deborah may not deduct self-employment tax.

The answer is C. Deborah may deduct 50% of the self-employment tax she paid as an adjustment to income on her Form 1040. A taxpayer can deduct one-half (not 100%) of self-employment tax paid as an adjustment on Form 1040. ###

43. Joe lost his job last year and withdrew money from a number of accounts. He paid the following penalties:
- $100 penalty for early withdrawal from a Certificate of Deposit (CD)
- $200 penalty from early withdrawal from a traditional IRA
- $50 late penalty for not paying his rent on time

How much of these listed amounts can Joe deduct as an adjustment to income on his Form 1040?
A. $0
B. $100
C. $200
D. $250

The answer is B. Early withdrawal penalties are tax-deductible if made from a time deposit account, such as a Certificate of Deposit. Taxpayers deduct any penalties on Form 1040, as an adjustment to income. ###

44. Chuck and Diana are married and file jointly. Chuck is self-employed and his profit was $50,000 in 2010. They pay $500 per month for health insurance coverage. Diana was a homemaker until March 1, 2010, when she got a job working for a local construction company. Diana was eligible to participate in an employer health plan, but she and Chuck didn't want to switch insurance providers, so she declined the coverage. Which of the following statements is TRUE?

A. No deduction is allowed in 2010 for self-employed health insurance.
B. Chuck and Diana may only deduct $1,000 in self-employed health insurance, which is for January and February, the two months they were not eligible to participate in an employer plan.
C. Chuck and Diana may deduct 100% of their insurance premiums because they declined the employer coverage.
D. Chuck and Diana may deduct 50% of their health insurance premiums on Chuck's Schedule C.

The answer is B. Chuck and Diana may only deduct $1,000 in self-employed health insurance for the two months that they were ineligible to participate in an employer plan. No deduction is allowed for self-employed health insurance for any month that the taxpayer has the option to participate in an employer-sponsored plan. This is true even if the taxpayer declines the coverage. Self-employed taxpayers may deduct 100% of health insurance premiums as an adjustment to income but only if they are unable to participate in an employer health plan. ###

45. In 2010, Thomas converted his traditional IRA to a Roth IRA. The IRA was made up only of deductible contributions and earnings at the time of the conversion and valued at $18,000. Thomas completed Form 8606 and does not elect to report all the income on the year of the conversion. How should the income be reported?

A. Thomas should include $9,000 in his taxable income in 2011 and $9,000 in his taxable income in 2012. B. Thomas should include $9,000 in his taxable income in 2010 and $9,000 in his taxable income in 2011. C. Thomas should include $18,000 in his taxable income in 2010.
D. Thomas should include $18,000 in income in 2011.

The answer is A. In a Roth conversion, any income as a result of the rollover is generally included in equal amounts over a 2-year period, beginning in 2011. This means the taxpayer should include one half of the amount in income in 2011 and the other half in income in 2012. A taxpayer must file Form 8606 to report a rollover from a qualified retirement plan to a Roth IRA.

Unit 1.8: The Standard Deduction and Itemized Deductions

More Reading:
Publication 502, *Medical and Dental Expenses*
Publication 529, *Miscellaneous Deductions*
Publication 600, *State and Local General Sales Taxes*
Publication 936, *Home Mortgage Interest Deduction*
Publication 547, *Casualties, Disasters, and Thefts*
Publication 526, *Charitable Contributions*
Publication 561, *Determining the Value of Donated Property*
Publication 587, *Business Use of Your Home*

Taxpayers may choose to take the "standard deduction" or "itemize" their deductions on their tax return. If the taxpayer chooses to itemize, then he must file a Schedule A along with his Form 1040. When taxpayers make the choice, they should use the type of deduction that results in the lower tax.

Some taxpayers are not eligible to use the standard deduction, such as nonresident aliens, dual-status aliens, and individuals who file returns for periods of less than 12 months. When a married couple files separate returns (MFS) and one spouse itemizes deductions, the other spouse must also itemize deductions, even if the other spouse has no expenses to itemize.

The Standard Deduction

The standard deduction is a dollar amount that reduces the amount of income that is taxed. The standard deduction is an amount that is based on the taxpayer's filing status.

Standard Deduction Amounts	
Filing Status	**2010**
Single	$5,700
Married Filing Jointly	$11,400
Married Filing Separately	$5,700
Head of Household	$8,400
Qualifying Widow(er)	$11,400

Example: Joel, 46, and Denise, 33, are filing a joint return for 2010. Neither is blind. They decide not to itemize their deductions. Their standard deduction in 2010 is $11,400.

An *increased* standard deduction is available to taxpayers who are:

* 65 or older and/or
* Blind or partially blind

*Note: Don't be confused by this concept. The "additional" standard deduction is not a credit or an itemized deduction. It is simply an increase over the regular standard deduction amount that Congress has decided to give to taxpayers who are over 65 and/or blind. The increased standard deduction amount in these cases is $1,100 per taxpayer for married filers and $1,400 for Single and Head of Household.

Example: Darius, 66, and Lisa, 59, are filing a joint return for 2010. Darius is over 65, and Lisa is blind. They do not itemize deductions. Because they are Married Filing Jointly, their base standard deduction is $11,400. Because Darius is over age 65, he can claim an additional standard deduction of $1,100. Because Lisa is blind, she can also claim an additional $1,100. Therefore, their total standard deduction is $13,600.

The standard deduction for a deceased taxpayer is the same as if the taxpayer had lived the entire year, with one exception: if the taxpayer died *before* his 65th birthday, the higher standard deduction for being 65 does not apply.

Example: Richard died on November 1, 2010. He would have been 65 if he had reached his birthday on December 12, 2010. He does not qualify for a higher standard deduction for being 65, because he died before his 65th birthday.

The standard deduction eliminates the need for taxpayers to itemize actual deductions, such as medical expenses, charitable contributions, and taxes. It is available to U.S. citizens and resident aliens who are individuals, married persons, and heads of household. In some cases, the standard deduction can consist of two parts: the "basic" standard deduction and an *additional* standard deduction amount for age, blindness, or both.

The additional amount for blindness will be allowed if the taxpayer is blind on the last day of the tax year, even if she did not qualify as "blind" the rest of the year. A taxpayer must obtain a statement from an eye doctor that states:

- The taxpayer cannot see better than 20/200 even while corrected with eyeglasses, or
- The taxpayer's field of vision is not more than 20 degrees (the taxpayer has disabled peripheral vision).

The additional amount for age will be allowed if the taxpayer is at least age 65 at the end of the tax year.

Example: Max and Wendy are both 30 years old and file jointly for 2010. They decide not to itemize their deductions. Max is blind, so he and Wendy are allowed an additional $1,100 as a standard deduction amount. They then enter $12,500 ($11,400 + $1,100) on their Form 1040. Their standard deduction is $12,500.

Standard Deduction for Dependents

A dependent is also allowed a standard deduction. If a dependent is claimed on another person's return, his standard deduction amount is the larger of:

- $950, or
- The dependent's *earned* income (such as wages) plus $300 (but not more than the regular standard deduction amount, generally $5,700).

Example: Georgia is single, 22, and a full-time student. Her parents claimed her as a dependent on their 2010 tax return. She has no itemized deductions, so she will take the standard deduction. Georgia has interest income of $120, taxes withheld from her wages totaling $35, and wages of $780. Her standard deduction is $1,080 ($780 + $300).

However, the standard deduction may be higher if the dependent is 65 or older or blind.

202

Example: Amy is 19, single, and blind. She is claimed on her parents' 2010 return. Amy has interest income of $1,300 and wages from a part-time job of $2,900. She has no itemized deductions. The base amount is $3,200 ($2,900 + $300, which is her wages plus $300). Because Amy is also blind, she is allowed an additional standard deduction amount of $1,400. So her standard deduction is figured as follows: $2,900 + $300 + $1,400 = $4,600.

Itemized Deductions

Itemized deductions allow taxpayers to reduce their taxable income based on specific personal expenses. If the total itemized deductions are greater than the standard deduction, they will result in a lower taxable income and lower tax.

In general, taxpayers benefit from itemizing deductions if they have mortgage interest, large unreimbursed medical expenses, or other large expenses such as charitable contributions. Itemized deductions are taken *instead of* the standard deduction. Generally, the taxpayer may choose whether to take itemized deductions or the standard deduction, and may take whichever deduction gives her the highest benefit.

However, the following taxpayers are forced to itemize:

- Married Filing Separately and one spouse itemizes: the other spouse is also forced to itemize.
- A nonresident or dual-status alien during the year (who is not married to a U.S. citizen or resident).

If either situation applies, the taxpayer must itemize personal deductions. He cannot choose the standard deduction.

Example: Shannon files as Married Filing Separately. Her spouse Grant will itemize his deductions. Shannon cannot use the standard deduction; she is also forced to itemize her deductions.

Medical and Dental Expenses (Subject to the 7.5% Limit)

Medical and dental expenses are deductible only if taxpayers itemize their deductions. Further, taxpayers can deduct only the amount of unreimbursed medical expenses that exceeds 7.5 percent of their Adjusted Gross Income (AGI). Qualified medical expenses include expenses paid for:

- The taxpayer
- The taxpayer's spouse
- Dependents (who must have qualified as dependents at the time the medical services were provided or at the time the expenses were paid)

*Exception: If a child of divorced or separated parents is claimed as a dependent on either parent's return, each parent may deduct the medical expenses he or she individually paid for the child. There is also an exception for medical expenses paid on behalf of former spouses pursuant to a divorce decree. A taxpayer may also deduct medical expenses that were paid on behalf of an adopted child, even before the adoption is final. The child must qualify as a dependent and must be a member of the taxpayer's household during the year the medical expenses were paid.

Example: Colby and Carmen are divorced. Their son Raymond lives with Carmen, who claims him as a dependent. Carmen deducts Raymond's standard medical and dental bills. Colby deducts the emergency bill he paid when Raymond broke his arm.

A taxpayer can deduct medical expenses paid for a dependent parent. All the standard rules for a dependency exemption apply, so a dependent parent would not have to live with the taxpayer in order to qualify.

Example: Julie pays all the medical expenses for her mother Rose, who is her dependent. Rose does not live with Julie. The medical expenses are still deductible on Julie's tax return as an itemized deduction if the 7.5% limit is reached.

Taxpayers may deduct unreimbursed medical and dental expenses and long-term care insurance premiums. Even vehicle mileage may be deducted if the out-of-pocket expenses were used for medical reasons, such as transportation to and from a medical appointment.

The standard mileage rate allowed for out-of-pocket expenses when used for medical reasons is 16.5 cents per mile. The taxpayer can also deduct parking fees and tolls.

A taxpayer can deduct only the amount of medical and dental expenses that is more than 7.5% of Adjusted Gross Income (AGI). In this section, the term "7.5% limit" is used to refer to 7.5% of Adjusted Gross Income. A taxpayer must subtract 7.5% (.075) of her Adjusted Gross Income from gross medical expenses to figure the medical expense deduction.

Example: Tracy's Adjusted Gross Income is $40,000. She had actual medical expenses totaling $2,500. Tracy cannot deduct any of her medical expenses because they are not more than 7.5% of her Adjusted Gross Income (7.5% of which is $3,000).

Example: Olivia's Adjusted Gross Income is $100,000. In 2010, she paid for a knee operation. She had $10,000 of out-of-pocket medical expenses related to the surgery. In this case, $2,500 would be allowed as an itemized deduction, the amount in excess of the $7,500 base ($100,000 X .075 = $7,500).

Qualifying Medical Expenses

Qualifying medical expenses include the costs of diagnosis, cure, mitigation, treatment, or prevention of disease, and the costs for medical (not cosmetic) treatments. They include the costs of equipment, supplies, and diagnostic devices needed for these purposes. They also include dental expenses and vision care, such as the cost of prescription eyeglasses and contact lenses, as well as transportation costs to obtain medical care. Medical expenses also include amounts paid for qualified long-term care insurance.

The cost of items such as false teeth, laser eye surgery, hearing aids, crutches, wheelchairs, and guide dogs for the blind or deaf are deductible medical expenses.

In some cases, even veterinary care can be deducted as a medical expense. The IRS allows taxpayers to include the cost of service animals in medical expenses. An animal trained to assist persons with other physical disabilities may also be deducted. Guide dogs or other service animals to be used by a visually-impaired or hearing-impaired person are considered "medical devices" for the purpose of this rule. Specifically, amounts paid for the care of these specially-trained animals are deductible as medical expenses.

Qualifying medical expenses include medical insurance premiums that the taxpayer has paid with after-tax dollars. A taxpayer can include only the medical and dental expenses paid during the year, regardless of when the services were provided. If a taxpayer pays medical expenses by check, the day a taxpayer mails the check is generally accepted as the date of payment. If a medical expense is paid by credit card, the date the credit card is charged is accepted as the date of payment.

If a taxpayer (or a dependent) is in a nursing home, and the primary reason for being there is medically related, the entire cost, including meals and lodging, is a medical expense (Publication 502).

Medical care expenses must be primarily to alleviate or prevent a physical or mental defect or illness. Medical expenses do NOT include expenses that are merely "beneficial" to general health, such as vitamins, spa treatments, gym memberships, or vacations. In addition, over-the-counter medications cannot be deducted as medical expenses on Schedule A.

Medically Related Legal Fees

A taxpayer can deduct legal fees that are necessary to authorize treatment for a mental illness. However, legal fees for the management of a guardianship estate, or legal fees for conducting the affairs of a person being treated are not deductible as medical expenses.

Medical Expenses of Deceased taxpayers

An election can be made to deduct medical expenses paid by a deceased taxpayer. This is legal for one year after the date of the taxpayer's death. The expenses may be treated as if paid when the medical services were provided (even if the medical expenses are not actually paid until after the taxpayer's death). In some cases the taxpayer's Form 1040 must be amended. Form 1040X is the correct form to submit an amended tax return. The medical expenses of a deceased taxpayer are still subject to a 7.5% floor.

> **Example:** Anne had heart surgery in November 2009 and incurred $20,000 in medical bills. Anne died on January 2, 2010. The 2009 medical bills were still unpaid at the time of her death. The executor of Anne's estate may elect to deduct her medical expenses in 2009, even though the medical expenses are paid at a later date.

Cosmetic Surgery

Cosmetic surgery is only deductible if it is used to correct a defect or disease. Cosmetic procedures simply for the enhancement of someone's physical appearance are not deductible medical expenses.

Example: Olga undergoes surgery to remove a breast as part of treatment for cancer. She pays a surgeon to reconstruct her breast. The surgery to reconstruct the breast corrects a deformity directly related to the disease. The cost of the surgery is includable in her medical expenses.

Example: Miles is two years old and was born with a congenital deformity. His parents pay for cosmetic surgery to correct the deformity. The surgery is deductible as a medical expense because it corrects a defect.

Medically Related Meals, Lodging, and Transportation

A taxpayer can deduct the cost of meals and lodging at a hospital or similar institution if the principal reason for being there is to receive medical care. The taxpayer can deduct the cost of lodging if all of the following requirements are met:

- The lodging is primarily for medical care.
- The medical care must be provided by a doctor, hospital, or a medical care facility.
- There is no significant element of personal pleasure or recreation.

The IRS imposes a $50 limit per night, (per person), for lodging for medically-related issues (Publication 502).

Capital Improvements for Medical Reasons

Capital improvements such as home improvements are usually not deductible by the taxpayer. However, a home improvement may qualify as a deductible medical expense if its main purpose is to provide a medical benefit to the taxpayer or to dependent family members.

The deduction for capital improvements is limited to the excess of the actual cost of the improvements over the increase in the Fair Market Value of the home. Home improvements that qualify as deductible medical expenses include:

- Wheelchair ramps
- Lowering of kitchen cabinets
- Railings and support bars
- Elevators

Tenants may deduct the entire cost of disability-related improvements, since they are not the owners of the property.

Example: Jay has a heart condition. He cannot easily climb stairs or get into a bathtub. On his doctor's advice, he installs a special sit-in bathtub and a stair lift on the first floor of his rented house. The landlord did not pay any of the cost of buying and installing the special equipment and did not lower the rent. Jay can deduct the entire amount as a medical expense.

Medical Transportation Expenses

A taxpayer may deduct transportation costs related to medical care. The actual cost for a taxi, bus, train, or ambulance can be deducted. If a taxpayer uses his own car for medical transportation, he may deduct actual out-of-pocket expenses such as gas and oil, or he may deduct the standard mileage rate of 16.5 cents a mile for medical expenses. With either method, the taxpayer may also include expenses for tolls and parking fees.

Deductible Taxes

Taxpayers can deduct certain taxes if they itemize their deductions. To be deductible, the tax must have been imposed on the taxpayer and paid by the taxpayer during the tax year. Taxes that are deductible include:

- State, local, and foreign income taxes
- Real estate taxes
- Personal property taxes
- State and local sales taxes

State and local taxes: State and local income taxes include withheld taxes, estimated tax payments, or other tax payments such as a prior year refund of a state or local income tax that taxpayers applied to their estimated state or local income taxes.

Motor vehicle taxes: Some taxpayers who purchased a new motor vehicle in 2009 did not have to pay their state or local sales or excise taxes until 2010. In these instances, they may be eligible to deduct the amount paid on their 2010 income tax return.

Foreign income taxes: Under the foreign earned income exclusion or the foreign housing exclusion, these taxes can be deducted on income that is not exempt from U.S. tax. Generally, income taxes paid to a foreign country can be deducted as:

- An itemized deduction on Schedule A, OR
- A credit against U.S. income tax

A taxpayer can choose between claiming the Foreign Tax Credit, or claiming any foreign tax paid on Schedule A as an itemized deduction. The taxpayer may use whichever method results in the lowest tax.

Sales Taxes: The Tax Relief Act extended the provision that allows taxpayers to elect to deduct state and local sales taxes in lieu of state and local income taxes.

Real Estate Taxes

State, local, or foreign real estate taxes that are based on the assessed value of the taxpayer's real property, such as the taxpayer's house or land, are deductible. Real estate taxes are reported to the taxpayer on Form 1098, *Mortgage Interest Statement*. A taxpayer may deduct real estate taxes on any real estate property she owns. Real estate taxes paid on foreign property are also deductible.

If a portion of a taxpayer's monthly mortgage payment goes into an escrow account, the taxpayer can only deduct the amount actually paid out of the escrow account during the year to the taxing authority. Some real estate taxes are not deductible, including taxes for local benefits, itemized charges for services, and homeowners' association fees.

If a property is sold, the real estate taxes must be "pro-rated" between the buyer and the seller according to the number of days that each owned the property. It doesn't matter who actually paid the real estate taxes. If, for example, the buyer paid all the taxes including delinquent taxes on a property, the amounts paid while the buyer was not the LEGAL owner must be added to the property's basis, rather than deducted on the taxpayer's current year return.

> **Example:** Mandy bought her home on September 1. The property tax was already overdue on the property when Mandy decided to purchase it. The real estate taxes on the home were $1,275 for the year and were paid by Mandy as a condition of the sale. Since Mandy did not own the home during the time the property tax was due, then the amount paid must be added to the basis of the residence. Mandy cannot deduct the $1,275 on her Schedule A as an itemized deduction.

Personal Property Taxes (DMV Fees)

Personal property taxes are deductible if they are:
- Charged on personal property
- Based only on the value of the personal property, and
- Charged on a yearly basis, even if collected more or less than once a year.

The most common type of personal property tax is a DMV fee. In order to be deductible, the tax must be based on the value of a property, such as a boat or car.

> **Example**: Genevieve makes the following tax payments: state income tax, $2,000; real estate taxes, $900; homeowners' association fee, $250. Genevieve's total tax deduction is $2,900 ($2,000 + $900 = $2,900). The $250 homeowners' association fee is not deductible.

Mortgage Interest and Other Deductible Interest

Certain types of interest are deductible as itemized deductions. To deduct mortgage interest, the taxpayer must be legally liable for the debt. The types of interest a taxpayer can deduct as an itemized deduction on Form 1040, Schedule A are:
- Investment interest
- Home mortgage interest (including certain points and mortgage insurance premiums)
- Mortgage interest on a second home or vacation home, with a maximum of two homes

Home Mortgage Interest

Home mortgage interest is interest paid on a loan secured by a taxpayer's home. The loan may be a mortgage, a second mortgage, a home equity loan, or a line of credit. A taxpayer is allowed to deduct the interest on a primary residence and one second home. A home can be a house, condominium, mobile home, house trailer, or houseboat that has sleeping, cooking, and toilet facilities.

A second home can include any other residence a taxpayer owns and treats as a second home. A taxpayer does not have to actually use the home during the year in order to get a deduction of the mortgage interest paid on a second home. Home mortgage interest and points are reported to a taxpayer on **Form 1098**, *Mortgage Interest Statement,* by the financial institution to which the taxpayer made the payments.

Home mortgage interest is only deductible if the mortgage is secured debt. The taxpayer must be legally liable for the debt in order to deduct the mortgage interest.

An empty lot (bare land) does not qualify for a Mortgage Interest Deduction. In order for interest to be deductible as home mortgage interest, the loan must be secured by an actual home. If the taxpayer is planning to build a house, the taxpayer can start deducting mortgage interest once construction begins.

*Note: Although a taxpayer may deduct real estate taxes on *more than* two properties, a taxpayer may not deduct mortgage interest on more than two homes.

A taxpayer may deduct late charges on the loan as mortgage interest.

Qualified Mortgage Insurance Premiums

Taxpayers can deduct Private Mortgage Insurance (PMI) premiums paid during the tax year on Schedule A. The following qualifications are required in order to deduct PMI:

- The borrower bought or refinanced the home
- The AGI is $100,000 or less ($50,000 if Married Filing Separately): full deduction
- The AGI is more than $100,000 ($50,000 if Married Filing Separately): reduced deduction
- The AGI is more than $109,000 ($54,500 if Married Filing Separately): no deduction

Payments made during 2010 for qualified mortgage insurance can be treated as home mortgage interest.

Home Mortgage Points

Points are the charges paid by a borrower to secure a loan. They are actually pre-paid interest that a buyer pays at closing in order to secure a lower interest rate. They are also called:

- Loan origination fees (including VA and FHA fees)
- Maximum loan charges
- Premium charges
- Loan discount points
- Prepaid interest

Only points paid as a form of interest can be deducted. Points paid to refinance a mortgage are generally not deductible in full the year the taxpayer paid them, unless the points are paid in connection with the improvement of a main home. Some loan fees do not qualify as "points." Points paid for specific services, such as home appraisal fees, document preparation fees, VA funding fees, or notary fees are not interest and are not deductible.

In order to deduct points in the year paid, the taxpayer must meet these requirements:

- The mortgage must be secured by the taxpayer's main home, and the mortgage was used to buy or build the home.
- The points are an established practice in the area the loan is funded, and the amount paid is not an excess or unusual amount for the area.

- The total points paid are not more than the total un-borrowed funds.
- The points must be computed as a percentage of the loan principal, and the points must be listed on the settlement statement.

Although this seems like a long list of restrictions, most homebuyers still qualify to take the deduction for points on the purchase of their primary residence. The deduction for points is reported on Schedule A.

Limits on the Mortgage Interest Deduction

If all of the taxpayer's mortgages fit into one or more of the following three categories, he can deduct the interest:

- Any mortgage the taxpayer obtained on or before 1987 (grandfathered debt.)
- Any mortgage obtained after 1987 to buy or improve a home (called home acquisition debt), but only if the mortgage debt totaled $1 million or less ($500,000 if MFS).
- A home equity mortgage, even if used for expenses other than to improve the home (called home equity debt), but only if the home equity line is $100,000 or less. The limit is $50,000 if MFS.

Example: Tamara borrowed $800,000 against her primary residence and $500,000 against her secondary residence. Both loans were used solely to acquire the residences. The loan amounts add up to $1,300,000. Since the total loan amount exceeds the $1 million limit for home acquisition debt, Tamara's Mortgage Interest Deduction is limited.

Home Equity Debt

The interest paid on a home equity line of credit is deductible by the taxpayer if certain rules are met. There is a limit on the amount of debt that can be treated as home equity debt. Home equity debt is not deductible if it exceeds the property's Fair Market Value.

Example: Carla bought her home for cash ten years ago. The Fair Market Value of her home is $80,000. Carla did not have a mortgage on her home until last year, when she took out a $45,000 loan, secured by her home, to pay for her daughter's college tuition and her father's medical bills. This loan is home equity debt. Since the $45,000 loan is secured by her home (and the loan amount is less than $100,000 in equity debt), the mortgage interest on the equity line is deductible.

The interest on home equity indebtedness is deductible by the taxpayer no matter how the proceeds are used.

Example: Jerry and Ashley obtained a home equity loan totaling $90,000. They used the loans to pay off gambling debts, overdue credit payments, and some nondeductible medical expenses. Jerry and Ashley can deduct the interest on their loans because the total of the home equity loans does not exceed $100,000.

> **Example:** Chad bought his home in 2003. Its FMV now is $110,000, and the current balance on Chad's original mortgage is $95,000. Shaky Bank offers Chad a home mortgage loan of 125% of the FMV of the home. To consolidate some of his other debts, Chad agrees to take out a $42,500 home mortgage loan [(125% × $110,000) – $95,000] with Shaky Bank. Chad's home equity line exceeds the Fair Market Value of the home. Therefore, his Mortgage Interest Deduction relating to his equity line is limited. For tax purposes, Chad's qualified home equity debt is limited to $15,000. This is the amount that the FMV of $110,000 exceeds the amount of home acquisition debt of $95,000.

Deductible Investment Interest

If a taxpayer borrows money to buy property held for investment, the interest paid is investment interest. The deduction for investment interest expense is limited to the amount of net investment income. A taxpayer cannot deduct interest incurred to produce tax-exempt income (such as the purchase of municipal bonds). Investment interest expense is calculated on IRS **Form 4952**, *Investment Interest Expense Deduction.*

> **Example:** Andy borrows money from a bank in order to buy $3,000 worth of short-term bonds. The bonds mature during the year and Andy makes $400 in investment interest income. He also has $210 in investment interest expense, which he paid on the loan originally taken out to buy the bonds. Andy must report the full amount of $400 as investment interest income. The $210 in investment interest expense is a deduction on **Schedule A.**

A taxpayer can "carry over" to the next tax year the amount of investment interest that he could not deduct because of the passive activity rules. The interest carried over is treated as investment interest paid or accrued in that next year.

> **Example:** Jackson borrows money from a bank in order to buy $10,000 worth of U.S. gold coins. During the year, the coins lose value and he has no investment income. Jackson has $326 in investment interest expense, which he paid on the loan originally taken out to buy the coins. He had no other investment income. Jackson may not take a deduction for the investment interest expense, because he has no investment income to offset it. Jackson must "carry over" to the next tax year the amount of investment interest that he could not deduct because of this limit.

Investment income is any income that is produced by property that is held for investment. A taxpayer must first determine net investment income by subtracting her investment expenses (other than interest expense) from the investment income.

Nondeductible Interest

Interest that cannot be deducted includes:
- Interest on personal car loans
- Other personal loans
- Annual fees for credit cards
- Credit card investigation fees
- Loan fees for services needed to get a loan
- Interest on a debt the taxpayer is not legally obligated to pay

- Finance charges for nonbusiness credit card purchases
- Personal interest (to be discussed later)
- Service charges
- Interest to purchase or carry tax-exempt securities
- Late payment charges paid to a public utility

A taxpayer cannot deduct fines and penalties paid to any government entity for violations of the law, regardless of their nature.

Charitable Contributions

Charities need funds to operate their tax-exempt programs. Most of the time, these contributions come from taxpayers. A charitable contribution is a donation to a qualified organization. Taxpayers must itemize deductions to be able to deduct a charitable contribution. Taxpayers can deduct contributions to qualifying organizations that:

- Operate exclusively for religious, charitable, educational, scientific, or literary purposes, or
- Work to prevent cruelty to children or animals, or
- Foster national or international amateur sports competition

Other qualifying organizations include:

- War veterans' organizations
- Certain nonprofit cemetery companies or corporations

Qualified donations also include donations for public purposes to the federal government of the United States, to any state, or to an Indian tribal government (example: a donation to the state capital's yearly children's toy drive).

To be deductible, contributions must be made to a qualifying organization, not to an individual. Taxpayers can only deduct a contribution in the year it is actually made.

Non-Qualifying Organizations

Not all nonprofit organizations that accept donations qualify as "charities." Even if an organization is a nonprofit, that doesn't automatically mean that contributions to the organization are deductible by donors.

There are some organizations that still qualify as nonprofit groups for tax purposes, but they do not qualify as charitable organizations for the purposes of a deductible contribution. The following are examples of donations that do not qualify:

- Gifts to civic leagues, social and sports clubs, labor unions, and Chambers of Commerce
- Gifts to groups run for personal profit
- Gifts to political groups
- Gifts to homeowners' associations
- Direct donations to needy individuals
- Any gifts to political groups or candidates for public office
- The cost of raffle, bingo, or lottery tickets, even if the raffle is part of a qualified organization's fundraiser

212

- Dues paid to country clubs or similar groups

Even though these groups may have nonprofit status, they do not qualify for a deductible contribution for the taxpayer. An exemption from tax does not automatically grant an entity to accept donations that are deductible to the grantor.

> **Example:** Renee ran a 10K organized by the Chamber of Commerce. She paid the race organizers a $30 entry fee and received a "free" T-shirt and pancake breakfast after the race. Renee did not make a contribution to a qualifying organization. She paid the Chamber of Commerce, which is not a qualifying charitable organization. Therefore, none of her entry fee is tax deductible as a charitable expense. If the race had been organized by the qualifying organization itself, part of her entry fee may have been deductible.

Qualified Cash and Non-Cash Contributions

In order to claim a deduction for noncash donations, the donated items must be in good condition. The taxpayer must get a receipt from the receiving organization and keep a list of the items donated. In most cases, the taxpayer will be able to claim a deduction for the Fair Market Value of the contribution (generally what someone would be willing to pay at a garage sale or thrift store). No deduction is allowed for items that are in poor or unusable condition, meaning the charity must be able to use the items (Publication 4302). Deductible items include:

- Cash donations.
- Fair Market Value of used clothing and furniture in good condition.
- Unreimbursed expenses that relate directly to the services the taxpayer provided for the organization. Only out-of-pocket expenses that are directly related to the donated services can be deducted. The value of time or services donated cannot be deducted.
- Part of a contribution above the Fair Market Value for items received such as merchandise and tickets to charity balls or sporting events.
- Transportation expenses, including bus fare, parking fees, tolls, and either the cost of gas and oil or a standard mileage deduction of 14 cents per mile in 2010.

> **Example:** Virgil is an attorney who donates his time to his local church for their legal needs. In 2010, he spent 10 hours drafting documents for his church, which is a qualified organization. He also has $200 in out-of-pocket expenses because he purchased a new printer and office supplies for the church. The printer and office supplies were delivered directly to the church rectory for its use. Virgil can take a charitable deduction for $200, the amount he spent on behalf of his church. He cannot take a deduction for the "value" of his time.

Non-Qualified Contributions

Amounts that may not be deducted include:

- The cost of raffle, bingo, or lottery tickets
- Tuition
- The value of a person's time or service
- Blood donated to a blood bank or to the American Red Cross

213

- Car depreciation, insurance, general repairs, or maintenance
- Direct contributions to an individual
- Sickness or burial expenses for members of a fraternal society
- Part of a contribution that benefits the taxpayer, such as the Fair Market Value of a meal eaten at a charity dinner

Recordkeeping Requirements for Charitable Contributions

There are very strict recordkeeping requirements for charitable contributions. Taxpayers must keep records to prove the amounts of cash and noncash contributions they make during the year.

Cash Contributions of $250 or Less

Cash contributions include those paid by cash, check, debit card, credit card, or payroll deduction. For a contribution by cash or check, the taxpayer must maintain a record of the contribution. It must be either a bank record or a written receipt from the organization. If the value of the individual donation is *less than* $250, the taxpayer must keep at least a canceled check or credit card slip, a receipt, or some other reliable written record or evidence.

A taxpayer cannot deduct a cash contribution, regardless of the amount, unless he or she keeps ONE of the following.

- A bank record that shows the name of the qualified organization, the date of the contribution, and the amount of the contribution. Bank records may include:
    - A canceled check,
    - A bank or credit union statement, or
    - A credit card statement.
- A receipt (or a letter or other written communication) from the qualified organization showing the name of the organization, the date of the contribution, and the amount of the contribution.

Example: Gary donates $10 per week to the Humane Society. He always pays by check, and he keeps the cancelled check as a record of his contribution. This is a valid method of recordkeeping for small donations under $250.

Cash Donations OVER $250

For cash donations OVER $250 dollars, the taxpayer can claim a deduction only if he has a receipt or written acknowledgement from the organization. A canceled check is not sufficient. The taxpayer must also provide the date of the contribution. The receipt (or acknowledgment) must meet certain tests. It must include:

- The amount of cash the taxpayer contributed
- Whether the qualified organization gave any goods or services as a result of the contribution (other than certain token items and membership benefits)

- A description and good faith estimate of the value of any goods or services provided in return by the organization (if applicable)

The taxpayer must obtain the receipt on or before:

- The date the taxpayer files her tax return for the year she makes the contribution, or
- The due date, including extensions, for filing the return.

If a charitable gift is made via an automatic payroll deduction, the taxpayer does NOT need an acknowledgement letter unless any single deduction exceeds $250. In that case, the taxpayer may save a copy of her pay stub.

Noncash Contributions

Noncash Contribution Donations Less Than $500

For each single contribution of at least $250 but not exceeding $500, the taxpayer must have all the documentation described for noncash contributions less than $250. In addition, the organization's written acknowledgement must state whether the taxpayer received any goods or services in return and a description and good faith estimate of any such items.

Noncash Contribution Donations of More Than $500

If a taxpayer's total deduction for all noncash contributions for the year is over $500, he must also file **Form 8283,** *Noncash Charitable Contributions.* If any single donation is valued at over $5,000, the taxpayer must also get an appraisal.

*Special "$500 Rule" for Donated Vehicles, Boats, and Airplanes

Special rules apply to any donation of a vehicle. This rule also applies to the donation of a boat or airplane. If the taxpayer donates a vehicle to a charity and the taxpayer claims a deduction of more than $500, the taxpayer can only deduct the smaller of:

- The gross proceeds from the sale of the vehicle, or
- The vehicle's Fair Market Value on the date of the contribution.

> **Example:** Kevin donates his used motorcycle to his church fundraiser. The FMV ("Blue Book" value) of the motorcycle is $2,500. The church sells the motorcycle 60 days later; the organization sends Kevin a Form 1098-C showing the proceeds from the sale of the donated item. The church was only able to sell the motorcycle for $1,700. Therefore, Kevin may only deduct $1,700 on his Schedule A, Form 1040 (the smaller of the FMV or the gross proceeds from the sale). He must attach a copy of Form 1098-C, *Contributions of Motor Vehicles, Boats, and Airplanes*, to his tax return.

Form 1098-C will show the gross proceeds from the sale of the vehicle. If the taxpayer does not attach Form 1098-C, he cannot deduct a contribution over $500 for a donated vehicle. Unless documented with Form 1098-C (or comparable documentation), the maximum value that can be taken for a vehicle donation is $500. Vehicles that are not in working condition may have zero donation value.

*Exceptions to the "$500 Rule" for Donated Vehicles

There are two exceptions to the strict rules regarding vehicle donations. This is called "Significant Intervening Use" and allows the donor to take a special exception for the value of the vehicle. It applies when the charity uses the vehicle for its own use, or otherwise sets the vehicle aside for specific purposes for a needy individual.

Exception 1: The vehicle is used by the organization. If the charity takes the vehicle for its own use, the taxpayer can deduct the vehicle's FMV.

Exception 2: The vehicle is given (or sold) to a needy individual. If the charity gives or sells the vehicle directly to a needy person, the taxpayer generally can deduct the vehicle's FMV at the time of the contribution.

> **Example:** Bonnie donates a used van to a charity that delivers meals to needy individuals. The charity uses her donated van every day for that purpose. Since this qualifies as "Significant Intervening Use," Bonnie may take a deduction for the FMV of the van at the time of the donation. The charity must have provided a written receipt and a statement to substantiate the "Significant Intervening Use."

Volunteering Expenses

Taxpayers may not deduct the "value of their time" when they volunteer for an organization. However, travel expenses such as transportation, meals, and lodging are deductible. Expenses that are incurred on behalf of the charitable organization are deductible as "out-of-pocket" expenses. Travel expenses can be deducted in actual expenses, or the taxpayer may use the standard mileage rate for charitable miles, which is 14 cents per mile in 2010.

> **Example:** Charles volunteered for the Boy Scouts in 2010. He was the den leader and regularly paid out-of-pocket expenses for travel, gas, and parking while performing duties and picking up supplies on behalf of the Scouts. Charles was not paid for his work. Charles may deduct his out-of-pocket costs related to the volunteer work, but he may not take a deduction for the value of his time.

> **Example:** Francine regularly volunteers at her local animal shelter. She uses her own car to travel back and forth to the shelter. She is not reimbursed for mileage. Francine also fosters kittens on behalf of the shelter. She pays for food and other supplies out-of-pocket while she's fostering the kittens. Once the kittens are old enough for adoption, she returns them to the animal shelter so that they may be adopted by the public. Francine may deduct her mileage and her out-of-pocket costs as a charitable contribution.

The 50 Percent Limit

There are limits to the amounts that can be claimed as a deductible donation. A taxpayer may not take a deduction for charitable contributions that exceed 50% of Adjusted Gross Income. In other words, if a taxpayer had $20,000 in gross income in 2010, the maximum she could deduct as a charitable contribution in 2010 would be $10,000 (50% of AGI).

There is a reduced limit of 30% or 20% that applies to certain organizations. This means that for certain nonprofit organizations, a taxpayer's contribution cannot exceed 20% of his AGI.

Examples of 50% limit organizations include churches, hospitals, most schools, state or federal government units, and animal welfare organizations. Also included are corporations, trusts, or foundations organized solely for charitable, religious, educational, scientific, or literary purposes, or to prevent cruelty to children or animals, or to foster certain national or international amateur sports competition.

Organizations Subject to the 30 Percent Limit

Certain organizations only qualify for the "30% limit." This means that the deductible amount of the contribution cannot exceed 30% of the taxpayer's AGI. A 30% limit applies to the following organizations:

- Veterans' organizations
- Fraternal societies (ex. Freemasons, Kiwanis)
- Nonprofit cemeteries

In addition, the 30% limit applies in the following cases:

- Gifts for the actual use of any organization (such as the donation of a table that the organization uses for itself)
- Any gift of appreciated property (such as stocks)

Appreciated property, also called "capital gain property," may be given to an organization that is normally a "50%" organization, such as a church. However, capital gain property is always subject to the 30% limit (or 20% limit), regardless of the organization type that actually receives the donation. This means that the donation of capital gain property will always be subject to limitations.

> **Example:** Howard's Adjusted Gross Income is $50,000. During the year, he gave appreciated stocks with an FMV of $15,000 to his synagogue, which is a 50% limit organization. Howard also gave $10,000 cash to a veteran's organization. The $15,000 gift of capital gain property is subject to the special 30% limit, even though it was given to a religious organization. The $10,000 gift is subject to the other 30% limit. However, both gifts are fully deductible by Howard because neither is more than the 30% limit that applies ($15,000 in each case) and together they are not more than the 50% limit of Howard's AGI ($50,000 x 50% = $25,000).

Charitable gifts of appreciated property held long-term are subject to a lower deductibility ceiling—30% of AGI—with a five-year carryover of any excess deduction (example: a gift of appreciated stock).

20 Percent Limit

The 20% limit applies to all gifts of capital gain property (appreciated property) to qualified organizations that are NOT 50 percent organizations.

> **Example:** Henry's Adjusted Gross Income is $23,000. During the year, he gave stocks with an FMV of $10,000 to his fraternal society, Kiwanis, which is a 30% limit organization. Henry makes no other donations during the year. The $10,000 donation of capital gain property is subject to the special 20% limit because it is capital gain property that was donated to a 30% limit organization. The donation is not fully deductible by Henry, because it exceeds 20 percent of his AGI ($23,000 x 20% = $4,600). Therefore, the maximum deduction for charitable contributions that Henry can take is limited to $4,600. He must carry over the remaining $5,400 to a future tax year.

Any contributions made by the taxpayer and carried over to future years retain their original character. For example, contributions made to a 30% organization are always subject to the 30% limit of AGI.

Charitable Contribution Carryovers

A carryover is simply an amount that a taxpayer is unable to deduct in the current year. Charitable contributions are subject to a five-year carryover period. The taxpayer can deduct the unused contribution for the next five years until it is used up, but not beyond that time.

A carryover of a "qualified conservation contribution" can be carried forward for 15 years. A qualified conservation contribution is the donation of a qualified real property interest (e.g., an easement) to an organization that uses it exclusively for conservation purposes.

> **Example:** Taylor owns 200 acres of wetlands. Taylor decides to donate the property to the Wildlife Conservation Society, a 501(c)(3) organization. The property is then used for wildlife conservation and research only. This is a "qualified conservation contribution" eligible for a 15-year carryover.

Non-Business Casualty and Theft Losses

The rules regarding non-business casualty losses are very complex. A "casualty loss" is an unexpected loss. A casualty loss does not include normal wear and tear or progressive deterioration from age or insect damage. The loss must be caused by a sudden, unexpected, or unusual event (e.g., car accident, fire, earthquake, flood, vandalism, theft). Lost or mislaid property is NOT considered a casualty loss.

Sometimes, a casualty loss will create a gain for the taxpayer. For example, this happens when the insurance reimbursement is more than the taxpayer's basis in the property. If the taxpayer has a gain, he may have to pay tax on it. In some cases, the gain can be deferred until the property is later sold.

A taxpayer must have proof of the casualty or theft in order to deduct it. The taxpayer must also prove that her losses were actually caused by the event. In the case of a casualty loss, the taxpayer must be able to prove:

- The type of casualty loss (car accident, fire, storm, etc.) and the date of occurrence

- That the taxpayer was the legal owner of the property, or at least legally liable for the damage (such as leased property where the lessee is responsible for damage)
- Whether insurance reimbursement exists

> **Example:** Gregory rents a car from Good Rentals, Inc. He signed a contract stating he would be responsible for any damage. The rental car is stolen and now Gregory is responsible for paying back Good Rentals. Gregory's car insurance does not have rental car coverage, so he is liable for the full amount. Gregory may deduct the loss as a casualty loss, subject to the applicable rules.

Personal casualty losses are calculated on IRS Form 4684, and the amount is then transferred to Schedule A as an itemized deduction.

Nondeductible losses include:

- Damage done by pets
- Slow insect damage to trees, clothing, or household items
- Any fire willfully set by the taxpayer (arson)
- Lost property
- Progressive deterioration
- Termite or moth damage
- Losses in real estate value from market fluctuations
- Accidental breakage of china, dishes, or other items during regular use

Special Rules for Deducting Personal Casualty Losses

Each personal casualty or theft loss is limited to the excess of the loss over $100. In addition, a 10%-of-AGI limit applies to the net loss. The "$100 Rule" and "10% Rule" apply to non-business casualty losses. Losses on business property are not subject to these rules. Personal casualty losses are also subject to the "Single Event Rule."

Generally, events closely related in origin are considered a "single event." It is a "single casualty" when the damage is from two or more closely related causes, such as wind and flood damage caused by the same storm. A single casualty may also damage two or more pieces of property, such as a hailstorm that damages both a taxpayer's home and his car parked in the driveway. Only a single $100 reduction applies. If a taxpayer has more than one casualty loss during the year, reduce each loss separately. Then the taxpayer must reduce the total of all losses by 10% of Adjusted Gross Income.

> **Example:** A fire damaged Dick's house in June, causing $3,000 in damage. In September, storm damaged his house again, causing $5,000 in damage. Dick must reduce each loss by $100 (Publication 547).

1. The $100 Rule

After a taxpayer has figured the casualty loss on personal-use property, she must reduce that loss by $100. This reduction applies to each total casualty or theft loss. It does not matter how many pieces of property are involved in an event; the taxpayer only has to reduce the losses for each EVENT by $100.

> **Example:** Sonny has a $750 deductible on his car insurance. He has a car accident in 2010, incurring $6,000 of damage. The insurance company pays Sonny for the damage minus the $750 deductible. The amount of Sonny's casualty loss is based solely on his deductible. Sonny's actual casualty loss is only $650 ($750 – $100) because the first $100 of a casualty loss on personal-use property is not deductible.

2. The 10% Rule

Personal casualty losses are further reduced by AGI. The taxpayer must reduce the total of all casualty losses on personal-use property by 10%. This rule does not apply to a net disaster loss within a federally declared disaster area.

Reporting a Casualty Loss or Gain

Taxpayers use **Form 4684**, *Casualties and Thefts*, to report a gain or loss from a personal casualty or theft. Form 4684 must be attached to the taxpayer's return. The taxpayer may claim a deductible loss on personal-use property only if she itemizes deductions. Sometimes, taxpayers will have a gain from casualty losses because the insurance reimbursement will exceed their basis. However, if a taxpayer has a gain on damaged property, she can postpone reporting the gain if the insurance reimbursement is spent to restore the property.

To determine a taxpayer's deduction for casualty losses:

1. Calculate the *lesser* of the FMV or adjusted basis of the item prior to the loss
2. Subtract any payments/reimbursements from insurance
3. Subtract $100 for each event (2010)
4. Subtract 10% of the taxpayer's AGI

> **Example:** Many years ago, Al bought a vacation cottage for $18,000. A storm destroyed the cottage in 2010. The FMV of the cottage in 2010 was $250,000. Al received $146,000 from his insurance company. He had a gain of $128,000 ($146,000 – $18,000 basis). Al spent the full $146,000 to rebuild his cottage. Since he used the insurance proceeds to rebuild his cottage, he can postpone reporting or recognizing the gain until the cottage is sold.

Although casualty losses are treated differently depending on whether the loss occurred to business property or personal property, all casualty losses are still reported on Form 4684.

Decrease in FMV

A decrease in the value of property because it is near an area that suffered a casualty cannot be taken into consideration. Casualty losses are deductible only for actual damage caused to a property.

> **Example:** In 2010, Nicole purchased a condo for $200,000. Two months after the purchase, a hurricane destroyed five other properties on her block. A resulting appraisal showed that all of the properties within a five-mile radius had declined in Fair Market Value by 15% because people were afraid to purchase homes in "hurricane territory." The reduction in the home's Fair Market Value is not a deductible casualty loss.

Insurance Reimbursements

Taxpayers can deduct qualified casualty losses to their home, household items, and vehicles. A taxpayer may not deduct casualty and theft losses that are covered by insurance unless he files a claim for reimbursement. The taxpayer must reduce his casualty loss by the amount of the insurance reimbursement. If the taxpayer decides not to file an insurance claim but has a deductible, he may still claim the amount of the insurance deductible, since that amount would not have been covered by the policy anyway.

> **Example:** Caitlyn has homeowners' insurance on her home. In 2010, she has a small fire and incurs $8,000 in damage. She does not want her insurance premium to go up, so she declines to file a claim and pays for the damage out-of-pocket. Her insurance policy carries a $1,500 deductible. Caitlyn cannot deduct the loss because she declined to file an insurance claim. However, she is allowed to deduct $1,500, the amount of the deductible, because her insurance would not have covered that amount in any case.

> **Example:** Louis has a car insurance policy with a $1,000 deductible. He has a car accident in 2010 and has $2,600 worth of damage. Louis doesn't want his insurance to go up, so he refuses to file an insurance claim. If Louis had filed a claim with his insurance company, his insurance would not have covered the first $1,000 of an auto collision, so the $1,000 is deductible as a casualty loss (still subject to the $100 and 10% rules).

Rules for Determining Fair Market Value and Adjusted Basis

A casualty loss is limited to the LESSER of the FMV of the property, or the property's adjusted basis right before the loss. The cost of replacement property is not part of a casualty or theft loss. Usually, a property's basis is its cost. For property that is acquired by inheritance or by gift, basis is figured differently (to be covered in a later unit).

> **Example:** Don purchased an antique vase at an auction for $600. Later, he discovered that the vase was actually a rare collectible and its Fair Market Value was $20,000. The vase was stolen two months later during a robbery. Don's casualty loss is limited to the $600 he paid for it, which is his basis in the property. Don cannot claim a casualty loss deduction for $20,000 (the value of the item).

> **Example:** Raquel bought a new leather sofa four years ago for $3,000. In April, a fire destroyed the sofa. Raquel estimates that it would now cost $5,000 to replace it. However, if she had sold the sofa before the fire, she probably would have received only $900 for it because the sofa was already four years old. Raquel's casualty loss is $900 (still subject to the $100 and 10% rules), the FMV of the sofa before the fire. Her loss is not $3,000 and it is not $5,000, the replacement cost.

Theft Losses

A theft loss may be deducted in the year that the theft is discovered. It doesn't matter when the theft actually occurred. Qualifying theft losses include:

- Ponzi investment schemes
- Burglaries
- Embezzlement by an employee
- Identity theft
- Mail fraud
- Blackmail, kidnapping for ransom

Some theft losses are not deductible. If the taxpayer has theft losses from his own illegal activity, the losses are not deductible.

Decline in value of stock: A taxpayer may not deduct the decline in value of stock as a casualty loss, even if it is related to accounting fraud. There is an exception for Ponzi scheme losses. However, the taxpayer may deduct these losses as capital losses, and the regular rules for capital losses apply.

The cost of insurance: The cost of insurance or other protection is not deductible as a casualty loss. This rule applies to non-business assets only.

Example: Jordan pays for renters insurance to cover the furniture and appliances in his home from theft or other disaster losses. Jordan may not deduct the cost of the renters insurance as a casualty loss.
Example: Sydney is self-employed and owns a florist's shop. She pays for hazard insurance on the shop. Sydney may deduct the cost of the insurance on her shop as a regular business expense.

Recovered property: If a taxpayer takes a deduction for stolen property and the property is later recovered by the police, she must report the recovery as income in the year the property is recovered. However, she must only report the amounts that actually reduced tax in an earlier year.

Business Casualty Losses

If income-producing property (such as rental property) is subject to a casualty loss, the amount of the taxpayer's loss is the adjusted basis in the property minus any salvage value and minus any insurance or other reimbursement received. A business-related casualty loss is treated much differently than a personal casualty loss. Business casualty losses are covered more extensively in Book 2, Businesses (for Part Two of the EA Exam).

Miscellaneous Itemized Deductible Expenses

Miscellaneous deductible expenses include all other categories of expenses that do not fall into the major categories of medical, taxes, interest, or charitable contributions. These "miscellaneous" expenses are further divided into two very important categories, which are:

- Miscellaneous expenses subject to the 2% of AGI limit, and
- Miscellaneous expenses deductible in full (not subject to the 2% AGI limit)

Miscellaneous Expenses Subject to the 2% Limit

A taxpayer may deduct certain expenses as miscellaneous itemized deductions on Schedule A (Form 1040). The taxpayer may ONLY claim the amount that exceeds 2% of her AGI. There are many common types of miscellaneous expenses that are subject to the 2% limit. Some examples are:

- Credit or debit card fees incurred when paying income tax charged by the card processor
- Union dues and fees
- Professional society dues
- Uniforms for work
- Small tools and supplies used for business
- Professional books, magazines, and journals
- Employment-related educational expenses
- Job-hunting expenses
- Investment counseling fees
- Investment expenses
- Safe deposit box rental for investment documents
- Tax counsel and assistance
- Fees paid to an IRA custodian

Investment expenses are allowed as a deduction if the expenses are directly connected with the production of investment income. Investment expenses are included as a miscellaneous itemized deduction on Schedule A (Form 1040), and are allowable deductions after applying the 2% limit.

> **Example:** Craig's AGI is $45,000. He must first figure out the 2% limit before he can start deducting these expenses (2% X $45,000 = $900). Craig has $1,100 in miscellaneous deductible work-related expenses. He can therefore only deduct $200 of those expenses ($1,100 - $900 = $200).

Unreimbursed Employee Business Expenses

An employee may deduct certain work-related expenses as itemized deductions. These expenses are reported on Form 2106, *Employee Business Expenses*, and the amount is transferred to Schedule A. The taxpayer can deduct only unreimbursed employee expenses that are:

- Paid or incurred during the tax year,
- For carrying on the business of being an employee, and
- Ordinary and necessary.

An expense does not have to be required to be deductible. However, it must be a common expense that would be accepted in the taxpayer's trade or profession. Employee business expenses are deductible if they are for the convenience of an employer, or required as a condition of employment. A taxpayer may deduct the following items as unreimbursed employee expenses:

- Business liability insurance premiums
- Damages paid to a former employer for breach of an employment contract
- Depreciation on an asset the employer requires for work

223

- Dues to professional societies
- Educator's expenses (the teacher credit)
- A home office used regularly and exclusively in a taxpayer's work
- Job search expenses
- Legal fees related directly to a job
- Licenses and regulatory fees
- Malpractice insurance
- Occupational taxes and research expenses of a college professor
- Rural mail carriers' vehicle expenses
- Subscriptions to professional journals
- Tools and supplies used for work
- Travel, transportation, meals, and lodging related to the taxpayer's work
- Union dues
- Work clothes and uniforms (if required and not suitable for everyday use)
- Work-related education
- Employee meals and entertainment

An employee may deduct unreimbursed business-related meals and entertainment expenses he has for entertaining a client, customer, or another employee. The limit on deductible meals and entertainment is 50% (the same for self-employed taxpayers and businesses). The taxpayer must apply the "50% limit" before applying the "2% of Adjusted Gross Income" limit. The taxpayer can deduct meals and entertainment expenses only if they meet the following tests:

- The main purpose of the meal or entertainment was the active conduct of business,
- The taxpayer conducted business during the entertainment period, and
- The taxpayer had more than a general expectation of some other specific business benefit at a future time.

Figuring Deductible Meals

A taxpayer can figure her deductible meal expense using either of the following methods:

Actual cost: Using the actual cost method, the taxpayer keeps track of her receipts and actual costs incurred.

The standard meal allowance: Taxpayers may choose to use the standard per diem rate in order to account for meals. This makes recordkeeping easier and eliminates the need to keep every meal receipt. The standard meal allowance is used for daily meals and incidental expenses (M&IE) while the taxpayer is away from his tax home overnight. However, some rules must be followed in order to take the standard meal allowance. The employee must still keep records to prove the time, place, and business purpose of the travel. The standard meal allowance (per diem) is the federal M&IE rate. The allowance amount varies based on federal rates (you do not need to know all the per diem meal allowance rates for the EA Exam). Regardless of the method used, the taxpayer can generally deduct only 50% of the cost of meals (there are some exceptions for transportation workers).

Nondeductible Employee Meals or Entertainment

There are cases where an employee cannot deduct certain types of entertainment, even if it is substantially business-related. The taxpayer cannot deduct dues (including initiation fees) for membership in any country club or social club.

This is an IRS rule that applies specifically to country clubs. The purpose of a club (not its name) will determine whether or not a taxpayer can deduct the dues. Generally, the taxpayer cannot deduct any expense for the use of an "entertainment facility." Examples include a yacht, hunting lodge, fishing camp, swimming pool, tennis court, bowling alley, car, airplane, apartment, hotel suite, or home in a vacation resort.

Example: Alejandro is an employee of Yarrow Plastics, Inc. He regularly entertains big clients at Rich Guy's Country Club, where he takes clients golfing and closes many contracts. Alejandro's membership dues to Rich Guy's Country Club do not qualify as a deductible business expense, even if he uses the club substantially for business use.

Entertainment Facilities and Employee Business Expenses

A taxpayer can deduct out-of-pocket expenses, such as for food and beverages, catering, gas, and fishing bait that the taxpayer provided during entertainment at a facility. The taxpayer may also deduct the cost of transportation to a meal or an event. These are not considered expenses for the use of an entertainment facility.

Example: Stanley rents a summer cottage on the river that he occasionally uses for entertaining clients. He cannot deduct the cost of renting this facility. He can, however, deduct the out-of-pocket costs of entertaining a client, which include meals and beverages during the actual entertainment or business meeting.

Deducting an Work-Related Home Office

An employee can deduct expenses for the business use of his home if certain rules are followed and tests are met. The home office must be used by the employee for the *convenience of the employer* in order to be deductible.

The space does not need to be marked off by a permanent partition, but the space needs to be exclusively and regularly used for business. The area used for business can be a room or other separately identifiable space, such as a shed or garage. If an area is not exclusively or regularly used in the employee's profession, the taxpayer cannot claim a deduction for the business use space.

If an employee is not required to work from home, she will not meet the convenience-of-the-employer test and cannot claim a deduction for the business use of the home (Publication 587).

Example: Kathleen is employed as a teacher. The school provides her with an office where she can work on her lesson plans, grade papers and tests, and meet with parents and students. The school does not require her to work at home. Kathleen prefers to use her home office and does not use the one provided by the school. She uses this home office exclusively and regularly for the administrative duties of her teaching job. Since the school provides Kathleen with an office and does not require her to work at home, she does not meet the "convenience-of-employer" test and cannot claim a deduction for her home office.

Example: Glenn is a tool salesman working for Tremendous Tools Co. He is on the road most of the time, and his home is the only fixed location for selling tools. Glenn regularly uses the right half of his basement for storage of inventory and product samples. The expenses for the space are deductible as an "employee-related" home office expense.

Example: Martha is a tax preparer and uses her study to prepare tax returns during tax season. She also uses the study to exercise on her treadmill. The room is not used exclusively in Martha's profession, so she cannot claim a deduction for the business use.

There is a special rule for "multiple offices." If a taxpayer has a home office and also uses an office at her regular workplace, the home office may still qualify for a deduction. If the employee meets with patients, clients, or customers in her home in the normal course of business, even though she also carries on business at another location, the employee can deduct expenses for that part of the home. The following tests must be met if there are multiple offices:

- The space must be used exclusively and regularly for business
- The taxpayer must physically meet with patients, clients, or customers on the premises (not just over the phone)

The use of the home office must be substantial and integral to the conduct of business.

Calculating the Home Office Percentage

Generally, the home office deduction depends on the percentage of the home that is used for business. A taxpayer can use any reasonable method to compute business percentage, but the most common methods are to:

- Divide the area of the home used for business by the total area of the home, or
- Divide the number of rooms used for business by the total number of rooms in the home if all rooms in the home are about the same size.

Taxpayers may not deduct expenses for any portion of the year during which there was no business use of the home.

Example: Polly is a self-employed bookkeeper, and she has a qualified home office. The entire square footage of her home is 1,200 square feet. Her home office 240 square feet, so therefore, her home office percentage is 20% (240 ÷ 1,200) of the total area of her home. Her business percentage is 20%.

226

Deductible Employee Travel Expenses

An employee may not deduct commuting expenses, which are the expenses incurred when going from a taxpayer's home to his main workplace. However, there are numerous instances where an employee may deduct mileage or other travel expenses relating to his employment. For 2010, the standard mileage rate for business use is 50 cents per mile. Deductible employee travel expenses include:

- Getting from one work location to another in the course of business
- Visiting clients or customers
- Going to a business meeting away from the regular workplace
- Traveling from a first job to a second job in the same day
- Getting from a taxpayer's home to a temporary workplace

Any amounts reimbursed by the employer would not be deductible. A taxpayer can deduct travel expenses related to a temporary work assignment. Travel expenses paid in connection with an indefinite work assignment are NOT deductible. Examples of deductible travel expenses include:

- The cost of getting to a business destination (air, rail, bus, car, etc.)
- Meals and lodging while away from home
- Taxi fares
- Baggage charges

"Tax Home" For the Purpose of Employee Travel Expenses

To determine the deductibility of employee travel, the employee must determine her "tax home." Generally, a taxpayer's tax home is her regular place of business, regardless of where the taxpayer maintains her residence. A taxpayer may deduct work-related expenses of traveling away from home for her profession or job.

Example: Grant is a railroad conductor. He leaves his home terminal on a regularly scheduled round-trip run between two cities and returns home 16 hours later. During the run, Grant has six hours off at his turnaround point. Grant stops, eats a meal, and rents a hotel room to get necessary sleep before starting the return trip. Grant is considered to be away from his tax home. His travel expenses are deductible (Publication 463).

Multiple Business Locations

If a taxpayer has multiple business locations, his "tax home" is the main place of business. If the taxpayer does NOT have a regular or main place of business because of the nature of the taxpayer's work, then her tax home may be the place where she actually lives.

Example: Crystal is a guitarist in a rock band. She travels with her band to multiple playing locations and venues, and also works as a freelance musician. Crystal has no regular place of business. She maintains a primary residence in Los Angeles. Crystal's tax home is in Los Angeles.

If a taxpayer does not have a regular place of business or post of duty and there is no place where he regularly lives, the taxpayer is considered a transient (an itinerant) and his tax home is wherever he works. As a transient, the taxpayer cannot claim a travel expense deduction because he is never considered to be traveling away from home.

Conventions

A taxpayer may deduct the cost of travel and attendance to conventions. In order for the travel cost to be deductible, the convention must be in the U.S. or in the "North American area" (including Canada and Mexico). For cruises, there is a $2,000 cap on deductions. A deduction is not allowed for conventions focused exclusively on investments or financial planning.

Job Search Expenses

A taxpayer may deduct job search expenses, if the expenses relate to the same profession. Expenses incurred can be deducted, even if the taxpayer does not find a new job. However, a taxpayer may not deduct the costs of searching for a job in a brand new occupation.

If the job search qualifies, the taxpayer can deduct costs for using an employment agency or career counselor, and for traveling to interviews. The taxpayer may also deduct the cost of printing, preparing, and mailing resumes.

Job-Related Education

The cost of courses designed to maintain or improve the skills needed for a present job (or required by an employer or the law) is deductible as an employee business expense. The taxpayer may also choose to take an education credit.

If a taxpayer has a regular job and then enrolls in work-related education courses on a temporary basis, she can deduct the round-trip costs of transportation between her home and school. This is true regardless of the location of the school, the distance traveled, or whether the taxpayer attends school on non-work days.

Deductible Uniforms

The cost of uniforms and other special work clothes required by an employer can be deducted as work-related expenses. The uniforms must NOT be suitable for everyday use. The taxpayer may also deduct the cost of upkeep, including laundry and dry cleaning bills.

Examples of employees who may deduct their uniforms include delivery workers, firefighters, health care workers, law enforcement officers, letter carriers, professional athletes, and transportation workers (air, rail, bus, etc.). Musicians and entertainers can deduct the cost of theatrical clothing and accessories that are not suitable for everyday wear. An employee can deduct the cost of protective clothing, such as safety shoes or boots, safety glasses, hard hats, and work gloves.

Full-time active-duty military personnel cannot deduct the cost of their uniforms. However, they may be able to deduct the cost of insignia, shoulder boards, and related items.

Nondeductible Expenses

A taxpayer cannot deduct the following expenses:

- Commuting expenses
- Political contributions
- The cost of entertaining friends
- Lost or misplaced cash or property
- An attorney's fee to prepare a will (This is considered a personal legal expense, so it is not deductible.)
- Brokers' commissions that are paid on an IRA or other investment property
- Burial or funeral expenses, including the cost of a cemetery lot
- Campaign expenses, lobbying expenses, illegal bribes or kickbacks
- Check-writing fees
- Athletic or country club dues and health spa expenses
- Fees and licenses, such as car licenses, marriage licenses, and dog tags
- Fines and penalties, such as parking tickets
- Investment-related seminars
- Life insurance premiums
- Losses from the sale of a primary residence, furniture, personal car, etc.
- Personal disability insurance premiums
- Legal expenses related to personal, living, or family expenses (divorce fees, etc.)
- Professional accreditation fees
- Residential telephone lines
- Expenses of attending stockholders' meetings
- Expenses of earning or collecting tax-exempt income

Miscellaneous Itemized Deductions (Not Subject to the 2% Limit)

There are also some expenses that are NOT subject to the 2% limit. A taxpayer can fully deduct the expenses that fall under this category on Schedule A, without regard to any percentage of income limits. The expenses that are NOT subject to the "2% Rule" are:

1. Gambling losses to the extent of gambling winnings (Taxpayers must have kept a written record of their losses.)

2. Work-related expenses for individuals with a disability that enable them to work, such as attendant care services at their workplace.

> **Example:** Erin has a visual disability. She requires a large screen magnifier at work in order to see well enough so she can perform her work. Erin purchased her screen magnifier for $550. She may deduct the cost of the screen magnifier as an itemized deduction NOT subject to the 2% floor.

3. Amortizable premium on taxable bonds: If the amount a taxpayer pays for a bond is greater than its stated principal amount, the excess is called a "bond premium." If this occurs, the excess is treated as a miscellaneous itemized deduction that is not subject to the 2% limit.

4. Casualty or theft losses from income-producing property: A taxpayer can deduct a casualty or theft loss as a miscellaneous itemized deduction not subject to the 2% limit if

the damaged or stolen property was income-producing property (property held for investment, such as stocks, notes, bonds, gold, silver, vacant lots, and works of art).

5. A taxpayer can deduct the federal estate tax attributable to income "in respect of a decedent" that the taxpayer includes in gross income. Income "in respect of a decedent" is income that a deceased taxpayer would have received had the death not occurred, and which was not properly includable in the decedent's final income tax return.

Summary: Itemized Deductions

Medical and Dental Expenses

Deductible medical and dental expenses are reported and calculated on Schedule A. Qualified medical and dental expenses are expenses the taxpayer paid during the tax year for himself, his spouse, and his dependents.

Taxes

Deductible taxes are reported on Schedule A. Taxpayers can deduct the following:

1. State and local income taxes
2. State, local, or foreign real estate taxes
3. State and local personal property tax payments

Deductible Interest

Deductible interest is reported on Schedule A. The taxpayer should receive Form 1098, *Mortgage Interest Statement*, which shows the deductible amount of interest she paid during the tax year. Only taxpayers who are legally liable for the debt can deduct the interest. Taxpayers can treat amounts paid in 2010 for qualified mortgage insurance as home mortgage interest.

Only points paid as a form of interest can be deducted on Schedule A. This interest, even if it qualifies for home mortgage interest, must generally be spread over the life of the mortgage. However, if the loan is used to buy or build a taxpayer's main home, the taxpayer may be able to deduct the entire amount in the year paid. See Publication 17 for more information.

Points paid to refinance a mortgage are generally not deductible in full the year the taxpayer paid them, unless the points were paid in connection with the improvement of a main home and certain conditions were met.

Charitable Deductions

Qualified charitable contributions are reported on Schedule A. The contributions to qualifying organizations that taxpayers can deduct include cash donations, dues paid to qualified organizations, Fair Market Value of used goods, and unreimbursed volunteer and travel expenses that relate directly to the services the taxpayer provided for the qualifying organization. Any donation over $250 requires a receipt from the organization. Any noncash donation over $500 must be reported using IRS Form 8283, Noncash Charitable Contributions. If any single noncash donation is valued at over $5,000, the taxpayer must also get an appraisal.

Unit 1.8: Questions

1. All of the following factors determine the amount of a taxpayer's standard deduction EXCEPT _____.

A. The taxpayer's filing status
B. The taxpayer's gross income
C. Whether the taxpayer is 65 or older, or blind
B. Whether the taxpayer can be claimed as a dependent

The answer is B. The standard deduction amount depends on the taxpayer's filing and dependent status, and whether the taxpayer is blind or at least 65 years old. ###

2. Sara and James are both 25, and they have been married for two years. What is their standard deduction?

A. $11,400
B. $8,400
C. $5,700
D. $3,650

The answer is A. Sara and James meet the requirements for the standard deduction for most people. Their standard deduction is $11,400. ###

3. Brenda is 22, single, and recently graduated from college. She provides all of her own support. What is her standard deduction for the tax year?

A. $5,700
B. $8,400
C. $5,400
D. $3,650

The answer is A. Brenda meets the requirements for the standard deduction for most people. Her standard deduction is $5,700. ###

4. Which of the following taxpayers is required to itemize deductions?

A. Sophie, who files a joint return with her husband, who died during the year
B. Andrea, who claims one dependent and files Form 1040
C. Gabrielle, whose itemized deductions are more than the standard deduction
D. Samir, whose wife files a separate return and itemizes her deductions

The answer is D. Married taxpayers who file separately and whose spouses itemize deductions must also itemize their deductions. ###

5. Brianne and her husband Clark are both over the age of 65 and legally blind. They file their returns as Married Filing Separately and do not itemize their deductions. What is Brianne's standard deduction?

A. $0
B. $8,500
C. $7,900
B. $15,800

The answer is C. This is calculated by multiplying $1,100 by 2 (she is blind and 65) to get $2,200, which is added to her standard deduction of $5,700. Brianne and Clark are allowed to use the standard deduction because neither is itemizing. If one of them had chosen to itemize, the other would have been forced to as well. ###

6. All of the following are deductible medical expenses EXCEPT _____.

A. Transportation for medical care
B. Transportation to a medical conference related to the chronic disease of a dependent
C. Smoking-cessation programs
D. Nonprescription nicotine gum and patches

The answer is D. Nonprescription medications are not deductible as medical expenses on Schedule A. Taxpayers may deduct transportation related to medical care. The cost of smoking programs and prescription drugs are also deductible. ###

7. Which of the following qualifies as a deductible medical expense?

A. Nonprescription ointment for treating poison oak
B. Premiums for life insurance
C. Prescription hearing aids and eyeglasses
D. Cost of childcare while a parent is in the hospital

The answer is C. Life insurance premiums, childcare, and non-prescription medicines are not deductible. Only the cost of the prescription hearing aids and eyeglasses would qualify as deductible medical expenses. ###

8. Christine and Luis file jointly. In 2010, they have an Adjusted Gross Income of $95,400 and $6,620 in unreimbursed medical and dental expenses. The total of Luis and Christine's deductible medical expenses on Schedule A is _____.

A. $6,620
B. $6,300
C. $5,620
D. $0

The answer is D. The total of Luis and Christine's medical expenses, $6,620, is less than $95,400 x 7.5% = $7,155. Only the portion of total medical expenses that exceeds 7.5% of the taxpayer's AGI is deductible on Schedule A. ###

9. All of the following home improvements may be itemized and deducted as medical expenses EXCEPT:

A. Cost of installing porch lifts and other forms of lifts
B. The cost of lowering cabinets to accommodate a disability
C. The cost of making doorways wider to accommodate a wheelchair
D. An elevator costing $4,000 that adds $5,000 to the FMV of the home

The answer is D. The deduction for capital improvements is limited to the excess of the actual cost of the improvements over the increase in the Fair Market Value of the home. Since the elevator adds value to the home, it cannot be deducted as a medical expense. ###

10. Justin had the following medical expenses for himself in 2010:

- $450 for contact lenses
- $800 for eyeglasses
- $9,000 for a broken leg, of which $8,000 was paid for by his insurance
- $200 for prescription drugs
- $1,900 for a doctor-prescribed back brace
- $200 for childcare while in the hospital

What is his medical expense deduction before the imposition of the income limit?
A. $1,900
B. $4,350
C. $4,550
D. $12,350

The answer is B. His medical expense deduction before limitations is $4,350. The babysitting is not deductible, even though it was incurred while he was obtaining medical care. The amounts reimbursed by insurance are not deductible as medical expenses. ###

11. Which of the following items is NOT a deductible medical expense?

A. Dental implants to replace broken or missing teeth
B. Contact lenses
C. Guide dog expenses for a blind person
D. Over-the-counter aspirin

The answer is D. The cost of medical items such as false teeth, prescription eyeglasses or contact lenses, laser eye surgery, hearing aids, crutches, wheelchairs, and guide dogs for the blind or deaf are all deductible medical expenses. Over-the-counter medicines are not deductible. ###

12. Jesse is in the process of adopting a child. In 2010, the child lived with Jesse and he provided all of the child's support. However, the adoption is not final. Which of the following statements is TRUE?

A. Jesse can include medical expenses that he paid before the adoption becomes final, if the child qualified as his dependent when the medical services were provided or paid.
B. Jesse cannot claim the medical expenses because the adoption is not final.
C. Jesse must save his receipts and, once the adoption becomes final, he may amend his tax return.
D. A taxpayer may only claim medical expenses for a biological child or a stepchild.

The answer is A. Jesse can include medical expenses that he paid before the adoption becomes final, as long as the child qualified as a dependent when the medical services were provided or paid (Publication 502). ###

13. All of the following expenses do not qualify as deductible medical expenses, EXCEPT:

A. Non-corrective cosmetic surgery
B. Maternity clothes
C. Final burial expenses
D. Smoking-cessation programs

The answer is D. A taxpayer may deduct the cost of a smoking-cessation program and prescription drugs used to alleviate nicotine withdrawal. However, the taxpayer may not deduct non-prescription nicotine gum or nicotine patches. ###

14. Which of the following is a deductible medical expense?

A. Acupuncture for back pain
B. Karate lessons for an overweight person
C. Marriage counseling
D. Teeth whitening

The answer is A. In this instance, only acupuncture qualifies as an IRS-allowed medical expense. Medical care expenses must be primarily to alleviate or prevent a physical or mental defect or illness. They do not include expenses that are merely beneficial to general health, such as vitamins, gym classes, or vacations. ###

15. Dora's AGI is $40,000. She paid medical expenses of $3,500. Taking into account the AGI limit, how much can Dora deduct on her Schedule A?

A. $0
B. $500
C. $2,313
D. $2,500

The answer is B. Dora can deduct only $500 of her medical expenses because that is the amount that exceeds 7.5% of her AGI. Dora's AGI is $40,000, 7.5% of which is $3,000. ###

16. Which of the following taxes can taxpayers deduct on Schedule A?

A. Federal income tax
B. Real estate taxes
C. Tax on alcohol and tobacco
D. Foreign sales tax

The answer is B. Taxpayers can deduct real estate taxes on Schedule A. ###

17. Which of the following expenses are deductible on Schedule A?
A. Stamp taxes
B. Parking ticket obtained while getting emergency medical care
C. Drivers' license fees
D. Personal property taxes paid on a speedboat

The answer is D. Only the property taxes paid on the boat would be deductible. Parking tickets and fines are never deductible. Drivers' license fees and stamp taxes are not deductible. ###

18. Ryan is having money troubles and agrees to sell his home to Janie. Janie agrees to pay all the delinquent real estate taxes on the residence, totaling $2,000. How must Janie treat the property tax payment of $2,000?
A. Janie may deduct the taxes as an itemized deduction on her Schedule A.
B. Janie may not deduct the taxes. She must add the taxes paid to her basis in the property.
C. The taxes may be pro-rated and deducted over the life of her loan.
D. Janie may deduct the taxes paid as an adjustment to income.

The answer is B. Janie can only deduct the property taxes that are legally imposed on her. A person cannot deduct property taxes unless she is the legal owner of the property. Property taxes paid during a purchase may be added to the buyer's basis if the taxes are for the time period that the property was owned by the seller (Publication 17).
 ###

19. Which of the following taxes is NOT deductible on Schedule A?

A. Property tax on a vacation home
B. Special assessments to improve the sidewalks
C. DMV fees (personal property taxes) based on the vehicle's value
D. Property taxes paid on a home in Mexico

The answer is B. The assessment to improve sidewalks is not deductible. Many states, cities, and counties also impose local benefit taxes for improvements to property, such as assessments for streets, sidewalks, and sewer lines. These taxes cannot be deducted, but they can be added to the property's basis (Publication 551). ###

20. For a tax to be deductible, all of the following must be true EXCEPT _____.

A. The tax must be imposed during the tax year.
B. The taxpayer must be legally liable for the tax.
C. The tax must be paid during the tax year.
D. The tax must be paid by the taxpayer.

The answer is A. Taxpayers can deduct tax imposed during a prior year, as long as the taxes were paid during the current tax year. ###

21. Christopher and Angie file a joint return. During the year, they paid:

- $2,180 in home mortgage interest that was reported to them on Form 1098
- $400 in credit card interest
- $1,500 paid to the bank for specific services (e.g. appraisal fee, notary fee, and preparation costs for the mortgage)
- $2,000 in interest on a car loan

How much can Christopher and Angie report as deductible interest?
A. $4,880
B. $4,080
C. $2,180
D. $0

The answer is C. Only their home mortgage interest ($2,180) is deductible. The other types of interest are all personal interest that is not deductible. ###

22. Nathaniel owns a home, and he also has a vacation home in the mountains that he did not use at all during the tax year. Which of the following statements is true?

A. Only the mortgage interest and property tax on his main home is deductible.
B. Both the mortgage interest and property tax on his main home and the second residence is deductible.
C. The mortgage interest on both homes is deductible, but the property tax on the vacation property is not.
D. The mortgage interest and property tax on his main home is deductible, and the property tax on the second home is deductible. Any mortgage interest on the second home is not deductible.

The answer is B. Both the mortgage interest and property tax on his main home and the second residence are deductible. The mortgage interest on a second home is deductible. The interest must fit the same requirements for deductibility as interest on a primary residence. Real estate taxes paid on a taxpayer's primary and second residence are deductible (Publication 17). ###

23. For the Mortgage Interest Deduction, which of the following choices would qualify as a home?

A. An empty lot where the taxpayer plans to build his main home
B. A sailboat with a camp stove
C. A vacation cabin without running water
D. An RV with a small kitchen, bathroom, and sleeping area

The answer is D. A qualified home includes a house, condominium, cooperative, mobile home, house trailer, boat, or similar property that has sleeping, cooking, and toilet facilities.###

24. Harvey refinanced his home and paid closing costs in 2010. He used the proceeds from the refinance to put on a new roof and also to pay off one of his credit cards. He paid the following fees:

- $400 Loan origination fee (points)
- $500 Home appraisal fee
- $45 Document prep fee
- $60 Loan closing fee
- $70 Title insurance

How much of the fees Harvey paid to the bank for the loan is *fully deductible* in 2010?
A. $0
B. $400
C. $900
D. $945
E. $1,005

The answer is A. Harvey may not fully deduct any of the expenses listed. He cannot "fully deduct" the points because the home loan is a refinance, not a purchase. Deductible fees are limited to home mortgage interest and certain real estate taxes. Points that represent interest on a refinancing are generally amortized over the life of the loan. Fees that are not associated with the acquisition of a loan (other than fees representing interest for tax purposes) generally only affect the basis of the home. Fees related to the acquisition of a loan, such as a credit report fee, are not deductible (Publication 936). ###

25. Ingrid is single with the following income and expenses:

- Wages $70,000
- Interest income $3,000
- Mortgage interest paid $24,000
- Investment interest expense $5,000
- Personal credit card interest $3,400
- Car loan interest $1,200
- Late fees on her mortgage $50

What is Ingrid's total allowable deduction for interest expense on her Schedule A?

A. $24,000
B. $27,000
C. $27,050
D. $32,400

The answer is C. The answer is: $24,000 + $3,000 + $50 = $27,050. The deduction for investment interest expense is limited to investment income. Late fees paid on a qualifying mortgage are deductible as interest. However, late fees for neglecting to pay property tax are NOT deductible. The remaining amount of interest expense must be carried over to the next tax year, and may be used to offset income in future tax years. The credit card interest is not deductible. ###

26. Alexander and Melinda are married and file joint tax returns. They have the following interest expenses in the current tax year. How much deductible interest do they have after limitations?

- $10,000 in mortgage interest on a main home
- $2,000 in mortgage interest on a second home
- $4,600 in interest on a car loan
- $600 in credit card interest
- $3,000 in margin interest expense
- $2,400 in investment income

A. $10,000
B. $12,000
C. $14,400
D. $15,000

The answer is C. The answer is figured as follows: $10,000 + $2,000 + $2,400 = $14,400. The mortgage interest on both homes is deductible. The interest on the auto loan and credit cards is not deductible. The margin interest expense is deductible, but limited to the amount of investment income, which is $2,400. Investment interest is deductible by individuals only to the extent of investment income. The remaining investment interest expense may be carried over to a future tax year. ###

27. All of the following are deductible charitable contributions that Larissa made to a qualifying battered women's shelter EXCEPT _____.

A. Fair Market Value of the used kitchen appliances, in good condition, she donated to the shelter
B. $35 of the $50 admission Larissa paid for a shelter fundraising dinner (the Fair Market Value was $15)
C. Fair Market Value of the hours Larissa spent staffing the shelter
D. Larissa's transportation costs for driving to and from her shift at the shelter

The answer is C. Larissa cannot deduct the value of her volunteer hours. The value of a person's time and service is not deductible. ###

28. Which taxpayer is required to fill out **Form 8283** and attach it to his or her return?

A. Lenny, who made a single cash contribution of $650 to a qualified organization
B. Hunter, whose deductible cash contributions totaled $550
C. Marilyn, whose non-cash contributions totaled $250
D. Debra, whose non-cash contributions totaled $600

The answer is D. Debra would be required to fill out **Form 8283** and attach it to her return. That is because any noncash donation over $500 must be described on Form 8283. ###

29. Julia made the following contributions last year:

- $600 to St. Martin's Church (The church gave her a receipt)
- $32 to the SPCA
- $40 to a family whose house burned
- $50 for lottery tickets at a fundraiser
- $100 for playing bingo at her church
- Furniture with a Fair Market Value of $200 to Goodwill

The amount that Julia can claim as deductible cash contributions is $____ .

A. $672
B. $632
C. $72
D. $32

The answer is B. Julia's donations to her church and to the SPCA are her only deductible cash contributions. Lottery tickets and bingo (or any type of gambling) is not a charitable contribution, even if the proceeds go to a qualifying organization. The donation of furniture to Goodwill is not a cash contribution, and therefore would not be included in the calculation. Non-cash contributions are reported separately from cash contributions. ###

30. Amelia donates $430 in cash to her church. What is required on the receipt to substantiate the donation correctly for IRS recordkeeping requirements?

A. The reason for the contribution
B. Amelia's home address
C. The amount of the donation
D. Amelia's method of payment

The answer is C. A taxpayer can claim a deduction for a contribution of $250 or more only if she has a receipt from the qualified organization. The receipt (acknowledgment) must include:
- The amount of cash contributed
- Whether the qualified organization gave the taxpayer any goods or services in return
- A description and good faith estimate of the value of any goods or services provided in return by the organization (if applicable)

A receipt for the donation must also show the amount, the date, and the name of the organization that was paid. ###

31. Mindy donates her used car to a qualified charity. She bought it three years ago for $15,000. A used car guide shows the FMV for this type of car is $5,000. Mindy's friend Buck offered her $4,500 for the car a week ago. Mindy gets a Form 1098-C from the organization showing the car was sold for $1,900. How much is Mindy's charitable deduction?

A. $15,000
B. $5,000
C. $4,500
D. $1,900

The answer is D. Mindy can only deduct $1,900 for her donation. She must attach Form 1098-C and Form 8283 to her return. This is because she is only allowed to take the lesser of the car's FMV, or the amount for which the charity was able to sell the car. ###

32. Oscar donated a nice leather coat to a thrift store operated by his church. He paid $450 for the coat three years ago. Similar coats in the thrift store sell for $50. What is Oscar's charitable deduction?

A. $0
B. $50
C. $400
D. $450

The answer is B. Oscar's donation is limited to $50. Generally, the FMV of used clothing and household goods is far less than their original cost. For used clothing, a taxpayer should claim as the value the price that buyers of used items actually pay in used clothing stores, such as consignment or thrift shops (Publication 561). ###

33. Kendra made $1,500 in noncash (property) contributions to a qualified charity. What form must she file and attach to her tax return in addition to Schedule A?

A. Form 8283
B. Form 2815
C. Form 1098-C
D. Form 1065

The answer is A. If a taxpayer's total deduction for all noncash contributions for the year is over $500, she must file **Form 8283,** *Noncash Charitable Contributions.* Taxpayers report their charitable contributions on Schedule A (Form 1040). If any single gift or group of similar gifts is valued at over $5,000, the taxpayer must also get an appraisal of the item or items from a qualified appraiser. ###

34. Laney pays $105 for a ticket to a church dinner. All the proceeds go to the church. The ticket to the dinner has an FMV of $20, the cost of the dinner. At the dinner, Laney buys $35 worth of raffle tickets, which the church is selling as a fundraiser. She doesn't win any raffle prizes. What is Laney's deductible charitable contribution to her church?

A. $85
B. $120
C. $140
D. $195

The answer is A. To figure the amount of Laney's charitable contribution, she must subtract the value of the benefit received ($20) from the total payment ($105). Therefore, Laney can deduct $85 as a charitable contribution to the church. The cost of raffle tickets or other wagering activity is never deductible as a charitable contribution. ###

35. Vera and Jack are married and file jointly. They contributed $15,000 in cash from their savings to their synagogue during 2010. They also donated $3,000 to a private foundation that is a nonprofit cemetery organization. A 30% limit applies to the cemetery organization. Their Adjusted Gross Income for 2010 was $30,000. Vera and Jack's deductible contribution for 2010 and any carryover to next year is:

A. $18,000 with zero carryover to next year
B. $15,000 with $2,100 carryover to next year
C. $7,500 with $2,100 carryover to next year
D. $15,000 with $3,000 carryover to next year

The answer is D. Vera and Jack cannot deduct more than $15,000, which is 50% of their income of $30,000. The remaining amount must be carried forward to a future tax year. ###

36. During a fundraising auction at his local church, Lyle pays $600 for a week's stay at a beachfront hotel. He intends to make the payment as a contribution, and all the proceeds go to help the church. The FMV of the stay is $590. What is Lyle's charitable contribution?

A. $0
B. $10
C. $590
D. $600

The answer is B. Lyle can only deduct $10, because he received the benefit of staying at the property. Only the *excess* contribution over the FMV of the item qualifies as a charitable contribution. ###

37. Maya is a church leader and she supervises the group on a prayer trip. She is responsible for overseeing the setup of the trip and really enjoys the activities. She also oversees the breaking down of the campsite and helps transport the group home. Which of the following statements is TRUE?

A. Maya may not deduct her travel expenses because she enjoyed the trip. Therefore, it is a vacation and is not deductible.
B. Maya may deduct her out-of-pocket expenses.
C. Maya may deduct only the travel expense to and from the campsite.
D. None of the above is true.

The answer is B. A taxpayer may claim a charitable contribution deduction for out-of-pocket expenses incurred while away from home performing services for a charitable organization only if there is no significant element of personal pleasure in the travel. However, a deduction will not be denied simply because the taxpayer enjoys providing services to a charitable organization.

The taxpayer is still allowed to take a charitable contribution deduction for the expenses if she is on-duty in a genuine and substantial sense throughout the trip. Since Maya had substantial supervisory and leadership duties throughout the trip, her out-of-pocket expenses are deductible. ###

38. Deductions to the following organizations are subject to the 50% limitation on deductible contributions:

A. Churches
B. Hospitals
C. Fraternal societies such as the Kiwanis and the Lions Club
D. Both A and B.

The answer is D. The 50% limit applies to the total of all charitable contributions made during the year. This means that the deduction for charitable contributions cannot exceed 50% of a taxpayer's AGI. A 30% limit applies to veterans' organizations, fraternal societies, nonprofit cemeteries, and certain private non-operating foundations. ###

39. Nancy donates $300 in cash to her local food bank. What type of documentation is required for her donation?

A. No documentation
B. A canceled check
C. A self-prepared statement
D. A receipt for each donation showing the amount, date, and who was paid

The answer is D. A taxpayer can claim a deduction for a contribution of $250 or more only if she has an acknowledgment or receipt of the contribution from the charity. The receipt must reflect the amount, date, and the name of the organization that was paid (Publication 17). ###

40. Jose spent the entire day attending his church organization's regional meeting as a chosen representative. He spent $50 on travel to the meeting and $25 on materials for the meeting. In the evening, Jose went to the movies with two other meeting attendees. He spent $50 on movie tickets. The charity did not reimburse Jose for any of his costs. How much can Jose deduct as a charitable expense?

A. $25
B. $50
C. $75
D. $150

The answer is C. His charitable contribution is $75 ($50 + 25 = $75). Jose can claim his travel and meeting expenses as charitable contributions, but he cannot claim the cost of the evening at the movies (Publication 526). ###

41. Ted pays a babysitter $100 to watch his children while he does volunteer work at the Red Cross. He also has $50 in transportation expenses of which $10 was reimbursed by the organization. What is Ted's deductible expense?
A. $0
B. $40
C. $50
D. $150

The answer is B. Only Ted's transportation costs are deductible ($50 - $10 reimbursement = $40). A taxpayer cannot deduct payments for child care expenses as a charitable contribution, even if they are necessary so he can do the volunteer work. ###

42. In March 2010, Sunny does volunteer work for 15 hours in the offices of a local homeless shelter. The full-time receptionist is paid $10 an hour to do the same work Sunny does. Sunny makes $15 per hour as a cashier at her regular job. Sunny also has $16 in out-of-pocket expenses for bus fare to the shelter. How much can Sunny deduct on her taxes as a charitable contribution?

A. $16
B. $150
C. $225
D. $241

The answer is A. A taxpayer cannot deduct the "value" of her time or services as a charitable deduction. However, a volunteer may deduct out-of-pocket expenses and the costs of gas and oil or transportation costs for getting to and from the place where she volunteers. Sunny cannot use the standard mileage rate because she did not use her own car for transportation. ###

43. Oliver pays $70 to see a special showing of a movie at a church fundraising event. The regular price of a movie ticket is $8. Pre-printed on the ticket it says "Contribution:$100." How much is Oliver's charitable deduction?

A. $8
B. $62
C. $70
D. $100

The answer is B. If the regular price for the movie is $8, the taxpayer contribution is $62 ($70 payment-$8 regular price). If a taxpayer pays MORE than FMV to a qualified organization for merchandise, goods, or services, the amount paid that is more than the value of the item can be a charitable contribution. No matter what the ticket says, the taxpayer may never deduct more than his actual contribution. ###

44. All of the following are nonprofit organizations. However, not all of them qualify as deductible contributions. Sam donated to each nonprofit listed. What is his total qualified deduction for 2010?

Amount	Organization
$100	Catholic church
$120	County animal shelter
$75	Salvation Army
$25	Red Cross
$50	Political contribution
$300	Chamber of Commerce
$670	**Total Contributions**

A. $320
B. $370
C. $220
D. $670

The answer is A. The contributions to the political organization and the Chamber of Commerce are not deductible on Schedule A. The deduction is figured as follows: ($100 + $120 + $75 + $25 = $320). ###

45. Dane participated in a fundraising bingo event for his local church. All the money collected by the church, a qualified organization, went to feed the homeless. Dane purchased $300 in bingo cards and won movie tickets valued at $60. What is Dane's charitable deduction?

A. $0
B. $60
C. $240
D. $300

The answer is A. Dane may not deduct any amount as a contribution. Deducting the cost of raffle, bingo, or lottery tickets is specifically prohibited by IRS Publication 17, even if the money goes to a qualified charity. The cost of raffle, bingo, or lottery tickets is never deductible as a charitable contribution. ###

46. Martin contributes to many organizations. In 2010, he contributes $5,000 in cash to his church and $4,000 to his local Chamber of Commerce. He also contributes land with a Fair Market Value of $16,000 to his church. Martin has a basis of $5,000 in the land. His taxable income for the year is $45,000. What is the maximum amount he can deduct for charitable contributions?

A. $9,000
B. $18,500
C. $22,500
D. $25,000

The answer is B. The contribution to the Chamber of Commerce is not a deductible contribution. The $5,000 contribution in cash is fully deductible, but gifts of appreciated property (the land) are subject to a maximum deduction of 30% of the taxpayer's contribution base.

However, charitable gifts of appreciated property held long-term are subject to a lower deductibility ceiling: 30% of AGI, with a five-year carryover of any excess deduction. So, Martin figures his charitable contribution as follows:

($45,000 x 30%) = $13,500
($5,000 + $13,500) = $18,500
Carryover = $2,500
($16,000 - $13,500 = $2,500)

47. Patrice's antique Persian rug was damaged by a new kitten before it was housebroken. Patrice estimates the loss at $4,500. Her AGI for the year is $50,000. How much of the casualty loss may she deduct?

A. $0
B. $4,500
C. $3,000
C. $2,900

The answer is A. A casualty loss is not deductible if the damage is caused by a family pet. Because the damage was not unexpected and unusual, the loss is not deduct-deductible as a casualty loss. ###

48. Ben's garage caught fire in 2010. The garage is not attached to his primary residence. Ben estimates the property damage at $6,000. He declines to file an insurance claim because he fixes the damage himself. Ben pays $3,000 for the cost of the materials. His insurance company has a $1,000 deductible for any casualty loss claim filed. What is Ben's deductible casualty loss before any deductions or income limitations?

A. $0
B. $1,000
C. $3,000
D. $6,000

The answer is B. If a taxpayer's property is covered by insurance, he cannot deduct a loss unless he files an insurance claim for reimbursement. However, if the taxpayer declines to file an insurance claim, the IRS limits eligible casualty losses to the amount that is not normally covered by insurance, such as the amount of the insurance deductible. ###

49. Isaac's home was damaged by a tornado. He had $90,000 worth of damage, but $80,000 was reimbursed by his insurance company. Isaac's employer had a disaster relief fund for its employees. Isaac received $4,000 from the fund and spent the entire amount on repairs to his home. What is Isaac's deductible casualty loss **before** applying the deduction limits?

A. $0
B. $4,000
C. $6,000
D. $10,000

The answer is C. Isaac's casualty loss before applying the deduction limits is $6,000. Isaac must reduce his unreimbursed loss ($90,000 - $80,000 = $10,000) by the $4,000 he received from his employer. Isaac's casualty loss before applying the deduction limits is $6,000 ($10,000 - $4,000) (Publication 547). ###

50. All of the following may be claimed as miscellaneous itemized deductions EXCEPT _____.

A. Unreimbursed commuting expenses to and from work
B. Professional society or union dues
C. Expenses of looking for a new job
D. Work-related expenses for individuals with a disability

The answer is A. The expenses of commuting to and from work are not deductible. These costs are personal expenses. A taxpayer cannot deduct commuting expenses to a primary workplace no matter how far his home is from his regular place of work. A taxpayer cannot deduct commuting expenses even if he works during the commuting trip (Publication 463). ###

51. All the following miscellaneous itemized deductions are subject to the 2% of AGI limit EXCEPT _____.

A. Investment counsel fees
B. Professional society dues
C. Expenses of looking for a new job
D. Work-related expenses for individuals with a disability

The answer is D. Work-related expenses for individuals with a disability are not subject to the 2% AGI limit. ###

52. Lola uses her home office while she works as a translator for an online translating company. Lola meets the requirements for deducting expenses for the business use of her home. Her home office is 240 square feet (12 feet × 20 feet) and her home is 1,200 square feet. What is Lola's "business use" percentage in order to figure her allowable deduction?

A. 5%
B. 10%
C. 15%
D. 20%

The answer is D. Lola uses 20% of her home for business. Her office is 20% (240 ÷ 1,200) of the total area of her home. Therefore, her business percentage is 20%. ###

53. Simon's AGI is $75,000. Therefore, the first_____ of miscellaneous employee work-related expenses are not deductible.

A. $1,000
B. $1,500
C. $5,625
D. Some other amount.

The answer is B. Simon's employee work-related expenses are subject to the 2% limit of Adjusted Gross Income. Therefore, Simon must figure his deduction on Schedule A by first subtracting 2% of his Adjusted Gross Income (75,000 x 2% = $1,500) from the total amount of these expenses. ###

54. Marissa works as a bookkeeper for A+ Bookkeeping. She was hired as a bookkeeper in 2006, but this year, her employer changed his educational requirements. Now all the bookkeepers are required to take three additional courses in order to keep their current positions. Marissa incurred the following expenses when she took these courses:

$100 Required supplies
$550 Tuition
$120 Required books
$50 Credit card interest from paying for tuition
$65 Bus passes to and from school
$885 Total educational expenses

What is Marissa's deductible work-related educational expense on her Schedule A **before** the 2% limitation?

A. $550
B. $670
C. $835
D. $885

The answer is C. Marissa may deduct all the costs as work-related educational expenses, with the exception of the credit card interest, which is a personal expense and not deductible. ###

55. Which of the following expenses does NOT qualify as a deductible transportation expense?

A. Getting from one client to another in the course of a taxpayer's business or profession
B. Commuting expenses
C. Traveling overseas to sign a business contract with a foreign supplier
D. Going to a business meeting out-of-state

The answer is B. A taxpayer can include in business expenses amounts paid for transportation primarily for and essential to business or trade. A taxpayer cannot deduct personal commuting expenses, no matter how far her home is from her regular place of work (Publication 17). ###

56. Which of the following will qualify for a deduction on Schedule A as an employee business expense?

A. The employer reimburses expenses under a tuition reimbursement (nontaxable) program.
B. Taking classes that maintain or improve skills needed in the taxpayer's present work.
C. Taking classes that are required by a taxpayer's employer or the law to keep her present salary, status, or job. The required education must serve a bona fide business purpose to the taxpayer's employer.
D. Both B and C.

The answer is D. Both B and C are correct. A taxpayer can deduct the costs of qualifying work-related education as business expenses. Choice "A" is incorrect because any amounts that are reimbursed by an employer cannot be deducted by the taxpayer.###

57. What form is used to figure a taxpayer's unreimbursed employee business expenses?

A. Form 1040-EZ
B. Form 2106
C. Form 8821
D. Form W-2

The answer is B. Generally, the taxpayer must figure the gross expenses on Form 2106, *Employee Business Expenses*, and attach it to her Form 1040. ###

58. Connor is deaf. He purchased a special device to use at work so he can identify when his phone rings. He paid for the device out-of-pocket, and his employer did not reimburse him. How should Connor report this on his tax return?

A. Connor may deduct the purchase as an itemized deduction, subject to the 2% floor.
B. Connor may deduct the purchase as an itemized deduction, NOT subject to the 2% floor.
C. Connor may not deduct the purchase because he is not totally disabled.
D. Connor may not deduct the purchase because he is not self-employed.

The answer is B. Connor may deduct the expenses for the computer as impairment-related work expenses. The deduction is not limited. If a taxpayer has a physical or mental disability that limits employment, he can choose to deduct the expense as a miscellaneous itemized deduction, NOT subject to the 2%-of-income floor.###

59. During the year, Leon paid $350 to have his tax return prepared. He also paid union dues of $450 and paid an attorney $3,000 to draft his will. What is Leon's miscellaneous itemized deduction on his Schedule A before the 2% limitation?

A. $350
B. $450
C. $800
D. $3,800

The answer is C. The attorney fees for drafting the will are not deductible. The tax preparation fees and union dues are deductible and subject to a 2% of AGI floor. ###

60. All of the following expenses may be deducted on Schedule A as a miscellaneous itemized deduction, except:

A. Cost of a safe deposit box
B. Union dues
C. Cosmetic surgery
D. Travel costs from one workplace to another workplace on the same day

The answer is C. Cosmetic surgery is not a deductible expense unless it is to correct a medical defect or disability (such as a disfigurement). Commuting costs are not deductible, but the travel costs between two separate workplaces are deductible as an employee-work expense. The commuting costs between a taxpayer's main workplace and his home are not deductible. Union dues and the cost of a safety deposit box are deductible expenses on Schedule A. ###

61. Abby has the following income and losses in 2010:
    1. $45,000 in wages
    2. $10,000 in gambling winnings
    3. $13,000 in gambling losses
    4. $1,500 attorney fees for a divorce

How should these transactions be treated on her tax return?

A. Report $55,000 in taxable income and $10,000 in miscellaneous itemized deductions on Schedule A, NOT subject to the 2% floor.
B. Report $53,000 in taxable income and $13,000 in miscellaneous itemized deductions, subject to the 2% floor.
C. Report $55,000 in taxable income and $13,000 in miscellaneous itemized deductions on Schedule A, subject to the 2% floor.
D. Report $45,000 in taxable income and $14,500 in miscellaneous itemized deductions on Schedule A, NOT subject to the 2% floor.

The answer is A. The full amount of income must be reported on Form 1040 ($45,000 + $10,000 = $55,000). The gambling losses are deductible only up to the amount of gambling winnings; a taxpayer must report the full amount of gambling winnings on Form 1040. The taxpayer then may deduct gambling losses on Schedule A (Form 1040). Gambling losses are not subject to the 2% of income limitation, but taxpayers cannot report more gambling losses than they do gambling winnings. ###

Unit 1.9: Tax Credits

More Reading:
Publication 972, *Child Tax Credit*
Publication 503, *Child and Dependent Care Expenses*
Publication 596, *Earned Income Credit*
Publication 970, *Tax Benefits for Education*

A tax credit directly reduces tax liability. A tax credit is usually more valuable than a tax deduction of the same dollar amount. It is important to understand this distinction for the EA Exam. A tax deduction will reduce income that is subject to tax, but a tax credit will actually reduce tax *liability*—the amount the taxpayer is required to pay the IRS.

In some cases (such as the Earned Income Credit or EIC), a tax credit is refundable. This can create a tax refund—even if the taxpayer does not owe any tax! There are two types of tax credits:

- **Refundable credits**
- **Nonrefundable credits**

Nonrefundable Tax Credits

A nonrefundable credit is a dollar-for-dollar reduction of the tax liability. A nonrefundable credit can reduce a taxpayer's tax liability down to zero, but not beyond that. Most tax credits are "nonrefundable" credits. Nonrefundable tax credits include the following:

1. Child and Dependent Care Credit
2. Lifetime Learning Credit
3. Credit for the Elderly or Disabled
4. Child Tax Credit
5. Foreign Tax Credit
6. Residential Energy Efficient Property Credit
7. Retirement Savings Contribution Credit
8. Mortgage Interest Credit
9. Energy-Efficiency Credits

Refundable Tax Credits

A refundable tax credit can produce a tax refund; even if the taxpayer does not owe any tax. Refundable tax credits that can reduce tax liability below zero include the following:

1. American Opportunity Credit (partially refundable)
2. Additional Child Tax Credit
3. Earned Income Credit (*heavily tested on the EA Exam)
4. Adoption Credit (refundable in 2010 for the first time)
5. First-Time Homebuyer Credit
6. Making Work Pay Credit
7. Credit for Excess Social Security Tax or Railroad Retirement Tax Withheld

Child and Dependent Care Credit

The Child and Dependent Care Credit is calculated using Form 2441. The Child and Dependent Care Credit is a nonrefundable credit that allows taxpayers to reduce their tax liability by a percentage of their dependent care expenses. The credit may be claimed by taxpayers who work and pay for daycare (or adult care services) for someone who is their dependent or spouse.

The credit can range from 20%-35% of a taxpayer's qualifying expenses. The percentage is based on the taxpayer's income. Since this credit is nonrefundable, it cannot exceed the amount of income tax on the return; that is, it can reduce an individual's tax to $0, but it cannot result in a refund.

Because the Child and Dependent Care Credit is a nonrefundable credit, only taxpayers with taxable income can claim the credit. In order to qualify, the expenses must be incurred in order for the taxpayer to work. It can be full-time or part-time work.

Some taxpayers receive dependent care benefits from their employers, which may also be called "Flexible Spending Accounts" or "reimbursement accounts." Taxpayers usually can exclude these benefits from their income. Employer-provided dependent care benefits are reported on the employee's Form W-2. All taxpayers who receive employer-provided dependent care benefits are required to complete **Form 2441,** *Child and Dependent Care Expenses*, to determine if they can exclude these benefits from their taxable income. A taxpayer must pass five eligibility tests in order to qualify for this credit:

1. Qualifying person test
2. Earned income test
3. Work-related expense test
4. Joint return test
5. Provider identification test

Qualifying Person Test

To meet the *qualifying person test*, the taxpayer's expenses must be for the care of a qualifying individual. In most cases, this is the taxpayer's child. However, expenses paid for the care of other dependents (such as a dependent parent who requires in-home care) are also allowable. A qualifying person is:

- A dependent child under the age of 13
- A spouse who is unable to care for himself or herself (a disabled spouse)
- Any other dependents who are unable to care for themselves

Only a custodial parent can take the Child and Dependent Care Credit. If the child is not being claimed as a dependent by the taxpayer because the noncustodial parent is taking the exemption under the special rules for children of divorced and separated parents, only the custodial parent may treat the child as a qualifying person for this credit.

> **Example:** Samuel paid someone to care for his wife Janet so he could work. Janet is permanently disabled and requires an in-home care aide. Samuel also paid to have someone prepare meals for his 12-year-old daughter Jill. Both Janet and Jill are qualifying persons for the credit. (Publication 503)

Dependent Care: the Earned Income Test

The next test is the earned income test. The taxpayer (AND spouse if married) must have earned income during the year. A taxpayer may claim daycare expenses while he or she is seeking employment. However, the taxpayer must have earned income for the year in order to take this credit. For couples filing MFJ, this means both spouses must work. This credit is not available to taxpayers who file separately.

A spouse is exempted if she is a full-time student or is disabled (explained below). Childcare expenses that are incurred so that the taxpayer may volunteer for a charity or other tax-exempt organization do NOT qualify for the credit. Earned income includes:

- Wages, Salaries, Tips
- Other taxable employee compensation
- Earnings from self-employment, including self-employment income earned by a general partner in a partnership
- Strike benefits
- Disability pay reported as wages

The taxpayer's spouse is treated as having earned income for any month he or she is:

- A full-time student, or
- Disabled

In either case, for the purposes of the credit, the spouse's income is considered to be $250 for each month. If, in the same month, the taxpayer and spouse are either full-time students or unable to care for themselves, only one of them can be treated as having earned income in that month (up to $500, or $250 for each).

Example: Jessica and Quincy are married. Quincy worked full-time all year and earned $40,000 in 2010. Jessica attended school full-time from January 1 to June 30. She was unemployed during the summer months and did not attend school the rest of the year. Jessica should be treated as having earned income for the months she attended school full-time, which were January through June of the tax year.

Example: Patsy is a stay-at-home mom. Her husband works and had earned income for the tax year. They have a young son. Patsy volunteers 12 hours a week at a local autism information hotline. She and her husband pay a caregiver to stay with their son during the hours she does her volunteer work. They do not qualify for the Dependent Care Credit because the caregiver expense is not work-related; that is, Patsy is not using it in order to work or to look for work. Also, to qualify for the credit, Patsy and her husband must BOTH have earned income for the tax year. Since Patsy does not have a job (and is not disabled or a full-time student) then the expenses would not qualify.

Work-Related Expense Test

Qualifying expenses must be "work related," meaning that the childcare must be incurred while a taxpayer is working or searching for work. Daycare expenses incurred during a short, temporary absence from work, such as for vacation or a minor illness, may still qualify as childcare expenses. An absence of two weeks or less is considered a short, temporary absence.

Example: Ernie and Grace have full-time jobs. They pay $45 to a babysitter once a week so they can go out to eat on a date. Since this is not a work-related expense, it is not qualifying childcare for the purposes of the Child Care Credit.

Example: Darcy works only three days a week. While she works, her six-year-old child attends a daycare center. Darcy pays the center $150 for three days a week or $250 for five days a week. Sometimes Darcy pays the $250 so she can run errands or do other tasks. However, the extra charge for daycare during the time Darcy is not working is not a qualifying expense. Darcy's deductible expenses are limited to $150 a week, which is the amount of work-related daycare expense.

The following expenses qualify as work-related:

- Cost of care outside the home for dependents under 13; for example, preschool or home daycare, before or after-school care for a child in grade school.
- Cost of assistive care for any other qualifying person; for example, dependent care for a disabled adult.
- Household expenses that are at least partly for the well-being and protection of a qualifying person; for example, the services of a housekeeper or cook.

Preschool expenses are deductible for children below the first grade. Private school tuition for kindergarten (or a higher grade) is not a qualifying expense, but after-school care at a private school may still qualify as a deductible expense.

Example: Roger's 10-year-old child attends a private school. In addition to paying for tuition, Roger pays an extra fee for the before-school and after-school program so Roger can go to work. Roger can count the cost of the before and after-school program when figuring the credit, but not the cost of tuition.

Example: Emily is single and her elderly mother Lorraine is her dependent. Lorraine is completely disabled and must be in an adult daycare so she does not injure herself. Emily pays $8,000 per year for Lorraine to be in the daycare. Emily may take the Dependent Care Credit, because Lorraine is disabled and incapable of self-care.

Examples of childcare expenses that do not qualify include:

- Education, such as expenses for a child to attend kindergarten or a higher grade
- The cost of sending a child to an overnight camp
- The cost of transportation not provided by a care provider
- A forfeited deposit to a daycare center

Example: Ellen is divorced and has custody of her 12-year-old daughter Terri. Terri takes care of herself after school. In the summer, Ellen spends $2,000 to send Terri to an overnight camp for two weeks. The cost of sending a child to an overnight camp is not considered a work-related expense. Ellen does not have any qualifying expenses for the purpose of this credit.

Care expenses do not include amounts paid for food, clothing, education, or entertainment. Small amounts paid for these items, however, can be included if they are incidental and cannot be separated from the cost of care.

> **Example:** Krista takes her three-year-old child to a nursery school that provides lunch and educational activities as part of its preschool childcare service. The meals are included in the overall cost of care, and they're not itemized on her bill. Krista can count the total cost when she figures the credit.

Payments for child care made to an individual will not qualify for the credit if the payment is made to a family member who is either:

- The taxpayer's own child under age 19
- Any other dependent listed on the taxpayer's tax return

There is a limit on the amount of work-related expenses taxpayers can include in figuring the Child and Dependent Care Credit. The limit is:

- $3,000 for expenses paid for one qualifying person, or
- $6,000 for two or more qualifying persons

No matter how many dependents a taxpayer has, the credit cannot be more than $6,000 in a single tax year. This child or dependent care must make it possible for a taxpayer to work or to seek employment. The credit is based on a percentage of the amount actually paid for care expenses.

Taxpayers may combine costs for multiple dependents. For example, if a taxpayer pays daycare for three qualifying children, the $6,000 limit does not need to be divided equally among them.

> **Example:** Lee has two children. His qualifying daycare expenses for his first child are $3,200. Lee's qualifying expenses for his second child are $2,800. He is allowed to use the total amount, $6,000, when figuring his credit (Publication 17).

> **Example:** Diego and Valeria both work and have three children. They have $2,000 in daycare expenses for their son Miguel; $3,000 for their son Cesar; and $4,000 for their daughter Cecilia. Their total childcare expenses are $9,000, but they may only use the first $6,000 as their basis for the Child Care Credit.

> **Example:** Lori is a single mother with a dependent child. Her son Noah is five years old. Lori takes Noah to daycare five days per week so she can work. Lori makes $46,000 in wages and spends $5,200 per year on daycare for Noah. The maximum that Lori can claim as a dependent care credit is $3,000, even though her actual expenses exceed that amount.

Joint Return Test

The joint return test specifies that married couples who wish to take the credit for child and dependent care must file jointly. However, a married taxpayer can be "considered unmarried" for tax purposes if they qualify for Head of Household filing status.[26] Taxpayers who file separately are not eligible for the Child and Dependent Care credit.

---

[26] In this case, the taxpayer will still be eligible for the Dependent Care Credit if they file as Head of Household. The taxpayer who claims the Dependent Care Credit must be the custodial parent.

Provider Identification Test

Finally, the provider identification test requires that taxpayers provide the name, address, and Taxpayer Identification Number (TIN) of the person or organization who provided the care for the child or dependent. If the daycare provider is an individual, the Social Security Number should be provided. If the care provider is a business or an organization, then the Employer Identification Number (EIN) must be provided. If the provider is a tax-exempt organization (church, school, etc.), it is not necessary to provide identification – a taxpayer may enter "TAX-EXEMPT."

If a daycare provider refuses to supply the taxpayer with identification information such as a Social Security Number, the taxpayer may still claim the credit. She must report whatever information she has about the provider (such as the name and address) and attach a statement to **Form 2441** explaining the provider's refusal to supply the information. Returns that do not include the provider information cannot be filed electronically.

Education Credits

Education credits are for postsecondary education expenses (college). Education credits reduce the amount of tax due. The amount of the credit is based on qualified education expenses the taxpayer paid during the tax year. There are two education credits:

- The American Opportunity Credit and
- The Lifetime Learning Credit

IRS **Form 8863,** *Education Credits (American Opportunity and Lifetime Learning Credits),* is used to claim both of the education credits.

There are general rules that apply to these credits, as well as specific rules for each credit. For example, taxpayers can take education credits for themselves, their spouse, and their dependents who attended an eligible educational institution during the tax year. Eligible educational institutions include colleges, universities, vocational schools, or community colleges. Taxpayers can claim payments that were prepaid for the academic period that begins in the first three months of the next calendar year.

> **Example:** Tom paid $1,500 in December 2010 for college tuition for the spring semester that begins in January 2011. He can use the $1,500 paid in December 2010 to compute his credit for 2010. Tom can deduct the education credit on his 2010 return, even though he won't start college until 2011. Taxpayers who pre-pay qualified expenses for an academic period that begins in the first three months of the following year can use the prepaid amount in figuring the credit.

All of the following conditions will DISQUALIFY a taxpayer from claiming education credits:

- If the taxpayer can be claimed as a dependent on someone else's tax return
- If the taxpayer files as Married Filing Separately
- If the taxpayer's Adjusted Gross Income (AGI) is above the limit for the taxpayer's filing status

- If the taxpayer (or spouse) was a nonresident alien for any part of the tax year[27]

To claim the credit for a dependent's education expenses, the taxpayer must claim the dependent on her return. The taxpayer doesn't necessarily have to pay for all of her dependent's qualified education expenses herself.

In some circumstances, eligible students can claim education credits for themselves even if their parents actually paid the qualified tuition and related expenses. This would be the same as if the parent had given the student a gift. If a taxpayer does not claim an exemption for a dependent who is an eligible student, the student can claim the American Opportunity or Lifetime Learning Credit.

> **Example:** Donna has a 19-year-old son named Trent, who is a full-time college student and her dependent. Trent's grandmother paid his tuition directly to the college. For purposes of claiming an education credit, Donna is treated as receiving the money as a gift and paying for the qualified tuition and related expenses. Since Donna claims Trent as a dependent, she may still claim an education credit. Alternatively, if Trent claims himself on his own return (and his mother does not), he might be able to claim the expenses as if he paid them himself (Publication 970).

If a taxpayer has education expenses for more than one student, he can take the American Opportunity Credit and the Lifetime Learning Credits on a "per student" basis. This means that a taxpayer may claim the American Opportunity Credit for one student and the Lifetime Learning Credit for another student on the same tax return.

> **Example:** Reed pays college expenses for himself and for his dependent daughter, who is 18. Reed qualifies for the Lifetime Learning Credit, and his daughter qualifies for the American Opportunity Credit. He can choose to take both credits on his tax return because he has two eligible students.

Qualified Education Expenses

Qualified education expenses are tuition and certain related expenses required for enrollment or attendance at an eligible educational institution. For tax year 2010, "qualified tuition and related expenses" has been expanded to include the cost of course materials for the American Opportunity Credit. These materials are eligible even if the college does NOT require them to attend the school.

Tuition expenses are reported to the taxpayer on Form 1098-T, *Tuition Statement*, issued by the school.

Non-qualifying Expenses

Qualified tuition and related expenses do not include expenses such as:

- Insurance
- Medical expenses (including insurance and student health fees)

---

[27] In a case when one spouse is a U.S. citizen or a resident alien and the other spouse is a nonresident alien, the taxpayers ELECT to treat the nonresident spouse as a U.S. resident. If the taxpayers make this choice, both spouses are treated as residents for income tax purposes and for withholding purposes.

- Room and board
- Transportation or personal, living, or family expenses

Any course of instruction or other education involving sports, games, or hobbies, is not a qualifying expense *unless* the course is part of the student's degree program.

> **Example:** Eli is a college sophomore who is studying to be a dentist. This year, in addition to tuition, he pays a fee to the university for the rental of the dental equipment he will use in the program. Eli's equipment rental fee is a qualified education expense.

Excluded Amounts

Taxpayers who pay qualified higher education expenses with tax-free funds cannot claim a credit for those amounts. Qualified expenses must be reduced by the amount of any tax-free educational assistance taxpayers receive. The taxpayer must reduce his qualified educational expenses by any of these tax-free educational benefits:

- Pell grants
- Employer-provided educational assistance
- Veteran's educational assistance
- Tax-free portions of scholarships and fellowships
- Any other nontaxable payments received as educational assistance (other than gifts or inheritances)
- Refunds of the year's qualified expenses paid on behalf of a student (e.g., if the student dropped a class and received a refund of tuition)

> **Example:** Faith received Form 1098-T from the college she attends. It shows her tuition was $9,500 and that she received a $1,500 scholarship. She had no other scholarships or non-taxable payments. Her maximum qualifying expenses for the education credit would be $8,000 ($9,500 - $1,500).

> **Example:** In 2010, Jackie paid $3,000 for tuition and $5,000 for room and board at her university. She was also awarded a $2,000 scholarship and a $4,000 student loan. The scholarship is a qualified scholarship that is excludable from Jackie's income—in other words, it is tax-free. For purposes of the education credit, she must first subtract the tax-free scholarship from her tuition (her only qualified expense). A student loan is not considered tax-free educational assistance because it must be paid back—it isn't income, it's a loan. To calculate her education credit, Jackie only had $1,000 in qualified expenses ($3,000 tuition - $2,000 scholarship).

American Opportunity Tax Credit

The American Opportunity Credit allows taxpayers to claim a credit of up to $2,500 based on qualified tuition and related expenses paid for each eligible student. The credit covers 100% of the first $2,000 and 25% of the second $2,000 of eligible expenses *per student*, up to the amount of tax.

Example: Jack is a single father who has two dependent daughters, Vanessa and Jasmine. Vanessa is a freshman in college. Jack paid $4,500 in qualified education expenses for Vanessa in 2010. Jasmine is a senior in college. Jack paid $5,300 in qualified expenses for Jasmine. Jack can claim a $5,000 American Opportunity Tax Credit on his return. This is because Jack is allowed to claim the full credit ($2,500) for each one of his daughters. The credit is calculated as 100% of the first $2,000 in expenses, and 25% of the second $2,000 of eligible expenses.

Forty percent of the American Opportunity Credit is now a refundable credit, which means the taxpayer can receive up to $1,000 even if no taxes are owed. The American Opportunity Credit is available for the first four years of college per eligible student (generally, freshman through senior years). Graduate school programs do not qualify. Under the current law, the American Opportunity tax Credit only applies for amounts paid in 2010.

Example: Toby had receipts for books and supplies his first year at college. He spent $1,291 for books, lab supplies, and equipment he needed for his introductory chemistry and geology courses. The school does not require that these books and equipment be purchased from the college in order to enroll. Regardless, these are qualified expenses for the American Opportunity Credit under a modification of the rules in 2010.

To be eligible for the American Opportunity Credit, the student must meet these basic requirements during the 2010 time period:

- Be enrolled in a program that leads to a degree, certificate, or other recognized educational credential
- Be enrolled at least half time for at least one academic period
- Be enrolled as a student in the first four years of college only
- Have no felony conviction for possessing or distributing a controlled substance

The credit phases out for married couples filing joint returns with income between $160,000-$180,000 and for Single filers with income between $80,000-$90,000. Couples with income above $180,000 and Single filers with income above $90,000 do not qualify for the credit.

If the student doesn't meet all of the conditions for the American Opportunity Credit, the taxpayer may still be able to take the Lifetime Learning Credit instead.

Lifetime Learning Credit

The Lifetime Learning Credit is not based on a student's workload. It is allowed for one or more courses, even if the student is not a degree candidate. Unlike the American Opportunity Credit, a taxpayer may claim the Lifetime Learning Credit for courses at any postsecondary school, regardless of the number of years she has attended in the past. This credit can be claimed an unlimited number of years, regardless of the number of courses taken, student workload, and educational goals. It is eligible for students who are merely acquiring or improving their existing job skills.

The Lifetime Learning Credit can be up to $2,000 per tax return (not per student!), depending on the amount of eligible expenses and the amount of tax liability. The credit is

20% of the first $10,000 of eligible expenses paid for all students, up to the amount of tax on the return. The Lifetime Learning Credit is not refundable. Books and other course materials are only eligible expenses if they are required by the college as a condition of enrollment or attendance.

The taxpayer can take the Lifetime Learning Credit even if the student is not enrolled at least half-time. The student does not have to be in a degree program, and a felony drug conviction does not disqualify the student.

Example: Colleen spent three months in prison for a felony cocaine conviction. She now attends Creek Community College, an eligible education institution. She paid $4,400 for the course of study, which included tuition, equipment, and books required for the course. The school requires that students pay for the books and equipment when registering for the course. The entire $4,400 is an eligible educational expense under the Lifetime Learning Credit. Colleen does not qualify for the American Opportunity Credit because she has a drug conviction.

Example: Zoe, a designer, enrolls in an advanced photography course at a local community college. Although the course is not part of a degree program, she enrolls in it to improve her job skills. The course fee she pays is considered qualified tuition for the purpose of claiming the lifetime learning credit.

Example: Lai works full-time and takes one course a month at night school. Some of the courses are not for credit, but she is taking them to advance her career. The education expenses qualify for the Lifetime Learning Credit, but not the American Opportunity Credit.

For 2010, the phase-out for Single is between $50,000-$60,000. For joint filers, the phase-out is $99,999-$120,000 or more (no credit is allowed). All education tax credits are claimed on **Form 8863**.

Foreign Tax Credit

This credit applies to taxpayers who have paid foreign taxes to a foreign country on foreign-sourced income and are subject to U.S. tax on the same income. U.S. citizens and residents compute their U.S. taxes based on their worldwide income. This sometimes results in U.S. citizens having to pay tax twice on the same income: once to the U.S. government and once to the government of the foreign country where the income was sourced.

The Foreign Tax Credit was created to help taxpayers avoid this double taxation. It allows taxpayers to take a credit for taxes paid to a foreign government.

U.S. citizens and resident aliens are eligible for the Foreign Tax Credit (FTC). Non-resident aliens are not eligible for the credit. Foreign tax paid is reported by the financial institution to taxpayers on Form 1099-INT or Form 1099-DIV.

There are two ways to claim the Foreign Tax Credit. If the total foreign tax paid does not exceed $300 (or $600 for filing status MFJ), taxpayers may claim the credit directly on Form 1040. Besides the dollar limitations, all of the foreign source income must be "passive category income" (which includes most interest and dividends) and reported on a qualified payee statement. A qualified payee statement includes Form 1099-INT, Form 1099-DIV, Schedule K-1 (for Forms 1041, 1065, 1065-B, 1120S), or similar substitute statement.[28]

If the tax paid exceeds $300 (or $600 for MFJ), then taxpayers must file **Form 1116, Foreign Tax Credit**.

Example: Bronson, who is single, owns a number of foreign stocks. In 2010, Bronson received a 2010 Form 1099-DIV that shows $279 of foreign taxes paid. Bronson paid no other foreign taxes. He is eligible to claim the $279 Foreign Tax Credit on Form 1040, and does not have to complete Form 1116.

Example: Yusuf and Fatima are married and will file jointly. Their Form 1099-DIV shows a foreign tax paid of $590. The couple is not required to complete Form 1116, because their foreign taxes are less than $600.

Example: Dacia is a shareholder of a French corporation. She receives $300 in earnings from the corporation. The French government imposes a 10% tax ($30) on Dacia's earnings. She must include the gross earnings ($300) in her income. The $30 of tax withheld is a qualified foreign tax for the purposes of the foreign tax credit.

In most cases, it is to the taxpayer's advantage to take the Foreign Tax Credit. However, taxpayers have the option to itemize foreign taxes as "Other Taxes" on Schedule A. They may choose either the deduction OR the credit, whichever gives them the lowest tax, for all foreign taxes paid. Taxpayers cannot claim both the deduction and a tax credit on the same return. However, a taxpayer may "alternate" years, taking a credit in one year and a deduction in the next year.

The taxpayer may even change her credit to a deduction and vice versa by amending her tax return. This credit is nonrefundable, so it can drop tax liability to zero, but not below that.

Non-Qualifying Expenses for the Foreign Tax Credit

The following expenses do not qualify for the Foreign Tax Credit. However, some may still qualify for the foreign tax deduction (covered under the unit for itemized deductions):

- Any taxes that the taxpayer does not legally owe or that would be refunded by the foreign nation if the taxpayer filed a claim
- Any taxes on already-excluded income (such as the Foreign Earned Income Exclusion)
- Taxes on foreign oil or gas extraction income

---

[28]This election is not available to estates or trusts.

- Taxes from international boycott operations
- Taxes of U.S. persons controlling foreign corporations or partnerships
- Taxes imposed by sanctioned foreign countries or countries that are involved with international terrorism (Cuba, the Sudan, North Korea— if interested, you can see a full list of excluded nations in Publication 514)
- Interest or penalties paid to a foreign country

The Foreign Tax Credit is a nonrefundable credit, and the taxpayer is allowed a one-year carryback and a ten-year carry-forward of any unused credit.

Taxpayers may not claim a tax credit for taxes paid on any income that has already been excluded from income using the Foreign Earned Income Exclusion or the Foreign Housing Exclusion.

Do not confuse the Foreign Tax Credit and the Foreign Earned Income Exclusion! The Foreign Earned Income Exclusion is completely different from the Foreign Tax Credit. The Foreign Earned Income Exclusion applies to income that is earned while a taxpayer is living and working overseas. The Foreign Tax Credit applies to any type of foreign earned income, including investments.

The Child Tax Credit and the Additional Child Tax Credit

The Child Tax Credit is unique because it has two components: a nonrefundable credit and a refundable credit. Taxpayers who cannot benefit from the *nonrefundable* credit may be able to qualify for the *refundable* "Additional Child Tax Credit."

- **Child Tax Credit:** This is a *nonrefundable* credit that allows taxpayers to claim a tax credit of up to $1,000 per qualifying child, which reduces their tax liability. Taxpayers whose tax liability is zero cannot take the Child Tax Credit because there is no tax to reduce. However, a taxpayer may be able to take the Additional Child Tax Credit, which is refundable, even if his tax liability is zero.
- **Additional Child Tax Credit:** This is a refundable credit that may result in a refund even if the taxpayer doesn't owe any tax. The Additional Child Tax Credit is claimed on **Form 8812**, *Additional Child Tax Credit*. Taxpayers who claim the Additional Child Tax Credit must claim the Child Tax Credit as well, even if they do not qualify for the full amount.

Both credits are very similar, but they are both considered separate credits. The Child Tax Credit is claimed directly on Form 1040. It cannot be claimed on Form 1040EZ.

The maximum amount taxpayers may claim for the nonrefundable Child Tax Credit is $1,000 for each qualifying child. The amount actually claimed on Form 1040 depends on the taxpayer's tax liability, Modified Adjusted Gross Income (MAGI), and filing status. The amount of the credit may be reduced if the taxpayer's MAGI is above the threshold amounts shown below based on the following filing statuses:

- Married Filing Jointly - $110,000
- Single, Head of Household, or Qualifying Widow(er) - $75,000
- Married Filing Separately - $55,000

The credit is phased out incrementally as the taxpayer's income increases. The credit is reduced by $50 for each $1,000 of Modified Adjusted Gross Income that exceeds the threshold amounts listed above.

> **Example**: Cordell and Roxana file jointly and have two children who qualify for the Child Tax Credit. Their MAGI is $86,000 and their tax liability is $954. Even though their AGI is less than the threshold limit of $110,000, they can only claim $954, reducing their tax to zero. Because Cordell and Roxana cannot claim the maximum Child Tax Credit, they may still be eligible for the Additional Child Tax Credit.

> **Example:** Stan files as Head of Household and has three children who qualify for purposes of the Child Tax Credit. Stan's MAGI is $54,000 and his tax liability is $4,680. Stan is eligible to take the full credit of $1,000 per child ($3,000) because his MAGI is less than $75,000 and his tax liability is greater than $3,000.

Definition of a Qualifying Child for the Child Tax Credit

To be eligible to claim the Child Tax Credit, the taxpayer must have at least one qualifying child. To qualify, the child must:

- Be claimed as the taxpayer's dependent
- Meet the relationship test: must be the son, daughter, adopted child, stepchild, foster child, brother, sister, stepbrother, stepsister, or a descendant of any of them (for example, a grandchild, niece, or nephew).
- Meet the age criteria: *under* the age of 17 at the end of the year.
- Not have provided over half of his or her own support
- Have lived with the taxpayer for more than six months of the tax year (there are special rules for divorced, separated, or unmarried parents)[29]
- Be a U.S. citizen, U.S. national, or resident of the U.S. (being a resident of Canada or Mexico does not qualify). Foreign-born adopted children will still qualify if they lived with the taxpayer *all year*, even if the adoption is not yet final.
- The taxpayer cannot file a Form 2555 (relating to foreign earned income)

> **Example:** Ed's son Jeff turned 17 on December 30, 2010. He is a citizen of the United States and has a valid SSN. According to the Child Tax Credit rules, he is not a qualifying child because he was not under the age of 17 at the end of 2010.

---

[29] There are special rules for children of divorced or separated parents, as well as children of parents who never married. In most cases the custodial parent will claim the dependency exemption for a qualifying child. The noncustodial parent, however, may be entitled to claim the dependency exemption for a child and thus the Child Tax Credit and Additional Child Tax Credit. A custodial parent's release of the dependency exemption will also release the Child Tax Credit and the Additional Child Tax Credit, if either applies, to the noncustodial parent. Noncustodial parents must attach **Form 8332** to their return each year the exemption is claimed.

> **Example:** Laura's adopted son Nash is 12. He is a citizen of the United States and lived with Laura for the entire tax year. Laura provided all of her son's support. Nash is a qualifying child for the Child Tax Credit because he was under the age of 17 at the end of the tax year; he meets the relationship requirement; he lived with Laura for at least six months of the year; and Laura provided his complete support.

*Note: Do not confuse the Child Tax Credit with the Child and Dependent Care Tax Credit!

Additional Child Tax Credit

The Additional Child Tax Credit is for certain individuals who do not qualify for the full amount of the nonrefundable Child Tax Credit. The Additional Child Tax Credit is *refundable*, so it can produce a refund, even if the taxpayer does not owe any tax.

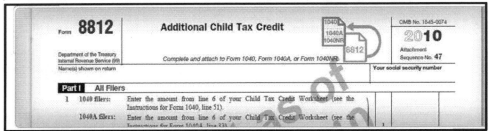

Like the Child Tax Credit, the Additional Child Tax Credit allows eligible taxpayers to claim up to $1,000 for each qualifying child after subtracting the allowable amount of Child Tax Credit. For taxpayers with earned income over $3,000, the credit is based on the lesser of:

- 15% of the taxpayer's taxable earned income that is more than $3,000 or
- The amount of unused child tax credit (caused when tax liability is less than allowed credit)

> **Example**: May and Dmitri have two qualifying children, a MAGI of $66,000, and a tax liability of $850. Because their tax liability is less than the full amount of the Child Tax Credit, they may be able to take the Additional Child Tax Credit of up to $1,150 ($2,000 - $850). Since the Additional Child Tax Credit is refundable, it will produce a refund of $1,150, even when a taxpayer doesn't owe any tax.

Nontaxable combat pay counts as earned income for calculating the Additional Child Tax Credit.

Adoption Credit

In 2010, a maximum credit of up to $13,170 can be taken for qualified expenses paid to adopt a child. For a special needs child, the credit is allowed even if the taxpayer *does not have* any adoption expenses. In order to take the credit, **Form 8839**, *Qualified Adoption Expenses*, must be attached to the taxpayer's Form 1040. There is a new documentation requirement in 2010, and the taxpayer is required to submit the final adoption paperwork, along with the date that the adoption was finalized. The forms cannot be e-filed, and a tax return claiming the adoption credit must be mailed along with the required paperwork.

The Adoption Credit phases out ratably between $182,520 and $222,520. A taxpayer cannot claim the Adoption Credit if AGI is over $222,520. The phase-out ranges are the same for all taxpayers. There is not a separate phase out for single or MFS filers. The Adoption Credit is now a fully refundable credit.

"Qualified" adoption expenses are directly related to the adoption of a child. These include:

- Adoption fees
- Court costs
- Attorney fees
- Travel expenses related to the adoption
- Re-adoption expenses to adopt a foreign child

Qualified adoption expenses DO NOT include:

- Illegal adoption expenses
- A surrogate parenting arrangement
- The adoption of a spouse's child
- Any amounts that were reimbursed by an employer or any other organization

An "eligible child" for the purposes of the credit is:

- Under 18 years old, or
- Disabled (of any age)

Until the adoption becomes final, the taxpayer may take the credit in the year *after* expenses were paid. Once the adoption becomes final, a taxpayer can take the credit in the year the expenses were paid.

Foreign Adoptions: Special Rules

If the adoption is for a foreign child, then the taxpayer may only take the credit in the year the adoption becomes final. The Adoption Credit cannot be taken for a child who is not a United States citizen or legal U.S. resident (green card holder) until the adoption becomes final. Any expenses paid in the year after the foreign adoption is finalized can be taken in the year they were paid.

Example: Jude and Jada adopt a baby from China. They have $3,000 in adoption expenses in 2009 and $7,000 in adoption expenses in 2010. The adoption becomes final in November 2010. They may take the Adoption Credit in 2010 for the combined expenses from 2009 and 2010 ($10,000 in total adoption expenses).

The Adoption Credit is not available for any expenses that were already reimbursed by an employer.

Special Needs Children: Special Rules

In the case of an adoption of a "special needs" child, the taxpayer may claim the full Adoption Credit regardless of actual expenses paid or incurred. A child has special needs if

- The child otherwise meets the definition of eligible child,
- The child is a United States citizen or resident,

- o   A state determines that the child cannot or should not be returned to his or her parent's home, and
- o   A state determines that the child probably will not be adopted unless assistance is provided.

The credit and exclusion for qualifying adoption expenses are each subject to a dollar limit and an income limit.

Employer-Provided Adoption Assistance

Amounts reimbursed by an employer as part of a qualified benefit arrangement may be excludable from gross income. If a taxpayer has enough qualifying expenses and can take both the adoption credit and an exclusion, this dollar amount applies separately to each.

> **Example:** Kara adopted a baby in 2010. She paid $15,500 in adoption expenses. Kara's employer paid $4,000 of her qualifying adoption expenses under an employer-provided adoption assistance plan. Kara may claim an Adoption Credit of $11,500 ($15,500 - $4,000) and also exclude the $4,000 of adoption assistance from her employer.

Making Work Pay Credit

The Making Work Pay credit is for those who earned income from a job, equal to the lesser of 6.2% of earned income or $400 ($800 if MFJ). 2010 is the final year for this refundable credit. A taxpayer cannot claim this credit if:

- Modified Adjusted Gross Income is $95,000 ($190,000 if MFJ) or more,
- If the taxpayer is a nonresident alien, or
- Can be claimed as a dependent on someone else's return

In order to qualify for the credit, the taxpayer must have a valid Social Security Number. Pensioners (those who receive pension or annuity income) do not qualify for the Making Work Pay credit, unless they also receive earned income. The credit is claimed on Schedule M (Form 1040A or 1040). Taxpayers who file Form 1040-EZ can use a worksheet and claim the credit directly on their return. Many working taxpayers are eligible for the Making Work Pay Tax Credit in 2010. Most workers received the benefit of the Making Work Pay Credit through larger paychecks, reflecting reduced federal income tax withholding during 2010.

Earned Income Tax Credit

(*Tested very frequently. Make sure you understand the details of the EITC)

The Earned Income Tax Credit (EITC or EIC) is the most frequently tested credit on the EA Exam. It is tested on both Part 1 and Part 3 (as part of due diligence requirements). EITC is a fully refundable federal income tax credit for low-income individuals. EITC is increased for taxpayers who have a qualifying child. This means that the EITC may give the taxpayer a refund, even if he doesn't owe any tax. The EITC is claimed on Schedule EIC, *Earned Income Credit*. This must be attached to the taxpayer's Form 1040. The EITC may not be claimed on Form 1040-EZ.

266

Advance EITC (AEITC)

Advance EITC allowed taxpayers to receive part of the Earned Income Credit in each paycheck. This "advance" credit is sometimes called the AEITC. Congress repealed the Advance EITC in 2010 so after December 31, 2010, workers will no longer receive Advance EITC in their paychecks. However, there are still taxpayers who received Advance EITC in 2010, which means it may be tested on this year's exam. The maximum Advance EITC workers could receive from their employers in 2010 was $1,830.

Any taxpayer who received Advance EITC in 2010 is *required* to file a tax return, regardless of his income amount.

Rules for Qualifying for the Earned Income Credit

There are very strict rules and income guidelines for the EITC. A taxpayer must have *earned* income in order to qualify for the EITC. Investment income does not qualify. In fact, investment income must not exceed $3,100 in 2010, or it will disqualify the taxpayer from claiming the EITC.

To claim the EITC, the taxpayer must meet ALL of the following tests:

- Must have a valid Social Security Number (an ITIN or ATIN is not valid for EITC). Any qualifying child must also have a valid SSN.
- Must have earned income from wages or self-employment (nontaxable combat pay qualifies.)
- Filing status cannot be MFS.
- Must be a U.S. citizen or legal resident all year (or a nonresident alien married to a U.S. citizen or resident alien filing MFJ).
- Cannot be a dependent of another taxpayer.

Qualifying Income for EITC

Only earned income (such as wages) qualifies for the EITC. Examples of non-qualifying income for the EITC include interest and dividends, pensions and annuities, Social Security and railroad retirement benefits, alimony, welfare benefits, workers' compensation benefits, unemployment compensation, and veterans' benefits.

However, military personnel can elect to include their nontaxable combat pay in earned income for the purposes of qualifying for the EITC. Qualifying "earned income" also includes:

- Tips
- Union strike benefits
- Long-term disability benefits received prior to minimum retirement age
- Net earnings from self-employment

Inmate wages do NOT qualify as earned income when figuring the Earned Income Credit. This includes amounts for work performed while in a prison work release program or in a halfway house.

Taxpayers Without a Qualifying Child

Low-income taxpayers without children may still qualify for the EITC in certain cases, but the rules are stricter and the amount of the credit is less. Any taxpayer with a qualifying child may claim the EITC without any age limitations, but a taxpayer *without* a child can only claim the EITC if all of the following tests are met:

- Must be at least age 25 but under 65 at the end of the year,
- Must live in the United States for more than half the year, and
- Must not qualify as a dependent of another person
- Cannot file Form 2555 (related to foreign earned income)

EITC Thresholds and Limitations

In 2009, the EITC increased for taxpayers who had a third qualifying child. The rules also changed for how to determine a "qualifying child" for the EITC. Adjusted Gross Income (AGI) thresholds are as follows:

EITC 2010 Tax Year

Adjusted Gross Income (AGI) must not exceed:

- $43,352 ($48,362 MFJ) with three (or more) qualifying children
- $40,363 ($45,373 MFJ) with two qualifying children
- $35,535 ($40,545 MFJ) with one qualifying child
- $13,460 ($18,470 MFJ) with no children

The maximum credit amount for tax year 2010:

- $5,666 with three or more qualifying children
- $5,036 with two qualifying children
- $3,050 with one qualifying child
- $457 with no qualifying children

Example: Graham is single and his AGI is $37,000. He has one qualifying child. Graham cannot claim the EITC because his AGI exceeds the income threshold for single filers ($35,535).

Four "Qualifying Child" Tests for the EITC

The definition of a "qualifying child" for the purposes of the EITC is different than the definition of a qualifying child for dependency. In order to qualify for the EITC, the taxpayer's qualifying child must meet the following four tests:

1. Relationship Test
2. Age Test
3. Residency Test
4. Joint Return Test

Relationship Test

There is a strict "relationship test" for the EITC. The child must be related to the taxpayer in the following ways:

- Son, daughter, stepchild, eligible foster child, adopted child, or a descendant of any of them (for example, a grandchild), or
- Brother, sister, half-brother, half-sister, stepbrother, stepsister, or a descendant of any of them (for example, a niece or nephew).

An adopted child is always treated as a taxpayer's own child. An "eligible foster child" must be placed in the taxpayer's home by an authorized placement agency or by court order.

In the case of a foreign adoption, special rules apply. To claim the EITC, the taxpayer must have a valid SSN. Any qualifying child listed on Schedule EIC *also* must have a valid SSN. An ATIN number is not sufficient for the purposes of the EIC. However, the taxpayer can elect to amend the tax return once an SSN is granted and the adoption is final.

> **Example:** Rusty is 31 and takes care of his younger sister Tiffany, who is 16. He has taken care of her since their parents died five years ago. Tiffany is Rusty's qualifying child for the purposes of the EITC.

Age Test for EITC

In order to qualify for the EITC, the child must meet the "age test." The child must be:
- Age 18 or younger, OR
- A full-time student, age 23 or younger, OR
- Any age, if permanently disabled

In addition, the qualifying child must be younger than the taxpayer claiming him (unless the child or person is permanently disabled).

> **Example:** Garth is 45 and supports his older brother Andy, who is 56. Andy lives with Garth and is profoundly retarded and permanently disabled. In this case, Andy meets the criteria to be Garth's "qualifying child" for the purposes of the EITC.

Residency Test and Joint Return Test

The qualifying child (dependent) may not file a joint return with a spouse, except to claim a refund.

> **Example:** Margaret's 18-year-old son and his 18-year-old wife had $800 of interest income and no other income. Neither is required to file a tax return. Taxes were taken out of their interest income due to backup withholding, so they file a joint return only to get a refund of the withheld taxes. The exception to the Joint Return Test applies, so Margaret's son may still be her qualifying child if all the other tests are met.

The child must have lived with the taxpayer in the United States for more than half of 2010 (this does not apply to newborn infants or temporary absences). U.S. military personnel stationed outside the United States are considered to meet the residency test for purposes of the EITC.

A child who was born or died in 2010 meets the residency test for all of 2010 if the child lived with the taxpayer the entire time he or she was alive in 2010.

> **Example:** Eleanor gave birth to a baby boy in March 2010. The infant died one month later. The child would still be a qualifying child for the purposes of the EITC because he meets the other tests for age and relationship.

First-Time Homebuyer Credit

The 2010 tax year is the last year that taxpayers can claim the First-Time Home-buyer Credit, as the rules and thresholds have changed. This credit only applies to homes purchased in the United States before May 1, 2010. No credit is allowed for a home bought after April 30, 2010 (after September 30, 2010, if a taxpayer entered into a written binding contract before May 1, 2010). The credit amount is the smaller of:

- $8,000 ($4,000 if Married Filing Separately), or
- 10% of the purchase price of the home.

In order to qualify as a "first-time homebuyer," the taxpayer must not have purchased a primary residence in the previous three years before the purchase of the home. The credit is fully refundable, meaning the credit will be paid out to eligible taxpayers even if they owe no tax.

If the taxpayer is married, both must be "first-time homebuyers" in order to take the credit. However, if two unmarried people purchase a home together and they later marry, the qualifying rules apply at the date of purchase.

If Taxpayer A (a first-time homebuyer) buys a house and then later that year marries Taxpayer B (not a first-time homebuyer), the credit is still allowed to Taxpayer A. Taxpayer A may take the maximum credit.

> **Example:** Malik and Eve were married in February 2010 and purchased a home together on March 1, 2010. Malik had not previously owned a home. Eve owned a home with her ex-husband two years ago. She does not qualify as a first-time homebuyer. Therefore, Malik and Eve do not qualify to take the First-Time Homebuyer Credit on their 2010 tax return.

> **Example:** Liam qualifies as a first-time homebuyer. On January 10, 2010, he buys a house. Liam has a girlfriend named Brooke. Brooke does not qualify as a first-time homebuyer. Liam and Brooke get married on September 30, 2010. Liam may still take the full amount of the First-Time Homebuyer Credit because the credit is determined on the date of purchase, not on the date of their marriage.

> **Example:** Darlene is a single first-time homebuyer, but she cannot qualify to purchase a home on her own. Darlene's father Alec co-signs on Darlene's loan. Alec does not qualify for the credit. Both names are on the mortgage. Darlene may claim the entire credit ($8,000 for purchase in 2010). Alec may not take the credit on his tax return.

Long-Time Homeowners

Changes to the law on November 9, 2009 authorized the Homebuyer Credit for long-time homeowners who purchased a replacement principal residence. For the first time, long-time homeowners who bought a replacement principal residence could also claim a homebuyer credit of up to $6,500 (up to $3,250 for MFS). They must have lived in the same principal residence for any five consecutive year period during the eight-year period that ended on the date the replacement home was purchased.

For the purpose of the Long-Time Homebuyer Credit, the taxpayer must have bought or entered into a binding contract on or before April 30, 2010 and closed on the home by June 30, 2010. For qualifying purchases in 2010, taxpayers have the option of claiming the credit on either their 2009 or 2010 return.

Members of the military serving outside the U.S. have an extra year to buy a principal residence in the U.S. and still qualify for the credit. Only one spouse must be overseas on official extended duty for either spouse to be eligible for the 2011 extension of time to purchase a principal residence and claim the credit.

Phase Out for the FTHB

A taxpayer is allowed the full credit if MAGI is $125,000 or less ($225,000 or less if Married Filing Jointly). The phase-out ranges for the credit:

- MFJ: $225,000 to $245,000
- Single, HOH, or QW: $125,000 to $145,000

Non-Qualifying Home Purchases

The following taxpayers do NOT qualify for the First-Time Homebuyer Credit:

- A homebuyer whose purchase was financed by tax-exempt mortgage revenue bonds
- Nonresident aliens do not qualify
- A homebuyer who disposes of the residence (or it ceases to be the taxpayer's principal residence) before the end of the year
- A homebuyer who acquires the home by gift or inheritance
- A homebuyer who acquires the home from a related person (this includes spouses, ancestors, and descendants, but excludes siblings)

The First-Time Homebuyer Credit is claimed on IRS **Form 5405** First-Time Homebuyer Credit.

The Saver's Credit (Retirement Savings Contributions Credit)

The Saver's Credit (previously called the Retirement Savings Contributions Credit) is a nonrefundable credit that taxpayers may claim if they made a contribution to a retirement plan. If the contribution is tax deferred, the taxpayer obtains the benefit of the tax deferral and a credit against their taxes; for example, a taxpayer may be able to claim this credit *as well as* a deduction for an IRA contribution. Such a "double" benefit is rarely allowed.

Eligibility for this credit is affected by Adjusted Gross Income, filing status, age, whether the taxpayer can be claimed as a dependent, and whether the taxpayer is a full-time student. For 2010, taxpayers cannot claim the Saver's Credit if their modified AGI exceeds:

- $55,500 for Married Filing Jointly
- $41,625 for Head of Household
- $27,750 for Single, Married Filing Separately, or Qualifying Widow(er)

271

> **Example:** Truman is 24 and earned $29,000 during the year. He is single and contributed $3,000 to his 401(k) plan at work. Truman is not eligible for the credit because his income exceeds the threshold limit of $27,750 (Publication 590).

Factors that Reduce the Eligible Credit

Even if taxpayers qualify for the credit, their eligible contributions will be reduced by certain distributions received during the "testing period." The testing period includes:

- The tax year,
- The two preceding tax years, and
- The period between the end of the tax year and the due date of the return, including extensions.

The types of distributions that reduce the eligible contributions include any distribution that is:

- Included in the taxpayer's gross income from a qualified retirement plan or from an eligible deferred compensation plan
- From a Roth IRA (does not include a qualified rollover contribution)

> **Example:** Luther is 28 years old. He is single, has an AGI of $25,000, and has contributed $1,500 to a 401(k) during the tax year. He has not received any distributions during the tax year or the two prior years.

If either spouse has a distribution during the testing period, *both* spouses must reduce their eligible contribution by that amount.

The credit is 10%-50% of eligible contributions up to $1,000 ($2,000 for MFJ). The credit is figured on **Form 8880**, *Credit for Qualified Retirement Savings Contributions*.

Residential Energy Credits

Taxpayers who purchase certain qualified energy-efficient improvements for their main home may be allowed a nonrefundable tax credit. There are two types of residential energy credits:

- Non-Business Energy Property Credit
- Residential Energy-Efficient Property Credit

These credits may *sound* similar, but the qualifying property and threshold amounts are different for each.

Non-Business Energy Property Credit

Taxpayers may be able to claim a credit of 30% of the cost of certain energy-efficient items placed in service in 2010. They must be installed in the taxpayer's primary residence in order to qualify. There are no income limits, so any taxpayer can claim the credit, regardless of his income thresholds.

Items can include energy-efficient windows, doors, insulation materials, and certain metal or asphalt roofs. Taxpayers cannot include the cost of installation for these items. Non-business energy items also include high-efficiency heat pumps, air conditioners, water heaters, and stoves that burn biomass fuel. Amounts paid for these *specific* items *can* include the cost of on-site preparation and installation.

The credit is limited to a total of $1,500 for tax years 2009 and 2010. This credit has a look-back provision, so if the taxpayer claimed a $1,000 credit in 2009, the taxpayer may only claim up to a $500 credit in 2010. The credit is calculated on **Form 5695**, *Residential Energy Credits*.

The Non-Business Energy Property Credit is a nonrefundable credit that reduces a taxpayer's tax liability. If the taxpayer has no tax liability, then she cannot use the credit and it is not carried over to the next year.

Example: Fletcher installed energy-efficient insulation in 2009 for a cost of $1,000. His Non-Business Energy Property Credit in 2009 was $300 ($1,000 X 30%). In 2010, he installed energy-efficient windows at a cost of $7,000. Because the maximum credit is $1,500 over two years, Fletcher's credit in 2010 will be reduced. His maximum credit in 2010 will be $1,200 ($7,000 X 30% = $2,100, limited to $1,500). Since Fletcher already claimed a $300 credit in 2009, the maximum he can claim in 2010 is $1,200 ($1,500-$300).

Residential Energy-Efficient Property Credit

This residential energy credit is also claimed on **Form 5695**, (Part II of the form). In the case of the Residential Energy Efficient Property Credit, NO CAP exists on the amount of credit that can be claimed by the taxpayer (except in the case of fuel cell property). The credit is only available for the following property:

- Solar electric property
- Solar water heating property costs
- Small wind energy property costs
- Geothermal heat pump property costs.
- Fuel cells (principal residence only)

This credit is also different because it applies to items installed at a principal residence *or* a second home (but does not apply to rental property). The residence must be in the United States. Also, the credit for fuel cells is only applicable to the taxpayer's primary residence. The maximum credit is 30% of qualifying costs. The credit may be applied to labor costs, assembly and installation, and any wiring that is needed to install the energy-efficient item in the home. No credit is allowed for equipment that is used to heat swimming pools or hot tubs.

The taxpayer must reduce his basis in the property by the amount of the credit. This credit is not refundable, but unused amounts can be carried over to the following year.

The item installed must be new and not used. This credit is not limited by Alternative Minimum Tax (AMT).

Credit for the Elderly or the Disabled

The Credit for the Elderly or the Disabled is calculated on **Schedule R** and reported on Form 1040 or Form 1040A. The credit applies only to elderly persons or disabled taxpayers. It is a nonrefundable tax credit that has such strict income limitations that tax practitioners rarely see anyone who qualifies for it. The EA Exam does not test this credit very often, but you should know that it exists, and the basic qualifications for the credit. In order to qualify for this credit, individuals must be:

- Age 65 or older OR
- Retired on permanent disability, receiving taxable disability income, and have not reached the mandatory retirement age[30]

A taxpayer with a permanent disability is defined as "unable to engage in substantial, gainful activity," (in other words, the taxpayer is unable to work). Working in a sheltered workshop setting,[31] however, is not considered substantial, gainful activity, and will not disqualify the taxpayer from claiming the credit.

> **Example:** Jeannie, 49, is on disability from her job as a construction worker. She now works as a full-time babysitter at minimum wage. Although Jeannie's disability forced her to retire from her previous job, she now works full-time. She cannot take the credit because she is engaged in a substantial, gainful activity.

Generally, disability income comes from an employer's disability insurance or pension plan. The disability payments replace wages.

Income Limits for the Credit for the Elderly or the Disabled

In addition to being a qualified individual, the taxpayer's total income must be within the following limits:

Taxpayers CANNOT take the credit IF filing status is:	AND AGI is equal to or exceeds:	OR nontaxable Social Security is equal to or more than:
S, HOH, or QW	$17,500	$5,000
MFJ and both spouses qualify	$25,000	$7,500
MFJ and only one spouse qualifies	$20,000	$5,000
MFS (did not live with spouse at any time during the year)	$12,500	$3,750

> **Example:** Cornelius is 67 years old and single. He received $12,000 in nontaxable Social Security benefits in the tax year. His AGI is $9,000. Even though Cornelius is a qualified individual, he is not eligible to claim the credit since his nontaxable Social Security benefits exceed $5,000.

Few taxpayers qualify for this credit because the income calculation includes the taxpayer's non-taxable Social Security and veterans' benefits, or other excludable pension, annuity, or disability benefits. Most taxpayers' Social Security benefits alone exceed the limit.

The Alternative Motor Vehicle Credit

This is a credit for alternative motor vehicles, such as qualified hybrid or advanced lean-burn technology vehicles. Taxpayers must use **Form 8910**, *Alternative Motor Vehicle Credit,* to claim this credit.

---

[30]Mandatory retirement age is the age set by a taxpayer's employer at which the taxpayer would have been required to retire, had the taxpayer not become disabled.

[31] A "sheltered workshop" is a workplace that provides an environment where physically or mentally challenged persons can acquire job skills and vocational experience.

Taxpayers may qualify for the Alternative Motor Vehicle Credit when they purchase a new hybrid vehicle. Used vehicles do not qualify. The credit varies based on the model and type of car. A taxpayer receives certification from the manufacturer indicating the credit amount. In order to qualify, the vehicle must be one of the four types listed below:

- Qualified hybrid vehicle
- Advanced lean burn technology vehicle
- Qualified alternative fuel vehicle
- Qualified fuel cell vehicle

Although used cars do not qualify for the credit, taxpayers may convert an existing vehicle to a qualified plug-in electric vehicle and take the credit based on the conversion. The credit for converting a vehicle to a qualified plug-in electric drive vehicle is the smaller of:

- $4,000, or
- 10% of the cost of the conversion.

Example: Becky converts her existing vehicle to a qualified plug-in electric vehicle on March 1, 2010. The cost of the conversion is $19,500. Becky's credit amount is $1,950 ($19,500 X 10% = $1,950).

Credit for Prior Year Alternative Minimum Tax (AMT)

The Alternative Minimum Tax, or AMT, is a separately figured tax that eliminates many deductions and credits, thus increasing tax liability. The AMT was originally adopted in order to prevent high income taxpayers from using elaborate deductions to reduce their income tax to zero. The AMT was designed to ensure that high income taxpayers pay at least a minimum amount of tax.

There is a special credit for prior-year minimum tax paid. This is because, with AMT, the taxpayer would be forced to pay taxes twice on the same items of income. A taxpayer can get a tax credit for Alternative Minimum Tax paid in a prior year. This credit is calculated on **Form 8801**, *Credit for Prior Year Minimum Tax.*

Mortgage Interest Credit

(*Not frequently tested) Taxpayers who hold qualified Mortgage Credit Certificates under a qualified state or local government program may claim a nonrefundable credit for mortgage interest paid. The credit is for homeowners who purchase low-income housing and was designed to help low-income individuals afford housing.

The credit only applies to taxpayers who are issued a Mortgage Credit Certificate (MCC) by their local or state government. The MCC will show the rate the taxpayer must use to figure his credit. Taxpayers use **Form 8396**, *Mortgage Interest Credit*, to calculate the amount of the credit.

Credit for Excess Social Security or Railroad Retirement Tax Withheld

This is a credit for workers who overpay their Social Security tax during the tax year. It usually happens when an employee is working two jobs and both employers withhold Social Security tax. If a taxpayer works for more than one employer during the year, each employer is required to withhold Social Security (or RRTA taxes). If the taxpayer's withholding for Social Security tax exceeds the annual maximum, he can request a refund of the excess amount. Social Security tax and Railroad Retirement Tax are both withheld at a rate of 6.2% of wages.

The maximum wage subject to Social Security taxes is $106,800 in 2010. If only one employer withheld too much Social Security or RRTA tax, the taxpayer must ask the employer to correct the error. The taxpayer cannot claim the excess as a credit against her income tax.

Example: Felix worked for two employers in 2010. He first worked for Tinkle Technology Co., where he earned $60,000. His employer correctly withheld Social Security tax of $3,720. Felix also worked for Branford Microchip Co. in 2010 and earned $55,000. $3,410 of Social Security tax was withheld from these wages. Because Felix worked for more than one employer and his total wages was more than $106,800, Felix can take a credit of $508.40 for the excess Social Security tax he overpaid.

A taxpayer claims this credit directly on **Form 1040** (line 69). This is a fully refundable credit.

Summary: Credits

Child and Dependent care credit: A nonrefundable credit for daycare and dependent care expenses. The credit is claimed on Form 2441. If the taxpayer is married, generally both spouses must be working or looking for work. Volunteer work does not count for this credit.

The American Opportunity Credit:
Total credit is $2,500 per student. The credit Is permitted for the first four years of postsecondary education (undergraduate). Generally, 40% of the credit is a refundable credit, which means taxpayers can receive up to $1,000 even if they owe no taxes.

Lifetime Learning Credit:
Total credit is $2,000 per return. There is no limit on the number of years that the taxpayer can claim the credit based on the same student's expenses. No portion of the credit is refundable. All education tax credits are claimed on Form 8863.

Adoption Credit:
The Adoption Credit is claimed on Form 8839, Qualified Adoption Expenses. In 2010, the Adoption Credit is refundable. The maximum Adoption Credit is $13,170 per child.

Earned Income Tax Credit:
To qualify for the Earned Income Tax Credit the taxpayer must have earned income from employment, self-employment or another source and meet ALL of the following rules:

- Have a valid Social Security Number
- Cannot file MFS
- Must be a U.S. citizen or resident
- Cannot be the qualifying child of another person
- Cannot file Form 2555 (related to foreign earned income)
- Adjusted Gross Income and earned income must meet certain limits
- Investment income must not exceed $3,100

Unit 1.9: Questions

1. Which of the following would be a qualifying child for the purposes of the child tax credit?

A. An 18-year-old dependent who is a full-time student
B. A six-year-old nephew who lived with the taxpayer for seven months.
C. A famous child actor who is 15 years old and provides over half of his own support.
D. A foster child who has lived with the taxpayer for four months.

The answer is B. in order to qualify for the child tax credit, the qualifying child must have lived with the taxpayer for more than six months (there are special rules for divorced, separated, or unmarried parents). The child must be under the age of 17, and cannot provide over half of his own support. ###

2. Eric and Jo are married and file jointly. They have two dependent children, Braden, age 14, and Shiloh, age 17. Assuming their Adjusted Gross Income is $109,000, what is their allowable Child Tax Credit?

A. $2,000
B. $1,200
C. $1,000
D. $0

The answer is C. Their modified AGI of $109,000 is less than the threshold of $110,000. Therefore, they are eligible for the maximum credit of $1,000. Only Braden is a qualifying child for the purposes of the Child Tax Credit. Shiloh is age 17, and does not pass the age test for this credit. A child must be *under* the age of 17 for the Child Tax Credit. ###

3. Which of the following individuals (all of whom have one qualifying child for the purposes of the Child Tax Credit) are eligible to claim the maximum $1,000 per child for the Child Tax Credit?

A. Fiona, who is Married Filing Separately with a MAGI of $60,000
B. Ken, who is a Qualifying Widower with a MAGI of $130,000
C. Nick, who is Single with a MAGI of $70,000
D. Stacy, who is Married Filing Jointly with a MAGI of $116,000

The answer is C. Nick may be able to take the full $1,000 credit for his child because his MAGI is not affected by the threshold limit of $75,000 for his Single filing status. ###

4. Beatrice has three dependent children, ages 2, 12, and 18. Assuming she meets the other criteria, what is the maximum Child Tax Credit she can claim on her 2010 tax return?

A. $1,000
B. $2,000
C. $3,000
D. $3,500

The answer is B. Beatrice can only claim $2,000. The maximum amount she can claim is $1,000 for each qualifying child. She only has two qualifying children, because one of her dependents is already over 17, and therefore no longer eligible for the credit. ###

5. Lauren and Ralph divorced in four years ago. They have one 12-year-old child, Amy, who lives with Lauren. All are U.S. citizens and have SSNs. Lauren and Ralph provide more than half of Amy's support. Lauren's AGI is $31,000, and Ralph's AGI is $39,000. The divorce decree does not state who can claim the child. Lauren signed Form 8332 to give the dependency exemption to Ralph. Which of the following statements is TRUE?

A. Ralph can claim Amy as a dependent along with the tax benefits.
B. Ralph and Lauren need to choose who can claim Amy as a dependent and any other tax benefits.
C. Ralph can claim Amy as a dependent and the Child Tax Credit. Lauren can use Amy to file as Head of Household and claim the Earned Income Credit and the Child and Dependent Care Credit as long as she meets the requirements for those specific benefits.
D. Neither Ralph nor Lauren can claim Amy as a dependent or can claim any of the other benefits.

The answer is C. Since Lauren signed Form 8332, the dependency exemption and the Child Tax Credit is given to Ralph, the non-custodial parent. However, Lauren can still file as Head of Household and claim the Earned Income Credit and Child and Dependent Care Credit based on Amy, as long as she otherwise qualifies for them. ###

6. Clyde is single and his Form 1099-DIV shows a total of $423 of foreign tax paid. What is the easiest way for Clyde to deduct his foreign taxes paid?

A. By completing Form 1116.
B. By claiming the tax directly on his Form 1040.
C. Foreign taxes are not deductible.
D. By deducting the tax paid on Schedule B.

The answer is A. Clyde needs to complete Form 1116 because his foreign taxes exceed $300. ###

7. Scott is 43 and unmarried. Scott's half-brother, Taylor, turned 16 on December 30, 2010. Taylor lived with Scott all year, and he is a U.S. citizen. Scott claimed Taylor as a dependent on his return. Which of the following is true?

A. Taylor is a qualifying child for the Child Tax Credit.
B. Taylor is NOT a qualifying child for the Child Tax Credit.
C. Taylor is not a qualifying child for the Child Tax Credit because siblings do not qualify.
D. Taylor only qualifies for the Child Tax Credit if he is a full-time student.

The answer is A. Taylor is a qualifying child for the Child Tax Credit because he was under age 17 at the end of 2010. Siblings can be qualifying children for the purposes of this credit. ###

8. Which of the following statements regarding the Foreign Tax Credit is correct?

A. The foreign tax credit is a refundable credit.
B. The foreign tax credit is available to US citizens and nonresident aliens.
C. Taxpayers may choose to take a deduction for foreign taxes paid, rather than the foreign tax credit.
D. Taxpayers can choose to claim both a deduction and a tax credit for foreign taxes paid, as long as the taxes were paid to different countries.

The answer is C. Taxpayers have the option to itemize foreign taxes on Schedule A. They may choose either the deduction OR the credit; whichever gives them the lowest tax, for all foreign taxes paid. Taxpayers cannot choose to claim both the deduction and a tax credit (on the same return). The taxpayer may change her credit to a deduction and vice versa by amending her tax return. This credit is nonrefundable, so it can drop tax liability to zero, but not below that. Form 1116 is used to report the Foreign Tax Credit. It must be attached to the taxpayer's Form 1040. ###

9. The Lifetime Learning Credit is different from the American Opportunity Credit. However, they do share some of the same requirements. Which of the following requirements is TRUE for both education credits?

A. There is no limit to the number of years the credits can be claimed.
B. Expenses related to housing are allowed as qualified education expenses.
C. The credits are available for only the first two years of postsecondary education.
D. To be eligible for either of the education credits, taxpayers must use any filing status other than Married Filing Separately.

The answer is D. Taxpayers who use the filing status of Married Filing Separately are not eligible to claim either the American Opportunity or Lifetime Learning credits.###

10. Which form is used to claim education tax credits?
A. Form 8863
B. Form 4136
C. Form 8812
D. Form 2441

The answer is A. IRS Form 8863 is used to claim all of the education credits. The American Opportunity Credit and the Lifetime Learning Credit are both claimed on IRS Form 8863. ###

11. Which of the following items is NOT tax-deductible as an education related expense for the Lifetime Learning Credit?

A. Required books
B. Childcare in order to attend class
C. Tuition
D. Required fees

The answer is B. Daycare is not a qualifying education expense. For purposes of the Lifetime Learning Credit, qualified education expenses are tuition and certain related expenses required for enrollment or attendance at an eligible educational institution. ###

12. Which of the following individuals is eligible for the American Opportunity Credit?

A. Betsy's son Garrett, who is enrolled full-time as a postgraduate student pursuing a Master's degree in biology.
B. Lucy, who is taking a ceramics class at a community college.
C. Doug, who was convicted of a felony for distributing a controlled substance.
D. Beth, who is taking at least one-half of the normal full-time course load required for a computer science associate's degree program, attending classes the entire school year in 2010.

The answer is D. Beth is eligible for the American Opportunity Credit because she is taking at least one-half of the normal full-time workload for her course of study for at least one academic period beginning during 2010. ###

13. In 2010, what is the maximum amount of the American Opportunity Credit?

A. $2,500 per tax return
B. $2,500 per student
C. $2,000 per tax return
D. $1,000 per student

The answer is B. In 2010 the maximum credit is $2,500 per student. The credit is *per student* per year, and the taxpayer's family may have more than one eligible student per tax return. ###

14. What is the maximum amount of the Lifetime Learning Credit in 2010?

A. $2,000 per student
B. $2,500 per student
C. $1,000 per student
D. $2,000 per tax return

The answer is D. The maximum credit is $2,000 *per tax return*. The credit is allowed for 20% of the first $10,000 of qualified tuition and fees paid during the year. The credit is per tax return, not per student, so only a maximum of $2,000 can be claimed each year. ###

15. Samira and Rishi are married and file jointly. Their daughter Amanda was enrolled full-time in college for all of 2010 and dropped out of college in 2011. Samira and Rishi obtained a loan in 2010 and used the proceeds to pay for tuition and related fees in 2010. They repaid the loan in 2011. Which year will they be entitled to claim an education credit?

A. They cannot claim an education credit.
B. 2010
C. 2011
D. 2012

The answer is B. Samira and Rishi are eligible to claim an education credit for the year 2010. The credit should be calculated for the year in which the taxpayer paid the expenses, not the year in which the loan is repaid. ###

16. Edwin is a professional bookkeeper. He decides to take an accounting course at the local community college in order to improve his skills. Edwin is not a degree candidate. Which educational credit does he qualify for?

A. The American Opportunity Credit
B. The College Credit
C. The Lifetime Learning Credit
D. The Mortgage Interest Credit

The answer is C. Edwin qualifies for the Lifetime Learning Credit. He does not qualify for the American Opportunity Credit because he is not a degree candidate. The "College Credit" does not exist. The Mortgage Interest Credit is not an education credit. ###

17. In 2010, Tyrone's parents paid $5,000 of their own funds to cover all of the cost of his college tuition. Tyrone also received a Pell grant for $3,000 and a student loan for $2,000. For the purposes of figuring an education credit, what are Tyrone's parents' total qualified tuition and related expenses?

A. $10,000
B. $7,000
C. $5,000
D. $2,000

The answer is D. The total qualified tuition payments are the net of the $5,000 tuition minus the grant of $3,000, which equals $2,000. The $3,000 Pell grant is tax-free, so it is not a qualified tuition and related expense.

18. Based on the Child and Dependent Care Credit rules, which of the following individuals meets the eligibility test for a "qualifying person"?

A. Jeremy, 5, who is taken care of by his mother at home all day
B. Destiny, 21, a full-time student supported by her parents
C. Leroy, 80, who lives at home with his son, who pays to have Leroy's meals delivered to the home daily
D. Leanne, 52, who is unable to care for herself, and is married to Jake, an employed construction worker

The answer is D. Leanne meets the qualifying person test because she is the spouse of someone who works, and she is unable to care for herself.###

19. Geraldine placed a $150 deposit with a preschool to reserve a place for her three-year-old child. Later, Geraldine changed jobs and was unable to send her child to the preschool. She forfeited the daycare deposit. Which of the following is TRUE?

A. The forfeited deposit is NOT deductible.
B. The forfeited deposit is deductible.
C. The forfeited deposit is a deduction on Schedule A.
D. The taxpayer may deduct the deposit only if she takes her child to another preschool.

The answer is A. The forfeited deposit is not for childcare and so is not a work-related expense. A forfeited deposit is not actually for the care of a qualifying person, so it cannot be deducted as a childcare expense and does not qualify for the Child and Dependent Care Credit. ###

20. Jeremiah paid daycare for his five-year-old son so he could work. His childcare expenses were $3,000 in 2010. He also paid a deposit of $100 to the daycare and an enrollment fee of $35. Jeremiah was reimbursed for $1,200 by his Flexible Spending Account at work. How much of the childcare expenses can he use to figure his Child and Dependent Care Credit?

A. $1,800
B. $1,900
C. $1,935
D. $3,135

The answer is C. Jeremiah's childcare expenses are figured as follows: ($3,000 + $100 + $35) - $1,200 = $1,935. If a taxpayer has a reimbursement under a Flexible Spending Account, those amounts are pretax. The taxpayer cannot use reimbursed amounts to figure his credit. Fees and deposits paid to an agency or a daycare provider are qualifying expenses if the taxpayer must pay them in order to receive care. Only a forfeited deposit would be disallowed. ###

21. Nina pays for daycare for each of the following individuals so she can work. All of the following are qualifying individuals for the purposes of the Child and Dependent Care Credit, EXCEPT:

A. Nina's husband, who is totally disabled.
B. Nina's son, age 13, who is Nina's dependent.
C. Nina's nephew, age 12, who is also Nina's dependent.
D. Nina's niece, who is 35, lived with her all year, and is completely disabled. Nina provided 100% of her support.

The answer is B. Nina's son does not qualify, because he is over the age limit for the credit. To qualify for the Dependent Care Credit, the qualifying person must be UNDER the age of 13, OR disabled. ###

22. Which of the following is NOT a qualifying expense for the purposes of the Child and Dependent Care Credit?

A. $500 payment to a grandparent for childcare while the taxpayer is gainfully employed
B. $300 payment to a daycare while looking for employment
C. $500 childcare expense while the taxpayer obtains medical care
D. $600 in daycare expense for a disabled spouse while the taxpayer works

The answer is C. Childcare costs to obtain medical care are not a deductible expense. Deductible daycare costs must be *work related* and for a child under 13, or a disabled dependent or spouse of any age. Childcare so that the taxpayer can volunteer, obtain medical care, run errands, or do other personal business is not "qualifying childcare." ###

23. What is the maximum amount of the Adoption Tax Credit for 2010?

A. $11,150
B. $12,150
C. $13,170
D. $13,550

The answer is C. The maximum credit for 2010 is $13,170 per child. If a taxpayer adopts two children, he will be eligible for the full credit on each child. ###

24. Which of the following expenses is NOT a qualified adoption expense for the purposes of the Adoption Credit?

A. Court costs
B. Re-adoption expenses to adopt a foreign child
C. Attorney fees for a surrogate arrangement
D. Travel expenses

The answer is C. The cost of a surrogate is not a qualified adoption expense. Qualified adoption expenses are expenses directly related to the legal adoption of an eligible child. These expenses include adoption fees, court costs, attorney fees, travel expenses (including amounts spent for meals and lodging) while away from home, and re-adoption expenses to adopt a foreign child. ###

25. Which tax form is used to claim the Adoption Credit?

A. Form 8839
B. Form 2815
C. Schedule A
D. Schedule C

The answer is A. To take the Adoption Credit, a taxpayer must complete Form 8839, *Qualified Adoption Expenses*, and attach it to Form 1040 or Form 1040A. ###

26. In 2010, Dylan and Hannah adopt a special needs child who is completely disabled. Their adoption expenses are $7,000, and their travel expenses related to the adoption are $1,200. What is their maximum Adoption Credit in 2010?

A. $7,000
B. $8,200
C. $13,170
D. None of the above.

The answer is C. Dylan and Hannah can take the full Adoption Credit of $13,170 in 2010, because they adopted a special needs child. There is a special rule for taxpayers who adopt special needs children. The full amount of the Adoption Credit is still allowed, even if the taxpayer does not have qualified adoption expenses. The determination of whether or not a child is special needs is made by the adoption authorities or the government agency overseeing the adoption. A child does not have to be disabled in order to qualify as "special needs." ###

27. Austin is a U.S. citizen, and he is adopting a foreign child. His income in 2010 was $31,000. The adoption is almost final, and he has an ATIN for the child. The child lived with Austin all year. Which of the following is true?

A. Austin can claim the Earned Income Tax Credit because his child is a qualifying child.
B. Austin cannot claim the Earned Income Tax Credit in 2010.
C. Austin cannot claim the Earned Income Tax Credit in 2010, but Austin can elect to amend the tax return once a SSN is granted and the adoption is final.
D. The Earned Income Credit is not applicable to foreign-adopted children.

The answer is C. To claim the EITC, the taxpayer must have a valid SSN issued by the Social Security Administration. Any qualifying child listed on Schedule EIC also must have a valid SSN. An ATIN is not sufficient for the purposes of the EIC. However, the taxpayer can elect to amend the tax return once an SSN is granted and the adoption is final. ###

28. To qualify for the Earned Income Credit, which of the following is TRUE?

A. The taxpayer must have a dependent child.
B. The taxpayer must be a U.S. citizen or legal U.S. resident all year.
C. The taxpayer's filing status can be MFS if the taxpayer does not live with his or her spouse.
D. The taxpayer must have a valid SSN or ITIN.

The answer is B. The taxpayer must be a U.S. citizen or legal resident all year. Taxpayers do not need to have a dependent child in order to qualify for the Earned Income Credit; however, the EITC is greatly increased if the taxpayer has a qualifying child. Single taxpayers who are low-income may still qualify for the credit. A taxpayer cannot claim the EITC if his filing status is MFS. A taxpayer must have a valid SSN in order to qualify for the EITC. An ITIN is not sufficient. ###

29. For those claiming the Earned Income Credit in 2010, the taxpayer's interest or investment income must be _____ or less.

A. $2,950
B. $3,100
C. $3,500
D. $4,000

The answer is B. For the purpose of the Earned Income Tax Credit (EITC), interest or investment income must be $3,100 or less. For the EA exam, you must memorize this number—the amount of investment income that disqualifies a taxpayer from claiming the EITC has been tested on numerous prior exams. ###

30. Monty and Belinda are married and living together. Monty earned $12,000 and Belinda earned $9,000 in 2010. They have two minor children and have decided to file Married Filing Separately tax returns, each claiming one child as a dependent. Which statement is TRUE?

A. They can both qualify for the Earned Income Credit on their MFS tax returns.
B. Based on the information, they qualify for the EITC on a joint tax return.
C. Monty can file "Single" and qualify for the EITC.
D. Belinda can file as "Head of Household" and claim the credit.

The answer is B. Since Monty and Belinda are married and live together, they can choose to file a joint return or each may choose to file separately. A taxpayer does not qualify for the EIC on a MFS return, so Monty and Belinda must file jointly in order to claim the credit. ####

31. Which of the following filing conditions would NOT prevent an individual from qualifying for the Earned Income Credit for the year 2010?

A. MFS filing status
B. A taxpayer with a qualifying child who is 23 and a full-time student
C. Investment income of $3,300
D. A taxpayer who is 68 years old without a qualifying child

The answer is B. All the other choices are disqualifying for the purposes of the EITC. At the end of the tax year, the child must be under age 19, OR under age 24 AND a full-time student, OR any age and disabled. ###

32. Jasmine is unmarried. She purchases her first home for $65,000 in January 2010. What is the amount of her First-Time Homebuyer credit?

A. $0
B. $6,500
C. $7,500
D. $8,000

The answer is B. The credit is 10% of the purchase price of the home, with a maximum available credit of $8,000 for either a single taxpayer or a married couple filing a joint return, or $3,750 for married persons filing separate returns. The answer is figured as $65,000 X 10% = $6,500. ###

33. On which tax form would a taxpayer claim the Credit for the Elderly or Disabled?

A. Schedule A
B. Form 8063
C. Schedule R
D. Form 8812

The answer is C. The Credit for the Elderly or Disabled must be claimed on Schedule R (Form 1040). The credit is not refundable. ###

34. Which of the following cars would NOT qualify for the Alternative Motor Vehicle Credit?

A: Hybrid vehicle
B: Advanced lean burn technology vehicle
C: Qualified gasoline burning vehicle
D: Qualified fuel cell vehicle

The answer is C. A gasoline burning vehicle is not a qualifying vehicle for the purposes of the Alternative Motor Vehicle Credit. The four qualifying vehicle types are hybrid vehicles, advanced lean burn technology vehicles, alternative fuel vehicles, and fuel cell vehicles. ###

35. The Residential Energy Efficient Property Credit is an enhanced energy credit for very specific energy systems or improvements. Which of the following items is NOT a qualifying item for the purposes of the credit?

A. Solar energy systems
B. Fuel cells
C. Small wind energy systems
D. Asphalt roofs

The answer is D. The Residential Energy Efficient Property Credit is a credit of 30% of the costs of solar energy systems, fuel cells, small wind energy systems, and geothermal heat pumps. There is no dollar limit on this credit. Asphalt roofs do not qualify for this credit, but they may qualify for the Personal Energy Property Credit, which is a different credit for energy-efficient items installed in a taxpayer's primary residence. ###

36. Which of the following taxpayers, who contributed to their employer's retirement plans, is eligible for the Retirement Savings Credit?

A. Franklin, who is Single and has an Adjusted Gross Income of $35,200
B. Sybil, who is Married Filing Jointly and has an Adjusted Gross Income of $49,500
C. Bert, who is Married Filing Separately and has an Adjusted Gross Income of $28,300
D. Carl, who is a Qualifying Widower and has a modified AGI of $29,000

The answer is B. Sybil qualifies for the credit because her AGI is not over $55,500, which is the threshold limit for Married Filing Jointly. Taxpayers who file as Single, Qualifying Widow(er), or Married Filing Separately (such as Franklin, Carl, and Bert) cannot qualify if they have an AGI that exceeds the AGI limits. ###

Unit 1.10: Basis of Property and Capital Gains (and Losses)

More Reading:
Publication 550, *Investment Income and Expenses*
Publication 551, *Basis of Assets*
Publication 4895, *Tax Treatment of a Property Acquired From a Decedent Dying in 2010*

Almost all property used for personal purposes is a capital asset. Investments are also capital assets. Examples include a home, furniture, jewelry, antiques, stocks, and bonds. The tax treatment of these assets varies based on whether the asset is personal-use or investment property. Almost everything a taxpayer owns and uses for personal purposes, pleasure, or investment is a capital asset, including:

- A home or vacation home
- Household furnishings
- Stocks or bonds (except when held by a professional securities dealer)
- Coin or stamp collections
- Gems and jewelry
- Gold, silver, coins, etc. (except when they are held for sale by a professional dealer)

When capital assets are sold, the difference between the asset's basis and the selling price is a capital gain or a capital loss. Losses from the sale of "personal-use" property, such as a main home or a car, are not deductible. However, losses from the sale of investments (such as stocks) are deductible up to a certain limit.

Investment property is a capital asset. Any gain or loss from its sale or trade is generally a capital gain or loss. Any gain or loss a taxpayer has from the sale is a "capital gain" or "capital loss." Stocks, stock rights (also called "stock options"), and bonds are also capital assets (except when held for sale by a securities dealer).

Property held for personal use only, rather than for investment, is a capital asset, and a taxpayer must report a gain from its sale as a capital gain. However, a taxpayer CANNOT deduct a loss from selling personal use property. Examples include a personal-use car or a television set.

Example: Liam owns a used 1999 Toyota. It is his personal-use vehicle. He purchased the car two years ago for $2,500. In 2010, he sells the car for $2,100. Liam cannot claim a loss from the sale of the car, since it is his personal-use vehicle.

Example: Mason sold his personal computer to his friend Adam for $750. Mason paid $5,000 for the computer five years ago. Mason used the computer to play games and to balance his checkbook. He did not use the computer for business. Mason cannot deduct a loss on the sale of his personal computer.

Capital gains and deductible capital losses are reported on **Form 1040, Schedule D,** *Capital Gains and Losses.* Schedule D is used most commonly to report gains and losses from stock sales, but it is also used to report other types of capital gains and losses.

> **Example:** Whitney collects antique coins as a hobby. She is not a professional dealer. In 2006, Whitney gets lucky and purchases an antique Roman coin for $50. In 2010, she is offered $1,000 for the coin, and she promptly sells it. Whitney has a capital gain and she must report it on Schedule D.

Noncapital Assets

On the other hand, assets held for business-use or created by a taxpayer for the purpose of earning revenue (author's writings, copyrights, inventory, etc.) are noncapital assets. Gains and losses from the sale of business property are reported on **Form 4797,** *Sales of Business Property* and (in the case of individual taxpayers) the amounts flow through to **Form 1040, Schedule D.** [32]

> **Example:** Tony is a sole proprietor of a fitness club. He also owns stock in a few companies as an investment. In 2010, Tony sold used fitness equipment from his club in order to make room for new equipment. Since the fitness equipment was business property, the sale of these assets is reported on **Form 4797,** *Sales of Business Property.*

The following assets are noncapital assets:

- Inventory (or any property held for sale to customers)
- Depreciable property used in a business
- Real property used in a trade or business (such as a commercial building or a residential rental)
- Self-produced copyrights, transcripts, manuscripts, drawings, photographs, or artistic compositions
- Accounts receivable or notes receivable acquired by a business
- Stocks and bonds held by professional securities dealers
- Business supplies
- Commodities and derivative financial instruments

Cost Basis

In order to understand capital gains and losses, you must understand the concept of "basis" and "adjusted basis." The basis of the asset is usually its cost. Cost basis is the amount of money invested into a property for tax purposes. Usually this is the cost of the item when it is purchased. Basis is figured differently when property is acquired by gift or inheritance. The cost basis of an asset can include:

- Sales taxes charged during the purchase
- Freight-in charges
- Installation and testing fees
- Delinquent real estate taxes that are paid by the buyer of a property
- Legal and accounting fees

---

[32] See Publication 544, *Sales and Other Dispositions of Assets,* for additional information on the sale of business property. Gains and sales of business property are covered more in Book 2.

All of these costs are added to an asset's basis. These costs are not deductible as an expense, whether or not the asset is business-use or personal-use.

> **Example:** Rashid purchases a new car for $15,000. The sales tax on the vehicle was $1,200. He also paid a delivery charge to have the car shipped from another dealership to his home. The freight charge was $210. Therefore, Rashid's basis in the vehicle is $16,410 ($15,000 + $1200 + $210).

Basis of Real Property (Real Estate)

The basis of real estate usually includes a number of costs in addition to the purchase price. If a taxpayer purchases real property (a house, a tract of land, a building), certain fees and other expenses become part of the cost basis. This also includes real estate taxes the seller owed at the time of the purchase, if the real estate taxes were paid by the buyer.

> **Example:** Landon purchases a home from Tina for $100,000. Tina lost her job and fell behind on her property tax payments. Landon agrees to pay the delinquent real estate taxes as a condition of the sale. The delinquent property tax at the time of purchase totaled $3,500. The IRS does not allow a taxpayer to deduct property taxes that are not his legal responsibility. Therefore, Landon must add the property tax to his basis. Landon's basis in the home is $103,500.

If a property is constructed rather than purchased, the basis of the property includes the expenses of construction. This includes the cost of the land, building permits, payments to contractors, lumber, and inspection fees. Demolition costs and other costs related to the preparation of land must be added to the basis of the land.

> **Example:** Wanda purchases an empty lot to build her home. The lot costs $50,000. Wanda also pays $2,000 for the removal of tree stumps before construction can begin. Therefore, Wanda's basis in the land is $52,000.

Adding Settlement Costs to Basis

Generally, a taxpayer must include settlement costs for the purchase of property in his basis. A taxpayer cannot include fees incidental to getting a loan. The following fees are some of the closing costs that can be included in a property's basis:

- Abstract fees
- Charges for installing utilities
- Legal fees (including title search and preparation of the deed)
- Recording fees
- Surveys
- Transfer taxes
- Owner's title insurance

Also included in a property's basis are any amounts the seller legally owes that the buyer agrees to pay, such as back taxes or interest, recording or mortgage fees, charges for improvements or repairs, and sales commissions.

How to Figure Adjusted Basis

This section discusses how to figure adjusted basis in property. Before figuring gain or loss on a sale or exchange, a taxpayer must usually make adjustments to the basis of the property. The result is the adjusted basis. The most common concepts when discussing basis are:

- **Cost basis:** The basis of property a taxpayer buys is usually its actual cost.
- **Adjusted basis:** Before figuring gain or loss on a sale, a taxpayer must usually make increases or decreases to the cost of the property. The result is the adjusted basis.

Example: Brian buys a house for $120,000. The following year, he paves the driveway, which costs him $6,000. Brian's *adjusted basis* is $126,000 ($120,000 original cost + $6,000 in improvements).

Basis "other than" cost

There are times when a taxpayer cannot use *cost* as the basis for property. In these cases, the Fair Market Value or the adjusted basis of the property can be used. Below are some examples of times when an asset's basis will be something other than cost:

Property Received for Services: If a taxpayer receives property in payment for services, the taxpayer must include the property's FMV in income, and this becomes the taxpayer's basis in the property. If two people agree on a cost beforehand, and it is deemed to be reasonable, the IRS will usually accept the agreed-upon cost as the asset's basis.

Example: Cassidy is an Enrolled Agent who prepares tax returns for a long-time client named Katie. Katie loses her job and cannot pay Cassidy's bill, which totals $450. Katie offers Cassidy a painting in lieu of paying her invoice. The Fair Market Value of the painting is approximately $520. Cassidy agrees to accept the painting as full payment on Katie's delinquent invoice. Cassidy's basis in the painting is $450, the amount of the invoice that was agreed upon by both parties.

The basis of gifted property and inherited property is also calculated on the basis "other than cost." In the case of inherited property, the cost basis is either modified or disregarded. Inherited property and gift property are covered later in this unit.

Basis After Casualty and Theft Losses

If a taxpayer has a casualty loss, she must decrease the basis of the property by any insurance proceeds. A taxpayer may increase her basis in the property by the amount spent on repairs that restore the property to its pre-casualty condition.

Example: Dale paid $5,000 for a car several years ago. It was damaged in a flood. He does not have flood insurance on the car. Dale spends $3,000 to repair the car. Therefore, his new basis in the car is $8,000 ($5,000 + $3,000).

Assumption of a Mortgage

If a taxpayer buys property and assumes an existing mortgage on it, the taxpayer's basis includes the amount paid for the property plus the amount owed on the mortgage. The taxpayer's basis includes the settlement fees and closing costs paid for buying the property. Fees and costs for getting a loan on the property (points) are not included in a property's basis.

> **Example:** Sondra buys a building for $20,000 cash and assumes a mortgage of $80,000 on it. Therefore, her basis is $100,000.

Involuntary Conversions and Basis Adjustments

An involuntary conversion occurs when a taxpayer involuntarily gives up or exchanges property. An involuntary conversion can happen after a disaster, such as a house fire. Involuntary conversions may also occur after casualties, thefts, or the condemnation of property. If a taxpayer receives replacement property as a result of an involuntary conversion, the basis of the replacement property is figured using the basis of the converted property. A taxpayer may also have to figure gain if the amount of the insurance reimbursement exceeds his basis of the asset.

> **Example:** Paige receives insurance money of $8,000 for her shed, which was destroyed by an earthquake. Paige's basis in the shed was $6,000. She uses $6,000 to purchase a new shed. Paige needs to recognize a $2,000 gain, since she realized a gain of $2,000 from the conversion ($8,000 - $6,000) and only used $6,000 of the $8,000 insurance proceeds to replace the shed.

Basis of Property Received as a Gift

The basis of property received as a gift is figured differently than property that is purchased. To figure basis in property received as a gift, the taxpayer must know the adjusted basis of the property just before it was gifted, its Fair Market Value, and the amount of gift tax paid on it, if any. Gift taxes are always paid by the giver (donor), not the receiver (donee) of the gift.

Do NOT confuse this concept with the basis of "inherited property," which is property that is passed on to another person after the owner of the property has died. Inherited property will be covered later.

Generally, the basis of gifted property is the same in the hands of the donee as it was in the hands of the donor. This is called a "transferred basis." For example, if a taxpayer gives his son a car and the taxpayer's basis in the car is $2,000, the basis of the vehicle remains $2,000 for the son. However, some adjustments must be made in cases where the taxpayer pays gift tax, or other adjustments.

> **Example:** Alicia's father gives her 50 shares of ABC stock. The Fair Market Value of the stock is currently $1,000. Her father has an adjusted basis in the stock of $500. Alicia's basis in the stock, for purposes of determining gain on any future sale, is $500 (transferred basis).

FMV Less Than Donor's Adjusted Basis

If the FMV of the gifted property is less than the donor's adjusted basis, the donee's basis for gain is the same as the donor's adjusted basis. If the donee reports a loss on the sale of gifted property, the basis is the lower of the donor's basis or the Fair Market Value of the property on the date of the gift. The sale of gifted property can also result in no gain or loss. This happens when the sale is greater than the gift's FMV but below the donor's cost basis.

Example: Russell receives a gift of 100 shares of stock from his Uncle Hugh. Hugh's basis in the stock was $10,000 when he gave it to Russell. However, the FMV of the stock at the time of the gift is only $9,000. Russell sells the stock two months later for $9,500. Russell does not have any gain or loss for tax purposes. His basis for figuring gain is $10,000, ($9,500 -$10,000) = $500 loss. Russell's basis for figuring loss is $9,000, and ($9,500 -$9,000) = $500 gain. This is an example of a sale of gifted property resulting in **no gain or loss.** This happens when the sale ($9,500) is above the gift's FMV ($9,000) but below the donor's basis ($10,000).

Example: Charlie's grandmother Leslie bought 20 shares of Google stock many years ago. The stock currently has an FMV of $7,500, but Leslie's basis in the stock is only $1,000. Charlie's basis in the stock is the same as his grandmother's: $1,000. If Charlie sells the stock for $7,500, he must report a taxable gain of $6,500.

Example: Ricky's Aunt Roberta bought 100 shares of Business Corp. stock when it was at $92. Her basis for the 100 shares is $9,200. Roberta then gives the stock to Ricky when it is selling at $70 and has an FMV of $7,000. In this case, Ricky has a "dual basis" in the stock. He has one basis for purposes of determining a gain, and a different basis for determining a loss. Here are three separate scenarios that help illustrate how the gain or loss would be calculated when Ricky sells the gifted stock:

Scenario #1: If Ricky sells the stock for more than Roberta's basis, he will use the donor's basis to determine his amount of gain. For example, if he sells the stock for $10,100, he will report a gain of $900 ($10,100 - $9,200).

Scenario #2: If Ricky sells the stock for less than the FMV of the stock at the time of the gift, ($7,000 in the example), he must use that basis to determine the amount of his loss. For example, if the stock continues to decline and Ricky eventually sells it for $4,500, he can report a loss of $2,500 ($7,000 - $4,500).

Scenario #3: If Ricky sells the stock for an amount between the FMV and the donor's basis, there will be no recognized gain or loss. For example, if Ricky sells the stock for $8,000, there will be no gain or loss on the transaction.

Basis of Inherited Property

Property acquired from a decedent dying in 2010 does not have an automatic increase in basis. This is due to the sweeping law changes in December 2010. For decedents dying *before* 2010, the basis of property acquired from a decedent was the fair market value of the property at the time of the decedent's death. This is sometimes referred to as "step-up" basis.

Under the 2010 Tax Relief Act, however, the executor may elect out of the estate tax system. For deaths that occurred 2010 only, estates have the unusual option of either:

- Using the stepped-up basis (when the property is sold, the gain will be calculated based on the change in value from the date of death)
- Or by using the new "carryover basis" rules that *only* apply to the 2010 tax year (when the property is sold, a gain will be calculated based on the change in value from the basis of the decedent). See the unit on Estates for more detailed information on this topic.

The new exceptions regarding the basis of inherited property are outlined in The NEW IRS **Publication 4895**, *Tax Treatment of a Property Acquired From a Decedent Dying in 2010.*[33]

The rules for determining basis of inherited property are different than the rules for gifted property. This is called property "inherited from a decedent." This means that the original owner has died, and the property has passed on to another individual. Do not confuse "inherited property" with "gifted property." The tax treatment is very different for each one.

The basis of inherited property is generally the FMV of the property on the date of the decedent's death. However, this can vary if the personal representative of the estate elects to use an alternate valuation date or other acceptable method.[34]

Cash or property inherited from a deceased taxpayer is not considered income to the recipient. A taxpayer does not have to report inherited property as income on her tax return. However, if the taxpayer later earns income from the property (such as interest, dividends, or capital gain from the sale of the property) those amounts must be reported.

Determining Basis on Inherited Property

A taxpayer's basis in inherited property is generally the Fair Market Value of the property on the date of the decedent's death. However, there are some cases where the executor for the estate may choose an alternate valuation date. In most cases the "valuation date" for the estate is the date of death (to be covered later).

This results in a beneficial tax situation for anyone who inherits property from a deceased person. This is because the taxpayer who inherits the property generally gets an increased basis. Tax professionals call this a "stepped-up" basis. However, there are cases where this rule can work against taxpayers. Although most property such as stocks, collectibles, and bonds increase in value over time, there are also occasions where the value of the property drops. This would create a "stepped-down" basis.

---

[33] At the date of this book's printing in February, 2011, Publication 4895 was not yet available. You can also refer to Internal Revenue Code Section 1223(9) to review the holding period for inherited property

[34] There are special rules for property inherited in 2010. The Economic Growth and Tax Relief Reconciliation Act of 2001 ("EGTRRA") repealed the estate tax for decedents dying after December 31, 2009, and before January 1, 2011. This odd rule only applies to tax year 2010. The rules for estates will be covered later in the book in the dedicated study unit for estates.

Example #1: Sasha's uncle bought 300 shares of Giant Corp stock many years ago for $500. Sasha inherited the Giant Corp stock when her uncle died. On the date of her uncle's death, the value of the stock was $9,000. Therefore, Sasha's basis in the stock is $9,000. She later sells the stock for $11,000. She has a capital gain of $2,000 ($11,000 - $9,000). This is the concept of a "stepped-up" basis.

Example #2: With the same facts as above, if Sasha were to sell the stock for $8,000, she would have a loss of $1,000.

Example #3: Sasha's aunt also bought 100 shares of Enron stock many years ago for $10,000. Sasha inherited the Enron stock when her aunt died. On the date of her aunt's death, the value of the Enron stock was $150. Therefore, Sasha's basis in the stock is $150. She later sells the stock for $150. She cannot report a loss on the stock. That is because the basis of the stock was "stepped-down" for tax purposes. No one will receive a tax deduction for the loss in value of the stock.

Exception for an Alternate Valuation Date

Usually, the basis of an estate is figured on the date of death. However, there is a special rule that allows the executor of the estate to elect a different valuation date. If the executor makes this election, the valuation date is six months after the date of death. Usually the executor will make this election in order to reduce the amount of estate tax that must be paid. Choosing to take an alternate valuation date will also affect the basis of the property that is passed on to the beneficiaries of the estate.

Example: Sonny will inherit an antique vase from his cousin Patrick when he dies. Patrick dies on January 1, 2010. The executor of Patrick's estate chooses to use the alternate valuation date. On the date of Patrick's death, the antique vase had a value of $12,000. Six months later, the vase has a value of $11,000. Sonny must take the vase with a basis of $11,000.

If a federal estate tax return does not have to be filed for the deceased taxpayer, the basis in the beneficiary's inherited property is the FMV value at the date of death.

Basis of Securities

A taxpayer's basis in stocks or bonds is usually the purchase price, plus any additional costs like brokers' commissions. In order to compute gain or loss on a sale, taxpayers must provide their basis in the sold property. The basis of stock is usually its cost, but basis can also include charges such as brokers' commissions and other fees.

When a taxpayer sells securities, the investment company will send **Form 1099-B** showing the gross proceeds of the sale. **Form 1099-B** does not usually include how much taxpayers paid; they must keep track of this information themselves. If taxpayers cannot provide their basis, the IRS will deem it to be zero.

Selling Blocks of Stock

Many taxpayers own shares of stock they bought on different dates or for different prices. This means they own more than one block of stock. Each block may differ from the others in its holding period (long-term or short-term), its basis (amount paid for the stock), or both.

In directing a broker to sell stock, the taxpayer may specify which block, or part of a block, to sell; this is called *Specific Identification.* The Specific Identification method requires good recordkeeping; however, this method simplifies the determination of the holding period and the basis of the stock sold, giving the taxpayer better control and versatility in handling an investment.

If the taxpayer cannot identify the specific block at the time of sale, shares sold are treated as coming from the earliest block purchased; this method is called *First In, First Out (FIFO).*[35]

FIFO Example: Tia bought 50 shares of stock of Coffee Corp. in 2005 for $10 a share. In 2006, Tia bought another 200 shares of Coffee Corp. for $11 a share. In 2008, she bought 100 shares for $9 a share. Finally, in 2010, she sold 130 shares. She cannot identify the exact shares she disposed of, so she must use the stock FIFO method to figure the basis of the shares that she sold. Tia figures the basis as follows:

Shares purchased

Year	# of Shares	Cost per share	Total cost
2005	50	$10	$500
2006	200	$11	$2,200
2008	100	$9	$900

The basis of the stock that Tia sold is figured as follows:

50 shares (50 × $10) balance of stock bought in 2005	$500
80 shares (80 × $11) stock bought in 2006	$880
Total basis of stock sold in 2010	$1,380

Adjusted Basis of Securities

An "adjustment to basis" is an increase or decrease in the original basis of an asset. It may include commissions or fees paid to the broker at the time of purchase or sale. Stock is usually bought and sold in various quantities. The taxpayer is required to keep track of the basis per share of all stock bought and sold.

Events that occur after the purchase of the stock can require adjustments (increases or decreases) to the "per share" basis of stock. The original basis per share can be changed by events such as stock dividends, stock splits, and DRIP (Dividend Reinvestment Plan) accounts.

- Stock dividends are issued *in lieu* of cash dividends. These additional shares increase the taxpayer's ownership so the original basis is spread over more shares, which decreases the basis per share.

---

[35] Specific Identification and First In, First Out (FIFO) are common inventory methods that are also used by businesses. You will learn more about how these inventory methods are used by businesses in Part 2 of the EA Exam course books.

- Stock splits are decided by the corporation as a way to bring down the market price of stock. A two for one stock split will decrease the basis per share by half. The original basis of $200 for 100 shares becomes $200 for 200 shares.

Example: Pepper paid $1,100 for 100 shares of Jolly Ice Cream, Inc. stock (including the broker's commission of $25), so the original basis per share was $11 ($1,100/100). Pepper received 10 additional shares of stock as a nontaxable stock dividend. Her $1,100 basis must be spread over 110 shares (100 original shares plus the 10-share stock dividend). So, adding 10 shares means her basis per share decreases to $10 ($1,100/110).

Wash Sales

A "wash sale" occurs when a taxpayer sells or trades identical securities at a loss and within 30 days. A taxpayer cannot deduct losses from sales of securities in a wash sale. A "wash sale" is when a taxpayer sells securities and then turns around and:

- Buys identical securities,
- Acquires substantially identical securities in a taxable trade, or
- Acquires a contract or option to buy identical securities.

The wash sale rule time period actually lasts a total of 61 calendar days: the 30 days before the sale is made, the 30 days after the sale is made, and the day of the sale. To claim a loss as a deduction, the taxpayer needs to avoid purchasing the same stock (or similar security) during the wash sale period. For a sale on July 31, for example, the wash sale period includes all of July and August.

Example: Mary Ann buys 100 shares of American Great Products for $1,000 on July 5, 2007. On July 31, 2010, she sells the shares for $750, resulting in a $250 loss on the sale. She then buys another 100 shares on the same day, July 31, for $750. Mary Ann cannot claim the $250 loss on her 2010 tax return because she bought 100 shares of the same stock within 30 days of the sale. If she had waited until the 31st day *after* the date of sale, she could have taken the loss.

If a taxpayer's loss was disallowed because of the wash sale rules, she must add the disallowed loss to the basis of the new stock or securities. The result is an increase in the taxpayer's basis in the new stock or securities. This adjustment postpones the loss deduction until the disposition of the new stock or securities. (Wash sale rules do not apply to trades of commodity futures contracts and foreign currencies.)

Example: Carlos sells 1,000 shares of Big Corp stock on December 4, 2009 and takes a loss of $3,200. On January 1, 2010, he buys back 1,000 shares of Big Corp stock. Because of the IRS wash sale rules, all of the $3,200 loss is disallowed. He cannot take the loss until he finally sells those repurchased shares in some later year. He must add the disallowed loss to the basis of the newly-purchased shares, resulting in an increase to the basis.

For the purposes of the wash sale rules, securities of one corporation are not considered identical to securities of another corporation. Similarly, "preferred" stock of a corporation is not considered identical to the common stock of the same corporation.

If the number of shares of identical securities a taxpayer buys within 30 days is either more or less than the number of shares sold, the taxpayer must determine the particular shares to which the wash sale rules apply. A taxpayer does this by matching the shares bought with an equal number of the shares sold. A taxpayer must match the shares bought in the same order that he bought them, beginning with the first shares purchased.

Example: Chelsea bought 100 shares of Best Chocolate stock on September 24, 2009. On February 3, 2010, she sold those shares at a $1,000 loss. On February 10, 2010, Chelsea bought 100 shares of identical stock. Since she *repurchased* identical shares ten days after selling the stock, she cannot deduct her $1,000 loss. She must add the disallowed loss ($1,000) to the basis of the 100 shares she bought on February 10.

Example: During 2007, Cody bought 100 shares of Burton stock on three occasions. He paid $158 a share for the first block of 100 shares, $100 a share for the second block, and $95 a share for the third block. On December 23, 2009, Cody sold all 300 shares of Burton stock for $125 a share. On January 6, 2010, he repurchased 250 shares of Burton stock. He cannot deduct the loss of $33 a share on the first block because he bought 250 identical shares of stock within 30 days after the date of sale. In addition, Cody cannot reduce the gain realized on the sale of the second and third blocks of stock by this loss.

If a taxpayer sells stock and her spouse then repurchases identical stock within 30 days, the taxpayer has a wash sale. This is true even if the spouses file separately.

Basis after a Stock Split (Stock Dividend)

A stock split occurs when a corporation distributes more stock to its existing stock-holders. A stock split, such as a "2-for-1" split, is when a corporation issues one share of stock for every share outstanding. A "stock dividend" is similar to a stock split in that a cor-poration issues stock to its shareholders, but does not issue cash dividends.

The way to figure basis after a stock split or a stock dividend is to divide the tax-payer's adjusted basis of the old stock between the shares of the old stock and the new stock. Basically, this means that if the old stock was priced at $10 per share, after the split each share would be worth $5. This is because the corporation's assets did not increase, only the number of outstanding shares.

A stock dividend and a stock split are not taxable events. However, both of these types of distributions do affect the taxpayer's basis in her stock.

After a split, taxpayers need to recalculate their basis for the newly acquired shares. The new basis per share is the total cost of the shares divided by the new share count.

Example: Sean bought 100 shares of Mini Corp. for $50 per share. Sean's cost basis is $50 x 100 shares or $5,000. In 2010, Mini Corp. issues a stock dividend. Sean receives 100 addi-tional shares of stock. Therefore, his new basis in each individual stock is $25 = ($5,000 ÷ [100+100]).

Capital Gains and Losses

Long-term capital gains are generally taxed at a lower rate than ordinary income. Short-term capital gains are taxed at the ordinary rate. This is why taxpayers prefer to have long-term capital gains, rather than short-term capital gains. The capital gains tax rate depends on the holding period, type of asset, and the taxpayer's ordinary income bracket.

If a taxpayer sells securities through a broker during the year, he should receive Form 1099-B, *Proceeds from Broker and Barter Exchange Transactions*, by January 31 following the end of the tax year.

This statement shows the gross proceeds from the sale of securities. The IRS also receives a copy of Form 1099-B from the broker. Taxpayers use Form 1099-B to report capital gains and losses on Schedule D (Form 1040). Schedule D is used to report gain or loss on the sale of investment property and other capital gain distributions. Schedule D is also used to report gain from the sale of small business stock and collectibles.

Example: Corbin received a Form 1099-DIV. He received a total capital gain distribution of $170 in 2010. Corbin also received Form 1099-B that shows a net sales price of $1,200 on the sale of 600 shares of Cuddly Inc. He bought the stock on February 26, 2005 and sold it on September 25, 2010. His basis in Cuddly Inc., including commission, is $1,455. He has an overall loss on the stock, and a capital gain distribution. Corbin must use Schedule D to report his capital gain and losses. The loss from the stock and the capital gain distribution will "net" on the Schedule D.

The sale and income must be reported in the year the security is sold, regardless of when the taxpayer receives the proceeds from the stock sale.

The $3,000 Loss Limit and Loss Carryovers

Capital losses are always netted against capital gains. This follows the normal passive activity loss rules.[36] However, there is an exception for stock losses. *Up to $3,000 of excess capital losses is deductible against ordinary income in a tax year* ($1,500 for married taxpayers filing separately). The allowable loss is referred to as the deduction limit. Unused losses are carried over to later years. The carryover losses are combined with the gains and losses that actually occur in the next year. Short-term and long-term capital loss carryovers are reported on Schedule D.

The carryover retains its character as either long-term or short-term. A long-term capital loss carried over to the next tax year will reduce that year's long-term capital gains before it reduces that year's short-term capital gains.

Example: Arthur purchased stock in 2008 for $10,000. He sold the stock in 2010 for $2,000. Arthur has an $8,000 long-term capital loss. He also has $30,000 in wages in 2010. He may claim $3,000 of his long-term capital loss against his ordinary income, thereby lowering his gross income to $27,000 ($30,000 -$3,000). The remainder of the long-term capital loss must be carried forward ($5,000).

---

[36] Passive activity rules were covered in Unit 6 (Rental and Royalty Income).

Unused losses may be carried over year after year until they are all deducted. There is no limit on how many times a loss can be carried over during the taxpayer's life.

Figuring Capital Gain or Loss

A taxpayer figures gain or loss on a sale or trade of stock or property by comparing the amount realized with the adjusted basis of the property.

- Gain: If the taxpayer realizes more than the adjusted basis of the property, the difference is a gain.
- Loss: If the taxpayer realizes less than the adjusted basis of the property, the difference is a loss.

Example: Nadine purchased 50 shares of Big Auto stock in 2007 for $5,000. Then, in 2008, she purchased 75 shares of Huge Utility stock for $8,200. In 2010, Nadine sold all her stock. Her Big Auto stock sold for $2,000. Her Huge Utility stock sold for $13,000. Nadine's gains and losses are figured as follows:

Stock	Basis	Sale Price	Gain or loss
Big Auto	$5,000	$2,000	($3,000)
Huge Utility	$8,200	$13,000	$4,800
Net Capital Gain			**$1,800**

All of Nadine's gains and losses are long-term, because she held the stock for over one year.

The "amount realized" is the total of all money received for the property. The amount realized also includes any liabilities that were assumed by the buyer. If a taxpayer receives money as well as other property or services, these additional items must also be included in the amount realized.

A realized gain (or loss) is the amount realized that is above (or below in the case of a loss) the adjusted basis of the property. This amount is not necessarily taxable. There are many instances where a taxpayer may have a realized gain that is not a taxable event. We will go over a number of these instances in this chapter.

A recognized gain or loss is the actual amount that must be included in income (or deducted from income) for tax purposes.

Example: Rod trades Bartley Company stock with an adjusted basis of $7,000 for Cartwright Company stock with a Fair Market Value (FMV) of $10,000. Rod's amount realized is $10,000. His gain is $3,000 ($10,000 – $7,000).

Worthless and Abandoned Securities

Starting in 2008, taxpayers could choose to "abandon" securities. Stocks, stock rights, and bonds (other than those held for sale by a securities dealer) that became worthless during the tax year are treated as though they were sold on the last day of the tax year. This affects whether a taxpayer's capital loss is long-term or short-term.

Taxpayers report losses from worthless securities on Schedule D (Form 1040). This rule is helpful for a taxpayer who has a security that has declined in value so much that he wishes to take a loss on it rather than retain ownership.

A taxpayer may "abandon" a security and treat it as worthless on his tax return. To abandon a worthless security, a taxpayer must permanently surrender all rights to the security and receive no consideration in exchange for it.

Capital Gain Distributions and Mutual Funds

A mutual fund is a regulated investment company generally created by "pooling" funds of investors to allow them to take advantage of a diversity of investments and professional management. Mutual funds often sell profitable investments at certain times throughout the year. Owners of mutual funds may receive both Form 1099-DIV and Form 1099-B. Form 1099-DIV reports capital gain distributions from sales of stock held by the mutual fund. Profits of these sales are reported to the shareholders as capital gain distributions.

If taxpayers (shareholders) decide to sell any of their shares in the mutual fund itself, Form 1099-B will be issued. The taxable gain or loss from the sale or exchange of the taxpayer's shares in a mutual fund is reported on Form 1040, Schedule D.

Capital gain distributions are always taxed at long-term capital gains tax rates, *no matter how long* a taxpayer has personally owned shares in the mutual fund.

Capital gain distributions can be reported directly on Form 1040 if a taxpayer has no other capital gains to report. Otherwise, capital gain distributions must be reported on Schedule D along with a taxpayer's other gains and losses.

Special Rules for Small Business Stock

There is a special type of stock called Section 1244 Small Business Stock (also called qualified small business stock[37]). This is stock in qualifying domestic corporations that is subject to special tax rules that are favorable to the shareholder. Losses on small business stock are considered ordinary losses (rather than capital losses) and any gain on a 1244 stock is a capital gain.

This means that the losses are not subject to the capital loss limit ($3,000 per year), but gains are still given favorable capital gains rates. The amount that can be deducted as an ordinary loss is $50,000 ($100,000 for joint filers). Ordinary losses are more favorable to the taxpayer because she can deduct this loss against her ordinary gross income. Losses from the sale of qualifying small business stock are reported on **Form 4797, Sales of Business Property**.

In order to qualify, the shareholder must be an individual or partnership (other entities do not qualify for this specialized treatment). Only the original purchaser of the stock can claim an ordinary loss. So, if this stock is inherited or gifted to another person, the special treatment for losses does not apply.

---

[37] A "qualified small business" is a domestic C corporation, the gross assets of which do not exceed $50 million (without regard to liabilities).

Gains on qualified small business stock are given preferential treatment. This is intentional; Congress has passed this special exemption in order to stimulate investment in small U.S. corporations. The general rule is this:

- A taxpayer generally can exclude up to 50% of the gain from the sale or trade of qualified small business stock held for over five years.
- The exclusion can be up to 75% for stock acquired after February 17, 2009, and up to 100% for stock acquired after September 27, 2010. The stock must be held for over five years in order to qualify for this 100% exclusion of gain.

So, for example, if a taxpayer purchases qualified small business stock on September 28, 2010, he would have to wait until September 29, 2015 to sell the stock in order to receive the 100% exclusion from gain.

In order for stock to qualify as "qualified small business stock," the corporation must be a small business corporation at the time the stock is issued. Only stock in a domestic corporation qualifies for this special treatment. (Corporate shareholders, estates, or trusts do not qualify for this special loss recognition treatment on the stock they own.) Gains from qualified small business stock are reported on Schedule D (Form 1040).

Holding Period (Short-Term or Long-Term)

The "holding period" is a very important concept to understand for the EA Exam. When a taxpayer disposes of investment property, he must determine his holding period in order to figure gain or loss. The holding period determines whether any capital gain or loss was a short-term or long-term capital gain or loss. Holding periods vary based on whether the property is purchased, inherited, or acquired as a gift.

If a taxpayer holds investment property for more than one year, any capital gain or loss is long-term capital gain or loss. If a taxpayer holds property for one year or less, any capital gain or loss is short-term capital gain or loss. To determine how long a taxpayer has held an investment property, she should begin counting on the date *after* the day she acquires the property. The day the taxpayer disposes of the property is part of the holding period. This is very important—the EA Exam will usually have a few questions relating to holding period.

Example: Nina bought 50 shares of stock on February 5, 2009 for $10,000. She sold all the shares on February 5, 2010 for $20,500. Nina's holding period is NOT more than one year and she has a short-term capital gain of $10,500. The short-term gain is taxed at ordinary income rates. A long-term gain is taxed at preferential tax rates. If Nina had waited one more day, she would have received long-term capital gain treatment on her gains, and it would have saved her on income taxes.

Do not confuse the "trade date" with the "settlement date," which is the date by which the stock must be delivered and payment must be made.

> **Example:** Stuart bought 100 shares of Huge Corp. stock on March 1, 2009 for $1,200. To determine his holding period, Stuart must start counting his holding period on March 2, 2009 (the day after the purchase). He sells all the stock on March 2, 2010 for $2,850. Stuart's holding period has been one year and a day, and therefore, he will recognize a long-term capital gain of $1,650 ($2,850 - $1,200).

Stock acquired as a stock dividend (also called a stock split) has the same holding period as the original stock owned.

> **Example:** On March 10, 2006, Jamal bought 500 shares of Big Widgets Corporation stock for $1,500, including his broker's commission. On June 6, 2010, Big Widgets distributed a 2% nontaxable stock dividend (10 additional shares). Three days later, Jamal sold all his Big Widgets stock for $2,030. Although Jamal owned the 10 shares he received as a nontaxable stock dividend for only three days, all the stock has a long-term holding period. Because he bought the stock for $1,500 and then sold it for $2,030 more than a year later, Jamal has a long-term capital gain of $530 on the sale of the 510 shares.

Special Rule: Holding Period of Inherited Property

If a taxpayer inherits property, her capital gain or loss on any later disposition of that property is ALWAYS treated as a long-term capital gain or loss. This is true regardless of how long the beneficiary actually held the property. The taxpayer is considered to have held the inherited property for more than one year even if she disposes of the property less than one year after the decedent's death.

> **Example:** Warren inherits an acre of land from his father Rudolph, who died in March 2010. At the time of his father's death, the land had an FMV of $18,000. Rudolph's adjusted basis in the land was $5,000. After Warren received the property, he sold it two weeks later for $18,500. Warren gets a "stepped-up" basis in the property and may use the FMV at the time of his father's death ($18,000) as the basis in the land. Therefore, Warren has a $500 long-term capital gain ($18,500 - $18,000 = $500).

> **Example:** Joni purchases 100 shares of Successful Corp on January 10, 2010. Joni dies two weeks later, and her father Ronald inherits the stock on September 30, 2010. Ronald sells the stock two days later. Even though no one actually held the stock for over a year, Ronald gets long-term capital gain treatment on the sale, because the stock was inherited property.

The holding period of the deceased person does not matter. Inherited property is always considered long-term, regardless of how long the original owner held the property, or how long the person who inherited the property holds it.

Holding Period for Gifted Property

The holding period for a gift is treated differently than the holding period for inherited and purchased property. If a taxpayer receives a gift of property, then the holding period includes the donor's holding period. This concept is also known as "tacking on" the holding period.

Example: Mary received an acre of land as a gift from her Aunt Helen. At the time of the gift, the land had an FMV of $23,000. Helen's adjusted basis in the land was $20,000. Helen held the property for six months. Mary holds the land for another seven months. Neither held the property for over a year. However, Mary may "tack on" her holding period to her aunt's holding period. Therefore, if Mary were to sell the property, she would have a long-term capital gain or loss, because jointly they held the property for thirteen months, which is over one year.

Basis of a Non-Business Bad Debt

There are two kinds of bad debts—business and non-business. If someone owes you money that you cannot collect, you have a bad debt. Some non-business bad debts are deductible, and others are not. Business bad debt arises in a trade or business (such as when a customer fails to pay her bill) and it is treated differently than non-business bad debt. Business bad debt is covered in Part 2 of the EA Exam.

To deduct a bad debt, the taxpayer must have a basis in it—that is, the taxpayer must have already included the amount in income or must have already loaned out the cash. If a taxpayer loans money to someone in a true debtor-creditor relationship that is unrelated to a business, the loan is a non-business debt. The debt must be a valid and enforceable obligation.

Taxpayers must prove that they have taken reasonable steps to collect the debt and that the debt is worthless. A debt becomes worthless when it is certain that the debt will never be paid. It is not necessary to go to court if the taxpayer can show that a judgment from the court would be uncollectible. A partially worthless debt is not deductible.

The taxpayer may take a bad debt deduction only in the year the debt becomes worthless, but a taxpayer does not have to wait until the debt comes due, if there is proof that the debt is already worthless (for example, if the debtor dies or declares bankruptcy).

Example: In January 2010, Stephanie loans her friend Jed $14,000 to buy a car. Jed signs a note and promises to pay the entire debt back with interest on December 31, 2010. Jed has a bad car accident in March 2010 and cannot pay his debts so he files for bankruptcy. Stephanie does not have to wait until the debt comes due. The loan has become worthless, since there is no longer any chance the amount owed will be paid. Stephanie can take the deduction for non-business bad debt.

For a legitimate bad debt to be deductible, the intent of the loan must be genuine. The transaction must be a true loan and not a gift. If a taxpayer lends money to a relative or friend with the understanding that it will not be repaid, it is considered a gift and not a loan. There must be a true creditor-debtor relationship between the taxpayer and the person or organization that owes the money.

Loan Guarantees

A *loan guarantee* is not a true debtor-creditor relationship. If a taxpayer simply guarantees a debt (by co-signing on the loan) and the debt becomes worthless, the taxpayer cannot take a bad debt deduction. If the taxpayer makes a loan guarantee as "a favor" to friends and does not receive any consideration in return, the loan payments are considered a gift and are therefore not deductible as a bad debt. There must be a profit motive in order for the loan to qualify as a true debtor-creditor relationship.

> **Example:** Lucas and Jason are co-workers. Lucas, as a favor to Jason, co-signs on an auto loan at their local credit union. Jason does not pay the loan and declares bankruptcy. Lucas is forced to pay off the note in order to maintain his credit. However, since he did not enter into a formal guarantee agreement to protect an investment or to make a profit, Lucas cannot take a bad debt deduction.

When minor children borrow from their parents, there is no genuine debt. A bad debt cannot be deducted for such a loan.

A legitimate non-business bad debt is reported as a short-term capital loss on Schedule D, Form 1040. It is subject to the capital loss limit of $3,000 per year. This limit is $1,500 if a taxpayer is married filing a separate return.

Installment Sales and Understanding the Installment Method

An installment sale is a sale of property where at least one payment is to be received after the tax year in which the sale occurs. A taxpayer is generally required to report the sale under the "installment method." If the taxpayer decides not to use the installment method, he must report all the gain in the year of the sale. Installment sale rules do not apply to property that is sold at a loss.

Under the installment method, a taxpayer reports income each year and only part of the gain received. Installment sales are reported on **Form 6252**, *Installment Sale Income*, which is attached to Form 1040. A taxpayer may also be required to complete Schedule D or Form 4797.

If the property sold is a capital asset, the taxpayer must include the capital gain on Schedule D. If the property sold is long-term business property, then any income due to depreciation recapture is reported as ordinary income in the year of the sale. The recaptured amount is reported on Form 4797.

> **Example:** Raoul sells property at a contract price of $6,000 and his gross profit is $1,500. The gross profit percentage on the sale is 25% ($1,500 ÷ $6,000). After subtracting interest, Raoul reports 25% of each payment, including the down payment, as installment sale income. The remainder (balance) of each payment is the tax-free return of the property's basis.

Special Rules for No-Interest Loans

Interest earned on an installment agreement is called the "stated" interest. If interest is not charged or the interest rate is too low, there is a minimum amount of interest the seller is considered to have received. If the installment sale calls for payments in a later year and the sales contract provides for no interest, the taxpayer may have to figure unstated interest, even if it creates a loss on the sale. This "imputed" or "unstated" interest is taxable.

The rules regarding imputed interest were created in order to prevent a seller from increasing his sales price in order to offer a zero percent interest rate so he may profit from a lower tax liability. The taxpayer must use the Applicable Federal Rate (AFR) to figure the unstated interest on the sale. The AFR must be applied to all loans of six or more months duration.

The taxpayer then must report interest as ordinary income. Interest is generally not included in a down payment. However, the taxpayer may have to treat part of each later payment as interest, even if it is not called "interest" in the agreement with the buyer.

Dealer Sales are Not Installment Sales

Sales of property by a professional dealer who regularly sells the same type of personal property are NOT installment sales. This rule also applies to real property held for sale to customers in the ordinary course of a trade or business. The sale of inventory is never treated as an installment sale even if the seller receives payment after the year of sale. However, the rule does not apply to an installment sale of property used for farming (the taxation of farmers is covered in Part 2 of the EA Exam).

Related Party Transactions

Special rules apply to related-party transactions. These are business deals between two parties who are joined by a special relationship. If a taxpayer sells capital assets to a close family member or to a business entity that the taxpayer controls, he might not get all the benefits of the capital gains tax rates, and he may not be able to deduct his losses. The related party transactions were put into place to prevent related persons and entities from shuffling assets back and forth and taking improper losses.

"50% Control" Rule

If a taxpayer controls more than 50% of a corporation or partnership, then any property transactions between the taxpayer and the business would be subject to related party transaction rules.

In general, a loss on the sale of property between related parties is not deductible. When the property is later sold to an unrelated party, gain is recognized only to the extent it is more than the disallowed loss. If the property is later sold at a loss, the loss that was disallowed to the related party cannot be recognized. If a taxpayer sells or trades property at a loss (other than in the complete liquidation of a corporation), the loss is not deductible if the transaction is between the taxpayer and the following related parties:

- Members of immediate family, including a spouse, siblings or half-siblings, ancestors, or descendants (child, grandchildren, etc.). *Note: For the purpose of this rule, an uncle, nephew, stepchild, stepparent, or in-law is not considered a related party.
- A partnership or corporation that the taxpayer controls (a taxpayer "controls" an entity when he has over 50% ownership in it). This also includes partial ownership by other family members.
- A tax-exempt or charitable organization controlled by the taxpayer or a member of his family.
- Losses on sales between certain closely related trusts or business entities controlled by the same owners.

307

> **Example:** Hillary buys stock from her brother Leo for $7,600. Leo's cost basis in the stock is $10,000. He cannot deduct the loss of $2,400 because of the related-party transaction rules. Later, Hillary sells the same stock on the open market for $10,500, realizing a gain of $2,900. Hillary's reportable gain is $500 (the $2,900 gain minus the $2,400 loss not allowed to her brother).

> **Example:** Vicky purchases stock from her father for $8,600. Her father's basis in the stock is $11,000. Vicky later sells the stock on the open market for $6,900. Her recognized loss is $1,700 (her $8,600 basis minus $6,900). Vicky cannot deduct the loss that was disallowed to her father.

If a taxpayer sells multiple pieces of property and some are at a gain while others are at a loss, the gains will generally be taxable while the losses cannot be used to offset the gains.

Summary: Capital Gains, Wash Sales, Small Business Stock

Reporting a Capital Gain or Loss
To report a capital gain or loss on Form 1040, Schedule D the taxpayer will need to identify:
- Basis or adjusted basis. (Adjusted basis includes the original cost plus any increases or decreases to that cost (such as commissions, brokers' fees, depreciation, insurance reimbursements, etc.)
- Basis is the original cost of the asset.

Holding period:
- Short-term property is held one year or less.
- Long-term property is held more than one year.

Long-term capital gains are taxed at a lower rate than short-term gains.

Proceeds from a sale:
- Form 1099-B reflects gross or net proceeds for a stock or mutual fund.
- Form 1099-S usually reflects gross proceeds of real estate transactions. A taxpayer generally won't receive a 1099-S on the sale of a primary residence, but it could happen if the bank makes an error.

If a taxpayer has a capital loss for the year, he should claim a capital loss deduction on Form 1040. This deduction is limited to a maximum of $3,000 in capital losses ($1,500 if Married Filing Separately). Any unused losses can be carried over to the following year. The losses retain their holding period status as either long-term or short-term.

Unit 1.10: Questions

1. Kayla's cost basis for 600 shares of Fenway Corporation stock she purchased in December 2008 and then sold in September 2010 was $2,400. Kayla sold the 600 shares for $4,400 and paid a $100 commission. Her broker reported the gross proceeds of $4,400 on Form 1099-B. What was the sales price for the shares and the amount of capital gain?

A. $4,400 sales price and $2,000 gain
B. $4,400 sales price and $1,900 gain
C. $4,500 sales price and $2,100 gain
D. $4,300 sales price and $1,900 gain

The answer is B. The sales price was $4,400, which was $1,900 more than the adjusted basis of $2,500 ($2,400 cost + $100 commission) of the shares.###

2. Colin purchases 100 shares of Entertainment Company stock for $1,000 on December 1, 2009. He sells these shares for $750 on December 22, 2009. Colin has seller's remorse, and on January 19, 2010 he repurchases 100 shares of Entertainment Company stock for $800. Which of the following statements is TRUE?

A. Colin may report his capital losses from the first sale on Schedule D.
B. Colin has a reportable gain in 2010.
C. Colin may not deduct his stock losses and must add the disallowed loss to his basis.
D. Colin may report a $250 capital loss in 2010.

The answer is C. Because Colin bought substantially identical stock, he cannot deduct his loss of $250 on the sale. However, he may add the disallowed loss of $250 to the cost of the new stock, $800, to obtain his basis in the new stock, which is $1,050. This is called the "wash sale rule." ###

3. Which of the following taxpayers is required to file Form 1040 and Schedule D?

A. Blanche, who received one Form 1099-B and no Forms 1099-DIV
B. Lorraine, who received Forms 1099-DIV for capital gain distributions from three different mutual funds
C. Perry, who owns stock but whose only capital gain came from his mutual fund
D. All of the above

The answer is A. Only Blanche sold stock and received Form 1099-B. A form 1099-B is used to report the sale of stock or similar securities, and therefore, a Schedule D would be required. Since Perry did not sell any stock, and only had capital gains from a mutual fund, he may report the income directly on his Form 1040. Lorraine only had capital gain distributions, and she may also report the income on her Form 1040. ###

4. On March 11, 2010, Henry bought 1,000 shares of Greenbrae Corporation stock for $4 each, plus paid an additional $70 for his broker's commission. What is Henry's basis in the stock?

A. $1,000
B. $4,000
C. $4,070
D. None of the above

The answer is C. Henry's basis in the stock is $4,070 ([1,000 X $4] = $4,000 + $70). ###

5. Kevin paid his broker a $75 fee on the sale of his stock. His Form 1099-B shows $925 as the gross proceeds from the sale. What is the amount Kevin reports as his sales price on Schedule D?

A. $925
B. $1,000
C. $850
D. $75

The answer is A. The sales price is never adjusted on Schedule D. The broker's commission is added to the stock's basis or purchase price of the stock. ###

6. Brigit purchased 1,000 shares of Free Drive, Inc. The original basis in the 1,000 shares of stock she purchased was $5,100, including the commission. On February 14, 2010, she sold 500 shares for $3,300. What is the adjusted basis of the stock she SOLD?

A. $5,100
B. $2,550
C. $3,300
D. $3,255

The answer is B. Brigit's original basis in the total stock was $5,100, which is $5.10 per share, so her basis in the 500 shares she sold is 500 X $5.10, or $2,550. ###

7. Tariq bought two blocks of 400 shares of stock, the first in March 2007 for $1,200 and the second in March 2010 for $1,600. In June of 2010, he sold 400 shares for $1,500 without specifying which block of shares he was selling. Tariq's sold stock represents a _____.

A. Short-term loss of $100
B. Short-term gain of $300
C. Long-term loss of $100
D. Long-term gain of $300

The answer is D. The basis and holding period would automatically default to the original block of shares, so Tariq realized a long-term gain of $300. ###

8. Nikhil's adjusted basis in 500 shares of Wediku Corporation was $2,550. If Nikhil sold 500 shares for $3,300, then what is his reported sales price for the shares and the resulting gain or loss on Schedule D?

A. $3,300 sales price and $750 gain
B. $3,300 sales price and $700 gain
C. $3,255 sales price and $750 gain
D. $2,550 sales price and $750 loss

The answer is A. The sales price is $3,300, which is $750 more than the adjusted basis of the shares. ###

9. Consuela bought 40 shares of Giant Corporation for a total purchase price $1,540. She also paid a $20 broker's commission on the purchase. What is her initial basis PER SHARE?

A. $39
B. $38.50
C. $1,560
D. $77

The answer is A. Consuela's initial basis for this stock is $1,560, or $39 per share ($1,560 ÷ 40 shares). Cost basis includes the amount paid for the stock and any commission paid on the purchase. ###

10. On March 10, 2009, Hans bought 500 shares of Manufacturing Company stock for $1,500, including his broker's commission. On June 6, 2010, Manufacturing Company distributed Hans a nontaxable stock dividend of 10 additional shares. Three days later, Hans sold all his stock for $2,030. What is the nature of his gain on all the shares sold?

A. Long-term capital gain of $530
B. Long-term capital gain of $500, short-term gain of $30
C. Short-term capital gain of $530
D. None of the above

The answer is A. Although Hans owned the 10 shares he received as a nontaxable stock dividend for only three days, all the stock has a long-term holding period. Because he bought the stock for $1,500 and then sold it for $2,030 more than a year later, Hans has a long-term capital gain of $530 on the sale of the 510 shares.

11. Deirdre bought 100 shares of stock of Around Pound Corporation in 2004 for $10 a share. In January 2005 Deirdre bought another 200 shares for $11 a share. In July 2005 she gave her son 50 shares. In December 2008 Deirdre bought 100 shares for $9 a share. In April 2010 she sold 130 shares. Deirdre cannot identify the shares she disposed of, so she must use the stock she acquired first to figure the basis. The shares Deirdre gave her son had a basis of $500 (50 × $10). What is the basis of the stock Deirdre sold in 2010?

A. $880
B. $1,380
C. $1,300
D. $1,000

The answer is B. If a taxpayer buys and sells securities at various times in varying quantities and she cannot adequately identify the shares sold, the basis of the securities sold is the basis of the securities acquired first (FIFO). Deirdre figures the basis of the 130 shares of stock she sold as follows:

50 shares (50 × $10)	
Balance of stock from 2004:	$500
80 shares (80 × $11)	
Stock bought in January 2005	$880
Total basis of stock sold	**$1,380**

###

12. Julian owned one share of common stock that he bought for $45. The corporation distributed two new shares of common stock for each share held. Julian then had three shares of common stock. What is Julian's basis for each share?

A. $5
B. $45
C. $15
D. $135

The answer is C. Julian's basis in each share is $15 ($45 ÷ 3). If a taxpayer receives a nontaxable stock dividend, divide the adjusted basis of the old stock by the number of shares of old and new stock. The result is the taxpayer's basis for each share of stock. ###

13. Claire owned two shares of common stock. She bought one for $30 in 2006 and the other for $45 in 2007. In 2010, the corporation distributed two new shares of common stock for each share held. Claire had six shares after the distribution. How is the basis allocated between these six shares?

A. All six shares now have a basis of $12.50.
B. Three shares have a basis of $10 each and three have a basis of $15 each.
C. The shares are valued at $45 each.
D. Some other amount.

The answer is B. The shares now are valued as follows: three with a basis of $10 each ($30 ÷ 3), and three with a basis of $15 each ($45 ÷ 3). If a taxpayer receives a nontaxable stock dividend, he must divide the adjusted basis of the old stock by the number of shares of old and new stock. The result is the taxpayer's basis for each share of stock (Publication 550). ###

14. On her one-year anniversary at her new job, Faith's employer gave her stock with the condition that she would have to return it if she did not complete a full five years of service with her company. Her employer's basis in the stock was $16,000, and its Fair Market Value is $30,000. How much should she include in her income for the current year, and what would be her basis in the stock?

A. Income of $16,000; basis of $30,000.
B. Income of $10,000; basis of $30,000.
C. Income of $30,000; basis of $16,000.
D. Faith would not report any income or have any basis in the stock until she has completed five years of service.

The answer is D. The stock is restricted, so Faith does not have constructive receipt of it. She should not report any income until she receives the stock without restrictions. Constructive receipt does not require physical possession of the item of income. However, there are substantial restrictions on the stock's disposition because Faith must complete another four years of service before she can sell or otherwise dispose of the stock. ###

15. Stephen purchases a truck for $15,000. He puts $5,000 down in cash and finances the remaining $10,000 with a five-year loan. He then pays taxes and delivery costs of $1,300. He also pays $250 to install a protective bedliner. What is Stephen's basis in the truck?

A. $6,550
B. $10,000
C. $16,550
D. $16,300

The answer is C. Stephen's basis in the truck is the cost of both acquiring the property and preparing the property for use. Therefore, his basis is figured as follows: ($15,000 + $1,300 + $250) = $16,550. Any funds that are borrowed to pay for an asset are also included in the basis. ###

16. Melissa purchased 1,000 shares of Devil Foods Company stock in 2008 at $10 per share. She sold 900 shares on January 15, 2010 at $9 per share, resulting in a $900 loss. Melissa's husband George purchased 900 shares on February 10, 2010. George and Melissa keep their finances separate and will file separately (MFS) in 2010. Which of the following is TRUE?

A. Melissa may deduct the $900 capital loss on her tax return.
B. Melissa has a wash sale and her loss is not deductible.
C. George may deduct the loss on his separate tax return.
D. None of the above.

The answer is B. The loss is disallowed. Melissa has a wash sale, because her spouse repurchased identical securities within 30 days. It doesn't matter if they file MFS. If a taxpayer sells stock and her spouse then repurchases identical stock within 30 days, the taxpayer has a wash sale. ###

17. Dorian purchased 1,000 shares of Home-Town Mutual Fund on February 15, 2008 for $15 per share. On January 31, 2010, he sold all his shares for $3.75 per share. He also earned $45,000 in wages in 2010. He has no other transactions during the year. How should this transaction be reported on his tax return?

A. Dorian has a short-term capital loss of $11,250. He will be allowed to offset $11,250 of his wage income with the capital loss.
B. Dorian cannot claim a capital loss because he has no passive income. He must carry over the entire loss to a future tax year and offset capital gains.
C. Dorian may take a $3,000 capital loss on his 2010 tax return and the remainder of the losses will carry forward to the following year.
D. Dorian may take a $5,000 capital loss on his 2010 tax return and the remainder of the losses will carry forward to the following year.

The answer is C. Dorian cannot deduct all his stock losses in the current year. Dorian may take a $3,000 capital loss on his 2010 tax return and the remainder of the losses will carry forward to the following year. There is a $3,000 annual capital loss limitation that prevents taxpayers from claiming all their passive capital losses against active income. Unused capital losses carry forward indefinitely. ###

18. Mackenzie purchases an empty lot for $50,000. She pays $15,000 in cash and finances the remaining $35,000 with a bank loan. The lot also has a $4,000 lien against it for unpaid property taxes, which she also agrees to pay. Which statement below is CORRECT?

A. Mackenzie's basis in the property is $50,000, and she may deduct the property taxes on her Schedule A as property taxes paid.
B. Mackenzie's basis in the property is $19,000.
C. Mackenzie's basis in the property is $54,000.
D. Mackenzie's basis in the property is $46,000.

The answer is C. Her basis is figured as follows: ($50,000 + $4,000 = $54,000). Mackenzie may not deduct the delinquent property taxes on her Schedule A. This is because any obligations of the seller that are assumed by the buyer increase the basis of the asset, and are not currently deductible. Since Mackenzie did not legally owe the property taxes but she still agreed to pay them, she must add the property tax to the basis of the property. ###

19. Shannon and Dan are married and file jointly. Dan purchased qualified small business stock in 2007. Which of the following statements is correct?

A. If they incur a loss on qualified small business stock, they cannot deduct the loss.
B. They can claim an ordinary loss limited to $50,000 on their jointly filed return.
C. They can claim an ordinary loss limited to $100,000 on their jointly filed return.
D. If they incur a gain on qualified small business stock, they must treat it as ordinary gain.

The answer is C. They may claim up to $100,000 as an ordinary loss on the stock on their jointly filed tax return. Losses on small business stock are considered ordinary losses (rather than capital losses) and any gain on this stock is capital gain. This means that the losses are not subject to the capital loss limit of $3,000 per year, but gains are still given favorable capital gains rates. The amount that can be deducted as an ordinary loss is $50,000 ($100,000 for MFJ). ###

20. Which form is used to report LOSSES from the sale of qualified small business stock?

A. Form 4797
B. Form 2848
C. Schedule C
D. Schedule B

The answer is A. Unlike other stock dispositions that are reported on Schedule D, the losses from the sale of qualifying small business stock are reported on IRS Form 4797, *Sales of Business Property*. ###

21. What form is used to report an installment sale?

A. Form 6252
B. Schedule C
C. Schedule E
D. Form 2848

The answer is A. A taxpayer should use Form 6252 to report installment sale income from casual sales of real or personal property during the tax year. He also will have to report the installment sale income on Schedule D or Form 4797, or both. ###

22. Marilyn won the lottery and then made personal loans to several friends. The loans were a true debtor-creditor relationship, but not business related. She could not collect on many of these loans. How does Marilyn report these transactions?

A. The losses from the uncollectible loans are not deductible, since they were personal loans.
B. The losses are deductible as non-business bad debt on Schedule D.
C. The losses are deductible as a business expense on Schedule C.
D. The losses are deductible on Schedule A as casualty losses.

The answer is B. A non-business bad debt is reported as a short-term capital loss on Schedule D. It is subject to the capital loss limit of $3,000 per year. ###

23. Antonio purchased 100 shares in Foresthill Mutual Fund in 2010 for $750. He received a capital gain distribution of $120 in 2010. The $120 was reported on Form 1099-DIV. How should this be reported on his tax return?

A. Antonio must reduce his stock's basis by $120.
B. Antonio must report the $120 as interest income.
C. Antonio must report the $120 as a long-term capital gain.
D. Antonio must report the $120 as a short-term capital gain.

The answer is C. Mutual funds frequently distribute capital gains to shareholders. Capital gain distributions for mutual funds are always taxed at long-term capital gain tax rates, no matter how long a taxpayer has held the mutual fund shares. Capital gain distributions can be reported directly on Form 1040 if a taxpayer has no other capital gain to report. Otherwise, capital gain distributions are reported on Schedule D along with other gains and losses. ###

24. In 2009, Sergio sold land with a basis of $40,000 for $100,000. Sergio's gross profit was $60,000. He received a $20,000 down payment from the buyer and the buyer's note (contract) for the remaining $80,000. The buyer's contract provides for four annual payments of $20,000 each, plus 8% interest, beginning in 2010. What is the gain that Sergio must report each year under the "installment sale" method?

A. $10,000
B. $12,000
C. $25,000
D. $45,000

The answer is B. Sergio's gross profit percentage is 60%. Therefore, he must report a gain of $12,000 on the payment received in 2009 (when the first payment of $20,000 was received) and the remaining four payments in 2010, 2011, 2012, and 2013. ###

25. Fred bought ten shares of Jixi Corporation stock on October 1, 2009. He sold them for a $7,000 loss on October 1, 2010. He has no other capital gains or losses. He also has $20,000 of wage income. How must Fred treat this transaction on his tax return?

A. Fred may deduct the $7,000 as a long-term capital loss on his 2010 return.
B. Fred may deduct the $7,000 as a short-term capital loss on his 2010 return.
C. Fred may deduct $3,000 as a short-term capital loss to offset his wage income on his 2010 return. The remaining amount ($4,000) must be carried over to future tax years.
D. Fred may deduct $3,000 as a long-term capital loss to offset his wage income on his 2010 return. The remaining amount ($4,000) must be carried over to future tax years.

The answer is C. Fred has a short-term loss because he did not hold the stock for over one year. He may deduct $3,000 of the loss in 2010, netting against his wage income. The remaining amount ($4,000) must be carried over to future tax years. The carryover retains its character as either long-term or short-term. A long-term capital loss carried over to the next tax year will reduce that year's long-term capital gains before it reduces that year's short-term capital gains (Publication 17).###

26. Connor purchased Blue-Chip Corporation stock in 2008 and sold it in 2010. In 2010, he also traded in a copy machine that he had been using in his business since 2007 for a new model. On December 15, 2009, Connor's mother gifted him 35 shares of Energy Corp. stock that she had held for a few years. Connor sold the gifted stock two weeks after he received it from his mother. What is the holding period for these properties?

A. All short-term.
B. Blue-Chip stock and copy machine is long-term and Energy Corp. stock is short-term.
C. All the stocks are long-term; the copy machine is short-term.
D. All are long-term.

The answer is D. All the property is long-term property. If a taxpayer holds investment property for more than one year, any capital gain or loss is a long-term capital gain or loss. If a taxpayer holds a property for one year or less, any capital gain or loss is a short-term capital gain or loss. If a taxpayer receives a gift of property, then the holding period includes the donor's holding period. Since Connor's mother had already held the stock for a few years, it would receive long-term treatment in Connor's possession. ###

27. An individual taxpayer has capital gain distributions only, and no other capital gains. Which of the following satisfies the reporting requirements?

A. All capital gain distributions must be entered on Schedule B.
B. The amount is entered on Form 1040.
C. All capital gain distributions must be entered on Schedule D.
D. If there are no other capital gains, capital gain distributions must be combined with interest on Schedule B.

The answer is B. Capital gain distributions can be reported directly on Form 1040 if the taxpayer has no other capital gains to report. Otherwise, capital gain distributions are reported on Schedule D along with other gains and losses. ###

28. Ruben bought 100 shares of Excellent Corp. stock on October 1, 2009 when the share price was $26. He then sold them for $20 a share on October 1, 2010. How should this trade be reported, and what is the nature of Ruben's gain or loss?

A. Ruben has a short-term capital loss of $600.
B. Ruben has a long-term capital loss of $500.
C. This is a wash sale.
D. This is a short-term loss of $500.

The answer is A. Ruben has a short-term capital loss of $600 = (100 shares X $26)-(100 shares X $20). Ruben's holding period was not more than one year, which means that the loss must be treated as a short-term capital loss. To determine holding period, begin counting on the date after the date the taxpayer acquires the property (Publication 17). ###

29. When trying to determine the holding period for investment property, which of the following is important?

A. The cost of the property
B. In the case of gifted property, the amount of the gift
C. The date of acquisition
D. The amount realized in the transaction

The answer is C. To determine the holding period, a taxpayer must begin counting on the day after the acquisition date. If a taxpayer's holding period is not more than one year, the taxpayer will have a short-term capital gain or loss. The amount realized in the transaction has no bearing on the holding period. ###

Unit 1.11: Non-Recognition Property Transactions

> **More Reading:**
> Publication 523, *Selling Your Home*
> Publication 544, *Sales and Other Dispositions of Assets*

This unit covers non-recognition property transactions. These are transactions where a taxpayer sells or exchanges property without any tax consequences. Some of these transactions are nontaxable, some are tax deferred, and some are considered nontaxable exchanges.

Taxpayers who sell property *usually* have a realized gain or loss on the sale. Taxpayers may also have a realized gain or loss when they trade property. Whether or not the taxpayer must pay tax on the gain or loss depends on the type of transaction.

There are many instances where taxpayers who have a gain on property are not required to recognize the income on their tax return. This chapter will review the most common nontaxable exchanges, which are called "non-recognition property transactions." The three most common transactions that result in "non-recognition" treatment are:

- Like-kind exchanges (Section 1031 exchange)
- Involuntary conversions (Section 1033 exchange)
- Sale of a primary residence (Section 121, excluded gain)

Sometimes, these transactions are partially taxable.

Sale of Primary Residence

In many cases, a taxpayer may exclude the gain from the sale of her primary residence. The exclusion from gain is up to $250,000 from the sale of the home ($500,000 on a joint return in most cases). The exclusion only applies to a "main home." The main home can be a:

- House
- Houseboat
- Mobile home
- Cooperative apartment
- Condominium

A taxpayer's main home is the residence where the taxpayer lives most of the time. It does not have to be a traditional house. In order to qualify as a "home," it must have sleeping, kitchen, and bathroom facilities. Vacation homes and second homes do not qualify for this special non-recognition treatment.

> **Example:** Wayne owns and lives in a house in the city. He also owns a beach house, which he uses only during the summer months. The house in the city is his main home; the beach house is not. Wayne sells the beach house and has $100,000 in gain. It cannot be excluded.

Eligibility Requirements for the Exclusion

To be eligible for the exclusion, taxpayers must:

- Have sold the home that has been their main home
- Meet the ownership and use tests
- Not have excluded gain in the two years prior to the current sale of their home

Taxpayers must report the portion of the gain that exceeds the allowable exclusion amount: $250,000 for individual taxpayers or $500,000 for Married Filing Jointly.

Ownership Test and Use Test

To claim the exclusion on the gain from the sale of a home, a taxpayer must meet the *ownership test* and *use test*. This means that during the five-year period ending on the date of the sale, the taxpayer must have:

- Owned the home for at least two years (the ownership test), and
- Lived in the home as his or her main home for at least two years (the use test)

In order to qualify for the exclusion, the taxpayer must NOT have excluded gain on the sale of another home sold during the previous two years.

Example: From 2004 to August 2009, Lindsay lived with her parents in a house her parents owned. On September 1, 2009, she bought the house from her parents. She continued to live there until December 14, 2010, when she sold it because she wanted a bigger house. Lindsay does not meet the requirements for exclusion. Although she lived in the property as her main home for more than two years, she did not own it for the required two years. Therefore, she does not meet both the ownership and use tests.

There are special exceptions for Armed Forces, intelligence personnel, and Peace Corps volunteers in the application of the five-year period. We will cover these exceptions later in this unit.

The required two years of ownership and use do not have to be continuous. Tax-payers meet the tests if they can show that they owned and lived in the property as their main home for either 24 full months or 730 days (365 x 2) during the five-year period.

Example: Beginning in June 2005, Helena moved into a rented condominium. When the unit came up for sale, she bought the condo on December 1, 2007. In 2008, Helena became ill, so on April 14 of that year she moved into her daughter's home. On July 10, 2010, while still living in her daughter's home, she sold her condominium. Helena can exclude all the gain on the sale of her condo because she met the ownership and use tests. Her five-year period runs from July 11, 2005 to July 10, 2010, the date she sold the unit. She owned her condo from December 1, 2007 to July 10, 2010 (over **two years**). She lived in the apartment from July 11, 2005 (the beginning of the **five-year period**) to April 14, 2008 (over **two years**).

Example: Trinity bought and moved into a house in July 2006. She lived there for 13 months and then moved in with her boyfriend, and kept her house empty. They broke up in January 2009. She moved back into her own house in 2009 and lived there for 12 months until she sold it in July 2010. Trinity meets the ownership and use tests because during the five-year period ending on the date of sale, she owned the house for four years and lived in it for a total of 25 months.

Ownership and use tests can be met during different two-year periods. However, a taxpayer must meet both tests during the five-year period ending on the date of the sale. Short, temporary absences, even if the property is rented during those absences, are counted as periods of use. Short absences include vacations and trips. Longer breaks, such as a one-year sabbatical, do not.

> **Example:** Katarina bought her home on February 1, 2008. Each year, she left her home for a four-month summer vacation. Katarina sold the house on March 1, 2010. She may exclude the gain (up to $250,000). The vacations are short temporary absences and are counted as periods of use.

Married Homeowners

The ownership and use tests are applied somewhat differently to married home-owners. Married homeowners can exclude up to $500,000 if they meet all of the following conditions:

- They file a joint return
- *Either* spouse meets the ownership test (only one is required to own the home)
- Both individuals must meet the use test
- Neither individual must have excluded gain in the two years before the current sale of the home

If either spouse does not satisfy all these requirements, the couple cannot claim the maximum $500,000 exclusion. The exclusion amount must be figured as if the couple was unmarried. In order to qualify for the full $500,000 exclusion, the couple must file a joint tax return.

Under the ownership test, each spouse is treated as owning the property during the period that either spouse actually owned it. However, BOTH spouses must meet the "use test."

> **Example:** Leigh sells her main home in June 2010, and she has $350,000 of gain. She marries Kelly in September 2010. Leigh meets the ownership and use tests, but Kelly does not. Leigh can exclude up to $250,000 of gain on her tax return for 2010, whether she files MFJ or MFS. The $500,000 exclusion for joint returns does not apply in this case because Kelly does not meet the use test.

> **Example:** Zaid owns a home that he has lived in continuously for eight years. In June 2007, he marries Annabel. She moves in with her husband and they both live in the house until December 1, 2010 when the house is sold. Zaid meets the ownership test and the use test. Annabel meets the use test, because only Zaid is listed as the owner of the property. On a jointly filed return, they may claim the maximum $500,000 exclusion because they both meet the use test, and Zaid meets the ownership test.

In the case of an unmarried couple that lives and owns a home together, they would be able to take the $250,000 exclusion individually on their separate returns if they qualify for the use test and the ownership test. Sometimes this exclusion also applies to family members who own a home and live together.

Example: Greta and Sydney are twin sisters. They are both widowed and decide to purchase a home and live together. If they were to later sell the home, then the ownership and use tests would apply to them, as well. Each one would be able to claim an exclusion for their portion of the sale on their individual returns ($250,000 exclusion each).

Deceased Spouses and Home Sales

If a taxpayer's spouse dies, there are special rules. A taxpayer is considered to have owned and lived in a home during any period of time when the spouse owned and lived in it as a main home (this is provided that the taxpayer did not remarry before the date of sale). So, in effect, the holding period is "tacked on" for surviving spouses.

Beginning with home sales after 2007, a maximum exclusion ($500,000) by an unmarried surviving spouse is allowed if the surviving spouse sells the home within two years after the date of the spouse's death.

Example: Alice has owned and lived in her home since July 2001. She marries William in April 2009, and he moves in to the home with her. Alice dies six months later, and William inherits the property. He does not remarry. William sells the home on December 1, 2010. Even though William did not own or live in the house for two years, he is considered to have satisfied the ownership and use tests because his period of ownership and use includes the period that Alice owned and used the property before her death. Furthermore, William may qualify to exclude up to $500,000 of the gain because of the special rule that applies to surviving spouses.

This exclusion also applies to a home that is transferred by a spouse if the transfer is part of a divorce. In the case of a divorce, the receiving spouse is considered to have owned the home during any period of time that the transferor owned it.

Five-Year Test Period Suspension for Military Personnel

Taxpayers can choose to have the five-year test period for ownership and use suspended during any period the homeowner (or either spouse if married) served on "qualified official extended duty" as a member of the armed services or Foreign Service of the United States, as an employee of the intelligence community, or as a member of the Peace Corps. This means that the taxpayer may be able to meet the two-year use test even if he and/or his spouse did not actually live in the home during the normal five-year period required of other taxpayers.

Taxpayers are considered on "qualified official extended duty" if they serve at a duty station at least 50 miles from their main home or live in government quarters under government order. Taxpayers are considered to be on extended duty when they are called to active duty for more than 90 days or an indefinite period.

> **Example**: Fidel bought a home in 2001 and lived in it for two-and-a-half years. Beginning in 2004, he was on qualified official extended duty in the U.S. Army. He sold his home in 2010 and had a $12,000 gain. Fidel would normally not meet the use test in the five-year period before the sale (2005-2010). However, Fidel can disregard those six years. The test period consists of the five years before he went on qualified official extended duty.

This extension of time can also apply to taxpayers who have recently left the military.

Exception for the Disabled

There is an exception to the use test if, during the five-year period before the sale of the home, the taxpayer becomes physically or mentally unable to care for herself. The taxpayer must have owned and lived in the home for at least one year.

Under this exception, the taxpayer is still considered to have lived in the home during any time that she is forced to live in a medical facility (including a nursing home) because of medical reasons.

Reduced Exclusion

Taxpayers who owned and used a home for less than two years (meaning they do not meet the ownership and use test) may be able to claim a "reduced exclusion" under certain conditions. These include selling the home due to a change in place of employment, health, or unforeseen circumstances.

Unforeseen Circumstances

If a taxpayer does not meet the ownership and use tests, he can still claim the exclusion for "unforeseen circumstances." The IRS allows for broad interpretation in qualifying for a reduced exclusion under this rule. The IRS will accept that a home sale has occurred primarily because of "unforeseen circumstances" if any of these events occur during the taxpayer's period of use and ownership of the residence:

- Death or divorce
- Health reasons (for a spouse, child, or other related person, such as a father, sibling, etc. The related person does not have to be a dependent in order for the "special circumstances" to qualify for the exclusion.)
- Unemployment or a job change (The "job related" exclusion qualifies if the new job is at least 50 miles farther than the old home was from the former place of employment. If there was no former place of employment, the distance between the new place of employment and the old home must be at least 50 miles.)
- Multiple births resulting from the same pregnancy
- Damage to the residence resulting from a disaster, or an act of war or terrorism
- Involuntary conversion of the property

Any of these situations listed can involve the taxpayer, spouse, co-owner, or a member of the taxpayer's household to qualify. The regulations also give the IRS Commissioner the

323

discretion to determine other circumstances as unforeseen. For example, the IRS Commissioner determined the September 11, 2001 terrorist attacks to be an "unforeseen circumcircumstance."

This is called the "reduced exclusion," because the taxpayer must figure the amount of excluded gain based on the actual use of the home.

> **Example:** Justin purchased his new home in Florida in June 2009. Then he suddenly lost his job. He got a new job in North Carolina and sold his house in April 2010. Because the distance between Justin's new place of employment and the home he sold is at least 50 miles, the sale satisfies the conditions of the distance safe harbor. Justin's sale of his home is due to a change in place of employment, and he is entitled to claim a reduced exclusion of gain from the sale.

How to Figure the Reduced Exclusion

The "reduced exclusion" amount equals the full $250,000 or $500,000 (for married couples filing jointly) multiplied by a fraction. The numerator is the shorter of:

- The period of ownership that the taxpayer owned and used the home as a principal residence during the five-year period ending on the sale date, OR
- The period between the last sale for which the taxpayer claimed the exclusion and the sale date for the home currently being sold.

The denominator is two years (or the equivalent in months or days). Figure the amount of the reduced exclusion by determining the number of days the taxpayer actually owned and used the property, divided by either 730 days (two years) or 24 months (two years).

> **Example:** Caroline purchases her home on January 1, 2010 for $350,000. Her mother is diagnosed with terminal cancer, and Caroline must move to care for her. Even though Caroline does not claim her mother as a dependent, the move still qualifies as an unforeseen circumstance. Caroline sells her home on May 1, 2010 for $430,000, realizing a gain of $80,000. She qualifies for the reduced maximum exclusion, and part of her gain is nontaxable. She owned and occupied the home for 121 days (January 1-May 1). She may exclude $41,438 ($250,000 X [121 ÷ 730]). Therefore, Caroline's taxable gain is $38,562 ($80,000-$41,438). This amount would be a short-term capital gain since she owned the house for less than one year.

> **Example:** Leah, a single taxpayer, lived in her principal residence for one full year (365 days) before selling it at a $400,000 gain in 2010. She qualifies for the reduced exclusion because she is pregnant with triplets (multiple births exclusion). Leah can exclude $125,000 of gain ($250,000 X [365 ÷ 730]).

*Study Hint: The EA Exam will always have a few questions regarding the sale of a primary residence. If you are asked to figure a reduced maximum exclusion, you will be given the number of days or months. You must then remember the formula.

Land Sale Only and Adjacent Lots

If a taxpayer sells the land on which his main home is located but not the house it-self, he cannot exclude the gain. Similarly, the sale of a vacant plot of land with no house on it does not qualify for the Section 121 exclusion.

> **Example:** Theresa purchases an empty lot in 2008 for $90,000, intending to build her dream home. The construction was delayed and her house was never completed. In December 2010, Theresa sells the land for $150,000. She owned the property for over a year, so she has $60,000 of long-term capital gain. None of the gain can be excluded from income, because there is no residence on the property.

However, if a taxpayer sells a vacant lot that is *adjacent to his main home*, he may be able to exclude the gain from the sale under certain circumstances. The home sale exclusion can include gain from the sale of vacant land that was used as part of the principal residence, if the land sale occurs within two years before or after the sale of the home. The land must be adjacent to land containing the home, and all other requirements of Section 121 must be satisfied. The sale of the land and the sale of the home are treated as one sale for purposes of the exclusion.

> **Example:** Roman's main home was on three acres of land. He sold a portion of his lot, directly adjacent to his home, for $70,000 in 2010. Roman meets the ownership and use tests. Therefore, he may be able to exclude his gain.

Figuring the Gain or Loss

Once a taxpayer is determined eligible for the exclusion, to figure the gain or loss on the sale of his home, you must know the following:

- Selling price
- Amount realized
- Basis
- Adjusted basis

Selling Price: The selling price is the total amount the taxpayer received for his or her main home. It includes money, all notes, mortgages, or other debts taken over by the buyer as part of the sale, and the Fair Market Value of any other property or services that the seller received.[38] Real estate sales proceeds are reported on **Form 1099-S**, *Proceeds From Real Estate Transactions*. If a taxpayer does not receive a **Form 1099-S**, she must figure basis by using sale documents and other records.

Amount Realized: The amount realized is the selling price minus selling expenses. Selling expenses include commissions, advertising fees, legal fees, and loan charges paid by the seller, such as points.

> **Example:** Selling price - Selling expenses = Amount realized
> $250,000 - $4,000 = $246,000

If the selling price or amount realized is $250,000 or less ($500,000 or less if filing jointly) there is no need to figure the realized gain if the "ownership and use" tests are met.

---

[38] A loss on the sale of a personal residence is not deductible.

Basis: The basis in a home is determined by how the taxpayer *obtained* the home. For example, if a taxpayer purchases a home, the basis is the cost of the home. If a taxpayer builds a home, then the basis is the building cost plus the cost of land. If a taxpayer receives a home through an inheritance or as a gift, the basis is either its FMV or the adjusted basis of the home.

If the taxpayer inherited the home, the basis is its FMV on the date of the decedent's death, or the later alternate valuation date chosen by the representative for the estate.

Adjusted Basis: The *adjusted basis* is the taxpayer's basis in the home increased or decreased by certain amounts. Increases include additions or improvements to the home. In order to be considered a basis *increase*, an addition or improvement must have a useful life of more than one year (example: putting on a new roof or an additional bedroom). Repairs that simply maintain a home in good condition are not considered "improvements" and should not be added to the basis of the property. Decreases to basis include deductible casualty losses, credits, and product rebates.

Formula for figuring adjusted basis:

Basis + Increases - Decreases = Adjusted basis

Example: Immanuel purchased his home years ago for $125,000. In 2010, Immanuel added another bedroom to the property. The cost of the addition was $25,000. This *increased* the house's basis. Immanuel's adjusted basis is therefore $150,000.

If the *amount realized* is more than the adjusted basis of the property, the difference is a gain and the taxpayer may be able to exclude all or part of it. If the amount realized is less than the adjusted basis, the difference is a nondeductible loss.

Example: Pete sold his main home for $275,000. His selling expenses were $10,000. The amount realized on Pete's sale is $265,000 (selling price minus selling expenses). He purchased his home ten years ago for $180,000. Therefore, his gain on the sale of the house is $85,000 ($265,000 - $180,000). If Pete meets the ownership and use tests, then he can exclude all the gain from the sale of his home.

Proceeds from the sale of a main home that meet the ownership and use tests must be reported *only* if the gain is greater than the taxpayer's allowed exclusion: only the excess gain must be reported. Gain from the sale of a home that is not the taxpayer's main home will generally have to be reported as income.

In both cases, the non-excludable gain is taxable gain and must be reported on **Schedule D.** If the home was used for business purposes or as rental property, the gain would be reported on **Form 4797**.

If the taxpayer owns a home for one year or less, the gain is reported as a short-term capital gain. If the taxpayer owns the home for more than one year, the gain is reported as a long-term capital gain.

Part II	Long-Term Capital Gains and Losses—Assets Held More Than One Year					
(a) Description of property (Example: 100 sh. XYZ Co.)	(b) Date acquired (Mo., day, yr.)	(c) Date sold (Mo., day, yr.)	(d) Sales price (see page D-7 of the instructions)	(e) Cost or other basis (see page D-7 of the instructions)	(f) Gain or (loss) Subtract (e) from (d)
8						
Main Home	09/03/94	07/07/10	789,000	226,000	563,000
Section 121 Exclusion					(500,000)

If the amount realized is less than the adjusted basis, the difference is a loss. A loss on the sale of a primary residence cannot be deducted. A loss on the sale of business property can be deducted, but will be covered in Part 2 of the EA Exam.

The taxpayer cannot include the fees and costs for obtaining a mortgage in the home's basis. These fees are not deductible. They include any costs that the taxpayer would have had to pay even if he paid cash for the home rather than financing it. These fees include pest inspections, title fees, etc.

However, if a taxpayer pays "points" then the points can be deducted as mortgage interest on Schedule A. The IRS defines "points" as pre-paid interest paid by a home buyer at closing in order to obtain a mortgage, or to obtain a lower interest rate.

If the taxpayer took depreciation deductions because she used her home for business purposes or as a rental property, she cannot exclude the part of the gain equal to any depreciation allowed (or allowable) as a deduction. Section 121 applies only to the non-rental (or non-business) portion.

> **Example:** Erica owns a duplex. She lives in one side and rents out the other side. Both of the units are the same size. She purchased the duplex in 2004 for $200,000. In 2010, Erica sells the duplex for $340,000. She has a **total gain** of $140,000. Since only half of the duplex counts as her primary residence, she would have to split the gain based on the portion of the property that qualifies as her main home. Under Section 121, Erica may exclude one half of the gain ($70,000). The other half of the gain ($70,000) is long-term capital gain. The rental portion of the duplex is treated as a sale of rental property (business property). She must report $70,000 of gain on **Schedule D.** Erica also has the option to reinvest the proceeds of the sale of her rental property into a new property by executing a Section 1031 exchange (covered next).

Like-Kind Exchanges (Section 1031 exchange)

A like-kind exchange occurs when similar business property is exchanged. If a taxpayer trades business or investment property (such as a rental property) for similar property, he does not have to pay tax on the gain or deduct any loss until he disposes of the property he received. This is the concept of a Section 1031 exchange. To qualify for non-recognition treatment, the exchange must meet all of the following conditions:

- The property must be business or investment property. A personal residence does not qualify.
- The property must not be "held primarily for sale" (such as inventory).
- Securities (such as stocks and bonds) do not qualify for like-kind exchange treatment.

- Partnership interests do not qualify for like-kind exchange treatment.
- There must be an *actual exchange* of property (the exchange for CASH is treated as a sale, not an exchange).
- The property to be received must be identified in writing within 45 days after the date of transfer of the property given up.

The replacement property must be received by the earlier of:

- The 180th day after the date on which the original property was given up in the trade, or
- The due date, (including extensions), for the tax return for the year in which the transfer of the property relinquished occurs.

The most common type of 1031 exchange is an exchange of real estate. Taxpayers must report a like-kind exchange to the IRS on **Form 8824**, *Like-Kind Exchanges*.

Rules Regarding Acceptable Like-Kind Exchanges

Some trades are not eligible for like-kind treatment. For an exchange to qualify as a 1031 exchange, the property must be "like-kind" property. For example, the trade of real estate for real estate or personal property for personal property is a trade of "like-kind property." Real properties (real estate) are generally acceptable as "like-kind," regardless of whether the properties are improved or unimproved. For instance, an exchange of a rental property for farmland would be an acceptable trade.

In order for the exchange to qualify as a Section 1031 exchange, the property must be the same "class" of property. For example, the trade of an apartment house for a store building or a panel truck for a pickup truck qualifies as a trade of "like" property. However, the exchange of a semi-truck for a plot of land would not qualify as a Section 1031 exchange, even if both properties were business properties.

Example: Casey exchanges a private jet with an adjusted basis of $400,000 for an office building valued at $375,000. This exchange does not qualify as a 1031 exchange. Private property (the jet) cannot be exchanged with real property (the building).

The trade of a piece of factory machinery for a factory building is NOT a qualifying exchange. Real estate located *inside* the United States and real estate located *outside* the United States is not "like property." Also, any equipment or other business property used within the United States and property used outside the United States is not "like property."

Example: Rebecca exchanges 100 acres of farmland for an apartment building in the city. This exchange does qualify for like-kind treatment. Exchanges of real property generally qualify for like-kind treatment, even if the property is dissimilar in actual use.

A taxpayer cannot deduct a loss in a Section 1031 exchange transaction.

Unacceptable Trades

For the Enrolled Agent Exam, you must know which types of trades are considered "unacceptable trades" by the IRS. Properties are "like-kind" if they are of the same nature or character, even if they differ in grade or quality. Intangible assets, such as trademarks, may still qualify for like-kind exchange treatment. However, the following types of property will NOT qualify for Section 1031 treatment:

- Livestock of different sexes
- Securities, bonds, stocks, or notes
- Currency exchanges
- The exchange of partnership interests

What is "Boot"?

Although the Internal Revenue Code itself does not use the term "boot," this term is frequently used in the tax field and in the IRS publications to describe property that is not "like-kind" property. The receipt of "boot" will cause a realized gain on an otherwise non-taxable exchange.

Usually this occurs when two people exchange property that is unequal in value. A typical transaction involves one party exchanging property with another party who ex-changes property and cash in order to make up the difference. The party that receives cash will have a partially taxable exchange. The exchange is still valid, but the taxpayer who re-ceives boot may have to recognize a taxable gain. Boot received can be offset by qualified costs paid during the transaction.

Example: Cain wishes to exchange his rental property in a 1031 exchange. His relinquished rental property has an FMV of $60,000 and an adjusted basis of $30,000. Cain's replace-ment property has an FMV of $50,000, and he also receives $10,000 in cash as part of the exchange. Cain, therefore, has a realized gain of $30,000 on the actual exchange, but he is required to pay tax on only $10,000—the cash (boot) received in the exchange. The rest of his gain is deferred until he sells or disposes of the property at a later date.

If you receive boot in an exchange, its Fair Market Value is recognized as taxable gain. However, this gain cannot exceed the amount of gain that would have been recog-nized if the property had been sold in a taxable transaction.

Sometimes, boot is recognized when two people exchange property that is subject to a liability. Liabilities on property are "netted" against each other. The taxpayer is treated as having received "boot" only if she is relieved of a greater liability than the liability she assumes.

This is also called "debt reduction boot," and it occurs when a taxpayer's debt on the replacement property is less than the debt on the relinquished property. "Debt reduc-tion boot" most often occurs when a taxpayer is "trading down" in an exchange (acquiring a cheaper or less valuable property).

Basis of Property Received in a Like-Kind Exchange

The basis of the property received is generally the adjusted basis of the property transferred.

Example: Adrian exchanges rental real estate (adjusted basis $50,000, FMV $80,000) for another rental property (FMV $80,000). Adrian's basis in the new property is the same as the basis of his old property ($50,000). Basis should be increased by any amount that was treated as a dividend, plus any gain recognized on the trade. Basis should be decreased by any cash received and the FMV of any other (additional) property received.

Example: Peyton bought a new computer for use in her business. She paid $4,300 cash, plus she traded in her old computer for $1,360. The old computer cost $5,000 two years ago. Peyton took depreciation deductions of $3,950 on the old computer. Even though she deducted depreciation of $3,950, the $310 gain on the exchange ($1,360 trade-in allowance minus $1,050 adjusted basis) is not reported because it is postponed under the rules for like-kind exchanges.

The basis of any other or additional property received is its Fair Market Value on the date of the trade. The taxpayer is taxed on any gain realized, but only up to the amount of the money and the Fair Market Value of the "unlike" (or boot) non-qualified property received.

Example: Judy has a rental house with an adjusted basis of $70,000. In 2010, Judy trades the rental for an empty lot with an FMV of $150,000. Judy's basis in the empty lot is $70,000, which is the adjusted basis from her previous property.

Property plus Cash

If a taxpayer trades property and also pays money, the basis of the property received is the basis of the property given up, increased by the additional money paid.

Example: Jorge trades in a truck (adjusted basis $3,000) for another truck (FMV $7,500) and also pays $4,000 in cash. The basis in Jorge's new truck is $7,000 (the $3,000 basis of the old truck plus the $4,000 additional money he paid).

Transfers Between Related Parties

Like-kind exchanges are allowed between related parties and family members. However, if *either* party disposes or sells the property within two years after the 1031 exchange, the exchange is usually disqualified; any gain or loss that was deferred in the original transaction must be recognized in the year the disposition occurs. For the purposes of this rule, a "related person" includes close family members (spouses, siblings, parents, and children). There are some exceptions to this "two-year" rule:

- If one of the parties originally involved in the exchange dies, the two-year rule does not apply.
- If the property is subsequently converted in an involuntary exchange (such as a fire or a flood), the two-year rule does not apply.
- If the exchange is genuinely NOT for tax avoidance purposes, the subsequent disposition will generally be allowed.

Exchanges between related parties get close scrutiny by the Internal Revenue Service, because they are often used by taxpayers to evade taxes on gains.

Involuntary Conversions (Section 1033)

An involuntary conversion occurs when property is destroyed, stolen, condemned, or disposed of under the threat of condemnation. If a taxpayer receives an award, property, or insurance money in payment, then the taxpayer has an "involuntary conversion." Involuntary conversions are also called *involuntary exchanges.*

In order to qualify as an involuntary conversion, the property must be converted as a result of:

- Theft, destruction, or other natural disaster,
- Condemnation, or
- Threat of condemnation.

The destruction or condemnation must be beyond the taxpayer's control in order to qualify.

Gain or loss from an involuntary conversion of property is usually recognized for tax purposes unless the property is a main home. A taxpayer reports the gain or deducts the loss on his tax return in the year the gain or loss is realized. A taxpayer cannot deduct a loss from an involuntary conversion on personal-use property unless the loss resulted from a casualty or theft.

However, a taxpayer may be able to AVOID reporting a gain on an involuntary conversion. She does not have to report the gain if she receives property that is similar to the converted property. The gain on the involuntary conversion is then deferred until a taxable sale or exchange occurs.

If a taxable gain is realized from insurance proceeds or some other source, tax on the gain can be deferred by reinvesting the proceeds in property similar to the property that was subject to the involuntary conversion. The taxpayer has two years to make the reinvestment in similar property in order to postpone the recognition of the gain. This type of conversion is called a "Section 1033" conversion.

If a taxpayer reinvests in replacement property similar to the converted property, the replacement property's basis is the same as the converted property's basis on the date of the conversion. The taxpayer will have a "carryover basis" in the new property. Essentially, her basis in the new property will be its cost, reduced by any gain realized on the old property that was not recognized. The basis may be decreased by the following:

- Any loss a taxpayer recognizes on the involuntary conversion
- Any money a taxpayer receives that he does not spend on similar property
- The basis is increased by the following:
- Any gain a taxpayer recognizes on the involuntary conversion
- Any cost of acquiring the replacement property

Example: Denise owns a residential rental with an adjusted basis of $50,000. It is destroyed by a hurricane in 2010. The property is insured, so the insurance company gives Denise a check for $100,000. Denise buys a replacement property six months later for $100,000. Her "realized gain" on the involuntary conversion is $50,000 ($100,000 insurance settlement-$50,000 basis). However, Denise does not have to "recognize" any taxable gain because she reinvested all the insurance proceeds in another, similar property.

Example: Franco owns an apartment building in Florida with a basis of $150,000. The building was destroyed by a mudslide and Franco eventually received an insurance settlement of $300,000. A year later, Franco decides to purchase another apartment building in Hawaii for $290,000. Franco's "realized gain" on the involuntary conversion is $150,000 ($300,000 - $150,000 basis). Franco must recognize $10,000 of gain, because he received an insurance payment of $300,000, but only spent $290,000 on the replacement property ($300,000 - $290,000). Franco must report $10,000 in capital gain and his basis in the new property will be $150,000, which is calculated as the cost of the new property in Hawaii minus the deferred gain ($290,000 - $140,000 = $150,000). If Franco had used all the insurance proceeds and invested it in the new property, he would not have to report any taxable gain.

Example: Pauline paid $100,000 for a rental property five years ago. After factoring in her depreciation deductions, her adjusted basis in the property is $75,000 in 2010. The property is insured for $300,000 and is totally destroyed by a flood in June 2010. On December 15, 2010, Pauline receives a $300,000 payment from her insurance. She reinvests all the insurance proceeds, plus $5,000 more of her own savings, into a new rental apartment building. She qualifies to defer all of her gain. Her basis in the new rental property is $80,000, ($75,000 + $5,000).

Condemnations

A condemnation is an involuntary conversion. Condemnation is the process by which private property is legally taken from its owner for public use, such as by a local government. The property may be taken by the government or by a private organization that has the legal power to seize it.

The owner receives a condemnation award (money or property) in exchange for the property that is taken. A condemnation is like a forced sale, the owner being the seller and the government being the buyer.

Example: The federal government is authorized to acquire land for public parks. The government tells Trevor that it is condemning his farmland in order to use it as a public park. Trevor goes to court to try to keep his property. The court decides in favor of the government, which takes Trevor's property and pays him $400,000 in exchange. Trevor's basis in the farmland was $80,000. He decides not to purchase replacement farmland. Therefore, he has a taxable event, and $320,000 would need to be recognized as income ($400,000 - $80,000 = $320,000). If Trevor were to purchase replacement property, he would have a nontaxable Section 1033 exchange.

A condemnation award is the money that is paid for the condemned property. Amounts taken out of the award to pay debts on the property are considered paid to the taxpayer and are included in the amount of the award.

Example: The state condemned Gabriel's property in order to build a light rail system. The court award was set at $200,000. The state paid Gabriel only $148,000 because it paid $50,000 to his mortgage company and also $2,000 in accrued real estate taxes. Gabriel is considered to have received the entire $200,000 as a condemnation award.

Postponing Gain or Loss from an Involuntary Conversion

Gain or loss from an involuntary conversion is not recognized if the taxpayer receives similar property. The basis for the new property is the same as the basis for the converted property. The gain on the involuntary conversion is deferred indefinitely until a taxable sale or exchange occurs.

If a taxpayer has an involuntary conversion and then purchases replacement property, he can elect to postpone reporting gain on the conversion. The taxpayer can postpone reporting all the gain if the replacement property costs at least as much as the amount realized from the sale.

> **Example:** Ayah is a self-employed tax preparer. She bought an office copier for $1,500 in 2008 and deducted $780 depreciation. In 2010, a fire destroyed the machine and Ayah received $1,200 from her fire insurance, realizing a gain of $480 ($1,200 - $720 adjusted basis). She chose to postpone reporting the gain, but her replacement machinery cost only $1,000. The taxable gain under the rules for involuntary conversions is limited to the remaining $200 insurance payment. All the replacement property is depreciable business property, so the ordinary income that Ayah must recognize on her tax return is only $200.

The Replacement Period

To qualify for non-recognition treatment, the *replacement property* must be obtained within a certain time period. The taxpayer has two years to roll over the condemnation or insurance proceeds from the involuntary conversion into a new investment. The replacement property must be "similar or related in service or use."

The replacement period is longer for business-use real property (real estate) and real property held for investment. In this case, the replacement period is three years. In both cases, the replacement property must be purchased before the end of the tax year in which the replacement deadline applies.

Property Type	Replacement period
Most property except those noted below	Two years
Real property (investment property or property used in a business) includes residential rentals, office buildings, etc.	Three years
Sale of livestock due to weather-related conditions in a federal disaster area	Four years

> **Example:** Joel owns a bar and pool hall. In 2010, the building is condemned by the city because of the discovery of asbestos in the building. Joel has until December 31, 2013 to replace the condemned pool hall with a similar building.

Condemnation of a Primary Residence

If a taxpayer has a gain because his main home is condemned, he can generally exclude the gain as if he had sold the home (the Section 121 exclusion). The taxpayer can exclude up to $250,000 of the gain (up to $500,000 if MFJ).

> **Example:** Fred and Dominique are married and file jointly. They paid $100,000 for their home in 2001. The house is insured for $700,000. Their home is completely destroyed by fire in 2010, so they receive an insurance payment of $700,000. They have a realized gain on the conversion of $600,000 ($700,000 - $100,000). But $500,000 of the gain would be excluded under Section 121 (the exclusion for the sale of primary residence), leaving $100,000 as taxable long-term capital gain. Fred and Dominique can also choose to reinvest the insurance proceeds under the rules for involuntary conversions, and defer all the gain.

Summary: Non-Recognition Property Transactions

Section 121: Sale of Primary Residence

A main home is the place the taxpayer lived most of the time. The ownership and use tests require that, during the five-year period ending on the date of the sale, the taxpayers:

- Owned the home for at least two years (the ownership test), and
- Lived in the home as their main home for at least two years (the use test)

The required two years of ownership/use do not have to be continuous. The maximum that can be excluded is $250,000 or $500,000 for MFJ.

Section 1031 Exchange: Like-Kind Exchanges

Section 1031 only applies to business properties. Section 1031 does NOT apply to exchanges of inventory, stocks, bonds, notes, other securities or evidence of indebtedness, or partnership interests. Livestock of different sexes are not like-kind properties. Also, property used in the United States and property used outside the United States do NOT qualify as like-kind properties. The most common type of 1031 exchange is an exchange of real estate. Taxpayers must report a like-kind exchange to the IRS on **Form 8824,** *Like-Kind Exchanges.*

Section 1033: Involuntary Conversions

In order to qualify as an involuntary conversion, a property must be converted as a result of:

- Theft, destruction, or other natural disaster,
- Condemnation, or
- Threat of condemnation.

The gain on the involuntary conversion can be deferred if insurance or condemnation proceeds are reinvested. The taxpayer will have a "carryover basis" in the new property. Essentially, his basis in the new property will be its cost, reduced by any gain realized on the old property that was not recognized.

Unit 1.11: Questions
Sale of Primary Residence: Questions

1. Guy lived and owned his home for only six months. In 2010, he decided to move in with his new girlfriend, so he sold his home for $275,000. His selling expenses were $10,000. The adjusted basis in his home is $60,000. He cannot exclude any of his gain under Section 121. What is the amount of his gain on the sale?

A. $60,000
B. $215,000
C. $205,000
D. Some other amount

The answer is C. The correct answer is $205,000. The amount of the gain on the sale of Guy's house is $205,000, which is the result of subtracting the adjusted basis in the home from the amount realized. ($265,000 - $60,000 = $205,000). The amount should be reported on Schedule D as a short-term capital gain since he owned the house for less than a year. ###

2. Salvador meets the eligibility requirements for claiming the exclusion on the gain from the sale of his home. The selling price of the home is $195,000 and selling expenses are $15,000. What is the amount realized in this sale?

A. $195,000
B. $180,000
C. $15,000
D. $0

The answer is B. The amount realized on Salvador's sale is $180,000 (selling price minus selling expenses). If Salvador qualifies for the full Section 121 exclusion, he may exclude all of the gain, and it doesn't need to be reported. ###

3. Lucille owns a home in a Colorado ski area (the "ski home"). She stays at the ski home most weekends and spends the entire months of December, January, and February there. When she is not at the ski home, she lives in a four-room apartment that she rents in Denver. For over half the year, she lives in Denver. What is Lucille's primary residence for the Section 121 exclusion?

A. Her ski home in Colorado
B. Her apartment in Denver
C. She is considered a transient for tax purposes
D. None of the above

The answer is B. Lucille's main home is her rental apartment in Denver because she lives there most of the time. If she were to sell the ski home, she would not qualify for the Section 121 exclusion on the sale because it is not her primary residence. ###

4. In September 2008, Reilly and Martine bought a new home in Phoenix, but they had trouble selling their old home in Los Angeles. They moved into their new home and kept the old home on the market, hoping it would sell. Six months later, in March 2009, they sold their old home at a $40,000 gain. They had owned and lived in the old home for four years. They excluded all the gain on the sale of the old home. On October 1, 2010, Reilly and Martine sold the Phoenix home they purchased in September 2008 at a $15,000 gain. They sold their house because they wanted to live closer to the beach. Can Reilly and Martine exclude the gain on the October 2010 sale?

A. Yes, they can exclude all the gain.
B. No, they cannot exclude any of the gain.
C. They can exclude a portion of the gain.
D. None of the above.

The answer is B. Because Reilly and Martine had excluded gain on the sale of another home within the two-year period ending on October 1, 2010, they cannot exclude the gain on the new sale. The sale does not qualify for a partial exclusion because they moved simply because they chose to live elsewhere. ###

5. Uri bought his principal residence for $250,000 on May 3, 2009. He sold it on May 3, 2010, for $400,000 because he wanted to move to Hawaii. What is the amount and character of his gain?

A. Long-term ordinary gain of $650,000
B. Long-term capital gain of $150,000
C. Short-term ordinary gain of $250,000
D. Short-term capital gain of $150,000

The answer is D. Uri owned the home for one year or less, so the gain is reported as a short-term capital gain. He must start counting his holding period AFTER the date of purchase (Publication 17). ###

336

6. Heather, a single woman, bought her first home in June 2007 for $350,000. She lived continuously in the house until she sold it in July 2010 for $620,000. Which of the following is TRUE?

A. Heather may exclude up to $250,000 in gain. The remaining amount must be reported and will be taxed as a long-term capital gain on Schedule D.
B. Heather may exclude all the gain. There is no amount that needs to be reported.
C. Heather may not exclude any of the gain.
D. Heather may exclude $250,000 in gain. The remaining amount must be reported as a short-term capital gain on Schedule D.

The answer is A. Heather is able to exclude the maximum amount of gain ($250,000) from the sale of her home. Her gain is $270,000 ($620,000 - $350,000). Her taxable gain is $20,000 ($270,000 gain - $250,000 exclusion). The $20,000 taxable gain must be reported as a long-term capital gain on Schedule D. ###

7. Mitchell purchased his primary residence for $350,000 on January 1, 2008. On January 3, 2009, he sells the home for $320,000, incurring a loss of $30,000. How is this transaction reported?

A. Mitchell has a short-term capital loss that can be reported on Schedule D.
B. Mitchell cannot deduct any loss from the sale of his home on his return.
C. Mitchell has a long-term capital loss that can be reported on Schedule D.
D. Mitchell has a deductible casualty loss.

The answer is B. If a taxpayer has a loss on the sale of a primary residence, he cannot deduct it on his return. Losses from the sale of a main home are never tax-deductible. (Publication 17). ###

8. Geoff sold his main home in 2010 at a $29,000 gain. He meets the ownership and use tests to exclude the gain from his income. However, he used one room of the home for business in 2008 and 2009. His records show he claimed $3,000 in depreciation for a home office. What is Geoff's taxable gain on the sale, if any?

A. $0
B. $1,000
C. $2,000
D. $3,000

The answer is D. Geoff can exclude $26,000 ($29,000 - $3,000) of his gain. He has a taxable gain of $3,000. If a taxpayer took depreciation deductions because he used his home for business purposes or as a rental property, he cannot exclude the part of the gain equal to any depreciation allowed (or allowable) as a deduction (Publication 523). ####

9. Which of the following would generally NOT be acceptable as "unforeseen circumstances" for a taxpayer to take a reduced exclusion on the sale of his primary residence?

A. The home is condemned
B. A divorce
C. The birth of twin girls
D. A move to a warmer climate for general health

The answer is D. The move to a warmer climate would not qualify. All of the following events would be qualifying events in order to claim a reduced exclusion from a premature sale:

- A divorce or legal separation
- A pregnancy resulting in multiple births
- Serious health reasons (the person who is sick does not need to be the taxpayer's dependent—only a close family member, such as a parent or a child).
- The home is sold after being seized or condemned (such as by a government agency)
- The move is because of a new job or new employment

If any of these exceptions apply, then the taxpayer may figure a reduced exclusion based on the number of days the taxpayer owned and lived in the residence. ###

10. Dan and Grace were married in January 2007. They purchased their first home in March 2007 for $150,000. In February 2010, Dan and Grace legally separated, and Grace was granted total ownership of the home by the divorce court as part of the divorce settlement. The divorce became final on June 2010, and the Fair Market Value of the home at the time of the transfer was $370,000. Grace sells the house on December 23, 2010 for $480,000. What is Grace's taxable gain in the transaction?

A. $0
B. $80,000
C. $120,000
D. $210,000

The answer is B. Special rules apply to divorced taxpayers. Grace meets the ownership and use tests, and the basis in the property remains the same. Transfers related to a divorce are generally nontaxable, and the Fair Market Value of the property at the time of the divorce has no bearing on the taxable outcome. The gain is figured as follows:

Original cost	$150,000
Sale price	$480,000
Total realized gain	$330,000
Sec. 121 exclusion	($250,000)
Taxable gain	**$80,000**

The taxable portion of the gain would be reported on Schedule D as a long-term capital gain. ###

11. Alfred and Kaye are married and file jointly. They owned and used a home as their principal residence for 22 months. Alfred got a new job in another state and they sold their home in order to move for the new employment opportunity. What is the maximum amount that can be excluded from income under the rules regarding a "reduced exclusion"?

A. $22,727
B. $250,000
C. $458,333
D. $523,000
E. $500,000

The answer is C. In this case, the maximum reduced exclusion available to Alfred and Kaye is $458,333 [$500,000 x (22 months/24 months)]. They qualify for a reduced exclusion because Alfred is moving for a change in employment. The reduced exclusion applies when the premature sale is primarily due to a move for employment in a new location. ###

12. Shane and Phyllis move after living in their home for 292 days, because Phyllis became pregnant with triplets and they need a larger home. The gain on the sale of the home is $260,000. Since they have lived there for less than two years but meet one of the exceptions, what is the actual amount of their reduced exclusion? (Two years=730 days)

A. $60,000
B. $200,000
C. $260,000
D. $500,000

The answer is B. The couple has an exclusion of $200,000 (292/730 multiplied by the $500,000 exclusion available for married taxpayers). The remaining $60,000 would be considered taxable capital gain income and would be reported on Schedule D. This move qualifies for the "reduced exclusion," because multiple births from the same pregnancy are considered a "health related" move. ###

Like-Kind Exchanges: Questions

13. How should taxpayers report Section 1031 exchanges to the IRS?

A. Form 8824
B. Form 4787
C. Schedule C
D. Schedule D

The answer is A. You must report a like-kind exchange to the IRS on Form 8824, Like-Kind Exchanges. ###

14. Samson exchanged a rental building for another rental building. He had a basis of $16,000, plus he had made $10,000 in improvements prior to the exchange. He exchanged it for a building worth $36,000. Samson did not recognize any gain from the exchange on his individual tax return. What is Samson's basis in the new property?

A. $26,000
B. $36,000
C. $10,000
D. $16,000

The answer is A. Samson's basis in the new building is based on his basis in the old building, which was $16,000 + $10,000 = $26,000. ###

15. Which of the following transactions DO NOT qualify for a Section 1031 like-kind exchange?

A. An exchange of business city property and farm property
B. An exchange of one trademark for another trademark
C. An exchange of a business desk for a business printer
D. An exchange of inventory for different inventory

The answer is D. Inventory never qualifies for like-kind exchange treatment. The property must NOT be held "primarily for sale," such as merchandise, retail stock, or inventory. Generally, real property exchanges will qualify for like-kind treatment, even though the properties themselves might be dissimilar. ###

16. Alex is a flight instructor. He trades in a small plane (adjusted basis $300,000) for another, larger plane (FMV $750,000) and pays $60,000 in an additional down payment. He uses the plane 100% in his instruction business. What is his basis in the new plane?

A. $0
B. $300,000
C. $360,000
D. $700,500
E. $810,000

The answer is C. Alex's basis is $360,000—the $300,000 basis of the old plane plus the $60,000 cash paid (Publication 551). ###

17. Bailey exchanges his residential rental property (adjusted basis $50,000, FMV $80,000) for a different rental property (FMV $70,000). What is Bailey's basis in the NEW property?

A. $50,000
B. $70,000
C. $80,000
D. $100,000

The answer is A. His basis in the new property is the same as the basis of the old ($50,000). The basis of the property received is the same as the basis of the property given up. ###

18. Jacob exchanges a residential rental in Las Vegas with a basis of $100,000 for an investment property in Miami Beach valued at $220,000 plus $15,000 in cash. What is Jacob's taxable gain on the exchange, and what is the basis of the new property on Miami Beach?

A. Taxable gain: $15,000. Basis: $100,000.
B. Taxable gain: $0. Basis: $235,000.
C. Taxable gain: $15,000. Basis: $220,000.
D. Taxable gain: $15,000. Basis: $135,000.

The answer is A. Jacob's total realized gain on the exchange is $135,000 ([$220,000 + $15,000] - $100,000 basis in old property). Only the cash boot is taxable ($15,000). Jacob's basis in the new building will be $100,000 (the original basis in the land he gave up). ###

Involuntary Conversions: Questions

19. Benny owns a yacht that he uses for personal use. His purchase price was $150,000. The yacht is destroyed by a tsunami in 2010. Benny collects $175,000 from his insurance company and promptly reinvests all the proceeds in a larger, new yacht, which costs Benny $201,000. What is his basis in the new yacht?

A. $175,000
B. $176,000
C. $201,000
D. $226,000

The answer is B. The answer is figured as follows: ($175,000 - $150,000) = $25,000: deferred gain; ($201,000 - $25,000) = $176,000: new basis in the asset. Since Benny purchased replacement property, the basis of the replacement property is the cost of the new yacht ($201,000) MINUS his deferred gain ($25,000). ###

19. A tornado destroys Bryant's primary residence home on July 15, 2008. He wants to replace the home using a Section 1033 exchange for involuntary conversions. What is the latest year that Bryant can replace the property in order to defer any gain from the insurance reimbursement?

A. Bryant must have made the election by December 31, 2010.
B. Bryant is not required to make an election.
C. Bryant must make the election by July 15, 2011.
D. Bryant must make the election by December 31, 2012.

The answer is A. Bryant must acquire qualifying replacement property by December 31, 2010 (two years from the END of the gain year), and report the details on his 2010 tax return. ###

21. Christian owns an office building with a $400,000 basis. The building was completely destroyed by a fire in 2010. Christian receives insurance money totaling $600,000. He purchases a new office building for $450,000 and then invests the rest of the insurance proceeds in stocks. Which of the following statements is true?

A. Christian has $200,000 in taxable gain he must recognize on his tax return.
B. Christian has $150,000 in taxable gain he must recognize on his tax return.
C. Christian does not have a taxable gain, because he reinvested all the proceeds in qualifying investment property.
D. Christian has $50,000 in taxable gain he must recognize on his tax return.

The answer is B. Christian's realized gain is $200,000 ($600,000 - $400,000) and his taxable gain is $150,000. He purchased another building for $450,000, so he may defer $50,000 of the gain under Section 1033 for involuntary conversions. The remainder of the gain, $150,000 ($600,000 - $450,000), must be recognized because he did not reinvest the remaining proceeds into "like-kind" property. If Christian had reinvested all the proceeds in a new building, then all of his gain would have been deferred, and he would not have to pay taxes on any of the amount. ###

Unit 1.12: The Estate and Gift Tax

> **More Reading:**
> Publication 559, *Survivors, Executors, and Administrators*
> Publication 950, *Introduction to Estate and Gift Taxes*
> Publication 4895, *Tax Treatment of Property Acquired From a Decedent Dying in 2010.*

*Note: In 2010, the rules regarding estate taxes changed dramatically. President Obama signed the *Tax Relief, Unemployment Insurance Reauthorization, and Job Creation Act of 2010* (Tax Relief Act) into law on December 17, 2010. This bill provided estate tax relief and also changed the gift tax rules. The laws regarding estates for 2010 are extremely complex, but we will explain the main concepts in this unit.

The estate tax is imposed on certain transfers at death. For Part One of the EA exam, you will be required to understand how the estate and gift taxes affect individual taxpayers.

Requirements for the Executor of an Estate

After a person dies, an executor is usually chosen to manage the estate. Current IRS requirements require the executor of an estate to file the following tax returns:

- The final income tax return (Form 1040) for the decedent (for income received before death);
- Fiduciary income tax returns (Form 1041) for the estate during its administration; and
- *Estate Tax Return* (Form 706), if the Fair Market Value of the assets of the estate exceed $5 million, or Form 8939, if the executor elects out of the estate tax and elects to apply the new carryover basis rules.

Estates in General

For federal tax purposes, an estate is a separate legal entity that's created when a taxpayer dies. The Estate Tax is a tax on the right to transfer property at death. A person who inherits property is not taxed on the transfer. Instead, the estate is responsible for paying any tax before the property is distributed to the heirs. The deceased taxpayer's property may consist of cash and securities, a primary residence, other real estate, insurance, trusts, annuities, business interests, and other assets.

The Gross Estate

The Gross Estate consists of an accounting of everything the deceased taxpayer owned at the date of death. Generally, when valuing the estate, the Fair Market Value of these items is used, not necessarily what the deceased taxpayer paid for them.[39] The total of all of these items is called the "Gross Estate." Keep in mind that the Gross Estate will likely include non-probate as well as probate property.[40]

---

[39] See the election below on "electing out of the Estate Tax" for more information about property valuation on the date of death.

[40] Probate property is property that was directly owned by a decedent for which there is no named beneficiary or which is not jointly owned. Probate property passes in accordance with the decedent's will. If the deceased taxpayer doesn't have a will, then state law determines how the property passes to the heirs.

Income keeps the same character in the hands of a beneficiary as it had in the hands of the estate. For example, if the income distributed includes dividends, tax-exempt interest, or capital gains, it will receive the same tax treatment in the beneficiary's hands.

The Gross Estate does NOT include property owned solely by the decedent's spouse or other individuals. Lifetime gifts that are complete (no control over the gifts is retained) are not included in the Gross Estate.

Once the executor has accounted for the Gross Estate, certain deductions are allowed in order to calculate the taxpayer's "Taxable Estate." These deductions may include mortgages and other debts, estate administration expenses, property that passes to surviving spouses, and qualified charities.

After the Taxable Estate is computed, the value of lifetime taxable gifts is added to this number and the tax is computed.

An estate tax return is filed using Form 706, *United States Estate (and Generation-Skipping Transfer) Tax Return.* The due date for Form 706 for 2010 decedents' estates is the later of September 19, 2011 or nine months after the date of death.[41] The executor may request an extension of time to file Form 4768. However, the tax is still due by the due date and interest is accrued on any amounts still owed by the due date that are not paid at that time.

If applicable, the estate is required to pay estimated tax just like any other entity. Since the estate tax is optional in 2010, it is rare that the administrator of an estate would have to pay tax on an estate. Although it is still possible on very large estates (over $5 million), if the executor does not opt-out properly or for some reason prefers to pay the estate tax instead of opting for the modified basis rules that are in affect for the 2010 tax year.

In its current form, the estate tax only affects the wealthiest 2% of all Americans.

Deductions from the Gross Estate

Once the executor has accounted for the entire "Gross Estate," certain deductions (and in special circumstances, reductions in value) are allowed in arriving at the deceased person's "Taxable Estate." The allowable deductions used in determining the "Taxable Estate" include:

- Funeral expenses paid by the estate.
- Debts owed at the time of death.
- Medical expenses and taxes.
- Casualty and theft losses.
- Charitable Deduction: If the decedent leaves property to a qualifying charity, it is deductible from the gross estate.
- Mortgages and debt.
- Administration expenses of the estate.
- Losses during estate administration.
- The Marital Deduction (generally, the value of the property that passes from the estate to the surviving spouse).

---

[41] At the time of this book's printing in March 2011, the 2010 Form 706 was still not available on the IRS website. The IRS has been very late in providing forms and guidance for 2010 estates.

- The state Death Tax deduction (if applicable).

After the net amount is computed, the value of lifetime taxable gifts is added to this number and the tax is computed. Most relatively simple estates (such as estates comprised of cash, publicly-traded securities, and small amounts of other easily valued assets) do not have to file an estate tax return.

Income In Respect of a Decedent

"Income in Respect of a Decedent" is any taxable income that was earned but *not received* by the decedent by the time of death. "IRD" is NOT taxed on the final return of the deceased taxpayer. IRD is reported on the tax return of the person or entity that receives the income. This could be the estate, the surviving spouse, or some other beneficiary, such as a child. IRD income retains the same tax nature after death as if the taxpayer were still alive. For example, if the income would have been short-term capital gain to the deceased, it's taxed the same way to the beneficiary. IRD can come from various sources, including:

- Unpaid salary, wages or bonuses,
- Distributions from traditional IRAs and employer-provided retirement plans,
- Deferred compensation benefits,
- Accrued but unpaid interest, dividends, and rent, and
- The accounts receivable of a sole proprietor.

There is no "step-up" in basis for IRD. If IRD is paid to the estate, it is reported on IRS Form 1041. If IRD is paid directly to a beneficiary, it must be reported on the beneficiary's tax return.

Example: Carlos, the decedent, was owed $5,000 in wages upon his sudden death. The check for the wages wasn't remitted by his employer until three weeks later. The beneficiary of these wages is Carlos's daughter Rosalie. The wages are considered IRD, and Rosalie must recognize the same amount of income as Carlos would have recognized, in this case all $5,000 as ordinary income.

Example: Beverly died on April 30. Upon her death, she had accrued (but not yet received) $1,500 in interest on bonds and $2,000 in rental income. Beverly's beneficiary will include $3,500 in IRD in gross income when the interest and rent are received. The income retains its character as passive interest income and passive rental income.

Regardless of the decedent's accounting method, IRD is subject to income tax when the income is received by the beneficiary.

Reporting the Self-Employment Income of a Deceased Person

The death of one partner automatically terminates the tax year of the deceased partner. The deceased partner's share of the partnership income is reported on the final tax return. The earnings are only subject to self-employment tax through the month of death.

However, self-employment income reported on a Schedule C or Schedule F (from farming) is all subject to SE tax, even though the taxpayer is deceased. The business income that is reported on Form 1041 is not subject to self-employment tax.

Example: Louise is a self-employed bookkeeper on the cash basis and reports her income and expenses on Schedule C. On May 10, 2010, Louise dies while many of her clients' invoices are still unpaid. Louise's daughter Kim is also her executor. She notifies all of Louise's clients and also collects $2,400 in client payments that trickle in after Louise's death. The income that Louise earned before May 10 should be reported on her final Form 1040. The $2,500 is IRD and must be reported on Form 1041. The $2,500 received after Louise's death is not subject to self-employment tax.

Estates and Credits

Estates are allowed some of the same tax credits that are allowed to individuals. The credits are generally allocated between the estate and the beneficiaries. However, estates are not allowed the credit for the elderly or the disabled, the child tax credit, or the earned income credit.

The Personal Representative (or Executor)

When a taxpayer dies, a personal representative generally is required to settle the decedent's financial affairs. A personal representative of an estate is the executor or administrator in charge of the decedent's property. The personal representative is responsible for filing the final income tax return and the estate tax return when it is due.

The personal representative is responsible for determining the estate tax before the assets are distributed to any beneficiaries. The tax liability for an estate attaches to the assets of the estate itself, so if the assets are distributed to the beneficiaries before the taxes are paid, the beneficiaries may be held liable for the tax debt, up to the value of the assets distributed.

If there is no executor appointed to handle the estate, every person in actual or constructive possession of any property of the decedent is considered an executor and must file a return. Either the personal representative or a paid preparer must sign the appropriate line of the return.

Form 709 Signature Area

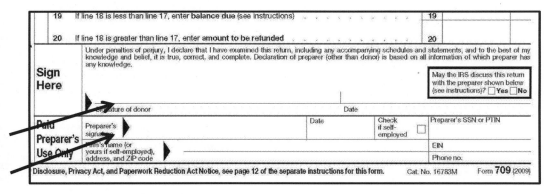

Transfers Between Spouses: the Marital Deduction

There are special rules and exceptions for transfers between spouses, which are generally not subject to federal gift or estate tax. The Marital Deduction allows spouses to transfer an unlimited amount of property to one another during their lifetimes or at death free of transfer taxes. The Marital Deduction is a deduction from the "Gross Estate" in order to arrive at the "Taxable Estate."

The unlimited Marital Deduction applies to both estate tax and gift tax. To receive an unlimited deduction, the spouse receiving the assets must be a U.S. citizen, a legal spouse, and have outright ownership of the assets.

Electing Out of the Estate Tax for the 2010 Tax Year

For the estates of decedents dying in 2010, the executor may *elect out* of the estate tax system and *instead* use the new carryover basis rules under the Economic Growth and Tax Relief Reconciliation Act of 2001 (EGTRRA). Under EGTRRA, a recipient's basis in assets acquired from the decedent who died in 2010 is the *lesser* of:

- The decedent's adjusted basis (carryover basis), or
- The Fair Market Value of the property on the date of the decedent's death.

However, there are two exceptions to this general rule:

- The executor can allocate up to $1.3 million, increased by unused losses and loss carryovers[42], to increase the basis of assets owned by the decedent at death; and
- The executor can also allocate an additional amount of up to $3 million to increase the basis of assets passing to a surviving spouse, either outright or in a *Qualified Terminable Interest Property trust.*

Also, the executor may increase the basis of certain property acquired from and owned by a decedent who died in 2010 and that passes to the decedent's surviving spouse by an additional amount of $3 million. The executor cannot, however, increase the basis in any property above its Fair Market Value at the time of death.

Form 8939 is used to elect out of the estate tax, to report the carryover basis of the decedent's property and to allocate the basis increase allowed under the optional carryover basis rules. If an executor decides to opt out of the estate tax, the due date for Form 8939 for 2010 estates is April 18, 2011.[43] Failure to furnish any information required on Form 8939 may result in a penalty of $10,000.

In addition, the executor must provide to each beneficiary a written statement that lists the information reported on Form 8939 related to the property that the beneficiary acquired from the decedent. The executor must furnish the beneficiaries with this statement no later than 30 days after the filing of Form 8939. Failure to provide each beneficiary with this statement can result in a penalty of $50 for each failure.

---

[42] Limited to $60,000 in the case of a decedent who is a nonresident alien, but with no loss or loss carryover increase.

[43] At the time of this printing, the IRS has not yet released the new Form 8939.

Basis of Estate Property

Property that is jointly owned by a decedent and another person will be included in full in the decedent's Gross Estate unless the executor can show that the other person contributed to some of the purchase price. To figure the surviving owner's new basis of property that was jointly owned, add the surviving owner's original basis in the property to the value of the part of the property included in the decedent's estate. Subtract from the sum any deductions for depreciation allowed to the surviving owner on that property.

If property is jointly held between husband and wife, there is only a "step-up" in basis of half the property's value (unless the executor "elects out" of the estate tax in 2010). If the decedent holds property in a community property state, half of the value of the community property will be included in the Gross Estate of the decedent, but the entire value of the estate will receive a 100% "step-up" in basis.

Special Election for Decedent's Medical Expenses

Medical expenses that were not paid before death are liabilities of the estate and are shown on the estate tax return (Form 706). However, if medical expenses for the decedent are paid out of the estate during the one-year period beginning with the day after death, the representative can elect to treat all or part of the expenses as paid by the decedent at the time they were incurred.

Final Tax Return (Form 1040)

The unpleasant task of filing a deceased taxpayer's final return usually falls to the executor of the estate, but if no executor is named, a survivor must do it. This is usually a spouse or a family member. The return is filed on the same form that would have been used if the taxpayer were still alive, but "deceased" is written after the taxpayer's name. The filing deadline is April 15 of the year following the taxpayer's death, just like regular tax returns (April 18 in 2011 because of the extended tax deadline this year).

The personal representative must file the final individual income tax return of the decedent for the year of death and any returns not filed for preceding years. If an individual died after the close of the tax year but before the return for that year was filed, the return for the year just closed will not be the final return. The return for that year will be a regular return and the personal representative must file it.

> **Example:** Stephanie dies suddenly on February 2, 2011. She had not yet filed her 2010 tax return. She earned $51,000 in wages in 2010. She also earned $13,000 in wages between January 1, 2010 and her death. Therefore, Stephanie's 2010 and 2011 tax return must be filed by her executor. Her 2011 return would be her last individual tax return.

If a refund is due on the taxpayer's final return(s), the taxpayer's representative must also file a copy of Form 1310, *Statement of Person Claiming Refund Due a Deceased Taxpayer*. Form 1310 is not required for a surviving spouse filing a joint return.

On a decedent's final tax return, the rules for a personal exemption and deductions remain the same as for any taxpayer. The full personal exemption may be claimed on the final tax return.

The Strange Estate Rules for 2010

The 2010 Tax Relief Act made significant changes to the applicable exclusion amounts for transfers after December 31, 2009 and created a special election for estates of decedents who died in 2010. The Act also established portability rules for decedents who die in 2011 and 2012; the rules allow a married couple to pass a decedent's unused exclusion to the surviving spouse.

The estate tax was retroactively reinstated for taxpayers who died in 2010. This means that the 2010 Tax Relief Act reinstated the estate tax for decedents who died after December 31, 2009. However, the 2010 Tax Relief Act also increased the applicable exclusion from tax to $5 million (up dramatically from 2009, when the exclusion was $3.5 million).

The 2010 Tax Relief Act also reduced the maximum tax rate for estates down to 35% (down from 45% for 2009). In addition, the 2010 Tax Relief Act allows executors of the estates of decedents dying in 2010 to completely elect out of the estate tax system and instead use the carryover basis rules enacted under the Economic Growth and Tax Relief Reconciliation Act of 2001 (EGTRRA).[44]

The 2010 Tax Relief Act did NOT change the exclusion amount or the maximum tax rate for gifts. The exclusion amount for gifts made in 2010 is still $1 million, and the maximum tax rate on gifts remains the same at 35%.

IRS Form 1041

IRS Form 1041 is used by a domestic decedent's estate, trust, or bankruptcy estate to report:

- The current income, deductions, gains, losses, etc. of the estate or trust[45];
- The income that is either accumulated or held for future distribution or distributed currently to the beneficiaries;
- Any income tax liability of the estate or trust; and
- Employment taxes on wages paid to household employees.

Form 1041 is also used to report the income that the deceased taxpayer had a right to receive but was unable to receive prior to his death (*frequently tested). Filing Form 1041 is the responsibility of the decedent's executor, surviving spouse, or surviving heirs. IRS Form 1041 is also used to report the earnings on the decedent's property after death. For example, dividends or interest earned must be reported, even though a taxpayer may have died. Usually, investment property will continue to earn revenues even after a taxpayer has died and they must be reported.

The due date for Form 1041 is the fifteenth day of the fourth month following the end of the entity's tax year. An extension of six months can be filed.

---

[44] If an executor chooses to elect out of the estate tax system for tax year 2010, he or she must make the election on a timely filed Form 8939, which is the form that will be used to report the basis of the assets acquired from a decedent. At the time of this book's release, Form 8939 was not yet available.

[45] The taxation of trusts is covered in Book 2.

The personal representative must file Form 1041 for any domestic estate that has:

- Gross income for the tax year of $600 or more, or
- A beneficiary who is a nonresident alien (any amount of income).

The personal representative files Schedule K-1 to report distributions to each beneficiary. Schedule K-1 provides the amount of income, deductions, and credits the beneficiary received during the year. The beneficiary is then required to report the distributions as income on his tax individual tax return.

The Gift Tax

The gift tax is imposed on the transfer of property by one individual to another. The tax applies whether the donor intends the transfer to be a gift or not. The gift tax is an excise tax that is imposed on the donor (under special arrangements the donee may agree to pay the tax instead) of the gift. This means that the *receiver* of the gift does not pay the tax. The *giver* pays the tax (if any). For gifts made in 2010, the maximum rate for the gift tax is 35%.

Gifts are frequently made to shift income legally to another family member, so that the donor will move into a lower tax bracket.

2010 Gift Exclusion Amounts

- The annual exclusion for gifts made to a donee during 2010 is $13,000.
- Unlimited gifts are allowed to a spouse as long as the spouse is a U.S. citizen.
- The annual exclusion for gifts made to spouses who are not U.S. citizens has increased to $134,000.
- The "lifetime exclusion" for 2010 is $1 million.

Example: Dan is single. In 2010, Dan gives his adult son Noah $15,000 to help start his first business. The money is not a loan, so Dan is required to file a gift tax return and report that he used $2,000 ($15,000 minus the $13,000 2010 gift exclusion) of his $1 million lifetime exemption.

The Marital Deduction

For U.S. estate and gift tax purposes, there are no tax consequences on gifts between spouses. The federal gift tax Marital Deduction is only available if the donee spouse (the person receiving the gift) is a U.S. citizen.

Gift-splitting

If a married couple makes a gift to another person, the gift can be considered as being one-half from one spouse and one-half from the other spouse. This is known as gift splitting. In 2010, gift splitting allows married couples to give up to $26,000 to a person without making a taxable gift. Both spouses must consent to split the gift. Married couples who split gifts must file a gift tax return, even if one-half of the split gift is less than the annual exclusion.

Example: Harold and his wife Margie agree to split gifts of cash. Harold gives his nephew George $21,000, and Margie gives her niece Gina $18,000. Although each gift is more than the annual exclusion ($13,000), by gift splitting they can make these gifts without making a taxable gift. In each case, because one-half of the split gift is not more than the annual exclusion, it is not a taxable gift. However, the couple must file a gift tax return. So even each individual gift totals more than $13,000 they can do this and it's not taxable

Example: Felicia gives her son James $24,000 to purchase a new car. Felicia elects to split the gift with her husband Rafael. One-half of the gift is deemed as coming from each spouse. Assuming they make no other gifts to James during the year, the entire $24,000 gift is tax free. With the election, Felicia's husband Rafael is treated as if he gave James half the amount, or $12,000. Since they have decided to split the gift, they are required to file a gift tax return.

Gift Tax Return Filing Requirements

There are many instances where a taxpayer is required to file a gift tax return. A gift tax return is required in the following instances:

- If the taxpayer gives more than $13,000 to one individual (except to a spouse or charity)
- If the taxpayer "splits gifts" with a spouse
- If a taxpayer gives a future interest to anyone other than a spouse

Generally, the following gifts are not taxable gifts and do not need to be reported on a gift tax return:

- Any gift that does not exceed the annual exclusion (for 2010, this is $13,000)
- Tuition or medical expenses paid for someone directly to an educational or medical institution (the educational and medical exclusions)
- Gifts to the taxpayer's spouse (as long as the spouse is a U.S. citizen)
- Gifts to a political organization for its use
- Gifts to qualifying charities
- A parent's support for a minor are not considered gifts if they are required as part of a legal obligation (such as by a divorce decree). They may be considered a gift if the payments are not legally required.

These gifts are not subject to any annual limits.

Example: In 2010, Esther decides to give her grandson $13,000 in cash. She also pays for her grandson's medical bills after he breaks his leg. She writes the check for $9,000 directly to the hospital. She also helps out by paying her grandson's college tuition. She writes a check totaling $15,000 directly to the college. Esther is not required to report any of these gifts. This is because the $13,000 gift is under the yearly exclusion amount. The other two payments made directly to the hospital and to the college are not considered gifts for tax purposes.

The Basis of Property Received as a Gift

For purposes of determining gain, a taxpayer generally takes a transferred basis when she receives property as a gift. This means that the taxpayer's basis in the property is the same as the donor's basis in the property. To figure the basis of property received as a gift, the taxpayer must know:

- The gift's adjusted basis (defined earlier) to the donor just before it was given to the taxpayer,
- The gift's FMV at the time it was given to the taxpayer, and
- Any gift tax paid on it.

Example: Darren's father gives him 20 shares of stock that are currently worth $900. Darren's father has an adjusted basis in the stock of $500. Darren's basis in the stock, for purposes of determining gain on any future sale of the stock, is $500 (transferred basis).

Generally, the "value" of the gift is its Fair Market Value on the date of the gift. The value of the gift may be less than its Fair Market Value to the extent that the donee gives the receiver something in return.

Example: Donald sells his son Jared a house for $10,000. At the time of the gift, the Fair Market Value of the house is $90,000. Donald has made a gift to his son of $80,000 ($90,000 - $10,000 = $80,000).

Summary: Estate Tax

The estate tax is a tax on the transfer of property after death. In 2010, the estate tax was repealed, but in December it was brought back retroactively to January 1, 1010. This is unprecedented; as an illustration, please note the table below in order to see how the rules for 2010 are different from the previous year and also for 2011. Estate tax returns are due nine months from the date of death, although the executor may request an extension of time to file.

The tax is still due on the due date. An estate tax return is filed on Form 706, *U.S. Estate Tax Return.*

Gift taxes are reported on Form 709, *United States Gift (and Generation-Skipping Transfer) Tax Return.*

Unit 1.12: Questions

1. Which of the following is NOT "Income in Respect of a Decedent"?

A. Wages earned before death, but still unpaid at the time of death
B. Vacation time paid after death
C. Taxable IRAs and retirement plans
D. A royalty check that was received before death, but not cashed

The answer is D. Since the royalty check was received before the taxpayer died, it is not considered IRD income. Income in Respect of a Decedent is taxable income earned but not received by the decedent by the time of her death. Since the check was received before death, it would not be "IRD" income for tax purposes. The fact that it was not cashed has no bearing on the nature of the income. ###

2. Mitchell died on July 1. Mitchell's nephew Bill asks his sister Jan to help him prepare the estate tax return. Jan is an Enrolled Agent, and Bill is the executor for the estate. Jan did not charge a fee to prepare the tax return. Who is required to sign the tax return?

A. Jan
B. Bill
C. Both Jan and Bill must sign
D. No one is required to sign the return

The answer is B. Bill is required to sign the tax return, but Jan is not. The personal representative must sign the tax return. If someone else prepares the tax return and does not charge a fee, then she is not required to sign the tax return (Publication 559 and Circular 230). ###

3. When is an estate tax return due?

A. Four months after the close of the taxable year
B. Six months after the close of the calendar year
C. Nine months after the date of death
D. Twelve months after the date of death

The answer is C. Estate tax returns are due nine months from the date of death, although the executor may request an extension of time to file. ###

4. Paula dies in 2010. Her gross estate is valued at $7.5 million. Her executor wants to elect out of the estate tax. Which form must be filed in order for the executor to elect out of the estate tax for the 2010 tax year?

A. Form 706
B. Form 8939
C. Form 709
D. Form 1041

The answer is B. Form 8939 is used to elect out of the estate tax, to report the carryover basis of the decedent's property, and to allocate the basis increase allowed under the optional carryover basis rules. If an executor decides to opt out of the estate tax, the due date for Form 8939 for 2010 estates is April 18, 2011. ###

5. The representative of an estate may request an extension of time to file an estate tax return and pay the tax.

A. True
B. False

The answer is B, False. An extension of time to file is NOT an extension of time to pay. The estate's representative (executor) may request an extension of time to file for up to six months from the due date of the return. However, the tax is still due by the due date and interest is accrued on any amounts still owed by the due date that are not paid at that time. ###

6. Nicky dies on May 5, 2010. On her final tax return, her personal exemption must be prorated for the portion of the year before her death.

A. True
B. False

The answer is B, False. On a decedent's final tax return, the rules for a personal exemption and deductions remain the same for any taxpayer. The full personal exemption may be claimed on the final tax return (Publication 559). ###

7. Which of the following items is NOT an allowable deduction from the Gross Estate?

A. Debts owed at the time of death
B. Medical expenses and taxes
C. Funeral expenses
D. None of the above

The answer is D. All of the items listed are deductible from the Gross Estate. The allowable deductions used in determining the "Taxable Estate" include:
•Funeral expenses paid by the estate.
•Debts owed at the time of death.
•Medical expenses and taxes.
•Casualty and theft losses.
•Charitable Deduction: If the decedent leaves property to a qualifying charity, it is deductible from the gross estate.
•Mortgages and debt.
•Administration expenses of the estate.
•Losses during estate administration.
•The Marital Deduction (generally, the value of the property that passes from the estate to the surviving spouse).
•The state Death Tax deduction (if applicable).

It is important to remember the distinction between these deductions, because many of these items are not deductible on the decedent's individual tax return, or the taxpayer's final return (such as funeral expenses). ###

8. Which form is used to report interest income that is distributed to a beneficiary?

A. Schedule K-1 (Form 1041)
B. Schedule B (Form 1041)
C. Form 1099-MISC
D. Form 1099-INT

The answer is A. A personal representative must file Schedule K-1 to report income that is distributed to each beneficiary. These schedules are filed with Form 1041. ###

9. Shelly died on February 28, 2011 before filing her 2010 tax return. She had earnings in 2010 and 2011. When is Shelly's FINAL tax return due?

A. December 31, 2011
B. April 15, 2010
C. April 18, 2011
D. April 15, 2012

The answer is D. Shelly's final tax return is due April 15, 2012. That is because she had earnings in 2010 and 2011, so she has a tax return due for both the 2010 and 2011 tax years. The personal representative must file the final income tax return of the decedent for the year of death and any returns not filed for preceding years. ###

10. The executor of Ophelia's estate is her sister Elaine. Elaine decides to make a distribution of 100% of the estate's assets before figuring and paying the estate's income tax liability. Which of the following is true?

A. The beneficiaries of the estate can be held liable for the payment of the liability, even if the liability exceeds the value of the estate assets.
B. No one can be held liable for the tax if the assets have been distributed.
C. The beneficiaries can be held liable for the tax debt, up to the value of the assets distributed.
D. None of the above.

The answer is C. The tax liability for an estate attaches to the assets of the estate itself, so if the assets are distributed to the beneficiaries before the taxes are paid, the beneficiaries can be held liable for the tax debt, up to the value of the assets distributed (Publication 559). ###

11. Delia's estate has funeral expenses for the cost of her burial. How should the executor deduct these costs?

A. Funeral expenses are an itemized deduction on Form 1040.
B. Funeral expenses are deducted on Form 1041.
C. Funeral expenses are deducted on Form 706.
D. Funeral expenses cannot be deducted as an expense.

The answer is C. No deduction for funeral expenses can be taken on Form 1041 or Form 1040. Funeral expenses must be claimed as an expense on Form 706 (Publication 559). ###

12. Dustin pays $15,000 in college tuition for his nephew Noah directly to Noah's college. Which of the following statements is CORRECT?

A. Because the payment is over $13,000, the gift is a taxable gift and a gift tax return is required.
B. The gift is not taxable, but a gift tax return is required.
C. The gift is taxable, but no gift tax return is required. Noah must report the income on his individual return.
D. The gift is not a taxable gift, and no gift tax return is required.

The answer is D. Because the payment qualifies for the educational exclusion, the gift is not a taxable gift. Tuition or medical expenses paid directly to a medical or educational institution for someone are not included in the calculation of taxable gifts. ###

13. Shawn, a single taxpayer, has never been required to file a gift tax return. In 2010, Shawn gave the following gifts:
1. $14,000 in tuition paid directly to a state university for his cousin
2. $13,500 paid to General Hospital for his brother's medical bills
3. $50,000 in cash donations paid to his city homeless shelter, a 501(c)(3)
4. $15,000 as a political gift paid to the Republican Party (not a qualified charity)
Is Shawn required to file a gift tax return?

A. No
B. Yes, because the donation to the political party is not an excludable gift
C. Yes, because the total of the gifts exceeded $13,000 for the year
D. Yes, because the gift to his nephew was in cash and was a reportable transaction over $10,000

The answer is A. None of the gifts are taxable, and no reporting is required. Tuition or medical expenses paid for someone directly to an educational or medical institution are not counted as taxable gifts (the educational and medical exclusions). Gifts to a political organization for its own use are not reportable and not counted as part of the gift tax limit, even though the political organization is not a qualified charity. ###

14. In which case must a gift tax return be filed?

A. A couple filing jointly give a gift of $13,000
B. A couple filing jointly give a gift of $15,000
C. A single individual gives a gift of $4,000 to an unrelated person
D. A wife gives a gift of $14,000 to her husband

The answer is B. This is an example of "gift splitting." A married couple may split gifts, but they are required to file a gift tax return. Gifts to a spouse generally do not require a tax return. In 2010, gift splitting allows married couples to give up to $26,000 to a person without making a taxable gift ($13,000 from each spouse). ###

15. In 2010, Jeffrey gives $25,000 to his girlfriend Sally. Which of the following statements is FALSE?

A. The first $13,000 of the gift is not subject to the gift tax.
B. Sally is required to file a gift tax return and pay tax on the gift.
C. Jeffrey is required to file a gift tax return.
D. If Jeffrey and Sally were married, then no gift tax return would be necessary.

The answer is B. Gift tax is paid by the donor, not the recipient, of the gift. Jeffrey is responsible for filing the gift tax return. The first $13,000 of the gift is not subject to gift tax because of the annual exclusion. The remaining $12,000 is a taxable gift. If Jeffrey and Sally were married, then no gift tax return would be necessary (the marital transfer rule). ####

Part 2: Businesses

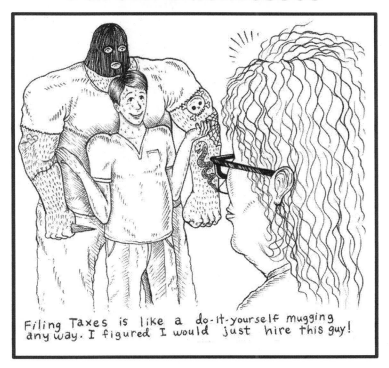

Tammy the Tax Lady ®

Tammy the Tax Lady is a registered trademark of Passkey Publications

Business Entities, Liability, Existence, & Taxation Snapshot

Character	Sole Proprietor-ship	C-CORP	S-CORP	LLC
Formation	No state filing required.	State filing required.	State filing required.	State filing required.
Existence	Automatically dissolved upon death.	Perpetual life.	Perpetual life.	Varies from state to state.
Liability	Sole proprietor has unlimited liability.	Shareholders are not responsible for the debts of the corporation.	Shareholders are typically not responsible for the debts of the corporation.	Members are not typically liable for the debts of the LLC.
Operational Requirements	None.	Board of directors, annual meetings, and annual reporting required.	Board of directors, annual meetings, and annual reporting required.	Some formal requirements, but less formal than corporations.
Management	Sole proprietor has full control of management and operations.	Managed by the directors, who are elected by the shareholders.	Managed by the directors, who are elected by the shareholders.	Members have an operating agreement that outlines management.
Taxation	Not a taxable entity. Sole proprietor pays all taxes on his/her individual return.	Taxed at the entity level. If dividends are distributed to shareholders, dividends are also taxed at the individual level.	No tax at the entity level. Income/loss is passed through to the shareholders.	If properly structured there is no tax at the entity level. Income/loss is passed through to members.
Pass Through Income/Loss	Yes	No	Yes	Yes
Double Taxation	No	Yes	No	No
Transferability of Interest	No	Shares of stock are easily transferred.	Yes	Varies

Unit 2.1: Entities and Recordkeeping Requirements

More Reading:
Publication 583, *Starting a Business and Keeping Records*
Publication 1779, *Independent Contractor or Employee*
Publication 334, *Tax Guide for Small Business*

There are several types of business entities that are available for taxpayers to use in order to form and run their businesses. Each business entity type has its own drawbacks, risks, and benefits. We will briefly go over business entities here. In later chapters, we will discuss individual business entity types more thoroughly.

Sole Proprietorship

An unincorporated business owned and controlled by one person is a sole proprietorship. A sole proprietorship may have many employees but only one owner. A sole proprietorship is the simplest business type, and the easiest to begin.

A sole proprietor must accept all the risks and liabilities of the business. If a sole proprietor does not have any employees, he does not even have to obtain an Employer Identification Number (EIN). A sole proprietorship cannot be transferred.

A sole proprietorship is taxed and reported on the taxpayer's personal income tax return. Income and expenses from the sole proprietorship are reported on **Form 1040, Schedule C,** *Profit or Loss from Business.* Losses are deducted "above the line" on Form 1040. Self-employed individuals who have net earnings of $400 or more from self-employment are required to pay self-employment tax by filing Schedule SE. Schedule SE is attached to their Form 1040. Farmers who are self-employed report their farming income on IRS Form 1040, Schedule F. Farmers are subject to specific IRS rules and will be covered in their own chapter later on.

Husband and Wife Businesses

Many small businesses are operated solely by a husband and wife, without incorporating or creating a formal partnership agreement. A husband and wife business may be considered a partnership whether or not a formal partnership agreement is made.

The *Small Business and Work Opportunity Tax Act* allows most businesses that are conducted by a husband and wife to be treated as a qualified joint venture. Therefore, the husband and wife may also choose to treat their qualified joint venture as a sole proprietorship on two separate **Schedules C**. This option is available only to married taxpayers who file joint tax returns.

Partnerships

A partnership is a business entity involving two or more people known as partners. A partnership must always have at least one "general partner." A general partner's actions can legally bind the entire business, meaning general partners are legally responsible for a partnership's debts and liabilities. A partnership tax return is filed on IRS **Form 1065.** Partners are not considered employees and are usually not issued a **Form W-2.** The partnership must furnish copies of **Schedule K-1** to its partners, showing the income and losses that is allocated to each partner.

A partnership is not a taxable entity. Instead, it has a reporting requirement. All of the income and losses from a partnership "flow through" to the partners, who are then responsible for reporting those amounts on their individual returns.

A *limited partner* is an investor who typically has no voice in the management of the partnership. A limited partner's liability is limited to her investment in the business. Only limited partners have passive income (not subject to self-employment tax), while general partners have active income. Only limited partners have limited liability. A limited partner has no obligation to contribute additional capital to the partnership, and therefore does not have an economic risk of loss in partnership recourse liabilities.

> **Example:** Dustin and Mark are father and son. Together they operate Junkyard Partnership. Each is active in the business, and each has an equal share in partnership interests and profits. In 2010, the Junkyard Partnership had $60,000 in net profits. The partnership must file a Form 1065, reporting its income and loss for the year. The partnership must also issue two Schedule K-1s—one to each partner (Dustin and Mark). Since they share profits and losses equally, Dustin and Mark will both have to report $30,000 in self-employment partnership income on their individual tax returns. Partnership income is reported on page 2 of **Schedule E**, *Supplemental Income and Loss (From rental real estate, royalties, partnerships, S corporations, estates, trusts, REMICs, etc.).*

A partnership can look very different depending on how it's structured—it can be anything from a small business run by a husband and wife, to a complex business organization with hundreds of general partners and limited partners as investors. A partnership may have individual partners, or corporate partners. A partnership can have an unlimited number of partners.

> **Example:** Samuel and Jane are brother and sister. Together they own Devil Dog Publishing. Devil Dog publishes a monthly magazine and newsletter for tattoo artists. Samuel writes most of the articles, and Jane takes care of the day-to-day running of the magazine, including paying the bills and securing advertising. Samuel and Jane are in a partnership and must file Form 1065.

An unincorporated organization with two or more members is generally classified as a partnership for federal tax purposes if its members carry on a business and divide its profits. However, a joint undertaking merely to share expenses is not a partnership. For example, co-ownership of rental property is not a considered a formal partnership unless the co-owners provide substantial services to the tenants.

> **Example:** Anderson and Sally are friends, and they own a rental property together. Each one owns a 50% interest. Anderson takes care of the repairs, and Sally collects and divides the rent. They do not have any other business with each other. The co-ownership of the rental property would not be considered a partnership for tax purposes. They would report their income and losses on **Schedule E,** based on their ownership percentage. So in this case, Anderson and Sally will divide the income and losses on their individual returns.

The partnership return must show the names and addresses of each partner and each partner's distributive share of taxable income. The return must be signed by a general partner. A limited partner may not sign the return or represent a partnership before the IRS.

Schedule E (Form 1040) 2010				Attachment Sequence No. **13**		Page **2**
Name(s) shown on return. Do not enter name and social security number if shown on other side.					Your social security number	

Caution. The IRS compares amounts reported on your tax return with amounts shown on Schedule(s) K-1.

Part II **Income or Loss From Partnerships and S Corporations** Note. If you report a loss from an at-risk activity for which any amount is **not** at risk, you must check the box in column (e) on line 28 and attach Form 6198. See page E-1.

27 Are you reporting any loss not allowed in a prior year due to the at-risk or basis limitations, a prior year unallowed loss from a passive activity (if that loss was not reported on Form 8582), or unreimbursed partnership expenses? If you answered "Yes," see page E-7 before completing this section. ☐ Yes ☐ No

28	(a) Name	(b) Enter P for partnership; S for S corporation	(c) Check if foreign partnership	(d) Employer identification number	(e) Check if any amount is not at risk
A			☐		☐
B			☐		☐
C			☐		☐
D			☐		☐

	Passive Income and Loss		Nonpassive Income and Loss		
	(f) Passive loss allowed (attach Form 8582 if required)	(g) Passive income from Schedule K-1	(h) Nonpassive loss from Schedule K-1	(i) Section 179 expense deduction from Form 4562	(j) Nonpassive income from Schedule K-1
A					
B					
C					
D					
29a	Totals				
b	Totals				
30	Add columns (g) and (j) of line 29a			**30**	
31	Add columns (f), (h), and (i) of line 29b			**31**	( )
32	**Total partnership and S corporation income or (loss).** Combine lines 30 and 31. Enter the				

If a Limited Liability Company (LLC) is treated as a partnership, for federal tax purposes it must file **Form 1065** and one of its general partners or owners must sign the return.

Partnership Definitions

General Partner: The partner with legal responsibility for the debts and liabilities of a partnership. Partnership income flows to the general partner and is subject to self-employment tax.

Limited Partner: A limited partner does not have an active role in the partnership and has limited liability for losses. A limited partner is generally just an investor. A limited partner's deductible losses are limited under the passive loss rules. Partnership income that flows to a limited partner (investor) is not subject to self-employment tax and is considered passive income.

Limited Partnership: A "limited partnership" is a partnership that has at least one limited partner. A limited partnership must have at least one general partner. Limited partnerships were created in the 1970s to allow investors to invest in businesses while reducing their own personal liability.

Limited Liability Partnership (LLP): A Limited Liability Partnership (LLP) is an entity formed under state law by filing articles of organization as an LLP. An LLP is not the same entity type as a Limited Liability Company (LLC). Generally, a partner in an LLP is not liable for the debt or malpractice of other partners and is only at risk for the partnership's assets. The partners in an LLP have unlimited personal liability for the responsibilities and commitments of the firm. Lawyers and other professionals regularly use the LLP entity type. The formation of an LLP is limited in many states to certain business types.

Limited Liability Company (LLC): A Limited Liability Company (LLC) is a legal entity. For IRS purposes, an LLC must file either as a corporation, partnership, or sole proprietorship. An LLC is a creation of state law that provides the liability protection of a corporation but the tax benefits of a partnership. Unlike a partnership, none of the members of an LLC are personally liable for its debts.

S Corporations

An S Corporation is a type of corporate structure that allows business owners to have the liability protection of a corporation but avoid the double taxation of a C Corporation. S Corporation status is only available to domestic corporations with U.S. shareholders. Nonresident aliens cannot own shares in an S Corporation. There is also a strict limit on the number of shareholders (a maximum of 100) that an S Corporation can have.

An eligible domestic corporation can avoid double taxation (once to the shareholders and again to the corporation) by electing to be treated as an S Corporation. In this respect, an S Corporation is taxed more like a partnership. In general, an S Corporation does not pay any income taxes; it is a "pass-through" entity.

An S Corporation's shareholders include their share of the corporation's separately stated items of income, deduction, loss, and credit, and their share of non-separately stated income or loss. An S Corporation is required to file a tax return every single year, regardless of income or loss, by filing IRS **Form 1120S**, *U.S. Tax Return for an S Corporation*. Shareholders who receive income from S Corporations will receive a Schedule K-1.

C Corporations

A corporation is considered an entity separate from its shareholders and must elect a board of directors who will be responsible for running the company. Each shareholder makes an investment or contribution of an asset (usually cash) or service for a percent ownership in the C Corporation. All corporations are required to have an Employer Identification Number (EIN). A C Corporation is an entity in the United States that can have an unlimited number of shareholders, both foreign and domestic. Most major companies are treated as C Corporations for federal income tax purposes.

The income of a C Corporation is taxed twice, once at the entity level and again as dividends when distributed to the owners. This is known as double taxation. C Corporations are covered at length later in the book.

Personal Service Corporations (PSC)

A Personal Service Corporation (PSC) is a corporation where the main work of the company is to perform services in the fields of health (including veterinary services), law, engineering, architecture, accounting, actuarial science, the performing arts, or consulting. Examples include law firms and medical clinics. The majority of the stock[46] is owned by employees, retired employees, or their estates. Unlike other corporations, a qualified Personal Service Corporation is always taxed at a flat rate of 35% on taxable income.

---

[46] Generally, a closely held corporation is a corporation where more than 50% of the value of its outstanding stock owned (directly or indirectly) by five or fewer individuals in the last half of the tax year.

Farmers

Farmers may receive income from many sources, but the most common source is the sale of livestock, produce, grains, and other products raised or bought for resale. This includes income from operating a livestock, dairy, poultry, fish, or fruit farm as well as income from operating a plantation, ranch, range, or orchard. It also includes income from the sale of crop shares. Self-employed farmers report their profit or loss from farming on IRS Schedule F.

Schedule F is for self-employed farmers, but if the farm is organized as a corporation or a partnership, the taxpayer needs to file the appropriate tax return for the specific entity type. Just like Schedule C taxpayers, farmers must report income and expenses, and pay regular income tax and self-employment tax on their net profits from farming.

Many special rules apply to farmers, including the payment of self-employment tax, inventory valuation, and estimated payments. These topics will be covered later in a dedicated chapter just for farmers.

Tax-Exempt Organizations

A nonprofit (tax-exempt) organization is an entity whose primary objective is to actively engage in activities of public or private interest without any profit motive. Just because an organization is tax-exempt doesn't mean that its donations are deductible by the donor. Most tax-exempt organizations rely on donations in order to sustain their activities.

To apply for tax exemption, most organizations must file Form 1023, *Application for Recognition of Exemption Under Section 501(c)(3) of the Internal Revenue Code.*

Because of the separation of church and state in the U.S., religious organizations such as churches, synagogues, and mosques are *not required* to apply for formal exemption. They are treated as tax-exempt organizations by default. Examples of organizations that are required to file for formal nonprofit exemption are animal rescue organizations, disaster relief organizations, child welfare organizations (such as boys and girls clubs), and conservation groups.

There are many restrictions on tax-exempt entities. In order to apply for tax exemption through the IRS, a "qualified organization" includes nonprofit groups that are religious, charitable, educational, scientific, or literary in purpose, or that work to prevent cruelty to children or animals.

Some entities do not qualify for tax exemption under 501(c)(3) of the Internal Revenue Code. Any entity that does not qualify as a 501(c)(3) may still qualify for nonprofit status. Organizations that do not qualify under IRC Section 501(c)(3) must file Form 1024, *Application for Recognition of Exemption under Section 501(a).*

Charities are all nonprofit organizations; however, not all nonprofit organizations are charities. Civic groups, Chambers of Commerce, and Rotary clubs are all examples of nonprofit groups that may qualify for tax-exempt status, but are not charities by definition.

Exempt organizations file Form 990 in order to report income and losses. Form 990 is usually an informational return only.

A nonprofit entity (exempt organization) cannot be classified as a partnership or a sole proprietorship. In order for an entity to qualify as an exempt entity, it must be organized as a community chest, corporation, trust, fund, or foundation.

Entity Classification Election Rules

A business entity may choose how it will be classified for federal income tax purposes. Businesses must use Form 8832, *Entity Classification Election*, to choose how they will be taxed.

Any LLC with a single owner will be disregarded as a separate entity for federal income tax purposes unless a Form 8832 is filed to elect classification as a corporation. A disregarded LLC with a single owner would file on Schedule C as a sole proprietorship.

Once a business entity chooses its classification, it cannot change the election within five years (60 months).

> **Example:** Kelly and Jim are married and own their own business. They decide to form an LLC for liability protection. Kelly files Form 8832, and she elects to classify their business as a partnership for tax purposes. A few months later, Kelly changes her mind and wants to switch classifications and be taxed as an S Corporation. Kelly must wait at least 60 months in order to change the election.

Employer Identification Number (EIN)

An Employer Identification Number is used for reporting purposes only. Taxpayers can apply for an EIN online or use IRS Form SS-4.

Most individuals file their tax returns using a Social Security Number (SSN). Sole proprietors who do not have employees are not required to have EINs. However, every partnership and corporation must have an Employer Identification Number. A sole proprietor that hires employees must also have an EIN. A sole proprietor may use the same Employer Identification Number for multiple businesses, as long as they are the same entity type.

However, if the sole proprietor decides to form a different business type such as a partnership or corporation, he will be required to request an EIN for each separate entity. A new EIN is required for any of the following changes:

- When a sole proprietor decides to incorporate or hire employees
- When a sole proprietor takes on a partner and becomes a partnership
- When a partnership becomes a sole proprietorship (for example, when one partner dies)
- When a sole proprietor files for Chapter 7 (liquidation)
- When a sole proprietor files for Chapter 11 (reorganization) bankruptcy
- When a taxpayer terminates one partnership and begins another partnership

Most businesses need an EIN. A business MUST apply for an EIN if any of the following apply:

- The business pays employees
- The business operates as a corporation, exempt organization, trust, estate, or a partnership
- The business files any of these tax returns:

- o Employment,
- o Excise, or
- o Alcohol, Tobacco and Firearms
- The business withholds taxes paid to a nonresident alien
- The business has a Keogh plan (a type of retirement plan)

An EIN can also be requested by any sole proprietor who simply wishes to protect her Social Security Number for privacy reasons. This way, a sole proprietor can give her EIN rather than her SSN to companies that need to issue her a Form 1099 for independent contractor payments.

The Tax Year

A "tax year" is an annual accounting period for keeping records and reporting income and expenses. Individuals file their tax returns on a calendar year. Businesses have the option to file their tax returns on either a calendar year or a fiscal year. A business adopts a tax year when it files its first income tax return (not including extensions).

Calendar year: A "calendar tax year" is 12 consecutive months beginning January 1 and ending December 31. Most partnerships operate on a calendar year, but there are exceptions (explained later).

Fiscal year: A "fiscal tax year" is 12 consecutive months ending on the last day of any month except December. A fiscal year-end doesn't have to fall on the same date each year. A "52/53-week" tax year is a fiscal tax year that varies from 52 to 53 weeks but does not have to end on the last day of the month. For example, some businesses choose to end their fiscal year on a particular day of the week (such as the last Friday in June). A fiscal year includes any tax year that lasts 12 months, but does not end in December.

Example: Paula works for the state of California. The state follows a fiscal year budget. Its fiscal year 2010 refers to the period from July 1, 2009 through June 30, 2010. This is a 12-month period not ending in December. Most federal and state government organizations use a fiscal year. Most large corporations also operate on a fiscal year basis.

Short tax year: A "short tax year" is a tax year of less than 12 months. A short period tax return is required when an entity changes its accounting period or dissolves. Even if a business is not in existence for a year, a tax return is still required. Requirements for filing the return and figuring the tax are generally the same as the requirements for a return for a full tax year (12 months) ending on the last day of the short tax year.

Example: Eduardo and Jared start a business partnership on January 1, 2010. They worked well together, but on October 1, 2010 Eduardo dies. Therefore, the partnership is no longer in existence. Jared decides to continue the business as a sole proprietor. He must request a new Employer Identification Number, since his business structure has changed. The partnership must be dissolved and the partnership tax return must be filed on a short tax year, based on the time the partnership was in existence (from January to October).

Example: Craig formed Bookworm Corporation in February 2010. He immediately started having financial troubles and dissolved his corporation in October 2010. Craig must file a corporate return showing a short tax year for the time that Bookworm Corporation was in existence.

IRS Form 1128, *Application to Adopt, Change, or Retain a Tax Year*, is used to request a change in the tax year reporting period. Form 8716, *Election to Have a Tax Year Other Than a Required Tax Year*, is used by partnerships and corporations to request a change from their "required tax year."

A "required tax year" is a tax year required under the Internal Revenue Code. A business adopts an accounting period (a "tax year") when it files its first tax return. Any business can adopt a calendar year, and in fact, most partnerships operate on a calendar year. However, it is also possible for a partnership to operate on a fiscal year. This usually happens when a partnership has a corporate partner.

If a partner owns more than 50% interest in the partnership, this creates a majority interest in the capital and partnership profits. The required tax year will be the tax year of this partner.

If there is no majority interest tax year, the partnership must use the tax year of all of the principal partners who have a more than 5% interest in the capital and partnership profits.

If there is no majority interest tax year and the principal partners don't have the same tax year, the partnership must use the tax year that has the *least aggregate* deferral of income to its partners (Publication 541).

If a business files its first tax return using the calendar tax year and later changes its business structure (such as moving from a sole proprietorship to a partnership), the business must continue to use the calendar year unless it receives IRS approval to change it (or is otherwise forced to change it in order to comply with the IRC).

Again, once a business has adopted a tax year, it must get IRS approval in order to change it by filing *Form 1128, Application to Adopt, Change, or Retain a Tax Year*. If an entity does not qualify for automatic approval, a ruling must be requested and a fee is required.

Section 444 Election

A Section 444 election is basically when a business makes a special request to the IRS for a tax year other than its required tax year. A partnership, S Corporation, or PSC can request to use a tax year other than its required tax year. A business makes a Section 444 election by filing Form 8716, *Election to Have a Tax Year Other Than a Required Tax Year*.

A business can request a Section 444 election if it meets all the following requirements:
- It is not a member of a tiered structure.
- It has not previously had a Section 444 election in effect.
- It elects a year that meets the deferral period requirement (explained next).

Understanding the Deferral Period

The determination of the deferral period depends on whether the business is retaining its tax year or adopting or changing its tax year with a Section 444 election.

Generally, a business can make a Section 444 election to retain its tax year only if the deferral period of the new tax year is three months or less. This deferral period is the number of months between the beginning of the retained year and the close of the first required tax year. If the business is requesting a change to a tax year other than its required year, the deferral period is the number of months from the end of the new tax year to the end of the required tax year. The IRS will allow a Section 444 election only if the deferral period of the new tax year is less than the shorter of:

- Three months, or
- The deferral period of the tax year being changed. This is the tax year immediately preceding the year for which the business wishes to make the Section 444 election. If the entity's tax year is the same as its required tax year, the deferral period is zero.

> **Example:** Golden Partnership uses a calendar year, which is also its required tax year. The partnership cannot make a Section 444 election because the deferral period is zero.

> **Example:** Davenport Partnership, a newly formed partnership, began operations on December 1, 2010. Davenport is owned by calendar-year partners. Davenport wants to make a Section 444 election to adopt a September 30 tax year. Davenport's deferral period for the tax year beginning December 1, 2010 is three months, the number of months between September 30 and December 31.

The Section 444 election remains in effect until it is terminated. If the election is terminated, another Section 444 election cannot be made for any tax year. The election also ends automatically when any of the following occurs:

- The entity changes to its required tax year.
- The entity liquidates.
- The entity becomes a member of a tiered structure.
- The IRS determines that the entity willfully failed to comply with the required payments or distributions.
- If the entity is an S Corporation, the Section 444 election will terminate if the corporation's S-election is terminated. However, if the S Corporation immediately becomes a Personal Service Corporation, the entity can continue the Section 444 election. This is also true in reverse; if a PSC becomes an S Corporation, it may continue to use the Section 444 election.

The Section 444 election *does not apply* to any business that establishes a genuine business purpose for a different period. For example, a seasonal business may elect a fiscal year based on a genuine business purpose. The deferral of income for the partners is not considered to be a legitimate "business purpose."

> **Example:** A calendar year corporation dissolved on July 22, 2010. Its final return is due by October 15, 2010 (the fifteenth day of the third month following the close of their short tax year). The return will cover the short period from January 1, 2010, through July 22, 2010.

Filing Extensions

Organizations and individuals may request an extension on the time they have to file their income tax return. April 15 of each year is the normal due date for filing most federal individual income tax returns. April 15 is also the due date for partnership tax returns.[47]

Corporate tax returns are due on March 15 (if the corporation is on a calendar year). Nonprofit organizations must file their information returns by May 15 if they are on a calendar-year reporting period. If the due date falls on a Saturday, Sunday, or legal holiday, the due

---

[47] Once again, individual and partnership returns are due on April 18 in 2011.

date is delayed until the next business day. Choosing to file an extension electronically does not require a taxpayer to file his return electronically.

The following forms are used by various entities to request a filing extension. Filing an extension does not grant the entity additional time to pay any tax due. The extension only grants the entity additional time to file. Any estimated tax due must be paid by the filing deadline, or else the entity will be subject to interest and penalties on the amount that is still due.

Sole Proprietors and Individuals: Form 4868: *Application for Automatic Extension of Time to File U.S. Individual Income Tax Return* (six month extension) to October 15th.

Nonprofit Organizations: Form 8868: *Application for Extension of Time to File an Exempt Organization Return* (three month extension, with the option to file for an additional three month extension).

Corporations and Partnerships: Form 7004: *Application for Automatic Extension of Time to File Corporate Income Tax Return* (six month extension). Form 7004 applies to Partnerships, C Corporations, and S Corporations and grants the entity an automatic six month extension to September 15.

Employee Classification

Employee classification is a very important issue to the IRS, and consequently, the subject is tested on the Enrolled Agent Exam. Misclassifying employees as independent contractors is a common problem that the IRS monitors very carefully. Businesses will often misclassify employees as independent contractors in order to avoid paying employment taxes and other taxes on the employees' wages.

Employers are required to accurately determine whether a person is an independent contractor or an employee. In the case of employees, employers must withhold income taxes, withhold Social Security and Medicare taxes, and pay unemployment tax on wages. An employer is not required to withhold or pay any taxes on payments to independent contractors. This is why so many employers will incorrectly classify a worker. The earnings of a person who is working as an independent contractor are subject to self-employment tax.

An employer must understand the relationship that exists between herself and the person performing the services. A person performing services for business may be:

- An independent contractor
- An employee (common-law employee)
- A statutory employee
- A statutory non-employee

The general rule is that an individual is an independent contractor if he has the right to control the result of his work. The IRS uses three characteristics to determine the relationship between a business and its workers:

- **Behavioral Control:** covers whether the business has a right to direct or control how the work is done.
- **Financial Control:** covers whether the business has a right to direct or control the financial and business aspects of the worker's job.
- **Type of Relationship:** relates to how the workers and the business owner perceive their relationship.

Employers who misclassify workers as independent contractors can end up with substantial tax penalties. They can face additional penalties for failing to pay employment taxes and for failing to file payroll tax forms. Examples of true independent contractors include: lawyers, mobile plumbers, independent bookkeepers, and auctioneers who follow an independent trade in which they offer their services to the public are usually considered independent contractors. However, whether such persons are truly employees or independent contractors depends on the facts in each case.

Example: Vera, an electrician, submitted a job estimate to a housing complex for electrical work at $16 per hour for 400 hours. She is to receive $1,280 every two weeks for the next ten weeks. Even if she works more or less than 400 hours to complete the work, Vera will receive $6,400. She also performs additional electrical installations under contracts with other companies that she obtains through advertisements placed in the local paper. Vera is an independent contractor.

Example: Donna is a salesperson employed full-time by Supercargo Dealership, an auto dealer. She works six days a week and is on duty in the showroom on certain assigned days and times. Lists of prospective customers belong to the dealer. She has to develop leads and report results to the sales manager. Because of her experience, she requires only minimal assistance in closing and financing sales and in other phases of her work. She is paid a commission and is eligible for prizes and bonuses offered by the dealership. The business also pays the cost of health insurance and group-term life insurance for Donna. Donna is an employee of the dealership.

Under common-law rules, anyone who performs services for an employer is an employee if the employer can control the employee's actions and the work that she does. This is the case even when the employer gives the employee freedom of action. What matters is that the employer has the right to control the details of how the services are performed. Generally, if an employer has behavioral control over the person, the person must be classified as an employee.

Statutory Employees

Some workers are classified as statutory employees. Statutory employees are still issued a form W-2 by their employers. Statutory employees report their wages, income, and allowable expenses on Schedule C, just like self-employed taxpayers. However, statutory employees are not required to pay self-employment tax, because their employers must treat them as employees for Social Security tax purposes. The following workers are typically considered statutory employees:

- Officers of nonprofit organizations
- A full-time traveling salesperson who solicits orders from wholesalers, restaurants, etc. on behalf of his employer. The merchandise must be for resale or for use in a business (e.g., food or cooking supplies sold to a restaurant)
- A full-time life insurance agent
- A commissioned truck driver engaged in distributing meat, vegetables, bakery goods, beverages (other than milk), or laundry or dry cleaning services
- A home worker performing work on material or goods furnished by the employer

Statutory Non-Employees Treated as Independent Contractors

There are two main categories of statutory non-employees: direct sellers and licensed real estate agents. They are treated as self-employed for all federal tax purposes, including income and employment taxes if:

- Payments for their services are directly related to sales, rather than to the number of hours worked, and
- Services are performed under a written contract providing that they will not be treated as employees for federal tax purposes.

Compensation for a statutory non-employee is reported on IRS Form 1099-MISC. The taxpayer then reports the income on Schedule C.

> **Example:** Adele works as a full-time real estate agent for Golden Gate Real Estate Company. She visits Golden Gate's offices at least once a day to check her mail and her messages. She manages dozens of listings and splits her real estate commissions with Golden Gate. She does not work for any other real estate company. Adele is a statutory non-employee. Golden Gate properly issues Adele a Form 1099-MISC for commissions and she files a Schedule C to report her income and expenses.

Directors of a corporation (members of the governing board) are also treated as statutory non-employees. If an exempt organization compensates board members for performing their duties as directors, the organization should treat them as independent contractors. (The director fee is reported on Form 1099-MISC.) This is the most common type of statutory non-employee that may be involved in an exempt organization.

Trust Fund Recovery Penalty (The 100% Penalty)

The Trust Fund Recovery Penalty (TFRP) is authorized under Section 6672 of the Internal Revenue Code. If income, Social Security, and Medicare taxes that a business withholds from employee wages are not deposited or paid to the United States Treasury, the Trust Fund Recovery Penalty may apply. The reason the Trust Fund Recovery Penalty is so important is because it can be assessed against company owners, employees, or company officers—anyone that the IRS determines is responsible for paying or collecting payroll taxes. Once the IRS asserts the penalty, it can take collection action against personal assets of anyone that is deemed a "responsible party."

The penalty is the full amount of the unpaid trust fund tax. The Trust Fund Recovery Penalty may be imposed on all persons who are determined by the IRS to be responsible for collecting, accounting for, and paying these taxes, and who acted willfully in not doing so. A responsible person can be an officer or employee of a corporation, an accountant, or even an unpaid volunteer director/trustee.

A "responsible person" also may include the person who signs checks for the corporation or who otherwise has authority to spend business funds, such as a bookkeeper.

The business does not have to have stopped operating in order for the TFRP to be assessed. The TFRP may be assessed against any person who:

- Is responsible for collecting or paying withheld income and employment taxes, or for paying collected excise taxes, and
- Willfully fails to collect or pay them.

A responsible person is a person or group of people who has the duty to perform and the power to direct the collecting, accounting, and paying of trust fund taxes. This person may be:

- An officer or an employee of a corporation
- A member or employee of a partnership
- A corporate director or shareholder
- A member of a board of trustees of a nonprofit organization
- Another person with authority and control over funds to direct their disbursement

For the IRS to determine that the individual willfully failed to pay the required taxes, the "responsible person":

- Must have been, or should have been, aware of the outstanding taxes, and
- Intentionally disregarded the law (no evil intent or bad motive is required).

Using available funds to pay other creditors when the business is unable to pay the employment taxes is an indication of willfulness.

Example: Jake was a supervisor at Barnaby Windows Corporation. His boss Stanley ran a very successful business and grossed over $7 million in sales annually. The business had 12 full-time employees as well as a number of independent contractors. Everything was going fine until late 2008, when Stanley's wife passed away from a sudden heart attack. Stanley began acting erratically and developed a drug problem. Jake ran the office as best he could, and since he had check-signing privileges to the bank account, he signed the employees' paychecks until the money ran out in late 2009. After that, the business closed and Stanley disappeared.

Jake found another job quickly and began working as a supervisor for another contractor. Everything was going great until the IRS showed up at his workplace. The IRS Revenue Agent confirmed that Jake had check-signing privileges at Barnaby Windows Corporation, his former employer, and told him he would be fully responsible for the unpaid payroll taxes that Stanley failed to pay in 2008 and 2009.

"But wait!" cried Jake. "I just did the best I could—I never stole any money—I just signed the employee paychecks!"

"Too bad," said the IRS. "You knew (or should have known) that the payroll taxes were not being remitted to the IRS. According to the law, that makes you responsible." (IRC Section 6672)

Understanding Employment Taxes and Self-Employment Tax

Employers must withhold federal income tax from employees' wages. Businesses withhold part of Social Security and Medicare taxes from employees' wages, and employers pay a matching amount.

Self-employment tax (SE tax) is a Social Security and Medicare tax primarily for individuals who work for themselves. It is similar to Social Security and Medicare taxes withheld from the pay of most wage earners. Self-employed persons (such as sole proprietors) therefore must pay the full amount of Social Security and Medicare taxes themselves.

At the end of the year, employers must complete Form W-2, *Wage and Tax Statement,* to report wages paid to employees. Form W-2s must be distributed or mailed to employees by January 31 after the end of the year.

Businesses are also required to send a copy of the W-2 to the Social Security Administration.

Employment Taxes	
Social Security portion	**2010**
Employer's portion	6.20%
Employee's portion	6.20%
Total for self-employed taxpayer	12.40%
Maximum earnings subject to Social Security taxes	$106,800

Medicare tax rate	**2010**
Employer's portion	1.45%
Employee's portion	1.45%
Total for self-employed individual	2.90%
Maximum earnings subject to Medicare taxes	No limit

Recordkeeping Requirements for Businesses

Adequate records are required to substantiate expenses and income to the IRS. Adequate records are important for a taxpayer to monitor business operations, verify his income and expenses, and to support the items on his tax return.

Taxpayers must keep records as long as they are needed for the administration of any provision of the Internal Revenue Code. Usually, this means that the business must keep records long enough to support income and deductions until the statute of limitations for the tax return has run out.

Generally, a taxpayer must keep records for at least three years from when the tax return was filed or within two years of the date the tax was paid (whichever is later). However, certain records must be kept for a longer period of time. If a taxpayer has employees, she must keep all employment tax records for at least four years (Publication 225).

Records relating to asset purchases must be kept indefinitely, at least until the asset is disposed of, or the statute of limitations for the tax return has run out, whichever is later.

Financial Statements & Analysis of Financial Records

Financial statements are the formal records of a business's financial activities. Financial statements are used in order to examine a business's financial health. There are many types of financial statements, but the two most common statements used for tax reporting purposes are the Income Statement and the Balance Sheet. As a tax professional, you will be required to use financial statements to help prepare tax returns.

The Income Statement

The Income Statement (also called the Profit and Loss Statement) is a financial statement that indicates how revenue is transformed into net income. The purpose of the Income

Statement is to show the profit or loss during a certain period, such as a fiscal year or a calendar year. The Income Statement shows income and expenses, with the profit or loss shown at the bottom of the statement.

Balance Sheet

The Balance Sheet (also called the Statement of Financial Position) is a summary of a business's assets, liabilities, and equity on a specific date, such as the very end of its financial year. A Balance Sheet is often described as a snapshot of a company's financial Balance Sheet accounts are also known as "real" accounts. These accounts represent things the business owns or owes (liabilities). Balances on the Balance Sheet are carried forward from year to year. This differs from Income Statement accounts, which are closed out at year-end and only reflect business operations within a specified period.

Business Accounting Periods and Tax Return Due Dates

Entity Type	Accounting Period	Due Date of Return
Sole Proprietorship	Adopts the same tax year as the owner, typically a calendar year	April 15[48] (same as individuals)
Partnership	Adopts the same tax year as the partners who own more than 50% of the business, usually the calendar year.	April 15, or the 15th of the 4th month following the end of the tax year
C Corporation	Fiscal or calendar year	March 15, or the 15th of the 3rd month following the end of the tax year
S Corporation	Calendar year unless a valid Section 444 election is made	March 15, or the 15th of the 3rd month following the end of the tax year
Exempt Entities	Fiscal or calendar year	May 15, or the 15th of the 5th month following the end of the tax year

---

[48] In 2011, the due date for individual and partnership returns is April 18 because of a holiday in the District of Columbia (Washington, D.C.)

Unit 2.1: Questions

1. How long must employers keep employment tax records?

A. At least four years after the employment tax becomes due
B. As long as the employee works for the company
C. Three years
D. Indefinitely

The answer is A. Employers must keep all employment tax records for at least four years after the tax becomes due or is paid, whichever is later (Publication 552). ###

2. A domestic LLC with at least two members that does NOT file Form 8832 is automatically classified as _____ for federal income tax purposes.

A. An S Corporation
B. A partnership
C. A Sole proprietorship
D. A Personal Service Corporation

The answer is B. A domestic LLC with at least two members that does not file Form 8832 is classified as a partnership for federal income tax purposes (Publication 541). ###

3. Which form must a Limited Liability Company (LLC) use in order to request to be taxed as a corporation for IRS purposes?

A. Form 8832
B. Form 2848
C. Form 3115
D. Schedule C

The answer is A. For federal tax purposes, an LLC must file Form 8832, *Entity Classification Election*, in order to be taxed as a corporation. An LLC may be classified for federal income tax purposes as a partnership, a corporation, or other entity. A domestic LLC with at least two members that does not file Form 8832 is automatically classified as a partnership for federal income tax purposes. ###

4. Corporation X was organized on April 1, 2010. It elected the calendar year as its tax year. When is the tax return due for Corporation X for this short tax year?

A. April 15, 2010
B. April 15, 2011
C. March 15, 2011
D. May 15, 2011

The answer is C. Its first tax return is due March 15, 2011. This short period return will cover April 1, 2010 through December 31, 2010. Corporate tax returns are due on the fifteenth day three months after the end of the corporation's taxable year. Since the corporation is on a calendar year, the tax return is due March 15. ###

5. Marmot Company is an LLC. It made the election to be taxed as a partnership on January 1, 2008. Later, the owners decide that they would rather be taxed as a corporation. What is the earliest date that Marmot Company can elect to be taxed as a corporation?

A. January 15, 2009
B. June 1, 2009
C. June 1, 2010
D. January 1, 2013

The answer is D. Eligible entities use Form 8832 to choose how they are classified for federal tax purposes. An entity cannot change an election within five years (60 months) after the effective date of its election. ###

6. Which of the following organizations does NOT require an EIN?

A. An estate
B. Real estate mortgage investment conduits
C. Nonprofit organizations
D. A sole proprietorship with no employees

The answer is D. A sole proprietorship without employees does not require an Employer Identification Number. The other choices listed all require an EIN. ###

7. A new Employer Identification Number (EIN) is required for all of the following events, EXCEPT:

A. A sole proprietor using his SSN who adds his brother as a partner.
B. A sole proprietor who uses his Social Security Number and does not have an EIN but needs to pay an employee.
C. A C Corporation that elects to be taxed as an S Corporation.
D. A partnership where one partner dies, leaving only one remaining owner.

The answer is C. C Corporations that elect to be taxed as S Corporations do not require a new EIN. A business MUST apply for an EIN if any of the following apply:
- The business begins paying employees.
- The business begins operating as a corporation, exempt organization, or a partnership.
- The business files any of these tax returns: Employment, Excise, or Alcohol, Tobacco and Firearms.
- The business withholds taxes on income paid to a nonresident alien.

When a sole proprietor is not required to have an EIN, he may file his tax return using only his Social Security Number. But a sole proprietor who starts a partnership must obtain a new EIN, because it is a different business entity type. ###

8. A sole proprietor will be required to obtain a new EIN in which of the following instances?

A. The business is subject to a bankruptcy proceeding.
B. The sole proprietor changes the name of her business.
C. The sole proprietor changes location.
D. The sole proprietor operates multiple locations.

The answer is A. A sole proprietorship is not required to obtain a new EIN when it changes location or its business name. A sole proprietor may operate many different businesses using the same EIN, as long as the businesses are also sole proprietorships. A sole proprietorship that is subject to a bankruptcy proceeding must obtain an EIN. ###

9. Which form is used to request an EIN?

A. Form SS-4
B. Form W-2
C. Form 1099-MISC
D. Form W-7

The answer is A. IRS Form SS-4 is used to request an Employer Identification Number. Taxpayers may also request an EIN by phone, online, or by fax. ###

10. In which of the following instances will a partnership NOT be required to obtain a new EIN?

A. The partners decide to incorporate.
B. The partnership is taken over by one of the partners and is subsequently operated as a sole proprietorship.
C. The general partner ends the old partnership and begins a new one.
D. The partnership adds other business locations.

The answer is D. A partnership is not required to obtain a new EIN simply to add business locations. In all of the other choices listed, the partnership would need to obtain a new EIN. ###

11. Which of the following date ranges is considered a fiscal tax year?

A. January 1, 2010 to December 31, 2010
B. February 15, 2010 to February 15, 2011
C. July 1, 2009 to June 30, 2010
D. May 1, 2010 to May 31, 2010

The answer is C. Answer C is the correct answer because a fiscal tax year is any tax year that is 12 consecutive months and ends on the last day of any month except December. Answer A is incorrect because this is a calendar year. Answer B is incorrect because a fiscal year must end on the last day of the month. Answer D is incorrect because it is not 12 consecutive months. ###

12. Which of the following dates would NOT be considered the end of an acceptable tax year?

A. January 31
B. April 15
C. December 31
D. The last Friday in February

The answer is B. April 15 is the normal IRS due date for individual tax returns, not the end of a tax year. Answer "A" is incorrect because January 31 is the last day of the month, which qualifies as a fiscal tax year-end. Answer "C" is incorrect because December 31 is a calendar year-end. Answer "D" is incorrect because a tax year that ends on the same day of the week every year is a 52/53-week tax year. ###

13. What is the definition of the calendar year?

A. A calendar year is always from January 1 to December 31.
B. A calendar year is always a 12-month period ending on the last day of any month.
C. A calendar year can end on any day of the month.
D. A calendar year starts on April 15 and ends on April 15 the following year.

The answer is A. A calendar year is always a 12-month period from January 1 to December 31. ###

14. A business must adopt its first tax year by what date?
A. The due date (including extensions) for filing a return
B. The due date (NOT including extensions) for filing a return
C. The date the EIN is established
D. The first time the business pays estimated payments

The answer is B. A business must adopt its first tax year by the due date (NOT including extensions) for filing a return for that year. A business adopts a tax year when it files its first income tax return. ###

15. Mandy and her friend Tammy work together, making beaded necklaces and selling them at craft shows. They run their business professionally and jointly, always attempting to make a profit, but they do not have any type of formal business agreement. They share with each other the profits or losses of the business. They made $24,900 in 2010 from selling necklaces, and they had $1,900 in expenses. Where and how is the correct way for Mandy and Tammy to report their income?

A. Report as "other income" on each taxpayer's Form 1040.
B. Each must report income and expenses on Schedule C.
C. Mandy and Tammy should calculate income and subtract expenses, and then report the net amount as "other income" on each individual Form 1040.
D. Mandy and Tammy are working as a partnership, and should report their income on Form 1065.

The answer is D. Mandy and Tammy are working as a partnership and should report their income on Form 1065. Income from partnership activities must be reported on Form 1065. Related expenses are deductible, and they are reported as deductions. Each partner would then receive a K-1 to report their individual items of expenses and income on their Form 1040. ###

Unit 2.2: Accounting Methods and Inventory Valuation

> **More Reading:**
> **Publication 538, *Accounting Periods and Methods***

A business must decide on its tax period and business structure (sole proprietorship, partnership, or corporation) before moving on to deciding which accounting method to use. An accounting method is a set of rules used to determine when income and expenses are reported. The most commonly used accounting methods are the cash method and the accrual method. A business may choose its accounting method with its first tax return.

A business owner may use different accounting methods if he has two *separate and distinct* businesses. According to the IRS, two businesses will not be considered *separate and distinct,* however, unless a separate set of books and records is maintained for each business.

Example: Blake is a self-employed Enrolled Agent. He prepares tax returns from January through April every year. He is also a motivational speaker and does speaking engagements on martial arts because he is an accomplished martial artist. He decides to report his tax preparation business using the accrual method and his martial arts business using the cash method. He keeps separate books and records for each business. Blake may use different accounting methods because he has two separate and distinct businesses with separate records.

Acceptable Accounting Methods

Businesses can report taxable income under any of the following accounting methods:

- Cash method

- Accrual method

- Hybrid method using elements of the accrual and cash method

- Special methods of accounting for certain items of income and expenses

Different rules apply to each accounting method. The most common accounting method is the *cash method*, which is used by most small businesses in the United States. The *accrual method* of accounting is used by most large corporations. The accrual method is considered the more "correct" method of recognizing income and expenses, because it reflects when income is actually earned.[49]

Cash Method

Most individual taxpayers and small businesses use the *cash method* of accounting, which is the simplest accounting method to use. However, the IRS restricts the usage of the cash method to small businesses. The following businesses may NOT use the cash method and are instead required to use the accrual method:

- Any corporation (or a partnership with the corporate partner) with average annual gross receipts exceeding $5 million
- Any tax shelter, regardless of size

---

[49] Accounting methods are covered in IRS Publication 538.

- Any business that carries or produces an inventory, unless the business has average annual gross receipts of $1 million or less
- Any corporation with long-term contracts

Example: Cameron and William Davis are both architects. Together, they form the Davis and Davis Architectural Corporation, which is a C Corporation. In 2010, the income for the corporation is $4.2 million. The Davis and Davis Corporation may still use the cash method of accounting because it has gross receipts under $5 million and does not carry any inventory.

Example: Corinne and her husband Doug run Bicycles-R-Us as a husband-and-wife partnership. Bicycles-R-Us designs and sells custom bicycles and always carries a substantial inventory. In 2010, Bicycles-R-Us had gross receipts of $2.3 million. Bicycles-R-Us cannot use the cash method of accounting because it produces an inventory and its average annual gross receipts exceed $1 million.

Exceptions: The following entities may use the cash method of accounting:
- A qualified family farming corporation with gross receipts of $25 million or less[50]
- Any corporation or partnership, other than a tax shelter, that meets the gross receipts test
- A qualified Personal Service Corporation
- Artists, authors, and photographers who sell works that they have created by their own efforts

If a business produces or sells merchandise, it usually has an inventory. Most businesses that keep an inventory are required to use the accrual method. There is an exception for small businesses that keep an inventory and have average annual gross receipts of $1 million or less. Taxpayers may also be required to capitalize certain costs, as explained later under the Uniform Capitalization Rules.

Example: Crape Company makes golf car parts. The company carries an inventory and manufactures the parts throughout the year. Crape's gross receipts have never exceeded $750,000. Therefore, Crape may continue to use the cash method of accounting.

Under the cash method, businesses deduct expenses only when they are actually paid, and report income only when it is actually received. The general rule is that expenses are only deductible if they apply to the current tax year, and taxpayers may not deduct expenses paid in advance. This means that businesses may not attempt to lower their taxable income by paying expenses years in advance. However, there is an exception called the "12-Month Rule."

The 12-Month Rule

An expense a taxpayer pays in advance is deductible only in the year to which it applies, unless the expense qualifies for the "12-Month Rule." This rule was instituted to prevent taxpayers from prepaying expenses years in advance in order to lower taxable income in the current year.

---

[50] Remember the $25 million exception for small farming corporations; it has been on multiple prior EA Exams.

However, in some cases, businesses may still deduct expenses that are paid in advance. Under the 12-Month Rule, the business is not required to capitalize amounts paid that do not extend beyond the earlier of the following:

- 12 months after the benefit begins, or
- The end of the tax year after the tax year in which payment is made.

> **Example:** Gerald is a calendar-year sole proprietor and pays $3,000 in 2010 for an insurance policy that is effective for three years (36 months), beginning on July 1, 2010. This payment does not qualify for the 12-month rule. Therefore, only $500 (6/36 x $3,000) is deductible in 2010, $1,000 (12/36 x $3,000) is deductible in 2011, $1,000 (12/36 x $3,000) is deductible in 2012, and the remaining $500 is deductible in 2013.

> **Example:** Bunny Partnership is a calendar-year business and pays $10,000 on July 1, 2010 for a business insurance policy that is effective for a 12-month period beginning July 1, 2010 and ending July 31, 2011. The 12-Month Rule applies. Therefore, the full $10,000 is deductible in 2010.

> **Example:** Roxanne is a sole proprietor and she rents an office for her tattoo business. She paid three years of rent in advance in order to get a substantial discount from her landlord. She cannot use the 12-Month Rule because the benefit she got from her payment exceeded the 12-month time period. She must amortize the expense for rent in the time period that applies to the payment.

Gross Receipts Test

An entity (other than a tax shelter) that meets the "gross receipts" test can generally use the cash method. An entity meets the test if its "average" annual gross receipts are $5 million or less. An entity's average annual gross receipts for a prior tax year are determined by adding the gross receipts for that tax year and the two preceding tax years and dividing the total by three.

Gross receipts for a short tax year are annualized. An entity that fails to meet the gross receipts test for any tax year is prohibited from using the cash method and must change to an accrual method of accounting, effective for the tax year in which the entity fails to meet the test.

> **Example:** Garrison LLP is a cash basis partnership that operates a clothing factory. Garrison Partnership prefers to use the cash method of accounting. Since Garrison LLP produces inventory, the average annual gross receipts must be $1 million or less for the three tax years ending with the prior tax year. Otherwise, the partnership will be forced to use the accrual method to figure its income and expenses.

> **Example:** Green Bay Company is trying to figure its average annual gross receipts. If gross receipts are $200,000 for 2008, $800,000 for 2009, and $1,100,000 for 2010, the company's average annual gross receipts for 2010 are $700,000 ([$200,000 + $800,000 + $1,100,000] ÷ 3 = $700,000).

The Concept of "Constructive Receipt"

Under the cash method, taxpayers include all income constructively received during the tax year. Income is "constructively received" when the amount is made available without restriction. A taxpayer does not need to have physical possession of the payment. Income is not considered to be constructively received if actual control of the income is restricted.

Example: Interest is credited to Nathan's bank account in December 2010, but he does not withdraw it until January 2011. Nathan must include the amount in gross income for 2010, not 2011. Nathan had ownership and control of the interest in 2010, so it is taxable in the year received.

Example: Better Jail Bonds LLP is a cash-basis partnership. They bill a customer on December 10, 2010. The customer sends them a check postdated to January 2, 2011. The check cannot be deposited until 2011 because it was postdated. Better Jail Bonds would include this income in gross income for 2011, since constructive receipt did not occur until 2011. If income is subject to restrictions, then it is only considered "constructively received" when the taxpayer has access to the funds.

Accrual Method

Under the accrual method of accounting, an entity reports income in the year earned and deducts or capitalizes expenses as they are *incurred*. The purpose of the accrual method of accounting is to match income and expenses in the correct year. Under the accrual method, a business records income when a sale occurs, regardless of when the business gets paid. Under the accrual method, income is reported on the EARLIEST of the following dates:

- When payment is received
- When the taxpayer earns the income
- When the income is due to the taxpayer
- When title has passed to the taxpayer[51]

Under the accrual method, expenses are reported as soon as they are incurred. It doesn't matter when the business actually pays for the expenses. The accrual method gives a more accurate picture of a business's financial situation than the cash method. This is because income is recorded when it is truly earned, and expenses are recorded when they are incurred.

Income earned in one period is accurately matched against the expenses that correspond to that period, so a business gets a better picture of net profits for each period. In formal accounting, this concept is called the "matching principle," and it is the reason why larger businesses use the accrual method.

Example: Ali's Computer Inc. is a calendar-year, accrual-basis sole proprietorship. The business sold a computer on December 28, 2010 for $2,500. Ali billed the customer in the first week of January 2011, but did not receive payment until February 2011. Ali must include the $2,500 in his 2010 income, the year he actually earned the income. This is because the company operates on the accrual method. Conversely, this also means that the business is allowed to deduct expenses as they are *incurred* (not necessarily when they are paid).

---

[51] Publication 538

Retailers who use the accrual method of accounting may account for the sale of goods when they actually ship the goods. Retailers may use this method for both tax and financial reporting purposes. Businesses can include advance payments in gross receipts for tax purposes in either:

- The tax year in which the business receives the advance payment; or
- The tax year in which the business actually ships the goods.

Shipping Terms and Transfer of Ownership

There are a few shipping terms that the IRS expects tax practitioners to understand. These terms are commonly used when shipping goods; it indicates the point at which the ownership of the goods transfers from shipper to buyer. The shipping terms dictate when a taxpayer will have to recognize income, or take an item out of inventory. This is especially important at the end of the year. The three most common terms are:

1. FOB destination: This means that the ownership of the goods passes to the buyer at the point of destination (when the goods arrive at the buyer's location).
2. FOB shipping point: This means that ownership of the goods passes to the buyer at the point of shipment, (when the goods leave the seller's premises). FOB shipping point is also called "FOB origin."
3. C.O.D. ("cash on delivery" or "collect on delivery"). This term refers to the collection of the payment upon delivery. The common abbreviations are C.O.D. or COD. COD title does not pass until payment is remitted for the goods.

Example: Happy Furniture Company is a calendar-year, accrual-basis corporation that manufactures custom household furniture. Under the accrual method, the company must accrue income when it actually sells the furniture, not when it receives the payment. For tax purposes, Happy Company does not accrue income until the furniture has been delivered and accepted by the buyer. In 2010, the company received an advance payment of $8,000 for an order of furniture to be custom manufactured for a total price of $20,000.
Happy Company shipped the furniture "FOB destination" to the customer on December 26, 2010, but it was not delivered and accepted by the customer until January 3, 2011. For tax purposes, Happy Company must include the $8,000 advance payment in gross income for 2010, and must include the remaining $12,000 of the contract price in gross income for 2011.

If a business uses the accrual method to report expenses, it is also required to use the accrual method to report income. Generally, advance payments for services to be performed in future years are taxable in the year the payments are received. But if there is an agreement that the service will be completed by the end of the next tax year, the recognition of that income can be postponed and included in income the next year. But the taxpayer cannot postpone the recognition of income beyond the next year.[52]

Postponement Not Allowed for Rents

Prepaid rent is always recognized when it is received, regardless of the accounting method used. An entity cannot postpone recognizing an advance payment in income if it will

---

[52] Publication 538

perform the service after the end of the tax year immediately following the year it receives the advance payment. A taxpayer can never postpone recording income from prepaid rent. This rule also applies if the business will perform the service at any unspecified future date.

An entity MAY postpone reporting income from an advance payment received for a service contract agreement on property it sells, leases, builds, installs, or constructs. This includes an agreement providing for replacement of parts or materials, such as a warranty agreement.

> **Example:** Sharon is in the television repair business as an accrual-based taxpayer. She received payments in 2010 for warranty service contracts under which she agrees to repair broken television sets. The television sets are manufactured and sold by another company. Sharon may include the warranty payments in gross income as she earns them, when she actually performs the services in the future.

Hybrid (Combination) Accounting Methods

Businesses may also choose to use a hybrid accounting method. A hybrid accounting method is a combination of cash and accrual. This means that the business may choose to use the accrual method to the extent that is required in order to comply with IRS regulations. Then, the business may use the cash method of accounting to account for the remainder of income and expenses. The following restrictions to the hybrid method apply:

- If an inventory is necessary to account for income, the business must use an accrual method for purchases and sales.
- If an entity uses the cash method for reporting income, it must use the cash method for reporting expenses.
- If an entity uses the accrual method for reporting expenses, the entity must use the accrual method for reporting income.

Any *combination* method that includes the cash method is treated as the cash method. Any hybrid method that clearly reflects income and expenses will generally be allowed. The hybrid method is often used by small businesses that carry inventories. These businesses may be required to use the accrual method to account for inventory, but then choose to use the cash method to account for other items of income and expense.

Switching Accounting Methods

A taxpayer is allowed to use any accounting method that clearly reflects income. If a business later wants to change its accounting method, it must receive prior IRS approval. The following accounting changes require prior approval from the IRS:

- Change from cash to accrual (or vice versa), unless the change is required by tax law, such as when a business's average gross receipts exceed $5 million
- Change in the method used to value inventory (change from LIFO to FIFO, for example)
- Change in accounting method to figure depreciation

Taxpayers must file Form 3115, *Application for Change in Accounting Method*, to request a change in either an overall accounting method or the accounting treatment of any item. However, IRS consent is not required for the following:

- Switching to straight-line depreciation from accelerated methods (once a taxpayer switches to straight-line for an asset, they cannot switch back)
- Making an adjustment in the useful life of an asset (a taxpayer cannot change the recovery time for MACRS or ACRS property, which is the depreciation method used for real property)
- The correction of an error
- A change in accounting method when the change is required by tax law

These exceptions are commonly tested on the Enrolled Agent's Exam.

Example: Gary is a general partner in Ultimate Partners LLC. He wishes to change his inventory method from LIFO to FIFO in 2010. Gary also discovered a big error in the useful life of a depreciable asset—the asset should have been depreciated over 15 years, rather than five. Ultimate Partners LLC must ask permission from the IRS to change inventory methods, but does not have to ask permission in order to correct the depreciation error.

Inventory Tracking and Valuation

Tracking of inventory is necessary in order to clearly show income when a business produces or sells products. Businesses must generally take a full physical inventory count at the beginning and the end of the tax year. Businesses must also take a physical inventory at reasonable intervals and the book amount for inventory must be adjusted to agree with the actual inventory. The reason why physical inventory counts are so important is because they are often the only way to catch certain irregularities such as theft, damaged goods, and obsolete products.

Example: Writher's Grocery Store takes a physical inventory once a month. During the physical inventory, store employees are required to record any damaged goods such as dented cans and ripped packaging. When the physical inventory is done, the manager does a reconciliation based on her records. At that time, she also discovers the amount of missing inventory due to theft. She then makes an adjustment to the books to record the theft losses and the damaged merchandise. The physical inventory count helps the store managers understand how much inventory they actually have.

If a taxpayer removes items from inventory for personal use, he is required to subtract the cost of personal use items from total purchases.

Inventory methods are frequently tested on the EA Exam. It is important that you understand the most common inventory valuation methods and the unique characteristics of each. The following are the most common inventory accounting methods.

Specific Identification Method

This method requires a detailed physical count. Entities use the Specific Identification Method when the business can identify and match the actual cost to the items in inventory. This method is most useful with a small inventory of high-dollar items; it is best used when inventory is highly specific, such as custom goods or rare items like artwork, diamonds or gemstones. The business simply accounts for each individual item as it is sold.

> **Example:** The Classic Custom dealership sells rare collectible and classic cars. Each car is inventoried and tracked individually by the license plate number. Expenses for each car are tracked on a separate spreadsheet. This is an example of Specific Identification inventory valuation.

Weighted Average Cost Method

This accounting method takes total inventory and divides it by the total amount of goods from beginning inventory and purchases. This method is also called simply the "Average Cost Method." This gives a "Weighted Average Cost per Unit." Essentially, this is an average cost for all the items in inventory.

This method is commonly used when a company has lots of similar goods, or many small, low-priced items that are difficult to account for individually. The formula for figuring average cost is:

Average Unit Cost = (Total Unit Cost)/ (Total Quantity of Units)
Inventory Value = (Average Unit Cost) x (Units of Current Inventory)

Example: The Weighted Average Cost Method

Anna owns a pet store. She purchases five dog leashes at $10 apiece. The following week, the price of the leashes goes up, and she purchases five more leashes at $20 apiece. Anna then sells five leashes the following week. The weighted average of Anna's inventory is calculated as follows:

Total cost of leashes:

(Five leashes at $10 each) = $50

(Five leashes at $20 each) = $100

Total number of units = 10 leashes

Weighted average = $150 / 10 = $15

$15 is the average cost per leash of the 10 leashes

FIFO (First In, First Out)

For taxation purposes, FIFO assumes that the assets that are remaining in inventory are matched to the assets that are most recently produced. FIFO is used by most major corporations to value their inventory.

With FIFO, the assumption is that inventory will be sold in the order that it is stocked, with the oldest goods sold FIRST and the newest goods sold LAST (like rotating stock in a grocery store).

The formula for figuring inventory based on the FIFO method is as follows:

Unit Cost per lot = (Cost/Quantity) for each lot
Inventory Value = (Unit Cost x Quantity) for each lot

In an economy of rising prices (during inflation), it is common for beginning companies to use FIFO for reporting the value of merchandise to bolster their balance sheets. FIFO generally produces a higher income.

Example: FIFO Method: Randall's Electronics sells car audio equipment. Beginning inventory on January 1 was 300 stereos at the wholesale cost of $20 each. The business is a cash-basis, calendar-year taxpayer. It calculates its beginning inventory and purchases as follows:

In January the business sold 1,200 stereos. On January 10 the business purchased 600 stereos at $20.10; on January 16 it purchased 400 stereos for $20.20; and finally on January 25 it purchased 500 stereos for $20.30. Under FIFO it is assumed that the oldest merchandise is sold first. Randall's Electronics had a beginning inventory of 300 stereos—those units are assumed to leave inventory first, followed by the units purchased on January 10 and January 16.

The total Cost of Goods Sold calculation is figured as follows:

300 x $20.00 = $ 6,000

600 x $20.10 = $12,600

300 x $20.20 = $ 6,600

Total 1,200 units sold. Total Cost of Goods Sold = $25,200

LIFO (Last In, First Out)

LIFO is a historical method of recording the value of inventory. The business records the last units purchased as the first units sold. In other words, LIFO assumes that the newest inventory is sold FIRST, with the oldest goods sold LAST.

Since the prices of goods and materials generally rise over time, this method records the sale of the most expensive inventory first and thereby can reduce taxes. Use of the LIFO method is highly regulated by the IRS. This is because using LIFO will often lead to a lower gross income for a company, and therefore, fewer income taxes.

A business must obtain permission from the IRS to switch to the LIFO method of inventory valuation. If a business has opted to use LIFO from its outset, however, it does not need to seek permission. The rules for using the LIFO method are very complex. The formula for figuring inventory using the LIFO method is as follows:

Unit Cost per lot = (Cost/Quantity) for each lot

Inventory Value = (Unit Cost x Quantity) for each lot

Example: LIFO Method: Dave's Decals sells auto decals and the company uses the LIFO method to calculate COGS. Using the LIFO method, the most recent inventory purchases are assumed to leave the inventory first. Beginning inventory on January 1 was 300 decals at the wholesale cost of $2 each. In January, Dave's Decals sold 1,200 decals. On January 16 the business purchased 400 decals for $3.10 and finally on January 25 it purchased 500 decals for $2.60. Here is how the Cost of Goods Sold is figured under LIFO:

January 25 purchase= 500 x $2.60 = $1,300

January 16 purchase= 400 x $3.10 = $1,240

Beginning inventory= 300 x $2.10 = $630

Total 1,200 units sold. Total Cost of Goods Sold in January = $3,170.

Most publicly traded companies use the FIFO method to value their inventories. However, there are a few large corporations that choose to use LIFO, including the well-known paint company Sherwin-Williams Corp. and Caterpillar Inc. (the tractor company). Companies choose to use LIFO primarily because it allows lowers gross income, and consequently, also lowers income tax.

The Difference between LIFO and FIFO*[53]

Economic Climate	FIFO	LIFO
Periods of Rising Prices (Inflation)	(+) Higher value of inventory	(-) Lower value of inventory
	(-) Lower cost of goods sold	(+) Higher cost of goods sold
Periods of Falling Prices (Deflation)	(-) Lower value of inventory	(-) Higher value of inventory
	(+) Higher cost of goods sold	(+) Lower cost of goods sold

Cost of Goods Sold (COGS)

The value of inventory is a major factor in figuring taxable income. The method used to actually value the inventory is very important. This is the issue of figuring the basis of the inventory.

Cost of Goods Sold (COGS) is determined by figuring all the costs that go into creating products that a business eventually sells. The costs included in COGS are those costs that are tied to the production of the goods. This includes the shipping costs in order to get the goods (raw materials) to the manufacturer in order to produce the inventory. Freight-in, express-in, and cartage-in on raw materials, supplies used in production, and merchandise purchased for resale are all part of Cost of Goods Sold. However, the postage or shipping costs to deliver a finished product to a buyer are NOT included.

For example, COGS for a shoe manufacturer would include the cost of the leather and thread, as well as wages for the workers that produce the shoes. The shipping cost of sending the finished shoes to retailers would not be included in the COGS equation.

The costs included in COGS will vary from one business type to another. The following methods are typically used:

- Cost
- Lower-of-cost or market
- Retail method

The equation for Cost of Goods Sold is as follows:
Beginning Inventory + Inventory Purchases – End Inventory = Cost of Goods Sold

The COGS attributed to a company's inventory are expensed *as the company sells* their goods. The way to figure COGS is to start with beginning inventory, add the materials purchased and used for production, and then subtract the ending inventory.

Costs Included in COGS

There are certain items and costs that must be allocated to the inventory, rather than expensed. If a business must account for an inventory, it must generally use an accrual method

---

[53] This concept has been on prior year exams.

of accounting. If a business is required to account for inventories, the following items should be included in the inventory valuation:

- Finished inventory products available for sale to customers
- Goods on consignment or contracted for sale where title has not passed to the buyer yet
- Raw materials (including freight) and work in progress
- Supplies that physically become part of the item so it can be sold (such as price tags, packaging, etc.)
- Any purchased merchandise (raw materials, etc.) if ownership has passed to the taxpayer, even if the taxpayer does not have physical possession of the goods yet
- Goods for sale on display or away from the taxpayer's place of business, if the taxpayer still has legal ownership of the goods
- Storage costs for unsold inventory
- Direct labor (including contributions to pension or annuity plans) for workers who produce the products.
- Factory overhead (for example, in a factory that produces goods, the overhead costs that are *directly related* to the production of the inventory would be included in COGS).[54]

Example: Doggie Delights Inc. is a cash-basis corporation that manufactures custom doggie sweaters. In January, Doggie Delights has $20,000 in overall sales. In the same month, the corporation also has a number of expenses, including wages for the sweater designers ($5,000) and the cost of raw materials, including yarn, appliqué, rhinestones, and other raw materials ($3,000). The wages and the cost of the raw materials are directly related to the production of the inventory (the sweaters) and must be included in the Cost of Goods Sold (COGS) calculation. All the other expenses that are NOT directly related to the manufacture of the sweaters would be expensed. The current expenses might include items like a receptionist's salary, ($1,500) telephone expense, ($130) advertising, ($1,200), and other costs that are not directly related to the manufacture of the goods. So, in this example, the income statement might look like this for the month of January:

Gross income from sales:	$20,000
COGS: ($5,000 + $3,000)	$8,000
Expenses: ($1,500 + $130 + $1,200)	$2,830
Net income for January	$9,170

The following items should NOT be included in a taxpayer's inventory:

- Goods that are consigned to the TAXPAYER by another vendor
- Goods ordered by the taxpayer, where ownership (title) has not yet passed to the taxpayer

---

[54] See Publication 535 for more information about COGS.

- Goods the taxpayer has sold, even if they have not arrived at their destination, if ownership has already passed to the buyer
- Freight charges to ship a finished item to a buyer or a customer

Inventory should not include the cost of assets, such as:

- Land, buildings, and equipment used in the business
- Notes, accounts receivable, and similar assets
- Supplies that do not physically become part of the item intended for sale

---

Example: Tiny Toys Inc. is a toy manufacturer. At the beginning of the year, Tiny Toys has $8,000 in inventory. During the year, Tiny Toys adds $24,000 in additional inventory purchased during year. At the end of the year, the owners do a final inventory count, and they calculate that they have $6,000 in ending inventory. The COGS for Tiny Toys is therefore $26,000.

Beginning Inventory + Purchases - Ending Inventory = Cost of Goods Sold

$8,000 beginning of year

+$24,000 inventory purchased

- $6,000 ending inventory

= $26,000 Cost of Goods Sold

Inventory is increased by merchandise or raw materials purchased. Labor costs are usually included in the COGS calculation only in manufacturing or mining businesses. In manufacturing, labor costs include the direct and indirect costs used in the fabrication of inventory or goods produced for eventual resale or retail sale to customers. Materials and supplies used in the actual manufacture of goods are also included in COGS.

Example: COGS Calculation: Sandy Beaches Company manufactures sandboxes for sale to retailers. The company starts with $12 million in inventory, makes $3 million in purchases of raw materials, and ends the period with $6 million in inventory. The company's cost of goods for the period would be $9 million ($12 million + $3 million - $6 million).

Sandy Beaches Company	Amount
Starting inventory:	$12,000,000
Purchases:	+$3,000,000
Ending inventory:	($6,000,000)
COGS:	**$9,000,000**

Valuing Inventory at Cost

To properly value inventory at cost, a business must include all direct and indirect costs associated with the inventory. Some businesses manufacture their own goods to sell. If so, the businesses deduct the Cost of Goods Sold (COGS) from their gross receipts. To determine these costs, the value of inventory at the beginning and end of the year must be calculated. There are several factors that go into determining COGS including:

- Inventory at the beginning of the year
- Inventory items withdrawn for personal use
- Labor costs and materials and supplies (generally a manufacturing cost)
- Inventory at the end of the year

- Inventory, net purchases, cost of labor, materials and supplies, and other costs added together

Lower-of-Cost or Market Method

Under the "lower-of-cost or market" method, the taxpayer must compare the market value of each item on hand with its cost and use the lower amount as its inventory value. This is a good way to record the actual value of inventory when the inventory loses value quickly, such as happens with fashion clothing. This method applies to the following:

- Goods purchased and on hand
- The basic elements of cost (direct materials, direct labor, and certain indirect costs) of goods being manufactured and finished goods on hand

Example of Lower-of-Cost or Market			
Graham makes leather motorcycle accessories at his factory. Under the lower-of-cost or market method, the following items would be valued at $600 in closing inventory.			
Inventory Item	**Cost**	**Market**	**Lower**
Leather jacket	$300	$500	$300
Motorcycle helmets	$200	$100	$100
Leather motorcycle chaps	$450	$200	$200
Total	**$950**	**$800**	**$600**

Graham must value each item in the inventory separately. He cannot value the entire inventory at cost ($950) and at market ($800) and then use the lower of the two figures.

Retail Method

Under the retail method, the total retail selling price of goods on hand at the end of the tax year in each department or of each class of goods is reduced to approximate cost by using an average markup expressed as a percentage of the total retail selling price.

For example, if a store always marks up its merchandise by 35%, then that percentage would be used as a basis for valuing its current inventory (Publication 538).

Reporting Obsolete Goods or Damaged Inventory

Goods that cannot be sold at normal prices or are unusable because of damage, imperfections, shop wear, changes of style, odd or broken lots, or other similar causes, should be valued at their actual selling price minus the direct cost of disposition, no matter which method is used to value the rest of the entity's inventory.

Reporting Thefts or Lost Inventory

Sometimes, a business will experience a theft loss or spoilage of inventory. There are several ways to claim a casualty or theft loss of inventory. In this case, a business may claim a casualty or theft loss of inventory simply by increasing the Cost of Goods Sold by properly reporting opening and closing inventories.

The business can also choose to take the loss separately as a casualty or theft loss. If the entity chooses to report a casualty loss, it must adjust opening inventory to eliminate the loss items and avoid counting the loss twice.

Uniform Capitalization Rules (UNICAP or UCR)

Under the Uniform Capitalization Rules (UCR), businesses must capitalize the direct costs for production of goods. In most cases, UCR also applies to businesses that purchase merchandise for resale to others. In essence, the UCR rules affect almost any business that carries or produces inventory. Businesses then recover the costs through depreciation, amortization, or Cost of Goods Sold when the property is used or sold. Under the UCR rules, most inventories that are produced for resale and the costs associated with the inventory must be capitalized rather than expensed.

This means that the costs that go into actually creating the inventory cannot be expensed and must be added to the basis of the inventory. Production expenses must be included in the basis of the property produced or in inventory costs rather than currently deducted. These costs are then recoverable through depreciation, amortization, or as Cost of Goods Sold. Most tangible goods are subject to the UCR.

The UCR also applies to films, sound recordings, videotapes, books, artwork, photographs, or similar property. However, *individual* freelance authors, photographers, and artists are EXEMPT from the Uniform Capitalization Rules.

Under the UCR, a business must capitalize expenses related to the property, such as taxes. Property acquired for resale is not subject to the Uniform Capitalization Rules if the average annual gross receipts for the business for the three prior tax years are $10 million or less. Businesses are subject to the Uniform Capitalization Rules if they do any of the following:

- Produce property for use in the business or activity.
- Produce property for sale to customers (the production of inventory).
- Purchase property for resale. (However, this rule does not apply to personal property if the business's average annual gross receipts are $10 million or less.)

Exceptions to the Uniform Capitalization Rules

The Uniform Capitalization Rules do NOT apply to the following:

- Resellers of personal property with average annual gross receipts of $10 million or less for the three prior tax years
- Non-business property (such as a hobby that produces occasional income)
- Research and experimental expenditures
- Intangible drilling and development costs of oil and gas or geothermal wells
- Property produced under a long-term contract
- Timber raised, harvested, or grown, and the underlying land
- Qualified creative expenses incurred as freelance (self-employed) writers, photographers, or artists that are otherwise deductible on their tax returns
- Loan originations

Unit 2.2: Questions

1. The following entities may not use the cash method of accounting, EXCEPT for:

A. A family farming corporation with gross receipts of $22 million
B. A "C" Corporation with gross receipts of $50 million
C. A tax shelter with $50,000 in gross receipts
D. A corporation with long-term contracts

The answer is A. A family farming corporation may use the cash method of accounting if its average annual gross receipts are $25 million or less (Publication 538). A tax shelter must always use the accrual method, regardless of its gross receipts. A corporation with long-term contracts must always use the accrual method. A C Corporation with gross receipts exceeding $5 million is required to use the accrual method of accounting. ###

2. Which of the following changes in accounting method DOES NOT require prior approval from the IRS?

A. A change from FIFO to LIFO inventory valuation
B. A change from the cash method to the accrual method
C. A change in the overall method of figuring depreciation
D. A correction of a math error in depreciating an asset

The answer is D. The correction of a math error does not require prior approval from the IRS. The taxpayer must file Form 3115, *Application for Change in Accounting Method*, to request a change in accounting method. Consent from the IRS is not required for the following changes:
- Correction of a math error for computing tax liability or other mathematical error
- A correction in depreciable life or correction of a depreciation error
- An adjustment to an asset's useful life. ###

3. Which form must be filed with the IRS in order to request a change in accounting method?

A. Form 1040X
B. Form 990
C. Form 1128
D. Form 3115

The answer is D. Taxpayers must file Form 3115 in order to request a change of accounting method with the IRS. ###

4. Helen Banner is the owner of Banner's Custom Lamps, Inc., a calendar-year, accrual-basis S Corporation. She sells five lamps to Sonny's Interior Design on December 21, 2010, billing Sonny's for $2,500. Sonny's Interior Design pays the invoice on January 15, 2011. Banner's Custom Lamps would include this income in which tax year?

A. 2010
B. 2011
C. 2012
D. None of the above

The answer is A. The income would be included in Banner's Custom Lamps' 2010 tax return, because Banner is using the accrual method of accounting for income and expenses. Under the accrual method, income is reported in the year earned and expenses are deducted in the year incurred. Since Banner sold the lamps in 2010, the income would be reported in 2010. ###

5. Benny owns a jewelry store. Which transaction below is NOT an example of "constructive receipt" of income in 2010?

A. Benny receives a check payment on December 31, 2010, but does not deposit the check in the bank until January 2, 2011.
B. Benny receives a direct deposit of funds to his bank account on December 15, 2010, but does not withdraw any of the funds until March 2011.
C. Benny receives a signed IOU from a delinquent account in November 2010. He finally receives payment on this account on January 10, 2011.
D. Benny receives a lump sum of cash to an escrow agent that is restricted for his use. It is an advance payment for a custom ring, but Benny cannot access any of the funds until the ring is delivered and inspected. On December 5, 2010, the ring is delivered and the restriction is lifted. Benny picks up the cash on January 9, 2011.

The answer is C. According to the "doctrine of constructive receipt," income is included in gross income when a person has an unqualified right to the funds. Constructive receipt must be more than just a billing, an offer, or a mere promise to pay. The amounts that were merely promised to Benny, therefore, do not have to be included in income for 2010. ###

5. A company can choose to compute taxable income under which of the following methods?

A. Hybrid method
B. Accrual method
C. Cash method
D. All of the above

The answer is D. A company can choose to compute its taxable income under any of the following methods, unless specifically prohibited by the IRS:

- Cash method
- Hybrid method
- Accrual method
- Special methods of accounting

Any accounting method that clearly reflects income is acceptable only if all items of gross income and expenses are treated the same from year to year. ###

7. Ray operates a retail store using the accrual method of accounting and reports income on Schedule C, *Net Profit or Loss from Business*. He plans to start a lawn care service to operate only in the summer months. Which of the following statements is TRUE?

A. The lawn care business is required to use the accrual method of accounting because Ray has already elected this method for his other business and all businesses operated by one individual must use the same method of accounting.
B. The lawn care business may use either the cash or accrual method of accounting so long as both businesses have separate and distinct records.
C. Ray may keep one set of records for both businesses, and use different methods of accounting for each one.
D. Ray must combine the income for both businesses and keep one set of record books for both.

The answer is B. A taxpayer may use different methods of accounting for two distinct and separate businesses. Separate accounting books must be kept for each business. ###

8. Which of the following entities may NOT use the cash method of accounting?

A. A partnership that produces inventory for sale to customers and has $1.2 million in average gross receipts
B. A C Corporation with $4.5 million in average gross receipts
C. A qualified family farming corporation with $14 million in average gross receipts
D. A sole proprietor with inventory and $900,000 in gross receipts

The answer is A. Generally, an entity cannot use the cash method if it has average annual gross receipts exceeding $5 million. If a company produces inventory, the threshold is gross receipts of $1 million. A qualified family farming corporation may use the cash method if its average gross receipts do not exceed $25 million. ###

9. The following are all acceptable methods of accounting for inventory except:

A. Specific Identification Method
B. Coupon Method
C. FIFO
D. LIFO

The answer is B. The "Coupon Method" does not exist. FIFO, LIFO, and Specific Identification are all acceptable inventory methods. ###

10. Jenny owns a small business selling makeup as a sole proprietor. Occasionally, she takes items out of inventory for her own personal use. In 2010, she took $250 worth of makeup for her own use. What is the proper tax treatment of this action?
A. Jenny must reduce the amount of her total inventory purchases by $250, the amount of the items removed for personal use.
B. Jenny may take an expense of $250 on Schedule C for the personal use items.
C. Jenny must increase the cost of her purchases by the value of her personal use items.
D. Jenny may deduct the $250 on Schedule A as an employee business expense.

The answer is A. Taxpayers are required to subtract the cost of personal use items from total purchases, if they remove items for personal use from business inventory. ###

11. Under the "lower-of-cost or market" method of valuing inventory, what is the value of the inventory as a whole, based on the table below?

Item	Cost	Market Value
Shirts	$200	$500
Shoes	$300	$200
Shorts	$225	$150
Total	**$725**	**$850**

A. $725
B. $850
C. $750
D. $550

The answer is D. To value inventory using the "lower-of-cost or market" method, compare the cost and the market value of each of the items in inventory, and choose the lower of the two to obtain the inventory's value. ###

12. Which of the following activities would make a taxpayer subject to the Uniform Capitalization Rules?

A. A taxpayer produces items as a hobby and occasionally sells them to family members
B. A taxpayer produces property for sale to wholesale retailers
C. A taxpayer acquires raw land and holds it for investment
D. A taxpayer refurbishes multiple automobiles for his own use

The answer is B. A taxpayer is subject to the Uniform Capitalization Rules if she produces real property or personal property for use in a trade or business. Producing items for personal use or as a hobby does not qualify. ###

13. Which of the following types of property are NOT exempt from the Uniform Capitalization Rules?

A. Qualified expenses of a writer, photographer, or performing artist
B. Timber and the underlying land
C. Services provided to customers
D. A company that produces automobiles

The answer is D. A company that produces automobiles would be subject to the UCR. Generally, the Uniform Capitalization Rules apply to a taxpayer that produces property for use or resale in a business. A company that provides services will not carry an inventory, so it is not subject to the UCR. Independent authors, writers, and artists are exempt from the UCR. ###

14. Chris is the owner-shareholder of Chris's Clothing Company, an S Corporation. He manufactures clothing for resale to the general public and also sells them to wholesale distributors. Chris is trying to figure out his inventory calculations in order to file his 2010 tax return. Which of the following items should be included in current inventory?

A. 2,000 T-shirts out on consignment for another retailer to sell
B. Large machinery used to manufacture the clothing
C. An order of fabric that is in transit, FOB destination (the title has not yet passed to Chris)
D. 1,000 shirts that were shipped COD to a retailer yesterday that have already arrived at the buyer's warehouse

The answer is A. Chris should include the consigned goods in his own inventory, since goods on consignment are not actually sold to the retailer. Merchandise sent COD is automatically included in inventory until it reaches the buyer, because title does not pass to the buyer until the item is delivered and paid for. The term "FOB" (also known as "Freight on Board") is commonly used when shipping goods to indicate the point at which the responsibility of the goods transfers from shipper to buyer. The buyer is responsible when shipped FOB shipping point and the seller is responsible when shipped FOB destination. Machinery and other fixed assets are not included in inventory. They are depreciated separately. ###

15. Which of the following practices is NOT an acceptable method of accounting for inventory?

A. The taxpayer accounts for inventory and includes only direct costs associated with manufacturing the goods.
B. The taxpayer has a theft loss of inventory when a disgruntled employee steals substantial amounts of merchandise. The taxpayer chooses to increase his Cost of Goods Sold (COGS) to account for the stolen items, and properly reports his beginning and closing inventory.
C. The taxpayer values his inventory using the "lower-of-cost or market" method, and chooses the lowest value for his inventory valuations.
D. The taxpayer has two businesses, and chooses to use LIFO for the first business and FIFO for the second one. He keeps a separate set of books for each business.

The answer is A. Taxpayers must include direct and indirect costs in inventory. Taxpayers may claim a casualty or theft loss of inventory through the increase in the Cost of Goods Sold by properly reporting opening and closing inventories. Taxpayers may choose to use different accounting methods for different businesses, so long as the businesses are kept separate and distinct accounting records are maintained for each. ###

16. Tuxedo House, a clothing retailer, had the following expenses in 2010. Based on the information below, what is Tuxedo House's Cost of Goods Sold?

Tuxedos purchased for resale $20,000
Freight-in $3,000
Freight-out to customers $6,000
Beginning inventory $15,600
Ending inventory $12,000

A. $23,000
B. $26,600
C. $28,600
D. $42,500

The answer is B. The COGS is calculated as follows: $26,600 ($15,600 beginning inventory + $20,000 purchases + $3,000 freight-in, minus $12,000 ending inventory). Freight-in and merchandise purchased for resale are part of the COGS, but freight-out is not included because it is an event that occurs after the merchandise is already finished and ready for sale. ###

17. All of the following activities are EXEMPT from the Uniform Capitalization Rules EXCEPT:

A. Resellers of personal property with average annual gross receipts of $10 million or less
B. Intangible drilling and development costs of oil and gas or geothermal wells
C. The expenses of a self-employed artist
D. The intangible film production costs of a corporate movie studio

The answer is D. *Self-employed* freelance authors, photographers, and artists are exempt from the Uniform Capitalization Rules, but the costs of a film production by a *corporate* movie studio must be capitalized. The Uniform Capitalization Rules do NOT apply to:

- Resellers of property with annual gross receipts of $10 million or less
- Non-business property
- Research and experimental expenditures
- Intangible drilling and development costs of oil and gas or geothermal wells
- Property produced under a long-term contract ###

18. Thomas purchases a bulk order of watches for his mail order business. The watches cost $5,000, and the sales tax on the watches is $350. What is the correct treatment of the sales tax paid on the watches?

A. Thomas may elect to deduct the sales tax on his tax return as a regular expense.
B. Sales tax paid on the watches must be added to the basis of the inventory.
C. Thomas cannot deduct the sales tax and cannot capitalize it.
D. Thomas may elect to deduct the sales tax as an itemized deduction on Schedule A.

The answer is B. Sales tax paid on inventory or a depreciable asset must be added to the basis of the asset. The sales tax increases the asset's basis. If the property is merchandise bought for resale (such as inventory), the sales tax is part of the cost of the merchandise and must be capitalized and then recovered in the "Cost of Goods Sold" calculation. ###

19. In which one of the following business situations does the Uniform Capitalization Rules apply?
A. The business sells clothing purchased wholesale, and has average annual gross receipts of less than $10 million
B. A famous self-employed artist creates paintings, and has average gross receipts of $9 million
C. The business sells office supplies purchased wholesale, and has average annual gross receipts of $11 million
D. The taxpayer is a photographer who produces photography for museums, and has average annual gross receipts of $5 million

The answer is C. Personal property acquired for resale is not subject to the Uniform Capitalization Rules if the average annual gross receipts for the three preceding tax years are $10 million or less. Generally, businesses must capitalize the wages paid to employees who produce tangible inventory. Costs paid or incurred by an individual (or a qualified employee-owner of a corporation) who is a writer, photographer, or artist are exempt from the Uniform Capitalization Rules. ###

20. Which of the following methods is not an acceptable method of calculating inventory costs?
A. The Specific Identification method
B. First In, First Out
C. Trade Discount Method
D. Weighted Average Cost

The answer is C. The "Trade Discount Method" is not a real method for valuing inventory. The Specific Identification Method, FIFO (First In, First Out) and Weighted Average Cost are all acceptable inventory valuation methods. ###

21. All of the following costs must be included in inventory EXCEPT:

A. Shipping raw materials to the business's factory
B. Shipping finished product orders to customers
C. Raw materials
D. Direct labor costs

The answer is B. Shipping finished products to customers is not an expense that should be included in inventory. This cost is a current expense and would be deductible as postage, rather than capitalized as a cost of inventory. ###

Unit 2.3: Business Income and Property Transactions

> **More Reading:**
> Publication 525, *Taxable and Nontaxable Income*
> Publication 544, *Sales and Other Dispositions of Assets*
> Publication 538, *Accounting Periods and Methods*

Business income includes any type of payment such as cash, checks, credit cards, property, or services exchanged. If there is a connection between any income received and a business, the income is considered business income. For example, fees received by a professional tax preparer are considered business income. Payments received in the form of property or services (bartering) must be included in income at their FMV. The definition of business income comes from the tax code, specifically IRC §61.

Just like individual taxpayers, businesses sometimes earn income that is exempt from tax. More often, businesses engage in transactions that *defer* income to a later date. An example is a Section 1031 exchange, which allows for deferral of income on the exchange of business or investment property. The following examples include common types of business income, but the list is not exhaustive. The most common type of business income is simply the payment for goods or services. This is how most businesses earn revenue. However, there are less common types of business income that must be reported. There are also some types of income that are not taxable, even to businesses.

Bartering Income

Bartering occurs when a taxpayer exchanges goods or services without exchanging actual money. An example of bartering is a plumber doing repair work for a dentist in exchange for dental services. The Fair Market Value of goods and services received in exchange must be included in income in the year received.

> **Example:** Ethan is a self-employed web designer. Ethan and a house painter are members of a barter club where members get in touch with one another directly and bargain. In return for Ethan's web design services, the house painter painted Ethan's home. Ethan must report the exchange as income on Schedule C. The house painter must include in income the Fair Market Value of the services Ethan provided.

Canceled Debt

If a business-related debt is canceled or forgiven, the business may have to include the canceled amount in income. Self-employed taxpayers report the amount on Schedule C or on Schedule F (Form 1040). A business is not required to realize income from a canceled debt to the extent that the payment of the debt would have led to a business deduction.

> **Example:** Barbells Partnership is a cash-basis business. The partnership orders computer repair services on credit. Later, Barbells Partnership has trouble paying its debts. The computer repair company forgives the repair bill. The partnership is not required to recognize the canceled debt as income because payment of the repair bill would have been deductible as a business expense anyway.

In the above example, a canceled business debt of a cash-basis taxpayer is not taxable; however, the canceled debt of an accrual-basis business is considered income, because the deduction for the expense would have already been recorded.

Real Estate Income (Rents and Hotels)

Self-employed real estate dealers or owners of a hotel or motel who provide services for guests must report their rental income and expenses on Schedule C, subject to self-employment tax. A taxpayer qualifies as a "real estate dealer" if he is primarily engaged in the business of selling real estate to customers. Rent received from real estate held for sale to customers is subject to SE tax. However, income received from real estate held for investment is NOT subject to SE tax. Rental income received from operating a hotel, motel, or boarding house is subject to SE tax if the owner provides substantial services such as maid or laundry service to the occupants.

If a taxpayer is not a professional "real estate dealer," he must report the rental income and expenses on Schedule E. The rental income is considered passive income not subject to self-employment tax.

> **Example:** Joe owns two residential rental properties. He manages them and collects rents. He also has a full-time job as a restaurant manager. He is not a real estate dealer. Joe must report his rental income and losses on Schedule E. Advance rental payments received under a lease must be recognized in the year it is received. This is true no matter what accounting method or period is used. This means that a taxpayer who owns rental properties and receives rent in advance cannot delay recognizing the income, even if the taxpayer is on the accrual basis.

Important Forms

- Schedule C, *Profit or Loss from Business* (used for professional real estate dealers)
- Schedule E, *Supplemental Income and Loss* (from rental real estate, royalties, partnerships, S Corporations, estates, trusts, REMICs, etc.)

Business Interest and Dividend Income

Businesses can earn interest just like individuals. This is especially true if the business lends money to other businesses and individuals. In any business, interest received on notes receivable that have been accepted in the normal course of business is reported as business income. A common example of this is when a C Corporation owns stock in another company. The C Corporation earns dividends and interest just like an individual.

Generally, dividends are considered passive income. However, dividends are business income to professional stockbrokers and securities dealers. For most sole proprietors, dividend income is non-business (passive) income.

Business-Related Court Awards and Damages

Court awards and settlements for injury or illness are generally not taxable to an individual. However, most other types of court awards and settlements are taxable income. There are certain court awards that are always included as business income. Here are some examples:

- Damages for:
  - Patent or copyright infringement,

- o   Breach of contract, or
- o   Interference with business operations.
- Compensation for lost profits
- Interest earned on any type of court award
- Punitive damages[55]

Amounts Not Considered Business Income

Not all income is taxable. Just like in the case of individual taxpayers, there are types of business-related income and property transfers that are not taxable or reportable. Some of these transactions may be partially taxable, and some are transactions where the recognition of income is delayed until a later date. Examples include:

- Issuance of stock from the sale of treasury stock
- Most business loans (these are debt, not income)
- Sales tax that is collected and then remitted to the state taxing agency
- Like-kind exchanges of property
- Gain from an involuntary conversion, if the gain is reinvested properly
- Consignments
- A volunteer workforce for an exempt entity
- Workers' compensation for injuries or sickness
- A pension, annuity, or similar allowance for personal injuries or sickness resulting from active service in the armed forces
- Refundable security deposits (if returned to the renter after returning the property)

There are other items of "income" that the Internal Revenue Code excludes from gross income, such as most types of compensation for physical injuries. For example, if a business owner or employee is injured by equipment and later receives a court settlement for the injury, the income is not taxable to the employee, but it is still deductible as a business expense by the company that issues the settlement.

Like-Kind Exchanges: 1031 Exchange

A Section 1031 exchange occurs when a business or individual exchanges business property for similar property. It is a situation where business income may be realized but not taxable. Instead, any income from a 1031 exchange is usually deferred until the property is later sold or disposed of. A Section 1031 exchange is also called a "like-kind" exchange. The advantage of this type of exchange is that an individual or business can sell property and replace it with similar property without having to recognize any income on the transaction.

Like-kind exchanges are also covered in Book 1 (Individuals), because Part One of the EA Exam deals with rental income. The most common type of 1031 exchange is an exchange of

---

[55] Punitive damages may be awarded in addition to compensatory damages for actual monetary losses. Punitive damages are subject to income tax, but not subject to self-employment tax (FICA).

real property (real estate). However, entities regularly exchange other types of business property, such as machinery, vehicles, and intangible assets, such as patents and copyrights. A Sec-Section 1031 exchange is the most common type of nontaxable exchange.

There are very strict rules and timetables in order for an exchange to qualify for this treatment. In a 1031 exchange, the exchanger has a maximum of 45 days after the sale to identify a list of potential replacement properties and 180 days after the sale to acquire one of those properties. Form 8824 is used to report like-kind exchanges.

To qualify as a "like-kind" exchange, the property traded and the property received must be both of the following:

- Business or investment property
- Like (alike or similar) property

Example: A corporation purchases a medical office building for $300,000. After four years, the Fair Market Value of the property is $350,000. If the corporation were to sell the property, it would have to recognize $50,000 in capital gain, plus it would also be forced to recognize any depreciation recapture as ordinary income. However, if the corporation decides instead to invest the proceeds from the sale of the building into another property, any gain would be deferred. This would be considered a like-kind exchange (a "non-recognition" property transaction).

If, as part of the exchange, the taxpayer also receives dissimilar property such as cash, gain is recognized to the extent of the other property and money received. "Boot" is all non-qualified property transferred in an exchange transaction. The most common example of "boot" is when two individuals exchange property that is unequal in value. One party may offer cash in order to make up the difference in value. Cash is always considered "boot." The addition of *unlike property* to the exchange will also be considered boot. This would be considered a "partially taxable" exchange.

Example: Stephen and Regina decide that they will exchange rental properties. Stephen's rental property is more valuable, so Regina agrees to exchange her rental property and an additional $10,000 in cash. Therefore, Stephen will be required to recognize $10,000 of gain on the transaction.

A business cannot take a loss on a 1031 exchange. This means that a business may potentially have to recognize gain (on a partially taxable exchange) but a loss is never recognized in a like-kind exchange transaction.

Qualifying Property for a 1031 Exchange

"Like-kind" property can be any property used in a trade or business or as an investment, including planes, boats, intangible assets, and vehicles, but it is most often associated with real estate. Generally, real property can be exchanged, even if the properties are substantially different. For example, an exchange of farmland for a commercial building will still qualify for non-recognition treatment. All of the following can be exchanged as "like-kind" property:

- Condos, raw land, apartment buildings, duplexes, commercial buildings, residential rentals, and retail buildings
- A single business property exchanged for two or more properties and vice versa
- Investment property exchanged for business property and vice versa

- Water rights, mineral rights, oil and gas interests, copyrights, trademarks, and other intangible assets (but NOT partnership interests or securities)
- Livestock (but not livestock of different sexes)

The IRS only allows business-use or investment property to qualify for Section 1031. Personal-use property does not qualify.

Non-Qualifying Property for a Section 1031 Exchange

Certain property does NOT qualify for Section 1031 exchange treatment. Section 1031 does not apply to exchanges of:

- Inventory, or any property purchased for resale
- Stocks, bonds, notes, or other securities
- Livestock of different sexes
- Real property in the United States and real property outside the United States
- Exchanges of shares of corporate stock in different companies
- Exchanges of partnership interests or LLC membership interests
- A personal residence, or personal-use property (such as a personal car)
- Land under development for resale
- Corporation common stock

> **Example:** Trevino owns a piece of raw land in Texas he wants to exchange. When the land sale closes, his escrow company holds the proceeds. Within 45 days Trevino identifies an apartment building he wants to buy in Florida and successfully negotiates a contract to buy the building. Within the required 180 days the escrow company releases the funds he needs to close the purchase, and the exchange transaction is complete. Trevino has successfully postponed any gain he had on the original property.

Related Party Exchanges

There are special rules for Section 1031 exchanges between related parties. For purposes of the like-kind exchange rules, the definition of related parties is:

- Family members (siblings, spouses, ancestors, and lineal descendants)
- An individual and an entity (corporation or partnership) where the individual owns either directly or indirectly more than 50% in value of the entity (this includes ownership by a spouse or close family member)
- Two entities in which the same individual owns directly or indirectly more than 50% of each
- An estate in which the taxpayer is either the executor or beneficiary of the estate
- A trust in which the taxpayer is the fiduciary and the related party is a beneficiary either of that same trust or a related trust or a fiduciary of a related trust

Section 1031 does not *prohibit* related-party exchanges, but it requires a longer holding period in order to deter taxpayers from exchanging assets with family members or related businesses, only to dispose of them immediately and shift the gain. For exchanges between related parties, there is a two-year holding period. The non-recognition treatment will be lost if either property in the exchange is disposed of within two years.

However, this rule does not apply if either party in the transaction dies, or if the property is subject to an involuntary conversion, such as due to a fire or other disaster.

Involuntary Conversions, IRC Section 1033, Deferred Gains

An involuntary conversion occurs when property is destroyed, stolen, or condemned. Involuntary conversions are also called involuntary exchanges. When property is involuntarily converted, the taxpayer may receive compensation, such as insurance proceeds. A "condemnation award" is the money paid to a taxpayer for condemned property, usually by the government.

The gains and losses that are sustained due to an involuntary conversion are considered outside the taxpayer's control, and therefore, receive special tax treatment. Sometimes, a taxpayer will have a gain on an involuntary conversion. This usually happens when the insurance proceeds exceed the taxpayer's basis of the property.

If the payment *exceeds* the taxpayer's basis of the property, the taxpayer has a gain. A taxpayer may elect to defer all or part of the gain by doing a Section 1033 exchange. The gain is not excluded—merely postponed until the taxpayer sells or disposes of the property at a later date. Any tax on the gain is deferred by *reinvesting* the proceeds in another (similar) property.

In the case of involuntary conversions, business and investment property is treated differently than personal use property. The loss on business or investment property that is subject to a casualty or condemnation is always its adjusted basis at the time of the loss, regardless of the property's fair market value.

If business property is only *partially* destroyed, the loss is the lesser of:
- The property's adjusted basis at the time of the loss OR
- The difference between the property's fair market value immediately before and after the loss occurrence

IRC Section 1033 defers gain only; if a taxpayer has a qualifying *loss* on business property, the loss is recognized. In order to defer the entire gain, the taxpayer must reinvest the entire proceeds in qualifying replacement property.

Example: The federal government is authorized to acquire land for building interstate railroads. The government informed Shannon that it would acquire one acre of her investment property in order to construct a railway line. The government took action to condemn Shannon's property, and she went to court to keep it. But the court decided in favor of the government, which took Shannon's property and paid her $350,000. The proceeds from this action are called a "condemnation award." Shannon's basis in the property was $300,000. This means that she has $50,000 in gain from the condemnation award. Condemnation awards are taxable income. However, Shannon may defer recognizing any income on the condemnation award if she reinvests the award proceeds in similar replacement property. This is considered a Section 1033 exchange.

To postpone reporting the gain from an involuntary conversion, the business must purchase or reinvest the replacement property within a certain period of time. This is the replacement period. The replacement period generally ends two years after the end of the first tax year in which any part of the gain on the condemnation or casualty is realized.

In general, a taxpayer has two years *after* the year that the involuntary conversion occurred to replace the property and make the reinvestment. However, there are special rules for certain types of property. For real estate, the replacement period is generally three years after the close of the year in which the gain is realized. There are also special rules for farmers that allow a longer replacement period (to be covered later).

Example: The Danbury Corporation experienced a flood that destroyed part of its machinery on January 28, 2010. Danbury Corporation's insurance company paid for 100% of the loss. The Danbury Corporation has until December 31, 2012 to replace or repair the machinery using the insurance proceeds it received. This is an involuntary conversion.

If the involuntary conversion property is not replaced within the allowed time period, an amended tax return would have to be filed, claiming the income as taxable.

The taxpayer's basis for the new property is the same as the basis for the converted property. The gain on the involuntary conversion is deferred until a taxable sale or exchange occurs (when the property is sold or disposed of).

Example: Garfield operates a clothing business. During the year, Garfield lost a delivery truck due to an accident. The truck had been partially depreciated, and the adjusted basis on the truck was $10,000. The insurance company sent a check for $55,000 to replace the damaged delivery truck. Two months later, Garfield uses all the insurance money to purchase a replacement truck, plus he pays an additional $2,000 out-of-pocket in order to purchase the new vehicle. The new truck is treated as having a "transferred basis" from the old truck for depreciation purposes. This means that the basis in the new delivery truck is $12,000 ($10,000 basis of the old truck + $2,000 additional out-of-pocket cost). This transaction does not have to be reported because it is a qualified involuntary conversion of business property.

Unit 2.3: Questions

1. In 2010, Bramble Partnership provided legal services to Andrews Corporation. Andrews Corporation then became insolvent. In lieu of payment, Bramble Partnership accepted a set of gold coins with a Fair Market Value of $5,000, and an electric scooter with a Fair Market Value of $2,000 and an adjusted basis of $1,000. What amount of income must Bramble Partnership report for this transaction?

A. $7,000
B. $6,000
C. $8,000
D. $5,000

The answer is A. Bramble Partnership must include the Fair Market Value of the coins ($5,000) and the Fair Market Value of the scooter ($2,000) as income. These would be considered compensation for services and must be included as income for the year. ###

2. Evelyn is a self-employed bookkeeper who performs services for a client, a small corporation. In exchange for her services, the corporation gives Evelyn 500 shares of stock with a Fair Market Value of $2,000. How would the transaction be reported?

A. Evelyn must report the stock as a capital gain.
B. This is not a taxable event. Evelyn would not have to recognize the income until she sold the stock.
C. Evelyn must recognize the stock as interest income.
D. Evelyn must include the Fair Market Value of the shares in her ordinary income.

The answer is D. Bartering is an exchange of property or services. Evelyn must include the Fair Market Value of property or services received in her gross income. Since the Fair Market Value of the stock is $2,000, she must include that amount in her income. ###

3. Which of the following would NOT be considered "income" for tax purposes?

A. Interest earned on a court award
B. Damages received in a suit or settlement for personal physical injuries
C. Barter income from consulting services
D. Legal damages awarded for copyright infringement

The answer is B. There are items of "income" that are excluded from gross income by provisions in the Internal Revenue Code. Gross income does not include certain types of compensation for physical injuries. ###

410

4. In which of the following transactions would taxable business income be recognized?

A. A like-kind exchange of business property
B. Damages awarded for a physical injury in the workplace
C. A $50,000 business loan
D. An accident settlement with punitive damages

The answer is D. Most court awards and settlements are taxable income, except for accident and injury awards. However, punitive damages are taxable. Punitive damages are sometimes awarded *in addition* to compensatory damages. ###

5. Which of the following property qualifies for 1031 like-kind exchange?

A. A personal residence
B. Inventory property
C. Corporation common stock
D. An empty lot held for investment

The answer is D. Real property held for investment qualifies for like-kind exchange treatment. A personal residence, inventory, and common stock do not qualify for Section 1031 treatment. ####

6. Big Time Tool Corporation rents large tools and machinery for use in construction projects. The company always charges a refundable security deposit and a nonrefundable cleaning deposit when someone rents a machine. Big Time Tool Corporation received the following amounts in 2010:

Rental income $50,000
Security deposits $4,050
Cleaning deposits $1,500

What amount should be included in the corporation's gross income?

A. $50,000
B. $51,500
C. $54,050
D. $55,550

The answer is B. The refundable security deposits are not taxable income, because those amounts are returned to the customer. The amounts included in gross income would be the rental income and the nonrefundable cleaning deposits ($50,000 + $1,500 = $51,500). ###

7. Bill owns rental property. On January 10, 2010, Bill's tenants accidentally burn down his rental home. The property had an adjusted basis of $26,000, and insurance pays Bill $31,000 for it. Bill bought replacement property similar in use to the converted property for $29,000 in January 2011. What is Bill's recognized gain in this transaction?

A. $5,000
B. $2,000
C. $7,000
D. $3,000

The answer is B. This transaction is treated as an involuntary conversion. Bill recognized a gain of $2,000 ($31,000 - $29,000), the unspent part of the payment from the insurance. Bill's unrecognized gain is $3,000, the difference between the $5,000 realized gain and the $2,000 recognized gain. The basis of the new property is figured as follows:

Cost of replacement property: $29,000
Minus: gain not recognized: $3,000
Basis of replacement property: $26,000
(Publication 551)###

8. Barbara exchanged an apartment building with an adjusted basis of $125,000 for a business office building. The Fair Market Value of Barbara's property is $500,000. The Fair Market Value of the business office building, the property Barbara receives, has an FMV of $475,000. What is Barbara's basis in the new building?

A. $125,000
B. $475,000
C. $500,000
D. $525,000

The answer is A. The basis of the new property is the same as the basis of the old ($125,000). The FMV of the buildings has no bearing on the basis in a nontaxable exchange situation (Publication 544). ####

9. Scott has a plane that he used in his business for two years. Its adjusted basis is $35,000, and its trade-in value is $45,000. Scott is interested in a new plane that costs $200,000. He trades his old plane for the new one and pays the dealer $155,000. What is Scott's basis for depreciation of the new plane?

A. $35,000
B. $155,000
C. $190,000
D. $200,000

The answer is C. Scott's basis would be $190,000 ($155,000 plus $35,000 adjusted basis of the old plane). Scott must report the exchange of like-kind property, even though no gain or loss is recognized, on Form 8824, *Like-Kind Exchanges* (Publication 544). ###

10. The Bargain Bin Company traded an older delivery truck having an adjusted basis of $11,000 and cash of $6,000 for a new truck with a Fair Market Value of $25,000. How much gain must the Bargain Bin recognize in this exchange, and what is its basis in the new truck?

	Gain	New Basis
A.	$0	$17,000
B.	$0	$25,000
C.	$8,000	$17,000
D.	$6,000	$25,000

The answer is A. The basis is $17,000 ($11,000 + $6,000). This exchange qualifies as a nontaxable exchange. The $6,000 in cash would be added to the basis of the new asset. Any gain is deferred on the exchange until the asset is later sold (or exchanged again). ###

11. Fran and Braden are mother and son. In March 2010, Fran and Braden completed a Section 1031 exchange. On January 2, 2011, Fran dies, and her property is inherited by her husband, who promptly sells it. Which of the following statements is TRUE?

A. Since one of the properties in the exchange has been sold before the two-year time limit for related parties, the Section 1031 exchange is disallowed, and both parties must pay tax on the transaction.
B. The exchange is still valid.
C. Since this was a related party exchange, then the Section 1031 exchange is still valid for Braden, but Fran's estate must pay tax on the exchange, since her husband disposed of the property before the two-year waiting period.
D. The non-recognition treatment is lost for both parties, but Fran's husband is liable for the tax on the exchange, since he was the owner of the property when it was sold.

The answer is B. On a related-party exchange, the non-recognition treatment will be lost if either property in the exchange is disposed of within two years. However, there are exceptions to this rule. The Section 1031 exchange will still be valid if either party in the transaction dies, or if the property is subject to an involuntary conversion, such as due to a fire or other disaster. ###

413

12. Which of the following property exchanges does NOT qualify as a like-kind exchange?

A: Exchange of an apartment building for an office building
B. Exchange of livestock of different sexes
C: Exchange of improved property for unimproved property
D: Exchange of farm machinery for factory machinery

The answer is B. The exchange of livestock of different sexes does not qualify. The exchange of real estate for real estate and the exchange of personal property for similar personal property are exchanges of like-kind property. ###

13. Hannah has a number of assets that she would like to exchange in a Section 1031 exchange. Which of the following trades qualifies as a nontaxable like-kind exchange?

A. The exchange of a vacant lot in the city with farmland in the country
B. The exchange of inventory with inventory of another corporation
C. The exchange of female cattle for male bulls
D. The exchange of real property outside the United States and real property located in the United States

The answer is A. The exchange of a vacant lot for a tract of farmland would qualify for like-kind exchange treatment. Section 1031 does not apply to exchanges of inventory, stocks, bonds, notes, other securities or evidence of indebtedness, or certain other assets. Properties are of like-kind if they are of the same nature or character, even if they differ in grade or quality. Personal properties of a like class are like-kind properties. However, livestock of different sexes are not like-kind properties. Also, property used predominantly in the United States and property used predominantly outside the United States are not like-kind properties. Inventory does not qualify for like-kind treatment. ####

14. Ron wants to transfer a partnership interest for another partnership interest and have the exchange qualify as nontaxable to him. Which circumstances will qualify the transaction?

A. Using the partnership as equity to purchase a different partnership interest.
B. Making sure the basis in both partnerships is the same.
C. No circumstances will qualify the transaction because partnership interests do not qualify for Section 1031 treatment.
D. Giving the partnership interest to the buyer in lieu of a salary.

The answer is C. The exchange of partnership interests does not qualify for Section 1031 treatment. Section 1031 does not apply to exchanges of inventory, stocks, bonds, notes, other securities or evidence of indebtedness, or certain other assets (Publication 17). ###

414

15. Special rules apply to like-kind exchanges between related persons. For the purposes of a Section 1031 exchange, what qualifies as a "related person" according to the IRS?

A: The taxpayer and the taxpayer's spouse
B: The taxpayer and a corporation in which the taxpayer has a 51% ownership
C: A partnership in which the taxpayer owns a 53% interest, and a partnership in which the taxpayer's spouse owns a 52% interest
D: All of the above

The answer is D. The taxpayer and a member of his immediate family are related persons for the purpose of like-kind exchanges. Any business where the taxpayer has beneficial ownership (over 50 percent) is also considered a "related party" for tax purposes. All of the answers are correct. ###

16. Steve is a self-employed carpenter who owns a compressor for use in his business. He trades the compressor (adjusted basis $3,000) for a large table saw (FMV $7,500) and pays an additional $4,000 cash to the seller in a qualified exchange. What is Steve's basis in the saw?

A. $7,000
B. $7,500
C. $4,000
D. $3,000

The answer is A. The basis of the saw is $7,000 (the $3,000 basis of the old asset plus the $4,000 paid). Cash paid is always added to the basis in a Section 1031 exchange. ###

Unit 2.4: Business Expenses and Employee Benefit Programs

More Reading:
Publication 535, *Business Expenses*
Publication 15-B, *Employer's Tax Guide to Fringe Benefits*
Publication 587, *Business Use of Your Home*
Publication 463, *Travel, Entertainment, Gift and Car Expenses*

Business expenses are the costs of carrying on a trade or business. These expenses are usually deductible if the business operates to make a profit. Some expenses must be treated differently than others, and some must be capitalized and depreciated.

Employee Compensation (Wages)

An employer can deduct wages paid to employees. In order to be deductible, the salary must be reasonable and for actual work performed by the employee. Vacation pay is deductible by the employer as employee compensation, even though it is not for actual work performed.

"Supplemental wages" refers to compensation paid *in addition* to an employee's regular wages. It includes, but is not limited to, bonuses, commissions, overtime pay, accumulated sick leave, severance pay, awards, prizes, back pay, retroactive pay increases, and payments for nondeductible moving expenses. Transfers of property to an employee can also be considered compensation, and the Fair Market Value of the property on the date of transfer is deductible by the business and taxable to the employee as wages. A gain or loss is recognized on the transfer of the difference between the FMV and the basis of the property.

Supplemental wages are taxable to the employee just like regular wages and deductible as a wage expense by the employer. Businesses are responsible for federal income tax withholding, Social Security and Medicare taxes, and Federal Unemployment Tax Act (FUTA) taxes.

These taxes are withheld from an employee's paycheck, and the business owner remits them to the IRS. Most businesses are then required to deposit these taxes electronically using the Electronic Federal Tax Payment System (EFTPS), although some very small businesses may still opt to pay employment taxes with their payroll tax returns.[56]

In order for a business to deduct employee compensation as a business expense, the expense must meet all of the following tests:

- The payments must be ordinary and necessary expenses directly related to the trade or business.
- The amounts must be reasonable. Reasonable pay is the amount that would ordinarily be paid by similar businesses in the same industry.

---

[56] There is an exception for very small businesses with less than $2,500 in employment taxes. If a business accumulates a liability for these taxes of less than $2,500 per quarter, the entity may submit payment of taxes due along with their timely filed payroll tax return (Form 941). A business can no longer use federal deposit coupons.

- There must be proof that services were actually performed (unless the compensation qualifies as supplemental wages, such as maternity leave, sick pay, or vacation pay).
- The expenses must have been paid or incurred during the tax year.

Fringe Benefits for Employees

A *fringe benefit* is a form of payment to employees. Fringe benefits are sometimes provided to independent contractors. There are many types of fringe benefits. Gifts of nominal value, such as turkeys, hams, or employee discounts, are not taxable to the employee and still remain deductible to the employer.

Cafeteria Plans

A cafeteria plan provides employees an opportunity to receive certain benefits on a pretax basis. The plan may make benefits available to employees, their spouses, and dependents. It may also include coverage of former employees. Participants in a cafeteria plan must be permitted to choose among at least one taxable benefit (such as cash) and one qualified benefit. A "qualified benefit" is a benefit that is nontaxable. The most common types of cafeteria plan benefits are health benefits, vision benefits, and dependent care benefits.

Generally, a cafeteria plan may not offer a benefit that defers pay. However, a cafeteria plan can include a qualified 401(k) plan as a benefit.

Employee Benefits Include:

- Accident, dental, vision, and medical benefits.
- Adoption assistance.
- Dependent care assistance ($5,000 per year or $2,500 if MFS). The exclusion cannot exceed the earned income of the employee (or the employee's spouse).
- Group term life insurance coverage (up to $50,000 of life insurance coverage may be provided as a nontaxable benefit to an employee; the cost of the insurance premium for coverage exceeding $50,000 would be taxable to the employee as wages).
- Health savings accounts.

Flexible Spending Arrangement

A Flexible Spending Arrangement (FSA) is a form of cafeteria plan benefit funded by salary reduction, which reimburses employees for expenses incurred for qualified benefits. An FSA may be offered for dependent care assistance, adoption assistance, and medical care reimbursements. The benefits are subject to an annual maximum and to an annual "use-or-lose" rule. An FSA cannot provide a cumulative benefit to the employee beyond the plan year (amounts do not carry over to the following year). The employee must substantiate her expenses, and then the distributions to the employee are tax-free. The most common FSA plans are for reimbursement of dependent care costs (daycare) and medical expenses.

Educational Benefits

An employer can offer employees educational assistance ($5,250 may be excluded per year, per employee). The employee may reimburse payments for tuition, fees and similar expenses, books, supplies, and equipment. The payments may be for either undergraduate- or graduate-level courses. The payments do not have to be for work-related courses. Qualified educational assistance cannot include payments for the following items:

- Meals, lodging, or transportation.
- Tools or supplies (other than textbooks).
- Courses involving sports, games, or hobbies UNLESS they:
  - Have a reasonable relationship to the business of the employer, or
  - Are required as part of a degree program.

If an employer pays more than $5,250 for educational benefits for an employee during the year, the excess is taxed as wages.

Employee Awards (Qualified and Non-Qualified Plan Awards)

Many companies give their employees awards for service. Employee awards can be nontaxable to the employee and still deductible by the employer, if certain requirements are met. An award can be given for service or safety achievement. An employee achievement award is one that meets all the following requirements:

- It is given to an employee for length of service or safety achievement.
- It is awarded as part of a meaningful presentation.
- It is not pay disguised as an award.

For a length-of-service award to qualify as nontaxable to the employee and still be deductible to the employer, the recipient of the award must have at least five years of service and not have previously received a length-of-service award in any of the prior four years. Awards of very small value (such as a framed certificate) are not included in this requirement. An employee award for safety achievement will qualify as an achievement award unless one of the following applies:

- It is given to a manager, administrator, clerical employee, or other professional employee.
- During the year, more than 10% of the employees have already received a safety achievement award (other than one of very small value).

An employer's deduction for employee achievement awards given to a single employee is limited to the following:

- $400 for awards that are not qualified plan awards
- $1,600 for all awards, whether or not they are qualified plan awards

A "qualified plan award" is an award that does not discriminate in favor of highly compensated employees. For example, if employee awards are only granted to highly compensated executives and not to regular "rank and file" employees, then the employee award cannot exceed the FMV of $400; otherwise, it will be partially taxable to the employee.

> **Example:** Big Time Bank offers employee awards for length of service. The award is an engraved gold watch valued at $1,200, which is given after five years of service. However, the awards are only granted to highly paid executives. The secretarial and customer service staffs are not eligible for the watch. The award is NOT a qualified plan award, because it discriminates in favor of the highly paid executives. In this case, a portion of the award would be taxable to the employee.

419

The exclusion for employee awards does NOT apply to awards of cash, gift certificates, or other cash equivalents. If an employee is given cash or gift cards, it would be taxable to the employee as wages.

Business Gifts: the $25 Limit

Companies are allowed to spend up to $25 per year *per employee*, tax-free, for a business gift. This does not include cash gifts. Any amount in excess of $25 is disallowed as a business deduction. The $25 limit for business gifts does not include incidental costs — for example, packaging, insurance, and mailing costs, or the cost of engraving jewelry. Any additional costs for postage and wrapping paper, etc. may be deducted separately by the business.

Example: Roggan Corporation gives each of its 75 employees a $25 fruit basket during the holidays. The company may take a tax deduction for the gifts ($1,875 = $25 X 75). The gift is not taxable to the employee, and the Fair Market Value of the gift is not included in the employee's wages.

A business may also deduct business-related gifts to clients and customers. The amount is still limited to $25 given to any person during the year. If a taxpayer and her spouse both give gifts, they are treated as one taxpayer for the purpose of the deduction, even if they both have separate businesses. A gift to the *spouse* of a business customer or client is generally considered an indirect gift to the customer or client.

Example: Hawaii Fruit Corporation gives a large fruit and nut basket to its best customer, Dominic's Produce Company. The fruit basket costs $57, and the shipping and mailing of the basket costs $17. Hawaii Fruit Corporation can deduct $25 for the basket and $17 for the cost of mailing, for a total gift deduction of $42.

Example: Juan is a salesman who sells tools to Hammer's Hardware Store. He gives Hammer's Hardware three fancy candy boxes to thank them for their patronage, one for each owner of the business. Juan pays $80 for each package, or $240 total. The three store owners take the packages home for their use. He can deduct a total of $75 ($25 limit × 3) for the packages. The remainder of the gift expense is disallowed.

Exceptions to the Gift Limit

Some items are considered promotional in nature and not subject to the regular gift limit. The following items are not considered "gifts" for purposes of the $25 limit:

- An item that costs $4 or less and has the business name clearly imprinted on the gift (examples include imprinted pens, desk sets, and plastic bags and cases)
- Signs, display racks, or other promotional materials to be used on the business premises of the recipient

Example: Betty's Beekeeper Company gives 150 imprinted pens to her customers and their employees. The pens cost $4 each and they are imprinted with Betty's business name, address, and phone number. She also gives ten of her best customers a beautiful wood rack to display her honeybee products in their stores. The display racks cost $100 each. None of these items is subject to the $25 gift limitation, since they are all promotional items and follow the IRS guidelines.

Transportation Benefits and Expenses

Employers may provide transportation benefits as a fringe benefit to their employees up to certain amounts without having to include the benefit in the employee's income. Qualified "transportation fringe" benefits include:

- Transit passes
- Qualified parking
- Transportation in a commuter highway vehicle (shuttle), rail, or ferry
- Cash reimbursements under a qualified reimbursement arrangement

The fringe benefit for parking passes in 2010 is $230 per month. The tax-free transit and vanpool benefit limit is also $230 per month.

Businesses may deduct mileage or other travel expenses for employees or owners. For 2010, the standard mileage rate for business use is 50 cents per mile. Deductible mileage expenses include:

- Getting from one client's location to another in the course of regular business
- Visiting clients or customers at their location
- Going to a business meeting away from the regular workplace
- Traveling to a temporary work site

Examples of deductible travel expenses include:

- The cost of getting to a business destination (air, rail, bus, car, etc.)
- Meals and hotels
- Taxi fares
- Baggage charges
- Tolls and bridge fees

Transportation costs can include airplane, train or bus tickets, travel agency costs, rental cars or taxis, etc. The receipts should show the amounts, dates, and destinations.

Actual Costs vs. Standard Mileage Rate

Most businesses may choose to use either the standard mileage rate or actual car expenses in order to figure the deduction for automobile expenses. A business owner is free to choose whichever method gives him a larger deduction. A taxpayer or employee cannot deduct the costs of driving a car or truck between her home and her main office or regular workplace. These costs are personal commuting expenses. The costs of driving to meet with clients or to do other business-related errands are deductible. Actual car expenses include the costs of the following items:

- Depreciation
- Lease payments
- Registration
- Garage rent, licenses, and repairs
- Gas, oil, and tires
- Insurance, parking fees, and tolls

If a business owner uses a vehicle for both business and personal purposes, he must divide (allocate) the expenses between business and personal use. In addition to using the standard mileage rate, a business can deduct any business-related parking fees and tolls. A business may also deduct the amounts reimbursed to employees for car and truck expenses (Publication 334). However, a business is prohibited from using the standard mileage rate if it:

- Uses a car for hire (such as a taxi or a shuttle)
- Operates five or more cars at the same time
- Claims a depreciation deduction using any method other than straight line
- Claims a Section 179 deduction on the car
- Claims the special depreciation allowance on the car
- Claims actual car expenses for a car that was leased

In any of the cases listed above, the business would be required to use actual costs, rather than the standard mileage rate.

Use of a Company Vehicle

The value of a vehicle for personal use by an employee is a taxable benefit. If an employer provides a car for an employee's personal use, the amount that can be excluded as a working condition benefit is the amount that would be allowable as a deductible business expense if the employee paid for its use. There are exceptions for emergency personnel such as police officers, who are required to use their emergency vehicles.

If an employer provides a vehicle to an employee for strictly business use, such as a delivery van that is used during working hours only, the use of the vehicle is nontaxable to the employee.

Travel on Cruise Ships: Special Rules

Business taxpayers can deduct up to $2,000 per year of expenses for attending conventions, seminars, or similar meetings held on cruise ships. All of these requirements must be met: the convention, seminar, or meeting must be directly related to the taxpayer's trade or business; the cruise ship must be a vessel registered in the U.S.; and all of the cruise ship's ports of call must be in the U.S.

Independent Contractors and Information Returns (Forms 1099)

Businesses may deduct payments to independent contractors. Businesses are required to report many of these payments to the IRS on Form 1099, which is used to report income other than wages (for which Social Security Administration Form W-2 is used instead). Businesses must issue Forms 1099 to recipients by January 31.

U.S. tax law requires businesses to submit a Form 1099 for every contractor paid at least $600 for services during a year. The amounts that businesses are required to report on Forms 1099 include:

- Commissions, fees, and other compensation paid to a single individual when the total amount is $600 or more during the year
- Interest, rents, annuities, and income items paid to a single individual when the total amount is $600 or more
- Royalties of at least $10
- Any fishing boat proceeds

422

- Gross proceeds of $600 or more paid to an attorney, whether or not the firm is incorporated
- Any amount paid to an individual who has had any federal income tax withheld under the backup withholding rules

---

Example: Tina is a bookkeeper who also owns a business office. In July, she hires a cleaning service for her office location. The cleaning service refuses to provide a Taxpayer Identification Number, so Tina is required to automatically withhold income tax on her payment to the cleaning service. The owner of the cleaning service gets mad and refuses to clean the office the following month. Tina is required to file a Form 1099-MISC for the cleaning service to report the backup withholding amounts.

If the business doesn't have a payee's SSN or EIN, backup federal income tax withholding would be required at a 28% rate.

Under current law, most payments to corporations are exempt from Form 1099 reporting requirements.[57] Also under current rules, there is no requirement for payments issued in exchange for property (such as purchases of merchandise or equipment).

Three copies of Form 1099 are made: one for the payor, one for the payee, and one for the IRS. Many businesses file thousands of Forms 1099 per year. Payors who file 250 or more Forms 1099 must file them electronically with the IRS.

If paper copies are filed, the IRS requires the payer to submit a copy of Form 1096, *Annual Summary and Transmittal of U.S. Information Returns*. Form 1096 is a summary of all the information forms being sent to the IRS. Businesses must file an additional Form 1096 for each type of information form they issue. For example, if a business filed two copies of a 1099-MISC and ten copies of a 1099-INT, the business would be required to file two Forms 1096, one for each TYPE of Form 1099 that was filed. If a business has employees, it must file quarterly employment tax returns (Form 941) in addition to making federal tax deposits of these taxes.

Some payments are not required to be reported on Form 1099-MISC, although they may be taxable to the recipient. A Form 1099-MISC is NOT required in the following circumstances:
- Payments to a corporation (usually)
- Payments for merchandise, telegrams, telephone, freight, storage, and similar items
- Wages paid to employees (these are reported on Form W-2, *Wage and Tax Statement*)
- Business travel allowances paid to employees (may be reportable on the employee's Form W-2)
- Cost of current life insurance protection (report on Form W-2 or Form 1099-R, *Distributions From Pensions, Annuities, Retirement or Profit-Sharing Plans, IRAs, Insurance Contracts, etc.*)
- Payments to a tax-exempt organization

Forms 1099-MISC should only be used for payments that are made in the course of a trade or business. Personal payments are not reportable.

---

[57] This 1099 reporting requirement currently does not apply to corporations receiving payments, but will change in 2012.

Example #1: Brett hires a painter to paint his home. The job costs $2,500. Brett is not required to report the payment to the painter, because it is for his personal residence. Personal payments are not reportable, and Brett cannot deduct the cost on his tax return.

Example #2: The following year, Brett calls the same painter to paint the interior of his business office, which he owns. The job costs $1,000. Since the cost is a business expense, Brett would be required to issue a 1099-MISC to the contractor. The $1,000 would be fully deductible on his business return as an expense.

Business Rent Expense

Businesses may deduct expenses for renting property. Rented property includes real estate, machinery, and other items that an entity uses to conduct business. The cost of acquiring a lease is not considered rent. It should be amortized.

Partial Business Use of Property

If a taxpayer has both business and personal use of rented property, he may deduct only the amount actually used for business. To compute the business percentage, compare the size of the property used for business to the entire size of the property. Use the resulting percentage to figure the business portion of the rent expense. Two commonly used methods for figuring the percentage are:

- Divide the area (length multiplied by width) used for business by the total area of the property
- If the rooms in the property are all about the same size, divide the number of rooms used for business by the total number of rooms

Example: Jasmine rents a business office to use as a studio for painting, and also to run her tutoring business. Her total rental payments for the year are $11,000. The office is 1,000 square feet; she uses 800 square feet for the tutoring business and the remaining 200 square feet as her painting area. Therefore, she uses the office 80% for her business and 20% for personal purposes. The deductible portion of the rent expense is $8,800 (80% × $11,000).

Home Office Deduction (Business Use of Home)

Taxpayers may be able to deduct certain expenses for the part of their home used for business. To deduct "business use of home" expenses, part of the taxpayer's home must be used regularly and exclusively as either:

- The principal place of business, and/or
- Exclusively as the place to meet with patients, clients, or customers in the normal course of business; or
- In direct connection with the business (if the taxpayer uses a separate structure that is not attached to the home).

Because of the "exclusive use" rule, taxpayers are not allowed to deduct business expenses for any part of their home that is used for both personal and business purposes. Self-employed people must fill out a special form to claim the home office deduction. Schedule C businesses must complete **Form 8829**, *Expenses for Business Use of Your Home*, and then transfer the total to their Schedule C when they file their income tax return (Form 1040).

424

Charitable Contributions by Businesses

Only individual taxpayers and C Corporations may deduct contributions to a qualified charitable organization. There are different rules for each entity. Self-employed taxpayers may not deduct charitable contributions as a business expense on their Schedule C or Schedule F. They are allowed to deduct the charitable contribution on their Schedule A as an itemized deduction. However, special rules apply to charitable contributions made by corporations. C corporations are permitted to deduct charitable deductions under IRC Section 170. However, the deduction is limited to 10% of taxable income. The rules for charitable contributions of corporations will be covered later, in the dedicated unit for corporations.

Business Travel, Meals, and Entertainment

To be deductible for tax purposes, business expenses deducted for travel, meals, and entertainment must be incurred while carrying on a genuine business activity. Generally, the business must be able to prove that entertainment expenses (including meals) are directly related to the conduct of business.

The 50% Limit for Meals and Entertainment

Only 50% of the cost of meals and entertainment is deductible as a business expense. Travel costs and transportation costs are 100% deductible. The 50% limit applies to business meals or entertainment incurred while:

- Traveling away from home (whether eating alone or with others) on business
- Entertaining customers at a restaurant or other location
- Attending a business convention or reception, business meeting, or business luncheon

Related expenses that are also subject to the 50% limit include:

- Taxes and tips on a business meal or entertainment activity
- Cover charges for admission to a nightclub
- Cost of a room in which the business holds a dinner or cocktail party

The 50% limit applies to meal and entertainment expenses incurred for the production of income, including rental or royalty income. It also applies to the cost of meals incurred while obtaining deductible educational expenses (such as meals during a continuing education seminar). The cost of transportation to a business meal or a business-related entertainment activity is NOT subject to the 50% limit.

Example: Karen is a business owner who takes her best client to lunch. The total restaurant bill is $88. Karen also pays cab fare of $10 to get to the restaurant. Her deductible expense for this event is $54, figured as follows:

Deductible meal expense	$88 X 50% =$44
Deductible travel expense	$10
Total deductible expense	**$54**

Meals NOT Subject to the 50% Limit

There are some examples where meals are not subject to the 50% limit. There are also certain employees and businesses that may take a larger percentage deduction on their meals and entertainment. The following meals are NOT subject to the 50% limit:

- Meals that are included in employees' wages as taxable compensation
- Meals that qualify as a *de minimis* fringe benefit, such as occasional coffee and doughnuts
- Meals furnished to employees when the employer operates a restaurant or catering service
- Meals furnished to employees as part of a teambuilding activity, such as a company picnic
- Meals that are required by federal law to be furnished to crew members of certain commercial vessels
- Meals furnished on an oil or gas platform or drilling rig located offshore or in Alaska

These meals would be 100% deductible by the employer.

There is also an exception for businesses subject to the U.S. Department of Transportation (DOT) "hours of service" limits. An individual or qualifying business can deduct 80% of meal expenses while traveling away from his tax home (as opposed to the general 50% limit) if the meals are subject to the DOT rules. This most often applies to interstate truckers, but can also apply to other professions. The following individuals are included in this exception:

- Interstate truck operators and bus drivers who are under DOT regulations
- Air transportation workers (such as pilots, crew, dispatchers, mechanics, and control tower operators) who are under Federal Aviation Administration regulations
- Railroad employees (such as engineers, conductors, train crews, dispatchers, and control operations personnel) who are under Federal Railroad Administration regulations
- Merchant marines who are under Coast Guard regulations

Businesses are also allowed to deduct employee's meals at the 80% rate when DOT hours of service regulations apply.

Meals and Lodging Provided to Employees

The Fair Market Value of meals or lodging an employer furnishes to an employee is nontaxable to the employee in certain circumstances. Under IRC §119, meals provided by an employer are not taxable to the employee if they are provided:

- On the employer's business premises, and
- For the employer's convenience.

Lodging is excludable from wages of the employee if it is provided:

- On the employer's business premises, and
- For the employer's convenience, and
- Required as a condition of employment.

Meals for the Convenience of the Employer

Meals are provided for the "convenience of the employer" if there's a substantial "non-compensatory" reason; that is, the intent is not to provide additional pay for the employee. Meals provided to employees for the "convenience of the employer" are 100% deductible by the employer, but are not taxable to the employees. To be considered "for the convenience of the employer," they must be taken on the business premises. The following situations illustrate meals furnished for the convenience of the employer:

- Workers need to be on call for emergencies during the lunch period (examples: paramedics, firefighters, doctors, police, and other emergency personnel)
- The nature of the business requires short lunch periods
- Eating facilities are not available in the area of work
- Meals are furnished to restaurant employees, before, during, or after work hours
- Meals are furnished to all employees on a regular basis, so long as meals are furnished to substantially all the employees for the convenience of the employer
- Meals are furnished immediately after working hours because the employee's duties prevented him or her from obtaining a meal during working hours

Example: Paramedic Transport, Inc. regularly provides meals to employees during working hours so that paramedics are available for emergency calls during the meal. The meals are therefore excludable from the employee's wages and still deductible by the employer.

Example: An employer has pizza delivered to the office at a group meeting because the business requires the meeting be kept short, and there are no alternative restaurants in the immediate area.

Infrequent (not routine) meals of minimal value may be excludable as a de minimis fringe benefit, regardless of the tests above. Cash provided for meals is generally not excludable under this Code section; however, under some limited situations it can be excluded as a de minimis fringe benefit.

Example: A computer manufacturer has an equipment breakdown in the evening. The engineers are required to work lengthy overtime to make repairs. After working ten hours, the engineers break for dinner because they know that they will continue to work late until the equipment is repaired. The supervisor gives each employee $10 for a quick meal. The meal is not taxable to the engineers because it was provided to permit them to work overtime in an *unusual situation*. The meal expense is deductible by the employer as a business expense as a de minimis fringe benefit.

Meal money calculated on the basis of number of hours worked (for example, $5 per hour for each hour worked over eight hours) is never excludable as a de minimis fringe benefit.

Example: A clothing retailer has a policy of reimbursing employees for breakfast or dinner when they are required to work an extra hour before or after their normal work schedule. The reimbursements are taxable to the employees as wages. This is because the employer has a regular policy that indicates payments are routinely made. In addition, the meal reimbursement does not enable the employee to work overtime, but is an *incentive* to do so.

The following do not qualify as *de minimis* fringe benefits:
- Cash (except for occasional, unusual, and *infrequent* meal money to allow overtime work or in unusual or emergency situations)
- Cash equivalent (i.e., savings bond, gift certificate for general merchandise at a department store)
- Certain transportation passes or costs
- Use of employer's apartment, vacation home, or boat
- Membership in a country club or athletic facility

Some of these benefits may be excludable under other provisions of the law.[58]

The Per Diem Rate for Meals and Travel

To ease recordkeeping requirements, a business may use the "per diem" rate as an alternative to the actual cost method. This is also called the "standard meal allowance" or just "standard allowance." The standard meal allowance is also called the "federal M&IE rate."

It allows a business to use a standard amount for daily meals and incidental expenses (M&E), instead of keeping receipts or other records of actual costs. The *per diem* rate makes recordkeeping easier for employers.

The per diem rate is the daily rate that employees or business owners use for expenses incurred while traveling for business. The rates differ based on domestic and foreign travel, and also vary by location. For example, the per diem rate in large cities like Los Angeles and New York is higher than for small cities. The per diem rates are published every year by the IRS in **Publication 1542**, *Per Diem Rates.*[59]

This standard allowance is a set amount that the IRS allows businesses to use in order to expense lodging, meals, and entertainment in connection with their business activities. If a taxpayer chooses to use the standard meal allowance, he still needs to prove the time, place, and business purpose of the travel and the meals. In order to be deductible, the IRS states that the travel expenses must be "ordinary and necessary" expenses incurred for business.

In order to deduct lodging expenses (hotel charges, etc.), the taxpayer must keep a record of the travel location, duration of the hotel stay, costs, and other expenses incurred. Additional records for laundry service, hotel Internet fees, telephone service, tips, and other charges should be shown separately. If the taxpayer is using the per diem rate for lodging, these extra charges are deductible in addition to the standard rate.

Taxpayers must keep a log of meal expenses and save receipts for amounts of $75 or more. If she does not want to keep track of the actual costs of meals, the taxpayer may instead use the standard meal allowance. However, if a business incurs a large meal expense (for example, an expensive meal with ten salespeople), it would be more beneficial for the business to use actual costs and keep receipts, rather than use the standard meal allowance.

Entertainment Expenses: Business-Related

A business is allowed to deduct business-related entertainment expenses that are incurred for entertaining a client, customer, or employee. However, the expense must be both "ordinary and necessary" and meet at least one of the following tests:

- Directly-related test
- Associated test

---

[58] Reference: *IRS Taxable Fringe Benefits Guide*

[59] If you are curious, you can also visit www.gsa.gov/perdiem for the U.S. General Services Administration, which updates the per diem rates every year. For locations outside the United States, go to www.state.gov/travel and select the option for "Foreign Per Diem Rates." You do not need to memorize any per diem rates for the EA Exam, but you do need to understand what "per diem" means and how it applies to business expenses.

An *ordinary* expense is one that is common and accepted in the taxpayer's trade or business. A *necessary* expense is one that is both helpful and appropriate for the business. An expense does not have to be required in order to be deductible.

If a business owner takes a client to a special event, the business may not deduct more than the face value of the ticket, regardless of the amount paid. Then the taxpayer must apply the 50% limitation for entertainment expenses.

Example: Erik wants to take his best two best clients to a basketball game, but the tickets are sold out. So Erik pays a private seller $390 for three tickets. The actual face value of each ticket is $52. Erik may only use the face value of the ticket as a basis for his deduction, and then he must further apply the 50% limit. Therefore, his deductible entertainment expense is $78, figured as follows:

Cost of three event tickets (face value only $52 X 3): $156
Then, apply the 50% limit ($156 X 50%): $78

Travel Expenses

If the travel includes some amount of personal travel, the taxpayer must keep records showing how much is related to business and then figure the amount of personal travel because that portion is not deductible as a business expense.

Businesses must determine the non-business portion of the expense by multiplying it by a fraction. The numerator of the fraction is the number of non-business days during the travel and the denominator is the total number of days spent traveling.

Lodging on an Employer's Premises

Some organizations provide lodging to their employees. The value of the lodging is not taxable to the employee if certain requirements are met. The lodging is instead treated like fringe benefits for employees. The value of lodging on an employer's premises can be excluded from an employee's income, if it is furnished for the employer's convenience and as a condition of employment.

Lodging can even be provided for the taxpayer, the spouse, and the taxpayer's dependents, and still not be taxable.

Example: Henry is a project supervisor for Franklin Construction. He is provided free hotel lodging at remote job sites, where he is required to stay for many months while timber is cleared and the grounds are prepared for construction projects. The value of the lodging is excluded from income, because it is for his employer's convenience. The cost of the hotel would be deductible by Franklin Construction as a business expense.

Accountable Plans

An "accountable plan" is a plan where an employer reimburses employees for business-related expenses such as mileage, meals, and travel expenses. The reimbursed amounts are deductible to the employer and not taxable to the employee.

For expenses to qualify under an accountable plan, the employee must follow guidelines in order to have the expenses reimbursed. An accountable plan requires employees to meet ALL of the following requirements:

- Have incurred the expenses while performing services as employees
- Adequately account for the expenses within a reasonable period of time
- Adequately account for their travel, meals, and entertainment expenses
- Provide documentary evidence of their travel, mileage, and other employee business expenses
- Return any excess reimbursement or allowance within a reasonable period of time if paid in advance

> **Example:** Dana is a saleswoman for Sunshine Cosmetics. She takes two potential clients out to dinner and pays for the meal. She also keeps track of her business mileage on a spreadsheet. The following week, she submits her receipts and the spreadsheet to Sunshine Cosmetics for reimbursement. Dana's employer reimburses her for the out-of-pocket expenses she incurred. This arrangement is an accountable plan. The reimbursement is not taxable to Dana.

Under an accountable plan, a business owner may *advance* money to his employees in anticipation of an expense; however, certain conditions must be met. The cash advance must be reasonably calculated to equal the anticipated expense. The business owner must make the advance within a reasonable period of time. If any expenses reimbursed under this arrangement are not substantiated, a business is not allowed to deduct those expenses under an accountable plan. Instead, the reimbursed expenses are treated as paid under a non-accountable plan and become taxable to the employee as wages.

Interest Expense

Entities can deduct interest paid or accrued during the tax year on debts related to the business. If the interest relates to a business expense or purchase, it is deductible. It does not matter what type of property secures the loan. A business must deduct interest as follows:

- Cash method: Under the cash method, a business can deduct only the actual interest paid during the tax year. A cash-method taxpayer cannot deduct a promissory note because it is a promise to pay and not an actual payment.
- Accrual method: Under the accrual method, a business can deduct only interest that has accrued during the tax year.

A taxpayer cannot receive a tax deduction by paying interest early. Interest paid in advance can only be deducted in the tax year in which it is DUE. If a business uses the accrual method, it cannot deduct interest owed to a related person who uses the cash method until payment is made and the interest is includible in the gross income of that person.

Insurance Expenses

A business can deduct premiums paid for business-related insurance. A business may also deduct health insurance premiums for its employees. The following types of insurance premiums are deductible as business expenses:

- Insurance that covers fire, storm, theft, accident, or similar losses
- Credit insurance that covers losses from business bad debts
- Group hospitalization and medical insurance for employees, including long-term care insurance

- Accident and health insurance premiums for an S Corporation's more-than-2% share-holder-employees, but the corporation must also include them in the shareholder's wages subject to federal income tax withholding
- Liability insurance or malpractice insurance
- Workers' compensation insurance
- Contributions to a state unemployment insurance fund
- Car insurance that covers vehicles used in a business

Employers may deduct the premiums on life insurance policies provided to their employees as a fringe benefit. The amount that the employer can provide tax-free to the employee is $50,000. The cost of premium coverage in excess of $50,000 is taxable to the employee. The business may deduct the premium just the way it would deduct the cost for any other employee benefit program.

If a business pays an insurance premium for years in advance, it can only deduct the portion that applies to the current tax year, regardless of whether it prepaid the entire amount. The 12-month rule applies.[60]

Health coverage for an employee's children under 27 years of age is now tax-free to the employee. The child does not have to be a dependent in order to qualify for this expanded benefit.[61]

These changes immediately allow employers with cafeteria plans to permit employees to begin making pre-tax contributions to pay for this expanded benefit. This also applies to self-employed individuals who qualify for the self-employed health insurance deduction on their federal income tax return.

Example: Gooey Chocolates Corporation is a cash-method business on a calendar year. On October 1, 2009, Gooey Chocolates pays $3,600 in advance for business insurance policy covering three years. The policy coverage begins October 1, 2009. Coverage ends September 30, 2012. Since the advance payment covers more than 12 months (36 months), then a portion of the $3,600 must be deducted ratably over the three-year period. The cost of the insurance policy must be amortized as follows:

Divide the policy cost by the coverage period to find the monthly premium amount:

($3,600 ÷ 36 = $100)

Multiply the months of coverage in each tax year by the monthly premium:

2009: deduction $300 ($3,600 ÷ 36 x 3).

2010: deduction $1,200: ($3,600 ÷ 36 x 12).

2011: deduction $1,200 ($3,600 ÷ 36 x 12).

2012: deduction $900 ($3,600 ÷ 36 x 9).

---

[60] The 12-month rule still applies. In some cases, businesses may still deduct expenses that are paid in advance. Under the 12-month rule, the business is not required to capitalize amounts paid that do not extend beyond the earlier of the following: (1) 12 months after the benefit begins, or (2) The end of the tax year after the tax year in which payment is made.

[61] The Affordable Care Act was enacted on March 23, 2010.

Example: Rick's Racing Bikes is a cash-method business on a calendar year. On May 1, 2010, Rick's Racing pays $2,000 for business insurance covering one year. The insurance policy begins May 1, 2010 and ends May 30, 2010. The 12-month rule applies. Rick's Racing may deduct the full $2,000 in 2010. The benefit does not extend beyond 12 months after the right to receive the benefit begins.

Taxes (Expense)

Generally, businesses can only deduct the taxes in the year for which they are paid and become due. This rule applies no matter what method of accounting the business uses. Even if a business uses an accrual method, the business generally cannot accrue real estate taxes until it pays them.

Not Deductible: Taxes for Local Improvements

Businesses cannot deduct taxes charged for local benefits and improvements that tend to increase the value of property. These include assessments for streets, sidewalks, water mains, sewer lines, and public parking facilities. A business must increase the basis of its property by the amount of the assessment. A business may deduct taxes for local benefits if the taxes are for maintenance, repairs, or interest charges related to those benefits. Examples such as water bills, sewerage, and other service charges are deductible as regular business expenses.

Example: Lawrence owns a business office on Main Street. In 2010, the city charges an assessment of $4,000 to each business on Main Street to improve the sidewalks. Lawrence cannot deduct this assessment as a current business expense. Instead, he must increase the basis of his property by the amount of the assessment.

Example: Waterfront City converts a downtown area into an enclosed pedestrian mall built to improve local businesses. The city assesses the full cost of construction, financed with 10-year bonds, against the affected properties. The city is paying the principal and interest with the annual payments made by the property owners. The assessments for construction costs are not deductible as taxes or as business expenses, but are depreciable capital expenses. The part of the payment used to pay the interest charges on the bonds is deductible as taxes.

Real Estate Taxes

In order for real estate taxes to be deductible, the taxing authority must calculate the property taxes on the assessed value of the real estate. If the property is sold, the deductible portion of the real estate taxes must be allocated between the buyer and the seller according to the number of days in the property tax year that each owned the property. The seller is treated as paying the taxes up to but not including the date of sale. The buyer is treated as paying the taxes beginning with the date of sale.

Taxes: Special Rules

A business cannot deduct federal income taxes. An entity may deduct state and local income taxes imposed as business expenses. A self-employed individual who reports income on Schedule C may deduct state and local income taxes only as an itemized deduction on Schedule A (Form 1040).

> **Example:** Reiner Corp. is a calendar-year C Corporation incorporated in Iowa. Iowa imposes a 10% state tax on Reiner's corporate earnings. In 2010, Reiner Corp. paid $12,000 in state income tax to Iowa. This state tax would be deductible as a business expense on the corporation's federal tax return (Form 1120).

Interest charged on unpaid income tax assessed on individual income tax returns is not a business deduction, even when the tax due is related to income from a trade or business. This interest should be treated as a business deduction only in figuring a Net Operating Loss deduction. Penalties on underpaid deficiencies and underpaid estimated tax are not deductible as interest.

Foreign Taxes

Generally, a business can take *either* a deduction or a credit for income taxes imposed by a foreign country. However, an individual cannot take a deduction or credit for foreign income taxes paid on income that is already exempt from U.S. tax under the foreign earned income exclusion or the foreign housing exclusion.

Employment Taxes (Social Security, Medicare, and FUTA)

Businesses must withhold various taxes from employee pay. Employers must withhold their employees' share of Social Security and Medicare taxes along with state and federal income taxes.

A business also needs to pay other employment taxes. These include the employer's share of Social Security and Medicare taxes, along with unemployment taxes. Businesses can deduct the employment taxes (payroll taxes) they must pay from their own funds as taxes. Employers may also be forced to pay state unemployment taxes or taxes to support a state disability fund. The business may deduct these payments as taxes.

> **Example:** A partnership pays its secretary $18,000 a year. However, after withholding various taxes, the employee receives $14,500. The business pays an additional $1,500 in employment taxes. The full $18,000 should be deducted as wages. The business can also deduct the $1,500 (employer's portion of the FICA) paid as taxes.

The Hire Act

Under the Hiring Incentives to Restore Employment Act (the Hire Act), enacted March 18, 2010, Congress has offered businesses an incentive to hire and retain unemployed workers.

The first incentive is a payroll tax exemption. This provides employers with an exemption from the *employer's share* (6.2 %) of social security tax on wages paid to qualifying employees, effective for wages paid from March 19, 2010 through December 31, 2010.

In addition, for each qualified employee retained for at least 52 consecutive weeks, businesses will also be eligible for a general business tax credit, referred to as the New Hire

Retention Credit,[62] of 6.2% of wages paid to the qualified employee over the 52 week period, up to a maximum credit of $1,000. The $1,000 maximum is *per worker*.

Taxable businesses and tax-exempt organizations qualify for the payroll tax exemption. The payroll tax exemption is claimed on Form 941, Employer's QUARTERLY Federal Tax Return, beginning with the second quarter of 2010.

Self-Employment Tax

Self-employed individuals can deduct one-half of their self-employment tax as a business expense in figuring Adjusted Gross Income. This deduction only affects income tax. It does not affect net earnings from self-employment or self-employment tax.

Section 199: The Domestic Production Activities Deduction (DPAD)

Companies can take a deduction known as the "Manufacturer's Deduction" for certain U.S.-based business activities. Congress passed the Domestic Production Activities Deduction in order to stimulate domestic manufacturing and farming. The deduction applies to activities related to installing, developing, improving or creating goods that are "manufactured, produced, or grown within the United States." This deduction also applies to the construction of real property in the United States and any qualified domestic film production (except for pornographic films.)

The DPAD is reported on IRS Form 8903, *Domestic Production Activities Deduction*. In 2010, the DPAD is equal to 9% of the lesser of:

- The business's qualified production activities income, or
- Taxable income determined without regard to the DPAD.

The deduction is limited to 50% of wages paid on Form W-2 by the company for the year. Therefore, if a company does not have any employees, it is not eligible for this deduction. This provision is to encourage domestic employment and to discourage outsourcing.

Eligible Activities for the DPAD

Only certain activities qualify for the DPAD. The activities must take place in the United States (Puerto Rico and U.S. territories also qualify). The following activities are "qualified production activities" eligible for claiming the DPAD:

- Manufacturing goods in the United States
- Selling, leasing, or licensing items that have been manufactured in the United States
- Selling, leasing, or licensing motion pictures that have been produced in the United States (not pornography)
- Construction of real property in the United States
- Engineering and architectural services relating to a U.S.-based construction project
- Software development in the United States
- The **production** of water, natural gas, and electricity in the United States (simply transmitting or distributing these goods does not qualify)
- The growth and processing of agricultural products and timber

---

[62] The credit is also reviewed in Unit 5, Business Credits

The deduction is available to individuals, trusts and estates, C Corporations, partnerships and other pass-through entities such as S Corporations and LLCs.

Not Qualified DPAD Activities

The following types of business are specifically excluded from claiming the DPAD:

- Construction services that are cosmetic in nature, such as drywall and painting
- Leasing or licensing items to a related party
- Selling food or beverages prepared at restaurants or dining establishments
- The transmission or distribution of electricity, natural gas, or water
- Any advertising, product placement, customer service businesses, and other tele-communications services

Business Bad Debts

There are two kinds of bad debts—business and non-business. Both are treated very differently under tax law. A non-business (personal) bad debt is only deductible a short-term capital loss on Schedule D (Form 1040). However, businesses may deduct a bad debt as a business expense, dollar-for-dollar, if certain requirements are met.

A business deducts its bad debts from gross income when figuring its taxable income. A business does not have to wait until a debt is due to determine whether it is worthless.

A debt becomes worthless when there is no longer any chance the amount owed will be paid. The business must take reasonable steps to collect the debt. Bankruptcy of a debtor is good evidence of the worthlessness.

If a business loans money to a client, supplier, employee, or distributor for a business reason and the loan later becomes worthless, the business may deduct the loan as a bad debt. The loan must have a *genuine business purpose* in order for this treatment to qualify.

> **Example:** Carol owns an eyeglass manufacturing company. One of her salesmen, Ivan, loses all his samples and asks Carol for a loan to replace them. Carol loans Ivan $3,000 to replace his samples and sample bags. Ivan later quits his job without repaying the debt. Carol has a business-related bad debt that she may deduct as a business expense.

Sometimes, an entity will recover an old debt that was previously written off as worthless. If a business recovers a bad debt later on, which was deducted in a prior year, the entity does not need to amend prior year tax returns. The taxpayer must include only the recovered portion as income in the current year tax return (Publication 535).

Casualties and Thefts of Business Property

A casualty is the damage, destruction, or loss of property resulting from an identifiable event that is sudden, unexpected, or unusual. Business casualty losses are reported on IRS Form 4684, *Casualties and Thefts*.

Business property and income-producing property are NOT subject to the $100 and 10% of AGI rules regulating casualty losses for personal use property. Business property that is subject to a casualty loss may be deducted without these limits (the $100 and 10% limit that applies to individuals and personal-use property).

Example: Tad has a fire at his home that destroys his couch and loveseat, which is personal-use property. The loss for his personal furniture is $5,000. This loss must be reduced by $100 and 10% of AGI before he can deduct the casualty loss. The same fire also damages a business asset, an expensive laptop that Tad had brought home that day in order to catch up on his work. The computer is completely destroyed and results in a business casualty loss of $3,000. This loss is not limited and is fully deductible.

If an entity has business or income-producing property such as rental property that is stolen or destroyed, the loss is figured as follows:

> **The taxpayer's adjusted basis in the property**
> **MINUS**
> **Any salvage value**
> **MINUS**
> **Any insurance or other reimbursement received**

Casualty Loss from Thefts

Many businesses are the victim of theft. Thefts can be perpetrated by an employee (embezzlement), by a customer, or by a stranger. In order to be deductible, the theft must be an illegal act. Fraud or misrepresentation also qualifies for a casualty loss. Theft includes the taking of money or property by the following means: blackmail, burglary, embezzlement, extortion, kidnapping for ransom, larceny, and robbery.

Example: Jeff owns a shop that sells sports memorabilia. Several years ago, Jeff purchased some signed football jerseys for display for $150, which is his adjusted basis in the property. Jeff's jerseys were stolen in 2010. The FMV of the jerseys was $1,000 just before they were stolen, and insurance did not cover them. Jeff's deductible theft loss is $150, which is his basis in the items.

Nondeductible Casualty Losses

A casualty loss is not deductible if the damage or destruction is caused by the following:

- Accidentally breaking articles such as glassware or china under normal conditions
- A family pet
- Arson by the taxpayer or someone paid by the taxpayer
- A car accident if the taxpayer's willful negligence caused it
- Loss of property due to progressive deterioration

Decline in Market Value of Stock Due to Accounting Fraud

A business or individual generally cannot deduct the normal decline in market value of stock acquired on the open market if the decline is caused by disclosure of accounting fraud or other illegal misconduct by the officers or directors of the corporation that issued the stock. However, the taxpayer can deduct as a capital loss the loss sustained when the taxpayer sells the stock or the stock becomes completely worthless. An individual taxpayer reports capital losses on Schedule D (Form 1040). There is also a special exception for stock and investment losses due to Ponzi schemes.

Ponzi Scheme Losses

A Ponzi scheme is when a business issues false financial statements in order to defraud investors. The classic example of a Ponzi scheme is where money collected from later "investors" is used to cover "income distributions" and "withdrawals" paid to earlier "investors" without any investments ever actually being made. Because there is no actual investment, the taxpayer who is a victim of a Ponzi scheme is actually the victim of theft, rather than a bad investment choice.

An investor loss from a Ponzi scheme may be treated as an ordinary theft loss, rather than a capital loss. This means that the loss will not be limited by the passive activity rules that other stock losses are subject to. The IRS will usually announce which Ponzi scheme losses are eligible for this special loss treatment. This rule applies to individuals as well as businesses that own stock that is deemed to be a "Ponzi Scheme."

Insurance and Other Reimbursements

If a business has property that is covered by insurance, it must file an insurance claim for reimbursement of the loss. Otherwise, the business cannot deduct this loss as a casualty or theft. The portion of the loss usually not covered by insurance (for example, a deductible) is not subject to this rule.

> **Example:** Howard and Bob are partners in Happy Flowers, a partnership. Howard uses a delivery van 100% in his business, and he has an accident causing $2,350 in damage to the van. Howard and Bob decide to pay the repair bill out-of-pocket so their business insurance costs won't go up. The auto insurance policy has a $500 deductible. Because the insurance would not cover the first $500 of an auto collision, only the $500 would be deductible. This is true even when Happy Flowers doesn't file an insurance claim, because the policy would never have reimbursed the deductible. Happy Flower's casualty loss deduction is limited to $500.

Net Operating Losses (NOL)

A Net Operating Loss (NOL) is when a business has tax deductions that exceed its income, resulting in a negative taxable income. This happens when a business has more expenses than revenues during a given tax year. By applying a Net Operating Loss to preceding tax years, a business can receive a refund of previously paid taxes. The NOL can also be used to reduce future tax payments. A business may choose whether or not to "carryback" or "carryforward" an NOL.

The NOL rules for individuals are the same as those for non-corporate taxpayers like sole proprietorships (also includes self-employed farmers). C Corporations have slightly different NOL rules (these will be covered in greater depth in the dedicated chapter for C Corporations). Estates and Trusts may also experience a Net Operating Loss.

Partnerships, Limited Liability Companies, and S Corporations don't really experience Net Operating Losses at the entity level. This is because these entities actually claim business losses which are subject to the passive activity rules, and then these losses are passed through to the individual partners (or shareholders, in the case of S Corporations).

The default election is to carry a Net Operating Loss back two years. This is called the carryback period. Then, the business would *carryforward* any remaining NOL for up to 20 years (the carryforward period). A business may also *elect* not to carryback an NOL and only carry it forward.

A valid election must be made in order to *forgo* the carryback period, and only carry an NOL forward. If a taxpayer fails to file a return on time and does not make the proper election, he is forced to carryback the NOL. A late election is not valid in this case. A business may not deduct any part of the NOL remaining after the 20-year carryforward period.

In order for an individual (or sole-proprietorship) to have a Net Operating Loss, the loss must be caused by the following expenses:

- Deductions from a trade or business that result in an overall loss
- Deductions from work as an employee (Form 2106)
- Casualty or theft losses (personal or business)
- Losses from rental property
- Moving expenses
- Losses from a farming business (special carryback rules apply to farmers, covered later[63])

An individual taxpayer may have a Net Operating Loss if his Adjusted Gross Income minus the standard deduction (or itemized deductions) is a negative number; this is most commonly caused by losses from a Schedule C business.[64]

Corporations, estates, and trusts may also have Net Operating Losses due to business losses or casualty losses. These entities will be covered later.

Longer Carryback Periods

In general, entities and individuals may carryback an NOL for two years, and carryforward the remainder for 20 years until the loss is all used up. There are certain instances where a business (or individual) will qualify for a longer NOL carryback period. The following are exceptions to the two year carryback rule:

- If the NOL is due to a farming loss, qualified farmers are eligible for a five-year carryback period.
- Federally declared disaster area losses have a three-year carryback period.
- Product liability losses have a ten-year carryback period. An example of this would be a business that sells an item that is later subject to a recall and lawsuits—the business is allowed to carryback the losses resulting from the product liability 10 years.

Reporting Net Operating Losses

In order to claim a refund from an NOL, an individual taxpayer may choose to amend a prior-year tax return, or the taxpayer may use IRS Form 1045. If the taxpayer chooses to

---

[63] The special carryback rules that apply to farmers will be covered more in a later unit dedicated to farming businesses.

[64] A taxpayer does not have to be a business in order to have a Net Operating Loss. It is also possible for an individual to have a casualty loss or other qualifying expenses (such as very high moving expenses) that will still result in a Net Operating Loss. (For more information, see Publication 536, *Net Operating Losses for Individuals, Estates, and Trusts*.). For Part 2 of the EA exam, you will only need to know about NOLs as they affect business taxpayers (but that still includes self-employed individuals who have an NOL on their Schedule C from business expenses).

amend a prior-year, use IRS Form 1040X. If the taxpayer is self-employed, then the Net Operating Loss does not change the amount of self-employment tax to any of the years to which it is carried forward or back.

An NOL carryback will only reduce tax. In the case of individual taxpayers, for a Net Operating Loss carryforward, the NOL carryforward is reported as a negative amount on the "other income" line of IRS Form 1040.

If a business or individual owes interest and penalties in a prior year, the NOL carryback will not abate them.

A C Corporation with a Net Operating Loss can file for a refund using Form 1139, or by amending their corporate tax return by using Form 1120X.

Example: The Towumme Corporation has been in business since 2009. In 2009, the company had net income of $30,000. However, in 2010, business slowed, and the Towumme Corporation had a Net Operating Loss of $50,000. The company decides to carryback its Net Operating Loss to 2009 in order to recover all the income taxes it paid in the prior year. In 2009, the Towumme Corporation also had a $1,200 estimated tax penalty for failing to remit estimated taxes on time. The corporation cannot recover the amount paid for the estimated tax penalty. An NOL carryback will not abate interest and penalties from a prior year.

There are rules that limit what items a business may deduct when figuring an NOL. The following items are not allowed when figuring an NOL:

- Any deduction for personal exemptions
- Capital losses in excess of capital gains
- The exclusion of gain from the sale of qualified small business stock
- Non-business deductions in excess of non-business income (hobby losses)
- Net Operating Loss deduction
- The Domestic Production Activities Deduction (DPAD)

Capital Expenses

Capital expenses are not really "expenses." They are costs that are not currently deductible, but are instead allocated to a capital asset account. Capital costs are actually part of a taxpayer's basis in the business. This means that capital expenses are treated like assets. The main costs that must be capitalized[65] are:

- The expenses of going into business (also called startup costs),
- The cost of business assets, and
- The cost of business improvements. An "improvement" is a cost that adds value to an asset, lengthens the useful life, or adapts the asset to a different use (example: a new roof, an addition of a bathroom to a rental, a new concrete floor in a factory, etc.)

---

[65] A "capitalized expense" is when a business classifies a cost as a long-term investment, rather than expensing it as a current expense. Certain costs and purchases must be capitalized according to current tax law. The most common capitalized costs are asset purchases (equipment and other assets). These cannot be deducted currently but instead must be depreciated over time.

Business Startup Costs

In 2010, Congress increased the amount allowed as a deduction for startup expenditures. Businesses may deduct up to $10,000 in startup expenses. If the startup expenses exceed $60,000, there is a dollar for dollar reduction until the deduction is eliminated.

> **Example:** Bronco Corporation has startup expenses of $61,000 in 2011. Bronco is $1,000 over the $60,000 threshold so it must reduce its deduction for start-up expenses by the amount that it is over the threshold. Bronco can deduct $9,000 of its start-up expenses: $10,000 minus the excess $1,000.

This expense would be claimed as an "other deduction" on business returns (such as Form 1065 or Form 1120), or as an "other expense" on Schedule C or Schedule F. Any remaining startup expenses would be capitalized and amortized ratably over 180 months (15 years) on Form 4562, *Depreciation and Amortization*. If a taxpayer completely disposes of a business before the end of the amortization period, he can deduct all the deferred startup costs. However, the business can deduct these deferred startup costs only to the extent they qualify as a loss.

> **Example:** Clean Water Inc. opened for business on November 1, 2010. Prior to opening, they incurred expenses for advertising and manager training. These costs amounted to $55,000 and were properly classified as startup costs. Since Clean Water had less than $60,000 of startup costs, the company is allowed to deduct the full $10,000, plus an additional $500 in amortization on its 2010 tax return [($55,000 - $10,000)/180 x 2 (months)].

Qualifying Startup Costs

Business *startup costs* are the expenses incurred before a business actually begins operations. Startup costs include any amounts paid in anticipation of the activity becoming an active trade or business. Startup costs do NOT include:

- Deductible interest,
- Taxes, or
- Research and experimental costs.

Startup costs are amounts paid or incurred for:

- Creating an active trade or business; or
- Investigating the creation or acquisition of an active trade or business.

Startup costs may include:

- An analysis or survey of potential markets
- Advertisements for the opening of the business
- Salaries and wages for employees who are being trained and their instructors
- Travel and other necessary costs for securing prospective distributors, suppliers, or customers
- Salaries and fees for executives and consultants, or for similar professional services

> **Example:** Moonlight Corporation received its charter on January 12, 2010. Later, Moonlight paid $15,500 in advertising for commercials before the business opened. Moonlight Corporation can elect to expense $10,000 as a startup cost immediately. It can then amortize the remaining $5,500 beginning in January 2010.

Qualifying Organizational Costs

In 2010, Congress increased the amount of deductible startup costs to $10,000. However, the deduction for organizational costs remained the same at $5,000 with a phase-out range of $50,000.

Amounts paid to organize a corporation, partnership, or other entity are considered a direct cost of creating a business. To qualify as an organizational cost it must be an expense:

- For the creation of the business
- Chargeable to a capital account
- Amortized over the life of the business
- Incurred before the end of the first tax year in which the entity is in business

Examples of qualifying organizational costs include:

- The cost of temporary directors
- The cost of organizational meetings
- State incorporation fees
- The cost of legal services, such as drafting the charter, bylaws, etc.
- Accounting services for setting up the corporation

Non-qualifying Organizational Costs

The following items are NOT qualifying organizational costs, and cannot be amortized:

- Costs for issuing and selling stock or securities, such as commissions, professional fees, and printing costs
- Costs associated with the transfer of assets to the corporation
- The cost of admitting or removing partners (other than at the time the partnership is first organized)
- The cost of making a contract concerning the operation of the partnership trade or business including a contract between a partner and the partnership
- The cost of issuing and marketing partnership interest such as brokerage, registration, and legal fees and printing costs (These "syndication fees" are capital expenses that cannot be depreciated or amortized.)

If a business is completely dissolved, disposed of, or sold at a later date, the business may deduct any remaining deferred organizational or startup costs on the final tax return.

In order to amortize startup or organizational costs, the business must attach Form 4562 to the tax return for the first tax year. If a business has both startup AND organizational costs, attach a separate statement to the return detailing both costs. Once a business makes an election to amortize startup and organizational costs, it is irrevocable. The election to amortize must be made by the due date of the return, *including extensions*.

If the business never materializes, then these costs are treated differently depending on the entity type. In the case of a corporation, all investigatory costs are deductible as a business loss. In the case of an individual, the costs incurred before making a decision to acquire a business are considered personal costs and are generally not deductible (this is only if the business never begins). This would include any costs incurred during a general investigation of a business.

Other Business Expenses

There are many types of expenses that are deductible for a business. Some expenses that would not be appropriate in one line of business may be completely acceptable in another. The deductibity of an expense may also depend on the facts and circumstances of the case. Here are some common business expenses:

- Advertising, including Internet and newspaper advertising
- Education and training for employees
- Environmental cleanup costs that are imposed on a business entity to clean up business waste (very common in construction businesses)
- Legal and professional fees to defend a business against a lawsuit (although legal fees to purchase an asset or legal fees to form a corporation are capital expenses)
- Business license fees
- Transportation and delivery costs for equipment or goods
- Penalties for nonperformance of a contract (although penalties for any violation of the law are never deductible)
- Subscriptions and memberships to trade magazines and professional organizations
- Utilities, supplies, and other expenses for items used in a business throughout the year

Nondeductible Expenses

There are many expenses that are not deductible by a business. Some are not deductible at all, and some must be capitalized. Any illegal activity or penalty for breaking the law is not deductible. The following costs are not business expenses:

- Charitable contributions (except for corporations, which are allowed charitable contributions)
- Any type of political contribution, kickbacks, or any cost that is incurred to try to influence legislation
- Lobbying expenses or any expenses related to influencing political legislation
- Any dues paid to country clubs, even if the club is used for business activity
- Any penalty paid to a government agency or fines for breaking the law (such as parking tickets)
- Repairs to equipment that add value to the asset or increase its useful life (these costs are considered improvements and must be capitalized)

Summary: Business Expenses

Business expenses are the cost of carrying on a trade or business. Expenses are usually deductible if the business is operated to make a profit. To be deductible, a business expense must be both ordinary and necessary. Business Expenses DO NOT include:

- Expenses used to figure the cost of goods sold,
- Capital Expenses* (these are generally depreciated), and
- Personal Expenses

*Start-up costs are generally capital expenses, but a business can elect to deduct or amortize certain business start-up costs.

Cost of Goods Sold

The following are types of expenses that go into figuring the cost of goods sold.

- The cost of products or raw materials, including freight and storage
- Direct labor costs (including contributions to pensions or annuity plans) for workers who produce the inventory or products
- Factory overhead

Under the uniform capitalization rules, the business must capitalize the direct costs production activities.

General Rules: Deductible Entertainment Expenses

Expenses to entertain a client, customer, or employee are deductible. Entertainment includes any activity generally considered to provide entertainment, amusement, or recreation, and includes meals provided to a customer or client. Tests to be met (1)Directly-related test (2)Associated test. A business generally can deduct only 50% of meal and entertainment expenses.

Unit 2.4: Questions

1. Artie is a self-employed accountant. He goes to a continuing education seminar out-of-state. He pays $400 for the seminar and $35 for a train ticket to the event. He also incurs $26 in restaurant meal expenses and $10 in taxi fare on the way to the restaurant. What is his deductible expense for this event?

A. $400
B. $435
C. $458
D. $465

The answer is C. The answer is $458 ($400 + $35 + $10 + [26 x 50%]). His meal expenses are subject to the 50% rule, but the taxi fare is fully deductible. The cost of the train ticket and the seminar are also completely deductible. ###

2. Kimberly is a sole proprietor and files a Schedule C. How should she report the $2,000 in charitable contributions she made on behalf of her business in 2010?

A. The contributions may be deducted on Schedule A as an itemized deduction.
B. The contributions may be deducted on Schedule C as a business deduction.
C. The contributions may not be deducted.
D. Up to 10% of the taxpayer's charitable contributions may be deducted on Schedule C.

The answer is A. Individual taxpayers can deduct contributions to a qualified organization, but only as an itemized deduction. Self-employed taxpayers may deduct these contributions on their Schedule A. The contributions cannot be deducted as a business expense on Schedule C. Only C corporations may deduct charitable contributions as a business expense. ###

3. Norman is the sole proprietor of Crusty Trucking Company. He is subject to the Department of Transportation rules for hours of service. In 2010, what percentage of his meals is he able to deduct while working as an interstate truck driver?

A. 50%
B. 75%
C. 80%
D. 100%

The answer is C. A taxpayer who is subject to the Department of Transportation's hours of service may deduct a larger percentage of his meal expenses when traveling away from his tax home. For the Department of Transportation (DOT) hours of service limits, multiply meal expenses incurred while away from home on business by 80% (2010 limits). ###

4. Which of the following tests is NOT required in order for entertainment expenses to be deductible?

A. Business was engaged in during the entertainment event.
B. The main purpose of the entertainment was the conduct of business.
C. There was more than just the general expectation of business benefit.
D. The taxpayer must prove that the entertainment produced a profitable venture or profitable event.

The answer is D. The taxpayer is not required to prove that the entertainment event actually produced a profit. The taxpayer must meet all the following tests in order to deduct an entertainment expense:
- Business was engaged in during the entertainment event.
- The main purpose of the entertainment was the conduct of business.
- There was more than just the general expectation of business benefit. ###

5. Which of the following tests are NOT true when determining whether an employee's pay is a legitimate business expense deductible by the business owner?

A. An employee can be a spouse, and her pay may still be deductible.
B. An employee must be paid according to job performance.
C. Vacation pay is deductible by the employer even though it is not for actual work performed.
D. Employee wages are deductible even if an employee is paid substantially less than his coworkers doing a similar job.

The answer is B. The test for the deductibility of wages by a business owner is not dependent on an employee's job performance. Section 162(a)(1) requires that the services be performed and that the amount be reasonable and incurred during the year. Vacation pay and sick pay are still considered "wages" even though the pay is not for actual work performed. ###

6. Jonathon owns a rental car company. He recently signed a contract with a vendor, which was finalized over dinner. The cost of the dinner was $250. Jonathon's own dinner was $50. The vendor ate a very expensive meal and also drank expensive liquor. The vendor's portion of the meal was $170. The remainder of the bill was for the tip and tax. How much of this expense is actually deductible by Jonathon as a business expense?

A. $25
B. $110
C. $125
D. $250

The answer is C. The entire meal amount is a qualified expense, but subject to the 50% meal and entertainment limitation. Therefore, the deductible portion of the expense is $125 ($250 X 50%). ###

7. Caliper Corporation purchased a machine to use in its business operations in July 2010. The cost of the machine was $250,000, not including $18,500 in sales tax. The entire purchase of the machine was financed with a small business loan. During 2010, Caliper Corporation paid interest of $10,500 on the loan. What is the proper treatment of this transaction?

A. Caliper Corporation should capitalize all the costs, including interest, on its 2010 tax return.
B. Caliper Corporation may take a deduction for the interest paid on the loan ($10,500). The other costs, including sales tax, should be capitalized and depreciated.
C. Caliper Corporation does not have a business expense for the purchase of the machine in 2010.
D. Caliper Corporation may deduct the sales tax and the loan interest as a business expense.

The answer is B. Caliper Corporation can take a deduction for the interest paid on the loan. However, the sales tax is not deductible. This is because taxpayers must add the cost of sales tax to the basis of a depreciable asset and depreciate the total over the useful life of the machine. The interest on a business loan, however, is a current expense and should be treated separately from the basis of the asset. ###

8. Anya is a music industry executive. In order to try to secure a client, she took two potential clients to a concert that was sold out. The normal ticket price was $210 per ticket, but she paid $500 to a ticket broker for three concert tickets. What is Anya's total deductible entertainment expense on Schedule C for the tickets?

A. $105
B. $210
C. $315
D. $500

The answer is C. A taxpayer may not deduct more than the face value of a ticket. Then the taxpayer must apply the 50% limitation for entertainment expenses. Therefore, the deductible expense that would be reflected as a business expense would be:
$210 x 3 (price per ticket) = $630
$630 X 50%= $315 ####

446

9. In 2010, Helton Partnership, a cash-basis entity, borrowed $50,000 to purchase machinery. $2,500 in interest on the loan was due in December 2010. Rather than pay the interest, the partnership refinanced the loan and the interest into a new loan amount totaling $53,800: the original loan amount plus interest and an additional $1,300 in loan origination fees. The first payment on the loan is due January 29, 2011. How much interest is deductible?

A. $0
B. $2,500
C. $2,800
D. $3,800

The answer is A. The partnership is on the cash basis; therefore, it can only deduct interest actually paid during the year. Since the partnership did not actually pay any interest, it does not have a deductible expense. The fact that the loan was refinanced has no bearing on the deductibility of the interest in the current tax year. ###

10. Marion owns a shoe shop. In 2010, she had the following income and expenses:

Repairs to business office floor $1,000
Tax on her business assets $2,000
Assessment for sidewalks $5,800
Utilities for her store $1,800

What is the tax treatment of the above expenditures?

A. Deduct repairs, property tax, and utilities as expenses. The assessment for sidewalks must be added to the basis of the property and depreciated.
B. All the above expenses are currently deductible.
C. The property tax must be deducted on Schedule A, and the rest of the expenses may be currently deducted as business expenses
D. Only the utilities and repairs may be currently deducted.

The answer is A. The repairs, property tax, and utilities are all deductible as current expenses. The property tax is deductible as a business expense (rather than on Schedule A) because it is assessed on business property. The assessments for streets, sidewalks, sewer lines, and other public services generally add value to the property and must be added to the basis of the property. ###

11. Delia, a self-employed real estate agent, traveled to a business convention by train. The train ticket cost $100. At the convention, she purchased a new computer that cost $2,100 for use in her business. She also purchased a computer game for $50. Delia spent $80 on meals and $90 on her hotel room during the convention. How much is deductible as a current business expense?

A. $190
B. $230
C. $2,280
D. $2,430

The answer is B. Delia may deduct the cost of her hotel room, one-half of her meals expense, and her train ticket to attend the convention.
$100 + $90 + (80 X 50%) = $230

The cost of the computer game is a personal expense and not deductible. The cost of the computer is not a current expense, but must be capitalized and depreciated over its useful life. ###

12. Samantha runs a Schedule C business on the cash basis. She paid the following insurance expenses in 2010:

State disability Insurance $1,500
Fire insurance for office building $1,000
Life insurance for herself $1,950

How much of the insurance expense is deductible on Schedule C as business expenses?

A. $1,500
B. $2,500
C. $2,950
D. $4,450

The answer is B. SDI, State Disability Insurance, is an employment tax that could be deducted as part of wages expense, or as an insurance expense. The fire insurance would also be deductible as an insurance expense. The cost of premiums for life insurance or loss of earning due to disability is not deductible, but the proceeds from these policies are generally tax-free as a result. However, an employer may deduct the cost of life insurance that is offered to an employee as part of a fringe benefit plan. If Samantha had employees and offered a life insurance policy to them, then the expense for the employee coverage would be deductible as a business expense. IRC Section 79 provides an exclusion for the first $50,000 of group term life insurance coverage provided under a policy carried directly or indirectly by an employer. ###

13. The Seaside Partnership made a business loan to Sugar Corporation, a supplier, in the amount of $10,000. After paying $2,000, Sugar Corporation defaults and the debt becomes worthless. How much may Seaside Corporation deduct as a business bad debt?

A. $0
B. $2,000
C. $8,000
D. $10,000

The answer is C. Loans to a client, customer, employee, or distributor for a business reason can be deducted as a business bad debt. The amount of the loan, minus what was repaid, would be the deduction on Seaside's tax return: $10,000 - $2,000 = $8,000. ####

14. Antonio is employed as an accountant by the GR Accounting Firm. When Antonio travels for his audit work, he submits his meal and travel receipts for reimbursement by the firm, which has an accountable plan for its employees. Which of the following statements is TRUE?

A. Under an accountable plan, the reimbursed amounts are taxable to Antonio and will be clearly listed on his Form W-2.
B. Under an accountable plan, Antonio may deduct his travel and meal expenses on his tax return, even though they have already been reimbursed by his employer.
C. Under an accountable plan, Antonio's employer may only deduct 50% of Antonio's meal expenses, even though Antonio was reimbursed in full for the expense.
D. Under an accountable plan, reimbursed expenses are usually taxable to the employee as wages, and the employer should deduct the expenses as wage expense.

The answer is C. The expenses for entertainment and meals must be reduced by 50%, regardless of whether the employer reimburses the employee for the full amount of the meals. Under an accountable plan, employee reimbursements are not included in the employee's income. The employer can deduct the expenses as current expenses on his tax return. ###

449

15. On January 1, 2010, Shreveport Partnership purchases a fire insurance policy for its business. The policy is for three years and is required to be paid in full the first year. Shreveport Partnership pays $1,800 for the policy. How much of this policy is deductible in 2010?

A. $0
B. $600
C. $800
D. $1,800

The answer is B. If a business pays an insurance premium in advance, it can only deduct the portion that applies to the current tax year, regardless of whether it prepaid the entire amount. Therefore, Shreveport Partnership may only deduct the part of the policy that applies to the current year, figured as follows: $1,800 ÷ 36 (months) =$50 per month; $50 X 12 = $600, the current year insurance expense ###

16. Bobby owns Bobby's Pawn Shop. He makes a business loan to a client in the amount of $5,000. Bobby also loans his brother Keith $1,000 so he can buy a car. His brother used to work sporadically at the shop as an employee. Both of the loans are now uncollectible. How much can Bobby deduct as a business bad-debt expense?

A. $1,000
B. $4,000
C. $5,000
D. $6,000

The answer is C. Only the loan to the client would be deductible as a business bad-debt expense. A loan to a client, customer, employee, or distributor for a business reason can be deducted as a business bad debt. Since Keith is a related person and not a regular employee, and the loan was for personal reasons, Bobby may not deduct the loan to his brother as a business bad debt. The loan to Keith would be a personal loan and may possibly qualify as a non-business bad debt and be deducted elsewhere, most likely on the taxpayer's Schedule D. But a personal bad debt is never deductible as a business expense. ###

17. Lily owns a dress shop. In 2008, she correctly deducted a $10,000 business bad debt after a fabric supplier defaulted on a loan. Then, in 2010, the fabric supplier wishes to do business with Lily again and repays $9,000 of the loan that was once in default. How must Lily report this payment?

A. Lily must amend her 2008 tax return to reflect the incorrect $10,000 bad debt deduction.
B. Lily must reflect this recovery of $9,000 as income in 2010.
C. Lily must reflect income of $9,000 in 2008 by going back and filing an amendment for that year.
D. Lily must amend her 2008 tax return, but she may still reflect $1,000 in bad debt deduction.

The answer is B. Lily is not required to amend her prior year return to report the recovery of the bad debt. Sometimes, an entity will recover an old debt that was previously written off as worthless. If a taxpayer recovers a bad debt that was deducted properly in a prior year, the taxpayer must include only the recovered portion as income in the current year tax return (Publication 535). ###

18. Which of the following benefits must be included in an employee's income?

A. Dependent care reimbursed under a qualified Flexible Spending Plan
B. Employee discounts on products
C. A holiday gift of $50 in gas cards
D. A holiday gift of a $25 canned ham

The answer is C. Gifts in cash (or cash equivalents, such as gift cards) must always be included in income. Cash gifts also include gift cards, gift certificates, and other cash value items. Excludable benefits that are qualified as fringe benefits and may be excluded from income include employee discounts, qualified transportation passes, parking, and de minimis holiday gifts. ###

19. Scotty owns Super Sausage Company. Scotty gives business gifts to ONE of his best customers, reflected as follows:

Glass display for Scotty's sausages: $500
Fruit basket: $50
20 imprinted pens: $35
Postage for the fruit basket $20

How much of the above can Scotty legally deduct on his tax return as a business gift expense?

A. $25
B. $525
C. $580
D. $605

The answer is C. There is a $25 limit per person per tax year for business gifts; however, there are exceptions to this rule. Incidental costs, such as packaging, insuring, and mailing, are not included in determining the cost of a gift for purposes of the $25 limit. Also, the following items are not considered gifts for purposes of the $25 limit:

- An item that costs $4 or less and has the business name imprinted on the gift
- Signs, display racks, or other promotional material to be used on the business premises of the recipient

Therefore, Scotty may deduct $580, figured as follows:

1. Glass display $500
2. Fruit basket $25 (only $25 is deductible as a gift expense)
3. 20 imprinted pens $35
4. Postage for basket $20
($500 + $25 + $35 + $20)=$580 ###

20. Nicholas owns a bookstore. In 2010, he has a loss of $4,000 due to water damage to his book inventory. His loss is completely covered by insurance. However, Nicholas will not be reimbursed by his insurance company until 2011. How should he treat this loss?

A. Nicholas should claim the entire loss as a casualty loss in 2010, and then claim the income from the insurance company reimbursement in 2011.
B. Nicholas must reduce the amount of his inventory loss in 2010. For 2011, he must include the insurance reimbursement as income.
C. Nicholas does not need to make any adjustments to his tax return, since he knows he will receive a reimbursement within a short period of time.
D. Nicholas must reduce his Cost of Goods Sold in 2010 to reflect the loss, and then claim the reimbursement as income in 2011.

The answer is C. Nicholas expects to be fully reimbursed for his loss, so no adjustments are necessary. If Nicholas was reimbursed by his insurance company and his reimbursement either exceeded his losses or was less than his losses, then an adjustment would be necessary (Publication 547). ###

21. The Pancake House has a qualified benefit plan for its employees. The following benefits were offered to the employees. Which of these is fully taxable to the employee?

A. Qualified group term life insurance of $50,000
B. Qualified dependent care of up to $5,000
C. A membership to the local athletic club, for the employee's health
D. Free transit passes

The answer is C. Memberships to athletic facilities are a taxable benefit. A workout area on the employer's premises is the exception. The other benefits are not taxable as part of a fringe benefit plan to employees. ###

452

22. Which of the following fringe benefits is subject to the 50% limitation for meals?

A. Meals in a restaurant during a business meeting
B. Meals catered at a business site during an employee picnic for management training
C. Meals provided to servers at a restaurant, for the convenience of the employer
D. Meals that are required by federal law to be furnished to crew members of certain commercial vessels

The answer is A. The 50% limit does not apply to any meals that are a de minimis benefit to the employee. Examples are coffee, doughnuts, occasional meals during employee parties and picnics. ###

23. Supplemental wages were paid to Dante in 2010. Which items listed below are not considered taxable wages to Dante?

A. Holiday bonus
B. Overtime pay
C. Vacation pay
D. Travel reimbursements under an accountable plan

The answer is D. Travel reimbursements considered part of an accountable plan are not included in an employee's wages. "Supplemental wages" refers to compensation that is paid to an employee in addition to his regular pay. These amounts are listed on the employee's W-2 and are taxable just like regular wages. ###

24. Mike borrowed $100,000 to purchase a machine for his business. The machine cost $90,000. The rest of the money went into Mike's business account and he purchased a jet ski with the money later in the year. However, the loan was secured entirely by his business assets. Which of the following statements is TRUE?

A. Mike cannot purchase personal items with a business loan; therefore, none of the interest is deductible.
B. All of the interest is deductible, because it is secured by his business assets.
C. Only the amount of interest allocated to the business machine would be deductible.
D. None of the answers is correct.

The answer is C. Generally, interest on a business loan is fully deductible. However, debt incurred for personal reasons is not deductible as a business expense. The amount of interest allocated to the business machine would be deductible, but not the amount for the jet ski, which is a personal expense. ###

25. Brenda rents a small storage unit for her business property on February 1, 2010. She is given a discount if she pays the full amount of the lease upfront, which is $1,620 for a three-year lease. What is Brenda's 2010 deductible expense for leasing the storage unit?

A. $495
B. $540
C. $560
D. $1,620

The answer is A. If a taxpayer pays for rent or a lease in advance, only the amount that applies to the current year is deductible. The balance must be deducted over the period over which it applies. The answer is figured as follows:
Deductible lease for 2010:

$1,620 / 36 (months) = $45 per month
$45 X 11 months (February-December 2010) = $495

26. All of the following expenses are deductible currently except:

A. Legal fees to acquire real property
B. Educational expenses related to business
C. Reimbursements for travel for employees
D. Legal fees incurred when a company successfully defends itself against a wrongful termination claim

The answer is A. Legal fees incurred to acquire real property are not currently deductible; they are capital expenses. These costs must be added to the basis of the asset and depreciated over its useful life. Other legal fees related to operating a business, or defending a business from a business-related lawsuit or employee matter are generally currently deductible. ###

27. Lollypop Company is having cash-flow difficulties, so it transfers a pickup truck to Bonnie, an employee, in lieu of wages. The company owes Bonnie $7,000 in wages. At the time of the transfer, the truck had a Fair Market Value of $7,000 and an adjusted basis to Lollypop Company of $5,500. How should this transaction be reported by Lollypop Company?

A. Wage expense of $7,000
B. Wage expense of $5,500
C. Wage expense of $2,500
D. Wage expense of $7,000 and gain on sale of $1,500

The answer is D. When property is transferred in lieu of wages or payment for other services, the employer is entitled to deduct its Fair Market Value at the time of the transfer. A gain or loss is realized if there is a difference between the Fair Market Value and the adjusted basis of the property. Lollypop Company will deduct $7,000 as wages and report the gain on the sale of the truck, figured as follows:
($7,000 - $5,500) = $1,500. ###

28. Alex is having financial difficulties, so he sells his office building to Cheryl, a real estate investor, who plans to use it as a business rental property. Alex was liable for $5,000 in delinquent real estate taxes on the property, which Cheryl agrees to pay. How should Cheryl treat this transaction?

A. Cheryl cannot deduct these taxes as a current expense; she must add the amount to the basis of the property.
B. Cheryl can deduct these taxes as a current expense on her Schedule A.
C. Cheryl can deduct these taxes as a current expense on her Schedule E.
D. Cheryl can deduct these taxes as a current expense on her Schedule C.

The answer is A. Cheryl may not deduct the taxes as a current expense, since they are delinquent real estate taxes and the person who is legally liable for the debt is Alex. However, the taxes may be added to the property's basis and depreciated as part of the purchase price, since Cheryl intends to use the property as a rental. ###

29. The Greenway Corporation files its tax return on time, but because of cash flow problems the corporation cannot pay the taxes due. Which of the following statements is true?

A. If Greenway is assessed interest and penalties on the delinquent taxes, then these penalties are deductible on next year's return.
B. Greenway cannot deduct any interest or penalties on its delinquent federal tax obligations.
C. Greenway can deduct penalties, but not the interest, on its delinquent federal tax obligations.
D. None of the above.

The answer is B. Penalties on late tax payments to the Internal Revenue Service are never deductible as a business expense, even if the penalties are related to business income. Generally, entities cannot deduct any fines or penalties. ###

30. Sandra owns a pottery business in Florida when she receives notice of a hurricane. She spends $300 to board up her business against the storm. The storm still causes $2,000 in damage to her inventory. What is the correct tax treatment of this loss?

A. Deduct $2,300 in business casualty losses.
B. Deduct $2,300 in personal casualty losses, after deducting the $500 "per loss" deduction amount, since the storm was not a business-related event.
C. Deduct $2,000 in business casualty losses. The $300 expense to board up the business is not deductible.
D. Deduct $2,000 in business casualty losses, and $300 as a business expense.

The answer is D. The cost of protecting a property against a casualty or theft is not actually part of the casualty loss. The amounts spent for protecting a business against losses are deductible as business expenses. A casualty loss is damage or loss of property resulting from an event that is sudden, unexpected, or unusual. The expenses that Sandra incurred to protect her business may be deductible instead as regular business expenses. ###

31. A partnership business may deduct all the following EXCEPT:

A. Federal income taxes
B. State income taxes
C. Foreign income taxes
D. Local income taxes

The answer is A. Federal income taxes are never deductible as a business expense. A corporation or partnership can deduct state and local income taxes as business expenses. An individual may deduct state and local income taxes only as an itemized deduction on Schedule A (Form 1040).

Generally, a business can take either a deduction or a credit for income taxes imposed by a foreign country. However, an individual cannot take a deduction or credit for foreign income taxes paid on income that is exempt from U.S. tax under the foreign earned income exclusion or the foreign housing exclu-exclusion.###

32. Garrett operates his printing business out of rented office space. He uses a van to deliver completed jobs to customers. Which of the following statements is FALSE?

A. Garrett can deduct the cost of round-trip transportation between customers and his print shop.
B. Garrett can deduct commuting costs between his home and his main or regular workplace.
C. Garrett can deduct the cost of mileage to deliver completed jobs to the post office to mail.
D. Garrett can deduct the costs to travel to his customers who are disabled and cannot come to his shop.

The answer is B. A taxpayer cannot deduct the costs of driving a car or truck between his home and his main or regular workplace. These costs are personal commuting expenses. The costs of driving to meet with clients or do other business-related errands are deductible. ###

33. Carrie is the sole proprietor of a flower shop. She drove her van 20,000 miles during the year. 16,000 miles were for delivering flowers to customers and 4,000 miles were for personal use. Carrie wants to use actual costs instead of the standard mileage rate. What is Carrie's percentage of business use for the van?

A. 10%
B. 20%
C. 80%
D. 90%

The answer is C. Carrie can claim only 80% (16,000 ÷ 20,000) of the cost of operating her van as a business expense. She cannot count the personal miles and therefore must prorate the mileage to reflect her percentage of business use (Publication 334). ###

34. The Banter Partnership paid the following penalties in 2010. Which are deductible?

A. A penalty paid to a local government for violating construction regulations
B. A penalty imposed by the IRS for late filing of a Form 1065 partnership return
C. A penalty for a parking violation
D. A penalty for late performance of a contract

The answer is D. Penalties paid for the performance (or nonperformance) of a contract are deductible. Penalties or fines paid to any government entity because of a violation of law are not deductible. ###

35. Which of the following costs qualify as business "startup costs"?

A. Costs associated with the transfer of assets to the corporation
B. Costs for issuing and selling stock or securities, such as commissions, professional fees, and printing costs
C. Research and experimental costs
D. A survey of potential markets

The answer is D. Startup costs are costs incurred in creating an active trade or business or investigating the creation or acquisition of an active trade or business. Startup costs include amounts paid for the following:

- An analysis or survey of potential markets, products, labor supply, transportation facilities, etc.
- Advertisements for the opening of the business
- Salaries and wages for employees who are being trained and their instructors
- Salaries and fees for executives and consultants, or for similar professional services

The other costs are all nondeductible costs. The costs associated with the transfer of assets to the corporation are capital expenses that cannot be amortized or deducted. ###

36. All of the following are excludable from wages except:

A. An outstanding employee achievement award valued at $300
B. Occasional snacks provided by the employer in the employee break room
C. Employer-provided vehicles that employees may also use for personal purposes
D. Meals furnished during work hours for the benefit of the employer

The answer is C. The value of a vehicle for personal use by an employee is a taxable benefit. If an employer provides a car for an employee's use, the amount that can be excluded as a working condition benefit is the amount that would be allowable as a deductible business expense if the employee paid for its use. There are exceptions for emergency personnel such as police officers, who are required to use their emergency vehicles. Employee achievement awards are exempt up to $1,600. Meals are exempt if either furnished for the employer's convenience or if *de minimis*. Snacks would usually be considered a de minimis benefit. ###

37. Giorgio, a self-employed businessman, spends $200 for a business-related meal. The tip was an additional $39. The taxi ride to attend the meal was $15.25. What is his final deduction on his Schedule C?

A. $119.50
B. $134.75
C. $239
D. $245

The answer is B. Taxpayers must apply the 50% limit after determining the amount that would otherwise qualify for a deduction. Taxes and tips are subject to the 50% limit. However, transportation costs to the business meal or activity are not subject to the limit and would be expensed as transportation costs, rather than meals and entertainment.
The answer is figured as follows:
($200 + $39 = $239) X 50%=$119.50
$119.50 + $15.25 = $134.75 ###

38. Actual car expenses include the costs of the following items EXCEPT:

A. Depreciation
B. Lease payments
C. Mileage
D. Registration

The answer is C. A taxpayer may choose to take the standard mileage rate OR actual expenses. A taxpayer may not take both. If a taxpayer does not choose to use the standard mileage rate, she may deduct actual car or truck expenses. ###

39. Paul, a self-employed businessman, gives a theater ticket to Belinda, who is one of his best customers. The ticket costs $15. Later in the same year, Paul gives a $30 gift basket to Evan, who is Belinda's husband. How much can Paul deduct as a gift expense?

A. $15
B. $45
C. $25
D. $0

The answer is C. There is a limit on the amount that can be deducted for business gifts. No more than $25 for business gifts given to any one person can be deducted during the year. A gift to the spouse of a business customer or client is generally considered an indirect gift to the customer or client. ###

40. Heart-Wise Ambulance Services provides meals and lodging for ten employees at the workplace as a condition of employment because the paramedics are not allowed to leave the premises when they are on a shift. The employees eat and sleep for free. Which of the following is TRUE?

A. All the costs of meals and lodging can be excluded from the employees' wages and deducted as an expense by the employer.
B. The meals and lodging are not taxable to the employee, but the employer can only deduct 50% of the meal expense.
C. The meals and lodging are taxable to the employee and deductible by the employer. The employee may then deduct the cost as an employee-business expense on Form 2106.
D. None of the above.

The answer is A. Employers may exclude the value of meals and on-site lodging from an employee's wages. Lodging provided for the convenience of the employer is also excludable from an employee's wages. Since the employees are required to remain on the employer's premises, the value of the meals and lodging is a nontaxable benefit to the employees. Meals provided to employees for the "convenience of the employer" are 100% deductible by the employer, but are not taxable to the employees. To be considered "for the convenience of the employer," they must be taken on the business premises, and there are also other restrictions (*IRS Taxable Fringe Benefit Guide*). ###

41. Which is NOT a true statement regarding a business "bad debt" expense?

A. The debt does not have to be due to be considered worthless.
B. A bad debt can result from a loan to a supplier.
C. Cash-basis taxpayers can take a deduction for amounts never received or collected.
D. A debt can arise from the guarantee of a debt that becomes worthless.

The answer is C. A cash-basis taxpayer cannot deduct a business bad debt if he has no basis in the debt. A cash-basis taxpayer cannot deduct amounts that were never received or collected (such as a customer who never paid a bill for services). However, a cash-basis taxpayer may take a bad debt deduction for losses actually incurred. For example, if the business makes a good-faith loan to a supplier and the supplier does not pay back the loan, then the lender has a bad debt that is deductible, because the lender has incurred a bona fide loss. ###

42. U.S. tax law requires businesses to submit a Form 1099 for every contractor paid at least _____ for services during a year.

A. $500
B. $600
C. $850
D. $1,000

The answer is B. U.S. tax law requires businesses to submit a Form 1099 for every contractor paid at least $600 for services during a year. This requirement usually does not apply to corporations receiving payments. Each payer must complete a Form 1099 for each covered transaction. ###

43. Bettina owns her own business, and she has an NOL in the current year. She is not a farmer. Bettina elects to carryback her losses to a previous period. How long may she carryback and carryforward her NOL?

A. Back 5 years, forward 20 years
B. Back 2 years, forward 20 years
C. Back 3 years, forward 25 years
D. Back 2 years, forward 5 years

The answer is B. A Net Operating Loss may be carried back two previous years, and the remaining loss may be carried forward to each of the subsequent 20 years. ###

44. With respect to Net Operating Losses occurring in 2010, which of the following statements is TRUE?

A. An NOL attributable to a farming business can be carried back five years ONLY if it is attributable to a President's declared disaster.
B. A business can elect to forgo the carryback period, but only if the business is a corporation.
C. Usually, an NOL is carried back two years and carried forward for three years.
D. If a business has an NOL, it must carryback the entire amount of the NOL to the previous two tax years, and then carryforward any remaining NOL for up to 20 years.

The answer is D. NOLs must be carried back to the earliest available tax year to reduce income in those years, and then carried forward for 20 years until the NOL is fully used by reducing income in the years to which it is carried. The taxpayer can elect to forgo a carryback period. If an NOL is not used by the end of the twentieth tax year, it expires. ###

45. Which event would create a genuine NOL?

A. Selling a personal used car for a loss
B. Selling a primary residence for a loss
C. Casualty loss from a fire on a personal residence
D. Large losses from the sale of stock

The answer is C. Only the casualty loss would potentially be a deductible loss. Losses from the *sale of* personal items would not be a deductible loss, but casualty and theft losses of personal property may create an NOL if all the income thresholds are met. Losses on the *sale of* a personal residence are not taxable. Losses from the sale of stock are *capital losses* and cannot be used to create an NOL. ###

46. Gabriel had an NOL in 2010. He is a qualified farmer, and all his income is from farming. What is the earliest year that he can carryback his losses?

A. 2002
B. 2005
C. 2006
D. 2007

The answer is B. The carryback period for farming losses is five years. The normal election is to carry a Net Operating Loss back two years. This is called the carryback period. Then, the business would carryforward any remaining NOL for up to 20 years (the carryforward period). Farming businesses are allowed a special exception to carryback their losses to the previous five years. ###

47. Which of the following does NOT qualify for the Domestic Production Activities deduction (Section 199)?

A. Manufacturing goods in the United States
B. Construction of buildings in the United States
C. Selling food or beverages prepared at restaurants or dining establishments
D. Software development in the United States

The answer is C. Selling food or beverages prepared at restaurants or dining establishments is specifically disallowed for the purpose of the DPAD. The following types of business are specifically excluded from claiming the DPAD:

- Construction services that are cosmetic in nature, such as drywall and painting
- Leasing or licensing items to a related party
- Selling food or beverages prepared at restaurants or dining establishments
- The transmission or distribution of electricity, natural gas, or water
- Any advertising, product placement, customer service businesses, and other telecommunications services

Most U.S.-based manufacturing qualifies for the DPAD. ###

48. The Hire Act enacted two provisions to encourage businesses to hire unemployed workers. One of the provisions allows for a payroll tax exemption from _____.

A. The employer's 6.2% share of social security tax on wages paid to qualifying employees
B. The employer and employee's share of social security tax on wages paid to qualifying employees.
C. The employer's 1.45% share of the Medicare tax on wages paid to qualifying employees.
D. None of the above.

The answer is A. The Hire Act enacted two provisions to encourage businesses to hire unemployed workers, one of which was a an exemption from the employer's 6.2% share of social security tax on wages paid to qualifying employees, effective for wages paid from March 19, 2010 through December 31, 2010.

Unit 2.5: Business Credits

More Reading:
Instructions for Form 3800
Publication 334, *Tax Guide for Small Business*

General Business Credit

There are many different business credits. Most of the credits discussed in this chapter are part of the "General Business Credit" (GBC). The General Business Credit is a combination of various business credits that are all claimed together on Form 3800, *General Business Credit.*

A business may be eligible for multiple credits in a single tax year, which combine to create the General Business Credit. Starting in 2010, the GBC includes the Small Employer Health Insurance Credit as specified by the 2010 Health Care Act.

Carryback and Carryforward

Normally, businesses can carryback unused business credits one year and carry them forward 20 years. However, effective in 2010, qualifying small businesses may take unused business credits and carry them back five years.[66] This applies to corporations, partnerships, and sole proprietorships, so long as the business's "average gross receipts" do not exceed $50 million. This means that most small businesses will be eligible for this special treatment.

Alternative Minimum Tax and Business Credits

In 2010, general business credits for an eligible small business can offset both regular tax and the Alternative Minimum Tax (AMT). This AMT provision is effective for any general business credits determined in 2010. It also applies to any carryback of business credits.

This is a one year initiative applicable only to the tax year 2010 (For fiscal year businesses, the effective tax year is the first tax year beginning on January 1, 2010).

Corporations whose stock is publicly traded are NOT eligible for this special AMT treatment. If a business is not an "eligible small business," then the General Business Credit may not offset AMT.

How to Report the GBC

Each individual business credit is computed individually on its own form. Then, the total amount is carried over to Form 3800. The credit is not refundable. Since it is an income tax credit, businesses may use the General Business Credit to offset any regular income tax liability, but not any employment tax liabilities (payroll taxes).

The General Business Credit for the year consists of carryforward credits from prior years plus the total of the current year credits. A business may also carryback business credits to a year in which it had tax. The General Business Credit is subtracted directly from the tax. Tax credits reduce an entity's tax liability dollar for dollar.

---

[66] The Small Business Jobs Act of 2010 created the new provisions for small businesses.

Unused business credits may be taken as a tax deduction if the business dissolves or, in the case of a sole proprietorship, when a business owner dies. The EA Exam will test some business credits, but it may be unnecessary to concentrate on the more obscure credits.

List of Business Credits

All of the following credits are part of the General Business Credit. The form a taxpayer uses to figure each credit is shown in parentheses. A taxpayer must also complete Form 3800.

*Agricultural Chemicals Security Credit (Form 8931) (*Obscure)*

This credit applies to qualified agricultural chemical security expenses paid or incurred by eligible agricultural businesses.

*Alcohol and Cellulosic Biofuel Fuels credit (Form 6478) (*Obscure)*

This credit consists of the alcohol mixture credit, alcohol credit, small ethanol producer credit, and cellulosic biofuel producer credit.

Alternative Fuel Vehicle Refueling Property Credit (Form 8911)

This credit is also called the Vehicle Refueling Property Credit. It applies to the cost of any qualified fuel vehicle refueling property placed in service in 2010. Taxpayers may claim a credit for the cost of installing clean fuel vehicle refueling property. The property qualifies for credit if it is used for business, or if it is installed at the taxpayer's primary residence.

The maximum credit allowable is:

- 50% of depreciable property, up to $50,000
- 50% of property installed at a taxpayer's primary residence, up to $2,000.
- 30% of depreciable property relating to hydrogen, up to $200,000

This credit reduces a taxpayer's basis.

Alternative Motor Vehicle Credit (Form 8910)

This credit consists of the following credits for certain fuel-efficient vehicles a business places in service:

- Qualified fuel cell motor vehicle credit
- Advanced lean burn technology motor vehicle credit
- Qualified hybrid motor vehicle credit
- Qualified alternative fuel motor vehicle credit
- Qualified plug-in electric drive motor vehicle conversion credit

This is a complex credit that is based on five different types of alternative motor vehicles that are placed into service during the year. This credit is unusual because it is allowed for both personal and business-use vehicles.

If the credit is claimed for a personal vehicle, the credit is a nonrefundable personal credit and will reduce the taxpayer's regular tax as well as the AMT. If the credit is claimed for a business use vehicle, the credit becomes part of the General Business Credit, so it is available for carryback and carryforward treatment.

A complete list of qualified vehicles by make and model is available on the IRS website (*Note: you will not be required to know the individual models for the EA Exam, but you should know the "general five" types of vehicles listed above, because this has been tested on prior exams.).

464

Biodiesel and Renewable Diesel Fuels Credit (Form 8864)

This credit applies to certain biodiesel fuels sold, used, or produced in the course of business. The credit is equal to one dollar for each gallon of biodiesel mixture used in the business. The credit is one dollar per gallon for biodiesel that is sold at retail. The credit is ten cents for each gallon of agri-biodiesel that is produced. Agri-biodiesel is an alternative fuel that may contain aviation fuel.

*Carbon Dioxide Sequestration Credit (Form 8933) (*Obscure)*

This credit is for carbon dioxide which is captured at a qualified facility and disposed of in a secure geological storage or used in a qualified enhanced oil or natural gas recovery project.

Credit for Employer Social Security and Medicare Taxes Paid on Employee Tips (Form 8846)

This credit is generally equal to an employer's portion of Social Security and Medicare taxes paid on tips received by food and beverage workers.   Restaurants   and   bars   are required to pay Social Security and Medicare taxes on their employees' tip income. Under IRC Section 45B, employers are allowed a credit for the taxes paid on those tips. An employer must meet both of the following requirements to qualify for the credit:

- The business has employees who received tips from customers for serving food or beverages.
- The business paid employer Social Security and Medicare taxes on these tips.

The credit applies only to tips received by food and beverage employees. It is NOT applicable to other tipped employees, such as hairdressers or bellhops. The credit is 100% of eligible amounts.

Minimum Wage Effect

This credit equals the Social Security and Medicare taxes paid on the tips received by employees. However, no credit is given for tips used to meet the federal minimum hourly wage rate. If, however, the employer pays each employee *at least* the minimum wage without including tips, then the employer can compute the credit on all reported tips.

*Credit for Employer Differential Wage Payments (Form 8932) (*Obscure)*

This is a credit to encourage employers to continue paying wages to employees who get called to active duty in the military for more than 30 days. The credit only applies to certain small businesses.

Credit for Employer-Provided Childcare Facilities and Services (Form 8882)

This credit applies to businesses that provide childcare for their employees or that provide childcare resource and referral service to workers. The credit is up to 25% of the cost of the childcare facility plus 10% of resource and referral costs. A business is limited to a credit of $150,000 per tax year.

*Credit for Increasing Research Activities (Form 6765) (*Obscure)*

This credit is designed to encourage businesses to increase the amounts they spend on research and experimental activities, including energy research.

Credit for Small Employer Pension Plan Startup Costs (Form 8881)

This credit applies to a company's startup costs of offering a new retirement plan to employees.[67] Plan types include defined benefit, defined contribution, 401(k), SIMPLE, or Simplified Employee Pension. This credit is only available to small employers. In order to qualify, the business, in the preceding year, must not have employed more than 100 employees with compensation of at least $5,000. The credit is 50% of eligible costs up to a maximum credit of $500 per year for the first three years of the retirement plan.

Disabled Access Credit (Form 8826)

This is a nonrefundable tax credit for a small business that pays or incurs expenses to provide access to persons who have disabilities. The expenses must allow the business to comply with the Americans with Disabilities Act. The Disabled Access Credit is equal to 50% of qualifying expenditures that exceed $250 but that do not exceed $10,250—for a maximum credit of $5,000 a year.

The only businesses eligible are ones whose gross receipts were $1 million or less for the preceding tax year or that had no more than 30 full-time employees.

Empowerment Zone and Renewal Community Employment Credit (Form 8844)

This credit provides businesses with an incentive to hire individuals who both live and work in a distressed community that has been identified as an "empowerment zone" or "renewal community." In 2010, the credit can be as much as $3,000 per qualified employee a year. (You will not need to know the specific geographic areas included in the credit for the EA Exam).

Energy Efficient Appliance Credit (Form 8909)

This credit is also called the Appliance Manufacturers' Credit and is available for manufacturers of certain energy-efficient dishwashers, clothes washers, and refrigerators. The credit is per machine and varies based on the type of machine.

Energy Efficient Home Credit (Form 8908)

This credit is available for eligible contractors of certain energy-efficient homes. Builders that construct new energy-efficient homes in the United States may claim a tax credit of $2,000 per unit. In order to qualify, the home's energy consumption must be at least 50% less than other comparable homes.

The credit can also apply to energy-efficient reconstruction of an older home. A manufactured home also qualifies for this credit if it meets a 30% reduced energy consumption standard. However, the tax credit for manufactured homes is smaller, at a maximum of $1,000 per unit.

---

[67] For more information, see Publication 560, *Retirement Plans for Small Business (SEP, Simple, and Qualified Plans)*.

Indian Employment Credit (Form 8845) (*Obscure)

This credit provides businesses with an incentive to hire certain individuals who live on or near an Indian reservation. To receive the credit, an employee or his spouse must be a member of an American Indian tribe. Businesses receive a credit for wages and health insurance costs paid to qualified employees up to $20,000 per employee a year (Publication 954).

Investment Credit (Form 3468)

The Investment Credit is the *total* of the following credits:

- **Rehabilitation Investment Credit:** This credit is given to businesses that rehabilitate pre-1936 buildings or certified historic structures. The credit is 10% (20% for a certified historic structure) of the qualified expenditures.
- **Energy Credit:** This credit is given to businesses that use solar energy to generate electricity or that use geothermal deposits to power their equipment. The credit is between 10% and 30% for qualified fuel cell and other solar energy property.
- Qualifying advanced coal project credit.
- Qualifying gasification project credit.
- Qualifying advanced energy project credit.
- Qualifying therapeutic discovery project credit.

The Investment credit allows businesses to take a deduction for a percentage of certain investment costs from their tax liability *in addition* to the normal allowances for depreciation. In effect, the credit subsidizes investment. In general, a business cannot claim the Investment Credit for property that is:

- Used mainly outside the United States
- Used by a governmental unit or foreign person or entity
- Used by a tax-exempt organization
- Used for lodging or in the furnishing of lodging ; or
- Any property that has already been expensed under Section 179 (accelerated depreciation) of the Internal Revenue Code.

*The Investment Credit has been tested on prior year EA exams.

Retention of Certain Newly Hired Individuals in 2010 Credit (Form 5884-B)

The new "HIRE" credit is new for 2010 and is designed to encourage the retention of new hires. This credit may apply if a business hired an employee after February 3, 2010, and before January 1, 2011, and the employee works for at least 52 consecutive weeks. The amount of the credit is the lesser of $1,000 or 6.2% of wages (the employer's share of the Social Security payroll tax on the employee's wages.)

Qualified Plug-In Electric Drive Motor Vehicle Credit (Form 8936)

This credit is for new qualified plug-in electric drive motor vehicles placed in service during the tax year. For vehicles acquired in 2010, the credit is $2,500 (plus, for a vehicle which draws propulsion energy from a battery with at least 5 kilowatt hours of capacity, $417, plus an additional $417 for each kilowatt hour of battery capacity in excess of 5 kilowatt hours). The total amount of the credit allowed for a vehicle is a maximum of $7,500. The credit amount depends on the vehicle's weight and battery capacity. Off-road vehicles and golf carts do not qualify.

Qualified Plug-In Electric Vehicle Credit (Form 8834, Part I only)

This credit applies to certain low speed vehicles, motorcycles, and three-wheeled vehicles purchased after February 17, 2009. The credit is 10% percent of the cost of the vehicle, with a maximum credit of $2,500. This credit is claimed on Form 8834, Part I only.

Small Business Health Care Tax Credit (Form 8941)

This is a new credit available to small businesses that pay health coverage for their employees. In 2010, the maximum credit is 35% of the insurance premiums paid by eligible small businesses. In 2014, this maximum credit will increase to 50% of premiums paid. This tax credit is available to employers who have fewer than 25 full-time equivalent employees and who pay wages averaging $50,000 or less per employee per year.

Work Opportunity Credit (WOC) (Form 5884)

This credit* (frequently tested) provides businesses with an incentive to hire individuals from targeted groups that have a particularly high unemployment rate or other special employment needs. There are 12 targeted groups, including veterans, ex-convicts, and welfare recipients.

In general, the credit can be claimed for a *percentage of* first-year wages and is typically 40% of the first $6,000 in first-year wages. The percentage varies by targeted group. The amount is increased to $12,000 of first-year wages for qualified veterans, with a maximum credit of $4,800. The credit is a percentage of the first $3,000 of wages, up to a maximum credit of $1,200 for summer youth.

If the employee is a long-term family assistance (welfare) recipient, the credit is 40% of first AND 50% of second year wages, up to $10,000 of wages (per qualifying employee). So, the maximum credit is $2,400 per employee. The targeted groups are:

- Qualified IV-A recipients (qualified recipients of TANF (Temporary Assistance for Needy Families.)
- Qualified veterans
- Ex-felons
- Employees ages 18-39 whose principal abode is in an empowerment zone, enterprise zone, renewal community, or rural renewal county
- Vocational rehabilitation referrals
- Summer youth employees
- Food stamp recipients
- SSI recipients
- Unemployed veterans and disconnected youths (only 2009-2010, must begin work before 2011)
- Hurricane Katrina employee

Unit 2.5: Questions

1. The General Business Credit is defined as:

A. A single business credit for small businesses
B. A set of several credits available to businesses
C. The credit for dependent care
D. A collection of charitable deductions for businesses

The answer is B. The General Business Credit consists of several credits available to businesses. The GBC is also the total of the carryforward of business credits from prior years plus the total current year business credits. ###

2. Farwell Corporation is a qualified small business for the purpose of the General Business Credit. The corporation could not use all of its credits in 2010. What is the carryback period for qualified small business in 2010?

A. The GBC may be carried back one year and carried forward 20 years.
B. The GBC may be carried back five years and carried forward 10 years.
C. The unused GBC cannot be carried over to another tax year.
D. The GBC may be carried back five years and carried forward for 20 years.

The answer is D. A new law allows an eligible small business to carry back general business credits five years and carry them forward 20 years. Previously, the credits could only be carried back one year. An "eligible small business" in this case is defined as follows:
- A corporation (whose stock is not publicly traded), a partnership, or a sole proprietorship, and
- The taxpayer must have $50 million or less in average annual gross receipts over the three preceding tax years. ###

3. In 2010, Meredith started a SIMPLE retirement plan for all ten of her employees and herself. It cost her $2,200 the first year in fees. Meredith's tax credit is:

A. $500
B. $1,500
C. $2,000
D. $2,200

The answer is A. The Credit for Small Employer Pension Plan Startup Costs applies to small businesses that start a new retirement plan for their employees. An employer may receive a credit of 50% of the first $1,000 of qualified startup costs for the first three years of the plan. The answer is $500, because only 50% of the first $1,000 qualifies for the credit. The maximum credit is $500 per year. ###

4. The new "Hire" Credit is designed to stimulate businesses to hire workers. How much is the maximum credit?

A. $500
B. $1,000
C. $5,000
D. $10,000

The answer is B. The amount of the credit is the lesser of $1,000 or 6.2% of wages (the employer's share of the Social Security payroll tax on the employee's wages.) This credit may apply if a business hired an employee after February 3, 2010, and before January 1, 2011, and the employee works for at least 52 consecutive weeks. ###

5. The Disabled Access Credit is:

A. A tax credit given to disabled taxpayers
B. A refundable credit given to businesses that pay expenses to provide wages to persons who have disabilities
C. A nonrefundable credit given to businesses that pay expenses to provide access to persons who have disabilities
D. A tax credit for medical insurance of disabled persons

The answer is C. The Disabled Access Credit is a nonrefundable tax credit for an eligible small business that pays expenses to provide access to disabled persons. The taxpayer must pay or incur the expenses to enable the business to comply with the Americans with Disabilities Act. The credit is taken on Form 8826. ###

6. Which of the following credits is part of the General Business Credit?

A. The Tuition and Fees Credit
B. The Earned Income Tax Credit
C. The Investment Credit
D. The Foreign Tax Credit

The answer is C. The Investment Credit is part of the General Business Credit. The other credits listed are not business credits; they are credits for individual taxpayers. ###

7. Dylan owns The Peach Pit Cannery. In 2010, he renovated his cannery to come into compliance with the Americans with Disabilities Act. The Peach Pit Cannery had gross receipts of $750,000 and spent $15,000 on disabled access upgrades. What is the current year Disabled Access Credit?

A. $2,500
B. $5,000
C. $10,000
D. $15,000

The answer is B. The amount of the Disabled Access Credit is 50% of the qualified expenses, but the maximum credit per year is $5,000. ###

8. Laura owns a business and hires four new employees. Which one is NOT a member of a targeted group for the purposes of the Work Opportunity Credit?

A. A qualified veteran
B. A qualified food stamp recipient
C. An ex-felon
D. A qualified student

The answer is D. According to Publication 954, targeted groups for the purposes of the Work Opportunity Credit include ex-felons, food stamp recipients, and veterans. A qualified student is not a member of the targeted groups. ###

Unit 2.6: Basis of Business Assets and Depreciation

> **More Reading:**
> Publication 946, *How to Depreciate Property IRS*
> Publication 544, *Sales and Other Dispositions of Assets*
> Publication 551, *Basis of Assets*

Basis of Business Assets

In order to understand the concept of depreciation, you must understand how the basis of business assets is calculated. The basis of a property also must be determined before a business can figure amortization, depletion, casualty losses, or gain or loss from the sale of a business asset.

There are many different kinds of business assets: land, buildings, machinery, furniture, trucks, patents, and franchise rights are all examples. Almost any asset used in a business can be considered a business asset.

Cost Basis of Business Assets

Certain events that occur during the period of ownership may increase or decrease the basis, resulting in an "adjusted basis." The basis of property is increased by the cost of improvements that add to the value of the property. The basis of property is decreased by depreciation and insurance reimbursements for casualty and theft losses.

The "basis of property" is usually its cost—the amount a business pays for an asset. The "cost basis" also includes sales tax and other expenses connected with a purchase. The basis of an asset includes amounts paid for the following items:

- Sales tax on the purchase
- Freight and postage charges to obtain the property
- Installation and setup fees
- Excise taxes
- Legal and accounting fees to obtain property (such as legal fees paid to a real estate attorney to purchase a plot of land)
- Revenue stamps and recording fees
- Real estate taxes (if assumed by the buyer)
- Settlement costs for the purchase of real estate
- The assumption of any liabilities on the property

Example: The Oceanside Partnership purchases a commercial building for $200,000 in cash and assumes a mortgage of $800,000 on it. The partnership also pays $5,500 in legal fees to a real estate attorney in order to handle the purchase. Oceanside's basis in the building is $1,005,500.

Example: Naomi pays $4,000 for a commercial dryer for her laundromat, Clean Time. The dryer's beginning basis is $4,000. Naomi also pays $500 for shipping and sales tax. The installation cost is $250. All these costs are added to the beginning basis, making it $4,750.

The basis of securities is the purchase price plus any costs of purchase, such as commissions and recording or transfer fees. Basis generally does not include interest payments. Interest payments on a loan may be deducted as an expense.

471

Taxpayers must fully capitalize the cost of business assets, including freight and installation charges. If a business buys property and assumes an existing mortgage on it, the basis includes the amount paid for the property plus the amount to be paid on the mortgage.

Increases to Basis

The costs of making improvements to an asset are capital expenses if the improvements:

- Add to the value of the asset,
- Appreciably lengthen the time a business can use it, or
- Adapt it to a different use.

These costs must be added to the basis of an asset. They cannot be expensed. Improvements are generally major expenditures, usually having a useful life of more than one year. Some examples are new electric wiring, a new roof, a new floor, new plumbing, bricking up windows to strengthen a wall, and lighting improvements.

Example: Jaime repairs a small section on one corner of the roof of a rental property. He can deduct the cost of the repair as a rental expense. However, the following year, Jaime must completely replace the roof. The new roof is an improvement because it increases the value and lengthens the life of the property. Jaime must capitalize and depreciate the cost of the new roof.

The following items also increase the basis of property:

- The cost of extending utility service lines to the property
- Impact fees
- Legal fees, such as the cost of defending and perfecting title
- Legal fees for obtaining a decrease in an assessment
- Zoning costs

Assessments for items such as paving roads and building ditches increase the value of an asset and therefore must be added to an asset's basis. A business cannot deduct assessments as taxes. However, a business can deduct charges for maintenance, repairs, or interest charges related to the improvements.

Loan Points

The term "points" is used to describe charges paid to obtain a home mortgage. Points are prepaid interest. Points are not added to the basis of an asset, regardless of why they are paid. A business cannot add the cost of points to the basis of the asset or any related property.

Demolition Costs

Demolition costs are added to the basis of an asset, which can be a difficult concept for EA candidates to understand. That means that demolition costs will *increase* basis, rather than decrease it. Demolition costs and other losses incurred by the demolition of any building are added to the basis of the land on which the demolished building was located. A business cannot claim the costs as a current deduction.

Example: Tony buys a lot with a badly damaged building on it for $25,000. He demolishes the building and prepares the land for a new structure. The demolition costs $13,000. He cannot deduct or expense the demolition costs. Tony's new basis in the land is $38,000.

Demolition costs INCREASE an asset's basis, because they must be added to the basis of the property. The costs associated with clearing land for construction also must be added to the basis of the land. For example, if a business pays to demolish an existing building and clear the lot of debris so new building can begin, all of the costs associated with the preparation of the land are added to the land's basis.

Decreases to Basis

A business must decrease the basis of any property by all items that represent a return of capital for the period during which the business holds the property. Depreciation, rebates, and casualty losses are all decreases to an asset's basis.

> **Example:** Kristin buys a copier that costs $1,200 to use in her business. She sends in a rebate receipt and gets a $50 rebate from the manufacturer. The correct way to account for this rebate is to reduce the basis of the asset to $1,150 ($1,200 - $50).

Examples of increases and decreases to basis:

Increases to Basis	Decreases to Basis
Putting an addition on a business	Exclusion from income of subsidies for energy conservation measures
Replacing an entire roof	Casualty or theft loss deductions and subsequent insurance reimbursements in excess of basis
Installing central air conditioning	Credit for qualified electric vehicles
Rewiring a rental property	Section 179 deduction
Assessments for local improvements	Deduction for clean-fuel vehicles and clean-fuel vehicle refueling property
Water connections, sidewalks, roads	Depreciation
Expenses to restore a property after a casualty loss	Nontaxable corporate distributions
Restoring damaged property or dilapidated property	Amortization
Legal fees	Rebates from a manufacturer or seller
Cost of defending and perfecting a title	
Zoning costs	

Class Life and MACRS

The Modified Accelerated Cost Recovery System (MACRS) is the current method of accelerated depreciation required by the United States income tax code. MACRS applies to most tangible property. Under MACRS, all assets are divided into classes that dictate the number of years over which an asset's cost will be recovered. For example, office equipment is depreciated with a class life of seven years, and water vessels are depreciated over ten years. Certain assets, such as computers, office furniture, and cars and trucks are assigned the same recovery period in all industries. Each MACRS class has a predetermined schedule that determines the percentage of the asset's cost that is depreciated each year.

The class life is also called the recovery period for the property. Depreciation spreads out the deduction over a period roughly consistent with the asset's useful economic lifetime, which is the recovery period.

Real property is depreciated under the straight-line method. Nonresidential buildings are depreciated over a 39-year recovery period using the straight-line method. Nonresidential buildings include commercial buildings like office buildings and shopping malls, as well as industrial buildings such as factories. Residential buildings (e.g., apartment complexes and residential rentals) are depreciated over a 27.5-year period using the straight-line method. The recovery period for buildings is the same regardless of what type of industry uses the building.

MACRS Class Life Table

Property Class	Asset Type
3-year property	Special handling devices for food and beverage manufacture
5-year property	Information systems, computers, typewriters, calculators, adding machines, copiers, automobiles, and trucks.
7-year property	All other business property not assigned to another class. Seven-year property includes office furniture, fixtures, and equipment.
10-year property	Assets used in petroleum refining and certain food products, vessels and water transportation equipment, trees or vines bearing fruit or nuts.
15-year property	Telephone distribution plants, improvements to land such as fences, roads, and bridges.
20-year property	Municipal sewers, Farm buildings that are not agricultural or horticultural structures.
27.5-year property	Residential rental property (apartment complexes)
39-year property	Nonresidential real property (office buildings, factories)

Other consistent acceptable methods of depreciation, such as the units-of-production method (covered later), and the income-forecast method, also may be used in some cases. Less accelerated depreciation methods, such as straight-line depreciation, are used to calculate depreciation for purposes of computing AMT income.

Election to Exclude Property from MACRS

Usually, assets are depreciated under the MACRS tables, which means that an asset is depreciated based on its useful life (the number of years it is deemed to be in service). However, there are other depreciation methods that are not based on years. If a business chooses to depreciate property under a method NOT based on a term of years (such as the unit-of-production method), it can elect to exclude that property from MACRS. It can make the election on Form 4562.

The business must make this election by the return due date for the tax year it places the property in service. However, if the business filed its return on time without making the election, the business can still do so by filing an amended return within six months of the return's due date.

We will go over the different types of depreciation methods (including methods that are not MACRS) later in this unit.

Depreciation in General

Depreciation is a tax deduction that allows a business to recover the cost of an asset. The amount allowed as an annual deduction roughly reflects the reduction in the value of the capital asset as it ages, which is called depreciation. A depreciable asset has value beyond the end of the year in which it is purchased. All tax depreciation is based on the original, historical cost of the asset and is not indexed for inflation.

A business must use **Form 4562**, *Depreciation and Amortization*, to report depreciation on a tax return. Even if a depreciation deduction is not taken, an adjustment to the basis must be made for the depreciation that "could have been" taken.

Most types of tangible property (except land) such as buildings, machinery, vehicles, furniture, and equipment are depreciable. Likewise, certain intangible property such as patents, copyrights, and computer software is depreciable. Raw land can never be depreciated. In order for a taxpayer to be allowed a depreciation deduction for a property, the property must meet all of the following requirements:

- The taxpayer must own the property.
- Taxpayers may depreciate capital improvements for property the taxpayer leases (for example, erecting a fence on leased property).
- A taxpayer must use the property in business or in an income-producing activity.
- The property must have a useful life of more than one year.

Example: Ron's Business Rentals made a down payment on a rental property and assumed the previous owner's mortgage. Ron owns the property and now may depreciate it.
Example: Harris's Doughnut Shop bought a new van that will be used only for business. Harris will be making payments on the van for the next five years. Harris owns the van and can depreciate it.

Even if a taxpayer meets the preceding requirements for a property, the following assets are not depreciable:

- Property placed in service and disposed of in the same year.
- Equipment that is used to build capital improvements.
- Section 197 intangibles. A business must amortize these costs.
- Term interest property. A "term interest" in property means a life interest in property, an interest in property for a term of years, or an income interest in a trust.

Salvage Value (Scrap Value)

An asset cannot be depreciated past the salvage value. The salvage of an asset is the estimated value of the property at the end of its useful life (also called the "scrap value"). The salvage value is based on the Fair Market Value of the asset once the business can no longer use it productively.

Salvage value is affected both by *how* a business uses the property and *how long* it uses it. If it is the business's policy to dispose of property that is still in good operating condition, the salvage value can be relatively large. However, if the business policy is to use property until it is no longer usable; its salvage value can be zero.

> **Example:** Cooper Trucking Inc. operates delivery trucks that deliver produce all across the country. Cooper Trucking purchases a new delivery vehicle in 2010 for $50,000. The MACRS class life of the truck is five years. At the end of five years, Cooper Trucking typically sells the used delivery trucks at auction for about $10,000. Therefore, the salvage value of the truck is $10,000. The basis of the truck is $50,000, but the *basis for depreciation* is $40,000. This is because the business expects to recover $10,000 at the end of the asset's useful life.

Most small businesses do not record a salvage value for their assets. However, most large businesses and corporations do track salvage value. This is especially true if the business has high-value depreciable assets, such as vehicles, airplanes, large machinery, or boats.

Placed-in-Service Date

Depreciation begins when a taxpayer places property into service for use in a trade or business or for the production of income. A business may begin to depreciate property as soon as it is placed into service.

> **Example:** Donald bought a machine for his business that was delivered in December 2010. However, it was not installed and operational until January 10, 2011. It is considered placed in service in 2011.

If the machine had been ready and available for use when it was delivered, it would be considered placed in service in 2010 even if it was not actually used until 2011.

> **Example:** On April 6, 2010 Sue bought a house to use as residential rental property. She made several repairs and had it ready for rent on July 5, 2010. At that time, she began to advertise it for rent in the local newspaper. The house is considered placed in service in July when it was ready and available for rent. She can begin to depreciate the rental property in July.

The property ceases to be depreciable when the business has fully recovered the property's basis, or when it is retired from use. In order to depreciate property correctly, the business must have the following information:

- The depreciation method for the property
- The class life of the asset
- Whether the property is "listed property"
- Whether the taxpayer elects to expense any portion of the asset
- Whether the taxpayer qualifies for any "bonus" first year depreciation
- The depreciable basis of the property

MACRS is the current method of accelerated asset depreciation required by the IRC and is the proper depreciation method for most property.

> **Example:** Natalie is a self-employed bookkeeper who is required to purchase bookkeeping and payroll software every year. Therefore, her bookkeeping software has a useful life of one year or less. She should not depreciate her payroll software. Instead, Natalie may deduct the yearly software cost as a business expense, since the item only has a useful life of one year.

Depreciation Methods

There are many depreciation methods that are acceptable to the IRS. A business may generally use any accepted method. Once a business chooses a depreciation method for an asset, it must generally use the same method for the life of the asset. However, a business may switch to the straight-line method at any time without IRS consent.

Straight-line Depreciation

Straight-line depreciation is the simplest and most often used depreciation technique. Straight-line can be used for any asset, and it must be used to amortize certain intangible assets. To figure out the deduction for straight-line, a business must first determine the basis, salvage value, and class life of the property. If the asset has a salvage value, a business must subtract the salvage value from the adjusted basis. The balance is the total depreciation the business can take over the useful life of the property. For an asset that originally cost $200 and has a five-year recovery period, the straight-line depreciation allowance would be $40 ([1 ÷ 5] x $200) each year for five years.

Straight-line Depreciation = (Cost - Salvage Value) ÷ Useful Life

A business may switch to the straight-line method at any time during the useful life of the property without IRS consent. After a business changes to straight-line, it cannot change back to the declining balance method or to any other method for a period of ten years without written permission from the IRS.

Example: On April 1, 2010, the Redstone Corporation purchases a computer system at the cost of $40,000. The system has a five-year class life under MACRS. There is no salvage value. Depreciation is figured as follows:

Depreciation for 2010 = ($40,000 ÷ 5 years) x (9 months ÷ 12) = **$6,000**

Depreciation for 2011 = ($40,000 ÷ 5 years) x (12 ÷ 12) = **$8,000** (this is a full year of depreciation)

Double-Declining Balance Method

The double-declining balance method is a common method of depreciation that uses a flat percentage depreciation rate over the class life of the asset. For example, if five years is the asset's cost recovery period, the double-declining balance method has a depreciation rate of [2 ÷ 5]. This is twice the straight-line depreciation rate, which explains the "double" in double-declining balance. Instead of spreading the cost of the asset evenly over its life, this system expenses the asset at a constant rate, which results in declining depreciation charges each successive period. Unless there is a change in the class life of the asset, the rate of depreciation generally will not change.

Example: For an asset that originally cost $200 and has a five-year recovery period, double-declining balance depreciation would be $80=([2 ÷ 5]x $200) in the first year; $48([2 ÷ 5]x[$200-$80]) in the second year; $28.80 ([2 ÷ 5]x[$200-$80-$48]) in the third year; and so on.

Businesses may also choose to depreciate an asset based on the 150% declining balance method. Both the double-declining balance and the 150% declining balance methods are referred to as "accelerated methods" because these declining balance methods concentrate a larger proportion of deductions in the early years of an asset's recovery period than do straight-line depreciation.

This is illustrated in the example above. For example, over the first two years of the asset's life, straight-line depreciation would allow only a cost recovery of $80, while double-declining balance depreciation would allow cost recovery of $128.

Unit-of-Production Method (Not MACRS)

This method allocates depreciation in proportion to the asset's use in operation. The asset is depreciated based on the number of units it can produce, rather than on a set number of years. For example, the depreciation deduction is figured by the number of units that a certain machine can produce.

This is also called the "units of activity" method, since it can be used to track the usage of an asset. For example, it can be used for depreciating airplanes based on air miles, delivery trucks based on miles driven, and machinery based on the number of units produced.

Under this method, depreciation is computed by dividing the total cost of the asset (minus salvage value) by its projected units-of-production capacity. Then, to find the periodic depreciation expense, a business multiplies the depreciation per unit of production by the number of units produced during the period.

Example: Big Corporation owns a machine that produces computer components. It was purchased for $500,000 and the machine is expected to produce a maximum of 240,000 units over its useful life. The salvage volume of the machine is $20,000. Using the units of production method, the machine's depreciable basis is $480,000 ($500,000 minus $20,000). Then, the depreciable basis is divided by the number of units that the machine is expected to produce ($480,000 divided by 240,000). This equals depreciation of $2 per unit produced. If the machine produces 30,000 components in the year 2010, the depreciation for the year will be $60,000 ($2 x 30,000 units). If the machine produces 25,000 parts in the next year, its depreciation for the year will be $50,000 ($2 x 25,000 units). The depreciation will be calculated similarly each year until the asset's accumulated depreciation reaches $480,000. At that point, even if the machine is still in use, it will be considered fully depreciated, and the depreciation will stop.

Section 179, Accelerated Depreciation Method

This section is heavily tested on the EA Exam. You must understand the Section 179 deduction, its thresholds, and the limits for the current year. The Section 179 deduction is a special depreciation allowance that allows certain small businesses to take a full deduction for property the first year they put the property into service.

Do not be confused by this. Section 179 is not a "business expense." Instead, it is "Bonus Depreciation" that allows a taxpayer to recover the full cost of an asset the first year the asset is put into service. So it functions *like* a business expense, but Section 179 is still a type of depreciation and there are special rules that apply to it.

Businesses can elect the Section 179 deduction *instead* of recovering the cost by taking depreciation deductions. Section 179 depreciation allows a business to immediately deduct the cost of property as an expense, rather than waiting for the property to be depreciated over time. This is generally limited to tangible, depreciable property that is acquired for use in the active conduct of a trade or business (such as machinery, computers, desks, etc.). However, the Section 179 deduction does apply to some limited intangible property, such as computer software. The 179 election may only be taken in the year the equipment is placed in use. To qualify for the Section 179 deduction, the property must meet all the following requirements:

- It must be tangible property (off-the-shelf computer software does qualify)
- It must be acquired for business use
- It must have been acquired by purchase (not as a gift)
- It can either be used or new property
- Must be over 50% business-use

The Section 179 deduction is elective, and businesses may still choose to use standard depreciation methods for all their assets instead of Section 179. The Section 179 deduction may not exceed taxable income for the year. For example, if the business's taxable income is $105,000, then the Section 179 deduction cannot exceed $105,000.

Section 179 Limits: 2010

The maximum Section 179 expense has been expanded in 2010 and is now $500,000. The deduction phase-out begins at $2 million on purchases of qualifying property. So for example, if a large corporation purchases $5 million worth of machinery and places it in service in 2010, the company is not eligible to take Section 179 on the property. However, it may still choose to use other depreciation methods.

Expanded Section 179 for Certain Real Property (QRP)

Also in 2010, there is a special rule that allows taxpayers to deduct up to $250,000 of Qualified Real Property (QRP) under Section 179. The taxpayer must elect to treat QRP as Section 179 property. This is the first time that businesses have been able to deduct any type of real property under Section 179. This special provision only applies to certain industries and property types[68] and includes the following real property:

- Qualified leasehold improvement property
- Qualified restaurant property (improvements to a restaurant building, such as a major renovation)
- Qualified retail improvement property (for example, an improvement of a retail clothing store, including major interior upgrades and other similar improvements)

The maximum amount of Section 179 expenses for QRP is limited to $250,000 (although a business is still eligible to deduct the full $500,000 limit for other qualifying property).

---

[68] Included in the Small Business Jobs Act of 2010 (9/27/10)

Example: Armando owns an Italian restaurant. In 2010, he did a major renovation to the interior of his restaurant. He changed all the booths and did a major kitchen remodel for a total cost of $260,000. He also purchased a computer for $5,000. Therefore, Armando has the following qualifying expenses for the Section 179 deduction:

Computer: $5,000

Qualifying Real Property: $260,000

Total asset purchases in 2010: $265,000

Since the limit for expensing QRP under Section 179 is $250,000, Armando may only expense $250,000 of the renovation. However, he may still take the Section 179 for the full cost of the computer, since the Section 179 limit for other qualifying property is $500,000 in 2010. Armando's allowable Section 179 deduction for 2010 is therefore $255,000 ($5,000 computer + $250,000 in allowable QRP). The remaining $10,000 that cannot be expensed can be carried over one year to 2011.

Assets Not Eligible for Section 179

Buildings and intangible assets (such as copyrights and patents) are not eligible for the Section 179 deduction. In general, land and land improvements, such as building structures and their components, do not qualify as Section 179 property (except for the partial QRP exceptions listed above). Land improvements include swimming pools, paved parking areas, wharves, docks, bridges, and fences. Buildings may be depreciated using regular MACRS straight-line depreciation.

Property acquired from a related person (that is, a spouse, ancestors, or lineal descendants) is not considered acquired by purchase and therefore does not qualify for the Section 179 deduction. However, property acquired from a related person is still eligible for standard depreciation methods.

Bonus Depreciation in 2010

In 2010, there is also an option for Bonus Depreciation. The *Tax Relief, Unemployment Insurance Reauthorization and Job Creation Act of 2010* provides for **100% depreciation** of assets placed in service in the period between September 9, 2010 through December 31, 2011. A **50% Bonus Depreciation** applies to purchases made between January 1, 2010 through September 8, 2010.

When applying these new depreciation provisions, Section 179 is generally taken first, followed by Bonus Depreciation – unless the business has no taxable income leftover to offset. This option only applies to NEW property. Used property does not qualify for Bonus Depreciation. Section 179 is still available for used property purchased in 2010.

Bonus Depreciation applies to tangible business property (including construction, mining, forestry, and agricultural equipment) with a MACRS recovery period of 20 years or less. This means that buildings do not qualify for Bonus Depreciation.

The biggest difference between Bonus Depreciation and Section 179 is that Bonus Depreciation only applies to new purchases, while Section 179 applies to both new and used equipment. Also, Bonus Depreciation is useful to very large businesses that spend more than

$2 million on equipment during the year. Bonus Depreciation is not subject to the same $2 million phase-out.

Listed Property

The IRS treats "listed property" differently, because taxpayers will often use these items for personal use in addition to business use. Deductions for listed property are subject to special rules and limits. Listed property includes cars and other vehicles used for transportation, as well as items used for entertainment, computers, and other telecommunication equipment. Listed property is any of the following:

- Passenger automobiles weighing 6,000 pounds or less (regular automobiles)
- Any other vehicle used for transportation, unless it is an excepted vehicle (*see next for a list of excepted vehicles)
- Items generally used for entertainment, recreation, or amusement (including photographic, phonographic, communication, and video-recording equipment)
- Computers and related equipment, unless used only at a regular business establishment and owned or leased by the person operating the establishment

Starting in 2010, cellular telephones are no longer considered listed property. Property that is 100% business-use, such as a desktop computer used exclusively at a business location, is not considered listed property. Computers and other related equipment used exclusively in a business location (including a qualified home office) are not subject to the listed property rules.

Excepted Vehicles

A vehicle used in a business of transporting persons (such as a tour bus or ambulance) or property for hire (such as a taxi cab) are not listed property. The following vehicles are NOT considered listed property:

- An ambulance or hearse
- A vehicle used directly in the trade or business of transporting persons or property for pay or hire, such as a taxi, shuttle, or other similar vehicles
- A truck or van that is a qualified non-personal use vehicle, such as a furniture delivery van that is only used for furniture delivery at a business location

The 50%-Use Test

If a taxpayer purchases listed property and places it in service during the year, the asset must be used more than 50% for business (including work as an employee) in order to claim a Section 179 deduction. Listed property meets the more-than-50%-use test for any year the business use is more than 50% of total use.

If the business use of the property is 50% or less, the taxpayer cannot take a Section 179 deduction and must instead depreciate the property using the straight-line method.

Example: Tania runs her own part-time catering business. She does not have a qualified home office because she runs her business from the kitchen table on her laptop computer. Tania's computer is therefore considered *listed property* because it is not used 100% in a qualified office in her home. Tania uses her computer 30% for her business, and the rest for personal use. Since she does not use the computer more than 50% for business, she cannot elect a Section 179 deduction. Tania may still take depreciation for the business-use portion under the straight-line method.

Depletion

Depletion is similar in concept to depreciation. Depletion is the method of cost recovery for mining and agricultural activities. Depletion refers to the exhaustion of a natural resource as a result of production, such as the "using up" of natural resources by mining, quarrying, or felling (of timber). Mineral property, timber, and natural gas are all examples of natural resources that are subject to the deduction for depletion. There are two ways of figuring depletion:

- Cost depletion
- Percentage depletion

Cost Depletion

"Cost depletion" is the basic method of computing depletion deductions. The method allocates the cost of a natural resource over the total anticipated reserve to yield cost depletion per unit (expressed in tons, barrels, etc.) A depletion deduction is then allowed each year based on the units exploited.

Cost depletion is figured by dividing the basis of the property by the total number of recoverable units. The number of units sold multiplied by this result is the deduction for depletion for the current year. Once a business figures the property's basis for depletion, the total recoverable units, and the number of units sold during the tax year, the business can figure the cost depletion deduction by taking the following steps:

Action	Result
Divide the property's basis for depletion by total recoverable units= **Rate per unit**	
Multiply the rate per unit by units sold= **Cost depletion deduction**	
Example: Brian bought a timber farm. In 2010 Brian determined that the timber could produce 300,000 units when cut. At the time of purchase, the adjusted basis of the timber is $24,000. Brian then cut and sold 27,000 units. Brian's depletion for each unit for the year is $.08 ($24,000 ÷ 300,000). His deduction for depletion is $2,160 (27,000 × $.08).	

Percentage Depletion

An alternative method of computing depletion is known as "percentage depletion." Under this method, a flat percentage of gross income from the property is taken as the depletion deduction. Percentage depletion may be used for most investments in depletable property; however, it may not be used for timber and its use for oil and gas properties is subject to strict limits. Mineral property includes oil and gas wells, mines, and other natural deposits, including geothermal deposits. The depletion deduction allows a business to account for the reduction of a product's reserves.

For mineral property, businesses generally must use the method that gives them a larger deduction. Businesses cannot use the "percentage" method to figure depletion for standing timber, soil, sod, dirt, or turf. They are required to use cost depletion.

To figure percentage depletion, businesses multiply a certain percentage, specified for each mineral, by gross income from the property during the year. The percentage depletion deduction cannot be more than 50% (100% for oil and gas property) of taxable income from the property figured without the depletion deduction and the Domestic Production Activities Deduction (DPAD).

Some businesses employ cost depletion at the outset of operations when a large number of units of the deposit are extracted and sold, and then convert to percentage depletion later, when percentage depletion yields a more sizable deduction.

Amortization

Amortization is used to write off the cost of an intangible asset investment over the projected life of the asset. Amortization is a method of recovering (deducting) the cost of an asset over a fixed period of time. It is similar to the straight-line method of depreciation.

Taxpayers must also amortize most business startup costs over time. Businesses figure yearly amortization by dividing the cost of the intangible asset by the useful life of the intangible asset.

Example: Sean spent $125,000 to purchase a copyright. The copyright has a remaining life of 15 years; the amortized amount per year equals $8,333.
Formula: Initial Cost ÷ Useful Life = Amortization per Year
Answer: ($125,000 ÷ 15 = $8,333 per Year)

Intangible Assets in General

Intangible assets include goodwill, patents, copyrights, trademarks, trade names, and franchises. The basis of an intangible asset is usually the cost to buy or create it. Intangible assets are treated just like physical assets. The basis of an intangible asset must be figured before the asset can be amortized.

Example: Charlotte purchases a copyright from another company. The copyright costs $12,000. The copyright has 15 years of useful life. She must amortize the copyright over 15 years (180 months). Therefore, the monthly amortization expense would be $66.67 ($12,000 ÷ 180).

The cost of intangible assets is amortized during the asset's useful life or legal life, *whichever is shorter.*

Example: On April 1, 2010, Frank buys a patent for $5,100. The patent has 17 years left on its useful life (the patent will expire in 17 years). He amortizes the patent under the straight-line method using its useful life. He divides the $5,100 basis by 17 years to get his $300 yearly deduction. He only owned the patent for 9 months during the first year, so he multiplies $300 by 9 ÷ 12 to get his deduction of $225 for the first year. Next year, Frank can deduct $300 for the full year.

Patents

The basis of a patent is the cost of its development, such as research and experimental expenditures, drawings, working models, and attorney and governmental fees. If the business can deduct research and experimental expenditures as current business expenses, it cannot include them in the basis of the patent. The value of an inventor's time spent on an invention is not part of the basis.

Copyrights

The basis of a copyright will usually be the cost of obtaining the copyright plus copyright fees, attorney fees, and clerical assistance. In the case of a purchased copyright, the basis is the cost of the copyright, plus any legal fees paid to obtain it.

Patents and copyrights are not eligible for Section 179 or any other accelerated depreciation method. Businesses can depreciate the cost of a patent or copyright only by using the straight-line method over its useful life. The "useful life" of a patent or copyright is the lesser of the life granted to it by the government or the remaining life when the business acquires it (if it is purchased or acquired from the original owner).

Example: Jackson purchases a patent for an electrical power strip to use in his business. He manufactures equipment and wishes to manufacture and sell the item to customers. The patent has nine years left on its useful life. Jackson may depreciate the cost of the patent over nine years.

However, if the patent or copyright becomes valueless before the end of its useful life, the remaining cost can be deducted as an expense.

Example: Joe purchases a patent for a popular toy design. The patent has a useful life of 10 years when Joe purchases it. However, two years after the purchase, the toy design is deemed hazardous to children, and all the toys are recalled. The patent is now considered worthless, and the remaining cost can be expensed.

Section 197 Intangible Assets

Generally, a business may amortize the capitalized costs of "Section 197 intangibles" over a 15-year period (180 months). These are assets that are not physical assets, and used in a business. Section 197 intangibles are created in connection with the *acquisition of a business* (when a buyer purchases another person's business, it may come with assets). The following assets are Section 197 intangibles and must be amortized over 180 months, when they are *part of a business acquisition*:

- Goodwill

- Going concern value: the value of a business based on its ability to continue to function and generate income even though there is a change in ownership
- Workforce-in-place: the value of employees already working in the business
- Business books and records, operating systems, or any other information base, including lists or other information concerning current or prospective customers (such as mailing lists)
- A patent, copyright, formula, or trademark
- A customer-based intangible: market share or any other value resulting from the future provision of goods or services because of relationships with customers in the ordinary course of business. For example:
  o An existing customer base
  o An existing circulation base
- Insurance in force
- A mortgage servicing contract
- A supplier-based intangible: the value resulting from the future acquisition of goods or services used or sold by the business because of business relationships with suppliers. For example:
  o A favorable relationship with distributors (such as favorable display space at a retail outlet)
  o A favorable credit rating or a favorable supply contract
- Any franchise license or trade name
- A contract for the use of any of the above

These are all intangible assets, and all of them have value that may be amortized. When these assets are acquired by purchase, the cost of the asset must be amortized over 15 years (180 months). These assets are not eligible for accelerated or Bonus Depreciation.

Intangibles that are NOT Section 197 Intangibles
The following assets are not Section 197 intangibles:
- Any interest in a corporation, partnership, trust, or estate (such as a stock interest in a corporation).
- Any interest under an existing futures contract, foreign currency contract, notional principal contract, interest rate swap, or similar financial contract.
- Any interest in land.
- Off-the-shelf computer software. Generally, "off-the-shelf" computer software placed in service during the tax year is depreciable and also eligible for Section 179. Examples of "off-the-shelf" computer software would be Microsoft Word and QuickBooks.
- Securities such as stocks and bonds.

Disposition of Business Assets and Section 1231
A business usually has many assets that can be disposed of in many ways. Assets can be sold, traded, exchanged, abandoned, or destroyed. In order to figure out how to report the disposition of an asset, taxpayers must first determine whether it is a capital asset, an ordinary income asset, or a Section 1231 asset.

First, the taxpayer must determine the character of the property. There are three types of property:

- Capital assets,
- Ordinary income assets, and
- Section 1231 assets.

Capital Assets: In general, capital assets are personal-use assets, collectibles, and investment properties. Capital assets also include stocks, bonds, and other securities (unless held by professional securities dealer). A personal residence and personal-use car are both examples of capital assets.

It is very important to understand the difference between a personal-use asset and a business asset, because the IRS specifically disallows recognition of most losses on personal-use property (except for casualty losses).

Example: Debbie owns her own home. She collects porcelain dolls as a hobby and owns 15 of them, which have appreciated in value (she is not a professional dealer). Debbie's home and collectibles are considered capital assets.

Ordinary Income Assets: The most common ordinary income assets are business inventory, accounts receivable, and other business assets that have not been held long enough for the holding period requirement to make them long-term (more than one year).

Example: In 2010, Ines purchases an expensive black-and-white copy machine for use in her business. The machine costs $6,000, but she realizes too late that she really needs a color copier. It was too late to return it, so, after three months Ines decides to sell the used black-and-white copier for $3,000. Since the copier was a business asset, it is not a capital asset. And since Ines did not own it for over a year, it is considered an ordinary income asset. The loss is therefore an ordinary loss.

Section 1231 Assets

Section 1231 gives special treatment for gains and losses on the sale of business assets. Section 1231 assets are business assets that have been held for over one year. Gains on Section 1231 assets are usually taxed at capital gains rates and losses are tax deductible as ordinary losses (except for depreciation recapture, which is taxed at ordinary income rates). This is the beneficial treatment that is afforded to business assets in the Internal Revenue Code.

Section 1231 assets include depreciable real property, non-depreciable real property, and long-term capital gain property that is held for the production of income but that is involuntarily converted by theft, casualty, or condemnation. In order to qualify as Section 1231 property, the property must have been held by the business for *over one year*. Here are some examples of Section 1231 assets:

- Machinery used in business
- A patent, copyright, or other intangible asset used in a business
- Hotels, office buildings, warehouses, residential apartment complexes, and other residential rental property
- Cattle and horses held for draft, breeding, dairy, or sporting purposes and held for TWO years or longer (does not include poultry)

486

- Any asset held for over one year that is used for the production of income and has been involuntarily converted

---

Example: Philip owns an antique vase that he purchased at auction two years ago. He also owns a residential rental that he purchased three years ago, as well as two vehicles. One is a pizza delivery van he bought five years ago that he uses exclusively in his pizza business. The other vehicle is his personal-use SUV that he uses for commuting and everyday tasks. Phillip's assets are categorized as follows:

Antique vase: A capital asset, because it is a collectible

Residential rental: Section 1231 rental property (held over one year and business-use)

Pizza delivery van/Section 1231 business property: (held over one year and business-use)

SUV: A capital asset, because it is a personal-use vehicle

When a 1231 asset is disposed of, the gain or loss is called a "Section 1231 gain or loss." The following transactions result in a Section 1231 gain or loss:

- Sales or exchanges of real property or
- Sales or exchanges of depreciable business property (such as machinery)

The property must be business-use property and held longer than one year. For the purpose of this rule, depreciable property includes amortizable Section 197 intangibles, such as patents and copyrights.

Example: Harwell Inc. manufactures shipping containers. Harwell has owned the land and the building that houses its manufacturing operations for many years. The land and the building are therefore Section 1231 assets, because they are used in a business and have been held for over one year. Harwell also has unsold shipping containers in inventory. The inventory is not a Section 1231 asset but rather an ordinary income asset. The sale of inventory always results in ordinary gain or loss.

A business may recognize a gain or loss if it:

- Sells property for cash

- Exchanges property for other property

- Receives money from a tenant for the cancellation of a lease

- Receives money for granting the exclusive use of a copyright

- Receives property to satisfy a debt

- Abandons property

- Receives insurance money in payment of damaged property

Usually, companies will depreciate assets to zero and continue to use the asset until it is no longer useful. However, if a company sells an asset for cash, the amount received is compared to the asset's adjusted basis in order to determine whether or not a gain or loss has occurred. If the business has a loss on the sale of a Section 1231 asset, the loss is treated as an *ordinary loss*. If the taxpayer has a gain, then the gain is treated as a long-term capital gain.

Example: Years ago, Superior Design Inc. purchased a high-end computer for $10,000. The company used the computer for six years and eventually sells it for $700. Superior Design had depreciated the computer down to its salvage value, which was estimated at $1,000. After the sale, the company has a loss of $300 on the sale of the computer ($1,000 salvage value minus $700 sale price). The computer is a Section 1231 asset and the loss is an ordinary loss.

Depreciation Recapture (Section 1245 and Section 1250)

Depreciation recapture occurs when a business sells previously depreciated property at a gain. If a business disposes of depreciable or amortizable property at a gain, the business may have to treat all or part of the gain (even if otherwise nontaxable) as ordinary income. Ordinary gain is taxed at the business's highest marginal rate.

Example: Jeff runs Cow Town farms, which is a calendar-year sole proprietorship. In February 2008, Jeff bought a tractor (5-year property) that cost $10,000. MACRS depreciation deductions for the tractor were $1,500 in 2008 and $2,550 in 2009. Jeff sells the tractor in May 2010 for $7,000. The MACRS deduction in 2010 is $893 (½ of $1,785). The gain on the sale of the tractor that must be treated as ordinary income is figured as follows:

Amount realized in the sale		$7,000
Original purchase price (basis)	$10,000	
Depreciation (MACRS deductions: $1,500 + $2,550 + $893)	$4,943	
Adjusted basis		$5,057
Gain realized		$1,943
Gain treated as ordinary income (lesser of line 3 or line 5)		**$1,943**

For business assets that are sold, the gain attributable to depreciation is "recaptured" as ordinary income. The balance of the depreciation is then capital gain.

Example: The Drake Partnership owns a $20,000 business machine that has been depreciated $12,000 over the years. Therefore, the partnership's adjusted basis in the machine is $8,000. In 2010, the partnership receives an offer to sell the machine at a healthy profit. The partnership sells the machine for $25,000, which was more than its original price. The partnership must recognize ordinary income from the sale of $12,000 and long-term capital gain of $5,000. The $12,000 is taxed as ordinary income from depreciation recapture.

Example: Years ago, Mabel purchased a residential rental for $125,000. Over the years, she claimed the proper amount of depreciation. In 2010, Mabel's adjusted basis in the rental property is $86,000. Her accumulated depreciation is $39,000. In December 2010, Mabel sells the property for $180,000 and recognizes $94,000 in taxable gain ($39,000 in ordinary gain from depreciation recapture, and $55,000 in long-term capital gain (Section 1231 gain). She will pay tax at a higher rate on the depreciation recapture ($39,000), but she will receive the benefit of long-term capital gain rates on the Section 1231 gain.

Section 1245 Property vs. Section 1250 Property

"Section 1245 property" is depreciable property that has been sold at a price in excess of its depreciated value. "Section 1250 property" is generally real property that was previously depreciated and subsequently sold at a gain. This is the important distinction between Section 1245 and Section 1250 property.

Congress' original justification for distinguishing Section 1250 property from Section 1245 property was that Section 1250 property was long-lived, often sold before the end of its useful life, that gains on such property contained a significant inflationary component, and that such gains should therefore be granted capital gains treatment. The difference between these properties deals with the tax treatment of gains upon disposition. The gain recognized on the sale or exchange of Section 1245 property attributable to any previously deducted depreciation allowance is taxed as ordinary gain.

For Section 1250 property, the recapture of depreciation as ordinary income is *limited to* the portion of previously deducted depreciation allowances that are in excess of deductions that would have been taken if they were computed using the straight-line method. Since most buildings are depreciated using only the straight-line method, then taxpayers generally get better treatment on depreciation recapture for Section 1250 property.

Section 1245 Property	Section 1250 Property
Personal property and business property.	Applies to real property (such as residential rentals and factory buildings)
All depreciation is recaptured as ordinary income.	Capital gain attributed to straight-line depreciation is subject to a special 25% maximum rate. This is called "unrecaptured Section 1250 gain."
Any remaining gain after subtracting the depreciation recapture is taxed at capital gain rates.	Any capital gain remaining after subtracting the 25% rate is subject to capital gains rates at a maximum of 15%.
*Note: Losses are never allowed on personal-use property, unless the loss is a casualty loss. Losses are allowed on business use property.	**Exception:** Any accelerated depreciation in excess of straight-line is recaptured as ordinary income.

Section 1245 Property

To be classified as Section 1245 property, the property must be depreciable (or amortizable) in nature. It can be personal tangible or intangible. There are some limited types of real property that count as Section 1245 property. In general, Section 1245 property is defined by the IRS as either:

- Personal (tangible or intangible) property, or
- Other tangible property (not including buildings) that is depreciable and that is:
- Used as an integral part of certain specified activities (manufacturing, production, extraction, or furnishing transportation, communications, electrical energy, gas, water, or sewage disposal services), or
- A facility used for the bulk storage of fungible commodities (examples of highly fungible commodities are crude oil, wheat, etc.)

So in this case, something like a grain silo would be considered Section 1245 property, rather than Section 1250 property (even if it was attached permanently to the land). Storage structures for oil and gas and other minerals would be considered Section 1245 property.

Section 1250 Property

Section 1250 property is depreciable real property that is NOT Section 1245 property. Thus, all personal property is Section 1245, while real property is either Section 1245 property or Section 1250 property, *depending on its use* by the taxpayer. In general, Section 1250 property consists of buildings (including their structural components), other inherently permanent structures, and land improvements of general use and purpose. Some examples of Section 1250 property include:

- Residential rentals
- Factory buildings
- Office buildings

Example: Several years ago, Crystal purchased a used binding machine at auction to use in her business. The cost of the machine was $1,000. Over the years Crystal claimed $400 in depreciation on the machine. In 2010, Crystal sold the machine for $1,100, which was more than what she originally paid. Her gain is figured as follows:

The sale price of the machine:	$1,100
MINUS adjusted basis ($1,000 - $400):	$600
Crystal's overall gain on the sale of the machine:	$500

The allocation of the gain is: $400 in ordinary income (this is the gain from depreciation recapture for Section 1245 property), and $100 in long-term capital gains (this is her gain after subtracting the recapture amount).

This is a very complex area of the Internal Revenue Code. In order to read more on the subject, you can also refer to **IRS Publication 544,** *Sales and Other Dispositions of Assets.*

Installment Sales

An installment sale is the sale of property where the seller receives at least one payment after the tax year of the sale. Each payment on an installment sale usually consists of the following three parts:

- Interest income
- Return of the seller's adjusted basis in the property
- Gain on the sale

If a sale qualifies as an installment sale, the gain must be reported under the *installment method* unless the business elects out of using the installment method. In that case, the business is forced to report all the gain in the year of the sale, even though it may not receive the remaining payments for many years.

Under the *installment method*, after the business has determined how much of each payment to treat as interest, he must treat the rest of each payment as if it were made up of two parts:

- A tax-free return of the adjusted basis in the property, and
- The gain (gain from an installment sale is reported on Form 6252)

A business should multiply the payments received each year (less interest) by the gross profit percentage. The result is considered installment sale income for the tax year. In certain circumstances, the business may be treated as having received a payment, even though it received nothing directly. A receipt of property or the assumption of a mortgage on the property sold may be treated as a payment.

Example: A business sells a machine at a contract price of $6,000, with a gross profit of $1,500, and it will receive payments over four years. The gross profit percentage is 25% ($1,500 ÷ $6,000). After subtracting interest, the business reports 25% of each payment, including the down payment, as installment sale income from the sale for the tax year it receives the payment. The remainder (balance) of each payment is the tax-free return of the machine's adjusted basis.

If the selling price is reduced at a later date, the gross profit on the sale will also change. The seller must then refigure the gross profit percentage for the remaining payments. The taxpayer will spread any remaining gain over future installments.

An installment sale may trigger recapture. If a business reports the sale of property under the installment method, any depreciation recapture under Section 1245 is taxable as ordinary income in the year of sale. This applies even if no payments are received in that year. If the gain is more than the depreciation recapture income, a business must report the rest of the gain using the rules of the installment method. The regular sale of inventory is not an installment sale even if the business receives a payment after the year of sale. Form 6252 is used to report installment sale income. An installment sale does not include:

- The sale of inventory
- A sale that results in a loss
- The sale of publicly traded property (such as stocks or bonds)
- The sale of depreciable property between related parties

The portion of each payment that is characterized as interest income is reported by the seller as ordinary income.

Example: In 2009, the Greenbelt Partnership sold land to a buyer under an installment sale. The land had a basis of $40,000, and the sale price was $100,000. Therefore, the gross profit was $60,000. Greenbelt received a $20,000 down payment and the buyer's note for $80,000. The note provides for four annual payments of $20,000 each, plus 8% interest, beginning in 2010. Greenbelt's gross profit percentage is 60%. Greenbelt reported a gain of $12,000 on each payment received in 2009 and 2010. In 2011, Greenbelt and the buyer agreed to reduce the purchase price to $85,000, and payments during 2011, 2012, and 2013 are reduced to $15,000 for each year. The new gross profit percentage is 46.67%. Greenbelt will report a gain of $7,000 (46.67% of $15,000) on each of the $15,000 installments due in 2011, 2012, and 2013.

Forms Used to Report Dispositions

Businesses must often use multiple forms to report a single disposition. The common forms a business uses to report dispositions are:

- Form 4797, *Sales of Business Property*
- Form 8824, *Like-Kind Exchanges*

491

- Form 6252, *Installment Sale Income*
- Form 4684, *Casualties and Thefts*
- Form 4797, *Sales of Business Property* (also used for condemned property)

Summary: Basis and Depreciation

Depreciation is a tax deduction that allows a business to recover the cost of property. It is an annual allowance for the wear and tear, deterioration, or obsolescence of the property. Most tangible property (except land), such as buildings, machinery, vehicles, furniture, and equipment are depreciable. Intangible property, such as patents and copyrights are amortizable. In order for a taxpayer to be allowed a depreciation deduction for a property, the property must meet all the following requirements:

- The taxpayer (or entity) must own the property.
- A taxpayer must use the property in business or in an income-producing activity.
- The property must have a useful life of more than one year.

Depreciation begins when a taxpayer places property in service. The property ceases to be depreciable when the taxpayer has fully recovered the property's cost or other basis or when the taxpayer retires it from service, whichever happens first.

Section 179

Section 179 is a type of accelerated depreciation that applies to both new and used equipment. If the business-use of any property is 50% or less, the taxpayer cannot take a Section 179 deduction. In 2010, the maximum Section 179 deduction is $500,000 with a phase-out at $2 million. In 2010, Section 179 also applies to specific types of real property. The Section 179 deduction for real property is limited to $250,000.

Bonus Depreciation

Bonus Depreciation and Section 179 are not the same thing.

- Bonus Depreciation applies to new equipment only.
- It is allowed for both regular and Alternative Minimum Tax purposes.
- It is elective; a business need not claim the depreciation bonus.
- It is not subject to the same $2 million phase-out as Section 179.
- 100% Bonus Depreciation applies to assets placed in service between September 9, 2010 and December 31, 2011. 50% Bonus Depreciation applies to assets placed in service between January 1, 2010 and September 8, 2010.

Unit 2.6: Questions

1. Which of the following vehicles used directly in a trade is considered "listed property" for tax purposes?

A. An ambulance
B. A passenger automobile weighing 6,000 pounds or less
C. A cellular phone
D. A van that transports property for hire

The answer is B. The IRS considers passenger automobiles weighing 6,000 pounds or less as listed property. The IRS no longer automatically considers cellular phones as listed property. ###

2. Jade purchases a condemned warehouse for her business, but it is in such bad condition that she decides to demolish it and build a new one. The demolition costs $15,600. How must Jade report these costs on her tax return?

A. The cost for the demolition is added to the basis of the land where the original demolished structure was located.
B. The demolition may be expensed on her tax return on Schedule E.
C. The demolition cost is an itemized deduction on her Schedule A.
D. The demolition cost must be amortized over 180 months.

The answer is A. Demolition costs or other losses related to the demolition of any building are added to the basis of the land (Publication 551). ###

3. What item would NOT be included in an asset's basis?

A. Sales tax
B. Installation charges
C. Recording fees
D. Interest paid on a loan to purchase the asset

The answer is D. Interest charges are not added to an asset's basis. Interest is a currently deductible expense. ###

4. Ian buys a building. He makes a $15,000 down payment in cash. He also assumes a mortgage of $180,000 on it and pays $1,000 in title fees and $2,000 in points. What is Ian's basis in the building?

A. $15,000
B. $195,000
C. $196,000
D. $198,000

The answer is C. Ian's basis is $196,000. The title fees, mortgage amount, and the down payment would all be added together to figure the original cost basis of the building. The points would not be included in the basis. Points are prepaid interest on a loan and are deducted as interest, rather than added to basis. ###

5. Levi owns a florist shop. He purchases two computers from his grandfather and places both in service in 2010 as part of a bona fide business transaction. The computers cost $350 each. Which of the following is true?

A. Levi can take a Section 179 deduction for both computers.
B. Levi can take regular MACRS depreciation on the computers.
C. Levi is not allowed to depreciate the computers since they were purchased from a related party.
D. None of the above.

The answer is B. The computers do not qualify as Section 179 property because Levi and his grandfather are related persons, meaning Levi cannot claim a Section 179 deduction. However, Levi may still depreciate the computers using MACRS depreciation. ###

6. Which of the following types of business property qualify for the Section 179 accelerated depreciation deduction?

A. A delivery truck
B. A business building
C. A residential rental property
D. A patent

The answer is A. To qualify for the Section 179 deduction, the property must be tangible personal property. Buildings, houses, and other real property generally do not qualify for Section 179 treatment. Intangible assets, such as patents and copyrights, must be amortized over their useful life. ###

7. Lou bought a cellular phone for $720 in 2010 and wants to take the Section 179 deduction. Based on his phone records, Lou uses the cell phone 45% for business use and 55% for personal use. What is Lou's Section 179 deduction for 2010?

A. $0
B. $324
C. $396
D. $720

The answer is A. When a taxpayer uses property for both business and non-business purposes, he can elect the Section 179 deduction ONLY if he uses the property more than 50% for business in the year the asset is placed into service. Lou may still choose to use another depreciation method for the business portion. ###

8. Mary purchases a video camera for her photography business and wants to take the Section 179 depreciation deduction. The video camera costs $1,100. She uses the property 80% for her business and 20% for personal purposes. What is Mary's Section 179 depreciation deduction?

A. $220
B. $660
C. $880
D. $1,100

The answer is C. The business part of the cost of the property is $880 (80% × $1,100). ###

9. Kerman Corporation is a calendar-year, cash-basis corporation that specializes in constructing office buildings. Kerman bought a truck on December 1, 2010 that had to be modified to lift materials to second-story levels. After the lifting equipment was installed, Kerman accepted delivery of the modified truck on January 10, 2011. The truck was placed in service on January 12, 2011, the date it was ready and available to perform the function for which it was bought. When can Kerman start depreciating the truck?

A. Never
B. 2009
C. 2010
D. 2011

The answer is D. Kerman may not depreciate the truck until it is placed in service for business use (Publication 946). ###

10. Which of the following property can a business NOT depreciate?

A. Property placed in service and disposed of in the same year
B. Intangible assets
C. Machinery
D. Buildings

The answer is A. Property placed in service and disposed of in the same year is not depreciated. Business property ceases to be depreciable when the taxpayer has fully recovered the property's cost or when the taxpayer disposes of it. If a business buys and then disposes of an asset in the same year, it would not be depreciated. ###

11. All of the following items DECREASE the basis of property except:

A. Casualty or theft loss deductions and insurance reimbursements
B. The cost of defending a title
C. Section 179 deduction
D. Depreciation

The answer is B. The cost of defending the title to a property or other legal fees INCREASES the basis of a property. INCREASES to basis include:

- The cost of improvements having a useful life of more than a year
- Assessments for local improvements
- Sales tax
- The cost of extending utility lines
- Legal fees, including the cost of defending or perfecting title
- Zoning costs

Decreases to basis include but are not limited to:

- Depreciation, amortization, and depletion deductions
- Nontaxable corporate distributions
- Insurance reimbursements for casualty and theft losses
- Easements
- Rebates from the manufacturer or seller ###

-

12. Priscilla's Pastries, a sole proprietorship, bought a building for $250,000 in cash in March 2009. Priscilla paid the title company $13,000 in settlement fees to purchase the property. She also assumed an existing mortgage of $35,000 on the property. Legal fees of $9,500 were incurred in a title dispute in 2010. What is Priscilla's basis in the building in December 2010?

A: $250,000
B: $285,000
C: $307,500
D: $309,500

The answer is C. The basis is $307,500 ($250,000 + $13,000 + $35,000 + $9,500). The settlement fees, mortgage assumed by the buyer, and the legal fees for defending a title are all included in the basis of the property. Priscilla cannot deduct the cost of the legal fees on her tax return as an expense. Instead, the amount must be added to the basis and depreciated under the straight-line method (MARCS for buildings). ###

13. Which of the following is NOT Section 1245 property?

A. Computer
B. Office building
C. Display shelving
D. Grain silo

The answer is B. Section 1245 property does NOT include real estate such as buildings and structural components; therefore, the office building would not be included. Storage structures such as oil and gas storage tanks, grain storage bins, and silos are not treated as buildings, but as Section 1245 property (Publication 225). ###

14. The maximum Section 179 expense a business can elect to deduct for Qualified Real Property placed in service in tax year 2010 is:

A: $179,000
B: $250,000
C: $500,000
D: $2 million

The answer is B. Also in 2010, there is a special rule that allows taxpayers to deduct up to $250,000 of Qualified Real Property (QRP) under Section 179. This special allowance for QRP is part of the maximum $500,000 Section 179 limit. So, for example, a taxpayer can have $250,000 of QRP and $250,000 of other business property to make up the $500,000 Section 179 maximum depreciation allowance (Publication 946). The overall maximum Section 179 deduction businesses can elect for property is $500,000. ###

15. Which of the following dispositions of depreciable property would trigger depreciation recapture?

A. Installment sale
B. Gift
C. Transfer at death
D. Section 1031 exchange where no money or unlike property is received

The answer is A. An installment sale can trigger recapture. If a business reports the sale of previously depreciated property under the installment method, any depreciation recapture under Section 1245 or 1250 is taxable as ordinary income in the year of sale (Publication 544). ###

16. The Friendship Partnership bought the Andrews Partnership. The goodwill and covenant not to compete associated with the purchase of this business was valued at $100,000. Per Section 197, what is the number of years over which goodwill can be amortized?

A. 5 years
B. 10 years
C. 15 years
D. 25 years

The answer is C. Goodwill is a Section 197 intangible. A business must amortize over 15 years the capitalized costs of Section 197 intangibles. ###

17. Which of the following would NOT qualify for a depletion deduction?

A. Oil well
B. Timber
C. Diamond mine
D. Gasoline refinery factory

The answer is D. A gasoline refinery would not qualify since it is not the depletion of a natural resource but is instead a factory that refines the product. Depletion is the exhaustion of natural resources, such as mines, wells, and timber, as a result of production. ###

18. Tom owns a construction business. He would like to switch all of his assets to straight-line depreciation for easier accounting and tracking of the assets. Which of the following statements is FALSE?

A. A business may switch to the straight-line method at any time during the useful life of the property without IRS consent.
B. A business must always request permission from the IRS to switch to the straight-line method.
C. When the change to straight-line is made, depreciation is figured based on the taxpayer's adjusted basis in the property at that time.
D. Tom can choose to switch all of his assets to straight-line no matter what type of depreciation method he has been using previously.

The answer is B. A business may switch to the straight-line method at any time during the useful life of the property without IRS consent. ###

Unit 2.7: Partnerships

More Reading:
Publication 541, *Partnerships*

A Partnership Defined

An unincorporated business with two or more members is generally classified as a partnership for federal tax purposes. A partnership is a pass-through entity. Its major advantage is that it is not taxed on its income. Instead, income and loss is figured on the partnership level, then distributed to the partners, and is only taxed at the individual partner level. In this respect, a partnership is similar to a sole proprietorship. In a partnership, all the deductions, losses, and credits "flow through" to the owners. In a partnership, each partner obtains a basis in his own partnership interest. A partner's basis can occur during the formation of a partnership, or it can be acquired by gift or purchase. The partner's basis increases when the partnership earns income. The partner's basis decreases when the partnership incurs a loss. Partnership basis is covered in more detail later in this unit.

A partnership reports income and loss on Form 1065, with its tax return due on the 15th day of the fourth month following the close of the tax year. Since most partnerships are calendar-year partnerships (rather than fiscal year), the partnership tax return is due on the same day as individual returns (normally April 15 but April 18 in 2011.) Partnerships are required to furnish a Schedule K-1 to each partner by the due date (including extensions) of the partnership tax return. The individual partners then report their share of partnership income on Schedule E of Form 1040. Schedule E is used to report many different types of activity, including income (or loss) from partnerships, rental real estate, royalties, Subchapter S Corporations, estates, and trusts.

Because partners are not considered employees of the partnership, no withholding is taken out of their distributions to pay the income and self-employment taxes on their Forms 1040. General partners of a partnership are considered to be self-employed and therefore must pay estimated payments just like other self-employed individuals.

A partnership may request a five-month extension to file, unlike individuals and corporations that may request a six-month extension. A calendar-year partnership requesting an extension to file a partnership tax return (Form 1065) will have an extension granted until September 15 instead of until October 15 as it used to be.

Every partnership must file an information return unless it has no activity whatsoever, with no income or loss during the year. The partnership return must show the names and addresses of each partner and each partner's distributive share of taxable income. The partnership return must be signed by a general partner. If a Limited Liability Company is treated as a partnership, it must file Form 1065 and one of its general partners must sign the return.

The partnership must furnish copies of Schedule K-1 to the partners by the partnership return due date or the extended due date. Limited partners are subject to self-employment tax only on guaranteed payments, such as salary and professional fees for services rendered.

The IRS requires partnerships with more than 100 partners (Schedules K-1) to file their returns electronically. Partnerships with 100 or fewer partners are not required to electronically file their returns. If a partnership fails to file electronically when it is required to do so, it must pay a penalty. There is an exception for partnerships that cannot file electronically (either because the e-file is rejected, or the return requires paper attachments, etc.)

Example: Lovett Partnership is a calendar-year, cash-basis partnership that is required to file a Form 1065 every year. The partnership has five partners, so it is also required to furnish each partner a Schedule K-1 for his or her share of partnership income. Profits and losses are passed through to the partners on Schedule K-1 and then taxed on the partners' individual tax returns.

Unlike a corporation, a partnership does not require any formal legal documents. A partnership must have at least two partners and at least one of them must be a "general partner." A joint undertaking merely to share expenses is not a partnership. For example, co-ownership of rental property is not a partnership unless the co-owners provide services to the tenants.

Example: Will and Todd are brothers, and they co-own a single residential rental that they inherited from their mother. They use a management company to run the property. Will and Todd are not partners, and their co-ownership of the property does not automatically create a partnership.

General Partnership vs. Limited Partnership

A partnership can either be a "general partnership" or a "limited partnership." In the case of a general partnership, all the partners have unlimited liability for partnership debts. This is not the case in a limited partnership. In a limited partnership, at least one partner is a "limited partner." Limited partners are only liable for partnership liabilities up to their investment in the partnership. Limited partners generally cannot participate in the management or the day-to-day administration of the partnership.

A limited partner has no obligation to contribute additional capital to the partnership and therefore does not have an economic risk of loss in partnership recourse liabilities. In this respect, a limited partner acts more like an investor than anything else. Limited partners are not subject to self-employment tax on their distributive share of income.

A limited partnership is formed under state limited liability law. A limited partnership can have an unlimited number of investors, but there must always be at least one general partner.

Limited Liability Company

A Limited Liability Company (LLC) is an entity formed under state law by filing articles of organization as an LLC. An LLC is not the same thing as an LLP (Limited Liability Partnership). Unlike a partnership, none of the members of an LLC are personally liable for its debts. An LLC may be classified for federal income tax purposes as a partnership, a corporation, or a disregarded entity. The owners of a Limited Liability Company are the ones that make the election on how they wish to be taxed. For example, a two-person LLC will automatically be taxed as a partnership if the owners do not make an election. A domestic LLC with two or more members will automatically be treated as a partnership for tax purposes if it does NOT file Form 8832, *Entity Classification Election*.

Limited Liability Partnership

A Limited Liability Partnership (LLP) is different from a Limited Liability Company (LLC). Usually, the owners of Limited Liability Partnerships offer professional services (attorneys, doctors, etc.) This entity type protects individual partners from liability for the malpractice of other partners. However, all the partners remain liable for the general debts of the partnership. A Limited Liability Partnership is an older entity type.

The Partnership Agreement

A partner's distributive share of income, gain, loss, deduction, or credit is generally determined by the partnership agreement. The term "partnership agreement" is very broad and refers to any agreement among the partners that defines income allocation. Any written document or oral agreement that bears on the underlying economic arrangement of the partners is considered to be part of the partnership agreement. Examples of such documents include:

- Loan and credit agreements
- Assumption agreements
- Indemnification agreements
- Subordination agreements
- Correspondence with a lender concerning terms of a loan
- Loan guarantees

A partnership agreement must be agreed on by all partners. It may be modified during the tax year and even after the tax year has closed. However, the partnership agreement cannot be modified after the due date for filing the partnership return for that year (not including extensions).

> **Example:** Terry and Dawn run a cash-basis, calendar-year partnership. They split the proceeds 50-50. In 2010, they both decide to alter the partnership agreement. They have until the due date of the partnership return (April 18, 2011) to change the partnership agreement. Filing for an extension does not give them additional time to change the partnership agreement after the tax year has closed.

A Partnership's Tax Year

A partnership generally must conform to the tax year of the partners. This means that, in general, partnerships report income on a calendar year. However, a partnership may request a fiscal year based on a legitimate business purpose. In order to qualify as a "legitimate business purpose," the partnership must be able to prove that the decision to adopt a different tax year is not simply to defer income.

A partnership may request filing on a fiscal tax year based on a "natural business year." This would be when a business closes its books after its busiest or most profitable period. A "natural business year" is a 12-month period where at least 25% of total gross receipts are received in the last two months of the year.

> **Example:** John and Kate run a seasonal business making pool equipment. Their busiest time of the year is during the summer months, and over 60% of their income is received during June and July. John and Kate may request a different tax year based on a legitimate business purpose—that is, the "natural tax year" of their seasonal business.

A partnership may also request a Section 444 election (explained previously in the unit on "Entities and Recordkeeping.")

Ineligible Organizations

Some organizations are prohibited from being classified as partnerships. The following organizations CANNOT be classified as partnerships:

- A corporation (although a corporation can be a partner in a partnership)
- Any joint-stock company or joint-stock association
- An insurance company
- Certain banks
- A government entity
- An organization required to be taxed as a corporation by the IRS
- Certain foreign organizations
- Any tax-exempt (nonprofit) organization
- Any Real Estate Investment Trust (REIT)
- Any organization classified as a trust or estate
- Any other organization that elects to be classified as a corporation by filing Form 8832

Family Partnerships

Members of a family can be legitimate partners and form a partnership together. However, family members will be recognized as partners only if ONE of the following requirements is met:

- If capital is a material income-producing factor, the family members must have acquired their capital interest in a bona fide transaction (even if by gift or purchase from another family member); actually own the partnership interest; and actually control the interest. This means that a family member who acquires a partnership interest from another family member needs to treat the activity as a bona fide business activity.
- If capital is NOT a material income-producing factor, the family members must have joined together in good faith to conduct a business. They must have agreed that contributions of each entitle them to a share in the profits and that some capital or service is provided by each partner.

For purposes of determining a partner's distributive share, an interest purchased by one family member from another family member is considered a gift from the seller. The Fair Market Value of the purchased interest is considered donated capital. For this purpose, members of a family include ONLY spouses, ancestors, and lineal descendants (grandson, daughter, son, stepson, etc.) Cousins, uncles, etc., would not be considered family members for this purpose.

Under the "related party transaction rules," an individual is considered as also owning the partnership interest directly or indirectly owned by his or her family. Members of a family, for figuring related persons for partnership interest, include only brothers, sisters, half-brothers, half-sisters, spouses, ancestors, parents, and lineal descendants (children, grandchildren). A loss on the sale or exchange of property between related persons is not deductible. This applies to both direct and indirect transactions.

Capital: Material or Not?

Capital is a material "income-producing factor" if a substantial part of the gross income of the business comes from the use of capital. Capital (investment) is an "income-producing factor" if the operation of the business requires substantial inventories or investments in plants, machinery, or equipment.

In general, capital is NOT an "income-producing factor" if the income of the business consists principally of fees, commissions, or other compensation for personal services performed by members or employees of the partnership.

Capital Interests

A "capital interest" in a partnership is an interest in its assets that is distributable to the owner of the interest in either of the following situations:

- The owner withdraws from the partnership
- The partnership liquidates

The right to share in earnings and profits is not a capital interest in the partnership.

> **Example:** Alexia and Aaron form a partnership in order to open a restaurant together. Aaron is an experienced restaurant manager, but he has no money to invest. Alexia owns the building and the restaurant equipment. Alexia's basis in the assets is $100,000. Therefore, Alexia has a "capital interest" in the partnership. Aaron does not.

Community Property

A husband and wife who own a business jointly can choose to classify the entity as a partnership for federal tax purposes by filing a partnership tax return. In a community property state, married couples can also choose to classify the entity as a sole proprietorship by filing a Schedule C (Form 1040) listing one spouse as the sole proprietor. A change in reporting position will be treated for federal tax purposes as a conversion of the entity.

Special Partnership Allocations

Unlike S Corporations that must report all income and expenses in proportion to stock ownership, partnerships allow more flexibility with income allocation. Special allocations of income, gain, loss, or deductions can be made between the partners.

For example, a partnership agreement may allocate all of the depreciation deductions to one partner. Additionally, a partnership agreement may specify that the partners may share capital, profits, and losses in different ratios. Stated differently, the sharing of profits does not have to coincide with the sharing of losses. Partnership agreements can be written to reflect whatever economic sharing and risk sharing arrangements the parties wish to execute.

> **Example:** Pandora and Jayne form a partnership to sell their clothing line. Pandora, who has design and sewing skills, goes into business with Jayne, who has the money to invest. Jayne contributes $100,000 in cash to the partnership. Pandora and Jayne agree to split the business profits 20/80 until Jayne recovers her entire investment; thereafter, profits are split 50/50.

Special allocations permit partners to assume different levels of risk and to set the timing of income in accordance with their preferences.

503

Such flexibility comes with some strings attached. Partners are not able to allocate tax benefits among themselves in a manner that is divorced from their allocation of economic profit or loss. A partner who is economically enriched by an item of partnership income or gain is required to shoulder the associated tax burden. Similarly, a partner who is economically hurt by an item of partnership loss is allocated the tax benefit of the loss. Tax allocations must conform to the economics of the partnership's transactions.

Partnership Startup and Organization Costs

Just like sole proprietorships and other businesses, partnerships are allowed to deduct a portion of their startup costs. The Small-Business Jobs Act of 2010 increased the partnership deduction for startup costs to $10,000, for this tax year only. This amount is phased out by the amount by which the total cost of startup expenditures exceeds $60,000. If the total costs exceed the phase-out, the deduction for startup costs is disallowed. In that case, all the partnership's startup costs may be amortized over 15 years (180 months).

Guaranteed Payments

Guaranteed payments are payments made to a partner by a partnership, which are determined without regard to partnership income. These are treated like "guaranteed pay" to a particular partner. Guaranteed payments are not the same as partnership distributions, because sometimes a partnership will be required to make a guaranteed payment to a partner, even if it has a loss. Guaranteed payments are usually outlined in a formal partnership agreement. The concept of guaranteed payments is tested heavily on the Enrolled Agent Exam.

Guaranteed payments are included in income in the partner's tax year in which the partnership's tax year ends. They are considered ordinary income to the partner and can cause a loss to the partnership. If so, the partner who receives a guaranteed payment would report the full amount of the payment as ordinary income on his individual tax return, and the partner would also report his distributive share of the partnership losses.

Example: Erica is a partner in the Baker Partnership. Under the terms of her partnership agreement, she is entitled to a guaranteed payment of $10,000 per year, regardless of how profitable the partnership is. In 2010, Erica's distributive share of partnership income is 10%. Baker Partnership has $50,000 of ordinary income after deducting Erica's guaranteed payment. She must include ordinary income of $15,000 ($10,000 guaranteed payment + $5,000 [$50,000 × 10%] distributive share) on her individual income tax return (Form 1040).

The partnership generally deducts guaranteed payments made to partners on Line 10 of Form 1065 as a business expense. They are also listed on Schedules K and Schedules K-1 of the partnership return. The individual partner then reports guaranteed payments on Schedule E (Form 1040) as ordinary income, along with her distributive share of the partnership's other ordinary income.

Contributions to a Partnership

When a partnership first forms, the partners will contribute property or cash in order to get a business started. Generally, no gain or loss is recognized when a partner contributes money or property to a partnership in exchange for his partnership interest. This is true whether the contribution occurs during partnership formation, or after the partnership has

504

already been in existence. However, there are some limited instances where a partner's contribution can create gain or loss recognition. Gain or loss must be recognized in the following situations:

- When property is contributed (in exchange for an interest in the partnership) to a partnership that would be treated as an investment company if it were incorporated. A partnership is treated as an investment company if over 80% of the value of its assets is held for investment in securities, such as stocks and bonds. This rule applies to limited partnerships and general partnerships, regardless of whether they are privately formed or publicly syndicated.

- Gain is also recognized if contributed property is then distributed to a different partner within seven years of the original contribution date. The contributing partner would recognize gain on the difference between the Fair Market Value and the adjusted basis of the property as of the contribution date. The character of the gain or loss will be the same that would have resulted if the partnership had sold the property to the distributee partner. This rule is designed to prevent partners from shifting assets around to each other in order to mask revenue.

Gain is also recognized when a partner contributes property to a partnership and then receives an immediate distribution. In this case, the transaction is a "disguised sale." A "disguised sale" is not treated as a contribution and a subsequent distribution. Instead, it is treated as a sale of property, if BOTH of the following tests are met:

- The distribution would not have been made if the initial contribution had not occurred.

- The partner's right to the distribution does not depend on the success of partnership operations.

When a partner contributes property to a partnership, the basis and the holding period of the asset are carried over. For example, if a partner contributes a building with an FMV of $100,000 and a basis of $50,000, the basis of the building in the hands of the partnership would be the same: $50,000.

Contribution of Services to a Partnership

A partner can acquire an interest in a partnership in exchange for services performed. If a partner receives a partnership interest as compensation for services, the partner must recognize the income as ordinary income. The Fair Market Value of a partnership interest that is transferred to an individual in exchange for services is treated as a guaranteed payment.

Example: Heidi is an attorney who contributes her services to a partnership in exchange for a 10% partnership interest. The Fair Market Value of the partnership interest is $3,000. Heidi is required to recognize $3,000 in ordinary income, and her basis in the partnership is $3,000. The payment is deducted by the partnership as a guaranteed payment and taxable to Heidi.

The FMV of the partnership interest received by a partner as compensation for services must be included in the partner's gross income in the first tax year in which the partner can transfer the interest.

Basis of Partner's Interest

The adjusted basis of a partner's partnership interest is ordinarily determined at the end of the partnership's tax year. However, if there has been a sale or exchange of all or part of a partner's interest or a liquidation of his entire interest in a partnership, the adjusted basis is determined on the date of sale, exchange, or liquidation. The basis of a partnership interest includes:

- The money or investment contributed by a partner
- Plus the adjusted basis of any assets/property the partner contributes
- Plus the amount of partnership liabilities the partner assumes

If the partner must recognize a gain as a result of her partnership contribution, this gain is included in the basis of her interest. Sometimes a partner will be required to recognize a gain when the partner contributes an asset to the partnership that is subject to liability. Any increase in a partner's individual liabilities because of his assumption of partnership liabilities is treated as a contribution of money to the partnership by the partner.

In a cash-basis partnership, any liabilities that are accrued but unpaid are not included in the basis calculation for each individual partner.

Loss Limitations

The amount of loss that a partner is allowed to deduct on her individual tax return is based directly on the partner's basis in the partnership. In general, a partner cannot deduct losses that exceed her partnership basis. Losses that are disallowed due to insufficient basis must be carried forward until the partner can deduct them in a later year.

Remember, however, that partnership debts can *increase* a partner's individual basis. So, for example, if a partner takes out a $50,000 loan in order to finance partnership operations and he personally guarantees the debt, then the partner is allowed to take losses due to his debt basis as well.

> **Example:** Rebecca invests $1,000 in the Andrews Partnership in return for a 10% partnership interest. The Andrews Partnership takes out a $500,000 loan and incurs $100,000 in losses during the first year. Rebecca's share of partnership liabilities would increase her basis to $51,000 [$1,000 cash investment + ($500,000 × 10%). Therefore, Rebecca's share of the loss is $10,000 ($100,000 × 10%). Rebecca is allowed to deduct the entire loss, because her partnership basis was increased by debt basis.

This only applies if the partner is at risk for the loss. If the partner does not have any personal liability to satisfy the debt, then losses are limited by the **at-risk rules.** The at-risk rules limit the deductibility of losses to the partner's basis *reduced* by their share of any nonrecourse debt. Basically, this means that a partner is prohibited from taking losses based on partnership liabilities unless the partner would be forced to satisfy the debt with their personal assets. This is what it means to be "at risk." The rules prevent abusive deductions from real estate and other tax shelter activities.

Understanding Partnership Liabilities

It is very important to understand the concepts regarding partnership liabilities. This is because partnership liabilities can affect individual partner basis. Gains and losses can also be triggered when liabilities are allocated to other partners. A partner (or related person) is considered to assume a partnership liability when:

- He or she is personally liable for it,
- The creditor knows that the liability was assumed by the partner or related person,
- The creditor can demand payment from the partner or related person, and
- No other partner or person related to another partner will bear the economic risk of loss on that liability immediately after the assumption.

The effect of liabilities on the individual partner's basis depends mainly on two factors:

- Whether or not the liability is recourse or nonrecourse
- Whether or not the partner is a general partner or a limited partner

Non-recourse liabilities

A non-recourse liability is when a creditor has no claim against the owner of the property. At most, the creditor may have a claim against an item of property. Non-recourse liabilities are usually secured by an asset, such as a house or car. An example of this would be a home loan where the bank's only recourse in case of default is to repossess the house. A partnership liability is considered a "non-recourse liability" if no partner has an economic risk of loss for that liability.

> **Example:** Reuben purchases a used van for use in his business. He is unable to make the payments. The loan is a non-recourse loan because the only thing the lender can do is repossess the vehicle. The lender cannot "go after" Reuben for the remainder of the loan or for any unpaid liability.

A partner's share of non-recourse liabilities is proportionate to her share of partnership profits. A partner's basis in a partnership interest includes the partner's share of a partnership liability only if the liability:

- Creates or increases the partnership's basis in any of its assets
- Gives rise to a current deduction to the partnership, or
- Is a nondeductible, noncapital expense of the partnership

Recourse liabilities

A partnership liability is a "recourse liability" when the individual partners have an economic risk of loss for that liability. A partner's share of a "recourse liability" would equal his economic risk of loss for that liability. A partner has an "economic risk of loss" if that partner would be obligated to make payments to a creditor.

Essentially, this means that a creditor would be able to pursue the individual partners in order to satisfy the debt. Partners generally share recourse liabilities based on their ratios for sharing losses. Limited partners are simply investors and are therefore not subject to this rule, so a limited partner's basis neither increases nor decreases in regard to the partnership's recourse liabilities.

Decreases in a Partner's Basis

A partner's basis can also decrease for a variety of reasons. If a partner's share of partnership liabilities decreases, this decrease is treated as a distribution of money to the partner by the partnership.

If contributed property is subject to a debt and the debt is assumed by the partnership, the basis of that partner's interest is reduced (but not below zero) by the liability assumed by the other partners.

This partner must reduce her basis because the assumption of the liability is treated as a distribution of money to that partner. The other partners' assumption of the liability is treated as a contribution by them of money to the partnership. A partner's individual partnership basis is *decreased* by the following items:

- The money and adjusted basis of property distributed to the partner by the partnership.
- The partner's distributive share of the partnership losses.
- The partner's distributive share of nondeductible partnership expenses that are not capital expenditures. This includes the partner's share of any Section 179 expenses, even if the partner cannot deduct the entire amount on his individual income tax return.
- The partner's deduction for depletion for any partnership oil and gas wells, up to the proportionate share of the adjusted basis of the wells allocated to the partner.

Example: Jeremy acquired a 20% interest in a partnership by contributing a moving van that had an adjusted basis to him of $8,000 and a $4,000 loan attached to it. The partnership assumed payment of the auto loan. The basis of Jeremy's interest is:

Adjusted basis of contributed property	$8,000
Minus: Part of mortgage assumed by other partners (80% × $4,000)	($3,200)
Basis of Jeremy's partnership interest	$4,800

---

*Note: A partner's basis can NEVER go below zero. So, in order to prevent a negative basis, a partner must recognize gain equal to the amount that the decrease in a partner share of liability exceeds his basis.

Example: Raymond acquired a 20% interest in a partnership by contributing an asset that had an adjusted basis to him of $8,000 and a $12,000 loan attached to it. Since the value of the asset is less than the amount of the liability, Raymond's partnership basis is zero. The $1,600 difference between the mortgage assumed by the other partners, $9,600 (80% × $12,000), and his basis of $8,000 would be treated as capital gain from the sale or exchange of a partnership interest. However, this gain would not increase the basis of his partnership interest. His partnership basis would remain zero.

Separately Stated Items

Partnership income is figured similarly to individual income. There are some deductions that are not allowed at the partnership level, and some items of income and loss must be separately stated on the tax return. These are called "separately stated items." The reason why these items are separately stated is because they "flow-through" to the partners with a specific character. For example, if a partnership makes a charitable contribution, it must list

508

the charitable contribution as a separately stated item. This is because the charitable contribution "flows-through" to the individual partners. The individual partners would then report their share of the charitable contribution on their Schedule A.

Separately stated items are heavily tested on the EA Exam. In order to figure taxable income, all the partnership income must first be divided into:

- Separately stated items, and
- Ordinary income or loss.

The IRC establishes which items must be "separately stated" on the partnership tax return. These items are separately stated so the IRS can ensure that the items retain their character as they are passed through to the partner level. The following items must be separately stated:

- Net short-term capital gains and losses
- Net long-term capital gains and losses
- Charitable contributions
- Dividends eligible for a dividends-received deduction
- Taxes paid to a foreign country
- Taxes paid to a U.S. possession (Guam, Puerto Rico, etc.)
- Section 1231 gains and losses
- Section 179 deductions and Bonus Depreciation
- Any tax-exempt income and expenses related to the tax-exempt income
- Investment income and related investment expenses
- Rental income, portfolio income, and related expenses
- Any recovery items (such as bad debt)

Any item of income that is not a separately stated item is classified simply as ordinary income. Ordinary income is not the same thing as "taxable income." Taxable income includes ordinary income, all the separately stated items, and any other adjustments, such as business expenses and cost of goods sold.

Example: The Stevenson Partnership operates as an accrual-based partnership. Its gross receipts for 2010 were $250,000. In addition to those gross receipts, the company also had the following items of income and expenses:

Liability insurance	($5,000)
Charitable contributions	($2,000)
Continuing education	($9,000)
Rental income	$25,000
Guaranteed payments to partners	($15,000)

The ordinary income for the Stevenson partnership is figured as follows:

Gross income:	$250,000
MINUS Liability insurance	$5,000
Continuing education	$9,000
Guaranteed payments to partners	$15,000
The ordinary income is therefore:	**$221,000**

The rental income and charitable contributions are NOT figured into the ordinary income of the partnership. Instead, these are separately stated items that pass through to the partners and retain their character (just like they would for a sole-proprietorship). Guaranteed payments are deductible to the partnership because they are treated like wages and are therefore deductible to the partnership and taxable to the partners.

Disallowed Deductions

There are a number of deductions that are allowed to individuals, but that cannot be claimed as expenses by partnerships. These deductions are instead passed through to the individual partners, and the partners may then take them on their own individual returns. The following deductions cannot be taken by a partnership:

- Personal exemptions
- Taxes paid to a foreign country or to a U.S. possession
- Charitable contributions
- Oil and gas depletion
- Net Operating Loss (NOL) carryback or carryover

Increases to Partnership Basis in General

Certain things will increase a partner's basis in the partnership. If a partner's share of partnership liabilities increases, this increase is treated as if the partner contributed money to the partnership. A partner's basis will be increased by the following items:

- The partner's additional cash contributions to the partnership
- The partner's increased share (or assumption of) partnership liabilities
- The partner's share of partnership income
- The partner's distributive share of the excess of the deductions for depletion over the basis of the depletable property

Example: Sam and Abdul have a partnership. Sam contributes a machine to his partnership that has an adjusted basis of $400 and an FMV of $1,000. Abdul contributes $1,000 cash. While each partner has increased his capital account by $1,000, which will be reflected in the partnership books, the adjusted basis of Sam's interest is only $400 and Abdul's partnership interest is $1,000.

Partnership Distributions

Every partner is taxed on his distributive share of income, whether or not it is actually distributed. Unless there is a complete liquidation of a partner's interest, the basis of property (other than cash) distributed to the partner is its adjusted basis to the partnership immediately before the distribution. However, the basis of the property distributed to the partner cannot be more than the adjusted basis of his interest in the partnership, reduced by any money received in the same transaction, as seen in the example below:

Example: The adjusted basis of Beth's partnership interest is $30,000. She receives a distribution of land that has an adjusted basis of $20,000 to the partnership. She also receives a distribution of $4,000 in cash. Her basis for the land is $20,000.

> **Example:** The basis of Mike's partnership interest is $10,000. He receives a distribution of $4,000 cash and a parcel of land that has an adjusted basis to the partnership of $8,000. His basis for the land is limited to $6,000 ($10,000 - $4,000, the cash he receives), since the total amount cannot exceed his partnership interest.

Distributions in Excess of Basis

If a partner has distributions that exceed her basis during any taxable year, the excess is treated as a capital gain to the partner. This occurs when a partner's share of the decrease in partnership liabilities during the taxable year and the cash distributions received by the partner during the taxable year exceed the basis of the partner's partnership interest.

However, if a partner's losses for the year exceed his basis, then the losses are limited to the basis of his partnership interest (there are some exceptions to this rule in a partnership liquidation). Any partnership losses and deductions that exceed the partner's basis may be carried forward indefinitely until the partner's basis in the partnership increases.

Figuring the Adjusted Basis of a Partnership Interest

The basis of an interest in a partnership is increased or decreased by certain items. Partnership distributions include the following:

- A withdrawal by a partner in anticipation of the current year's earnings
- A complete or partial liquidation of a partner's interest
- A distribution to all partners in a complete liquidation of the partnership

A partnership distribution is not taken into account in determining the partner's share of the partnership income or loss. If any gain or loss from the distribution is recognized by the partner, it must be reported on her return for the tax year in which the distribution is received. Money or property withdrawn by a partner in anticipation of the current year's earnings is treated as a distribution received on the last day of the partnership's tax year.

Effect on Partner's Basis

A partner's adjusted basis in his partnership interest is decreased (but not below zero) by the money and adjusted basis of property distributed to the partner. A partnership generally does not recognize any gain or loss because of distributions it makes to partners. The partnership may be able to elect to adjust the basis of its undistributed property.

However, certain distributions are treated as a sale or exchange. When a partnership distributes the following items, the distribution may be treated as a sale or exchange of property rather than a distribution:

- Unrealized receivables or substantially appreciated inventory items distributed in exchange for any part of the partner's interest in other partnership property, including money
- Other property, including money, distributed in exchange for any part of a partner's interest in unrealized receivables or substantially appreciated inventory items

Any gain or loss on a sale or exchange of unrealized receivables or inventory items a partner received in a distribution is treated as an *ordinary* gain or loss. [69] However, If the partner sells inventory items after holding them for five years, the type of gain or loss can be treated as a capital gain or loss.

> **Example:** Marcia was a partner in Big Toy Partnership, which was a business that sold children's toys. In 2010, the store closes and Marcia receives, through dissolution of the partnership, inventory that has a basis of $19,000. Within two years, she sells all the inventory for $24,000. The $5,000 gain is taxed as ordinary income. If she would have held on to the inventory for more than 5 years, her gain would have been capital gain, provided the inventory was a capital asset in her hands at the time of sale.

This treatment does not apply to the following distributions:

- A distribution of property to the partner who contributed the same property to the partnership
- Payments made to a retiring partner or successor in interest of a deceased partner that are the partner's distributive share of partnership income or guaranteed payments

Payments made in liquidation of the interest of a retiring or deceased partner in exchange for his interest in partnership property are considered a distribution, not a distributive share or guaranteed payment that could give rise to a deduction for the partnership.

Partner Debt Acquired by a Partnership

If a partnership acquires a partner's debt and extinguishes the debt by distributing it to the partner, the partner will recognize capital gain or loss to the extent the Fair Market Value of the debt differs from the basis of the debt. The partner is treated as having satisfied the debt for its Fair Market Value. If the issue price of the debt exceeds its FMV when distributed, the partner may have to include the excess amount in income as canceled debt.

Sale of a Partnership Interest

A partnership interest is a capital asset. Typically that means any gain or loss recognized on the sale of a partnership interest is treated as a capital gain or loss. Gain or loss is calculated as the difference between the amount realized and the adjusted basis of the partner's interest in the partnership. If the selling partner is relieved of any partnership liabilities, that partner must include the liability relief as part of the amount realized for his or her interest.

> **Example:** Selene became a limited partner in the Rincon Partnership by contributing $10,000 in cash on the formation of the partnership. The adjusted basis of her partnership interest at the end of 2010 is $20,000, which includes her $15,000 share of partnership liabilities. Selene sells her interest in the partnership for $10,000 in cash on December 31st, 2010. Selene realizes $25,000 from the sale of her partnership interest ($10,000 cash payment + $15,000 liability relief). She must report $5,000 ($25,000 realized − $20,000 basis) as a capital gain.

---

[69] For this purpose, inventory does not include real or depreciable business property, even if they are not held more than 1 year.

An exchange of partnership interests does not qualify as a nontaxable exchange of like-kind property. This applies regardless of whether they are general or limited partnership interests or interests in the same or different partnerships.

Liquidation of a Partnership

When a partnership dissolves or stops doing business, it is called a *partnership liquidation*. A partnership can dissolve when a partner dies, or when one partner drops out of the business. Generally, in a partnership liquidation, the following events are treated as occurring at the same time:

- All partnership liabilities become payable in full
- All of the partnership's assets have a value of zero, except for property contributed to secure a liability
- All property is disposed of by the partnership in a fully taxable transaction for no consideration
- All items of income, gain, loss, or deduction are allocated to the partners
- The partnership liquidates

The basis of property received in complete liquidation of a partner's interest is the adjusted basis of the partner's interest in the partnership reduced by any money distributed to the partner in the same transaction.

Sometimes, a partnership will dissolve with unamortized startup expenses. If a partnership is liquidated before the end of the amortization period, the unamortized amount of qualifying organizational costs and startup expenses can be deducted in the partnership's final tax year.

Liquidation at Partner's Retirement or Death

A payment made to a deceased or retiring partner in liquidation of his interest is considered a distribution, not a distributive share or guaranteed payment that could give rise to a deduction (or its equivalent) for the partnership. For income tax purposes, a retiring partner or "in interest of a deceased partner" is treated as a partner until his interest in the partnership has been completely liquidated.

Example: Tim's basis in his partnership interest is $20,000. In a distribution in liquidation of his entire interest, he receives a delivery truck and a utility trailer (neither of which is inventory or unrealized receivables). The truck has an adjusted basis to the partnership of $15,000 and an FMV of $15,000. The trailer has an adjusted basis to the partnership of $15,000 and an FMV of $5,000. To figure his basis in each property, Tim first assigns a basis of $15,000 to the truck and $15,000 to the trailer. This leaves a $10,000 basis decrease (the $30,000 total of the assigned basis minus the $20,000 allocable basis). He allocates the entire $10,000 to the trailer (its unrealized depreciation). Tim's basis in the truck is $15,000, and his basis in the trailer is $5,000 ($15,000 - $10,000).

Loss on Liquidating Distribution

In a partnership liquidation, the liquidating distributions are similar to regular distributions except the partner can recognize a loss on them. If the total basis of the cash and property received is less than the partner's basis in the partnership, then the partner may recognize a loss. A partner cannot recognize loss on a partnership distribution unless ALL of the following requirements are met:

- The adjusted basis of the partner's interest in the partnership exceeds the distribution.
- The partner's entire interest in the partnership is liquidated.
- The distribution is in money, unrealized receivables, or inventory items.

Partnership Termination

A partnership terminates when ONE of the following events takes place:

- All its operations are discontinued and no part of any business, financial operation, or venture is continued by any of its partners in a partnership.
- At least 50% of the total interest in partnership capital and profits is sold or exchanged within a 12-month period, including a sale or exchange to another partner.

The partnership's tax year ends on the date of termination. If a partnership is terminated before the end of its regular tax year, Form 1065 must be filed for the short period, which is the period from the beginning of the tax year through the date of termination. This is a "short tax year." The partnership return is due the fifteenth day of the fourth month following the date of termination.

If a business partnership breaks up and one of the former partners is insolvent and cannot pay any of the partnership's debts, sometimes existing partners will be forced to pay more than their share of the liabilities. If a partner pays any part of the insolvent partner's share of the debts, he can take a bad debt deduction.

Penalties

In 2010, the IRS increased late filing penalties on partnerships. The penalty for late filing is $195 per month, per partner, up to 12 months. So, for example, if a partnership has four partners and files its tax return two months late, it would be liable for a late filing penalty of $1,560 ($195 × 2 months × 4 partners).

This penalty will not be imposed if the partnership can show reasonable cause for its failure to file. Additional penalties may apply if the partnership fails to furnish Schedules K-1 to its partners, fails to supply a Tax Identification Number, or fails to furnish information on tax shelters. Reasonable cause exceptions also apply.

Summary: Partnerships

An unincorporated business with two or more members is automatically treated as a partnership for IRS purposes. Co-ownership of rental property is not considered a partnership. A joint undertaking merely to share expenses is not considered a partnership.

The distributive share of income from a partnership is subject to self-employment tax for general partners.

A partnership files IRS Form 1065 to report income and expenses. A partnership must also provide a Schedule K-1 to each partner reflecting the individual partner's distributive share of income and losses. A partnership can request a five month extension of time to file by filing **Form 7004,** *Application for Automatic Extension of Time to File Certain Business Income Tax, Information, and Other Returns.*

Unit 2.7: Questions

1. A domestic Limited Liability Company (LLC) with at least two members that does not file Form 8832, *Entity Classification Election*, is classified as:
A. A sole proprietorship

B. A partnership
C. A corporation
D. A joint venture

The answer is B. A domestic LLC with two or more members will be treated as a partnership for tax purposes if it does not file Form 8832, *Entity Classification Election*. ###

2. In 2010 Randall and Ellie formed Spring Lawn, Ltd., a calendar-year partnership, to provide yard maintenance to residential customers. Before they began operations in November 2010, they incurred legal fees of $2,000 and consulting expenses of $1,000 to draft the partnership agreement and file the required forms. They also paid a commission of $600 to a broker to market partnership interests. How much of these expenses may be deducted on Spring Lawn's partnership tax return for 2010?

A. $0
B. $600
C. $3,000
D. $3,600

The answer is C. The partnership may choose to deduct the amounts for legal fees and consulting expenses ($2,000 + $1,000 = $3,000). However, the amount paid in commissions to a broker to market partnership interests must be capitalized and cannot be amortized or depreciated. The costs for issuing and marketing interests in the partnership such as brokerage, registration, and legal fees and printing costs are not amortizable. The deduction for startup costs was increased by the Small Business Jobs Act of 2010. Partnerships are allowed to deduct up to $10,000 worth of startup costs. ###

3. Which of the following statements is TRUE?

A. The IRS requires partnerships with more than 100 partners to file their returns electronically.
B. The IRS requires all partnerships to file electronically.
C. The IRS requires limited partnerships with more than 10 partners to file their returns electronically.
D. The IRS requires partnerships with 100 or more partners to file electronically

The answer is A. The IRS requires partnerships with more than 100 partners (Schedules K-1) to file their returns electronically. Partnerships with **100 or fewer** partners are not required to electronically file their returns. ###

4. Which of the following statements regarding limited partnerships is correct?

A. A limited partner has an economic liability for damages and an economic risk of loss.
B. A limited partner does not have an economic risk of loss in partnership recourse liabilities.
C. A limited partner does not have an economic risk of loss in partnership recourse liabilities; however, a limited partner is required to contribute additional capital.
D. A limited partner is treated just like a general partner when it comes to recourse liability.

The answer is B. A limited partner generally has no obligation to contribute additional capital to the partnership and therefore does not have an economic risk of loss in partnership recourse liabilities. Thus, absent some other factor such as the guarantee of a partnership liability by the limited partner or the limited partner making the loan to the partnership, a limited partner generally does not have a share of partnership recourse liabilities (Publication 541). ###

5. Otto and Janelle form a cash-basis general partnership with cash contributions of $20,000 each. Under the partnership agreement, they share all partnership profits and losses equally. They borrow $60,000 and purchase depreciable business equipment. However, only Janelle is required to pay the creditor if the partnership defaults, so she has an economic risk of loss in the liability for the debt. What is Janelle's basis in the partnership?

A. $80,000
B. $60,000
C. $50,000
D. $20,000

The answer is A. This debt is included in Janelle's basis in the partnership because she has an economic risk of loss in the liability. Incurring it creates an additional $60,000 of basis in the partnership's depreciable property. Her basis in the partnership would be $80,000 ($20,000 + $60,000), while Otto's basis would be only $20,000 (Publication 541). ###

6. The adjusted basis of Hugo's partnership interest is $15,000. He receives a non-liquidating distribution of $8,000 cash and land that has an adjusted basis to the partnership of $10,000. What is the basis of the land in Hugo's hands?

A. $7,000
B. $10,000
C. $12,000
D. $15,000

The answer is A. Hugo's basis for the distributed property is limited to $7,000 ($15,000 - $8,000, the cash received). In a non-liquidating distribution, the basis of property (other than cash) distributed to the partner by a partnership is its adjusted basis to the partnership immediately before the distribution. However, the basis of the property to the partner cannot be more than the adjusted basis of his partnership interest in the partnership. ###

7. Bill owns a 75% capital interest in Taffy Partnership. Bill's wife Veronica is a 65% owner in Monty Partnership. Bill and Veronica file separate tax returns and keep all their books and records separate. Taffy Partnership sells Monty Partnership a factory machine for $7,600. Taffy Partnership's cost basis in the machinery is $10,000. What is Taffy Partnership's deductible loss?

A. $0
B. $2,400
C. $7,600
D. $10,000

The answer is A. Taffy Partnership's loss of $2,400 is not deductible. A loss on the sale or exchange of property between related persons is not deductible. This applies to both direct and indirect transactions. The fact that Bill and Veronica file separate tax returns does not change the fact that they are still related parties for the purposes of this transaction. ###

8. Lawrence owns a 65% capital interest in Red Reel Partnership. His brother Andrew owns a 90% interest in Blue Fish Partnership. Red Reel Partnership sells a delivery truck with an adjusted basis of $40,000 and a Fair Market Value of $65,000 to Blue Fish Partnership for $25,000. What is Red Reel Partnership's recognized loss?

A. $0
B. $15,000
C. $25,000
D. $40,000

The answer is A. Lawrence and his brother Andrew are related persons, and therefore the loss is disallowed. A loss on the sale or exchange of property between related persons is not deductible. This applies to both direct and indirect transactions. For these purposes, "related persons" includes a partnership and a person owning, directly or indirectly, 50% or more of the capital interest in the partnership. ###

9. Polly and Diane form P&D Partnership in 2010. Polly contributes $16,000 cash and Diane contributes equipment with a Fair Market Value of $15,000 and an adjusted basis of $5,000. What amount should Diane report as a gain as a result of this transaction?

A. $0
B. $3,000
C. $5,000
D. $8,000

The answer is A. Usually, neither the partner nor the partnership recognizes a gain or loss when property is contributed to the partnership in exchange for a partnership interest. This applies whether a partnership is being formed or is already operating. However, if an asset is encumbered by a liability, such as a mortgage, then there is a possibility that the partner will recognize a gain on the exchange (Publication 541). ###

10. Buck and June are equal partners in B&J Partnership. In 2010, the partnership breaks up. Buck is insolvent, and June becomes responsible for paying a portion of his partnership debt. Which of the following statements is TRUE?

A. June can take a bad debt deduction for any amount that she must pay that is not her share of the partnership liability.
B. Buck is not responsible for paying any of his liabilities after dissolution.
C. June cannot take a bad debt deduction for any debt that the partnership incurred.
D. None of the above.

The answer is A. If a business partnership breaks up and one of the former partners is insolvent and cannot pay any of the partnership's debts, existing partners may have to pay more than their share. If a partner pays any part of the insolvent partner's share of the debts, she can take a bad debt deduction for the amount she pays. ###

11. Daniel is a general partner in the Dustbowl Partnership. During the year, Daniel personally assumes $100,000 of the partnership's liabilities. Which of the following statements regarding partnership liabilities is TRUE?

A. The assumption of partnership debt by Daniel is treated as a distribution of cash to Daniel, and it decreases Daniel's partnership basis.
B. The assumption of partnership debt by Daniel increases his basis.
C. Daniel cannot assume partnership liabilities.
D. Only limited partners are allowed to assume partnership liabilities.

The answer is B. The assumption of partnership debt by Daniel *increases* his basis. If a partner's share of partnership liabilities increases, or a partner's individual liabilities increase because he assumes partnership liabilities, this increase is treated as a contribution of money by the partner to the partnership.###

12. Manny is permanently retiring from Sunnyside Partnership this year. His adjusted basis in the partnership is $50,000. He receives a distribution of $65,000 in cash. How would Manny report this transaction?

A. $15,000 gain upon distribution
B. $50,000 gain upon distribution
C. $65,000 capital gain
D. $65,000 ordinary income

The answer is A. Manny must recognize $15,000 worth of gain. This is the difference between his adjusted basis in the partnership and the amount of his distribution ($65,000 - $50,000). Upon the receipt of the distribution, the retiring partner or successor in interest of a deceased partner will recognize gain only to the extent that any money (and marketable securities treated as money) distributed is more than the partner's adjusted basis in the partnership (Publication 541). ###

13. Which of the following statements is TRUE about limited partners?

A. Limited partners do not have an economic risk of loss in partnership recourse liabilities.
B. Limited partners have legal liability and economic risk of loss, just like general partners.
C. Limited partners can always participate in the management of the partnership.
D. A true limited partner has an ongoing obligation to contribute additional capital.

The answer is A. Limited partners are only liable for partnership liabilities up to their investment in the partnership. Limited partners generally cannot participate in the management or the day-to-day administration of the partnership. A limited partner has no obligation to contribute additional capital to the partnership, and therefore does not have an economic risk of loss in partnership recourse liabilities. A limited partner generally does not have a share of partnership recourse liabilities. ###

14. Roadhouse Partnership forms in 2010. Roadhouse decides to treat its organizational costs as startup costs and elects to amortize. Which of the following costs would NOT be considered a qualifying cost for the election to amortize startup costs?

A. The costs of acquiring a building for the partnership
B. Legal fees to draft the partnership agreement
C. Accounting fees for services related to the organization or the partnership
D. The cost of training employees before the business opens

The answer is A. The expenses for acquiring or transferring assets to a partnership cannot be amortized. They must instead be included in the basis of a partnership interest. The other choices are all costs that may be amortized or deducted as qualifying startup or organizational costs. ###

15. When payments are made by a partnership to partners that are without regard to the partnership income, these payments are called:

A. Capital gains
B. Ordinary distributions
C. Passive income
D. Guaranteed payments

The answer is D. Guaranteed payments are those made by a partnership to a partner that are determined without regard to the partnership's income. A partnership treats guaranteed payments for services, or for the use of capital, as if they were made to a person who is not a partner. ###

16. Which form is used by a partnership to request an extension of time to file?

A. Form 7006
B. Form 1065
C. Form 7004
D. Form 8426

The answer is C. Form 7004, *Automatic Extension of Time to File Certain Business Income Tax, Information, and Other Returns,* is used by partnerships to extend their filing deadline for five months. ###

17. The R&R Partnership has two partners, Gil and Hassid. They share profits and losses 50/50. The R&R Partnership has the following activity during the year.

Gross income from services: $200,000
Business expenses: $30,000
Tax exempt interest income: $10,000
Rental income: $12,000
Charitable contributions made: $4,000

What is Hassid's share of the partnership income (EXCLUDING all the separately stated items)?

A. $85,000
B. $91,000
C. $100,000
D. $105,000

The answer is A. The share of the partnership income to Hassid does not include the separately stated items. Hassid's share of the partnership income is split evenly with Gil, so his portion is figured as follows: ($200,000 - $30,000 business expenses) = $170,000
$170,000 X 50% =$85,000

The rental income, tax exempt income, and charitable contributions are all separately stated items. They do not affect the calculation for ordinary income. ###

17. Sandra and Tina operate the Collins Partnership together and share profit and losses equally. During the year, the Collins Partnership had the following activity:

Gross income from operations: $75,000
Charitable contributions made: $3,000
Rental income: $5,000
Cost of Goods Sold: $10,000
Business expenses: $15,000

How much ordinary income should the Collins Partnership report, NOT including the separately stated items?

A. $65,000
B. $60,000
C. $55,000
D. $50,000

The answer is D. The ordinary income that the partnership must report is calculated as follows: $50,000 = ($75,000 - $15,000 - $10,000). Cost of Goods Sold and business expenses are deducted from the gross sales revenues. The charitable contributions and rental income have to be separately stated on the tax return. ###

18. Frances and Jennie are equal partners in a restaurant. In 2010, they purchase a new $30,000 pizza oven for the restaurant. They want to take the Section 179 deduction for the full cost of the oven. The partnership's taxable income before the Section 179 deduction is $25,000. There were no other qualifying Section 179 purchases during the year. What is the amount of Section 179 deduction that Frances can deduct on her individual tax return?

A. $0
B. $6,000
C. $12,500
D. $15,000

The answer is C. The Section 179 deduction for the $30,000 oven is limited by the partnership income. The Section 179 cannot exceed overall income for the year, so the deduction is limited to $25,000. Then the deduction is split between the two partners ($25,000 X 50%) = $12,500. Section 179 is a separately stated item on a partnership tax return. ###

20. Which of the following will INCREASE the basis of a partner's interest in a partnership?

A. A partner's share of tax-exempt income from muni bonds owned by the partnership
B. A decrease in the partner's share of liabilities
C. A distribution of $2,000 in cash to the partner
D. A property distribution with a FMV of $5,000

The answer is A. Income attributable to a partner will increase the partner's basis in his partnership interest. This includes tax-exempt income. ####

21. Lydia acquired a 50% interest in a partnership by contributing a building that had an adjusted basis to her of $80,000 and was subject to a $40,000 mortgage. The partnership then assumed payment of the mortgage. What is the basis of Lydia's partnership interest?

A. $20,000
B. $40,000
C. $60,000
D. $80,000

The answer is C. Since Lydia's contributed property is subject to a mortgage and the liability is assumed by the partnership, the basis of that partner's interest is reduced (but not below zero) by the liability assumed by the other partners. Lydia must reduce her basis because the assumption of the liability is treated as a distribution of money to her.

The other partners' assumption of the liability is treated as a contribution by them of money to the partnership.
Adjusted basis of contributed property (building) = $80,000. Minus: Part of mortgage assumed by other partners (50% × $40,000) = ($20,000). Basis of Lydia's partnership interest= $60,000 ####

22. The adjusted basis of Jo's partnership interest is $14,000. She receives a distribution of $8,000 cash and land that has an adjusted basis of $2,000 and a fair market value of $3,000. How much gain should Jo recognize on this distribution?

A. $0
B. $1,000
C. $2,000
D. $7,000

The answer is A. Because the cash received does not exceed the basis of her partnership interest, Jo does not recognize any gain on the distribution. Any gain on the land will be recognized when she sells it. The distribution decreases the adjusted basis of Jo's partnership interest to $4,000 [$14,000 – ($8,000 + $2,000)]. A partner generally recognizes gain on a partnership distribution only to the extent any money included in the distribution exceeds the adjusted basis of the partner's interest in the partnership. ###

23. The adjusted basis of Steve's partnership interest is $10,000. He receives a distribution of $4,000 cash and a machine that has an adjusted basis to the partnership of $9,000 and a Fair Market Value of $12,000. This was not a liquidating distribution. What is Steve's basis in the machine?

A. $5,000
B. $8,000
C. $12,000
D. $16,000

The answer is B. Steve's basis for the machine is limited to $5,000 ($10,000 – $4,000, the cash he receives). The basis of the machine is limited by Steve's basis in his partnership interest. Publication 541 states that; *unless* there is a complete liquidation of a partner's interest, the basis of any property distributed to the partner by a partnership is its adjusted basis to the partnership immediately before the distribution. However, the basis of the property to the partner cannot be more than the adjusted basis of his or her interest in the partnership reduced by any money received in the same transaction. ###

Unit 2.8: C Corporation Formation and Requirements

More Reading: Publication 542, *Corporations*

General Requirements

    A C Corporation is a corporation that is taxed under Subchapter C of the Internal Revenue Code. Most major companies are C Corporations. A corporation is a business entity that is created under state law. It owns property in its own name and it can be sued directly. However, the shareholders who own stock in a corporation do not own its individual assets. Individual shareholders are protected from legal liability except in very unusual circumstances.

    There are two types of corporate entities recognized by the IRS: C Corporations and S Corporations. The two are treated very differently under the Internal Revenue Code. The net income of a C Corporation is taxed, whereas the net income of an S Corporation is not taxed. An S Corporation is a "pass-through" entity, similar to a partnership. Although there are many benefits to S Corporation status, most major corporations do not qualify for the S-election. That is because publicly-traded companies may have thousands and thousands of shareholders, both foreign and domestic. An S Corporation is only allowed to have 100 domestic shareholders, among other limitations. We will cover S Corporations in a later unit.

    There are some key concepts that you must understand that set corporations apart from any other type of business entity.

Corporate Structure

    When a corporation is first formed, the Board of Directors determines the type of shares that the company will issue. In the case of a small corporation (such as a business with a single owner), the company may issue 1,000 shares of common stock upon its inception, and never issue any other stock or securities. In the case of a large corporation (such as a company that is publicly traded like Coca-Cola, Ford, or General Electric), the corporation will issue both equity securities (stocks) and debt securities (bonds).

    A corporation may have multiple classes of stock but must have common stock. Preferred stock is called "preferred" because when a corporation liquidates (or dissolves), the owners of preferred stock get preference over the claims of common stockholders. A corporation does not pay dividends on common stock unless it first pays dividends on preferred stock.

Corporation Filing Requirements

    A C Corporation files Form 1120, *U.S. Corporation Income Tax Return*. Some businesses are automatically treated as corporations for tax purposes.

    Corporations are always required to file a tax return, regardless of their taxable income. All domestic corporations in existence for any part of a tax year (including corporations in bankruptcy) must file an income tax return. A corporation generally must file Form 1120 to report its income, gains, losses, deductions, credits, and to figure its income tax liability. However, a corporation may file Form 1120-A if its gross receipts, total income, and total assets are each under $500,000. A corporation must file its income tax return by the fifteenth day of the third month after the end of its tax year.

A corporation must continue to file tax returns even if there is no business activity or profits. A corporation does not have to file after it has formally dissolved. The only exception to this filing requirement is for exempt entities, which are generally required to file another form, such as a Form 990. Exempt entities are covered in a later unit.

The following businesses formed after 1996 are automatically treated as corporations:

- A business formed under a federal or state law that refers to itself as a corporation
- A business formed under a state law that refers to itself as a joint-stock company or joint-stock association
- Insurance companies
- Certain banks that are insured by the FDIC
- A business owned by a state or local government
- A business specifically required to be taxed as a corporation by the IRC (for example, certain publicly-traded partnerships)
- Certain foreign businesses
- Any other business that elects to be taxed as a corporation and files Form 8832, *Entity Classification Election*

A corporation filing a short-period return (for example, a corporation that dissolves in the middle of the year) must generally file by the fifteenth day of the third month after the short period ends. This means that a calendar-year corporation must file its tax return by March 15 of the following year.

> **Example:** Greenbook Inc. is a domestic corporation with a fiscal year tax year-end of March 31. Greenbook must file Form 1120 by June 15.

> **Example:** Candy Cane Corporation's tax year ends December 31. It must file its income tax return by March 15.

Electronic filing is *mandatory* for C Corporations that have $10 million or more in assets and at least 250 or more returns of any type, including information returns such as Forms W-2 or Forms 1099.

Corporate Extension of Time to File

A corporation must file Form 7004, *Automatic Extension of Time to File Certain Business Income Tax, Information, and Other Returns,* to request a six-month extension of time to file a corporation income tax return.

Form 7004 does not extend the time for paying the tax due on the return. Interest, and possibly penalties, will be charged on any part of the final tax due not shown as a balance due on Form 7004. The interest is figured from the original due date of the return to the date of payment. Corporations can generally file Form 1120 and certain related forms, schedules, and attachments electronically. Certain corporations must electronically file Form 1120.

524

Corporate Refunds and Amended Returns

Corporations may use Form 1139, *Corporate Application for Tentative Refund,* or Form 1120X, *Amended U.S. Corporation Income Tax Return,* to apply for a refund. A corporation can get a refund faster by using Form 1139.

The corporation cannot file Form 1139 before filing the return for the corporation's capital loss year, but it must file Form 1139 no later than one year after the year it sustains the capital loss. If the corporation does not file Form 1139, it must file Form 1120X to apply for a refund. The corporation must file Form 1120X within three years of the due date, including extensions, for filing the return for the year in which it sustains the capital loss.

Personal Service Corporations

A corporation is a Personal Service Corporation if its principal activity during the prior tax year is performing personal services. Personal services include any activity performed in the fields of accounting, actuarial science, architecture, consulting, engineering, health (including veterinary services), law, and the performing arts. A corporation that provides these services will be considered a PSC if substantially all of its compensation is derived from providing personal services. Personal service corporations are taxed at a flat rate of 35%.[70]

A Personal Service Corporation cannot be classified as an S Corporation. A PSC must use a calendar tax year unless it has a valid Section 444 election in effect, or if it can show a substantial and genuine business purpose for a different tax year and has obtained IRS approval. A PSC is subject to the passive activity loss limitations and must file Form 8810, *Corporate Passive Activity Loss and Credit Limitations*, to compute the allowable passive activity loss and credit.

A person is considered an "employee-owner" of a Personal Service Corporation if both of the following apply:

- He or she is an employee of the corporation or performs personal services for, or on behalf of, the corporation on any day of the testing period.
- He or she owns any stock in the corporation at any time during the testing period.

Corporate Taxation

Corporations are subject to tax on their earnings, just like individuals. A C Corporation is not a pass-through entity and is therefore taxed in a variety of ways. There are special rules regarding corporate taxes and estimated payments. The following sections cover the most frequently tested issues regarding corporate taxes.

There are many benefits to incorporation. However, one of the main drawbacks of a C Corporation is the tax ramifications of this entity type. Unlike a partnership, a sole proprietorship, or an S Corporation, the earnings of a C Corporation are *taxed twice*. Corporate income is taxed when it is earned and then taxed again when it is distributed to shareholders as divi-

---

[70] The graduated corporate tax rates do not need to be memorized for the Enrolled Agent Exam. However, you must remember that Personal Service Corporations (PSCs) are taxed at a flat rate of 35%.

dends. A corporation does not receive a tax deduction for the distribution of dividends to its shareholders.

Unlike partnerships and S Corporations, income does not retain its character when it is passed through to shareholders of a C Corporation. A C Corporation is NOT a pass-through entity. So, for example, if a C Corporation has earnings from rental income, it must pay tax on the income at the corporate level. When the income is then distributed to a shareholder, the income does not retain its character as rental income. It is distributed merely as a dividend.

> **Example:** In 2010, ABC Corporation receives tax-exempt income from bonds. The C Corporation subsequently distributes the income to its shareholders as taxable dividends. Even though the income was originally tax-exempt, it does not retain its tax-exempt character when it passes to the shareholder. However, in the case of an S Corporation or a partnership, the income would have retained its character when it was passed through to the owners or S Corporation shareholders.

A corporation can have revenues from many different sources. A C Corporation must include income from all sources as "gross income." This means that the corporation's operating income is added to interest income, rental income, and gains and losses on property transactions. Tax-exempt income (such as municipal bond income) will retain its character as tax-exempt in the hands of the corporation. However, when a corporation distributes revenue to its shareholders, the revenue is taxed as a distribution to the shareholder, regardless of its original character.

> **Example:** Super Sailing Inc. is a calendar-year C Corporation with 20 equal shareholders. After deducting business expenses, Super Sailing has $150,000 in taxable net income in 2010. The Corporation also earns $4,000 in interest from municipal bonds. The $4,000 of tax-exempt bond interest is excluded from the corporation's taxable income. Super Sailing must pay tax on only $150,000 of gross income. In December 2010, Super Sailing also distributes $120,000 to its shareholders. The company cannot take a tax deduction for the distribution. Each shareholder has an equal stake in the company, so each shareholder receives $6,000 in dividend income ($120,000 ÷ 20 = $6,000). Each shareholder is required to recognize $6,000 in dividend income for tax year 2010.

Accounting Method for C Corporations

C Corporations may use any permissible accounting method for keeping track of income and expenses. Permissible methods include:

- Cash
- Accrual
- Any other method authorized by the IRS (such as a hybrid method)

A corporation with more than $5 million in average annual gross receipts is required to use the accrual method.[71] If a corporation produces inventory, then the accrual method is generally required for sales and purchases of merchandise, unless average gross receipts are $1 million or less.

---

[71] Family farming corporations have a higher threshold. They are allowed to use the cash method as long as their average annual gross receipts do not exceed $25 million. Family farming corporations will be covered in a later unit specifically for farmers.

Using the "Non-accrual Experience Method"

The "non-accrual experience method" is a method of accounting for bad debt. If a corporation uses the accrual method of accounting and qualifies to use the non-accrual experience method for bad debts, it is not required to accrue service-related income that it expects to be uncollectible. Accrual-method corporations are not required to maintain accruals for certain amounts from the performance of services that, on the basis of their experience, will not be collected, if:

- The services are in the fields of health, law, engineering, architecture, accounting, actuarial science, performing arts, or consulting; or
- The corporation's average annual gross receipts for the three prior tax years do not exceed $5 million.

This provision does NOT apply if the corporation charges interest on late payments, or if the business charges customers any penalty for failure to pay an amount timely. A business is permitted to use the non-accrual experience method only for amounts earned for performing services. A business cannot use this method for amounts owed from activities such as lending money, selling goods, or acquiring receivables.

Accumulated Earnings Tax

A corporation will be subject to the accumulated earnings tax if it does not distribute enough of its profits to shareholders. This rule was instituted by the IRS to prevent large corporations from "hoarding" income and not distributing it to their shareholders.

The accumulated earnings tax is imposed on a corporation that is formed or used to avoid income tax for its shareholders by permitting earnings and profits to accumulate instead of being divided or distributed. The tax is levied at a rate of 15% of accumulated taxable income.

A C Corporation is allowed to accumulate its earnings for a possible expansion or other bona fide business reasons. However, if a corporation lets earnings accumulate beyond the reasonable needs of the business; the earnings may be subject to the accumulated earnings tax. If the accumulated earnings tax applies, interest applies to the tax from the date the corporate return was originally due, without extensions.

An accumulation of $250,000 (or less) is generally considered "reasonable" for most businesses. For PSCs, the limit is $150,000. Reasonable "needs" of the business include the following:

- Specific, definite, and feasible plans for use of the earnings accumulation in the business
- The amount necessary to redeem the corporation's stock included in a deceased shareholder's gross estate, if the amount does not exceed the reasonably anticipated total estate and inheritance taxes and funeral and administration expenses incurred by the shareholder's estate

The absence of a bona fide business reason for a corporation's accumulated earnings may be indicated by many different circumstances, such as a lack of regular distributions to its shareholders or withdrawals by the shareholders classified as personal loans. However, actual moves to expand the business generally qualify as a *bona fide* use of the accumulated income. Examples of "qualified accumulations" include:

- The expansion of the company to a new area or a new facility
- Acquiring another business through the purchase of stock or other assets
- Providing for reasonable product liability losses

The fact that a corporation has an unreasonable accumulation of earnings is sufficient to establish liability for the accumulated earnings tax unless the corporation can show the earnings were not accumulated to allow its individual shareholders to avoid income tax.

Estimated Tax for C Corporations

Generally, a corporation must make estimated tax installment payments if it expects its estimated tax for the year to be $500 or more. Installment payments are due by the fifteenth day of the fourth, sixth, ninth, and twelfth months of the corporation's tax year. Corporations do not send estimated tax payments directly to the IRS. Corporations are generally required to use EFTPS.

There is no penalty for underpayment if tax is less than $500, or if each quarterly estimated tax payment is at least 25% of the corporation's current year tax.

Also, no underpayment penalty will apply if each estimated tax installment is at least 25% of the income tax of the prior year return. This provision will not apply in the following instances:

- If the prior tax year was a short year (less than 12 months)
- If the corporation did not file a return for the prior year
- If the prior year tax return showed zero tax liability
- If the corporation had at least $1 million of taxable income in any of the last three years

Example: Crazy Clowns Corporation's tax year ends December 31. Estimated tax payments are due on April 15, June 15, September 15, and December 15.

If a corporation overpays its estimated tax, it may apply for a refund of the overpayment. If the overpayment is at least 10% of its expected income tax liability AND at least $500, the corporation may complete **Form 4466**, *Corporation Application for Quick Refund of Overpayment of Estimated Tax.*

Electronic Federal Tax Payment System (EFTPS)

The corporation must enroll in EFTPS in the current tax year to make deposits of all tax liabilities (including Social Security, Medicare, withheld income, excise, and corporate income taxes). Any business or individual taxpayer can use EFTPS, a free service from the IRS. However, some financial institutions (such as banks and payroll companies) may charge a fee to enroll a business in EFTPS. A business can make payments at any time of the day or night.

Estimated tax payments can be scheduled weekly, monthly, or quarterly. Both business and individual estimated payments can be scheduled in advance. Businesses used to be able to deposit their payroll taxes using federal tax deposit coupons. However, beginning in 2011, the Financial Management Service (FMS), a bureau of the Treasury Department, is eliminating these deposit coupons (Form 8109). Beginning January 1, 2011, all federal tax deposits must be made using EFTPS.

There is an exception for very small businesses with less than $2,500 in employment taxes. If a business accumulates a liability for these taxes of less than $2,500 per quarter, the entity may submit payment of taxes due along with their timely filed payroll tax return (Form 941). However, these small businesses may still voluntarily make deposits by EFTPS.

Failure to File and Failure to Pay Penalties

The IRS will assess a late filing penalty of 5% of the unpaid tax for each month or part of a month the corporate return is late, up to 25%. This late filing penalty is in addition to late payment penalties and interest. The minimum penalty for a return that is over 60 days late is the smaller of the tax due or $135. The penalty will not be imposed if the corporation can show that the failure to file was for good cause.

If a corporation fails to make estimated tax payments, there is a late payment penalty of one half of one percent per month, up to a maximum of 25%.

The failure-to-file penalty cannot be more than 25% of the corporation's tax. It is reduced by the failure-to-pay penalty for any month both penalties apply.

Trust Fund Recovery Penalty-The "100% Penalty"

The IRS takes payroll taxes very seriously. If an employee of a corporation fails to properly remit payroll taxes to the IRS, he can be held liable for the unpaid payroll taxes. This penalty can be applied to an officer, an employee, or even a shareholder. Even volunteer (unpaid) directors have been held liable for this penalty—anyone who the IRS deems is a "responsible party" in the case.

The Trust Fund Recovery Penalty (TFRP) may be assessed against any person who:

- Is responsible for collecting or paying withheld income and employment taxes, or for paying collected excise taxes, and
- Willfully fails to collect or pay them.

An employee will not be considered a responsible person if her function was solely to pay the bills as directed by a superior, rather than to determine which creditors would or would not be paid. Similarly, if an employee (such as a bookkeeper) does not have check-signing privileges or access to bank funds, then that employee will not be deemed a "responsible person."

Corporate AMT, Alternative Minimum Tax

The corporate Alternative Minimum Tax (AMT) ensures that corporations pay at least a minimum amount of tax on their income. A corporation owes AMT if its tentative minimum tax is more than its regular tax. If a corporation's tentative minimum tax exceeds regular tax, the excess amount is payable in addition to the regular tax.

Corporate and individual minimum taxes were first put into the U.S. tax code in 1969. Initially, the minimum tax functioned much like an excise tax on specified tax preferences in excess of some fixed amount. Corporations use Form 4626, *Alternative Minimum Tax-Corporations*, to figure the tentative minimum tax of a corporation that is not a small corporation for AMT purposes.

Small corporations, with average gross receipts of $5 million or less, are exempt from corporate AMT. After the first year of qualification, the corporation is considered a "small corporation" if its average annual gross receipts for the prior three years do not exceed $7.5 million ($5 million if the corporation had only one prior tax year). Most corporations will automatically qualify for the exemption in their first year of existence.

If the corporation fails the $7.5 million test for any year, the corporation will become ineligible for the AMT exemption for that year and all subsequent years. If a corporation fails to qualify under the first year $5 million limit, it will never qualify for the AMT exemption even if its gross receipts remain under the $7.5 million exemption limit.

The starting point for the determination of income for AMT purposes is the corporation's regular taxable income. Regular taxable income is modified by a series of additional computations called "adjustments" and "preferences." Adjustments can either increase or decrease taxable income, whereas preferences are calculated on a property-by-property basis and only apply to the extent that they are positive.

Adjustments include a portion of accelerated depreciation on buildings and equipment, amortization of pollution control facilities, mining exploration and development expenses, income reported under the completed contract method of accounting, and installment sales income. Corporations use Form 8827, *Credit for Prior Year Minimum Tax*, to figure the minimum tax credit, if any, for Alternative Minimum Tax incurred in prior tax years and any minimum tax credit carry forward. A minimum AMT tax credit may be carried forward indefinitely.

Reconciliation of Book Income vs. Tax Income

Differences in accounting rules for financial reporting (book income) and tax reporting can lead to differences in the amount of income reported to shareholders and tax authorities. "Book Income" is used for financial reporting purposes (and also formal accounting purposes). Corporations report income that is currently recognized for tax purposes but not for financial accounting. For tax purposes, when a payment is received, a company generally recognizes it as income.

An example of these differences is rental payments that a company receives in advance. Under financial accounting rules, a company is required to recognize the advance rental payments as income pro-rata over the time period of the lease, while tax rules classify the entire amount as income in the current period. If the rental period spans more than one accounting period, a temporary difference arises but reverses in a later tax year, leading to a difference in that later tax year, which the company reports on another line on Schedule M-1 as "income recorded on books this year not included on this return."

The differences in book and taxable income are reconciled for tax reporting purposes in Schedule M-1 of Form 1120 by small corporations with less than $10 million in assets. Larger corporations with over $10 million dollars in gross assets use Schedule M-3.

Some examples of expenses that must be reconciled for tax reporting purposes and financial reporting purposes are:

- Charitable contribution carryover
- Travel and entertainment in excess of the allowable limit
- Income subject to tax not included in the books
- Federal income taxes paid or accrued depending on the accounting method used. Federal income taxes are deductible for accounting purposes, but not for tax purposes
- Advance rental income

Schedule M-3 gives the IRS additional information about tax return calculations and the differences between book income numbers and taxable income numbers. Schedule M-3 contains three main sections:

- Financial statement reconciliation
- Detail of income/loss items
- Detail of expenses/deductions

A domestic corporation with total assets of $10 million or more is required to file Schedule M-3, *Net Income (Loss) Reconciliation for Corporations With Total Assets of $10 Million or More,* along with its regular tax return.

Corporate Formation Section 351 Transfers

Once a business decides to form a corporate structure, a transfer of assets to the corporation usually takes place. A corporation is formed initially by a transfer of money, property, or services by prospective shareholders in exchange for stock in the corporation.

Transfers to a corporation have tax consequences to both the corporation and the individual shareholder. IRC Section 351 covers the transfers of property to corporations. The code section applies not only to transfers of property to large multinational corporations but also to transfers of property to small corporations, such as those formed when a partnership or sole proprietorship opts to become a corporation.

A corporation acquires capital investment by issuing shares of stock to shareholders. The stock represents the shareholder's ownership interest in the corporation. The money the corporation raises by issuing stock is called "contributed capital."

If a taxpayer transfers money or property to a corporation in exchange for stock and immediately afterwards the taxpayer controls the corporation, the exchange is not taxable. This rule applies both to individuals and to entities that transfer property to a corporation. The rule also applies whether the corporation is being formed or is already in operation. This non-recognition rule does NOT apply in the following situations:

- The corporation is an investment company.
- The taxpayer transfers the property in a bankruptcy proceeding in exchange for stock that is used to pay creditors.
- If the stock is received in exchange for the corporation's debt (other than a security) or for interest on the corporation's debt (including a security) that accrued while the taxpayer held the debt.

Both the corporation and any person involved in a nontaxable exchange of property for stock must attach to their income tax returns a complete statement of all facts pertinent to the exchange.

In order to be "in control" of a corporation, immediately after the exchange the transferors must own at least 80% of the total combined voting power of all classes of stock entitled to vote and at least 80% of the outstanding shares of each class of nonvoting stock.

> **Example:** Mandy owns an office building. Her basis in the building is $100,000. She organizes a corporation when the building has a Fair Market Value of $300,000. Mandy transfers the building to the corporation for all its authorized capital stock, which has a par value of $300,000. No gain is recognized by Mandy or the corporation.

> **Example:** Aaron and Pedro transfer property with a basis of $100,000 to a corporation in exchange for stock with a Fair Market Value of $300,000. This represents only 75% of each class of stock of the corporation. The other 25% was already issued to someone else. Aaron and Pedro must recognize a taxable gain of $200,000 on the transaction.

This non-recognition rule does NOT apply when services are rendered in exchange for stock. The value of stock received for services is income to the recipient.

> **Example:** Wayne is an architect. He transfers property worth $35,000 and renders services valued at $3,000 to a corporation in exchange for stock valued at $38,000. Right after the exchange, Wayne owns 85% of the outstanding stock. No gain is recognized on the exchange of property. However, Wayne must still recognize ordinary income of $3,000 as payment for services he rendered to the corporation.

Property of Relatively Small Value

This non-recognition rule does not apply when the property transferred is of a relatively small value when compared to the value of stock, and the main purpose of the transfer is to qualify for the non-recognition of gain or loss. Property transferred will not be considered to be of "small value" if its FMV is at least 10% of the FMV of the stock already owned or to be received by the transferor.

If a group of transferors exchanges property for corporate stock, each transferor does not have to receive stock in proportion to his interest in the property transferred. If a disproportionate transfer takes place, it will be treated for tax purposes in accordance with its true nature. It may be treated as if the stock were first received in proportion and then some of it used to make gifts, pay compensation for services, or satisfy the transferor's obligations.

Recognition When Money or Other Property is Received

If, in an otherwise nontaxable exchange of property for corporate stock, the taxpayer also receives money or property, she may have to recognize gain. The rules for figuring the recognized gain in this situation are similar to those for a partially nontaxable exchange (like-kind exchange). If the property the taxpayer gives up includes depreciable property, the recognized gain may have to be reported as ordinary income from depreciation. No loss can be recognized by the transferor.

Assumption of Shareholder Liabilities

If a corporation assumes a shareholder's liabilities, the exchange generally is not treated as if the shareholder received money or other property. There are two exceptions to this treatment:

- If the liabilities the corporation assumes are more than the shareholder's adjusted basis in the property transferred, gain is recognized up to the difference.
- However, if the liabilities assumed give rise to a deduction when paid, such as a trade account payable or a legitimate interest expense, no gain is recognized.

If there is no good business reason for the corporation to assume a shareholder's liabilities, or if the main purpose in the exchange is to avoid federal income tax, the assumption is taxable to the shareholder.

Example: Sheldon transfers machinery to a corporation for stock. Immediately after the transfer, Sheldon controls the corporation. He also receives $10,000 in the exchange. Sheldon's adjusted basis in the machinery is $20,000. The stock he receives has an FMV of $16,000. The corporation also assumes a $5,000 mortgage on the machinery for which Sheldon was personally liable. The liability assumed by the corporation is not treated as taxable to Sheldon. The recognized gain is limited to $10,000, the cash received.

If a corporation transfers its stock in satisfaction of indebtedness and the Fair Market Value of its stock is less than the indebtedness it owes, the corporation has income (to the extent of the difference) from the cancellation of indebtedness. For example, if stock is given to an individual in order to pay for a debt, the transfer does not qualify for non-recognition treatment.

Corporate Startup Expenses and Organizational Costs

Corporations can elect to amortize certain costs for organization. Startup and organizational costs can be amortized ratably over a 180-month period. The amortization period starts with the month the corporation begins operating. The cost must qualify as ONE of the following:

- A business startup cost
- An organizational cost for a corporation

The deduction for startup expenses is separate from the deduction for organizational costs. The $10,000 deduction for start-up expenses is reduced by the amount the corporation's total startup or organizational costs exceed $60,000. Any remaining costs must be amortized. If a corporation dissolves or is disposed of before the amortization period is up, the remaining startup costs can be deducted on the corporation's final return. These are costs that were paid before the corporation began operations. Start-up costs include expenses like:

- Advertising the business before it actually opens
- Wages for training new employees
- Wages paid to employees during training, and the costs of the training itself

Start-up costs DO NOT include research and development expenses.

A corporation can also deduct organizational costs. However, the deduction for organizational costs is $5,000 with a phase-out range of $50,000. To qualify as an organizational cost it must be:

- For the creation of the corporation
- Chargeable to a capital account
- Amortized over the life of the corporation
- Incurred before the end of the first tax year in which the corporation is in business

Examples of qualifying organizational costs:

- The cost of temporary directors
- The cost of organizational meetings
- State incorporation fees
- The cost of legal services for writing the corporate bylaws or the corporate charter

Organizational costs DO NOT include:

- Any costs associated with a stock issue, such as brokers' commissions on stock sales or the costs of printing stock certificates
- Any costs incurred for the transfer of assets to the corporation, (like the transfer of a building or other real estate).

Amortizable startup costs for purchasing an active trade or business include only investigative costs incurred in the course of a general search for or preliminary investigation of the business. These are costs that help a taxpayer decide whether to purchase a business.

Capital Expenditures

Capital expenditures are costs that cannot be deducted in the year in which they are paid or incurred, and must be capitalized. The general rule is that if the property acquired has a useful life longer than the taxable year, the cost must be capitalized. The capital expenditure costs are then amortized or depreciated over the life of the asset in question.

Capital expenditures create or add basis to the asset or property, which once adjusted will determine tax liability in the event of sale or transfer. The following items are capital expenses that CANNOT be amortized or deducted:

- Any costs associated with issuing and selling stock or securities, such as commissions, professional fees, and printing costs
- Costs associated with the transfer of assets to the corporation
- The cost of acquiring fixed assets or transferring fixed assets to a corporation
- Preparing an asset to be used in business (such as modifying machinery before a factory opens)
- Legal costs of establishing or maintaining one's right of ownership in a piece of property (such as applying for a patent)

Corporate Income and Loss

C Corporations are subject to their own unique tax rate schedules, both on regular income and also on capital gain. Unlike the capital gain of individuals, the capital gains of corporations are taxed at the same rate as ordinary income. Business income, gain from property transactions, interest income, royalties, and dividends are all included in corporate income. Some income may be excluded, like municipal bond interest (muni bonds).

Gains and losses from property transactions are handled the same way for corporations as they are for individuals. The rules regarding like-kind exchanges and involuntary conversions are also basically the same for corporations and non-corporate taxpayers.

Personal Service Corporations are subject to a flat tax of 35% regardless of their income. *Remember this percentage for PSCs, because it is frequently tested on the exam.

In 2010, a C corporation may have a maximum of $500,000 of Section 179 deduction.[72] In 2010, the Section 179 deduction starts to phase out at $2 million of qualifying property put into service.

---

[72] Small Business Jobs Act of 2010 (September 27, 2010)

Corporate Net Operating Losses (NOLs)

A corporation figures and deducts a Net Operating Loss (NOL) the same way an individual, estate, or trust does. The same two-year carryback and up to 20-year carryforward periods apply, and the same sequence applies when the corporation carries two or more NOLs to the same year. A corporation must carry back an NOL two years prior to the year the NOL is generated. If the NOL is not used in the prior two years, the remaining NOL can be carried forward for up to 20 years.

A corporation figures a Net Operating Loss the same way it figures taxable income. It starts with gross income and subtracts its deductions. If its deductions are more than its gross income, the corporation has an NOL. However, the following rules for figuring NOL apply:

- A corporation cannot increase its current year NOL by carrybacks or carryovers from other years where it has a loss.
- A corporation cannot use the Domestic Production Activities Deduction to create or increase a current year NOL.
- A corporation can take the deduction for dividends received, without regard to the aggregate limits that normally apply.
- A corporation can figure the deduction for dividends paid on certain preferred stock of public utilities without limiting it to its taxable income for the year.

If a corporation carries back an NOL, it can use either Form 1120X or Form 1139. A Personal Service Corporation may not carry back an NOL to any tax year in which a Section 444 election is in effect.

If a corporation carries forward its NOL, it enters the carryover on Schedule K, Form 1120. If the NOL available for a carryback or carryforward year is greater than the taxable income for that year, the corporation must modify its taxable income to figure how much of the NOL it will use in that year and how much it can carry over to the next tax year.

A corporation can make an election to waive the two-year carryback period and use only the 20-year carryforward period. To make the election, a corporation would attach a statement to the original return filed by the due date (including extensions) for the NOL year. A corporation can take different deductions when figuring an NOL. A corporation's NOL differs from individual, estate, and trust NOLs in the following ways:

- A corporation must make different modifications to its taxable income in the carryback or carryforward year when figuring how much of the NOL is used and how much is carried over to the next year.
- A corporation uses different forms when claiming an NOL deduction.

If a corporation reasonably expects to have a Net Operating Loss in its current year, it may automatically extend the time for paying income tax liability for the preceding year by filing IRS Form 1138, *Extension of Time For Payment of Taxes by a Corporation Expecting a Net Operating Loss Carry Back.*

Corporate Capital Gains and Losses

Corporations pay tax on their capital gain at the same rate as their ordinary income. The maximum corporate tax rate on capital gains is 35%. The losses are only allowed to the extent of capital gain.

In the case of corporations, a net capital loss is carried back three years. Then, the remaining loss is carried forward five years. Capital losses that are a result of foreign expropriation[73] may not be carried back, but may be carried forward for ten years. In the case of a Regulated Investment Company (RIC), net capital losses may be carried forward eight years.

The $3,000 loss limitation that applies to individual taxpayers does not apply to corporations. In other words, if a corporation has an excess capital loss, it simply cannot deduct the loss in the current tax year. Instead, it carries the loss back or forward to other tax years and deducts it from any net capital gains that occur in those years.

Any capital loss carryover becomes a short-term capital loss carryover. It does not retain its original identity as long term or short term. A C Corporation may not carry a capital loss from, or to, a year for which it is an S Corporation. A capital loss is carried back to prior years in the following order:

- Three years prior to the loss year
- Two years prior to the loss year
- One year prior to the loss year

Any loss remaining is carried forward for five years. A capital loss from another year cannot produce or increase a Net Operating Loss in the year in which it is carried back. In other words, corporations can carry capital losses only to years that would otherwise have a total net capital gain.

> **Carryback Example:** In 2010, a calendar-year corporation has a capital gain of $3,000 and a capital loss of $9,000. The capital gain offsets some of the capital loss, leaving a net capital loss of $6,000. The corporation treats this $6,000 as a short-term loss when carried back or forward. The corporation carries the $6,000 short-term loss back one year. In 2009, (the prior year) the corporation had a short-term capital gain of $8,000 and a long-term capital gain of $5,000. It carries back the loss and subtracts the $6,000 short-term loss (carryback) first from the net short-term gain. This results in a net capital gain of $7,000. This consists of a net short-term capital gain of $2,000 ($8,000 - $6,000) and a net long-term capital gain of $5,000.

Related Party Transactions

A taxpayer cannot deduct a loss on the sale or trade of property (other than in the complete liquidation of a corporation), if the transaction is between the taxpayer and a corporation in which the taxpayer owns more than 50% in value of the outstanding stock.

For tax purposes, two corporations are considered "related persons" if one shareholder owns, either indirectly or directly, more than 50% of the value of the stock outstanding in both corporations. The ownership by a taxpayer's spouse or immediate family members is included

---

[73] This is when a foreign nation "expropriates" a corporation's assets for its own use.

in this calculation. In addition, a loss on the sale or trade of property is not deductible if the transaction is directly or indirectly between the following related parties:

- A corporation or partnership owned by the same person (50% or more ownership).
- An S Corporation or a C Corporation owned by the same person (50% or more ownership).
- Two S Corporations if the same person owns more than 50% of the stock in each.
- An executor and a beneficiary of an estate (except in the case of a sale or trade to satisfy a pecuniary bequest).
- Two corporations that are members of the same controlled group (under certain conditions, however, these losses are not disallowed but must be deferred).
- Any Personal Service Corporation and any employee-owner of the corporation (such as partners in a law firm), regardless of the amount of stock or percentage of ownership in the corporation.

In the case of related party transactions, the following rules apply:

- Losses cannot be deducted on a sale or exchange of property between related parties.
- Deductions for expenses on transactions between related parties are disallowed.
- Like-kind exchanges are disallowed between related parties if either party disposes of the property within two years of the exchange.

Determining Related-Party Ownership

An individual is considered to own the stock owned, directly or indirectly, by or for his family. For this rule, "family" includes only brothers and sisters (including half-brothers and half-sisters), a spouse, ancestors, and lineal descendants (children, grandchildren, grandparents, etc.) In determining whether a person directly or indirectly owns any of the outstanding stock of a corporation, the following rules apply:

- Stock directly or indirectly owned by or for a corporation, partnership, estate, or trust is considered owned proportionately by or for its shareholders, partners, or beneficiaries.
- An individual is considered to own the stock that is directly or indirectly owned by or for her family.
- An individual owning any stock in a corporation is considered to own the stock that is directly or indirectly owned by or for his partner.

Example: Robert is a 90% owner in Hay Bale Corporation. His wife Eileen is a 55% owner of Terabyte Corporation. For tax purposes, Robert is considered a "related person" for the purposes of ownership in Terabyte Corporation. Therefore, for the related-party transaction rules, Robert is also considered a 55% owner in Terabyte Corporation and his wife Eileen is considered a 90% owner in Hay Bale Corporation.

Closely Held Corporations and the "At-Risk" Rules

A closely held corporation generally has a small number of shareholders (usually family), and no public market for its corporate stock. The corporate ownership and management often overlap. This is different from a publicly held corporation, because in a publicly held company, the shares of the corporation are traded publicly on the stock market. A corporation is considered to be "closely held" if all of the following apply:

- It is not a Personal Service Corporation.
- At any time during the last half of the tax year, more than 50% of the value of its outstanding stock is, directly or indirectly, owned by or for five or fewer individuals. "Individual" in this case includes certain trusts and private foundations.

The reason why this issue is important to the IRS is because of the application of the "at-risk" rules.[74] The amount "at-risk" generally equals:

- The money and the adjusted basis of property contributed by the taxpayer to the activity, and
- The money borrowed for the activity.

These rules dictate that losses are only allowed up to the amount of the entity's risk of financial loss. The amount that is considered "at risk" for the corporation includes any cash contributed to the activity plus debts for which the corporation is directly liable. The "at-risk" amount also includes the FMV of any property (adjusted for any liens or encumbered mortgages) that is pledged as security or collateral for the debts of the activity which is also at risk.

If the corporation does not have a risk of financial loss in the activity, then the losses are not deductible.

Example: Allworth Corporation is a closely held C Corporation with only two related shareholders (a father and son). Allworth Corp. invests $50,000 in a business venture, and also pledges the value of a factory building as collateral security for an additional $100,000 loan that is also invested into the business venture. Allworth's factory building has a Fair Market Value of $150,000 but is also secured by a lien of $125,000. Allworth Corp.'s amount "at-risk" in the business venture is only $75,000 ($50,000 plus the $25,000 ($150,000 - $125,000) equity in the building).

All of the following items increase an entity's amount "at-risk":

1. A contribution of additional cash (or property) to the venture.
2. Any recourse loan for which the corporation is liable for repayment.

The amount "at-risk" is decreased by the following items:

1. An investor's withdrawal of cash or property from the activity.
2. A nonrecourse loan where the corporation is not liable for repayment.

The amount at risk cannot be decreased below zero. If this occurs, suspended losses from prior years must be reduced.[75]

---

[74] The at-risk limits on business losses apply to individuals, estates and trusts, and closely held corporations.

[75] For more information about the "at-risk" rules, see IRS Publication 925, *Passive Activity and At-Risk Rules*.

Summary: Key Concepts

1. A corporation is a legal entity that is separate and distinct from its members and share-holders. A C Corporation enjoys perpetual life and limited liability.

2. A C Corporation is taxed twice: first at the corporate level and then at the shareholder level. Shareholders of a C Corporation cannot deduct corporate losses. A corporation must maintain a list of all its shareholders, and generally must conduct at least one shareholder meeting per year.

3. A C Corporation must file a charter, issue stock, and be overseen by a board of directors. A C Corporation may have a single owner-shareholder, or millions of shareholders.

4. Corporate existence starts when the articles of incorporation are filed with the state office that handles incorporations (e.g., usually the Secretary of State), along with any required filing fees.

5. If a corporation liquidates, it will recognize gain or loss on the sale or distribution of its assets. Corporate shareholders then recognize gain or loss on the surrender of their stock to the corporation.

6. A C Corporation may sell common or preferred stock with different voting rights. A corporation may also sell bonds. In this way, a corporation may find it easier to raise investment capital than other business entity types. The major stock exchanges (like the New York Stock Exchange and NASDAQ) will only list securities issued by corporations.

7. One of the major advantages of a C Corporation is the ability for shareholder-employees to receive tax-free employee fringe benefits that are 100% deductible to the corporation as a business expense.

8. A corporation is always free to select either a calendar or fiscal year as its tax year. The tax year is elected on the corporation's first tax return.

Unit 2.8: Questions

1. The Lucks Corporation incurred $40,000 in startup costs when it opened for business in 2010. Instead of deducting the costs, the corporation has elected to amortize them. What is the minimum period over which these expenses can be recovered?

A. 12 months
B. 36 months
C. 60 months
D. 180 months

The answer is D. Businesses can choose to amortize startup expenses. Corporations can elect to evenly deduct ("amortize") the expenses over 180 months. ###

2. The Crunchy Corporation has just been formed. It has organizational costs that the corporation wishes to amortize. Which of the following tests are NOT required in order for the corporation to amortize its costs?

A. The costs are for the creation of the corporation.
B. The costs are chargeable to a capital account.
C. The costs must be paid by EFTPS.
D. The costs could be amortized over the life of the corporation if the corporation had a fixed life.

The answer is C. Corporations can elect to amortize certain costs for setting up and organizing. Corporations can amortize an organizational cost only if it meets all the following tests:
- It is for the creation of the business and not for starting or operating the trade or business.
- It is chargeable to a capital account.
- It could be amortized over the life of the business if it had a fixed life.
- It is incurred by the due date of the return (excluding extensions) for the first tax year in which it is in business (Publication 535). ###

There is no such requirement that the costs are paid by EFTPS.

3. Bernie Moon forms Moon Enterprises LLC (Limited Liability Company) as a single-member LLC. What form must Moon Enterprises LLC file in order to elect to be taxed as a C Corporation?

A. Form 1065
B. Form 8832
C. Form 1120
D. Form 7004

The answer is B. A single-member LLC will be taxed as a sole proprietorship unless Form 8832, *Entity Classification Election*, is filed. ###

4. The accumulated earnings tax is a tax that is imposed on C Corporations that accumulate earnings beyond the reasonable needs of their business. Which of the following reasons would NOT be an example of a "qualified accumulation"?

A. The expansion of the company to a new area or a new facility
B. Acquiring another business through the purchase of stock or other assets
C. Allowing the shareholders to take loans from the corporation.
D. Providing for reasonable product liability losses

The answer is C. Allowing shareholders to draw personal loans from a corporation is not a valid reason for a corporation to accumulate earnings. In fact, this is one of the things that the IRS looks for when it imposes the accumulated earnings tax upon a corporation. The accumulated earnings tax is imposed when a corporation tries to avoid income tax by permitting earnings and profits to accumulate instead of being divided or distributed. The tax is levied at a rate of 15% of accumulated taxable income. The absence of a bona fide business reason for a corporation's accumulated earnings may be indicated by many different circumstances, such as a lack of regular distributions to its shareholders or withdrawals by the shareholders classified as personal loans. However, actual moves to expand the business generally qualify as a bona fide use of the accumulations. ###

5. Which of the following types of domestic business entities will automatically be taxed as a corporation?

1. A joint stock company
2. An insurance company
3. Any business formed under state law that refers to itself as a corporation
4. A single member Limited Liability Company (LLC)

A. All of the above
B. 1, 2, and 3 only
C. 3 only
D. 2 and 3 only

The answer is B. A single member LLC will be taxed as a sole proprietorship unless an election is made by filing Form 8832, *Entity Classification Election*. The rest of the choices are required to be taxed as corporations. ###

6. If a corporation's tentative minimum tax exceeds the regular tax, the excess amount is:

A. Payable instead of the regular tax
B. Carried back to abate losses from prior years
C. Payable in addition to the regular tax, unless a corporation is insolvent
D. Payable in addition to the regular tax

The answer is D. If a corporation's tentative minimum tax exceeds the regular tax, the excess amount is payable *in addition* to the regular tax. ###

7. Blair and Drew buy a building together for $100,000. Both organize a corporation when the property has a Fair Market Value of $300,000. Blair and Drew transfer the property to the corporation for 100% of its authorized capital stock, which has a par value of $300,000. How much gain is recognized by Blair?

A. $0
B. $50,000
C. $150,000
D. $300,000

The answer is A. No gain is recognized by Blair, Drew, or the corporation. If a person transfers property (or money and property) to a corporation in exchange for stock in that corporation and immediately afterward controls the corporation, the exchange is usually not taxable. A shareholder also generally does not recognize a gain or loss upon the transfer of property when a company is initially formed. ###

8. Bandy Corporation's fiscal tax year ends June 30. Not counting extensions, what is the due date for its tax return?

A. September 15
B. April 15
C. October 15
D. January 15

The answer is A. Bandy Corporation must file its income tax return by September 15. If the due date falls on a Saturday, Sunday, or legal holiday, the due date is extended to the next business day. Generally, a corporation must file its income tax return by the fifteenth day of the third month after the end of its tax year. ###

9. Which form must a corporation file in order to request an extension to file its tax return?

A. Form 7004
B. Form 2848
C. Form 2553
D. Form 8821

The answer is A. Corporations file Form 7004, *Automatic Extension of Time to File Certain Business Income Tax, Information, and Other Returns,* to request a six-month extension of time to file a corporation income tax return (Publication 542). ###

10. Lisa transfers property worth $35,000 and renders services valued at $4,000 to a corporation in exchange for stock valued at $38,000. Right after the exchange, Lisa owns 85% of the outstanding stock. How much income, if any, must Lisa recognize in this transaction?

A. $0
B. $4,000
C. $32,000
D. $35,000
E. $38,000

The answer is B. Lisa recognizes ordinary income of $4,000 as payment for services she rendered to the corporation. Normally, the exchange of money or property for a controlling interest in a corporation is treated as a nontaxable exchange. However, services are not included in this definition. The value of stock received for services is income to the recipient. ###

11. Nell transfers property with a basis of $200,000 and an FMV of $350,000 to a corporation in exchange for stock with a Fair Market Value of $300,000. This represents 65% of the stock of the corporation. How much gain is recognized by Nell on this transaction?

A. $0
B. $50,000
C. $100,000
D. $300,000

The answer is C. Nell must recognize a taxable gain of $100,000 ($300,000 FMV of stock minus $200,000 basis) on the transaction. IRC Section 351 provides that no gain or loss shall be recognized if property is transferred to a corporation solely in exchange for stock and immediately after the exchange the shareholder is in control of the corporation. However, Nell did not control the corporation after the transfer. In order to be in control of a corporation, the transferor must own, immediately after the exchange, at least 80% of the total combined voting power of all classes of stock entitled to vote and at least 80% of the outstanding shares of each class of nonvoting stock. Since Nell only has control over 65% of the shares, the exchange is taxable. ###

12. What is the penalty for a corporation that fails to make estimated tax payments?

A. One-half of one percent per month, up to a maximum of 25%
B. Five percent per month, up to a maximum of 25%
C. Five percent per month, up to a maximum of 35%
D. Five percent per month, up to a maximum of 100%

The answer is A. If a corporation fails to make estimated tax payments, there is a late payment penalty of one-half of one percent per month, up to a maximum of 25%. ###

13. Top Care Corporation is a calendar-year, cash-basis corporation. Top Care is required to make estimated tax payments. What are the due dates for the estimated payments?

A. April 15, June 15, September 15, and December 15
B. January 15, March 15, June 15, September 15, and December 15
C. March 1, June 1, September 1, and December 1
D. None of the above

The answer is A. Installments for corporations are due by the fifteenth day of the fourth, sixth, ninth, and twelfth months of the year. So, for example, a calendar-year corporation would have estimated tax due dates of April 15, June 15, September 15, and December 15. ###

14. Metro Corporation had a profitable year in 2010 and is required to make estimated payments during the year totaling $19,000. However, because of serious economic difficulties, Metro genuinely expects to post a loss in 2011. Which statement is true about Metro's required estimated payments?

A. Metro is NOT required to make estimated payments in 2011.
B. Metro must make estimated payments of at least 90% of the prior year's tax liability.
C. Metro is required to pay 100% of the prior year tax liability.
D. Metro must make a minimum estimated tax payment of $500.

The answer is A. Metro Corporation does not have to make estimated payments if it expects to post a loss during the year. A corporation must make installment payments of estimated tax only if it expects its estimated tax for the year to be $500 or more. If the corporation expects to have a loss for the year, it is not required to make estimated tax payments. ###

15. Which form is used for a C Corporation to receive a quick refund of overpayment of estimated tax?

A. Form 4466
B. Form 1120
C. Form 7004
D. Form 1040

The answer is A. A corporation may use Form 4466 in order to receive a quick refund of the corporation's overpayment of estimated tax. In order to use this form, the overpayment must be at least 10% of the expected tax liability and at least $500. ###

Unit 2.9: Corporate Deductions, Distributions, and Liquidations

More Reading:
Publication 542, *Corporations*

Corporate Deductions

Although a C Corporation recognizes income and loss similar to individuals and other businesses, there are numerous special provisions that apply only to corporations. This section will go over special provisions that are unique to C Corporations.

Charitable Deduction

Unlike other business entities, a C Corporation can deduct a limited amount in charitable contributions. S Corporations are not allowed this special deduction. C Corporations may deduct charitable contributions up to 10% of their taxable income. This is different from the rules that govern charitable contributions for individuals and other entities.

Corporations may only deduct charitable contributions that are made to qualified organizations. The rules regarding what qualifies as a "charitable organization" are the same for corporations as they are for individuals. The contribution is deductible if made to, or for the use of, a charity, church, or other qualifying or nonprofit organization. Corporations can carry over (with certain limits) any charitable contributions made during the year that are more than the 10% limit to the subsequent five years. Any charitable contribution not used within that period is lost. Corporations have no restrictions on the amount of charitable contributions that they can make. Any unused amounts would be a carryover.

A corporation using the accrual method of accounting can choose to deduct unpaid contributions for the tax year if the board of directors authorizes the contribution, and the corporation pays the contribution within 2.5 months after the close of its tax year. This choice is reported on the corporation's return for the tax year. A declaration stating that the board of directors adopted the resolution during the tax year must accompany the return. The declaration must include the date the resolution was adopted.

> **Example**: Larder Corporation is a calendar-year, accrual-based corporation. Larder's board of directors approves a charitable contribution of $5,000 to the United Way on December 15, 2010. Larder Corporation correctly deducts the contribution on its 2010 corporate tax return. Larder does not actually have to pay the contribution until March 15, 2011, 2.5 months after the close of its tax year.

A corporation using the cash method of accounting deducts contributions in the tax year they are paid.

A corporation figures its taxable income for the purposes of the charitable deduction *without* the following:

- The Dividends-Received Deduction (DRD)
- The Domestic Production Activities Deduction
- Any Net Operating Loss carryback to the tax year
- Any capital loss carryback to the tax year

Carryover of Excess Charitable Contributions

A corporation can carry over, within certain limits, to each of the subsequent five years any charitable contributions made during the current year that exceed the 10% limit.

> **Example:** The Bahamas Corporation has net income of $600,000 in 2010 before taking into account its charitable contribution. The corporation donated $80,000 to a qualified charity in 2010. It also has a Net Operating Loss carryover of $100,000 from a prior year. Therefore, the corporation's charitable deduction is limited to $50,000. The allowable contribution deduction is figured as follows:
>
> $$(\$600{,}000 - \$100{,}000 = \$500{,}000) \times 10\% = \$50{,}000$$

The charitable contribution that is not allowed in the 2010 tax year can be carried forward up to five years. If the Bahamas Corporation does not use the remainder at the end of five years, then the deduction is lost.

A corporation loses any excess contributions not used within that five-year period. A corporation cannot deduct a carryover of excess contributions to the extent it increases a Net Operating Loss carryover. No carryback is allowed for charitable contributions.

> **Example:** Gromwell Corporation, a calendar-year C Corporation, makes a large charitable contribution in 2005. The corporation has a carryover of excess contributions paid in 2005 and it does not use all the excess on its return for 2006. Gromwell Corporation can carry the rest over to 2007, 2008, 2009, and 2010. After that time, it can no longer carry over the 2005 charitable contribution excess if any remains.

Generally, no deduction is allowed for any charitable contribution of $250 or more unless the corporation gets a receipt from the donee organization. The written receipt or "acknowledgment" should show the amount of cash contributed or a description of the property contributed. The receipt or acknowledgment should also give a description and a good faith estimate of the value of any goods or services provided in return for the contribution, or state that no goods or services were provided in return for the contribution.

If a corporation (other than a closely held or Personal Service Corporation) claims a deduction of more than $500 for contributions of property other than cash, a schedule describing the property and the method used to determine its Fair Market Value must be attached to the corporation's return. In addition the corporation should keep a record of:

- The approximate date and manner of acquisition of the donated property
- The cost or other basis of the donated property held by the donor for less than 12 months prior to contribution
- Any donation of a used vehicle, boat, or similar property if it takes a deduction larger than $500 for the donated vehicle.

Closely held and Personal Service Corporations must complete and attach Form 8283, *Noncash Charitable Contributions*, to their returns if they claim a deduction of more than $500 for noncash contributions. For all other corporations, if the deduction claimed for donated property exceeds $5,000, the corporation must complete Form 8283 and attach it to its tax return. A corporation must obtain a qualified appraisal for all deductions of property claimed in excess of $5,000.

A qualified appraisal is not required for the donation of cash, publicly traded securities, or inventory.

Dividends-Received Deduction

A corporation can deduct a percentage of certain dividends received during its tax year. This is called the "Dividends-Received Deduction." The Dividends-Received Deduction is a tax deduction taken by a corporation on the dividends paid to it by other corporations in which it has an ownership stake. This deduction is designed to reduce the consequences of double taxation. The DRD is only available to C corporations; not LLCs, S corporations, Partnerships, or individuals.

Without this deduction, corporate profits would be taxed to the corporation that earned them, then to the corporate shareholder, and then *again* to the individual shareholder. The Dividends-Received Deduction complements the consolidated return regulations, which allow affiliated corporations to file a single consolidated return for U.S. federal income tax purposes.

Generally, if a corporation receives dividends from another corporation, it is entitled to a deduction of 70% of the dividend it receives. If the corporation receiving the dividend owns 20% of the other corporation, then the deduction increases to 80%. If, on the other hand, the corporation receiving the dividend owns more than 80% of the distributing corporation, it is allowed to deduct 100% of the dividend it receives, making the dividend essentially nontaxable to the receiving corporation.

Limitations on the Dividends-Received Deduction

The total deduction for dividends-received is based on the percentage of stock ownership from the distributing corporation:

Percentage of ownership	Dividends Received Deduction
Less than 20%	70%
20 - 80%	80%
Greater than 80%	100%

Example: The Quincy Corporation owns 25% of Lightstar Corporation. The Quincy Corporation has net income of $70,000 *before* taking into account its dividends-received. In 2010, Quincy received $100,000 in dividends from Lightstar. Quincy receives an 80% Dividends-Received Deduction, figured as follows: $80,000 = ($100,000 × 80%). Therefore, the Quincy Corporation only has to recognize $20,000 of the dividends received from Lightstar Corporation. In 2010, the Quincy Corporation's taxable net income is $90,000 ($70,000 + $20,000).

There are some other limitations on the Dividends-Received Deduction:

- The deduction is only available to C Corporations, not to individuals, LLCs, partnerships, or other entities.
- There is a 45-day minimum holding period for common stock.
- This deduction does NOT apply to dividends from preferred stock.
- If a corporation is entitled to a 70% Dividends-Received Deduction, it can deduct amounts only up to 70% of its taxable income.

547

- If a corporation is entitled to an 80% Dividends-Received Deduction, it can deduct amounts only up to 80% of its taxable income.

If a corporation is entitled to a 100% Dividends-Received Deduction, there is no taxable income limitation, and the corporation may deduct the full amount of the dividends received. Normally, a C Corporation can deduct dividend income it receives from other domestic corporations, but the deduction is limited to a total of either 70% or 80% of the corporation's taxable income. However, if the corporation has an NOL, this limit doesn't apply.

> **Example:** Jamestown Corporation owns 85% of the outstanding stock in Humboldt Corporation. In 2010, Jamestown Corporation receives $250,000 in dividends from Humboldt Corporation. Because Jamestown Corporation has over 80% ownership of Humboldt Corporation, the dividends are not taxable. Jamestown Corporation may claim the Dividends-Received Deduction for the dividends received from Humboldt Corporation.

Small business investment companies can deduct 100% of the dividends received from taxable domestic corporations.

Non-qualifying Dividends

In order to qualify for the Dividends-Received Deduction, the receiving corporation must hold the stock for a minimum holding period. Corporations CANNOT take a deduction for dividends received from the following entities:

- A real estate investment trust (REIT)
- A tax-exempt corporation
- A corporation whose stock was held less than 45 days
- Any corporation, if another corporation is under an obligation to make related payments for positions in substantially similar or related property

Dividends on deposits in domestic building and loan associations, mutual savings banks, cooperative banks, and similar organizations are interest income—not dividends. They do not qualify for this deduction. In figuring the limit for the Dividends-Received Deduction, a corporation must determine taxable income without the following items:

- The Net Operating Loss Deduction
- The Domestic Production Activities Deduction
- The deduction for dividends received
- Any adjustment due to the nontaxable part of an extraordinary dividend
- Any capital loss carryback to the tax year

Effect of NOL on the Dividends-Received Deduction

If a corporation has a Net Operating Loss (NOL) for a tax year, the Dividends-Received Deduction must be figured differently. The limit of 80% (or 70%) of taxable income does not apply. To determine whether a corporation has an NOL, a corporation must figure the Dividends-Received Deduction without the 80% (or 70%) of taxable income limit.

Example: ABC Corporation loses $25,000 from its own business operations in 2010. ABC Corporation also receives $100,000 in dividend income from a 20%-owned corporation. Therefore, ABC Corporation's taxable income in 2010 is $75,000 ($100,000 - $25,000) before the Dividends-Received Deduction. If ABC Corporation claims the full Dividends-Received Deduction of $80,000 ($100,000 × 80%) and combines it with an operations loss of $25,000, it will have an NOL of ($5,000). Therefore, the 80% of taxable income limit does not apply. The corporation can deduct the full $80,000.

Example: Redwood Corporation has a loss of $15,000 from business operations in 2010. Redwood's taxable income is $85,000 before the Dividends-Received Deduction. After claiming the Dividends-Received Deduction of $80,000 ($100,000 × 80%), its taxable income is $5,000. Because Redwood Corporation will NOT have an NOL after applying a full Dividends-Received Deduction, its allowable Dividends-Received Deduction is limited to 80% of its taxable income, or $68,000 ($85,000 × 80%).

Capital Contributions

Contributions to the capital of a corporation are not taxable to the corporation, whether or not they are made by the shareholders. If a shareholder contributes property to a corporation, the basis of the contributed property to the corporation is the same as the basis that the shareholder had in the property, increased by any gain that the shareholder recognized in the exchange. The basis of property contributed to capital by anyone other than a shareholder is zero.

Example: The city of San Jose gives Madera Corporation a plot of land as an enticement to locate its business operations in the city. Madera accounts for the property as a contribution to capital. The land has zero basis since the property was contributed by a non-shareholder.

Corporate Dividends and Distributions

Corporate distributions occur when money, stock, or other property is distributed to a shareholder in correlation to the shareholder's ownership of stock. Ordinary dividends are the most common corporate distribution and are taxable as ordinary income to the shareholder. This means these dividends are not capital gains.

Ordinary dividends are paid out of the earnings and profits of a corporation. They are reported to shareholders on Form 1099-DIV.

Example: Tobias is the only shareholder of Seaside Corporation, a calendar-year corporation. During the year, Seaside makes four $1,000 distributions to Tobias. At the end of the year (before subtracting distributions made during the year), the corporation has $10,000 of current year profits. Since the corporation's current year earnings and profits ($10,000) were more than the amount of the distributions it made during the year ($4,000), all of the distributions are treated as distributions of current year earnings and profits. The corporation must issue a Form 1099-DIV to Tobias by January 31 to report the $4,000 distributed to him as dividends. Seaside Corporation must use Form 1096, *Annual Summary and Transmittal of U.S. Information Returns*, to report this transaction to the IRS by February 28 (March 31 if filing electronically). The corporation does not deduct these dividends on its income tax return.

Distributions can take the form of stock, cash, or other property. A dividend that is not paid in cash can be distributed in the form of property, such as land, vehicles, or trademarks. A shareholder also may receive dividends through a partnership, an estate, a trust, or any other business that is taxed as a corporation. The most common kinds of distributions are:

- Ordinary dividends (in cash or in property)
- Capital gain distributions
- Stock distributions or stock dividends

Dividends are payments made by a company to its shareholders. When a corporation earns a profit, a corporation can reinvest the profit in the business (called retained earnings), or it can be paid to the shareholders as a dividend. Paying dividends is not considered an expense; rather, it is the division of an asset among shareholders. A corporation cannot deduct a dividend as a business expense. Many companies retain a portion of their earnings and pay the remainder as a dividend.

A distribution is calculated by adding the amount of any money paid to the shareholder plus the Fair Market Value (FMV) of any property transferred to the shareholder. The distribution amount is reduced by the following liabilities:

- Any liability of the corporation the shareholder assumes
- Any liability that the property is subject to upon distribution, such as mortgage debt on a building that the shareholder assumes

The amount of a distribution can never go "below zero," no matter how much liability a shareholder assumes on the distribution. The FMV of any distributed property becomes the shareholder's basis in that property.

Distributions from Earnings and Profits (E&P)

A corporate distribution to a shareholder is usually treated as a distribution of the corporation's earnings. Any part of a distribution from current-year earnings and profits or accumulated earnings and profits is reported as dividend income to the shareholder. Corporate earnings and profits (E&P) are not the same as taxable income.

Corporate distributions in excess of E&P are nontaxable to the corporate shareholder to the extent of the shareholder's stock basis. If a distribution is more than the adjusted basis of a shareholder's stock, he has a gain (usually a capital gain).

The amount of corporate E&P determines taxation of corporate distributions to shareholders. Taxable distributions of a C Corporation are deducted first from current E&P, and then from any accumulated E&P existing from prior years.

Corporate E&P is initially increased by the corporation's taxable income. The following transactions *increase* the amount of current corporate earnings and profits:

- Long-term contracts reported on the completed contract method
- Intangible drilling costs deducted currently
- Mine exploration and development costs deducted currently
- Dividends-Received Deduction

The following transactions reduce the amount of current corporate E&P:

- Corporate federal income taxes
- Life insurance policy premiums on a corporate officer

- Excess charitable contribution (over 10% limit)
- Expenses relating to tax-exempt income
- Excess of capital losses over capital gains
- Corporate dividends and other distributions

If a corporation cancels a shareholder's debt without repayment by the shareholder, the amount canceled is treated as a distribution to the shareholder. This type of corporate distribution is generally treated as a distribution of earnings and profits.

Corporate Gain from Property Distributions

A corporation will recognize a gain on the distribution of property to a shareholder if the FMV of the property exceeds the adjusted basis of the property. This is the same treatment the corporation would receive if the property were sold. However, for this purpose, the FMV of the property is the greater of the following amounts:

- The actual FMV
- The amount of any liabilities the shareholder assumed in connection with the distribution of the property

If the property was depreciable, the corporation may have to recognize gain as ordinary income from depreciation recapture.

Stock Distributions

Stock dividends occur when a corporation issues additional shares of its own stock to shareholders, rather than a cash dividend. "Stock rights," also known as "stock options," are distributions by a corporation of rights to acquire its stock. Stock rights allow shareholders to purchase additional shares at a set price, which may be offered to some or all shareholders.

A stock dividend is also called a "stock distribution." Both terms mean essentially the same thing. It is when a corporation gives additional shares of stock to its shareholders, rather than issuing a cash dividend.

Distributions of stock dividends and stock rights are generally tax-free to shareholders and not deductible by the corporation. However, stock and stock rights become taxable if any of the following apply to their distribution:

- The shareholder has the choice to receive cash or other property instead of stock or stock rights.
- The distribution gives cash or other property to some shareholders and an increase in the percentage interest in the corporation's assets or earnings and profits to other shareholders.
- The distribution is in convertible preferred stock.
- The distribution gives preferred stock to some shareholders and gives common stock to other shareholders.
- The distribution is of preferred stock.

A corporation cannot deduct the expenses of issuing a stock dividend. These expenses include printing, postage, cost of advice sheets, transfer agent fees, and any fees for listing on stock exchanges. The corporation must capitalize these costs.

Nondividend Distributions

If nondividend distributions are made to shareholders (land, other property, etc.), the corporation must report these distributions to the IRS on Form 5452, *Corporate Report of Nondividend Distributions*. A nondividend distribution reduces the basis of a shareholder's stock. It is not taxed until the shareholder's basis in the stock is fully recovered. The nontaxable portion is also called a "return of capital"; it is a return of the shareholder's investment in the company.

When the basis of the shareholder's stock has been reduced to zero, she must report any additional nondividend distributions as a taxable capital gain.

Distribution Reporting Requirements

A corporation must file Form 1099-DIV with the IRS for each shareholder who receives a dividend of $10 or more during a calendar year. A corporation must send Forms 1099-DIV to the IRS with Form 1096 by February 28 (March 31 if filing electronically) of the year following the year of the distribution.

The corporation is also required to furnish Forms 1099-DIV to shareholders by January 31 of the year following the close of the calendar year during which the corporation made the distributions.

The corporation is allowed to furnish Forms 1099-DIV early to shareholders. A business may furnish Forms 1099-DIV to shareholders any time after April 30 of the year of the distributions if the corporation has made its final distributions for the calendar year.

Constructive Distributions

A "constructive distribution" may occur when a corporation confers a benefit upon a shareholder. The IRS may re-categorize certain transactions as "constructive distributions," which makes the transaction nondeductible to the corporation. Since distributions are not deductible as a business expense by the corporation and are often taxable to the shareholder, it is a situation that corporations try to avoid.

Often, this transaction is initially categorized as something else, such as salaries or rent. However, the IRS may choose to disallow the expense and re-categorize the transaction as a "constructive distribution." Examples of "constructive distributions" include:

- **Unreasonable compensation:** If a corporation pays an employee-shareholder an unreasonably high salary considering the services actually performed, the excessive part of the salary may be treated as a distribution to the employee-shareholder.
- **Unreasonable rents:** If a corporation rents property from a shareholder and the rent is unreasonably more than the shareholder would charge to a stranger for use of the same property, the excessive part of the rent may be treated as a distribution to the shareholder.
- **Cancellation of a shareholder's debt:** If a corporation cancels a shareholder's debt without repayment by the shareholder, the amount canceled is treated as a distribution to the shareholder.
- **Property transfers for less than FMV:** If a corporation transfers (or sells) property to a shareholder for less than the FMV, then the transfer could be deemed a distribution.

- **Below market or interest-free loans**: If a corporation gives a shareholder an interest-free loan at a rate below the applicable federal rate, the uncharged interest may be treated as a constructive distribution to the shareholder, and therefore taxable to the shareholder and not deductible by the corporation.

Transfers of Property to Shareholders for Less than FMV

A sale or exchange of property by a corporation to a shareholder may be treated as a distribution to the shareholder. For a shareholder who is not a corporation, if the FMV of the property on the date of the sale or exchange exceeds the price he paid, the excess may be treated as a distribution to him.

The distribution of appreciated property by a corporation to a shareholder is treated as a taxable sale of that property. If a corporation (C Corporation or S Corporation) distributes property to a shareholder, the corporation must recognize gain (not loss) if the fair market value (FMV) of the property exceeds its adjusted cost basis.

Any property distribution is treated as if the corporation had sold that property to the shareholder. This transaction is taxable, and is reported on Form 1099-DIV and Form 5452. If the property was depreciable or amortizable, the corporation may also have to treat all or part of the gain as ordinary income from depreciation recapture (Publication 542).

A corporation cannot recognize any losses on a distribution of appreciated property (i.e., where the property's FMV is less than the adjusted cost basis). However, a corporation is allowed to recognize losses when depreciated property is distributed to shareholders in complete liquidation (when the corporation ceases operations).

Accumulated Earnings and Profits

"Accumulated earnings" are earnings and profits from prior years earned by a corporation that have not been distributed to its shareholders. Usually, corporations reinvest these earnings, rather than distribute them. If a corporation's current earnings and profits are less than the distributions made during the year, part or all of each distribution is treated as a distribution of accumulated earnings and profits. Accumulated earnings and profits are always earnings that the corporation accumulated before the current year.

If accumulated earnings and profits are reduced to zero, the remaining part of each distribution reduces the adjusted basis of shareholder's stock. If the corporation makes distributions to shareholders that exceed the adjusted basis of their stock, the distribution is treated as a capital gain from the sale or exchange of property and is taxable to the shareholder.

Stock Redemptions

A stock redemption occurs when a corporation buys back its own stock. The corporation acquires its own stock from a stockholder in exchange for property (usually by buying the stock back with cash). A stock redemption is considered to have occurred whether the stock acquired is canceled, retired, or held as treasury stock.

A shareholder is required to treat the amount realized on a stock redemption as either a dividend distribution or a sale of stock. Stock redemptions are generally treated as a dividend unless certain conditions are met. There are five main tests that determine whether or not the shareholder will receive capital gains treatment on redemption of stock. The five tests are as follows:

- The redemption is not equivalent to a dividend, meaning that the shareholder's proportionate interest and voting power in the corporation has been substantially reduced.
- There was a substantially disproportionate redemption of stock, meaning that the amount received by the shareholder is not in proportion to his stock ownership.
- The redemption was due to a complete termination of a non-corporate shareholder's interest.
- The redemption was part of a partial liquidation.
- The distribution is received by an estate. The estate may treat the stock redemption as a sale in order to pay death taxes.

The corporation must realize a gain from the redemption, as if the property were sold at the Fair Market Value to the shareholder. The corporation must recognize income on the distribution of depreciated property to the extent of depreciation or the amount realized (whichever is less). The corporation may not recognize a loss on a stock redemption unless:

- The redemption occurs in a complete liquidation of the corporation, or
- The redemption occurs on stock held by an estate.

Corporate Liquidations and Dissolution

Liquidating distributions are distributions received by a shareholder during a complete or partial dissolution of a corporation. When a corporation dissolves, it redeems all of its stock in a series of distributions. A corporate liquidation is treated as a sale of all outstanding corporate stock in exchange for a corporation's assets.

These distributions are often recognized by the shareholder as a return of capital. Shareholders will receive a Form 1099-DIV from the corporation showing the amount of the liquidating distribution. A liquidating distribution is not taxable to the shareholder until the shareholder recovers all of her basis in the stock. After the basis of the stock has been reduced to zero, shareholders must report the liquidating distribution as a capital gain.

If a dissolving corporation is filing a final return, the corporation can request a prompt assessment from the IRS after filing its final tax return. At the corporate level, the corporation recognizes gain or loss on the liquidation in an amount equal to the difference between the FMV and the adjusted basis of the assets distributed.

Gain or loss is recognized by the corporation on a liquidating distribution as if the corporation sold the assets to a buyer at Fair Market Value. A corporation is allowed to recognize losses during the liquidation, except for those losses with related parties.

"Complete liquidation" exists when the corporation ceases to be a going concern and its activities are merely for the purpose of winding up its affairs, paying its debts, and distributing any remaining balance to its shareholders. In certain cases in which the buyer is a corporation in control of the distributing corporation, the distribution may not be taxable. A corporate dissolution or liquidation is reported on Form 966, *Corporate Dissolution or Liquidation*.

554

The corporation must file an annual return for the year it goes out of business, even if it has no income or business activity in that year. (Exempt entities should not file Form 966, even if they are organized as corporations.) C Corporations must file Form 966 within 30 days after the resolution or plan is adopted to dissolve the corporation or liquidate any of its stock.

The fiduciary representing a dissolving corporation or a decedent's estate may request a prompt assessment of tax. The IRS ordinarily has three years from the date an income tax return is filed (or its due date, whichever is later) to charge any additional tax that is due. However, a personal representative of a decedent's estate may request a prompt assessment of tax after the return has been filed. This reduces the time for making the assessment to 18 months from the date the written request for prompt assessment was received. This request can be made for any income tax return of the decedent and for the income tax return of the decedent's estate.

Unit 2.9: Questions

1. Bartleby Corporation is a calendar-year corporation that uses the accrual method of accounting. What is the last day that the corporation can make a charitable contribution and still deduct it on its 2010 tax return?

A. December 31, 2010
B. April 15, 2011
C. January 15, 2011
D. March 15, 2011

The answer is D. A corporation using the accrual method of accounting can choose to deduct unpaid contributions for the tax year if the board of directors authorizes the contribution, and the corporation pays the contribution within 2.5 months after the close of its tax year. This choice is reported on the corporation's return for the tax year. ###

2. Which of the following statements about stock distributions is CORRECT?

A. Stock distributions must be treated as a cash distribution that is taxable to the shareholder.
B. Stock distributions are usually taxable to the corporation when distributed to shareholders.
C. Stock distributions are always deductible by a corporation as an expense.
D. Stock distributions are not taxable to shareholders and not deductible by the corporation.

The answer is D. Distributions by a corporation of its own stock are commonly known as stock dividends or stock rights. Stock rights are distributions by a corporation of rights to acquire the corporation's stock. Generally, stock dividends and stock rights are not taxable to shareholders. ###

3. Capital Cross Corporation is a calendar-year C Corporation. In 2010, Capital Cross has charitable contributions that it cannot use on the current year return. What is the final year that Capital Cross can *carryforward* its unused charitable contributions?

A. 2011
B. 2013
C. 2015
D. 2020

The answer is C. A corporation can carry over charitable contributions made during the year for five years. It loses any unused excess after that period. Corporate charitable contributions cannot be carried back, only carried *forward*. ###

4. April bought corporate stock in 2007 for $1,000. In 2008, she received a return of capital of $800. April did not include this amount in her income, but correctly reduced the basis of her stock to $200. She received another return of capital of $300 in 2010. The first $200 of this amount reduced April's basis to zero. How should she report the remaining $100 in distributions?

A. April must report $100 in long-term capital gain in 2010.
B. April does not have to report any additional return of capital.
C. April must report the $100 as ordinary income.
D. April must report any additional return of capital as a capital loss.

The answer is A. When the basis of a shareholder's stock has been reduced to zero, the shareholder must report any additional return of capital received as a capital gain. Since April has held the stock for more than one year, the gain is reported as a long-term capital gain. ###

5. Three years ago, Mark purchased 100 shares of Rock Star, Inc. for $10 per share. In 2010 Rock Star, Inc. completely liquidated and distributed $20,000 to Mark in exchange for all of his stock. Mark must report this distribution as:

A. A $20,000 long-term capital loss.
B. A $19,000 short-term capital gain.
C. A $19,000 long-term capital gain.
D. This transaction is nontaxable to Mark and does not have to be reported.

The answer is C. Mark had a $19,000 long-term capital gain. His basis in the stock was $1,000 [100 shares stock x $10]. So his gain is figured as follows: ($20,000 - $1,000). Gain or loss that is recognized to shareholders on distributions in a corporate liquidation is generally determined by the difference between the total of the money and property received by the shareholders and the basis of their stock surrendered. The gain or loss will be long-term or short-term depending on the length of time the stock has been held. Since Mark purchased the shares many years ago, his holding period exceeds one year and is therefore recognized as long-term capital gain and must be reported on his return. ###

6. Geraldine owns 1,000 shares of Kimball Corporation. Her shares were all acquired on January 1, 2005, and her basis in the stock is $20,000. Kimball Corporation completely liquidated in 2010 and distributed $56,000 in two payments to Geraldine. Geraldine received $16,000 in December 2010 and $40,000 in January 2011. How much gain or loss is recognized by Geraldine in 2010 and 2011?

A. $4,000 loss in 2010 and $40,000 gain in 2011
B. $4,000 loss in 2010 and $44,000 gain in 2011
C. No gain or loss in 2010 and $40,000 gain in 2011
D. No gain or loss in 2010 and $36,000 gain in 2011

The answer is D. The *liquidating distribution* is not taxable until the shareholder's stock basis ($20,000) has been recovered. Geraldine recovered $16,000 of her basis in 2010. This left a balance of $4,000 of her basis in 2010. Her recognized gain is $36,000 ($56,000 total distribution - $20,000 basis), and she will recognize no gain or loss in 2010. Geraldine will recognize $36,000 capital gain in 2011. ###

7. Ryan is a 5% shareholder in Prank Corporation, and he has an outstanding $10,000 loan that he owes to the corporation. In 2009, Ryan files bankruptcy and defaults on the loan. Prank Corporation cancels Ryan's debt in 2010. How should this cancellation of debt be reported?

A. The debt cancellation is a $10,000 taxable distribution to Ryan.
B. The debt cancellation is ordinary income to Ryan.
C. The debt cancellation is a charitable contribution to Ryan.
D. The debt cancellation is a $10,000 return of capital.

The answer is A. If a corporation cancels a shareholder's debt without repayment by the shareholder, the amount canceled is treated as a distribution to the shareholder. A corporate distribution to a shareholder is generally treated as a distribution of earnings and profits. ###

8. The Party Time Corporation distributes $75,000 in cash along with a delivery truck having a $40,000 adjusted basis and a $60,000 FMV to a shareholder. What gain, if any, must Party Time Corporation recognize?

A. $0
B. $20,000
C. $40,000
D. $60,000

The answer is B. A corporation will recognize a gain on the distribution of property to a shareholder if the FMV of the property is more than its adjusted basis ($60,000 FMV - $40,000 adjusted basis = $20,000). This is the same treatment the corporation would receive if the property were sold. ###

9. The Red Dog Corporation paid dividends to the following shareholders in 2010:

Marie: $1,000 in dividends
Rose: $90 in dividends
Laura: $9.75 in dividends
Timothy: $100 in dividends
The Red Dog Corporation is required to issue a Form 1099-DIV to which shareholders?

A. All shareholders must receive a Form 1099-DIV.
B. Marie and Rose only.
C. Timothy, Marie, and Rose only.
D. Only Marie.

The answer is C. A C Corporation is required to issue a Form 1099-DIV with the IRS for each shareholder paid dividends and other distributions on stock of $10 or more during a calendar year. ###

10. All of the examples below are considered corporate distributions EXCEPT?

A. Ordinary dividends
B. Capital gain distributions
C. Constructive distributions
D. Compensation to an employee-shareholder

The answer is D. Compensation or wages to an employee-shareholder is not considered a distribution. Instead, the wages would be treated as a business expense just like wages for any other business. The wages are deductible by the corporation and then taxable to the employee-shareholder as wages. ###

11. In 2008, Sabine purchased 100 shares of Vital Corporation stock for $50 per share. In 2010, Vital Corporation liquidated. After paying all of its outstanding liabilities, Vital Corporation distributed $10,000 in cash and appreciated property worth $90,000 to ALL of its shareholders. Sabine's portion of the distributed assets and cash was $12,000. How much capital gain must she report from this liquidating distribution in 2010?

A. $0 gain
B. $3,000 capital gain
C. $7,000 capital gain
D. $10,000 capital gain

The answer is C. The capital gain is figured as follows: Her basis is $5,000 ($50 x 100 shares). Then subtract her portion of the distribution from her basis: ($12,000 distribution - $5,000 basis). Sabine has a $7,000 capital gain. ###

12. Distributions of stock rights are generally tax-free to shareholders. Which of the following statements is FALSE?

A. Even if a shareholder has a choice to receive cash instead of stock rights, as long as the shareholder chooses to receive stock rights, the distribution will be tax-free.
B. Stock rights are distributions by a corporation of rights to acquire its own stock.
C. Stock rights are rights provided to a shareholder to purchase new shares.
D. Stock rights can be taxable in some circumstances.

The answer is A. If the shareholder has a choice to receive cash *instead of* stock rights, the distributions of stock and stock rights are taxable. Distributions by a corporation of its own stock are commonly known as stock dividends. Stock rights (also known as "stock options") are distributions by a corporation of rights to acquire its own stock. ###

13. Break Neck Corporation is an accrual-based, calendar-year corporation. On December 15, 2010, Break Neck's board of directors authorizes and elects to pay a charitable contribution of $25,000 to the Humane Society. The check is mailed to the Humane Society on February 23, 2011. When is the earliest Break Neck can deduct this charitable contribution?

A. 2010 tax return
B. 2011 tax return
C. 2012 tax return
D. Never

The answer is A. The corporation is on an accrual basis and therefore may deduct the charitable contribution on its 2010 tax return. Corporations reporting taxable income on the accrual method can elect to treat as paid during the tax year any contributions paid by the fifteenth day of the third month after the end of the tax year if the contributions were authorized by the board of directors during the tax year. ###

14. In 2010 Real Time Corporation made contributions totaling $20,000 to qualified charitable organizations. Due to the 10% limit, Real Time Corporation could only deduct $15,000 of the contributions on its return. Which of the following statements regarding the excess contributions of $5,000 is correct?

A. Excess charitable contributions can be carried back two years and carried forward 20 years.
B. Excess charitable contributions can be carried forward five years.
C. Excess charitable contributions can be carried back three years and carried forward ten years.
D. Excess charitable contributions can be carried forward 20 years.

The answer is B. The corporation can carry over excess charitable contributions made during the year that are more than its income and that are subject to the 10% limit to each of the subsequent five years. Any excess charitable contributions that are not used in a five-year period are lost. Charitable contributions made by a corporation cannot be carried forward indefinitely. A corporation cannot carry back excess charitable contributions. ###

15. Buffalo Corporation displays a collection of artwork in its main office. When the 75% owner retires, he is presented with his choice from the art collection. He selects a painting with a Fair Market Value of $250,000. Buffalo Corporation's basis in the painting is $100,000. How should the transaction be reported on the Buffalo Corporation's tax return?

A. No reporting is required.
B. $150,000 distribution
C. $150,000 taxable gain.
D. $250,000 taxable gain

The answer is C. The corporation must recognize a gain for any property distributed that has an FMV higher than its adjusted basis. This is the same treatment the corporation would receive if the property were sold. The answer is figured as follows:

FMV of distribution	$250,000
SUBTRACT adjusted basis	$100,000
Recognized gain	$150,000

###

16. The Farber Corporation owns 10% of the Lewisville Corporation. In 2010, Farber receives $10,000 in dividends on Lewisville stock. What is the amount of the Dividends-Received Deduction that Farber Corporation can take?

A. 10% Dividends-Received Deduction
B. 50% Dividends-Received Deduction
C. 70% Dividends-Received Deduction
D. 80% Dividends-Received Deduction

The answer is C. The dividends deduction for less-than-20% owned stock is the lesser of:
- 70 % of the dividends, or
- 70 % of the taxable income

If a company owns less than 20% of another company, it is able to deduct 70% of the dividends it receives. If the company owns more than 20% but less than 80% of the company paying the dividends, it is able to deduct 80% of the dividends received. If it owns more than 80% of the dividend-paying company, it is allowed to deduct 100% of the dividends it receives. ###

17. In 2010, Salvage Corporation has a $15,000 LOSS from operations. However, Salvage has received $100,000 in dividends from a 30%-owned corporation. Therefore, its taxable income is $85,000 before the Dividends-Received Deduction. What is the corporation's Dividends-Received Deduction?

A. $15,000
B. $68,000
C. $80,000
D. $100,000

The answer is B. The corporation will not have an NOL after applying the full Dividends-Received Deduction, so its allowable Dividends-Received Deduction is limited to 80% of its taxable income, or $68,000 ($85,000 × 80%). ###

18. Davidson Corporation owns 50% of Nguyen Corporation's outstanding common stock. Davidson has taxable income of $8,000, which includes dividends of $10,000. What is Davidson Corporation's taxable income after the Dividends-Received Deduction?

A. $0
B. $1,600
C. $6,400
D. $8,000
E. $10,000

The answer is B. Davidson Corporation cannot deduct the full $8,000 (80% × $10,000) because of taxable income limitations. The income limitations will affect the amount of the Dividends-Received Deduction, and therefore, taxable income. The deduction is limited to 80% of taxable income, which is $6,400 (80% × $8,000).

Taxable Income:	$8,000
Minus DRD:	$6,400
Income after DRD:	$1,600

###

19. The Surf's Up Corporation had a Net Operating Loss (NOL) of $110,000. Which of the following statements is TRUE?

A. The corporation can forgo the carryback period and choose to carry the entire loss forward to the next 20 years.

B. The corporation is required to carryback losses for two years and then forward 15 years.
C. The corporation can carryback losses five years and carry them forward 25 years.
D. A corporation cannot carryback losses. It can only carry them forward.

The answer is A. A corporation is not required to carryback losses. Any corporation entitled to a carryback NOL may *elect* to forgo the carryback period. Net Operating Losses can be carried back to the two years before the loss year and then forward to the 20 years following the loss year (Publication 542). ###

Unit 2.10: S Corporations

More Reading:
Form 1120S and Instructions

The rules governing S Corporations are found in "Subchapter S" of the Internal Revenue Code. An S Corporation has similarities to both a C Corporation and a partnership. An S Corporation is a pass-through entity, just like a partnership. Also like a partnership, an S Corporation is not taxed on its earnings. Instead, earnings and losses pass through to shareholders. Like a C Corporation, an S Corporation enjoys liability protection that a partnership does not. Although most large corporations are classified as "C Corporations," over 60% of corporate returns filed are S Corporations. An S Corporation reports income and loss on Form 1120S.

However, S Corporations have some drawbacks. Although they offer more liability protection, they are less flexible than partnerships and have a number of limitations. Unlike a partnership, there are some instances where an S Corporation is forced to pay tax on its earnings. There are also significant restrictions on the number and type of shareholders that an S Corporation can have. For example, the number of S Corporation shareholders is limited to 100. We will go over these restrictions in more detail later in the unit.

In order to become an S Corporation, the corporation must file an "S-election," and its shareholders must all consent to the election. The shareholders' consent is binding and may not be withdrawn after a valid S Corporation election is made. An S Corporation files an election on Form 2553, *Election by a Small Business Corporation*. Once the election is made, it stays in effect until it is terminated, either by the shareholders, or by "automatic termination" by failing to adhere to the IRS requirements for S Corporation status.

A business must elect S Corporation status within 2.5 months of the start of its tax year in order for the election to be effective at the beginning of the year. An election made AFTER the first 2.5 months of an S Corporation's tax year becomes effective on the first day of the following tax year. IRS consent is required for another election if the corporation wants to elect S status again within five years of the termination. A corporation can file Form 2553 late and still receive IRS approval to make the election retroactive to the beginning of the corporation's tax year. This is called a "late S-election." The IRS will generally accept a late S-election, as long as the following requirements are met:

- The entity must qualify for S Corporation status.
- The entity had intended to be classified as an S Corporation as of the effective date of the S Corporation election.
- The corporation failed to qualify as an S Corporation solely because it did not file Form 2553 in a timely manner.
- The entity applies for relief no later than six months following the due date of the tax return.
- The corporation either had reasonable cause or inadvertently failed to file Form 2553 in a timely manner.
- The corporation has not yet filed tax returns for the first tax year for which it intends to file as an S Corporation, or the corporation has filed its first tax return using Form 1120S and the shareholders properly reported their share of income in a manner consistent with the corporation's intention to be an S Corporation.

- No shareholder has reported inconsistencies with the S Corporation election.

If the S-election is made during the corporation's tax year for which it first takes effect, any individual stockholder who holds stock at any time during the part of that year before the election is made must also consent to the election, even though the person may have sold or transferred his stock before the election is made.

An S Corporation may choose to use the cash or accrual method of accounting if it meets the requirements. An S Corporation may not use the cash method if it is a tax shelter.

S Corporation Requirements

Foreign corporations cannot apply for S Corporation status; a company must be domestic in order to qualify as an S Corporation.

There are additional strict rules regarding eligibility for S Corporation status. In order to qualify as an S Corporation, a business must meet the definition of a "small business corporation," per IRC Section 1361. The main requirements for S Corporation status are:

- It cannot have more than 100 shareholders.
- Shareholders must be U.S. citizens or residents and must be physical entities (persons), so corporate shareholders and partnerships are excluded. However, certain tax-exempt corporations, estates, and certain kinds of trusts are permitted to be shareholders in an S Corporation. An S Corporation IS ALLOWED to own a partnership interest or own stock in a C Corporation.
- An S Corporation can only have one class of stock, but that stock can be voting or nonvoting. Variation in voting rights is permitted. The difference in voting rights allows one group of shareholders to retain voting control, while still allowing other shareholders to benefit from corporate earnings.
- Profits and losses must be allocated to shareholders proportionately to each one's interest in the business.
- Nonresident aliens cannot be shareholders in an S Corporation.
- Shareholders of an S Corporation must give written consent for the S election.

> **Example:** A husband and wife own 90% of an S Corporation and their son owns the remaining 10%. The son announces his marriage to a nonresident alien, to whom he gifts one-half of his stock. The S Corporation's status is revoked, because a nonresident alien cannot hold stock ownership in an S Corporation.

For the purpose of the 100-shareholder limit, related persons are considered one shareholder. Spouses are automatically treated as a single shareholder. Families, defined as individuals descended from a common ancestor, plus spouses and former spouses of either the common ancestor or anyone lineally descended from that person, are considered a single shareholder as long as any family member elects such treatment. When a shareholder dies, the deceased shareholder's spouse and the estate are still considered one shareholder for the purpose of the shareholder limit.

A husband and wife cannot be considered a single shareholder if they divorce, or if the marriage is dissolved for any other reason than death. Therefore, a shareholder's divorce can potentially increase the number of shareholders and exceed the 100-shareholder limit. The following entities CANNOT elect S Corporation status:

- A bank or thrift institution that uses the reserve method of accounting for bad debts
- An insurance company
- A Domestic International Sales Corporation (DISC)
- Any foreign entity

Filing Requirements

An S Corporation files its tax return on IRS Form 1120S, *U.S. Income Tax Return for an S Corporation*. Individual items of income, deductions, and credits pass through to individual shareholders on Schedule K-1.

An S Corporation is always required to file a tax return, *regardless* of income or loss. The filing requirement ends only when the corporation is totally dissolved. The IRS mandates electronic filing for S Corporations with $10 million or more in assets and that continually file 250 or more returns of any type (W-2, 1099, K-1). The tax return for an S Corporation is due on the fifteenth day of the third month following the date the corporation's tax year ended. In the case of a calendar-year corporation, the tax return would be due March 15.

S Corporations may apply for a six-month extension of time to file. Form 7004, *Automatic Extension of Time to File Certain Business Income Tax, Information, and Other Returns,* is used to request an extension.

Shareholders are required to pay estimated tax for their individual returns. S Corporations are only required to pay estimated tax if corporate-level taxes apply. A corporation that has dissolved must generally file by the fifteenth day of the third month after the date it dissolved. If the due date falls on a Saturday, Sunday, or legal holiday, the corporation can file on the next business day.

The S Corporation return must be signed and dated by the president, vice president, treasurer, assistant treasurer, chief accounting officer, or any other corporate officer authorized to sign. If a return is filed on behalf of a corporation by a receiver, trustee, or assignee, the fiduciary must sign the return instead of the corporate officer. Returns and forms signed by a receiver or trustee in bankruptcy on behalf of a corporation must be accompanied by a copy of the order or instructions of the court authorizing signing of the return or form.

If an employee of the corporation completes Form 1120S, the paid preparer's space should remain blank. Anyone who prepares Form 1120S but does not charge a preparation fee should not sign the "paid preparer" space.

Stock Requirements

A C Corporation is not allowed to own stock in an S Corporation. However, an S Corporation can own stock in a C Corporation. An S Corporation can only have one class of stock. All the stock of an S Corporation must possess identical rights to distribution and liquidation proceeds. Only differences in voting rights are permitted; voting and nonvoting stock can still be considered identical stock for the purposes of the stock requirement.

Permitted Tax Year

An S Corporation may always use a calendar year, or any other tax year for which the corporation establishes a bona fide business purpose. An S Corporation may also make a Section

444 election in order to have a tax year other than the permitted tax year. An existing S Corporation may elect as its tax year:

- A calendar year
- A fiscal year duly elected and approved by the IRS under Section 444
- A fiscal year with a legitimate business purpose
- A certain 52-53-week year (fiscal year)
- An ownership tax year (the tax year that coincides with <50 % ownership of the corporation)

A new S Corporation must use Form 2553, *Election by a Small Business Corporation*, to elect a tax year. An existing S Corporation that wishes to *change* its existing tax year may use Form 1128, *Application to Adopt, Change, or Retain a Tax Year*, to apply for a change in tax year.

However, Form 8716, *Election to Have a Tax Year Other Than a Required Tax Year*, is used to apply for a tax year change under Section 444.

Income and Expenses

Income and expense items retain their character when they are passed through to S Corporation shareholders. Passive activity loss limitations do not apply to S Corporations, and instead apply to individual shareholders. Items of income, gain, loss, deduction, or credit are allocated to a shareholder on a daily basis, according to the number of shares of stock held by the shareholder on each day of the corporation's tax year.

The adjusted basis of a shareholder's S Corporation stock is calculated as follows:

How to Figure the Adjusted Basis of a Shareholder's Stock
+ Share of all income items that are separately stated, including tax-exempt income
+ Share of all non-separately stated income items
+ Share of deduction for excess depletion of oil and gas properties
- Distribution of cash or property to the shareholder (not wages)
- Share of all loss and deduction items that are separately stated
- Share of all non-separately stated losses
- Share of nondeductible expenses
= Adjusted basis in S Corporation stock at the end of the year

S Corporations: Separately Stated Items

Net income or loss is passed through to Subchapter S Corporation shareholders on a pro rata basis (similar to a partnership). Some items must be separately stated on an S Corporation's tax return. These separately stated items affect the tax liability of the individual shareholders. Items that must be separately stated include but are not limited to:

- Net income or loss from rental real estate activity
- Portfolio income or loss that includes:
    o Interest income
    o Dividend income
    o Royalty income
- Capital gain or loss
- Section 1231 gain or loss

- Charitable contributions
- Section 179 expense deduction
- Foreign taxes paid or accrued
- Expenses related to portfolio income or loss
- Credits, such as:
    o Low-income housing credit
    o Qualified rehabilitation expenses
    o Other credits
- Investment interest expense
- Tax preference and adjustment items needed to figure a shareholder's AMT

An S Corporation is not eligible for a Dividends-Received Deduction. Unlike a C Corporation, an S Corporation is not allowed to take a deduction for charitable contributions. Instead, charitable contributions are separately stated and passed through to the individual shareholders. The individual shareholders may then take a deduction for charitable contributions on their individual Schedules A (Form 1040).

Limited Taxation of S Corporations

In general, S Corporations are not subject to taxation and are primarily pass-through entities. S Corporations are not subject to income tax, Alternative Minimum Tax, or accumulated earnings tax. However, in certain cases, S Corporations are subject to taxes. A Subchapter S Corporation may have to pay income tax due to:

- Excess net passive investment income
- Built-in gains
- Investment credit recapture
- LIFO recapture

Excess Net Passive Investment Income

S Corporations, which have been C Corporations previously and have earnings and profits (E&P) accumulated from years in which they had C Corporation status, may have to pay tax at the corporate level on Excess Net Passive Income (ENPI). Additionally, if the corporation has passive investment income for three consecutive tax years, it may LOSE its S-status.

If an S Corporation, (which was formerly a C Corporation with accumulated E&P), has passive investment income in excess of 25% of its gross receipts for three consecutive taxable years, the S- election is terminated as of the beginning of the fourth year.

> **Example:** For 2007, 2008, and 2009, Snakeskin Corporation, a calendar-year S Corporation, earned passive investment income in excess of 25% of its gross receipts. If Snakeskin Corporation holds accumulated E&P from years in which it was a C Corporation, its S-election would be terminated as of January 1, 2010. This would be considered an *involuntary termination*, and the corporation would be taxed as a C Corporation moving forward.

The purpose of this tax is to discourage a C Corporation with accumulated earnings and profits (E&P) from becoming or functioning as a holding company in order to obtain favorable tax treatment as an S Corporation. For this purpose, "passive investment income" includes interest, dividends, and royalties.[76] The ENPI tax is imposed on S Corporations that meet BOTH of the following conditions:

- The corporation has accumulated E&P from the years it was a C Corporation at the end of that taxable year; AND
- The corporation's passive investment income exceeds 25% of its gross receipts.

If income is generated in the ordinary course of business, it is non-passive income (or active income); therefore, it is not included in "passive investment income."

Note: The exception for self-created property applies only when the corporation created the property and does NOT apply when the property is created by the shareholder and contributed to the corporation.

Example: Trailblazer Inc. is an S Corporation with accumulated E&P from Subchapter C years. In 2010, Trailblazer's first taxable year as an S Corporation, it has gross receipts of $75,000:

$5,000 is royalty payments from Trademark A

$8,000 is royalty payments from Trademark B

$62,000 is gross receipts from regular operations

Trailblazer created Trademark A, but Trailblazer did not create Trademark B or perform significant services with respect to the development or marketing of Trademark B. Because Trailblazer created Trademark A, the royalty payments from Trademark A are derived in the ordinary course of business and are not considered passive income for purposes of determining Trailblazer's passive investment income. However, the royalty payments for Trademark B are included within the definition of royalties for purposes of determining Trailblazer's passive investment income. Trailblazer's passive investment income for the year is $8,000.

If the corporation has always been a Subchapter S Corporation, the ENPI tax does not apply.

The tax on Excess Net Passive Income is figured as follows:

Equals = passive investment income in excess of 25% of gross receipts for the year,

Divided by ÷ the passive investment income for the year,

Multiplied by × the net passive investment income for the year

---

The tax rate on Excess Net Passive Income is 35%. This tax is applied on passive income from activities such as royalties, rents, dividends, and interest. The tax is applied against the lesser of:

- Excess Net Passive Income, or
- Taxable income figured as though the corporation were a C Corporation.

Built-in Gains Tax

A C Corporation that elects to be taxed as an S Corporation is taxed at the highest corporate rate, 35%, on all gains that were "built-in" at the time of the S-election, if the gains were recognized during the "recognition period." The built-in gains tax[77] is imposed on assets sold by an S Corporation that it held when it was converted from a C Corporation, unless the assets are held by the S Corporation for a certain period of time. The statutory period is gener-

---

[76] IRC §§1362(d)(3)(C) and 1375(b)(3).

[77] Not in IRS literature, but in actual practice, this tax is widely called the "BIG TAX" (in all-caps). It is also referred to as the "BIG TAX" in financial circles.

ally 10 years after conversion but was reduced to seven years for gains recognized in 2009 and 2010.[78]

The built-in gains tax usually applies to S Corporations that were once C Corporations. However, this tax can apply also to an S Corporation that acquires an asset from a C Corporation in which the basis is transferred (such as a related party transaction). The built-in gains tax may apply to the following S Corporations:

- An S Corporation that was a C Corporation before it elected to be an S Corporation.
- An S Corporation that acquired an asset with a basis determined by reference to its basis (or the basis of any other property) in the hands of a C Corporation (a transferred-basis acquisition).

The built-in gains tax requires an S Corporation to measure the amount of unrecognized appreciation that existed at the time an S-election is made. The amount of unrecognized gain is determined for each asset. The net of unrecognized built-in gains and built-in losses is the company's unrecognized built-in gain. The S Corporation then pays taxes at the highest corporate rate based on the recognized built-in gain. The amount of the tax is a deduction for the shareholders. The tax is reported on page two of Form 1120S.

The built-in gains tax does not apply following the tenth year that the S Corporation is in existence. An S Corporation passes through all net income or losses to shareholders, so an S Corporation does not accumulate Earnings and Profits (E&P) like a C Corporation. However, an S Corporation may have accumulated earnings and profits carried over from prior years if it was previously a C Corporation.

Built-in Gains Tax
The formula is as follows:
The combined FMV of assets – the combined basis of assets
= net unrealized built-in gains

The Built-in Gains Tax only applies to corporations that elected S status after 1986, and it only affects property dispositions for seven years after the date of S-election (also called the recognition period). The applicable recognition period is the seven-year period beginning:

- For an asset held when the S Corporation was a C Corporation, on the first day of the first tax year for which the corporation is an S Corporation, or
- For an asset with a basis determined by reference to its basis in the hands of a C Corporation, on the date the asset was acquired by the S Corporation.

An S Corporation must figure the built-in gains tax separately for the group of assets it held at the time its S-election became effective and for each group of assets it acquired from a C Corporation. For tax years beginning in 2009 or 2010, no tax is imposed if the S Corporation's seventh year of the applicable recognition period ended before the tax year.

Investment Credit Recapture

If a C Corporation claims the General Business Credit, then the S Corporation is responsible for the recapture. Business credit recapture is the responsibility of the entity that claims the credit. If the company is an S Corporation when the credit originates, the credit

---

[78] Note: In 2011, this statutory holding period is lowered even further, to five years after conversion from a C Corporation to an S Corporation.

passes through to the shareholders and they must report the recapture on IRS Form 4255, *Recapture of Investment Credit*.

LIFO Recapture Tax

For corporations accounting for inventory using LIFO (Last In, First Out) in the final year before making an S Corporation election, a calculation for a LIFO recapture tax is required. This tax is a corporate-level tax, instituted to account for built-in gains on older inventory, gains that might otherwise not be recognized during the seven-year recognition period.

The taxable "LIFO recapture amount" is the amount (if any) by which the inventory amount of the inventory assets under the First in, First Out method exceeds the inventory amount of such assets under the LIFO method.

The term "inventory assets" refers to the stock in trade of the corporation, or other property of a kind that would properly be included in the inventory of the corporation if on hand at the close of the taxable year.

The LIFO recapture tax is paid in four equal installments, beginning on the due date of the final C Corporation return. The three subsequent installments are due on the due date of the first three S Corporation returns. If the LIFO value is higher than the FIFO value, no negative adjustment is allowed.

Passive Activity Loss Rules

An S Corporation that engages in rental activity or an S Corporation with a shareholder who does not materially participate in S Corporation activities is subject to passive activity loss rules. There are two types of passive activities:

- Business activities in which the shareholder does not materially participate during the year
- Rental activities, even if the corporation materially participates in them

If the passive activity loss rules apply, the shareholders' at-risk amount must be reduced by the full amount allowable as a current deduction.

S Corporation Basis

S Corporation shareholders must pay taxes on their share of the corporation's current year income or loss is taxed whether or not the amounts are distributed. Those items increase or decrease the basis of the shareholder's S Corporation stock as appropriate.

Generally, S Corporation distributions, except dividend distributions, are considered a return of capital and reduce the shareholder's basis in the stock of the corporation. The part of any distribution that is more than the stockholder's basis is treated as a gain from the sale or exchange of property.

S Corporation distributions are not treated as dividends except in certain cases in which the corporation has accumulated earnings and profits from years before it became an S Corporation.

S Corporations issue Schedule K-1 to individual shareholders. The shareholders then must report their distributive share of the S Corporation's income, gain, loss, deductions, or credits on their individual Forms 1040. Corporate distributions may be made in either cash or property. S Corporation distributions are not treated as dividends.

A shareholder's deduction for her share of losses is limited to the adjusted basis of her stock and any debt the corporation owes the shareholder. Any loss or deduction not allowed because of this limit is carried over and treated as a loss or deduction in the next tax year.

Computing Stock Basis

In computing stock basis, the shareholder starts with his initial capital contribution to the S Corporation or the initial cost of the stock purchased (the same as a C Corporation). That amount is then increased or decreased based on the flow-through amounts from the S Corporation. Income will increase stock basis.

A shareholder's basis in his S Corporation stock varies based on how the stock was acquired (by purchase, gift, or inheritance). In general, this is how shareholder basis is determined in S Corporation stock.

How Stock is Acquired	How Stock Basis is Determined
Purchase	If the shares were purchased outright, initial basis is the cost of the shares.
S Corporation capitalized	If the shares were received when the S Corporation was formed under IRC §351, the basis in the stock is equal to the basis of the property transferred to the corporation, reduced by the amount of property received from the corporation, increased by gain recognized on the transfer, and decreased by any boot received (IRC §358).
Prior C Corporation	Initial basis in S Corporation stock is the basis in the C Corporation stock at the time of conversion.
Gift	The recipient's basis in shares received by gift is generally the donor's basis (IRC §1015). Suspended passive activity losses can increase the basis of a gift (IRC §469).
Inheritance	The basis of inherited stock is its Fair Market Value at the date of death, or, if elected, the alternate valuation date (IRC §1014).
Services rendered to the S Corporation	Basis in stock received in exchange for services is measured by the stock's Fair Market Value, rather than by the value of the services (Treas. Reg. §1.61-2).

The basis adjustment rules under IRC §1367 are similar to the partnership rules. However, while a partner has a unitary basis in his partnership interest, the adjustments to the basis of stock of an S Corporation are applied on a separate share basis. A loss, deduction, or distribution will decrease stock basis. Here are the rules for figuring shareholder basis in an S Corporation:

- A non-dividend distribution in excess of a shareholder's stock basis is taxed as a capital gain on the shareholder's personal return, usually a long-term capital gain.
- Nondeductible expenses reduce a shareholder's stock and debt basis before loss and deduction items. If nondeductible expenses exceed basis, they do not get carried forward.

- If the current year has different types of losses and deductions that exceed the shareholder's basis, the allowable losses and deductions must be allocated pro rata based on the size of the particular loss and deduction items.
- A shareholder is not allowed to claim losses and deductions in excess of stock and debt basis. Losses and deductions not allowable in the current year are suspended due to basis limitations.
- Suspended losses and deductions due to basis limitations retain their character in subsequent years. Any suspended losses or deductions in excess of stock and debt basis are carried forward indefinitely until basis is increased in subsequent years or until the shareholder permanently disposes of the stock.
- In determining current year allowable losses, current year loss and deduction items are combined with the suspended losses and deductions carried over from the prior year, though the current year and suspended items should be separately stated.
- A shareholder is only allowed debt basis to the extent she has personally lent money to the S Corporation. A "loan guarantee" is not sufficient to allow the shareholder debt basis.
- Part or all of the repayment of a reduced basis debt is taxable to the shareholder.
- If stock is sold, suspended losses due to basis limitations are lost forever. The sales price does not have an impact on the stock basis. A stock basis computation should be reviewed in the year stock is sold or disposed of.

The order in which stock basis is increased or decreased is important. Since both the taxability of a distribution and the deductibility of a loss are dependent on stock basis, there is an "ordering rule" in computing stock basis. Stock basis is adjusted annually, on the last day of the S Corporation year, in the following order:

- Increased for income items and excess depletion
- Decreased for distributions
- Decreased for nondeductible, non-capital expenses and depletion
- Decreased for items of loss and deductions

When determining the taxability of a non-dividend distribution, the shareholder must consider solely his stock basis (debt basis is not considered). A shareholder's basis can never be reduced below zero. Losses can be carried forward to future years.

Rules Regarding Debt Basis

S Corporation shareholders are required to compute both **stock basis** and **debt basis**. The amount of a shareholder's basis is very important. For losses and deductions that exceed a shareholder's stock basis, the shareholder is allowed to deduct the excess up to his basis in loans he personally made to the S Corporation. Debt basis is computed similarly to stock basis but there are some differences.

If a shareholder has S Corporation losses and deductions in excess of stock basis and those losses and deductions are claimed based on debt basis, the debt basis of the shareholder will be reduced by the claimed losses and deductions. If an S Corporation repays reduced basis debt to the shareholder, part or all of the repayment is taxable to the shareholder. Unlike a C

Corporation, each year the shareholder's basis in an S Corporation will go up or down based upon the S Corporation's operations.

It is important to understand that the shareholder's Schedule K-1 reflects the S Corporation's income, loss, and deductions that are allocated to each individual shareholder. The K-1 does not state the taxable amount of a distribution. The taxable amount of distributions *is contingent* on the shareholder's stock basis. It is the shareholder's responsibility to track her individual basis. If a shareholder receives a non-dividend distribution from an S Corporation, the distribution is tax-free to the extent it does not exceed her stock basis.

At-Risk Limitations

The amount of loss that is deductible on a shareholder's tax return is limited to the shareholder's at-risk basis. Limits apply to a shareholder's distributive share of a loss from an S Corporation. These limits determine the amount of the loss each partner or shareholder can deduct on his own return. These limits and the order in which they apply are:
The adjusted basis of:

- Cash and the adjusted basis of property that the shareholder contributed to the S Corporation, and
- Any loans the shareholder makes to the corporation, or any amounts that are borrowed for use by the S Corporation for which the shareholder is directly liable.

Losses Flow Through

If a shareholder is allocated losses from an S Corporation, he must have adequate stock basis to claim that loss. In addition, even when the shareholder has adequate basis to claim the S Corporation loss, he must also consider at-risk limitations and passive activity limitations and therefore may not be able to claim the loss.

Reasonable Wages

S Corporations are corporations that elect to pass corporate income, losses, deductions, and credits through to their shareholders for federal tax purposes. Shareholders of S Corporations report the flow-through of income and losses on their personal tax returns and are assessed tax at their individual income tax rates. Sometimes, an S Corporation will choose to pay little or no wages to employee-shareholders. This is because wages are subject to employment tax, while ordinary income (distributions) passing through to S Corporation shareholders is not subject to employment taxes. However, the issue of "reasonable compensation" is one of the main reasons why an S Corporation is audited by the IRS.

If an S Corporation is not paying a "reasonable" salary to a shareholder-employee, distributions to that shareholder may be recharacterized as wages subject to payroll taxes.

S Corporations should treat payments for services to officers as wages and NOT as distributions of cash and property or loans to shareholders. Courts have consistently held that S Corporation employee-shareholders should receive wages that are subject to federal employment taxes (FICA).

The IRC states that any officer of a corporation (including S Corporations) is an employee of the corporation for federal employment tax purposes. S Corporations should not attempt to avoid paying employment taxes by having their officers treat their compensation as cash distributions, payments of personal expenses, or loans rather than as wages.

An officer of a corporation is an employee of the corporation. The fact that an officer is also a shareholder does not change the requirement that payments to the corporate officer be treated as wages. If cash or property did go to the employee-shareholder, a salary amount must be determined and the level of salary must be reasonable and appropriate.

There are no specific guidelines for reasonable compensation in the Code or in IRS regulations. Various courts that have ruled on this issue have based their determinations on the facts and circumstances of each case.

Some factors considered by the courts in determining reasonable compensation for officers of an S Corporation include:
- Training and experience
- Duties and responsibilities
- Time and effort devoted to the business
- Dividend history
- Payments to non-shareholder employees
- Timing and manner of paying bonuses to key people
- Amounts that comparable businesses pay for similar services
- Compensation agreements
- The use of a formula to determine compensation

The Treasury regulations provide an exception for an officer of a corporation who does not perform any services or performs only minor services and receives no compensation. Such an officer would not be considered an employee for tax purposes.

Health Insurance Premiums for S Corporation Shareholders

Health and accident insurance premiums paid on behalf of at least 2% S Corporation shareholder-employees are deductible by the S Corporation as fringe benefits and are reportable as wages for income tax withholding purposes on the shareholder-employee's Form W-2.

This rule applies to shareholders that have at least 2% corporate stock ownership or greater.[79] In the case of a 2% shareholder of an S corporation the business must include the value of accident or health benefits provided to the shareholder in wages subject to federal income tax withholding. However, the S Corporation can exclude the value of these health benefits from the employee's wages subject to Social Security, Medicare, and FUTA taxes.

A 2% shareholder-employee is eligible for an AGI deduction for amounts paid during the year for medical care premiums if the medical care coverage is established by the S Corporation. Previously, the term "established by the S Corporation" meant that the medical care coverage had to be in the name of the S Corporation.

Since 2008, the IRS has stated that if the medical coverage plan is in the name of the shareholder and not in the name of the S Corporation, a medical care plan can still be considered to be established by the S Corporation if:
- The S Corporation either paid or reimbursed the shareholder for the premiums, and

---

[79] For more information on this topic, see Publication 15-B.

- Reported the premium payment as wages on the shareholder's Form W-2.

Schedule K-1 (Form 1120S) and Form 1099 cannot be used as an alternative to Form W-2 to report this additional compensation.

The S Corporation treats the fringe benefit as a wage expense. The shareholder treats the fringe benefit as compensation.

> **Example:** Victory Inc., an S Corporation, provides fringe benefits such as health insurance to its two owner-shareholders. Victory paid $5,000 in insurance premiums. The corporation treats the shareholders as having received the health insurance as additional compensation and includes the insurance expenditure as W-2 wage income. The shareholders report the health insurance as income.

*Note: Health insurance coverage for regular employees (who are NOT shareholders/owners of the S Corporation) is fully deductible as a business expense and is generally not taxable to the employees. This rule about health insurance premiums being treated as wages only applies to shareholders owning more than 2% of the S corporation's stock.

The S Corporation cannot take a deduction for amounts during a month in which the owner-shareholder is eligible to participate in any subsidized health plan maintained by another employer (or the spouse's employer).

> **Example:** Franklin is the single owner-shareholder in an S Corporation. He pays the health insurance for himself and his wife. Franklin's wife works full-time for an employer who has offered to provide family health coverage. Franklin and his wife declined the coverage because they don't want to switch doctors. Because Franklin has the option to participate in an employer plan (through his wife), he cannot deduct the health insurance premiums provided by his S Corporation.[80]

For the purpose of this rule, long-term care insurance is treated similar to health insurance. The same rules discussed above apply to the premiums for those policies.

The Accumulated Adjustments Account (AAA)

If a C Corporation elects to become an S Corporation, sometimes it will have an AAA account. The Accumulated Adjustments Account (AAA) is an account the S Corporation maintains to track undistributed income that has been taxed during the period its S-election is in effect. The AAA is a corporate account and does not belong to any particular shareholder. This account only applies to S Corporations that *were once* C Corporations.

S Corporations with accumulated E&P must maintain the AAA to determine the tax effect of distributions during S years and the post-termination transition period. It is not mandatory to track AAA if the S Corporation does not have prior year C Corporation earnings and profits (E&P) (IRC Section 1368).

Nevertheless, if an S Corporation without accumulated E&P engages in certain transactions where an AAA account is required, such as a merger into an S Corporation with accumulated E&P, the S Corporation must be able to calculate its AAA at the time of the merger. Therefore, it is recommended that the AAA be maintained by all S Corporations. The AAA may have a negative balance at year end (IRC Section 1368).

---

[80] This rule does not apply to C Corporations.

Corporate Distributions

Distributions from an S Corporation with no accumulated earnings and profit are treated as a nontaxable return of capital. If an S Corporation distributes property, the distribution may be treated as a gain from the sale of property. The type of gain is determined when the final year-end reconciliations are made, and the shareholder has adjusted his stock basis for any increases. The type of gain is determined before any decreases attributable to the current year are deducted.

Distributions up to the shareholder's adjusted stock basis are treated as a nontaxable return of capital. Distributions that *exceed* the shareholder's adjusted stock basis are reported as a capital gain, and must be reported on the individual shareholder's Schedule D.

The amount of an S Corporation distribution is equal to the sum of all cash and the Fair Market Value of the property received by a shareholder. If an S Corporation distributes *appreciated* property, (such as stocks), the S Corporation and the shareholder must treat the distribution as a sale to the shareholder.

Distributions from an S Corporation are not subject to payroll tax. Withdrawals from an S Corporation in the form of dividends are subject to federal taxes at the ordinary income tax rates. Distributions in the form of wages are subject to payroll tax and income tax on the shareholder level.

Distributions from an S Corporation must be paid to all shareholders on the same date, based on each shareholder's individual ownership percentage. This is also called a "pro rata distribution."

Termination of an S-Election

Once the election is made, it stays in effect until it is terminated. The S Corporation election will terminate automatically if the corporation fails to maintain IRS requirements for an S Corporation. For example, if an S Corporation admits a nonresident alien as a shareholder, the S Corporation election will be terminated. An S Corporation election will also be automatically terminated in any of the following cases:

- The corporation no longer qualifies as a "small business corporation." This termination of an election is effective as of the day the corporation no longer meets the definition of a small business corporation. Attach to Form 1120S for the final year of the S Corporation a statement notifying the IRS of the termination and the date it occurred.
- The corporation, for each of three consecutive tax years,
    - Has accumulated earnings and profits, and
    - Derives more than 25% of its gross receipts from passive investment income. The election terminates on the first day of the first tax year beginning after the third consecutive tax year. In addition, the corporation must pay a tax for each year it has Excess Net Passive Income.
- The S-election may be willingly revoked by the shareholders. An S-election can be revoked only with the consent of the majority shareholders. This means that, at the time the revocation is made, the revoking shareholders hold more than 50% of the corporation's stock (including nonvoting stock).
- An S-election will be terminated if the corporation creates a second class of stock.

A shareholder revocation may specify an effective revocation date that is on or after the day the revocation is filed. If no date is specified, the revocation is effective at the start of a tax year if the revocation is made on or before the fifteenth day of the third month of that tax year. If no date is specified and the revocation is made after the fifteenth day of the third month of the tax year, the revocation is effective at the start of the next tax year.

To voluntarily revoke an S-election, the corporation must file a statement of revocation with the IRS center where it filed its election to be an S Corporation. The statement must be signed by each shareholder who consents. A revocation may be rescinded before it takes effect.

> **Example:** On May 1, 2010, Zander Corporation, a calendar-year S Corporation, exceeded 100 shareholders. The shareholders decided to do business going forward as a C Corporation. Zander Corporation must file a final Form 1120S reporting the date of the termination of its "S status."

Involuntary Terminations

An S Corporation may involuntarily lose its S status and revert to a C Corporation. The IRS allows some leeway in this case. If the IRS deems that the revocation was inadvertent, (that the shareholders did not mean to revoke their S-election, or that the revocation was accidental) the corporation will be given the chance to correct the error and retain its S-election status.

> **Example:** In 2010, Morrison Corporation, a calendar-year S Corporation, inadvertently terminates its S status. The S Corporation shareholders immediately correct the problem. Therefore, the S Corporation status is considered to have been continuously in effect, and no termination is deemed to have occurred. Only a single S Corporation tax return will need to be filed for tax year 2010.

A terminating event will be considered "inadvertent" if the event was not within the control of the corporation, and the shareholders did not plan to terminate the election. In order to qualify after a terminating event, ALL of the following must occur:

- The S-election must have involuntarily terminated either because:
    - The corporation no longer qualified as a small business corporation, or
    - It had accumulated earnings and profits from past C Corporation activities.
- The IRS must agree that the termination was inadvertent.
- The corporation must take reasonable and immediate steps to correct the issue.
- The shareholders and the corporation must agree to any adjustments proposed by the IRS.
- The corporation must request a private letter ruling for any inadvertent termination relief.

If the status of an S Corporation is terminated, either because the shareholders elect to become a C Corporation or because a "terminating event" occurs (such as the shareholders exceeding the maximum of 100), the S Corporation cannot elect to become an S Corporation again for at least five years.

The IRS may choose to waive the five-year restriction. If the S Corporation election was terminated during the tax year and the corporation reverts to a C Corporation, the entity must file Form 1120S for the S Corporation's short year by the due date (including extensions) of the C Corporation's short year return.

Termination of a Shareholder's Interest

A shareholder may sell or liquidate her stock interest in an S Corporation. The sale is treated the same way as the sale of stock in a C Corporation. The shareholder reports the sale of the stock on Schedule D. The gain or loss that is recognized by the shareholder is the difference between the shareholder's basis and the sale price of the stock.

If a shareholder in an S Corporation terminates his interest in a corporation during the tax year, the corporation, with the consent of all affected shareholders (including those whose interest is terminated), may elect to allocate income and expenses as if the corporation's tax year consisted of two separate short tax years, the first of which ends on the date of the shareholder's termination.

To make this election, the corporation must attach a statement to a timely filed original or amended Form 1120S for the tax year for which the election is made. The corporation must state that it is electing to treat the tax year as if it consisted of two separate tax years.

The statement must also explain how the shareholder's entire interest was terminated (e.g., sale or gift), and state that the corporation and each affected shareholder consent to the election. A single statement may be filed for all terminating elections made for the tax year. If this election is made, the taxpayer should write "Section 1377(a)(2) Election Made" at the top of each affected shareholder's Schedule K-1.

Unit 2.10: Questions

1. Close family members can be treated as a single shareholder for S Corporation purposes. A "family member" in this instance includes:

A. A nonresident alien spouse
B. A first cousin
C. A shareholder's son
D. A brother-in-law

The answer is C. A shareholder's son can be considered a single "family unit" for the purposes of the "single shareholder" rule for S Corporations. Spouses are automatically treated as a single shareholder. An S Corporation cannot have a nonresident alien member, so a nonresident alien spouse would not qualify. Families, defined as individuals descended from a common ancestor, plus spouses and former spouses of either the common ancestor or anyone lineally descended from that person, are considered a single shareholder as long as any family member elects such treatment. ###

2. All of the following statements about S Corporations are true EXCEPT:

A. S Corporations cannot have more than 100 shareholders.
B. S Corporations can own stock in a C Corporation.
C. S Corporations have only one class of stock.
D. An S Corporation can also be an insurance company.

The answer is D. An S Corporation cannot be an insurance company. An S Corporation can only have one class of stock, and it cannot have more than 100 shareholders. An S Corporation can own shares in a C Corporation, but a C Corporation cannot own shares in an S Corporation. ###

3. A C Corporation can elect to become an S Corporation EXCEPT in which of the following circumstances?

A. The C Corporation has 50 shareholders.
B. The C Corporation is incorporated in Canada.
C. The C Corporation has common stock with voting and non-voting rights.
D. The C Corporation is on a fiscal year with a legitimate business purpose.

The answer is B. Only domestic U.S. corporations are allowed to elect S-status. A C Corporation can elect to become an S Corporation if it otherwise qualifies. An S Corporation can only have one class of stock, but differences in voting rights are allowed. An S Corporation can have a fiscal year if it has a legitimate business purpose for doing so. ###

4. All S Corporations, regardless of when they became an S Corporation, must use a "permitted tax year." A permitted tax year is any of the following EXCEPT:

A. The calendar year
B. A tax year elected under Section 444
C. A 52-53-week tax year
D. A short tax year

The answer is D. A short tax year is only applicable when a corporation is dissolving or in its first year. All S Corporations, regardless of when they became S Corporations, must use a "permitted tax year." ###

5. A calendar-year S Corporation operating on the accrual basis has the following income items and expenses. What is the income of this S Corporation, NOT counting the separately stated items?

Gross receipts	$300,000
Interest income	$25,000
Royalty income	$10,000
Salary paid to shareholder	$20,000

A. $55,000
B. $280,000
C. $320,000
D. $345,000

The answer is B. The interest income and royalty income are separately stated items. The gross receipts subtracted from the salary paid to a shareholder equal the non-separately stated income. The amount is figured as follows: ($300,000 - $20,000 = $280,000). ###

6. What is the total amount of separately stated income items of the following calendar-year S Corporation operating on the accrual basis? Use the following information:

Rental real estate income	$ 300,000
Interest income	$25,000
Royalty income	$10,000
Section 1231 gain	$20,000
Gross receipts	$700,000

A. $355,000
B. $345,000
C. $700,000
D. $720,000

The answer is A. All of the income, except for the total gross receipts listed at the bottom, must be separately stated on the S Corporation's tax return.
The total of the separately stated items is figured as follows:

Rental real estate activities:	$300,000
Interest income	$25,000
Royalty income	$10,000
Section 1231 gain	$20,000
Total	$355,000

####

7. Which of the following items is NOT a separately stated item on an S Corporation return?

A. Charitable contributions
B. Net short-term capital gains or losses
C. Interest income
D. Interest expense on a business loan

The answer is D. Charitable contributions, interest income, and short-term capital gains and losses are all separately stated items. The interest on a business loan is not a pass-through item; it is simply a business expense, as it would be for any other entity. ###

8. Which of the following statements is FALSE about the tax on Excess Net Passive Income of S Corporations?

A. A Subchapter S Corporation is subject to tax on ENPI if its passive income is more than 25% of gross receipts, and at the end of the year, the Subchapter S Corporation has accumulated earnings and profits from when it was a C Corporation.
B. If the corporation has always been a Subchapter S Corporation, the ENPI tax does not apply.
C. The penalty tax on ENPI can be up to 50% of gross receipts.
D. The tax rate on ENPI is 35%.

The answer is C. There is no 50% tax on Excess Net Passive Income. The tax rate on ENPI income is 35%. A Subchapter S Corporation is subject to tax on ENPI if its passive income is more than 25% of gross receipts, and at the end of the year, the Subchapter S Corporation has accumulated earnings and profits from when it was a C Corporation. ###

9. S Corporations are generally not subject to taxation and are primarily pass-through entities. But in certain cases, S Corporations are subject to taxes. Which of the following taxes does NOT apply to S Corporations?

A. Excess net passive investment income
B. Built-in gains tax
C. Self-employment tax
D. LIFO recapture

The answer is C. S Corporations are not subject to self-employment tax. Self-employment tax only applies to individuals. The S Corporation may have to pay income tax due to:
- Excess net passive investment income
- Built-in gains
- Investment credit recapture
- LIFO recapture

###

10. On January 15, 2010, Elliott decides to terminate his corporation's S-status, switching to a C Corporation. He later changes his mind and wishes to elect S Corporation status again. How long does Elliott have to wait to elect S Corporation status again?

A. 18 months
B. Two years
C. Four years
D. Five years

The answer is D. A corporation must generally wait five years to make another election. IRS consent is required for another election by the corporation on Form 2553. ###

11. In January 2010, Mike and Sandy are shareholders in Walker Company, a calendar-year C Corporation. Mike owns 65% of the corporate stock and Sandy owns the remainder. Mike decides that he wants to convert to an S Corporation. Regarding the conversion, which of the following statements is FALSE?

A. Mike and Sandy must both consent to the conversion to the S Corporation.
B. The election to become an S Corporation is taken on Form 2553.
C. Mike may choose (on his own) to convert the C Corporation to an S Corporation because he owns more than 50% of the stock.
D. Mike and Sandy cannot be nonresident aliens in order to elect S Corporation status.

The answer is C. All the shareholders must consent to the election, even though the person may have sold or transferred his other stock before the election is made. An S Corporation may not have a nonresident alien shareholder. ###

12. Which of the following events would cause the termination of an S Corporation's status?

A. A shareholder who has a zero basis in her stock.
B. An S Corporation that has a nonprofit corporation 501(c)(3) shareholder.
C. The S Corporation issues two shares of stock to a C Corporation.
D. An S Corporation that owns 70% of the stock in a C Corporation.

The answer is C. An S Corporation cannot issue stock to a C Corporation. However, an S Corporation may own stock in a C Corporation. S Corporation shareholders must be U.S. citizens or U.S. residents, and must be physical entities (persons), so corporate shareholders and partnerships are excluded. Certain small business trusts can be shareholders. However, certain tax-exempt corporations, notably 501(c)(3) corporations, are permitted to be shareholders. ###

13. Which of the following will prevent a C Corporation from qualifying for S Corporation status?

A. The corporation owns a 20% interest in a foreign partnership.
B. The corporation has a shareholder that is an estate.
C. The corporation sells a share of stock to a nonresident alien.
D. The corporation files a tax return 60 days late.

The answer is C. Nonresident aliens cannot be shareholders in an S Corporation. An S Corporation may own a partnership interest or own stock in a C Corporation. Estates are allowed to own stock in an S Corporation. ###

14. Bettendorf Company is a calendar-year corporation that wishes to elect S Corporation status in 2010. What is the latest date that Bettendorf Company can file Form 2553 to elect S status in 2010?

A. March 15
B. April 15
C. February 15
D. December 31

The answer is A. An eligible corporation must make an S-election within two months and 15 days of its tax year (or within 2.5 months of its inception) to become an S Corporation. Since Bettendorf is a calendar-year corporation, its tax year begins January 1. It must make the election on or before March 15. ###

16. On January 1, 2010, Gloria, Kristin, and Nancy are all equal shareholders in Fairview Corporation, a calendar-year C Corporation that has been in existence for four years. On March 1, 2010, Gloria sells her entire stock interest in the corporation to an unrelated party named Irving. Irving immediately wants to convert the corporation to an S Corporation. What is required in order for the corporation to convert to S-status?

A. Irving may convert the corporation into an S Corporation as long as Kristin and Nancy consent.
B. Gloria must also consent to the election, along with Kristin and Nancy.
C. Irving may convert the corporation to an S Corporation on his own.
D. The corporation cannot convert to S-status until it has been in existence for five years.

The answer is B. In order for the election to be made, Gloria must also consent to the election, even though she has sold all of her shares to Irving. If the S-election is made during the corporation's tax year for which it first takes effect, any individual stockholder who holds stock at any time during the part of that year before the election is made must also consent to the election, even though the person may have sold or transferred her stock before the election is made. All the shareholders must consent to the election, even though the person may have sold or transferred his other stock before the election is made. ###

17. Greenhouse Corporation is an S Corporation. It has four shareholders: Jordan, Mai, Simon, and Nora. The corporation has 10,000 shares outstanding. The shareholders have the following ownership:

Shareholder	Ownership
Jordan	4,500 shares
Mai	2,000 shares
Simon	2,000 shares
Nora	1,500 shares
Total	**10,000 shares**

Nora and Jordan wish to terminate the S-election, but Mai and Simon do not. What statement is TRUE?
A. Jordan can elect to terminate the corporation's S-status on his own.
B. All of the shareholders must agree to terminate the election.
C. Nora and Jordan have enough stock ownership to terminate the election.
D. At least 75% of the shareholders with active ownership must agree to the termination.

The answer is C. An S-election may be revoked if shareholders holding *more than* 50% of the stock agree to the termination. Since Nora and Jordan own more than 50% of the outstanding stock, they can elect to revoke the S-election. ###

18. Sydney owns 50% of Fantasy Inc., a calendar-year S Corporation. In January 2010, Sydney's stock basis is $3,000. At the end of 2010, Fantasy Inc. has $2,000 in income and distributes a large machine with an FMV of $7,000 to Sydney. How much income must Sydney report on her individual tax return for this distribution?

A. $0
B. $3,000
C. $5,000
D. $6,000

The answer is B. Sydney is required to recognize capital gain on the distribution of the machine. She must report $3,000 in income on her personal tax return. The distribution is figured as follows:

Sydney's adjusted basis	$3,000
S Corp income X 50%	$1,000
Adjusted basis 12/31/10	$4,000
Distribution	
FMV of machine	$7,000
Less shareholder's basis	$4,000
Her capital gain	**$3,000**

###

19. Danielle is a 50% owner in Lilliputian Corporation, an S Corporation. Danielle's basis is $5,000 in the corporation. At the end of 2010, Lilliputian Corporation reports $10,000 in ordinary income. In December 2010, Lilliputian makes a distribution to Danielle of appreciated property. It is a rare motorcycle originally purchased for $1,000 but now worth $8,000. How much income does Danielle have to report on her individual return?

A. $0
B. $1,000
C. $2,000
D. $8,000

The answer is A. If an S Corporation distributes appreciated property, the S Corporation and the shareholder will treat the distribution as a sale to the shareholder. The distribution lowers Danielle's stock basis to $2,000.

Danielle's adjusted basis	$5,000
S Corporation income × 50%	$5,000
Adjusted basis 12/31/10	$10,000
Distribution	
FMV of property	$8,000
Less: Shareholder's basis	$10,000
Capital gain	$0
####	

20. Francisco is the single shareholder in his S Corporation. At the beginning of the year, his stock basis was $50,000. The corporation had zero income in 2010. The corporation distributed property to Francisco with an FMV of $75,000 and an adjusted basis of $62,000. What is the treatment of the distribution?

A. $50,000 as a return of capital and $25,000 taxable capital gain
B. $50,000 as a return of capital and $12,000 taxable capital gain
C. $60,000 as a return of capital and $15,000 taxable capital gain
D. $62,000 as a return of capital and $0 taxable gain

The answer is A. The distribution is figured as follows:

Francisco's adjusted basis:	$50,000
S Corporation income	$0
Adjusted basis 12/31/10:	$50,000
Distribution	
FMV of property:	$75,000
Less: Shareholder's basis:	$50,000
Capital gain:	$25,000

Francisco must report $25,000 in capital gain income on his personal tax return. The distribution reduces the shareholder's basis in his stock, and the remaining amount exceeding the basis is treated as capital gain. ###

21. A corporation may NOT elect to be an S Corporation if:

A. It is a domestic corporation.
B. It has voting and nonvoting stock.
C. It has two classes of stock.
D. It is a C Corporation for less than five years.

The answer is C. A corporation may not elect S Corporation status if it has two classes of stock. A corporation may have both voting and nonvoting stock because they're not considered different classes of stock. A corporation must be a domestic corporation in order to qualify for S Corporation status. ###

Unit 2.11: Farmers and Farming Corporations

More Reading:
Publication 225, Farmer's Tax Guide

There are many special tax rules specific to farming businesses. The tax laws reflect the understanding that farming is an unpredictable business, and special tax provisions have been added to reflect Congress' understanding of this unique business.

Farming businesses report income and loss on Schedule F, *Profit or Loss from Farming*. Farming businesses are primarily engaged in crop production, animal production, or forestry and logging. A farm includes stock, dairy, poultry, fish, fruit, and tree farms. It also includes plantations, ranches, timber farms, and orchards.

Farmers are considered self-employed and must pay self-employment tax on their earnings. Sole proprietor farmers report their income on Schedule F (Form 1040). A farming business may also be organized as a partnership or a corporation.

Certain "associated" businesses are not considered "farming businesses" and instead must file on Schedule C. Examples of businesses that are NOT considered "farming businesses" include:

- Veterinary businesses
- Businesses that supply farm labor
- Businesses that raise or breed dogs, cats, or other household pets
- Businesses that are only in the business of breeding
- Businesses that provide agricultural services such as soil preparation and fertilization

Examples of TRUE farming businesses include:

- Fruit and tree nut farming, crop farming
- Forest nurseries and timber tracts
- Aquaculture farms (such as salmon, clam, and oyster farming)
- Beef cattle ranching and farming
- Crop shares for use of the farmer's land (but only if the farmer materially participates in the activity).

The rent received for the use or rental of farmland is generally rental income, NOT farm income. Passive income from the rental of farmland is not subject to Self-Employment tax. However, if the farmer *materially participates* in farming operations on the land, the rent is considered farm income. If the farmer does NOT materially participate in operating the farm, this income is passive income and is reported on Form 4835, *Farm Rental Income and Expenses*.

Form 4835 is used to report farm rental income based on crops or livestock produced by a tenant. This form is used to report *passive* income only.

Special Rules for Estimated Taxes

Self-employed farmers[81] must complete Schedule SE (Self-Employment Tax) to figure out how much they should pay in taxes for Social Security and Medicare. A farmer is usually self-employed if he operates his own farm, or rents farmland from others to engage in the business of farming.

Special rules apply to the payment of estimated tax by individuals who are qualified farmers (and fishermen). If two-thirds of the business's gross income comes from farming, the business qualifies under the special rules for estimated tax.

A qualified farmer does not have to pay any estimated tax if she files her 2010 tax return and pays all the tax due by March 1, 2011. If a farmer is required to pay estimated tax, he may choose to make only one estimated tax payment (also called the "required annual payment") by January 15 (*in 2011, the date is Jan 18, 2011 because of Martin Luther King's birthday). In order to qualify for this special treatment, the taxpayer must have at least two-thirds of his income from farming or fishing activity. On past EA Exams, the IRS has required the candidate to figure the amount of farm-source income in order to qualify for this special treatment regarding estimated tax payments.

"Farm income" does not include any of the following:
- Wages received as a farm employee
- Income received under a contract for grain harvesting with workers and machines furnished by the taxpayer
- Gains received from the sale of farm land and depreciable farm equipment
- Gains from the sale of securities, regardless of who owns the securities

If the taxpayer is a qualified farmer (or fisherman), he can either:
- Pay all his estimated tax by the fifteenth day after the end of his tax year (usually January 15)
- File his return and pay all the tax owed by the first day of the third month after the end of his tax year (usually March 1).

Accounting Methods for Farming

Farming businesses are allowed to use any acceptable accounting method, including special methods of accounting allowed just for farming businesses. Almost all farming businesses operate using the cash method of accounting. Farmers generally choose an accounting method when they file their first income tax return that includes a Schedule F, *Profit or Loss from Farming*. Farmers are allowed to use the following accounting methods:

---

[81] Qualified farmers and fishermen are allowed to pay their Self-Employment tax in a single estimated payment. If two-thirds of the taxpayer's gross income for 2009 OR 2010 is from farming or fishing, then the taxpayer is only required to make a single estimated payment. The due date of the estimated payment for the tax year 2010 is January 18, 2011. Therefore, the due date for the first three installments of estimated tax do not apply to farmers and fishermen. This is a special rule in the tax code specifically for this business type. Farmers and fishermen also have the option to SKIP the January estimated payment; if they file their tax return AND pay their *entire balance due* by March 1, 2011. No other business is afforded this type of special treatment.

- Cash method
- Accrual method
- Special methods (the Crop method)
  - **The Crop method** is a special inventory valuation method that is only allowed for farming businesses. If crops are not harvested and disposed of in the same tax year they are planted, with IRS approval a farmer may use the crop method of accounting. Under the crop method, the farmer may deduct the entire cost of producing the crop, including the expense of seed or young plants, in the year income is realized from the crop. This method is not allowed for timber.
- Combination (hybrid) method: the IRS allows businesses to use a hybrid combination of the cash method and the accrual method. Under a hybrid accounting method, companies may use the accrual accounting method to satisfy tax requirements and the cash basis method for all other transactions.

Example: Ernie is a self-employed farmer who uses the accrual method of accounting. He keeps his books on the calendar-year basis. Ernie sells grain in December 2010, but he is not paid until January 2011. Ernie must include the sale and also deduct the costs incurred in producing the grain on his 2010 tax return.

Example: Miguel is also a self-employed farmer, but he uses the cash method of accounting. Miguel sells livestock in December 2010, but he is not paid until January 2011. Since Miguel uses the cash method and there was no constructive receipt of the sale proceeds until 2011, he does not report the income from the livestock sale on his 2010 return. Under this method, Miguel would include the sale proceeds in income in 2011, the year he receives payment.

The accrual method is required only for certain large farm corporations and partnerships. The following farming businesses MUST use the accrual method of accounting:

- A corporation (*other than* a family farming corporation) that had gross receipts of more than $1 million for any tax year
- A family farming corporation that had gross receipts of more than $25 million for any tax year
- A partnership with a corporate partner
- A tax shelter (of any size or income)

Special Rule for Family Farming Corporations

Farming businesses are required to use the accrual method if they reach a gross receipts' threshold of $1 million (because farming businesses typically carry inventory). However, a special exception exists in the law for *family farming* corporations. Qualified family farming corporations are still allowed to use the cash method as long as their average annual gross receipts are $25 million or less.

A family farming corporation is a business where the owners are related persons. A family farming corporation must meet at least ONE of the following requirements:

- Members of the same family own at least 50% of the corporation's stock
- Members of two families have owned, either directly or indirectly, at least 65% of the corporation's stock

589

- Members of three families have owned, either directly or indirectly, at least 50% of the corporation's stock

> **Example:** Dave and Raymond are brothers. They are also the two sole shareholders of Da-Ray Farms Corporation, which is a qualified family farming corporation. Da-Ray Farms raises cattle, and in 2010, it has $20 million in gross receipts. Since Da-Ray is a qualified family farm, the entity is allowed to use the cash method of accounting.

Farm Inventory Methods

Farmers may use the same inventory methods that are available to other businesses, such as cost, lower of cost or market, etc., which were covered earlier in the book under inventory methods. However, there are two other inventory methods that are unique to farming businesses:

- Farm-price method
- Unit-livestock-price method

Farm-Price Method: Under the farm-price method, each item, whether raised or purchased, is valued at its market price LESS the cost of disposition. The costs of disposition include broker's commissions, freight, hauling to market, and other marketing costs. If a farming business chooses to use the farm-price method, it must use it for the entire inventory, except that livestock can be inventoried under the unit-livestock-price method.

Unit-Livestock-Price Method: The unit-livestock-price method is an easier inventory method that allows farmers to group livestock together, rather than tracking costs on each individual animal. A farmer may classify livestock according to type and age, and then use a standardized unit price for each animal within a class. The unit price should reasonably approximate the costs incurred in producing the animal. If a farming business uses the unit-livestock-price method, it must include all raised livestock in inventory, regardless of whether it is held for sale or for draft, breeding, sport, or dairy purposes. This method accounts only for the costs incurred while raising an animal to maturity. It does not provide for any decrease in the animal's market value after it reaches maturity.

Farm Inventory in General

All livestock purchased primarily for sale must be included in inventory. If the livestock was purchased primarily for draft, breeding, sport, or dairy purposes, the farmer can choose to depreciate it, or include the livestock in inventory. However, the business must be consistent from year to year, regardless of the method chosen.

If a farmer values his livestock inventory at cost or the lower-of-cost or market, he does not need IRS approval to change to the unit-livestock-price method. However, if he values his livestock inventory using the farm-price method, then he must obtain permission from the IRS to change to the unit-livestock-price method.

All harvested and purchased farm products held for sale, such as grain, hay, or tobacco, must be included in inventory. Supplies acquired for sale or that become part of the items held for sale must be included in inventory. A business may expense the cost of supplies consumed in operations during the year.

Livestock held primarily for sale must be included in inventory. Livestock held for draft, breeding, or dairy purposes can either be depreciated or included in inventory (*commonly tested concept).

Uniform Capitalization Rules

Farming businesses are subject to the uniform capitalization rules. A farmer can determine costs required to be allocated under the uniform capitalization rules by using the farm-price or unit-livestock-price inventory method. This applies to any plant or animal, even if the farmer does not hold or treat the plant or animal as inventory property.

Farming inventory should include all items held for sale, or for use as feed, seed, etc., whether raised or purchased, that are unsold at the end of the year. Generally, currently growing crops are *not required* to be included in inventory. However, if the crop has a pre-productive period of more than two years, the farmer may have to capitalize (or include in inventory) the costs associated with the crop.

If a farming business uses the accrual method of accounting, it is subject to the following uniform capitalization rules:

- The rules apply to all costs of raising a plant, even if the pre-productive period of raising a plant is two years or less.
- The rules apply to all costs related to animals.

Examples of items that must be included in inventory:

- Eggs in the process of hatching
- Harvested farm products that are held for sale, such as grain, cotton, hay, or tobacco
- Supplies that become a physical part of an item held for sale (such as containers or other packaging)
- Any livestock that is held primarily for sale* (frequently tested on the EA Exam)
- Fur-bearing animals (such as mink or chinchilla) that are being held for breeding

Sales of Farm Products and Farm Assets

Taxpayers must report farming income on Schedule F (Form 1040). Farmers use this schedule to figure the net profit or loss from regular farming operations. Income from farming is reported on Schedule F and includes amounts received from cultivating, operating, or managing a farm for profit. Income reported on Schedule F does NOT include gains or losses from sales or other dispositions of the following farm assets:

- Land
- Depreciable farm equipment
- Buildings and structures
- Livestock held for draft, breeding, sport, or dairy purposes (this is livestock that is NOT held primarily for sale)

If a farmer sells assets that are not held primarily for sale (such as those listed above), the sale must be reported on Form 4797, *Sales of Business Property*. The sale of depreciable equipment, buildings, land, and other depreciable property must be reported on Form 4797, rather than Schedule F. The same rules apply to the sale of livestock "held for draft, breeding, sport, or dairy purposes." In this case, the sale may result in ordinary or capital gains or losses. Farmers should always report these sales on Form 4797, *Sales of Business Property*.

However, when a farmer sells flowers, timber, grains, or other products raised on a farm, the entire amount is reported on Schedule F. This would be similar to any other self-employed taxpayer selling regular inventory and reporting the sales proceeds on Schedule C. When a farmer sells farm products bought for resale, his profit or loss is the difference between his basis in the item (usually cost) and any payment received for it.

> **Example:** In 2009, Oscar bought 20 feeder calves for $6,000 for resale. He sold them in 2010 for $11,000. Oscar reports the $11,000 sales price, subtracts his $6,000 basis, and reports the resulting $5,000 profit on his 2010 Schedule F.

Dispositions of Farm Property and Real Estate

When a farmer disposes of real property used in a farming business, his taxable gain or loss is usually treated as ordinary income or capital gain under the rules for Section 1231 transactions. When a farmer disposes of depreciable property at a gain, he may have to recognize all or part of the gain as ordinary income under the depreciation recapture rules. Any gain remaining after applying the depreciation recapture rules is a Section 1231 gain, which may be taxed as a capital gain.

When a farming business sells property, the taxable gain is either treated as ordinary income or as a capital gain (which is generally taxed at lower rates). Just like other businesses, assets that are held for longer than one year are subject to long-term capital gains treatment.

The sale of farming business property is also subject to the Section 1231 rules. When a farming business disposes of depreciable property (Section 1245 property or Section 1250 property) at a gain, the taxpayer may have to recognize ordinary income under the depreciation recapture rules. Any gain remaining after applying the depreciation recapture rules is a "Section 1231 gain," which then may be taxed as a capital gain. Gains and losses from farming property are reported on Form 4797, *Sales of Business Property,* rather than on Schedule F.

Section 1231 Transactions Specific to Farming Businesses

Gain or loss on the following farm-related transactions is subject to Section 1231 treatment:

1. Sale or exchange of cattle or horses held for draft, breeding, dairy, or sporting purposes and held for 24 months or longer.

2. Sale or exchange of other livestock held for draft, breeding, dairy, or sporting purposes and held for 12 months or longer. Other livestock includes hogs, mules, sheep, and goats, but does not include poultry.

3. Sale or exchange of depreciable property used in the farming business and held for longer than one year. Examples include farm machinery and trucks.

4. Sale or exchange of real estate used in the farming business and held for longer than one year. Examples are a farm or ranch, including barns and sheds.

5. Sale or exchange of unharvested crops.

6. Sale from cut timber.

7. The condemnation of business property held longer than one year. Condemnations of business property usually qualify for non-recognition treatment if replacement property is purchased within a certain time period, under the involuntary conversion rules.

Postponing Gain Due to Disaster-Area Provisions

There are special rules for farmers regarding the postponement of gain due to weather conditions. If a farmer sells or exchanges *more* livestock, including poultry, than he *normally would* in a year because of a drought, flood, or other weather-related condition, he may postpone reporting the gain from the *additional* animals until the following year. The taxpayer must meet all the following conditions to qualify:

- The principal trade or business must be farming.
- The farmer must use the cash method of accounting.
- The farmer must be able to show that she would not have sold or exchanged the additional animals this year except for the weather-related condition.
- The area must be designated as eligible for assistance by the federal government.

The livestock does not have to be raised or sold in the affected area for the postponement to apply. However, the sale must occur solely because the weather-related condition affected the water, grazing, or other requirements of the livestock. The farmer must figure the amount to be postponed separately for each generic class of animals—for example, hogs, sheep, and cattle.

> **Example:** Yolanda is a calendar-year farmer, and she normally sells 100 head of beef cattle a year. As a result of drought, she sells 135 head during 2010 and realizes $70,200 from the sale. On August 9, 2010, because of drought, the affected area is declared a disaster area eligible for federal assistance. The income Yolanda can postpone until 2010 is $18,200 [($70,200 ÷ 135) × 35], which is the portion of the gain attributed to the additional animals that she sold over her normal amount.

A weather-related sale or exchange of livestock (other than poultry) held for draft, breeding, or dairy purposes *may* also qualify as an involuntary conversion. Livestock that is sold or exchanged because of disease may not trigger taxable gain if the proceeds of the transaction are reinvested in replacement animals within two years of the close of the tax year in which the diseased animals were sold or exchanged. This would qualify as an involuntary conversion.

Postponing Gain from a Weather-Related Condition

To postpone gain, the farmer must attach a statement to his tax return for the year of the sale. The statement must have the following information for each class of livestock for which the taxpayer is postponing gain:

- A declaration that the postponement of gain is based on Section 451(e) of the IRC
- Evidence of the weather-related conditions that forced the early sale or exchange of the livestock
- An explanation of the relationship of the area affected by the weather-related condition to the farmer's early sale or exchange of the livestock
- The number of animals sold in each of the three preceding years
- The number of animals the farmer would have sold in the tax year had he followed normal business practices in the absence of weather-related conditions
- The total number of animals sold and the number sold because of weather-related conditions during the tax year

- A computation, as described earlier, of the income to be postponed for each class of livestock

In order to postpone gain, the farmer must file this statement along with the tax return by the due date of the return, including extensions. However, for sales that qualify as an involuntary conversion, the farmer can file this statement at any time during the replacement period.

Crop Insurance and Disaster Payments

Insurance proceeds, including government disaster payments, are taxable in the year they are received. This includes payments for the inability to plant crops because of a drought or other natural disaster. The farmer can elect to postpone reporting the income until the following year if he meets all of these conditions:

- The farming business must use the cash method of accounting.
- Crop insurance proceeds were received in the same tax year the crops are damaged.
- Under normal business practices, the farming business would have reported income from the damaged crops in the year following the year the damage occurred.

A statement must be attached to the tax return indicating the crops that were damaged and the total insurance payment received.

In order to make this election to postpone income, the farmer must be able to prove that the crops would have been harvested or otherwise sold in the following year.

Sometimes, farmers choose to forgo the planting of crops altogether. These farmers may then receive agricultural program payments from the government. An agricultural program payment is reported on Schedule F, and the full amount of the payment is subject to Self-Employment tax.

Unit 2.11: Questions

1. Isaac is a calendar-year, self-employed farmer on the cash basis. For the purposes of the estimated tax for qualified farmers, all of the following statements are true EXCEPT:

A. A qualified farmer does not have to make any estimated payments if he files by April 15 and pays all his taxes with his return.
B. A taxpayer is a qualified farmer if at least two-thirds of his previous year's gross income is from farming.
C. The required annual estimated tax payment for farmers is due on the fifteenth day after the close of the tax year.
D. The required annual payment is two-thirds of the current year's tax or 100% of the previous year's tax.

The answer is A. If a farmer waits until April 15 to file his return, he must pay estimated taxes just like any other business. If the taxpayer is a qualified farmer, he can either:
- Pay all his estimated tax by the fifteenth day after the end of his tax year (this date is usually January 15)
- File his return and pay all the tax owed by the first day of the third month after the end of his tax year (usually March 1)

A qualified farmer does not have to pay any estimated tax if he files his tax return AND pays all the tax due by March 1. If a farmer is required to pay estimated tax, he may also choose to make only one estimated tax payment (also called the "required annual payment") by January 18, 2011. ###

2. Examples of "income from farming" include the following EXCEPT:

A. Income from operating a livestock, dairy, poultry, bee, fruit, or tree farm
B. Beef cattle ranching and farming
C. Crop shares for the use of the farmer's land
D. Gains received from the sale of depreciable farm equipment

The answer is D. Gross income from farming does not include the gains from the sale of depreciable farm assets. That is because the sale of depreciable assets is usually a capital gain or loss, rather than ordinary income from operations. ###

3. Which of the following regarding farm inventory is FALSE?

A. Livestock held primarily for sale should not be included in inventory.
B. Currently growing crops are not required to be included in inventory.
C. All harvested and purchased farm products held for sale or for feed or seed, such as grain, hay, silage, concentrates, cotton, or tobacco, must be included in inventory.
D. Supplies acquired for sale or that become a physical part of items held for sale must be included in inventory.

The answer is A. Livestock held primarily for sale MUST be included in inventory. Livestock held for draft, breeding, or dairy purposes can either be depreciated OR included in inventory (Publication 225). ###

4. The following businesses engaged in farming MUST use an accrual method of accounting EXCEPT:

A. A farming business that had gross receipts of $5.5 million
B. A family farming corporation that had gross receipts of $20 million
C. A partnership with a corporation as a partner
D. A qualified farming business that is also a tax shelter

The answer is B. A family farm corporation that had gross receipts of $25 million or less is allowed to use the cash method of accounting to report expenses and income. All of the other entities listed are required to use the accrual method. ###

5. The following inventory valuation methods are all acceptable methods for valuation of farm inventory EXCEPT:

A. Cost
B. Retail coupon method
C. Farm-price method
D. Unit-livestock-price method

The answer is B. The retail coupon method does not exist. All of the other inventory valuation methods listed are allowed for farming businesses. ###

6. Joel is a qualified farmer who usually sells 500 beef cattle every year. However, because of a severe drought, he was forced to sell 800 beef cattle. Which of the following statements is TRUE?

A. Joel may choose to postpone all the gain in this transaction.
B. Joel may choose to postpone a portion of his gain in this transaction.
C. Joel must use the accrual method of accounting.
D. Postponement of gain is not allowed.

The answer is B. Joel may postpone a portion of his gain to the following year. If a farmer sells or exchanges more livestock, including poultry, than he normally would in a year because of a drought, flood, or other weather-related condition, he may postpone reporting the gain from the *additional* animals until the next year. The farmer must use the cash method of accounting in order to postpone gain in this manner. ###

7. Kathy is a qualified farmer. In 2010, she sells an old tractor that was used in her business. On which form should this sale be reported?

A. Schedule F
B. Schedule C
C. Form 4797
D. Form 4868

The answer is C. Sale of depreciable equipment is reported on Form 4797. The resulting gain or loss is capital gain or loss. ###

8. Jon owns a farming business and has income from the following sources:

Income from milk production: $50,000
Sale of old dairy cows: $20,000
Sale of feed: $15,000
Sale of used machinery: $4,000

How much of the income should be reported on Jon's Schedule F, *Profit or Loss from Farming*?

A. $50,000
B. $65,000
C. $74,000
D. $85,000

The answer is B. Gross income from farming activity is reported on Schedule F, and includes farm income, farm rental income, and gains from livestock that were raised specifically for sale on the farm, or purchased specifically for resale. The sale of old dairy cows and the sale of used machinery do not qualify. The sale of depreciable machinery is not reported on Schedule F, and likewise, the sale of livestock used for dairy purposes results in a capital gain (or loss) and is not reported on Schedule F. Instead, these amounts would be reported on Form 4797, *Sales of Business Property*. Therefore, the income reported would be from milk production and sale of feed ($50,000 + $15,000 = $65,000) (Publication 225). ###

9. Oliver is a farmer and has decided to refrain from growing any crops in 2010. He receives agricultural program payments for this activity. How should these payments be reported?

A. As "other income" on the taxpayer's individual Form 1040
B. On Schedule E, *Supplemental Income and Loss*
C. As farm income, but not subject to Self-Employment tax
D. As farm income on Schedule F, subject to Self-Employment tax

The answer is D. An agricultural program payment is reported on Schedule F, and the full amount of the payment is subject to Self-Employment tax. ###

10. Which of the following statements about farmers is TRUE?

A. Gross income from farming includes capital gains from the sale of equipment.
B. A farmer will not be charged an underpayment penalty for unpaid estimated taxes if his tax return is filed by March 1 and all tax due is paid.
C. A farmer does not have to report income from insurance payments.
D. An individual who owns livestock as a hobby and grows a large garden can be considered a farmer for tax purposes.

The answer is B. If at least two-thirds of an individual's gross income is from farming, then no underpayment penalty will be assessed if all estimated tax payments are made by January 15, OR no penalty will be assessed if the taxpayer's return is filed by March 1 and all tax due is paid. ###

11. For the purposes of the estimated tax exemptions for farmers, what type of income is not included in "farming income"?

A. Gains from the sale of timber
B. Income from the sale of grain
C. Gross income from a farming corporation
D. Gains from sale of investment stock owned fully by the farming corporation

The answer is D. Income from farming does not include the gains from the sale of securities, regardless of who owns the securities. ###

12. Luke is a qualified farmer. A bull calf was born on his farm on 2009. Luke spent $750 in feed for the calf and it was sold for $5,000 for breeding use in 2010. How much is Luke's gain from the sale of the bull calf?

A. $0
B. $4,250
C. $4,750
D. $5,000

The answer is D. The basis of livestock is generally cost. However, since the bull calf was born on the farm, the basis of the calf is $0. The cost of the feed is deductible, and is listed on the return as a regular business expense and as a deduction from gross income. The cost of the feed is not "added" to the basis of the calf. The sale of livestock held for breeding is not included in regular farming income. Special rules apply to the sale of livestock held for draft, breeding, sport, or dairy purposes. In this case, the sale resulted in a capital gain of $5,000. Farmers report these sales on Form 4797, *Sales of Business Property*. ###

13. Hope is a qualified farmer who grows soybeans. In 2010, her soybean crop was destroyed by flood. If the crop had not been destroyed, she would have harvested it in 2011. Hope receives federal disaster payments in 2010. Which of the following is TRUE?

A. Hope can choose to postpone the income from this disaster payment until 2011.
B. Disaster payments are not taxable income.
C. Hope must report the income on her 2010 return.
D. Hope may delay recognition of the gain for two years.

The answer is A. She can delay recognizing income on the payment until the following year. Payments for disaster relief may be included in income in the tax year following the year in which they were awarded. In order to make this election, the farmer must be able to prove that the crops would have been harvested or otherwise sold in the following year. ###

Unit 2.12: Exempt Organizations

More Reading:
Publication 4220, *Applying for 501(c)(3) Tax-Exempt Status*
Publication 557, *Tax-Exempt Status for Your Organization*
Publication 598, *Tax on Unrelated Business Income of Exempt Organizations*

Exempt organizations are also called "nonprofit" organizations. To seek recognition of exemption from federal tax, organizations generally must request permission from the IRS. A tax-exempt organization is one that does not have to pay income taxes. However, tax-exempt status does NOT mean that the organization can automatically receive contributions that are fully deductible by the donor.

"Tax exempt" does not necessarily mean "tax deductible." While the IRS defines more than 20 different categories of tax-exempt organizations, contributions to groups in only a few of these categories are tax deductible to the donor. Only contributions made to certain tax-exempt organizations, most notably 501(c)(3) organizations, are deductible on the donor's federal income tax return. There are many exempt organizations, such as a Chamber of Commerce, that are tax exempt, but do not qualify to receive contributions that are deductible to the donor.

A tax-exempt organization cannot be organized as a partnership or a sole proprietorship. An organization that is operated primarily for profit also does not qualify for tax-exempt status.

A tax-exempt organization may be organized as a corporation, trust, community chest, private foundation, or religious group. Tax-exempt organizations are organized primarily for religious, charitable, scientific, educational, or literary purposes. Organizations created to prevent cruelty to animals or children also qualify.

Tax-exempt organizations must file an annual information return, Form 990, *Return of Organization Exempt from Income Tax*. Churches and certain religious organizations, as well as certain state and local government entities, are exempt from the annual return filing requirement.

Exempt Organizations with Employees

Every tax-exempt entity must have an EIN whether or not it has employees. Religious organizations are NOT REQUIRED to file an application for exemption in order to be recognized as tax exempt by the IRS. Religious entities are also not required to file annual information returns (Form 990). However, religious entities may still have to file informational returns if they have employees or nonrelated business income.

Even if an organization is not required to file Form 990 (such as a church or other religious organization), any entity with employees is still responsible for filing employment tax returns. Churches must still withhold payroll taxes from the wages of their employees even though churches are generally exempt from paying income tax.

Example: Trinity Methodist Church is not required to file an application for exemption in order to be recognized as tax-exempt by the IRS. Trinity applies for an EIN as an exempt entity and begins regular worship. In 2010, Trinity Church hires three employees: a part-time choir master, a receptionist, and a bookkeeper. Although Trinity does not have to file Form 990, Trinity is still required to file employment tax returns and remit and collect employment taxes from the employees it has hired.

If a tax-exempt organization has employees, the entity is responsible for federal income tax withholding and Social Security and Medicare taxes on the employees' wages. In addition, some exempt organizations are also responsible for Federal Unemployment Tax (FUTA). The basic requirements for tax and wage reporting compliance, calculating withholding, making deposits, and keeping tax and reporting records apply to exempt organizations just like any other businesses.

Applying for Exempt Status

To be recognized as tax-exempt under Section 501(c)(3) of the Internal Revenue Code, an organization must be organized and operated exclusively for exempt purposes, and none of its earnings may benefit any private shareholder or individual. The organization must NOT be operated for the benefit of private interests. In addition, it may not attempt to influence legislation as a substantial part of its activities, and it may not participate in any campaign activity for or against political candidates. There are two forms that are used by nonprofit organizations to request exemption. In order to apply for recognition of exempt status by the IRS under Section 501(c)(3) of the IRC, entities use Form 1023, *Application for Recognition of Exemption*.

Organizations that do not qualify for exemption under Section 501(c)(3) may still qualify for tax-exempt status. They can file Form 1024, *Application for Recognition of Exemption Under 501(a)*.

In order to qualify for tax exemption, most organizations must request exemption from the IRS by the end of the fifteenth month after it was created, with a 12-month extension available. An organization is not required to file Form 1023 unless its annual gross receipts are more than $5,000.

An organization must file Form 1023 to request formal exemption within 90 days of the end of the year in which it exceeds this threshold. However, a private foundation is always required to request exemption regardless of the amount of its gross receipts.

Example: An animal rescue organization that was created on January 1, 2003 but did not exceed the $5,000 gross receipts threshold until September 30, 2010 must file Form 1023 to request formal tax-exemption by March 31, 2011.

Retroactive Exemption Allowed

An organization that files its application before the deadline may be recognized as tax-exempt from the date of its creation. This is called a "retroactive exemption." An organization that files an application after the deadline may also be recognized as tax-exempt from the date of the application. An exempt organization may request a retroactive exemption when it files Form 1023.

Filing Requirements for Exempt Entities

Every organization must file an annual information return, unless it is specifically exempt from the filing requirement. The organizations that are NOT required to file a yearly Form 990 are:

- Churches and their affiliated organizations
- Government agencies

Small tax-exempt organizations with gross receipts under $25,000 are still required to file Form 990-N, *Electronic Notice for Tax Exempt Organizations Not Required to File Form 990*. This form is also called an "e-postcard" because it is filed electronically and is so short. There is no paper version of Form 990-N. A small tax-exempt organization may also voluntarily choose to file a long form (Form 990) instead.

Exempt Entities: Financial Activity	Filing requirement
Gross receipts normally < $25,000	Form 990-N (e-postcard)
Gross receipts < $500,000 and Total assets < $1.25 million	Form 990-EZ or 990
Gross receipts ≥ $500,000, or Total assets ≥ $1.25 million	Form 990
Private foundation (regardless of financial activity)	Form 990-PF

*Note: Any organizations eligible to file the e-postcard may opt to file a full return (Form 990).

The annual information return for a tax-exempt entity is due by the fifteenth day of the fifth month after the accounting period ends. For a calendar-year entity, the due date is May 15. If the organization has been dissolved, the return is due by the fifteenth day of the fifth month after the dissolution.

Extensions of Time to File

An exempt entity may request a three-month extension of time to file by filing Form 8868, *Application for Extension of Time to File an Exempt Organization Return*. The organization may also apply for an additional three-month extension if needed. When filing a request for the first three-month extension, neither a signature nor an explanation is required. However, when filing an additional three-month extension, both a signature and an explanation are required.

An organization must file Form 990 electronically if it files at least 250 returns during the calendar year and has total assets of $10 million or more at the end of the tax year. A private foundation is required to file Form 990-PF electronically if it files at least 250 returns during the calendar year.

Section 501(c)(3) organizations must make their application (Form 1023) and the three most recent annual returns (Form 990) available to the public. The IRS also makes these documents available for public inspection and copying. Private foundation returns are subject to the same disclosure rules. These documents must be made available at the organization's principal office during regular business hours (Publication 4220).

Penalties for Late Filing and Failure to File

An exempt organization that fails to file a required return must pay a penalty of $20 a day for each day the return is late. The same penalty will apply if the organization gives incorrect information on the return. The maximum penalty for any year is the smaller of:

- $10,000, or
- 5% of the organization's gross receipts for the year.

For an organization that has gross receipts of over $1 million for the year, the late filing penalty is $100 a day, up to a maximum of $50,000.

If the exempt organization is subject to this penalty, the IRS may specify a date by which the return or correct information must be supplied by the organization. Failure to comply with this demand will result in a penalty imposed upon the manager (or officer) of the organization, or upon any other person responsible for filing a correct return. The penalty is $10 a day for each day that a return is not filed after the period given for filing. The maximum penalty imposed on an individual in connection with one return is $5,000. This penalty is in addition to the late filing penalty imposed on the organization itself.

An organization's exempt status may be revoked for failure to file. Failure to file an annual information return for three years in a row will result in the automatic revocation of exempt status. In this case, the organization would be required to reapply for exemption.

No penalty will be imposed if reasonable cause for failure to timely file can be shown.

501(c)(3) Organizations

The most common types of exempt organizations are 501(c)(3) organizations. These are entities that are organized solely for charitable, educational, or religious purposes. These entities are exempt if they meet ALL the following criteria:

- Organized and operated exclusively for religious, charitable, scientific, literary purposes; public safety testing; prevention of cruelty to children or animals; or fostering national or international amateur sports competition;
- No part of the entity's net earnings benefit any private shareholder or individual; and
- The organization is prohibited from trying to influence legislation, spread any political propaganda, or engage in lobbying activities.

The following organizations are generally qualified "501(c)(3)" organizations:

1. Charitable organizations that conduct activities that promote relief of the poor, the distressed, or the underprivileged, advancement of religion, advancement of education or science, erection or maintenance of public buildings, eliminating prejudice and discrimination, and combating community deterioration and juvenile delinquency.

2. Educational organizations including schools such as a college or a professional or trade school, symphonies, forums, panels, or similar programs.

3. Religious organizations: The term "church" includes synagogues, temples, mosques, and similar types of organizations. Other religious organizations, such as mission organizations, speakers' organizations, nondenominational ministries, ecumenical organizations, or faith-based social agencies, may also qualify for exemption. However, these other ancillary religious organizations must apply for exemption from the IRS.

Other Section 501(c) Organizations

Not all tax-exempt organizations are 501(c)(3) organizations. There are other organizations that qualify for tax-exempt status, but may or may not qualify to accept donor-deductible contributions. Other examples of nonprofit entities that are NOT 501(c)(3) organizations include:

- 501(c)(4) Civic leagues and social welfare organizations
- 501(c)(5) Labor unions, agricultural, and horticultural organizations
- 501(c)(6) Business leagues, etc. (Grassroots lobbying organizations)
- 501(c)(7) Social and recreation clubs
- 501(c)(8) and 501(c)(10) Fraternal beneficiary societies (Rotary clubs)
- 501(c)(4), 501(c)(9), and 501(c)(17) Employees' associations
- 501(c)(12) Local benevolent life insurance associations
- 501(c)(13) Nonprofit cemetery companies
- 501(c)(14) Credit unions and other mutual financial organizations
- 501(c)(19) Veterans' organizations
- 501(c)(20) Group legal services plan organizations
- 501(c)(21) Black lung benefit trusts
- 501(c)(2) Title-holding corporations for single parents
- 501(c)(25) Title-holding corporations or trusts for multiple parents
- 501(c)(26) State-sponsored high-risk health coverage organizations
- 501(c)(27) State-sponsored workers' compensation reinsurance organizations

To be exempt under Internal Revenue Code Section 501(c)(7), a social club must be organized for pleasure, recreation, and other similar nonprofit purposes, and substantially all of its activities must be for these purposes. A club will not be recognized as tax-exempt if its charter or any written policy statement provides for discrimination against any person based on race, color, or religion. It should file Form 1024 to apply for recognition of exemption from federal income tax.

Private Foundations

Every organization that qualifies for tax-exempt status under Section 501(c)(3) of the IRC is further classified as either a public charity or a private foundation. Tax-exempt entities are automatically presumed to be private foundations, unless they are specifically excluded.

For some organizations, the primary distinction between a classification as a public charity or a private foundation is the organization's source of financial support. Generally, a public charity has a broad base of support while a private foundation has very limited sources of support.

This classification is important because different tax rules apply to the operations of each. Deductibility of contributions to a private foundation is more limited than deductibility of contributions to a public charity.

A private foundation is a charitable organization that is set up as a holding entity for donated assets. Private foundations receive less preferential tax treatment than public charities and religious organizations because they are not always seen as being operated for the good of the public. Private foundations are required to file an information tax return (Form 990-PF) every single year.

Some organizations are automatically excluded from being classified as private foundations. As listed in Section 509(a)(1) of the Internal Revenue Code, these organizations are NOT considered private foundations:

- Any church
- An educational organization, such as a school or college
- A hospital or medical research organization operated in conjunction with a hospital
- Endowment funds operated for the benefit of colleges and universities
- Any domestic governmental organization
- A publicly-supported organization
- Organizations organized and operated exclusively for testing for public safety

Any exempt organization will NOT be considered a private foundation if it receives more than one-third of its annual support from its own members and/or the general public.

Unless it falls into one of the categories specifically excluded, the organization will be treated as a private foundation by the IRS. In addition, certain nonexempt charitable trusts are also treated as private foundations. Organizations that fall into the excluded categories are institutions such as hospitals or universities and those that generally have broad public support.

There is an excise tax on the net investment income of domestic private foundations. Certain foreign private foundations are also subject to a tax on investment income derived from United States' sources. This excise tax must be reported on Form 990-PF, and must be paid annually or in quarterly estimated tax payments if the total tax for the year is $500 or more. There are several restrictions on private foundations, including:

- Restrictions on self-dealing between private foundations and their contributors
- Requirements that the foundation annually distribute income for charitable purposes
- Limits on their holdings in private businesses
- Provisions that investments must not jeopardize the carrying out of exempt purposes
- Provisions to assure that expenditures further exempt purposes, rather than private purposes

*Remember: All private foundations must file Form 990-PF, *Return of Private Foundation*, every year regardless of their income.

More on Prohibited Activities

Depending upon the nature of its exemption, a tax-exempt organization will jeopardize its tax-exempt status if it engages in certain prohibited activities. Charitable organizations may not intervene in political campaigns or conduct substantial lobbying activities. Under the Internal Revenue Code, all Section 501(c)(3) organizations are prohibited from directly or indirectly participating in any political campaign on behalf of or in opposition to any candidate for public office.

Contributions to political campaign funds or public statements of position (verbal or written) made on behalf of the organization in favor of or in opposition to any candidate for public office violate the prohibition against political campaign activity. Violating this prohibition may result in denial or revocation of tax-exempt status. Voter education or registration activities are not prohibited, but any activity with evidence of bias that favors one candidate over another, opposes a candidate in some manner, or has the effect of favoring a candidate will constitute prohibited participation or intervention.

Individuals, including clergy, are allowed to speak for themselves—even on important political issues. But religious leaders cannot make partisan comments in official publications or at official functions. A religious body may invite a candidate to speak at its events as long as it provides equal opportunity to all candidates seeking the same office.

The Unrelated Business Income Tax (UBIT)

An exempt organization must be operated primarily for a tax-exempt purpose. However, an exempt organization may engage in income-producing activities unrelated to the tax-exempt purpose as long as these activities are not a substantial part of the organization's regular activities. Unrelated business activities are subject to federal tax. Nonprofit organizations must pay the "Unrelated Business Income Tax" (UBIT) on unrelated business income. For most organizations, an activity is considered an "unrelated business" and subject to UBIT if it meets three requirements:

- It is a trade or business,
- It is regularly carried on, and
- It is not substantially related to furthering the exempt purpose of the organization.

Unrelated business income is income from a trade or business, regularly carried on, that is not substantially related to the charitable, educational, or other purpose that is the basis for the organization's exemption. An exempt organization that has $1,000 or more of gross income from an unrelated business must file Form 990–T.

Tax-exempt organizations must make quarterly payments of estimated tax on unrelated business income. An organization must make estimated tax payments if it expects its tax for the year to be $500 or more. Form 990-T of a tax-exempt organization must be filed by the fifteenth day of the fifth month after the tax year ends.

An employees' trust must file Form 990-T by the fifteenth day of the fourth month after its tax year ends. A tax-exempt organization's Form 990-T is not available for public inspection.

Example: A university enters into a multi-year contract with a sports drink company to be the exclusive provider of sports drinks for the university's athletic department and concessions. As part of the contract, the university agrees to perform various services for the company, such as guaranteeing that coaches make promotional appearances on behalf of the company (e.g., attending photo shoots, filmed commercials, and retail store appearances). The university itself is a qualified non-profit organization, but the income received from the exclusive contract would be subject to UBIT (Rul. 81-178). The university is required to file a Form 990-T.

> **Example:** A college negotiates discounted rates for the soft drinks it purchases for its cafeterias in return for an exclusive provider arrangement. Generally, discounts are considered an adjustment to the purchase price and do not constitute gross income to the purchaser. Thus, the amount of the negotiated discount is not includable in UBIT. The college is not required to file a Form 990-T.

Recordkeeping and Disclosure Requirements

Tax-exempt organizations are required to keep books and records detailing all activities, both financial and non-financial. Financial information, particularly information on its sources of support (contributions, grants, sponsorships, and other sources of revenue) is crucial to determining an organization's private foundation status.

A donor cannot claim a tax deduction for any contribution of cash, checks, or other monetary gifts unless the donor maintains a record of the contribution or a written communication from the charity (such as a receipt or a letter) showing the name of the charity, the date of the contribution, and the amount of the contribution.

Important Forms for Exempt Organizations

- Form 990, *Return of Organization Exempt From Income Tax*
- Form 990-EZ, *Short Form Return of Organization Exempt From Income Tax*
- Form 990-PF, *Return of Private Foundation*
- Form 990-T, *Exempt Organization Business Income Tax Return*
- Form 1023, *Application for Recognition of Exemption Under Section 501(c)(3) of the Internal Revenue Code*
- Form 1024, *Application for Recognition of Exemption under Section 501(a)*
- Form 1041, *U.S. Income Tax Return for Estates and Trusts*
- Form 8283, *Noncash Charitable Contributions*
- Form 8868, *Extension of Time to File an Exempt Organization Return*

Unit 2.12: Questions

1. Which of the following organizations do not qualify for tax-exempt status?

A. A charitable organization
B. A religious organization
C. A private foundation
D. An educational partnership

The answer is D. A partnership does not qualify for exemption from income tax. A tax-exempt organization cannot be organized as a partnership or sole proprietorship. ###

2. Cat Rescue Inc. is a nonprofit organization that helps prevent cruelty to animals. It is required to file Form 990 in 2010. Cat Rescue Inc. is on a calendar year. What is the due date of its tax return, not including extensions?

A. April 15
B. March 15
C. May 15
D. October 15

The answer is C. Since Cat Rescue is on a calendar year, its tax return is due May 15. Each tax-exempt organization is required to file by the fifteenth day of the fifth month after its fiscal year ends. ###

3. Which of the following statements is TRUE?

A. Any exempt organization that qualifies for tax-exempt status with the IRS receives contributions that are fully deductible by the donor.
B. A church is not required to file an annual information return (Form 990).
C. A religious entity does not have to file payroll tax returns if it has employees.
D. A church may be organized as a sole proprietorship.

The answer is B. A religious organization is not required to file an annual information return. However, a religious organization with employees is still responsible for filing employment tax returns. Churches must still withhold payroll taxes from the wages of their employees even though churches are generally exempt from paying income tax. Neither nonprofit nor tax-exempt status means that the organization can receive contributions that are fully deductible by the donor. "Tax exempt" does not necessarily mean "tax deductible."###

4. Most organizations seeking recognition of exemption from federal income tax must use specific application forms prescribed by the IRS. Which form must be filed in order to request recognition as a 501(c)(3) nonprofit organization by the IRS?

A. Form 1023
B. Form 1024
C. Form 1040
C. Form 990

The answer is A. The form currently required by the IRS to apply for 501(c)(3) status is Form 1023, *Application for Recognition of Exemption Under Section 501(c)(3) of the Internal Revenue Code.* ###

5. Which of the following exempt organizations is NOT required to file an annual information return?

A. A church with gross receipts exceeding $250,000
B. An exempt literary organization with $6,000 in gross receipts
C. A Chamber of Commerce with $26,000 in gross receipts
D. A private foundation with income less than $5,000

The answer is A. Only the church would not be required to file a tax return. Every organization must file a Form 990 unless specifically exempt. Most federally tax-exempt nonprofits that have incomes of more than $25,000 must file an information return, and all private foundations must file, regardless of income. ###

6. Of the organizations listed below, which organization would NOT qualify for tax-exempt status under the Internal Revenue Code?

A. A Christian church with only eight members
B. A political action committee
C. A trust for a college alumni association
D. A local boys club

The answer is B. A political action committee would not qualify. In general, if a substantial part of an organization's activities includes attempting to influence legislation, the organization's exemption from federal income tax will be denied. Organizations that offer voter information or promote voter registration and are nonpartisan may still qualify for exemption. ######

7. The Blue Lake Sailing Club is a social club promoting the social activity of sailing. Which of the following is TRUE?

A. The Blue Lake Sailing Club may apply and be recognized as exempt from federal income tax.
B. A social club cannot qualify for IRS exemption.
C. This type of organization only qualifies for exemption if it is organized as a religious organization.
D. None of the above.

The answer is A. The sailing club can apply for exemption from income tax. To be exempt under Internal Revenue Code Section 501(c)(7), a social club must be organized for pleasure, recreation, and other similar nonprofit purposes and substantially all of its activities must be for these purposes. A club will not be recognized as tax exempt if its charter or any written policy statement provides for discrimination against any person based on race, color, or religion. It should file Form 1024 to apply for recognition of exemption from federal income tax. ###

8. The local Catholic church has two employees: Martha, who works as a secretary in the church rectory, and Jack, who is the church custodian. Which return must the church file in order to fulfill its IRS reporting obligations?

A. Form 990
B. Form 8300
C. Employment tax returns
D. All of the above

The answer is C. Exempt churches, their integrated auxiliaries, and conventions or associations of churches are not required to file information returns. However, every employer, including an organization exempt from federal income tax that pays wages to employees is responsible for withholding, depositing, paying, and reporting federal income tax, Social Security and Medicare (FICA) taxes, and also for filing employment tax returns. ###

9. Which of the following organizations may request exempt status under the Internal Revenue Code as a charitable organization?

A: A Catholic school
B: A Hindu organization
C: A children's rescue organization
D: All of the above

The answer is D. Nonprofit organizations that are exempt from federal income tax under Section 501(c)(3) of the Internal Revenue Code include entities organized exclusively for religious, charitable, scientific, testing for public safety, literary or educational purposes, fostering national or international amateur sports competition, or for the prevention of cruelty to children or animals.###

10. A 501 (c)(3) charitable organization (which is organized as a corporation) has annual gross receipts of $121,000 and assets of less than $500,000 in 2010. What is the easiest form that the organization qualifies to file?

A. Form 990-N
B. Form 990-EZ
C. Form 990-PF
D. Form 1120

The answer is B. A charitable organization does not file Form 1120, even if it is organized as a corporation. A charitable organization that has less than $200,000 in gross receipts and less than $500,000 in assets may file Form 990-EZ. ###

11. Which form is used for an exempt organization to request an extension of time to file?

A. Form 8868
B. Form 7004
C. Form 990
D. Form 4797

The answer is A. Form 8868, *Application for Extension of Time to File an Exempt Organization Return*, is used to request an extension of time to file. ###

12. A charitable organization has $2,000 in unrelated business income in the current year. How is this income reported?

A. The organization must file a business tax return for the unrelated business income.
B. The organization is required to file Form 990-T.
C. The organization will have its exempt status revoked.
D. The organization must file Schedule C to correctly report the business income.

The answer is B. An exempt organization that has $1,000 or more of gross income from an unrelated business must file Form 990–T (Publication 596). ###

Unit 2.13: Retirement Plans for Businesses

> **More Reading:**
> **Publication 560, *Retirement Plans for Small Business***

Employers set up retirement plans as a fringe benefit to their employees. Self-employed taxpayers are also allowed to set up retirement plans for themselves. There are numerous retirement plans that employers can choose from.

In Part One of the EA Exam, we cover retirement plans from the perspective of the individual taxpayer. For Part Two of the EA Exam, you must understand retirement plans from the perspective of the employer who provides the retirement plan to his employees.

Retirement plans offer employers and their employees a "tax-favored" way to save for retirement. Businesses can deduct retirement contributions they make on behalf of their employees. Earnings on retirement contributions are generally tax-free until distribution.

Employer contributions to an employee retirement plan are an ordinary business expense. A C Corporation would deduct the expense on Form 1120.

The rules are a little different for other entity types. Any business, such as a sole proprietorship or a partnership, can always deduct retirement plan contributions made on behalf of employees. This is true even if the business has a net operating loss for the year. However, in the case of a sole proprietorship or partnership, if the owners of the business contribute to *their own* retirement accounts, then they must take the deduction on Form 1040.

Sole proprietors and partners deduct retirement contributions for *themselves* on Form 1040. In order for a sole proprietor or a partner to make retirement contributions, they must have self-employment income. Self-employment income for the purpose of this deduction means net profits from a Schedule C or Schedule F, self-employed income from a partnership, or wages as a shareholder-employee in an S-corporation.

Example: Tamara is self-employed and reports her income and losses on Schedule C. Tamara owns a dress shop. She has a retirement account set up for herself and her five employees. In 2010, Tamara's dress shop showed a loss on her Schedule C. She has no other income. Tamara made regular contributions to her employees' retirement accounts in 2010, and she may deduct these contributions to her employees' accounts as a business expense. However, Tamara cannot make a contribution for herself in 2010, because she has no self-employment income. Since her business showed a loss, she has no qualifying income for the purpose of her own retirement plan contribution.

Simplified Employee Pension (SEP)

A Simplified Employee Pension (SEP) plan provides the simplest and least expensive method for employers to make contributions to a retirement plan for themselves and their employees. The business owner is also allowed to contribute to her own SEP. A SEP allows employees to make contributions on a tax-favored basis to Individual Retirement Accounts (IRAs) owned by the employees.

A SEP may be established as late as the due date (*including extensions*) of the company's income tax return for the year the employer wants to establish the plan. Employers must make their contributions to the plan by the due date of the employer's tax return, including extensions. With a SEP, there is no "plan document," and there is no annual reporting requirement with the IRS. Contributions to a SEP can vary from year to year, so it is a very flexible option for small employers.

A SEP can be set up for an individual person's business even if he participates in another employer's retirement plan.

> **Example:** Billy works full time for the post office as a mail carrier. But he also runs a small catering business with his wife. They have self-employment income from the business. Billy may set up a SEP for himself and his spouse, even though he is already covered by the post office employer plan.

Under a SEP, employers make contributions to a traditional Individual Retirement Arrangement (called a SEP-IRA) set up for each eligible employee. A SEP-IRA is owned and controlled by the employee, and the employer makes contributions to the financial institution where the SEP-IRA is maintained. SEPs are exclusively funded by contributions of the employer.

A SEP-IRA must be set up for *each eligible employee*. This means that every eligible employee must have his own SEP-IRA. However, a SEP-IRA does not need to be set up for "excludable employees" (covered next).

A SEP does not require employer contributions every year, but it cannot discriminate in favor of Highly Compensated Employees (HCEs). HCEs are defined as employees owning more than 5% of the company or who are paid more than $110,000 (in 2010). This means that a business cannot choose to fund the retirement plans of its highly-paid executives, while ignoring the retirement plans of its other workers.

Employee Eligibility: SEP

For the purposes of a SEP, an "eligible employee" is an individual who meets all the following requirements:

- Has reached age 21
- Has worked for the employer in at least three of the last five years
- Has received at least $550 in compensation in 2010

If an employer sets up a SEP, then all the employees who are "eligible employees" must also be allowed to participate. An employer can use *less restrictive* participation requirements than those listed, but not *more restrictive* ones.

Money withdrawn from a SEP-IRA (and not rolled over to another plan) is subject to income tax for the year in which an employee receives a distribution. If an employee withdraws money from a SEP-IRA before age 59½, a 10% additional tax generally applies.

As with other traditional IRAs, employee participants in a SEP-IRA must begin withdrawing minimum distributions from their accounts by April 1 of the year following the year the participant reaches age 70½.

Excluding Employees from a SEP Plan

The following employees can be excluded from coverage under a SEP:

- Employees already covered by a union agreement
- Nonresident alien employees who have received no U.S. source wages, salaries, or other personal services compensation
- Transient employees who leave within three years

> **Example:** Quincy Company decides to establish a SEP for its employees. Quincy has chosen a SEP because its industry is cyclical in nature, with good times and down times. In good years, Quincy can make larger contributions for its employees, and in down times it can reduce the amount. Quincy knows that under a SEP, the contribution rate (whether large or small) must be uniform for all employees. The financial institution that Quincy has picked to be the trustee for its SEP has several investment funds for employees to choose from. Individual employees have the opportunity to divide their employer's contributions to their SEP-IRAs among the funds available to Quincy employees.

Contribution Rules and Limits: SEP

Contributions to a SEP must be made in cash; an employer cannot contribute *property* to a SEP. However, plan participants may be able to transfer or "roll over" certain property from one retirement plan to another. When employers contribute to a SEP, they must contribute to the SEP-IRAs of all participants who had qualified compensation, including employees who die or terminate employment before the contributions are made.

A SEP-IRA cannot be a Roth IRA. Employer contributions to a SEP-IRA will not affect the amount an individual can contribute to a Roth or traditional IRA. To deduct SEP contributions for a year, the business must make the contributions by the due date (including extensions) of its tax return for the year. Unlike traditional IRAs or Roth IRAs, employee contributions to a SEP-IRA are excluded from income, rather than deducted from it.

Contribution Limits: SEP

Contributions made for 2010 to an employee's SEP-IRA cannot exceed the lesser of:

- 25% of the employee's compensation, OR
- $49,000 (in 2010)

> **Example:** An employee, Annie, earned $21,000 for 2010. The maximum contribution her employer can make to Annie's SEP-IRA is $5,250 (25% × $21,000).

In 2010, the maximum employer contribution to a SEP for any eligible employee is $49,000.

> **Example:** Sylvia earned $210,000 for 2010. Because of the maximum contribution limit for 2010, the employer can only contribute $49,000 to Sylvia's SEP-IRA.

Distributions from a SEP

Employers cannot prohibit distributions from a SEP-IRA. Employers also cannot make contributions conditional that any part of the contribution must be kept in the employee's account after the business has made its contributions.

SEP Rules	Rules for Employers	Rules for Employees
Eligibility	Any business or self-employed individual may set up a SEP.	All employees who have worked for the business for three out of the last five years and earned at least $550 in the current year.
Contribution Thresholds	25% of compensation up to $49,000. Vesting is immediate.	Only employers and self-employed individuals can contribute to the plan. Employees cannot contribute to a SEP. Vesting is immediate.
Pros	Contributions can vary from year to year. Inexpensive to set up and administer.	Employers cannot prohibit distributions from a SEP, because vesting is immediate.
Drawbacks	A SEP must cover all qualifying employees. Employers cannot discriminate in favor of Highly Compensated Employees. Only employers can contribute to the plan.	Employees cannot contribute.

Savings Incentive Match Plan for Employees (SIMPLE IRA and SIMPLE 401K)

If a business has 100 or fewer employees (who earned $5,000 *or more* during the preceding calendar year); it can set up a SIMPLE retirement plan. In addition, the business cannot currently have another retirement plan.

A SIMPLE IRA plan provides the employer and his employees with a simplified way to contribute toward retirement. SIMPLE IRA plans have lower start-up and annual costs.

Under a SIMPLE plan, employees can choose to make retirement plan contributions by reducing their own salary, rather than receiving these amounts as part of their regular pay. In addition, businesses will contribute matching or non-elective contributions. SIMPLE plans can only be maintained on a calendar-year basis. An employer may initially set up a SIMPLE IRA plan as late as October 1.

SIMPLE plans are not qualified retirement plans.[82] For purposes of the 100-employee limitation, all employees employed at any time during the calendar year are taken into account, regardless of whether they are eligible to participate in the SIMPLE IRA plan. A SIMPLE IRA must be set up for *each employee* with contributions under the plan. Employees must receive notice of their right to participate, to make salary reduction contributions, and to receive employer contributions.

A SIMPLE plan can be structured as an IRA or a 401(k) plan. An employer cannot maintain another qualified plan if it already has a SIMPLE plan (***Exception**: An employer may have another retirement plan if the other plan is targeted to a union workforce).

If a business maintains a SIMPLE plan for at least one year and later, fails to meet the 100-employee limit, the business is allowed a two-year grace period to establish another plan.

---

[82] A "qualified" retirement plan is one that complies with IRS law so that taxes are deferred on contributions and earnings thereon until withdrawn.

SIMPLE IRA

Unlike a SEP, SIMPLE IRAs allow employee contributions and they mandate an employer match to employee contributions. A SIMPLE IRA has a lower contribution threshold than a SEP. In 2010, annual contributions to an SIMPLE IRA are limited to $11,500 ($14,000 if 50 or older). This does not include the amount of the employer-matching contribution (which can be up to 3% of the employee's wages).

Example: Regina works for the Skidmore Tire Company, a small business with 75 employees. Skidmore Tire has decided to establish a SIMPLE IRA plan and will make a 2% non-elective contribution for each of its employees. Under this option, even if Regina does not contribute to her own SIMPLE IRA, she would still receive an employer non-elective contribution to her SIMPLE IRA equal to 2% of salary. Regina has a yearly salary of $40,000 and has decided that this year he cannot afford to make a contribution to his SIMPLE IRA. Even though she does not make a contribution this year, Skidmore must make a non-elective contribution of $800 (2% of $40,000). The financial institution partnering with Skidmore on the SIMPLE IRA has several investment choices, and Regina has the same investment options as the other plan participants.

A SIMPLE IRA is an inexpensive retirement plan option for businesses that have a small number of employees. An employee may not "opt out" of participation in SIMPLE. A SIMPLE IRA plan may only be maintained on a calendar-year basis.

SIMPLE IRA plans operate on a calendar-year basis. An employer can set up a SIMPLE IRA plan effective on any date from January 1 through October 1 of a year, provided the employer did not previously maintain another SIMPLE IRA plan.

This requirement does not apply if the employer is a new employer that started operations October 1. A new employer may set up a SIMPLE IRA plan as soon as administratively feasible after the business comes into existence.

If an employer previously maintained a SIMPLE IRA plan, the employer can set up a SIMPLE IRA plan effective only on January 1 of any given year.

Example: Rockland Quarry Company is a small business with 50 employees. Rockland has decided to establish a SIMPLE IRA plan for all of its employees and will match its employees' contributions dollar-for-dollar up to 3% of each employee's salary. Under this option, if a Rockland employee does not contribute to his SIMPLE IRA, then that employee does not receive any matching employer contributions.

Elizabeth is an employee of Rockland Company. She has a yearly salary of $50,000 and decides to contribute 5% of her salary to her SIMPLE IRA. Elizabeth's yearly contribution is $2,500 (5% of $50,000). The Rockland matching contribution is $1,500 (3% of $50,000). Therefore, the total contribution to Elizabeth's SIMPLE IRA that year is $4,000 (her $2,500 contribution plus the $1,500 contribution from Rockland).

Withdrawals from a SIMPLE IRA

Distributions from a SIMPLE IRA are subject to income tax for the year in which they are withdrawn. If a participant takes a withdrawal from a SIMPLE IRA before age 59½, a 10% additional penalty generally applies. If the withdrawal occurs within two years of beginning participation, the 10% tax is increased to 25%. SIMPLE IRA contributions and earnings may be rolled over tax-free from one SIMPLE IRA to another. A tax-free rollover may also be made from a SIMPLE IRA to another type of IRA, or to another employer's qualified plan, after two years of beginning participation in the original plan.

SIMPLE IRA Rules	Rules for Employers	Rules for Employees
Eligibility	Any employer with 100 employees or less. The employer cannot maintain another retirement plan in addition to the SIMPLE IRA.	All employees who have earned over $5,000 in any two years prior and who will earn at least $5,000 in the current year.
Contribution Thresholds	Employer matching is mandatory up to 3% of employee compensation. The employer portion is limited to a maximum of $4,900, regardless of the employee's contribution.	An employee can contribute up to $11,500 in addition to an employer match up to 3% of the employee's salary. A self-employed individual can contribute $11,500 plus the equivalent employer match to his or her own account. Employees over 50 may contribute 14,000 in 2010.
Pros	Employees can make contributions. Vesting is immediate.	Employees can make contributions. Vesting is immediate.
Drawbacks	Employer matching is mandatory.	Employees with higher salaries may prefer a retirement plan option that allows them to contribute more.

SIMPLE 401(k) Plan

A SIMPLE plan can also be structured as a 401(k). A SIMPLE 401(k) is structured like a traditional 401(k). Generally, a SIMPLE 401(k) plan has recurring fees. However, just as with the SIMPLE IRA plan, there is a two-year grace period for growing businesses. Under a SIMPLE 401(k) plan, an employee can elect to defer some compensation. But unlike a regular 401(k) plan, the employer must make either:

- A matching contribution up to 3% of each employee's pay, or
- A non-elective contribution of 2% of each eligible employee's pay.

No other contributions can be made. The employees are totally vested in any and all contributions, but withdrawals are subject to a possible 10% penalty if the employee is under age 59½. Participant loans are permitted with a SIMPLE 401(k).

Pros and Cons of a SIMPLE 401(k):
The plan is not subject to the discrimination rules that everyday 401(k) plans are.
Employees are fully vested in all contributions.
The straightforward benefit formula allows for easy administration.
The plan offers optional loans, and hardship withdrawals add flexibility for employees.
No other retirement plans can be maintained.
Withdrawal and loan flexibility adds an administrative burden for the employer.

SIMPLE Vesting Rules

Employee and employer contributions are always 100% vested—that is, the money an employee has put aside plus employer contributions and earnings from investments cannot be forfeited, and the employee has the right to withdraw at any time, even though those withdrawals may be subject to penalty. Employees can also move (rollover) their SIMPLE IRA assets from one SIMPLE IRA plan to another.

SIMPLE Reporting Requirements

SIMPLE IRA plans are not required to file annual financial reports with the government. Distributions from the plan are reported by the financial institution making the distribution to both the IRS and the recipients of the distributions on Form 1099-R, *Distributions from Pensions, Annuities, Retirement or Profit-Sharing Plans, IRAs, Insurance Contract*s. The financial institution/trustee handling the SIMPLE IRA provides the IRS and participants with an annual statement containing contribution and Fair Market Value information on Form 5498, *Individual Retirement Arrangement Contribution Information*.

SIMPLE IRA contributions are not included in the "Wages, tips, other compensation" box of Form W-2, *Wage and Tax Statement*. However, salary reduction contributions must be included in the boxes for Social Security and Medicare wages.

SIMPLE 401(k) plans DO have a reporting requirement. The plan must file Form 5500 annually.

401(k) Plans in General

A 401(k) Plan is a defined contribution plan that is a cash or deferred arrangement. Employees can elect to defer receiving a portion of their salary which is instead contributed on their behalf, before taxes, to the 401(k) plan.

401(k) plans have become a common retirement savings vehicle for small businesses. With a 401(k) plan, an employee can choose to defer a portion of his salary. So instead of receiving that amount in his paycheck today, an employee can contribute the amount into a 401(k) plan sponsored by his employer. Sometimes the employer will match employee contributions.

These deferrals are accounted separately for each employee. Deferrals are made on a pretax basis but if the plan allows they can be made on an after-tax (Roth) basis at the employee's choosing.

Many 401(k) plans provide for "employer matching" contributions. Employer contributions and pretax deferrals (plus earnings) are not taxed by the federal government or by most state governments until they are distributed later to the employee. So the earnings on the account grow tax-free.

401(k) plans can vary significantly in their complexity. However, many financial institutions administer 401(k) plans, which can lessen the administrative burden on individual employers of establishing and maintaining these plans.

401(k) Plan Rules	Rules for Employers	Rules for Employees
Eligibility	Any business or employer is eligible to set up a 401(k) plan.	All employees who have worked at least 1,000 hours in the past year.
Contribution Thresholds	The maximum contribution for 2010 is $49,000. The vesting period is determined by the employer.	An employee can contribute up to $16,500 ($22,000 if age 50 or older.)
Pros	Employees and employers can make contributions to this plan. Employer matching is not required.	Employees can make contributions.
Drawbacks	This type of plan can be expensive to administer.	Employer contributions can take years to vest.

A 401(k) plan can include cash or elective deferral. Elective deferral is when an employer diverts part of the employee's pretax earnings to a retirement plan. The employee may designate the amount that will be deducted.

Qualified Plans

There are two basic kinds of qualified plans—**defined contribution plans** and **defined benefit plans**—and different rules apply to each. An employer is allowed to have more than one type of qualified plan, but maximum contributions cannot exceed yearly limits.

All qualified plans are subject to federal regulation under the Employee Retirement Income Security Act (ERISA). Although the federal government does not require an employer to establish any type of retirement plan, it does provide minimum federal standards for qualified plans. ERISA mandates minimum funding requirements to ensure that retirement benefits will be available to employees who retire. The act also requires that retirement plan funding be certified by an actuary.

ERISA covers qualified retirement plans, health, and other welfare benefit plans (e.g., life, disability, and apprenticeship plans). Among other things, ERISA provides that those individuals who manage plans (and other fiduciaries) must meet certain standards of conduct. The law also contains detailed provisions for reporting to the government and for disclosure to participants. In addition, there are provisions aimed at assuring that plan funds are protected and that participants who qualify receive their benefits.

ERISA also mandates that qualified plans meet specific requirements regarding who is actually eligible, which employees are covered, vesting, how the plan is communicated to employees, and funding of the plan.

Defined Contribution Plan

We have already reviewed a few types of defined contribution plans. A defined contribution plan provides an individual account for each participant in the plan. It provides benefits to a participant largely based on the amount contributed to that participant's account. Benefits are also affected by any income, expenses, gains, losses, and forfeitures of other accounts that may be allocated to an account.

In these plans, the employee or the employer (or both) contribute to the employee's individual account under the plan, sometimes at a set rate, such as 3 percent of earnings annually. These contributions generally are invested on the employee's behalf. The employee will ultimately receive the balance in their account, which is based on contributions plus or minus investment gains or losses. The value of the account will fluctuate due to the changes in the value of the investments.

In a defined contribution plan, an employee's retirement benefits depend on his or her contributions, rather than years of service or earnings history. Examples of defined contribution plans include 401(k) plans, 403(b) plans, and 457 plans, all of which are similar.

Defined Benefit Plan

A defined benefit plan promises a specified monthly benefit at retirement. Fewer and fewer companies are offering defined benefit plans because they are costly to administer and not flexible. Contributions to a defined benefit plan are not optional.

The benefits in most traditional defined benefit plans are protected by federal insurance. Most federal and state governments offer defined benefit plans to their employees.

Contributions for self-employed taxpayers are limited to 100% of compensation. If the business does not have any income for the year, then no contribution can be made. Contributions are based on actuarial tables.

Employees enrolled in defined benefit plans can often receive a greater benefit at retirement than under any other type of retirement plan. On the employer side, businesses can generally contribute (and therefore deduct) more each year than in defined contribution plans. However, defined benefit plans are often more complex and likely more expensive to establish and maintain than other types of plans. A defined benefit plan can be administered through a Keogh.

Defined Benefit Plan Rules	Rules for Employers	Rules for Employees
Eligibility	Any business or employer.	All employees who have worked at least 1,000 hours in the past year.
Contribution Thresholds	There is no set limit for defined benefit plans. However, contributions are limited to 100% of compensation.	Employees cannot contribute to this type of plan.
Pros	Vesting is determined by the employer. Shareholder-employees of closely held corporations can contribute and deduct more per year than in a defined contribution plan.	Employees are guaranteed a fixed payout for life after retiring.
Drawbacks	This type of plan can be expensive to administer. Annual reporting is required. Future benefits are dependent on contributions and the fund's performance. An actuary is required to determine the contribution and deduction limit.	Employer contributions can take years to vest. Fixed income could be inadequate in future years in a defined benefit plan.

Employer Credit for Pension Startup Costs

Employers can claim a tax credit for pension startup costs. The credit equals 50% of the cost to set up the plan, up to a maximum of $500 per year for each of the first three years of the plan.

Employers can choose to start claiming the credit in the tax year before the tax year in which the plan becomes effective. In order to qualify for this credit, the employer must have had 100 or fewer employees who received at least $5,000 in compensation for the preceding year.

This credit is part of the General Business Credit, which can be carried back or forward to other tax years if it cannot be used in the current year. The credit is reported on Form 8881, *Credit for Small Employer Pension Plan Startup Costs*.

Retirement Savings Contributions Credit

Retirement plan participants (including self-employed individuals) who make contributions to their own retirement plan may *also* qualify for the Retirement Savings Contribution Credit. The credit is 10%-50% of eligible contributions up to $1,000 ($2,000 for MFJ).

Retirement Plan Reporting Requirements

Form 5500, *Annual Return/Report of Employee Benefit Plan*, is used to report information concerning employee benefit plans. Any administrator of an employee benefit plan subject to ERISA must file an information return about the benefit plan every year.

Form 5500 is intended to assure that employee benefit plans are operated and managed in accordance with certain prescribed standards. The requirements for completing Form 5500 vary according to the type of plan. Plan administrators must file an annual return, Form 5500, by the last day of the seventh month after the plan year ends.

Prohibited Transactions

A prohibited transaction is a transaction between a plan and a disqualified person that is prohibited by law. Disqualified persons who take part in a prohibited transaction must always pay a tax, even if they correct the error. A 15% excise tax is always charged on a prohibited transaction. If the transaction is not corrected within the taxable period, an additional tax of 100% of the amount involved is imposed on the "disqualified person." Prohibited transactions include the following:

- A transfer of plan income or assets to a disqualified person
- Any act of a fiduciary by which plan income or assets are used for his/her own benefit
- The receipt of money or property by a fiduciary for his or her own account from any party dealing with the plan in a transaction that involves plan income or assets
- The sale, exchange, or lease of property between a plan and a disqualified person
- Lending money between a plan and a disqualified person
- Furnishing goods or services between a plan and a disqualified person

Example: A plan fiduciary had a prohibited transaction by investing in a life insurance company's group annuity contract, resulting in a 10% commission paid to his company on the investment. This qualifies as a prohibited transaction between a plan fiduciary and a retirement plan.

A "disqualified person" is defined as ANY ONE of the following:
- A fiduciary of the retirement plan
- A person providing services to the plan
- An employer, any of whose employees are covered by the plan
- An employee organization, any of whose members are covered by the plan
- Any individual, either indirectly or directly, who owns 50% or more of the ownership of the company who administers the retirement plan
- A member of the family of any individual described in the above bullet points.
- A corporation, partnership, trust, or estate that has any direct or indirect ownership and holds 50% or more of any of the following:
  - The combined voting power of all classes of stock entitled to vote or the total value of shares of all classes of stock of a corporation
  - The capital interest or profits interest of a partnership
  - The beneficial interest of a trust or estate
- An officer, director, 10% or more shareholder, or Highly Compensated Employee of the entity administering the plan

If a prohibited transaction is *not corrected* during the taxable period, the taxpayer usually has an additional 90 days after the day the IRS mails a notice of deficiency for the 100% tax to correct the transaction. This correction period (the taxable period plus the 90 days) can be extended if ONE of the following occurs:
- The IRS grants a reasonable time needed to correct the transaction
- The taxpayer petitions the U.S. Tax Court

Early Distributions: The 10% Penalty

If a distribution is made to an employee under the plan before she reaches age 59½, the employee may have to pay a 10% additional tax on the distribution. Distributions before an individual is at least 59½ are called early distributions.

There are several exceptions to the "age 59½ rule." An individual will not have to pay the additional 10% penalty in following situations:
- The taxpayer has unreimbursed medical expenses that are more than 7.5% of her Adjusted Gross Income
- The distributions are not more than the cost of the taxpayer's medical insurance
- Disability or death
- Distributions in the form of an annuity
- Distributions are not more than qualified higher education expenses
- Distributions are used to buy, build, or rebuild a first home (up to $10,000 of distributions)
- Distributions are used to pay the IRS due to a levy
- Distributions are made to a qualified reservist (an individual called up to active duty)

Even though these distributions will not be subject to the penalty, they will still be subject to income tax. Distributions that are properly rolled over into another retirement plan are not subject to either income tax or the 10% additional penalty.

> **Example:** Lauren is 43 years old and she takes a $5,000 distribution from her traditional IRA account. Lauren does not meet any of the exceptions to the 10% additional tax, so the $5,000 is an early distribution. Lauren must include the $5,000 in her gross income for the year of the distribution and pay income tax on it. Lauren must also pay an *additional* penalty tax of $500 (10% × $5,000).

Summary: Retirement Plans

Simplified Employee Pension (SEP)

Contributions to a SEP are tax deductible, and a business pays no taxes on the earnings on the investments. Contributions can vary. There is no filing requirement.

Sole proprietors, partnerships, and corporations, including S Corporations, can set up SEPs. Employers may be eligible for a tax credit of up to $500 per year for each of the first three years for the cost of starting the plan. Administrative costs are low.

An eligible employee is an employee who:

- Is at least 21 years of age, and
- Has performed service for a business in at least three of the last five years.

All eligible employees must participate in the plan, including part-time employees, seasonal employees, and employees who die or terminate employment during the year.

Excludible Employees

The SEP may also cover the following employees, but there is no requirement to cover them:

- Employees covered by a union contract;
- Nonresident alien employees who did not earn income from the business;
- Employees who received less than $550 in compensation during the year.

SIMPLE Plan

SIMPLE IRA plans may be established only by employers that had no more than 100 employees who earned $5,000 or more in compensation during the preceding calendar year. For purposes of the 100-employee limitation, all employees employed at any time during the calendar year are taken into account, regardless of whether they are eligible to participate in the SIMPLE IRA plan.

In 2010, annual contributions to an SIMPLE IRA are limited to $11,500 ($14,000 if 50 or older). This does not include the amount of the employer-matching contribution (which can be up to 3% of the employee's wages).

Qualified Plans

There are two kinds of qualified plans—defined contribution plans and defined benefit plans.

Defined Benefit Plans: promise a specified monthly benefit at retirement.

Defined Contribution Plans: did not promise a specified benefit at retirement. In these plans, the employee or the employer (or both) contribute to the employee's individual account under the plan, sometimes at a set rate, such as 5 percent of earnings annually. Examples of defined contribution plans include 401(k) plans, 403(b) plans, employee stock owner-ownership plans, and profit-sharing plans.

A 401(k) Plan is a common defined contribution plan that is a cash or deferred arrangement. Employees can elect to defer receiving a portion of their salary which is instead contributed on their behalf, before taxes, to the 401(k) plan. Sometimes the employer will match employee contributions.

Characteristics Of Defined Benefit And Defined Contribution Plans		
Character	Defined Benefit Plan	Defined Contribution Plan
Employer Contributions and/or Matching Contributions	Employer funded. Federal rules set amounts that employers must contribute.	There is no requirement that the employer contribute, except in SIMPLE and safe harbor 401(k)s, SIMPLE IRAs, and SEPs. The employer may choose to match a portion of the employee's contributions or to contribute without employee contributions.
Employee Contributions	Employees generally do not contribute.	Many plans require the employee to contribute.
Managing the Investment	The employer must ensure that the amount in the plan plus investment earnings will be enough to pay the promised benefit.	The employee often is responsible for managing the investment of his or her account, choosing from investment options offered by the plan. In some plans, plan officials are responsible for investing the plan's assets.
Amount of Benefits Paid Upon Retirement	A promised benefit is based on a formula, often using a combination of the employee's age, years worked for the employer, or salary.	The benefit depends on contributions made by the employee and/or the employer and investment earnings on the contributions.
Type of Retirement Benefit Payments	Traditionally, these plans pay the retiree monthly annuity payments that continue for life.	The retiree may transfer the account balance into an Individual Retirement Account (IRA) from which the retiree withdraws money. Some plans also offer monthly payments through an annuity.
Guarantee of Benefits	The federal government, through the Pension Benefit Guaranty Corporation (PBGC), guarantees some amount of benefits.	No federal guarantee of benefits.

Unit 2.13: Questions

1. "Prohibited transactions" are transactions between a retirement plan and a disqualified person. Which of the following is EXEMPT from the prohibited transaction rules?

A. A fiduciary of the plan
B. A person providing services to the plan
C. An employer whose employees are covered by the plan
D. A disqualified person who receives a benefit to which he is entitled as a plan participant

The answer is D. If a person is qualified to receive a plan benefit, then the transaction is not a prohibited transaction. A prohibited transaction is a transaction between a plan and a disqualified person that is prohibited by law. Certain transactions are exempt from being treated as prohibited transactions. For example, a prohibited transaction does not take place if a disqualified person receives a benefit to which she is entitled as a plan participant or beneficiary. ###

2. Sarah runs her own business. She set up a new qualified defined benefit plan for her ten employees. In 2010, Sarah can receive a maximum tax credit of _____ for qualified retirement plan startup costs.

A. $100
B. $500
C. $1,000
D. $2,000

The answer is B. The maximum yearly credit amount is $500. Employers may claim a tax credit of 50% of the first $1,000 of qualified startup costs if starting a new qualified defined benefit or defined contribution plan, SIMPLE plan, or Simplified Employee Pension. This credit is reported on Form 8881, *Credit for Small Employer Pension Plan Startup Costs.* ###

3. Angel is a sole proprietor whose tax year is the calendar year. Angel made a contribution to his SIMPLE IRA on April 15, 2011. What is the earliest he can deduct this contribution?

A. His 2010 tax year return.
B. His 2011 tax year return.
C. The contribution is not deductible on his tax return because it was made late.
D. None of the above.

The answer is A. Taxpayers can deduct contributions for a particular tax year if they are made by the due date of the federal income tax return for that year. Angel may deduct the contribution made in 2011 on his 2010 tax return. ###

4. Maura is 26 years old and began participating in a SIMPLE retirement account on March 10, 2009. She took an early distribution from the account on December 26, 2010. She does not qualify for any of the exceptions to the early withdrawal penalty. The distribution amount was $10,000. What is the *penalty* amount that Maura must pay on the early distribution?

A. $1,000
B. $1,500
C. $2,500
D. $3,000

The answer is C. Early withdrawals generally are subject to a 10% additional tax. However, the additional tax is increased to 25% if funds are withdrawn within two years of beginning participation in a SIMPLE IRA. The answer is ($10,000 × 25% = $2,500) ###

5. Brenda owns the Berry Company, a sole proprietorship with 107 employees. Which of the following plans is NOT available for Brenda's company?

A. A qualified plan
B. A defined benefit plan
C. A SIMPLE IRA
D. None of the above

The answer is C. Brenda cannot set up a SIMPLE IRA for her employees, because her company exceeds the 100-employee threshold. Employers can set up a SIMPLE IRA plan only if they have 100 or fewer employees who received $5,000 or more in compensation for the preceding year. Employees include self-employed individuals who received earned income and leased employees. Once employers set up a SIMPLE IRA plan, they must continue to meet the 100-employee limit each year they maintain the plan. ###

6. Marcelo runs Perez Body Shop and sets up a SEP-IRA for all of his employees. He is allowed to stipulate in his benefits handbook that employees cannot withdraw from their SEP IRA while they are still employed by Perez Body Shop.

A. True
B. False

The answer is B, False. Employers cannot prohibit distributions from a SEP-IRA. Also, employers cannot make their contributions contingent on the condition that any part of them must be kept in the account. ###

7. Bonny & Clyde Partnership has 15 employees. The partnership contributes to its employees' retirement accounts. How is this transaction reported?

A. The business can take the deduction for its contributions to its employees' retirement accounts on Form 1065, *Partnership Income Tax Return*.
B. The business cannot take a deduction for its contributions to its employees' retirement accounts. Instead, the amounts contributed are added to the partnership basis.
C. The individual partners are allowed to deduct contributions to the employee retirement plans on their individual returns.
D. None of the above.

The answer is A. Employer contributions to an employee retirement plan are an ordinary business expense. A partnership enters the deductible contributions under a qualified pension, profit-sharing, annuity, SEP, or SIMPLE IRA plan, and under any other deferred compensation plan on Form 1065. ###

8. Rotary Inc. decides to establish a SEP for its employees. Which of the following statements about Rotary Inc.'s retirement plan is FALSE?

A. In good years, Rotary can make larger contributions for its employees, and in down times it can reduce the amount.
B. Individual employees have the opportunity to divide their employer's contributions to their SEP-IRAs among the funds made available to Rotary employees.
C. Under a SEP, the contribution rate can be different for all employees based on length of service and sales performance.
D. SEPs are exclusively funded by contributions of the employer.

The answer is C. Under a SEP, the contribution rate (whether large or small) must be uniform for all employees. Employers may distribute less when they have less income, but the plan cannot discriminate, and all the employees must be provided with uniform coverage under the plan. ###

9. Which of the following statements regarding a SEP-IRA is TRUE?

A. Money can be withdrawn from a SEP-IRA by the employee at any time without penalty.
B. Money can be withdrawn from a SEP-IRA by the employee at any time, but a penalty may apply.
C. An employee must wait at least two years to withdraw money from a SEP-IRA.
D. An employee must wait at least three years to withdraw money from a SEP-IRA.

The answer is B. Although a penalty may apply, participants are allowed to withdraw money from a SEP-IRA at any time. Withdrawals can be rolled over tax-free to another SEP-IRA, to another traditional IRA, or to another employer's qualified retirement plan. ###

10. What types of employers CANNOT establish a SEP?

A. A self-employed taxpayer without any employees
B. A corporation
C. A nonprofit entity with 5 employees
D. All of the above can establish a SEP.

The answer is D. Any employer can establish a SEP. Self-employed taxpayers can also establish a SEP for themselves. ###

11. The Goody Company has started a SEP plan for its employees. The company currently has four employees. Which of the following employees is the company NOT REQUIRED to cover under the SEP plan?

A. Faye, 45 years old, a full-time employee for the last five years
B. Larry, 25 years old, a part-time employee for the last three years
C. Randolph, 20 years old, a full-time employee for the last three years
D. Max, 42 years old, a seasonal employee for the last six years

The answer is C. Randolph is not an automatically eligible employee because he is not at least 21 years old. For the purposes of a SEP, an "eligible employee" is an individual who meets all the following requirements:

- Has reached age 21
- Has worked for the employer in at least three of the last five years
- Has received at least $550 in compensation

An employer can use less restrictive participation requirements than those listed, but not more restrictive ones. ###

12. Leah is a sole proprietor with two employees. She establishes a 401(k) SIMPLE plan. Leah has a net loss in 2010 on her Schedule C. Which of the following is TRUE?

A. Because the business shows a loss, she is prohibited from contributing to her retirement account, as well as the retirement accounts of her employees.
B. Because the business shows a loss, she is prohibited from contributing to her retirement account, but she may contribute to the retirement accounts of her employees.
C. Leah may make a retirement contribution to her own retirement account as well as the accounts of her employees.
D. None of the above.

The answer is B. Leah is self-employed, so she must have compensation in order to contribute to her own retirement plan. However, she is not prohibited from contributing to her employees' retirement plan, even if the business has a loss. ###

13. Theresa is a small business owner who maintains a SEP plan for her employees. Which of the following employees can be excluded from the plan, if Theresa chooses?

A. Stan, a 32-year-old part-time employee who has worked for Theresa for five years
B. Aldo, a 42-year-old seasonal employee and U.S. resident alien who has worked for Theresa for three years
C. Noel, a 21-year-old part-time employee who is also a union member
D. Millie, a 55-year-old full-time employee who has worked for Theresa for four years

The answer is C. Employers may choose to exclude employees covered by a union agreement. Since Aldo is a RESIDENT alien, he still qualifies to participate. Only nonresident aliens may be excluded. ###

14. A 401(k) plan can include what type of contribution arrangement?

A. Cash
B. Elective deferral
C. Both A and B
D. Property and cash

The answer is C. A 401(k) plan can include cash or elective deferral. Elective deferral is when an employer deducts part of the employee's pretax earnings to a retirement plan. The employee designates the amount that will be deducted. ###

15. Which of the following is not a requirement of ERISA (the Employee Retirement Income Security Act)?

A. ERISA requires that employers follow certain standards for retirement plans.
B. ERISA requires employers to set up retirement plans for their employees.
C. ERISA requires minimum funding standards for retirement plans.
D. ERISA covers two types of pension plans: defined benefit plans and defined contribution plans.

The answer is B. ERISA does not require that employers set up retirement plans for their employees. All of the other answers are correct. ###

16. What is the due date for Form 5500?

A. The last day of the seventh month after the plan year ends
B. The last day of the twelfth month after the plan year ends
C. April 15
D. January 15

The answer is A. Plan administrators must file an annual return, Form 5500, *Annual Return/Report of Employee Benefit Plan,* by the last day of the seventh month after the plan year ends. ###

17. Josie works full time for a company, and she participates in her employer's retirement plan. Josie also has her own side catering business. She does not have any employees. Can Josie set up a SEP for self-employment income, even though she is already participating in her employer's plan?

A. Yes, Josie can still set up a SEP for her catering business.
B. No, Josie cannot set up a SEP because she is covered by an employer plan.
C. No, Josie cannot set up a SEP because she is a prohibited individual.
D. Josie can set up a SEP only if she hires employees.

The answer is A. Yes, Josie can set up a SEP. A SEP can be established for a person's independent business activity even if she participates in her existing employer's retirement plan. ####

Unit 2.14: Trust and Estate Income Tax

More Reading:
Publication 559, *Survivors, Executors, and Administrators*
Publication 950, *Introduction to Estate and Gift Taxes*
Publication 4895, *Tax Treatment of Property Acquired From a Decedent Dying in 2010.*

Estates and trusts are separate legal entities that are defined by the assets that they hold. An estate is created when a taxpayer dies. The estate tax is imposed on certain transfers at death. Estates are allowed an exemption of $600.

A trust, on the other hand, is created while the taxpayer is alive (or by a taxpayer's last will). A trust is a legal entity that can hold title to property for the benefit of one or more persons or entities. A trust is also defined as an agreement that determines how an individual's property will be distributed during his or her lifetime and also upon death.

Estates and trusts are generally required to obtain an Employer Identification Number (EIN), just like any other entity.

For Part Two of the EA Exam, you will be required to understand the differences between estates and trusts, and how these two entities are taxed.

New Rules for Estates in 2010

*Note: In 2010, the rules regarding estate taxes changed dramatically. President Obama signed the *Tax Relief, Unemployment Insurance Reauthorization, and Job Creation Act of 2010* (Tax Relief Act) into law on December 17, 2010.[83] This bill provided estate tax relief, and also changed the gift tax rules. The laws regarding estates for 2010 are extremely complex.

An estate is a separate legal entity for federal tax purposes. A decedent's estate is created when a taxpayer dies. The Estate Tax is a tax on the right to transfer property at death. The taxpayer's property may consist of cash and securities, a primary residence, other real estate, insurance, trusts, annuities, business interests and other assets.

In 2010, the estate tax was repealed and then reinstated. This has created an extremely unusual situation for the 2010 tax year. In 2010, executors have the option to either apply the estate tax, or "opt out" of the estate tax. The executor is allowed to choose which method is most advantageous to the estate and its beneficiaries. There are tax consequences for each choice, which we shall cover next.

The Retroactive Estate Tax in 2010

The 2010 Tax Relief Act retroactively reinstated the estate tax for estates of decedents who died in 2010 and provides for an exclusion amount of $5 million and a maximum estate tax rate of 35% (reduced from 45% for 2009). This means that the first $5 million of an estate does not get taxed, so the estate tax only affects the wealthiest 2% of Americans.

---

[83] If an executor chooses to elect out of the estate tax system for tax year 2010, the executor must make the election on a timely filed Form 8939, which is the form that will be used to report the basis of the assets acquired from a decedent. At the time of this book's release, Form 8939 was not yet available.

Also, the 2010 Tax Relief Act allows executors of the estates of decedents who died in 2010 to completely *elect out* of the estate tax system and use the new carryover basis rules enacted under the Economic Growth and Tax Relief Reconciliation Act of 2001 (EGTRRA).

If the executor makes the election to opt out, the recipient's basis in property acquired from a decedent who died in 2010 is the *lesser* of:

- The decedent's basis in the property,
- Or the Fair Market Value of the property at the time of the decedent's death.
- This is sometimes referred to as "carryover" basis.

This election applies only to estates of decedents who died during 2010. In addition, if the executor makes this *opt out election*, the executor may still increase the basis of property acquired by a decedent who died in 2010 by $1.3 million ($60,000 in the case of a decedent who is not a United States citizen). However, the executor may not increase the basis in any property above its Fair Market Value at the time of the decedent's death.

The 2010 Tax Relief Act did NOT change the exclusion amount or the maximum tax rate for gifts. The exclusion amount for gifts made in 2010 is still $1 million and the maximum tax rate on gifts remains the same at 35%.[84]

Requirements for the Executor of an Estate

After a person dies, an executor is usually chosen to manage the estate. Current IRS requirements require the executor of an estate to file the following tax returns:

- The final income tax return (Form 1040) for the decedent (for income received before death);
- Fiduciary income tax returns (Form 1041) for the estate during administration; and
- Estate Tax Return (Form 706), if the Fair Market Value of the assets of the estate exceed $5 million, or Form 8939, if the executor opts out of the estate tax and elects to apply the new carryover basis rules.

An estate may have an income tax filing requirement for each year that it has $600 or more of gross income or has a beneficiary who is a nonresident alien, from the date of death until the final distribution of the assets to the beneficiaries. The tax is figured on the estate's income in a manner similar to that for individuals.

Every estate with an income tax filing requirement must file Form 1041. The fiduciary of a domestic decedent's estate, trust, or bankruptcy estate uses Form 1041 to report:

- The income, deductions, gains, losses, etc. of an estate or trust;
- The income that is either accumulated, held for future distribution, or distributed to the beneficiaries;
- Any income tax liability of the estate or trust; and
- Employment taxes on wages paid to household employees.

When completing Form 1041, the executor must take into account any items that are *Income in Respect of a Decedent (IRD)*. In general, IRD is income that a decedent was entitled to receive but that was not includible in the decedent's final income tax return (such as a check received after death). IRD includes:

- All income of a decedent that was received after death,

---

[84] The taxation of gifts is covered in Book One.

- Income to which the decedent had a contingent claim at the time of his or her death (such as income that was earned, but not yet paid, like accrued interest)

Some examples of IRD for a decedent are:

- Salary payments that are payable to the decedent's estate (not received by the tax-payer before death),
- Uncollected interest on U.S. savings bonds, and
- Proceeds from the completed sale of farm produce.

The IRD retains the same character it would have had if the decedent had lived and received such amount.

So, for example, if a deceased taxpayer's estate earns interest income, when the interest income is passed on to the beneficiaries, it retains its character as passive interest income.

> **Example:** Fred owns many profitable apartment buildings in New York. On March 30, 2010, Fred dies. His assets (that now are part of his estate) include all the apartment buildings. The estate is being managed by Fred's tax attorney who was named the executor in Fred's will. The beneficiary of the estate is Fred's daughter Ashley. After Fred's death, the apartment buildings continued to generate rental income. While the tax attorney is preparing Fred's assets for distribution, the rental income must be reported. Any rental income that was received after Fred's death must be reported on Form 1041. As the executor of the estate, Fred's attorney will be required to file Form 1041 until all the estate assets are finally distributed to Ashley. Sometimes this can take several years, especially when there are substantial real estate assets.

The Gross Estate

The Gross Estate consists of an accounting of everything the deceased taxpayer owns at the date of death. Generally, when valuing the estate, the Fair Market Value of these items is used, not necessarily what the deceased taxpayer paid for them.[85] The total of all of these items is called the "Gross Estate." The includible property may consist of cash and securities, real estate, insurance, trusts, annuities, business interests, and other assets. Keep in mind that the Gross Estate will likely include non-probate as well as probate property.[86]

The Gross Estate includes the value of all property in which the taxpayer had an interest at the time of death. The Gross Estate also includes the following:

- Life insurance proceeds payable to the estate (this includes a policy that will be paid to the decedent's heirs);
- The value of certain annuities payable to the estate (or heirs); and
- The value of certain property transferred within three years before the taxpayer's death.

Income keeps the same character in the hands of a beneficiary as it had in the hands of the estate. For example, if the income distributed includes dividends, tax-exempt interest,

---

[85] See the section on "electing out of the estate tax" for more information about property valuation on the date of death.

[86] Probate property is property that was directly owned by a decedent for which there is no named beneficiary or which is not jointly owned. Probate property passes in accordance with the decedent's will. If the deceased taxpayer doesn't have a will, then state law determines how the property passes to the heirs.

or capital gains, they will keep the same character in the beneficiary's hands for purposes of the tax treatment given those items.

The Gross Estate does NOT include property owned solely by the decedent's spouse or other individuals. Lifetime gifts that are complete (no control over the gifts are retained) are not included in the Gross Estate.

Once the executor has accounted for the Gross Estate, certain deductions are allowed in order to calculate the taxpayer's "Taxable Estate." These deductions may include mortgages and other debts, estate administration expenses, property that passes to surviving spouses, and qualified charities. After the Taxable Estate is computed, the value of lifetime taxable gifts is added to this number and the tax is computed. The tax is then reduced by the Unified Credit (explained later).

An estate tax return is filed using Form 706, *United States Estate (and Generation-Skipping Transfer) Tax Return*. The due date for Form 706 for 2010 decedents' estates is the later of September 19, 2011 or nine months after the date of death.[87] The executor may request an extension of time to file on Form 4768. Just like any other entity type, if taxes are due, then they must be estimated and paid with the extension request, or late-payment penalties will apply.

Generation-skipping Transfer Tax (GST tax)

The Generation-Skipping Transfer tax (GST tax) is imposed on a taxpayer's transfers of property to younger generations (grandchildren or great-grandchildren). The technical term is "skip persons." According to the IRS, a skip person is either:

- A person who is assigned to a generation which is two or more generations below the generation of the transferor, or
- A trust in which all interests are held by skip persons or a trust in which no person holds an interest and from which no distribution may be made to a non-skip person (IRC § 2613).

The GST tax is generally imposed at the highest estate tax rate. However, *the 2010 Tax Relief, Unemployment Insurance Reauthorization, and Job Creation Act* provides that the GST tax rate is 0%.[88]

Although the GST tax is 0% for 2010, there are some limits to the amount of assets that can be transferred:

- The GST tax exemption for 2010 (also for 2011) is $5 million for individuals ($10 million if MFJ).
- The gift tax exemption in 2010 is only $1 million.[89]

---

[87] At the time of this book's printing in March 2010, the 2010 Form 706 was still not available on the IRS website. The IRS has been very late providing forms and guidance for 2010 estates.

[88] Section 302(c) of the 2010 Tax Act: (c) Modification of Generation-Skipping Transfer Tax. — In the case of any Generation-Skipping Transfer made after December 31, 2009 and before January 1, 2011, the applicable rate determined under Section 2641(a) of the Internal Revenue code of 1986 *shall be zero*.

[89] Gift taxes are covered and tested on Part One of the EA Exam.

Estate Termination

As mentioned previously, an estate is created when a taxpayer dies. The estate officially terminates when all of the assets and income of the deceased taxpayer have been distributed, and all of the liabilities have been paid. If an estate's existence is unnecessarily prolonged, the IRS can step in and terminate the estate after a reasonable period for completing the final duties of administration.

If an estate or trust has a loss in its final year, the loss can be passed through to the beneficiaries, allowing them a deduction on their returns. Losses cannot be passed through to beneficiaries in a non-termination year.

The Taxation of Trusts

A trust is an entity created under the state law in which it was formed. A trust involves the creation of a fiduciary relationship between a grantor, a trustee, and a beneficiary for a stated purpose (usually for the transfer of assets). A trust may be created during an individual's life (an inter-vivos trust) or at the time of death under a will (a testamentary trust). The primary benefit of a trust is that it can be created to hold property for the benefit of other persons. In some cases, trusts can also be used to legally avoid some taxes. A trust can also be created for the benefit of a disabled individual. The creation of a trust involves three parties:

- The grantor: The person who contributes property to the trust.
- The trustee (or fiduciary): The person or entity charged with the fiduciary duties associated with the trust.
- The beneficiary: The person who is designated to receive the trust income or assets.

Example: An elderly individual is having medical problems and decides to put his assets in a trust. He asks his attorney to create the trust and manage the assets. The elderly person then names his grandson as the beneficiary of the trust. In this common scenario, the elderly person is the **grantor**, the lawyer is the **trustee**, and the grandson is the **beneficiary**.

Sometimes, a trust is used to transfer property in a controlled manner. For example, a wealthy parent wishes to transfer ownership of assets to his child, but does not want the child to waste all the assets (or spend all the money). The assets could be transferred to a trust, and the parent could be the grantor and the trustee. The child would be the beneficiary. That way, the parent still has control over the assets, and the child is prevented from using them all up.

The accounting period for a trust is generally the calendar year. The due date for a calendar-year trust is April 15. Trusts must file IRS Form 1041, *U.S. Income Tax Return for Estates and Trusts*, in order to report activity.

A trust figures its gross income similar to that of an individual taxpayer. Both trusts and estates are allowed a personal exemption in computing tax liability. Estates are allowed a personal exemption of $600. A trust that distributes all its income currently is allowed an exemption of $300. All other trusts are allowed an exemption of $100 per year.

Most deductions and credits allowed to individuals are also allowed to trusts. However, there is one major distinction: a trust is allowed a deduction for its distributions to beneficiaries. For this reason, a trust is sometimes called a "pass-through" entity. The beneficiary, and not the trust, pays income tax on his or her distributive share of income. Schedule K-

1 (Form 1041) is used to report income that a trust distributes to beneficiaries. The income must then be reported on the beneficiaries' individual income tax returns.

A trust is required to file a tax return if it has:

- Any *taxable* income for the year (after subtracting the allowable exemption amount),
- Gross income of $600 or more (regardless of whether or not the income is taxable), or
- A beneficiary who is a nonresident alien.

> **Example:** The Smith Family Trust has $400 in tax-exempt interest from muni bonds during the year. There is no other income. Normally, the trust would not be required to file because the income earned by the trust is tax-exempt. However, the Smith Family Trust has a beneficiary who is a nonresident alien. Therefore, the trust is required to file a Form 1041.

Distributable Net Income of a Trust (DNI)

Distributable Net Income (DNI) is trust income that is currently available for distribution. If the beneficiary receives a distribution in excess of DNI, only the DNI is taxed. The Income Distribution Deduction (IDD) is allowed to trusts (and estates) for amounts that are paid, credited, or required to be distributed to beneficiaries. The Income Distribution Deduction is calculated on Schedule B (Form 1041) and is limited to DNI. This amount, which is figured on Schedule B (Form 1041), is used to determine how much of the income distributed to a beneficiary will be includible in his or her gross income.

A Simple vs. Complex Trust

When it comes to income distribution, there are two types of trusts: a simple trust and a complex trust. The Internal Revenue Code defines a simple trust as a trust that:

- Distributes all of its income currently; and
- Makes no distributions from principal; and
- Makes no distributions to charity.

Any trust that is not a "simple trust" is automatically defined as a complex trust. The IRS defines a complex trust as a trust that:

- Is allowed to accumulate income;
- Makes discretionary distributions of income;
- Can make mandatory (or discretionary) distributions of principal; and/or
- Makes distributions to charity.

A trust may be a simple trust one year, and a complex trust in another year. For example, if a simple trust fails to distribute all its income in the current year, it becomes a complex trust.

Trust Types (e.g., grantor, irrevocable, tax shelters)

A Grantor Trust

A grantor trust is a valid legal entity under state law, but it is not recognized as a separate entity for income tax purposes. With a grantor trust, the person who gives the assets to the trust is treated as the owner and retains control over the trust. In the eyes of the IRS, the "grantor" is considered the owner of the trust for income tax purposes.

The grantor (also known as trustor, settlor, or creator) is the creator of the trust relationship and is usually the owner of the assets initially contributed to the trust. The grantor establishes the terms and provisions of the trust relationship between the grantor, the trustee, and the beneficiary. These will usually include the following:

- The rights, duties, and powers of the trustee;
- Distribution provisions;
- Ability of the grantor to amend, modify, revoke, or terminate the trust agreement;
- The designation of a trustee or successor trustees; and
- The designation of the state under which the trust agreement is to be governed.

> **Example:** The John Doe Trust is a "grantor-type trust." John Doe is the grantor. During the year, the trust sold 100 shares of ABC stock for $1,010 in which it had a basis of $10 and 200 shares of XYZ stock for $10 in which it had a $1,020 basis. The trust does not report these transactions on Form 1041. Instead, a schedule is attached to Form 1041 showing each stock transaction separately and in the same detail as John Doe (grantor and owner) will need to report these transactions on his Schedule D (Form 1040). The trust may not net the capital gains and losses, nor may it issue John Doe a Schedule K-1 (Form 1041) showing a $10 long-term capital loss.

- **Revocable Trust:** A revocable trust is a trust in which the grantor retains the right to end the trust. Trust assets are subject to the estate tax upon the grantor's death. A revocable trust is treated as a grantor trust for income tax purposes. This type of trust is generally created only to manage and distribute property. Many taxpayers use this type of trust instead of a will.
- **Revocable Living Trust:** A revocable living trust is an arrangement created during the life of an individual and can be changed or ended at any time during the individual's life. A revocable living trust is generally created to manage and distribute property. Many people use this type of trust instead of (or in addition to) a will. Because this type of trust is revocable, it is treated as a grantor type trust for tax purposes.

Non-Grantor Trust

A "non-grantor trust" is any trust that is not a grantor trust. A non-grantor trust is considered a separate legal entity from the individual or organization that created it. The trust's income and deductions are reported on Form 1041. If a non-grantor trust makes distributions to a beneficiary, in general those distributions carry any taxable income to the beneficiary.

Irrevocable Trusts: An irrevocable trust is a trust that cannot be revoked after it is created. The transfer assets into this type of trust are generally considered a "completed gift" subject to gift tax.

Disability Trust: A qualified disability trust is a non-grantor trust created solely for the benefit of a disabled individual under age 65. In 2010, a qualified disability trust can claim an exemption of up to $3,650. This is a specific exception to the regular exemption for trusts, which Congress passed in order to help taxpayers with disabilities.

Charitable Trusts: A charitable trust is a trust devoted to qualified charitable contribution purposes. Charitable trusts are irrevocable, which means that once a trust has been created, the grantor of the property cannot go back and claim control of the assets. A charitable trust is generally created for the purpose of legally avoiding tax on charitable gifts.

> **Example:** Hugo creates a charitable trust whose governing instrument provides that the Catholic Church, (a qualified religious organization) and the SPCA (a 501(c)(3) charity) are each to receive 50% of the trust income for 10 years. At the end of the 10-year period, the corpus will be distributed to the Red Cross, also a 501(c)(3) organization. Hugo is allowed an income tax deduction for the value of all interests placed in trust.

Abusive Trust Arrangements

Certain trust arrangements purport to eliminate taxes in ways that are not permitted under the law. These are called "abuse trusts." Abusive trust arrangements often use trusts to hide the true ownership of assets and income or to disguise the substance of transactions. These arrangements frequently involve more than one trust, each holding different assets of the taxpayer (for example, the taxpayer's business, business equipment, home, automobile, etc.) Some trusts may hold interests in other trusts, purport to involve charities, or are foreign trusts.

When trusts are used for legitimate business, family, or estate planning purposes, either the trust, the beneficiary, or the transferor to the trust will pay the tax on the income generated by the trust. Trusts cannot be used to transform a taxpayer's personal, living, or educational expenses into deductible items. A taxpayer cannot use a trust to avoid tax liability by ignoring either the true ownership of income and assets or the true substance of transactions. Participants and promoters of abusive trust schemes may be subject to civil or criminal penalties.

Unit 2.14: Questions

1. What is included in the Gross Estate?

A. The Gross Estate of the decedent consists of an accounting of everything the taxpayer owns at the date of death.
B. The Gross Estate of the decedent consists of an accounting of everything the taxpayer owns six months after the date of death.
C. The Gross Estate of the decedent consists of an accounting of everything the taxpayer owns at the date of death, including income that the taxpayer owned but has not yet received.
D. None of the above.

The answer is A. The Gross Estate of the decedent consists of an accounting of everything the taxpayer owns at the date of death. The total of all of these items is the "Gross Estate." ###

2. The calculation for the Gross Estate does NOT include which of the following?

A. Life insurance proceeds payable to the decedent's heirs
B. The value of certain annuities payable to the estate
C. Property owned solely by the decedent's spouse
D. The value of certain property transferred within three years before the taxpayer's death

The answer is C. The Gross Estate does NOT include property owned solely by the decedent's spouse or other individuals. ###

3. What is the due date for Form 706 for a decedent who died in 2010?

A. The later of April 15, 2011 or nine months after the date of death
B. The later of September 19, 2011 or nine months after the date of death
C. The later of September 19, 2011 or twelve months after the date of death
D. Twelve months after the date of death

The answer is B. The due date for Form 706 for 2010 decedents' estates is the later of September 19, 2011 or nine months after the date of death. ###

4. The Franklin Trust is required to distribute all its income currently. What is the exemption amount for the Franklin Trust?

A. $0
B. $100
C. $300
D. $600

The answer is C. A trust that distributes all its income currently is allowed an exemption of $300. All other trusts are allowed an exemption of $100 per year. ###

5. Which trust is NOT required to file a tax return?

A. A trust with any taxable income for the year
B. A trust with gross income of $1,000
C. A trust with a beneficiary who is a nonresident alien
D. A trust with $100 in gross income for the year and a single U.S. citizen beneficiary

The answer is D. A trust with $100 in gross income for the year and a single U.S. citizen beneficiary would typically not be required to file a tax return. ###

6. Which of the following is NOT a characteristic of a simple trust?

A. The trust may distribute assets to charity.
B. The trust distributes all its income currently.
C. The trust makes no distributions from principal.
D. The trust makes no distributions to charity.

The answer is A. A simple trust may not distribute assets to charity. That is a characteristic of a complex trust. The Internal Revenue Code defines a simple trust as one that distributes all its income currently, makes no distributions from principal, and makes no distributions to charity. Any trust that is not a "simple trust" is automatically defined as a complex trust. ###

7. Which estate is NOT required to file Form 1041?

A. An estate with gross income of $600
B. An estate with $700 in exempt income
C. An estate with $200 in gross income and a beneficiary who is a nonresident alien
D. An estate with $500 in gross income and a beneficiary who is a resident alien

The answer is D. An estate with $500 in income and a beneficiary who is a resident alien is not required to file a tax return. Resident aliens (green card holders) are taxed the same way as citizens. An estate with a nonresident alien beneficiary would be required to file Form 1041, regardless of the amount of income earned. The fiduciary must file Form 1041 for a domestic estate that has:
•Gross income for the tax year of $600 or more, or
•A beneficiary who is a nonresident alien.
###

Part 3: Representation

Tammy the Tax Lady®

Tammy the Tax Lady is a registered trademark of PassKey Publications

Unit 3.1: Practices and Procedures

> **More Reading:**
> Circular 230, *Regulations Governing the Practice of Attorneys, Certified Public Accountants, Enrolled Agents, Enrolled Actuaries, Enrolled Retirement Plan Agents, and Appraisers before the Internal Revenue Service*
> Publication 470, *Limited Practice Without Enrollment*

"Practice Before the IRS"

"Practice before the IRS" includes all matters connected with a presentation before the Internal Revenue Service, or any issues relating to a client's rights, privileges, or liabilities under laws or regulations administered by the IRS. "Practice" includes:

- Communicating with the IRS on behalf of a taxpayer regarding his rights or liabilities
- Representing a taxpayer at conferences, hearings, or meetings with the IRS
- Preparing and filing documents for the IRS (not including the preparation of tax returns)
- Corresponding and communicating with the IRS
- Rendering written advice regarding any entity, transaction, plan, or arrangement

Actions That Are Not "Practice Before the IRS"

Preparing a tax return, furnishing information at the IRS's request, or acting as a witness for a taxpayer do not constitute "practice" before the IRS. Simply exchanging information with the Internal Revenue Service is not considered practice before the IRS.

A tax preparer is a person who prepares tax returns for compensation. An unenrolled return preparer does not have to be a CPA, Enrolled Agent, or attorney. A few states, such as California and Oregon, require tax return preparers to have minimum education requirements and to register with a state agency.

> **Example:** Danny is an unenrolled tax return preparer who prepares about 50 returns per year for clients and friends. In 2010, he is contacted by his friend Ariel. Ariel wants Danny to represent her before the IRS in the examination of her tax return. Danny did not prepare the return, and therefore cannot represent Ariel before the IRS. However, Danny can appear as a witness on her behalf and also furnish information to the IRS.

Individuals who are not practitioners may appear before the IRS as witnesses or communicate to the IRS on a taxpayer's behalf and appear as a witness—but they may not advocate for the taxpayer.

"Practice before the IRS" does NOT include the representation of clients in the U.S. Tax Court. The U.S. Tax Court has its own, separate regulations for admission to practice before it.

All individuals who practice before the IRS are subject to the provisions in Circular 230, *Regulations Governing the Practice of Attorneys, Certified Public Accountants, Enrolled Agents, Enrolled Actuaries, Enrolled Retirement Plan Agents, and Appraisers before the Internal Revenue Service*. In addition to using this study guide, it is important that all EA Exam candidates read Circular 230 before taking Part 3 of the EA Exam.

Special Circumstances and Unenrolled Individuals

There are some exceptions to the general rule regarding enrolled practitioners (CPAs, Enrolled Agents, and attorneys). Because of a "special relationship" with the taxpayer, the following *unenrolled* individuals can represent some taxpayers before the IRS. This rule usually applies to representatives for a business entity, such as an officer of a corporation. However, a family member may also "practice" before the IRS on behalf of another family member.

An individual: Any individual may always represent *himself* before the IRS and does not have to file a written declaration of qualification and authority. A disbarred individual may also represent himself before the IRS.

A family member: An individual family member may represent members of her immediate family. Family members include a spouse, child, parent, brother, or sister of the individual.

An officer: A bona fide officer of a corporation (including parents, subsidiaries, or affiliated corporations), association, organized group, or, in the course of his official duties, an officer of a governmental unit, agency, or authority may represent the organization he is an officer of before the IRS.

A partner: A general partner may represent the partnership before the IRS.

An employee: A regular full-time employee can represent her employer. An employer can be an individual, partnership, corporation (including parents, subsidiaries, or affiliated corporations), association, trust, receivership, guardianship, estate, organized group, governmental unit, agency, or authority.

A fiduciary: A trustee, receiver, guardian, personal representative, administrator, or executor can represent the trust, receivership, guardianship, or estate.

> **Example:** Jim is not enrolled to practice before the IRS. However, Jim's daughter Ginny is 20 and is being audited by the IRS. Jim is allowed to represent Ginny before the IRS, because of the family relationship. A father is allowed to represent his child before the IRS.

If an unenrolled return preparer does not meet the requirements listed above for "limited representation," the preparer must file Form 8821, *Tax Information Authorization*. Form 8821 does not grant a preparer any rights representation. Instead, Form 8821 allows the unenrolled return preparer to obtain and share information from the IRS (such as tax transcripts and copies of tax returns).

Enrolled Practitioners

Tax professionals and unenrolled individuals (in the limited circumstances listed above) are allowed to represent taxpayers before the IRS. Enrolled Agents, attorneys, Enrolled Actuaries, and Certified Public Accountants may all represent taxpayers before the IRS by virtue of their licensing.

Attorneys

Any attorney who is not currently under suspension or disbarment from practice before the IRS and who is a member in good standing of the bar of the highest court of any state, possession, territory, commonwealth, or in the District of Columbia may practice before the

IRS. A student attorney who receives permission to practice before the IRS by virtue of his status as a law student under Section 10.7(d) of Circular 230 is also allowed to practice before the IRS.

Certified Public Accountants (CPAs)

Any CPA who is not currently under suspension or disbarment from practice before the IRS and who is duly qualified to practice as a CPA in any state, possession, territory, commonwealth, or in the District of Columbia may practice before the IRS. A student CPA candidate who receives permission to practice before the IRS by virtue of her status as a CPA student under Section 10.7(d) of Circular 230 is also allowed to practice before the IRS.

Enrolled Agents

Any Enrolled Agent may practice before the IRS, as long as he is not disbarred or suspended from practice. An Enrolled Agent (EA) is a federally-authorized tax practitioner who is empowered by the U.S. Department of the Treasury to represent taxpayers before all administrative levels of the Internal Revenue Service for audits, collections, and appeals. Some Enrolled Agents are allowed to represent taxpayers in the U.S. Tax Court.

Enrolled Actuaries (Limited Practice)

Any individual who is enrolled as an actuary by the Joint Board for the Enrollment of Actuaries may practice before the IRS. The practice of Enrolled Actuaries is limited to certain Internal Revenue Code sections that relate to their area of expertise, principally those sections governing employee retirement plans.

Enrolled Retirement Plan Agents (Limited Practice)

The Enrolled Retirement Plan Agent, or ERPA, is a new classification of a professional allowed to practice before the IRS. An ERPA is similar to an Enrolled Agent. The rules governing ERPAs are set forth in Circular 230.

Unenrolled Return Preparers (Limited Practice)

Any individual other than an attorney, CPA, Enrolled Agent, or Enrolled Actuary who prepares a return and signs it as the return preparer is an unenrolled return preparer. An unenrolled return preparer may represent the taxpayer only concerning the tax liability for the year or period covered by the return that he prepared.

An unenrolled return preparer is permitted to represent taxpayers only before the Examination Division of the IRS and is not permitted to represent taxpayers before the Appeals, Collection, or any other division of the IRS. An unenrolled preparer cannot practice before appeals officers, revenue officers, and counsel. Also, an unenrolled preparer cannot execute claims for refund, receive refund checks, execute consents to extend the statutory period for assessment or collection, execute closing agreements, or execute waivers of restriction on assessment or collection of a deficiency in tax.

Unenrolled preparers may still be subject to IRS penalties for failing to adhere to the tax code. They can be fined for negligence, inadequate disclosure, and accuracy-related errors.

An unenrolled preparer may not appear before the IRS without the taxpayer present.

Volunteer Students at Tax Clinics (Allowed by Special Order)

Students volunteering in a Low Income Taxpayer Clinic (LITC) and the Student Tax Clinic Program (STCP) may represent taxpayers before the IRS. A taxpayer may authorize a student/volunteer who works in these programs to represent her under a special order issued by the Office of Professional Responsibility. This program is also called VITA, the Volunteer Income Tax Assistance program.

Authorization for Special Appearances

The Office of Professional Responsibility can authorize an individual who is not otherwise eligible to practice before the IRS to represent another person in extraordinary circumstances. The prospective representative must request this authorization in writing from the Office of Professional Responsibility. However, it is granted only when extremely compelling circumstances exist. If granted, the Office of Professional Responsibility will issue a letter that details the conditions related to the appearance and the particular tax matter for which the authorization is granted.

The authorization letter from the Office of Professional Responsibility should not be confused with a letter from an IRS center advising an individual that he has been assigned a Centralized Authorization File (CAF) number (an identifying number that the IRS assigns representatives). The issuance of a CAF number does not indicate that a person is either recognized or authorized to practice before the IRS. It merely confirms that a centralized file for authorizations has been established for the representative under that number.

Example: Josie is not a tax return preparer. In 2010, Josie's husband dies and she is named the executor of her husband's estate. She files a Form and, indicating a fiduciary relationship. Josie is assigned a CAF number, because she is an authorized representative for the estate, and therefore eligible for a CAF number. Josie is not an enrolled practitioner but is allowed to represent the estate by virtue of her role as the executor and surviving spouse.

The Centralized Authorization File (CAF)

The IRS has a centralized computer database called the CAF system that contains information on the authority of taxpayer representatives. A CAF number is assigned to a tax practitioner when a Form 2848 or Form 8821 is filed. This number represents a file that contains information regarding the type of authorization that taxpayers have given representatives for their accounts. When a practitioner submits a power of attorney document to the IRS, it is processed for inclusion in the CAF.

A CAF number also enables the IRS to automatically send copies of notices and other IRS communications to a representative.

Mandatory New Tax Preparer Registration

In 2010, the Internal Revenue Service approved new registration, testing, and continuing education of tax return preparers. These new regulations affect the 2010 filing season. As it stands currently, Enrolled Agents, CPAs, and attorneys will be exempt from *some* of these new rules.

Starting in 2010, all unenrolled preparers are required to register and take an exam. The IRS now requires the following:

- Registration with the IRS by all paid tax return preparers who must also obtain a Preparer Tax Identification Number (PTIN). Tax preparers who register will be subject to a limited tax compliance check to make sure that they have filed their own personal and business tax returns.
- A minimum competency test and continuing professional education for all paid tax return preparers except attorneys, Certified Public Accountants (CPAs), and Enrolled Agents who are active and in good standing with their respective licensing agencies.

To avoid business interruption for existing preparers and clients, existing preparers have approximately three years to meet the competency testing requirement. There would be two levels of competency examinations for: (1) Wage and non-business Form 1040 series and (2) Wage and Small Business Form 1040 series.

Part of this new legislation includes formally extending the ethical rules found in Treasury Department Circular 230 to apply to all paid preparers. This expansion would allow the IRS to suspend or discipline tax return preparers who engage in unethical or disreputable conduct.

The tax return preparer registration will be effective for a three-year period and requires preparers to renew their registration every three years. In addition, the IRS plans to require all signing paid tax return preparers be subject to verification of personal and business tax compliance every three years.

New IRS PTIN Requirement

Starting January 1, 2011, use of the PTIN will be mandatory on all federal tax returns and claims for refund prepared by a paid tax preparer. The PTIN is a nine-digit number that preparers must use when they prepare and sign a tax return or claim for refund. Previously, PTIN use was optional in place of the preparer's Social Security Number. Mandatory use of the PTIN is part of a broader effort by the IRS to regulate the tax return preparation industry and improve services for taxpayers.

This new rule also applies to individuals who prepare portions of tax returns or claims for a refund. Paid preparers must apply for a new or renewed PTIN through a new signup system at www.irs.gov/taxpros. Tax professionals may also opt to use a paper application, Form W-12, *IRS Paid Preparer Tax Identification Number (PTIN) Application*, which takes about four to six weeks to process.

Any preparer who obtained a PTIN prior to the new signup system launch on September 28, 2010 must renew his existing PTIN. Generally, preparers with existing PTINs will be permitted to retain their numbers if the information they provide during the signup process matches what the IRS currently has on file. Preparers who do not have an existing PTIN will be required to sign up for one. The PTIN application must be accompanied by a required fee.

Persons Who Are Not Considered "Tax Preparers"

A person who merely gives an opinion about events that have *not happened* (such as tax advice for a business that has not been created) is not considered a tax preparer for the purpose of IRS penalties.

If there is no prior agreement for compensation, the individual who prepares the return is not considered an "income tax preparer" for IRS purposes. This is true even if the individual receives a gift or a favor in return. The agreement for compensation is the deciding factor for whether or not a person will be considered a preparer for IRS purposes.

> **Example:** Terri is a retired accountant. She prepares tax returns for her family members. Terri does not prepare tax returns for compensation. Sometimes, a family member will give Terri a gift in return. Terri does not ask for any gifts or expect them. Terri is not a "tax return preparer" for IRS purposes.

An individual will not be considered an income tax return preparer in the following instances:
- A person who merely gives an opinion about events that have not happened (such as tax advice for a business that has not been created).
- A person who merely furnishes typing, reproducing, or mechanical assistance.
- An employee who prepares a tax return or claim for refund for his employer. This also applies to an officer or general partner of a business. For example, a general partner who prepares a tax return for his own partnership is not considered an "income tax preparer."
- Any fiduciary who prepares a tax return or claim for refund for a trust or estate.
- An unpaid volunteer who provides tax assistance under a VITA program.
- An unpaid volunteer who provides tax assistance to the elderly under Section 163 of the Internal Revenue Code, also called Tax Counseling for the Elderly (TCE).
- Any official or employee of the IRS who is performing official duties by preparing a tax return for a taxpayer or business who requests it.

> **Example:** Thomas is a CPA. His neighbor Cain consults with Thomas about a business he is thinking about starting. Thomas gives Cain an opinion regarding the potential business and taxes. In this case, Thomas is not considered a "tax preparer" for the purpose of IRS preparer penalties. This is because Thomas is merely giving an opinion about events that have not happened yet.

An employee who prepares a tax return for his employer or for another employee is not a "preparer" for the purposes of Circular 230. The employer (or the individual with overall supervisory responsibility) has the responsibility for accuracy of the return.

> **Example:** Claudia is a full-time bookkeeper for Creative Candies Corp. Claudia is an employee, and she prepares the payroll checks and payroll tax returns for all of the employees of Creative Candies. As a full-time employee, Claudia is not considered a "tax preparer" for the purpose of IRS penalties. Her employer, Creative Candies Corp., is ultimately responsible for the accuracy of the payroll tax returns.

Preparation of tax returns outside the U.S. is included in these rules. Tax preparers who work overseas on U.S. tax returns are still subject to Circular 230 regulations.

Employer of Preparers

A tax preparer is also someone who employs other preparers. For example, if an Enrolled Agent owns a franchise that employs ten tax preparers, the EA, as the owner of the business, is the one who is actually liable for any preparer penalties. The employees of the business generally are not considered "tax preparers" for the purpose of IRS penalties.

Any person who employs tax return preparers is required to retain records detailing the name, identifying number, and principal place of work of each income tax return preparer employed. The records of the income tax preparers must be made available upon request to the IRS. They must be retained and kept available for inspection for at least three years following the close of period for each tax return. The "return period" means the 12-month period beginning July 1 each year.

Employment (Payroll) Tax Returns

Individuals who employ income tax preparers must keep records of all employment taxes and employment records for at least four years after filing the fourth quarter for the year (payroll tax returns). All employer tax records must be made available for IRS review. Necessary records include:

- The Employer Identification Number (EIN)
- Amounts and dates of all wage, annuity, and pension payments, and amounts of tips reported (if applicable)
- The Fair Market Value of in-kind wages paid
- Names, addresses, Social Security numbers, and occupations of employees and recipients
- Any copies of Form W-2 that were returned undeliverable
- Dates of active employment
- Periods for which employees were paid sick leave
- Copies of employees' and recipients' income tax withholding allowance certificates (Forms W-4)
- Dates and amounts of tax deposits
- Copies of all employment returns filed
- Records of fringe benefits provided, including substantiation

The "Substantial Portion" Rule

If more than one individual is involved in the preparation of a tax return, the preparer who has the primary responsibility for the accuracy of the return is considered to be the income tax preparer. Only the person who prepares all or a substantial portion of a tax return shall be considered the "preparer" of the return. A person who merely gives advice on a portion or a single entry on the tax return is considered to have prepared only that portion. In order to identify who is responsible for a "substantial portion" of the return, the following guidelines may be used. Generally, a portion of a tax return is not considered to be "substantial" if it involves only minor dollar amounts:

- Less than $2,000, or
- Less than 20% of the Adjusted Gross Income on the return.

Usually, a single schedule would not be considered a "substantial portion" of a tax return, unless it represents a major portion of the income.

Example: Greg and Bill are partners in a tax practice. In March, Greg takes a short vacation, and Bill finishes a few of the returns that Greg had left on his desk. Later, one tax return comes up for audit and it is determined that the return has a gross misstatement. Greg prepared the Schedule C on the return, and Bill prepared and finished the rest of the return. The Schedule C represents 95% of the income and expenses shown on the return. Therefore, for the purpose of any potential penalty, Greg is considered the "preparer" of this return, since he prepared the schedule that represents the majority of the income and expenses on the return.

IRS Power of Attorney and Disclosure Authorization

When a taxpayer wishes to use a representative, she must fill out Form 2848, *Power of Attorney and Declaration of Representative.* This form authorizes another person to represent a taxpayer before the IRS. The form must be signed by the taxpayer. The representative must be eligible to practice before the IRS in order to complete Form 2848.

Only "natural persons" may practice before the IRS, which means that an entity such as a corporation or partnership is not eligible. For example, an Enrolled Agent who fills out Form 2848 on behalf of a client must use his own name, rather than the name of his business. The person representing the taxpayer must be qualified, and the duty may not be delegated to an employee.

Example: Michael is an Enrolled Agent who runs a tax practice and employs two unenrolled preparers. While Michael is out of town, a former client named Fannie comes in and requests representation for an IRS appeal. Michael has a power of attorney for Fannie, but his employees do not. Michael is the only person who may represent Fannie before the IRS. The duty of audit representation cannot be delegated to Michael's employees.

U.S. citizenship is not required to practice before the IRS, and in fact, many Enrolled Agents work abroad helping expatriate taxpayers with their tax liabilities overseas.

Example: Janice is an Enrolled Agent who operates Janice Jones's Accounting Corporation. When Janice prepares a Form 2848 for a taxpayer, she must represent her client as an individual. Janice is granted permission to represent her client, but her corporation is not.

Example: Paul is not an Enrolled Agent or a tax professional. However, Paul is a fiduciary for his grandmother's estate. Therefore, Paul is qualified to represent his grandmother's estate before the IRS. Paul may fill out and submit IRS Form 2848.

A qualified representative can represent a taxpayer before the IRS *without* the taxpayer present, as long as the proper power of attorney is signed and submitted to the IRS. Any authorized representative, other than an unenrolled preparer, can usually perform the following acts:

- Represent a taxpayer before any office of the IRS
- Record an interview or meeting with the IRS
- Sign an offer or a waiver of restriction on assessment or collection of a tax deficiency, or a waiver of notice of disallowance of claim for credit or refund
- Sign consents to extend the statutory time period for assessment or collection of a tax
- Sign a closing agreement
- Receive but never endorse or cash a refund check drawn on the U.S. Treasury

A signed IRS Form 2848, *Power of Attorney and Declaration of Representative* (or other acceptable power of attorney, such as a durable power of attorney), is required in order for a tax professional to represent a taxpayer before the IRS. A signed Form 2848 is not required when the taxpayer is deceased and is being represented by a fiduciary or executor. Form 2848 is used by:

- CPAs, Enrolled Agents, Enrolled Actuaries, and attorneys
- Unenrolled preparers, if specifically permitted, in very limited circumstances (such as a family member representing a taxpayer, or an executor representing an estate).

A Power of Attorney is valid until revoked. It may be revoked by the taxpayer or withdrawn by the representative. It may also be superseded by the filing of a new power of attorney for the same tax and tax period.

A power of attorney ends upon death. A power of attorney is automatically rescinded when another power of attorney is filed. A newly filed power of attorney concerning the same matter will revoke a previously filed power of attorney. For example, if a taxpayer changes preparers and the second preparer files a power of attorney on behalf of the taxpayer, the old power of attorney on file will be rescinded, unless the taxpayer specifically requests that the old power of attorney remain active.

Non-IRS Powers of Attorney (Durable Power of Attorney)

The IRS will accept a non-IRS power of attorney, but it must contain all of the information present on a standard IRS Form 2848.

Example: Ronald signs a durable power of attorney that names his neighbor Edwin as his attorney-in-fact.[90] The power of attorney grants Edwin the authority to perform all acts on Ronald's behalf. However, it does not list specific tax-related information such as types of tax or tax form numbers. Shortly after Ronald signs the power of attorney, he is declared incompetent. Later, a federal tax matter arises concerning a prior year return filed by Ronald. Edwin attempts to represent Ronald before the IRS, but is rejected because the durable power of attorney does not contain required information. If Edwin attaches a statement (signed under the penalty of perjury) that the durable power of attorney is valid under the laws of the governing jurisdiction, he can sign a completed Form 2848 and submit it on Ronald's behalf. If Edwin can practice before the IRS, he can name himself as the representative on Form 2848.

If a practitioner wants to use a different power of attorney document other than Form 2848, it must contain the following information:

- The taxpayer's name, mailing address, and Social Security Number.
- The name and mailing address of the representative.
- The types of tax involved and the tax form number in question.
- The specific periods or tax years involved.
- For estate tax matters, the decedent's date of death.
- A clear expression of the taxpayer's intention concerning the scope of authority granted to the representative.

---

[90] Attorney-in-fact: A person who holds power of attorney and therefore is legally designated to transact business and other duties on behalf of another individual.

- The taxpayer's signature and date. The taxpayer must also must attach to the non-IRS power of attorney a signed and dated statement made by the representative.

IRS Form 8821, Disclosure Authorization

Any third party may be designated to receive tax information. Form 8821, *Tax Information Authorization,* authorizes any individual, corporation, firm, organization, or partnership to receive confidential information for the type of tax and periods listed on Form 8821. IRS Form 8821 is used by unenrolled preparers, banks, employers, and other institutions to receive financial information on behalf of an individual or a business.

Form 8821 is only a disclosure form, so it will not give an unenrolled preparer any power to represent a taxpayer before the IRS. Form 8821 only may be used to obtain information, such as copies of tax returns.

Representative Signing in Lieu of the Taxpayer

A representative named under a power of attorney is generally not permitted to sign a personal income tax return unless both of the following are true:
- The signature is permitted under the Internal Revenue Code and the related regulations.
- The taxpayer specifically permits signature authority in the power of attorney.

For example, the regulation permits a representative to sign a taxpayer's return if the taxpayer is unable to sign for any of the following reasons:
- Disease or injury (for example, a taxpayer who is completely paralyzed, or has a debilitating injury)
- Continuous absence from the United States (including Puerto Rico) for a period of at least 60 days prior to the date required by law for filing the return
- Other good cause if specific permission is requested of and granted by the IRS

When a return is signed by a representative, it must be accompanied by a power of attorney authorizing the representative to sign the return.

Summary: Practice Before the IRS

"Practice" before the IRS does not include the preparation of tax returns. An unenrolled preparer may represent a taxpayer in a limited fashion, and:
- Only to the examination function of the IRS, and
- Only with respect to a tax return he prepared.

Unenrolled preparers are prohibited from certain actions. An unenrolled return preparer cannot perform any the following:
- Execute closing agreements with respect to a tax liability
- Extend the statutory period for tax assessments or collection of tax
- Execute waivers of restriction on assessment or collection of a deficiency in tax
- Carry out or request claims for a refund
- Receive checks of any client refund
- Receive client checks and then subsequently remit the amounts to the IRS

Unit 3.1: Questions

1. For taxpayers who want someone to represent them in their absence at an examination with the IRS, all of the following statements are correct except:

A. The taxpayer must furnish that representative with written authorization on Form 2848, *Power of Attorney and Declaration of Representative*, or any other properly written authorization.
B. The representative can be an attorney, Certified Public Accountant, or Enrolled Agent.
C. The representative can be anyone who helped the taxpayer prepare the return.
D. Even if the taxpayer appointed a representative, the taxpayer may attend the examination or appeals conference and may act on his own behalf.

The answer is C. Only certain persons are allowed to represent a taxpayer before the IRS. Usually, only an attorney, Certified Public Accountant, or Enrolled Agent may represent a taxpayer before the IRS without the taxpayer present. ###

2. Attorneys and CPAs licensed to practice in a particular state must _____ in order to practice before the IRS.

A. Be in good standing in that state and may practice before the IRS only in that state
B. Be in good standing in that state and may practice before the IRS in any state
C. Take the EA Exam in order to practice outside the state in which she is licensed
D. None of the above

The answer is B. Any attorney or Certified Public Accountant who is not currently under suspension or disbarment from practice before the IRS and who is licensed in good standing in any state, possession, territory, commonwealth, or the District of Columbia may practice before the IRS (Publication 947). Enrolled Agents may practice in any state. ###

3. Which of the following statements is TRUE?

A. A parent has authority to represent her child before the IRS only if the child is present.
B. A parent has authority to represent her child before the IRS without the child present.
C. A parent cannot represent her child before the IRS without an enrolled practitioner present.
D. None of the above.

The answer is B. A parent may represent a child before the IRS. A family member may represent, without compensation, a taxpayer before the IRS. The taxpayer does not have to be present. ###

4. Denise and Gabriela are best friends. They are not family members. Gabriela is going to appear before the IRS for an examination. Denise wants to appear as a witness on her best friend's behalf. Denise is not an enrolled preparer, but she still wants to appear before the U.S. Tax Court. Which of the following statements is TRUE?

A. Denise may represent Gabriela before the U.S. Tax Court.
B. Denise may advocate for Gabriela to the best of her ability.
C. Denise may appear before the IRS as a witness and communicate information.
D. Denise may not appear before the IRS in any capacity.

The answer is C. Simply appearing as a witness before the IRS is allowed and not considered "practice before the IRS." Individuals who are not practitioners may appear before the IRS as witnesses or communicate to the IRS on a taxpayer's behalf and appear as witnesses—but they may not advocate for the taxpayer. ###

5. Generally, federal government employees may practice before the IRS.

A. True
B. False

The answer is B, False. An individual employed by the federal government generally cannot practice before the IRS. State and local government employees generally may not practice before the IRS if their employment discloses information relating to federal taxes. However, regardless of the situation, an individual may always represent himself or a family member before the IRS. ###

6. Which of the following individuals DOES NOT qualify as an enrolled practitioner under Circular 230?

A. Certified Public Accountant
B. Enrolled Actuary
C. Attorney
D. Unenrolled student volunteers at a VITA site
E. A recognized fiduciary of an estate

The answer is E. All of the practitioners listed qualify to represent a taxpayer before the IRS, under certain circumstances. However, a fiduciary of an estate is not "enrolled to practice" before the IRS. The fiduciary only has the right to represent the estate before the IRS—NOT other taxpayers or entities. Student volunteers at a VITA site are given a special exemption to represent taxpayers before the IRS. VITA is the IRS's Volunteer Income Tax Assistance program, designed specifically to help low income taxpayers. ####

7. Matthew is a full-time employee for Parkway Partnership. He is not an EA, attorney, or a CPA. Parkway requests that Matthew represent the partnership in connection with an IRS audit. Which of the following statements is TRUE?

A. Matthew is allowed to represent the partnership before the IRS.
B. Matthew is not allowed to represent the partnership before the IRS.
C. Matthew is only allowed to represent individual partners before the IRS.
D. None of the above.

The answer is A. Matthew is a full-time employee for Parkway Partnership, so in that capacity he may represent his employer before the IRS. Representing a taxpayer (or an entity) before the IRS during an audit is considered "practice before the IRS." Practice before the IRS is limited to Enrolled Agents, CPAs, and attorneys, with a few exceptions, such as the one listed here. ###

8. Which of the following parties is QUALIFIED to act as an official representative for a taxpayer before the IRS?

A. An unenrolled preparer who did not prepare the tax return in question
B. A taxpayer's neighbor who is not a CPA, attorney, or EA
C. A shareholder of a corporation in which the taxpayer owns only 1% of the stock
D. A student attorney

The answer is D. A student attorney who receives permission to practice before the IRS by virtue of his status as a law student under Section 10.7(d) of Circular 230 is allowed to practice before the IRS. ###

9. Barry helps his friend Jose, who does not speak very good English. Barry appears before the IRS and translates for Jose at an IRS examination. Which of the following is TRUE?

A. Barry is practicing before the IRS.
B. Jose must sign Form 2848, authorizing Jose to represent him.
C. Barry is not considered to be "practicing before the IRS."
D. The IRS prohibits unrelated persons from being present at an IRS examination.

The answer is C. In general terms, Barry is merely assisting with the exchange of information and is not advocating on Jose's behalf. An example of an individual assisting with information exchange but not practicing would be a taxpayer's friend serving as a translator when the taxpayer does not speak English (*IRS Manual Chapter 25*). Simply appearing as a witness or communicating information to the IRS does not constitute "practice before the IRS." ###

10. Which form is used for a tax professional to apply for a new PTIN?

A. Form W-7
B. Form W-9
C. Form W-12
D. Form 2815

The answer is C. Tax professionals are required to apply for (or renew) their PTIN in order to prepare 2010 tax returns. The preparer may apply online or use Form W-12.###

11. A Centralized Authorization File (CAF) is _____.

A. A CAF is an automated file containing information regarding the authority of an individual appointed under a power of attorney or person designated under a tax information authorization.
B. A CAF is a file containing a practitioner's own personal tax return files.
C. A CAF is an automated list of disbarred tax preparers.
D. A CAF is an automated file of taxpayer delinquencies.

The answer is A. The CAF contains information on third parties authorized to represent taxpayers before the IRS and/or receive and inspect confidential tax information on active tax accounts or those accounts currently under consideration by the IRS. ###

12. Which of the following is considered a "paid preparer" for the purpose of the Circular 230 regulations?

A. A full-time bookkeeper working for an employer who prepares payroll tax returns
B. A retired CPA who prepares tax returns for free for his family members
C. A person who merely furnishes typing, reproducing, or mechanical assistance
D. A full-time secretary who also prepares tax returns for pay part-time from home during tax season

The answer is D. A tax preparer is anyone who prepares tax returns for compensation. A person who prepares and signs a tax return WITHOUT compensation (such as for a family member) is not considered a tax return preparer for the purposes of the preparer penalties. An employee who prepares a tax return for his employer or for another employee is not a "preparer" for the purposes of Circular 230. The employer (or the individual with supervisory responsibility) has the responsibility for accuracy of the return. ####

13. How long is a Power of Attorney authorization valid?

A. For one year
B. For three years.
C. Until it is revoked.
D. Until the due date of the next tax return.

The answer is C. A Power of Attorney is valid until revoked. It may be revoked by the taxpayer or withdrawn by the representative or may be superseded by the filing of a new power of attorney for the same tax and tax period. A Power of Attorney also ends upon the taxpayer's death. ###

Unit 3.2: Rules of Enrollment

More Reading: Publication 947, *Practice Before the IRS and Power of Attorney*

Qualifying for Initial Enrollment

There are two tracks to become an Enrolled Agent, which are outlined in Treasury Department Circular 230. An Enrolled Agent may receive her designation by passing a three-part exam administered by Prometric, or may become an Enrolled Agent by virtue of past employment with the IRS.

The IRS may waive the requirement for former IRS employees to pass the EA and ERPA[91] exams, but will NOT waive the requirement for the Enrolled Actuary exam. Individuals must prove that they can become Enrolled Agents by virtue of technical experience with the IRS. Factors considered with the second track are the length and scope of employment and the recommendation of the superior officer.

Track I: Exam Track

For the first track, an EA candidate must apply for a Preparer Tax Identification Number (PTIN) and apply to take the Special Enrollment Examination (or the SEE, also known as the "EA Exam"). The candidate then must do the following:

- Achieve passing scores on all parts of the SEE
- Apply for enrollment on Form 23
- Pass a background check

Track II: Previous Experience with the IRS

For the second track, an EA candidate must possess the years of past service and technical experience specified in Circular 230. He then must:

- Apply for enrollment on Form 23
- Pass a background check

Applicants can apply to take the EA Exam by filing Form 2587, *Application for Special Enrollment Examination*. Once the candidate passes all three parts of the EA exam, he must file Form 23, *Application for Enrollment to Practice before the Internal Revenue Service*, in order to obtain his Treasury card.

The Director of Practice is responsible for administering and enforcing the regulations governing practice before the IRS, and the Director also makes the determinations on applications for enrollment to practice.

Denial of Enrollment

Any individual engaged in practice before the IRS who is involved in disreputable conduct is subject to disciplinary action. Disreputable acts alone may be grounds for denial of enrollment, even after the candidate has passed the EA Exam. The Director of the Office of Professional Responsibility (OPR) must inform the applicant why she is denied an application for enrollment.

---

[91] ERPA: Enrolled Retirement Plan Agent

The applicant may file a written appeal within 30 days after receiving the notice of denial of enrollment. The appeal must be filed along with the candidate's reasoning why the enrollment application should be accepted. The appeal must be filed with the **Secretary of the U.S. Treasury** (not with the IRS).

A decision on the appeal will be rendered by the Secretary of the Treasury, or his delegate, as soon as practicable. Again, an Enrolled Agent who is denied enrollment and wishes to challenge the denial must file a written appeal with the Secretary of the Treasury, NOT with the Office of Professional Responsibility. Remember this distinction because it is often tested on the EA Exam.

The Office of Professional Responsibility (OPR)

The Office of Professional Responsibility is responsible for administering and enforcing the regulations governing practice before the IRS. These regulations are published in Circular 230. The OPR's responsibility includes making determinations on applications for enrollment to practice before the IRS and conducting disciplinary proceedings relating to enrolled individuals.

Roster of Enrolled Agents and Enrolled Retirement Plan Agents

The Office of Professional Responsibility maintains a roster of Enrolled Agents and Enrolled Retirement Plan Agents. The roster includes enrolled individuals who are in inactive or retired status. The roster has the following information:

- Current Enrolled Agents:
    - Who have been granted enrollment to practice
    - Whose enrollment has been placed in inactive status for failure to meet the continuing education requirements for renewal of enrollment
- Inactive Enrolled Agents:
    - Who are in inactive retirement status
    - Whose offer of consent to resign from enrollment has been accepted by the Office of Professional Responsibility
- Other individuals (and employers, firms, or other entities, if applicable) censured, suspended, or disbarred from practice before the IRS or upon whom a monetary penalty was imposed
- Disqualified appraisers
- Enrolled Retirement Plan Agents (ERPAs):
    - Who have been granted active enrollment to practice
    - Whose enrollment has been placed in inactive status
    - Whose enrollment has been placed in inactive retirement status
    - Whose offer of consent to resign from enrollment has been accepted by the Office of Professional Responsibility

This roster may be available for public inspection in a manner prescribed by the Secretary of the Treasury.

Renewal of Enrollment

Application for renewal is based on the last digit of the Enrolled Agent's Social Security Number or Tax Identification Number. If an EA does not renew her enrollment, she may not practice as an Enrolled Agent. A prerequisite for renewal is completing the necessary continuing professional education requirements.

Enrolled Agents must renew their enrollment status every three years. As part of the application process, the IRS will check the candidate's filing history to verify that she has filed and paid all federal taxes on time. A non-complying Enrolled Agent will be given an opportunity to state the basis for the noncompliance with the possible consequence of being placed on the roster of inactive Enrolled Agents for a three-year period.

The schedule for the IRS renewal process is listed below. If the candidate's Social Security Number ends in:

- 0, 1, 2, or 3 – Due date of renewal: 1/31/13 (CPE Reporting period 01/01/10 to 12/31/12)
- 4, 5, or 6 – Due date of renewal: 1/31/11 (CPE Reporting period 01/01/08 to 12/31/10)
- 7, 8, or 9 (or no SSN)– Due date of renewal: 1/31/12 (CPE Reporting period 01/01/09 to 12/31/11)

EAs who do not have an SSN must use the "7, 8, or 9" renewal schedule. Enrolled Agents may be enrolled to practice even if they are citizens of a foreign country. These EAs help many individuals overseas who have a U.S. tax liability and a filing requirement. There are Enrolled Agents throughout the U.S. and overseas—wherever the IRS has an outpost.

Renewal Requirements

The IRS will send a reminder notice when an EA is due for renewal. If the practitioner does not receive a reminder notice, he must still file Form 8554, *Application for Renewal of Enrollment to Practice before the Internal Revenue Service,* to renew status. To apply for renewal, an Enrolled Agent must:

- Fill out Form 8554 and enclose a check or money order for $125 (this amount will change in 2011) made payable to the Internal Revenue Service. This fee is non-refundable, even if the application is denied.
- Complete 72 hours of Continuing Professional Education (CPE) over the three-year enrollment cycle to remain active. Each year EAs must take a *minimum* of 16 hours of CPE including at least two hours of Ethics CPE.
- If the EA has retaken and passed the Special Enrollment Examination (SEE) since the last renewal, she is only required to take 16 hours of CPE during the last year of the renewal cycle.

An Enrolled Agent is required to complete a minimum of 72 hours of continuing education credit during each enrollment cycle. An Enrolled Agent cannot complete all of his CPE just before his renewal date. The application for renewal is required to maintain active renewal status. Not receiving notice of the renewal requirement from the Director of Practice does not excuse the agent from having to re-apply.

Enrolled Agents who fail to comply with the requirements for eligibility for renewal of enrollment will be notified by the Office of Professional Responsibility through First Class mail. The notice will explain the reason for noncompliance. The Enrolled Agent has 60 days from the date of the notice to respond.

Continuing Professional Education (CPE) for Enrolled Agents

Any individual who receives initial enrollment during the enrollment cycle (basically, a new EA) must complete at least two hours of CPE during each month of the enrollment cycle. Enrollment for any part of a month is considered enrollment for an entire month.

If a candidate takes more than two hours of ethics courses during a single year, the additional ethics courses will count toward the yearly requirement. However, an Enrolled Agent may not take additional ethics courses in the current year and neglect to take them in future years. Ethics courses must be taken every year.

In order to qualify as professional CPE, the course of learning must be designed to enhance professional knowledge in federal taxation or federal tax-related matters. Courses related to state taxation do not qualify for the IRS requirement. To qualify as a CPE sponsor, a program presenter must be ONE of the following:

- An accredited educational institution, or
- Be recognized for continuing education purposes by the licensing body of any state, or
- Be recognized as a professional organization or society, or
- File a sponsor agreement for approval.

CPE Coursework

All continuing education programs are measured in terms of contact hours. The shortest recognized program is one contact hour. In order for a course to qualify for CPE credit, the course must have at least 50 minutes of continuous participation. A qualified course may also be longer than an hour; for example, a course lasting longer than 50 minutes but less than 80 minutes will still count only as one contact hour.

Individual segments at conferences, conventions, and the like will be considered one total program. For example, two 90-minute segments (180 minutes) at a continuous conference will count as three contact hours. For a university or college course, each semester hour credit will equal 15 contact hours and a quarter-hour credit will equal ten contact hours.

For Enrolled Agents who are also writers or instructors, continuing education credit will be awarded for publications on federal taxation or federal tax-related matters including accounting, tax preparation software, and taxation or ethics, provided the content of such publications is current and designed for the enhancement of the professional knowledge of an individual enrolled to practice before the Internal Revenue Service. The maximum credit for publications may not exceed 25% of the continuing education requirement of any enrollment cycle.

For those practitioners who are instructors, one hour of continuing education credit will be awarded for each contact hour completed as an instructor, discussion leader, or speaker. Two hours of continuing education credit will be awarded for actual subject preparation time for each contact hour completed as an instructor, discussion leader, or speaker at such programs.

It is the responsibility of the individual claiming such credit to maintain records to verify preparation time. The maximum credit for instruction and preparation may not exceed 50% of the continuing education requirement for an enrollment cycle.

CPE Waiver

A waiver of CPE requirements may be requested in extraordinary circumstances. The discretion to grant a waiver lies in the hands of the Office of Professional Responsibility. Qualifying circumstances include:

- Health issues
- Active deployment for military personnel
- Absence from the United States for employment or other reasons
- Other reasons on a case-by-case basis

The request for a waiver must be accompanied by appropriate documentation, such as medical records or military paperwork. If the request is denied, the Enrolled Agent will be placed on the inactive roster. If the request is accepted, the individual will receive an updated enrollment card reflecting his renewal.

CPE Recordkeeping Requirements

CPE sponsors must maintain records to verify the participants who attended and completed the program for a period of three years following completion of the program.

In the case of conferences, conventions, and the like, records must be maintained to verify completion of the program and attendance by each participant at each segment of the program. Individuals applying for renewal of enrollment must also retain their CPE records for three years following the date of renewal. Required CPE record information includes:

- The name of the CPE sponsoring organization
- The location of the program
- The title of the program and description of its content
- Written outlines, course syllabi, textbooks, and/or electronic materials provided or required for the course
- The dates attended
- The credit hours claimed
- The name of the instructor, discussion leader, or speaker, if appropriate
- The certificate of completion and/or signed statement of the hours of attendance obtained from the sponsor

Unit 3.2: Questions

1. Enrolled Agents generally must complete continuing education credits for renewed enrollment. Which of the following describes the credit requirements?

A. A minimum of 72 hours must be completed in each year of an enrollment cycle
B. A minimum of 24 hours must be completed in each year of an enrollment cycle
C. A minimum of 80 hours must be completed, overall, for the entire enrollment cycle
D. A minimum of 16 hours must be completed in each year of the enrollment cycle, including two hours of ethics

The answer is D. A minimum of 16 hours of continuing education credit, including two hours of ethics, must be completed in each year of the enrollment cycle. An Enrolled Agent must complete a minimum of 72 hours of continuing education during each three-year period. ###

2. Generally, each individual who applies for renewal to practice before the IRS must retain information about Continuing Professional Education hours completed. How long must CPE verification be retained?

A. For one year following the enrollment renewal date.
B. For three years following the enrollment renewal date.
C. For five years if it is an initial enrollment.
D. The individual is not required to retain the information if the CPE sponsor has agreed to retain it.

The answer is B. Each individual applying for renewal must retain information about CPE hours completed for three years following the enrollment renewal date. ###

3. The form that exam candidates must fill out in order to apply to take the IRS Enrolled Agent's exam is:

A. Form 2587
B. Form 2848
C. Form 8115
D. Form 2115

The answer is A. Applicants can apply to take the Special Enrollment Examination by filing Form 2587, *Application for Special Enrollment Examination*. ###

4. Enrolled Agents applying for renewal of their enrollment must file which IRS form?

A. Form 8554
B. Form 2815
C. Form 2251
D. Form 8851

The answer is A. Applicants for renewal must file Form 8554, *Application for Renewal of Enrollment to Practice before the Internal Revenue Service*. To qualify for renewal, applicants must complete the necessary CPE hours during each three-year enrollment cycle. ###

5. After the initial enrollment renewal period, regular renewal enrollments are required every three years. This is known as an enrollment cycle. A minimum of how many hours of continuing education are required per three-year cycle?

A. 52
B. 72
C. 16
D. 97

The answer is B. In order to maintain their licenses, Enrolled Agents must complete 72 hours of continuing education within a three-year cycle based on the last digit of their Social Security Numbers. The IRS enforces a 16-hour minimum per year and requires two hours of ethics per year. ###

6. Enrolled Agents who do not comply with the requirements for renewal of enrollment will be contacted by the Office of Professional Responsibility. How much time does the Enrolled Agent have to respond to the OPR?

A. 30 days from the date of the notice to respond
B. 60 days from the date of the notice to respond
C. 90 days from the date of receipt to respond
D. 90 days from the date of the notice to respond

The answer is B. Enrolled Agents who fail to comply with the requirements for eligibility for renewal of enrollment will be notified by the Office of Professional Responsibility through First Class mail. The notice will explain the reason for noncompliance. The Enrolled Agent has 60 days from the date of the notice to respond. ###

7. Nathan, an Enrolled Agent, teaches various continuing education courses in tax law. What is the maximum credit for instruction and preparation that Nathan can take during his enrollment cycle?

A. 10%
B. 50%
C. 60%
D. 90%

The answer is B. The maximum credit for instruction and preparation may not exceed 50% of the continuing education requirement for an enrollment cycle. ###

8. To maintain active enrollment to practice before the IRS, each individual enrolled is required to have her enrollment renewed. The Office of Professional Responsibility will notify the individual of her renewal of enrollment and will issue her a card as evidence of enrollment. Which of the following statements about renewal of enrollment is correct?

A. A reasonable refundable fee may be charged for each application for renewal of enrollment filed with the Office of Professional Responsibility.
B. Failure by an individual to receive notification from the Office of Professional Responsibility of the renewal requirement will not be justification for the failure to renew enrollment in a timely manner.
C. Forms required for renewal may only be obtained from the National Association of Enrolled Agents.
D. The enrollment cycle is a three-year period and all Enrolled Agents must renew at the same time, no matter when they first became Enrolled Agents.

The answer is B. Application for renewal is required to maintain active renewal status. Not receiving notice of the renewal requirement from the Director of Practice does not excuse the agent from having to reapply. Failure to receive notification from OPR of the renewal requirement will not be justification for the failure to renew enrollment in a timely manner. The renewal fee is nonrefundable. The renewal forms are available on the IRS website. ###

10. Lee is an Enrolled Agent and also an author who writes tax articles regarding tax compliance issues. He can receive continuing credit education for his writing. What is the maximum amount of credit that Lee can take for his writing during his enrollment cycle?

A. 0%
B. 10%
C. 25%
D. 50%

The answer is C. For Enrolled Agents, continuing education credit will be awarded for publications on federal taxation or federal tax related matters including accounting, tax preparation software, and taxation or ethics, provided that the content of such publications is current and designed for the enhancement of the professional knowledge of an individual enrolled to practice before the IRS. The maximum credit for publications may not exceed 25% of the continuing education requirement of any enrollment cycle. ###

11. Andrea has been enrolled to practice before the IRS for many years. Her records show that she had the following hours of qualified CPE in 2010:

1. January 2010, 6 hours: General tax CPE
2. May 2010, 4 hours: Ethics
3. December 2010, 4 hours: General tax CPE

Based on these records, has Andrea has met her 2010 CPE requirements?

A. Yes, Andrea has met her 2010 minimum CPE requirements.
B. No, Andrea has met her ethics requirement, but not the overall minimum requirement for the year.
C. No, Andrea has not met her ethics requirement, but she has met the overall minimum requirement for the year.
D. None of the above.

The answer is B. The IRS enforces a 16 hour minimum per year, and requires two hours on ethics per year. Andrea has only completed 14 hours of CPE in 2010. She has met her ethics requirement, but she has not met the overall minimum requirement for the year. ###

12. How long must Enrolled Agents keep records of their CPE courses?

A. One year
B. Three years
C. Four years
D. Six years

The answer is B. Individuals applying for renewal of enrollment must retain their CPE records for three years following the date of renewal. ###

13. Under Circular 230, an applicant who wishes to challenge the Office of Professional Responsibility's denial of his application for enrollment is required to do which of the following?

A. File a written appeal with the Secretary of the Treasury
B. File a written appeal with the Director of the Office of Professional Responsibility
C. File a written appeal with the Commissioner of the IRS
D. Resubmit another application within 30 days

The answer is A. An Enrolled Agent who is initially denied enrollment and wishes to challenge the denial must file a written appeal with the Secretary of the Treasury, NOT with the Office of Professional Responsibility.###

Unit 3.3: Tax Preparer Responsibilities

More Reading:
Publication 4019, *Third Party Authorization, Levels of Authority*
Publication 947, *Practice Before the IRS and Power of Attorney*

Currently, any person may prepare a federal tax return for any other person for a fee. All tax return preparers are subject to some oversight, but the level of oversight depends on whether the tax return preparer holds a professional license, has been enrolled to practice before the IRS, chooses to file returns electronically, and the jurisdiction where he or she prepares returns.

The Treasury Department's Circular 230 sets forth regulations that govern Enrolled Agents, CPAs, attorneys, and others who practice before the IRS. It imposes professional standards and codes of conduct for tax preparers and tax advisors. It prohibits certain actions, requires other actions, and details penalties for ethical and other violations by tax preparers.

Central to the Circular 230 regulations is the mandate for practitioners to exercise due diligence when performing the following duties:

- Preparing or assisting in the preparing, approving, and filing of returns, documents, affidavits, and other papers relating to IRS matters.
- Determining the correctness of oral or written representations made by the client, and also for positions taken on the tax return.

Best Practices

Circular 230 also explains the broad concept of "best practices." Tax advisors must provide clients with the highest quality representation concerning federal tax matters by adhering to best practices in providing advice and in preparing documents or information for the Internal Revenue Service. Tax advisors who oversee a firm's practice of providing advice on federal tax issues or of preparing or assisting in the preparation of submissions to the Internal Revenue Service should take reasonable steps to ensure that the firm's procedures for all employees and managers are consistent with best practices. Best practices include the following:

- Communicating clearly with the client regarding the terms of the engagement.
- Establishing the facts, determining which facts are relevant, evaluating the reasonableness of any assumptions or representations, relating the applicable law (including potentially applicable judicial doctrines) to the relevant facts, and arriving at a conclusion supported by the law and the facts.
- Advising the client of the conclusions reached; for example, advising whether a taxpayer may avoid accuracy-related penalties if he relies on the advice provided.
- Acting with integrity in practice before the Internal Revenue Service.

The Duty to Advise

A practitioner who knows that her client has not complied with the revenue laws or who has made an error or omission in any return, document, affidavit, or other required paper has the responsibility to advise the client promptly of the noncompliance, error, or omission, as well as the consequences of the error.

Under the rules of Circular 230 §10.21, the tax practitioner is not responsible for fixing the noncompliance issue once she has notified the client of the issue. The tax professional is also not responsible for notifying the IRS of noncompliance.

> **Example:** James is an Enrolled Agent. James has a new client, Monique, who has self-prepared her own returns in the past. James notices that Monique has been claiming Head of Household on her tax returns, but she does not qualify for this status, because she does not have a qualifying person. James is required to promptly notify Monique of the error and tell her the consequences of not correcting the error. However, James is not required to amend her prior year tax returns to correct the error.

The §10.21 obligations are not limited to practitioners preparing returns, so the discovery of an error or omission in the course of a tax consulting or advisory engagement will also trigger its requirements.

> **Example:** Grant is an Enrolled Agent. He takes over another tax preparer's practice and realizes that the previous preparer has been taking Section 179 depreciation on assets that do not qualify for this bonus depreciation treatment. Grant must notify his clients of the error and the consequences of not correcting the error. Grant is not required to correct the error.

A tax professional may rely on the work product of another tax preparer. A practitioner will be presumed to have exercised due diligence if he relies on the work product of another person and to have used reasonable care in evaluating the work product of the other practitioner.

Other Duties and Prohibited Acts

Performance as a notary: A tax practitioner who is a notary public and is employed as counsel, attorney, or agent in a matter before the IRS or who has a material interest in the matter cannot engage in any notary activities related to that matter.

Negotiations of taxpayer refund checks: Tax return preparers must not endorse or otherwise negotiate (cash) any refund check issued to the taxpayer.

No delay tactics allowed: A practitioner must not delay the prompt disposition of any matter before the IRS.

No employment of disbarred persons: A tax practitioner may not knowingly employ a person or accept employment from a person who has been disbarred or suspended by the Director of Practice. This restriction applies even if the duties of the disbarred or suspended person would not include actual preparation of tax returns.

Conflicts of Interest § 10.29

A tax professional may represent conflicting interests before the IRS only if all the parties offer their consent in writing. If there's any possible conflict of interest, an interested person must disclose the existence of a financial interest and be given the opportunity to disclose all material facts. A conflict of interest exists if:

- The representation of one client will be directly adverse to another client; or
- There is a significant risk that the representation of one or more clients will be materially limited by the practitioner's responsibilities to another client, a former client, a third person, or by a personal interest of the practitioner.

The only requirements are that consent be obtained in writing and retained for at least 36 months from the date representation ends. At minimum, the consent should adequately describe the nature of the conflict and the parties the practitioner represents. The practitioner may still represent a client when a conflict of interest exists if:

- The practitioner reasonably believes that she will be able to provide competent and diligent representation to each affected client;
- The representation is not prohibited by law; and
- Each affected client waives the conflict of interest and gives informed consent, confirmed in writing.

The Privacy of Taxpayer Information: Section 7216

Internal Revenue Code §7216 is a **criminal provision** enacted by Congress that prohibits preparers of tax returns from knowingly or recklessly disclosing or using tax return information. The regulations are under Internal Revenue Code in Section 7216, *Disclosure or Use of Tax Information by Preparers of Returns.*

Strict privacy regulations concerning taxpayer information have been enacted and are currently being modified by the IRS. These regulations have been designed to give taxpayers more control over their personal information and tax records. The rules also instituted higher fines and a felony penalty for practitioners who knowingly disclose taxpayer information.

The Section 7216 rules limit a tax professional's use and disclosure of information obtained from the client. They basically restrict the use of the information to the preparation of the tax return. The regulations explain precise and limited exceptions in which a tax professional is permitted to disclose information obtained from a client.

Tax preparers must generally obtain written consent from taxpayers before they can disclose information to a third party, or use the information for anything other than the actual preparation of tax returns. The actual consent form must meet the following guidelines:

- Identify the purpose of the disclosure.
- Identify the recipient and describe the authorized information.
- Include the name of the preparer and the name of the taxpayer.
- Include mandatory language that informs the taxpayer that he is not required to sign the consent and if he does sign the consent, he can set a time period for the duration of that consent.
- Include mandatory language that refers the taxpayer to the Treasury Inspector General for Tax Administration if she believes that her tax return information has been disclosed or used improperly.
- If applicable, inform the taxpayer that his tax return information may be disclosed to a tax return preparer located outside the U.S.
- Be signed and dated by the taxpayer. Electronic (online) consents must be in the same type as the website's standard text and contain the taxpayer's affirmative consent (as opposed to an "opt out" clause).

These updated privacy regulations apply to paid preparers, electronic return originators (EROs), tax software developers, and other persons or entities engaged in tax preparation. The regulations also apply to most volunteer tax preparers, for example, Volunteer Income Tax

Assistance (VITA) and Tax Counseling for the Elderly (TCE) volunteers, and employees and contractors employed by tax preparation companies in a support role. The regulations provide a criminal penalty for disclosure of certain information. Violations could result in imprisonment for up to one year, a fine of not more than $1,000, or both, for *each violation*.

Allowable Disclosures

In certain circumstances, a preparer may disclose information to a second taxpayer who appears on a tax return. The preparer may disclose return information obtained from the first taxpayer if:

- The second taxpayer is related to the first taxpayer.
- The first taxpayer's interest is not adverse to the second taxpayer's interest.
- The first taxpayer has not prohibited the disclosure.

Example: Zach is an Enrolled Agent with two married clients, Serena and Tyler, who file jointly. Serena works long hours, so she is unavailable when Tyler meets with Zach to prepare their joint 2010 tax return. Later, Serena comes in alone to sign the return. She also has a quick question regarding the mortgage interest on a tax return. Zach is allowed to disclose return information to Serena because the tax return is a joint return, both of their names are on the return, and Tyler has not prohibited any disclosures.

A taxpayer is considered "related" to another taxpayer in any of the following relationships:

- Husband and wife, or child and parent
- Grandchild and grandparent
- General partner in a partnership
- Trust or estate and the beneficiary
- A corporation and shareholder
- Members of a controlled group of corporations

A tax preparer may also disclose tax return information that was obtained from a first taxpayer in preparing a tax return of the second taxpayer, if the preparer has obtained written consent from the first taxpayer. For example, if an unmarried couple lives together and splits the mortgage interest, the preparer may use or disclose information from the first taxpayer as long as the preparer has written consent.

The Definition of "Tax Return Information"

"Tax return information" is all the information tax return preparers obtain from taxpayers that is used to prepare tax returns. It also includes all biographical information, preparer worksheets, correspondence from IRS during the preparation, filing and correction of returns; statistical compilations of tax return information; and tax return preparation software registration information. All of this tax return information is protected by §7216 and its regulations.

When Disclosure Permission is Not Required

The tax preparer is NOT required to obtain disclosure permission from the client if the disclosure is made for any of the following reasons:

- A court order or subpoena issued by any court of record whether at the federal, state, or local level. The required information must be clearly identified in the document (subpoena or court order) in order for a preparer to disclose information.

- An administrative order, demand, summons, or subpoena that is issued by any federal agency, state agency, or commission charged under the laws of the state with licensing, registration, or regulation of tax return preparers.

- In order to report a crime to proper authorities. Even if the preparer is mistaken and no crime exists, if the preparer makes the disclosure in good faith, she will not be subject to sanctions.

- Confidential information for the purpose of peer reviews.

A tax preparer may disclose private client information to his attorney, or to an employee of the IRS, subsequent to an investigation of the tax return preparer conducted by the IRS.

> **Example:** Harry is a CPA who is being investigated by the IRS for misconduct. Harry has an attorney who is assisting in his defense. In reality, Harry was the victim of embezzlement because his bookkeeper was stealing client checks. Harry discovered the embezzlement when the IRS contacted him about client complaints. Harry may disclose confidential client information to his attorney in order to assist with his defense. Harry may also disclose confidential client information to the IRS during the course of the investigation.

A tax preparer may disclose tax return information to a tax return processor. For example, if a tax preparer uses an electronic or tax return processing service, she may disclose tax return information to that service in order to prepare tax returns or compute tax liability.

A tax preparer may also solicit additional business from a taxpayer in matters not related to the IRS (for example, if the preparer also offers other financial services such as bookkeeping or insurance services). However, the tax preparer must obtain written consent from the taxpayer in order to make these solicitations.

This also includes the disclosure of tax return information to third parties if the taxpayer agrees in a written consent.[92]

---

[92] In 2010, the IRS released Revenue Ruling 2010-4 and Revenue Ruling 2010-5. These proposed, temporary regulations enable tax return preparers to use or disclose tax return information without explicit taxpayer consent in certain limited circumstances. Tax preparers would be able to contact their clients regarding recent tax law developments that may affect those clients. They also would be able to disclose information in connection with the potential sale or purchase of a tax return preparer's business and during the process of conducting client conflict-of-interest checks. These proposed regulations would make it easier for preparers to contact clients to discuss their individual tax situations, without having to first obtain written consent to do so. Neither Revenue Ruling is final.

> **Example:** Juliet is an Enrolled Agent who also sells insurance. She obtains a written consent from her client Manuel. She sends Manuel a solicitation by mail for her insurance services. This is allowed because Juliet obtained written consent from Manuel in advance.

Third Party Designee

A taxpayer can choose a "third party designee" by checking the "yes" box on his tax return. This allows the IRS to discuss the taxpayer's return with a friend, family member, or any other person the taxpayer chooses. A third party designee authorization automatically expires on the due date of the next tax return.

The Third Party Designee (Checkbox) Authorization does not allow the designee to "represent the taxpayer." The authorization is also specific to the tax return upon which the designation appeared. Effective since January 1, 2004, the Third Party Designee (Checkbox) Authorization was expanded to mirror the authority of a Form 8821. The designee may address any issue arising out of the tax return for a period not to exceed one year from the due date of the tax return. The designee may also receive written account information including transcripts upon request.

The Third Party Designee (Checkbox) Authorization can co-exist with a Power of Attorney for the same tax and tax period.[93]

IRS Records Requests

Upon lawful request, a tax preparer must submit tax records to the IRS. If the requested information or records are not in the practitioner's possession, he must promptly advise the requesting IRS officer and provide any information the practitioner has regarding the identity of the person who may have possession or control of the requested information or records.

The tax practitioner must reasonably inquire about the identity of any person who may have possession of the requested records, but the practitioner is NOT required to make inquiry of any other person or independently verify any information provided by the practitioner's client regarding the identity of such persons.

If the Office of Professional Responsibility requests information concerning possible violations of the regulations by other parties, such as other preparers or taxpayers, the practitioner must furnish the information and be prepared to testify in disbarment or suspension proceedings.

A tax practitioner may not interfere with any lawful effort by the IRS to request or obtain records. A practitioner can be exempted from these rules if he believes in good faith and

---

[93] Please see Pub 4019 for a quick reference of third party authorizations.

on reasonable grounds that the information requested is privileged or that the request is of doubtful legality.

Confidentiality Privilege for Client Records

There is confidentiality protection granted to Enrolled Agents and their clients. The confidentiality protection for certain communications between a taxpayer and an attorney (privileged communications) applies to similar communications between a taxpayer and any federally authorized tax practitioner. This confidentiality privilege cannot be used in any proceeding with an agency other than the IRS. The protection of this privilege applies only to tax advice given to the taxpayer by any individual who is a federally authorized tax practitioner (CPA, EA, or attorney).

The confidentiality protection applies to communications that would be considered privileged if they were between the taxpayer and an attorney and that relate to:

- Non-criminal tax matters before the IRS, or
- Non-criminal tax proceedings brought in federal court by or against the United States.

The confidentiality privilege does NOT apply in criminal tax matters. However, attorneys retain a confidentiality privilege in all matters, including criminal and non-criminal matters before the IRS.

Return of Client Records

A tax practitioner is *required* to return a client's records whether or not fees have been paid. Client records are defined as any records belonging to the client, including any work product that the client has already paid for, such as a completed copy of a tax return. The practitioner must, at the request of a client, promptly return any and all records that are necessary for the client to comply with her federal tax obligations. The practitioner may retain copies of the records returned to a client.

A fee dispute does not relieve the practitioner of his responsibility to return client records. The practitioner must provide the client with reasonable access to review and copy any additional records retained by the practitioner under state law that are necessary for the client to comply with her federal tax obligations. Client records do NOT include the tax practitioner's work product. The practitioner is not required to give the client any tax return, claim for refund, schedule, affidavit, appraisal, or any other document prepared by the practitioner if he is withholding the documents because of a fee dispute.

> **Example:** Leroy is an Enrolled Agent. His client Samantha became very upset with Leroy because he told her she owed substantial penalties to the IRS in 2010. Samantha wanted to get a second opinion, and she did not want to pay Leroy for his time. Leroy is required to hand over Samantha's tax records, including copies of her W-2 forms and any other information she brought to his office. Leroy returns her original records, but he does not give her a copy of the tax return he prepared.

> **Example:** Clara is an Enrolled Agent. She does substantial tax work for a partnership, Greenway Landscaping. Greenway has been slow to pay in the past, so Clara asks that the owners of Greenway pay for the tax returns when they pick them up. Greenway refuses and demands the tax returns anyway. Clara decides to discontinue all contact with Greenway. Clara must return Greenway's original records, but she is NOT required to give Greenway work product that the owners have not paid for.

Tax preparers are required by law to furnish a copy of the tax return to the client at the same time that the return is presented for signature.

Tax Return List

Tax preparers are required to keep a copy or a list of all returns they have prepared for at least three years. Alternatively, preparers may also keep copies of the actual returns. If the preparer does not keep copies of the actual returns, the preparer is required to keep a list or card file of clients and tax returns prepared. At a minimum, the list must contain the taxpayer's name, identification number, tax year, and the type of return prepared. In actual practice, most tax preparers now keep scanned or digital copies of client tax returns rather than a list of the returns prepared.

Signature Requirements for Preparers

A paid preparer is required by law to sign the tax return and fill out the preparer areas of the form. The preparer must also include her appropriate identifying number (PTIN or SSN) on the return. Although the preparer signs the return, the taxpayer is ultimately responsible for the accuracy of every item on the return.

The preparer must give the taxpayer a copy of the return. A return preparer is required to manually sign the return or claim for refund after it has been completed and before it is presented to the taxpayer. If the original preparer is unavailable for signature, another preparer must review the entire preparation of the return or claim, and then must manually sign it.

For the purposes of the signature requirement, the preparer with primary responsibility for the overall accuracy of the return or claim is considered the preparer (if more than one preparer is involved). If a return is mechanically completed by a computer that is not under the control of the individual preparer, a manually signed attestation may be attached to the return.

For the purposes of penalties, a tax preparer must sign the return or claim for refund after it is completed and before it is presented to the taxpayer for signature. The manual signature requirement may be satisfied by a photocopy of the manually signed copy of the return or claim. The preparer must retain the manually signed copy. A valid signature is defined by state law and may be anything that clearly indicates the intent to sign.

A preparer may sign *on behalf of the taxpayer* in the client's signature area if certain standards are met. For example, regulations permit a representative to sign a taxpayer's return if the taxpayer is unable to sign the return because of disease or injury, or continuous absence from the United States. When a return is signed by a representative, it must be mailed and accompanied by a power of attorney (Form 2848).

A taxpayer may also assign an agent to sign her tax return. A parent may sign a tax return on behalf of a minor child. In the case of a joint tax return, both spouses must sign. If one spouse is deceased, the surviving spouse may sign the return and enter "filing as a surviving spouse" in the signature area of the return. If one spouse cannot sign because of disease or injury, the other spouse may sign on his behalf. A dated and signed statement should be attached to the return stating the reason the spouse cannot sign and that the disabled spouse has given permission for the other to sign. Paid tax preparers are also required to sign payroll tax returns.

The preparer's declaration on signing the return states that the information contained in the return is true, correct, and complete based on all information the preparer has.

Alternative Methods of Signing

The IRS allows preparers to sign Form 8878, *IRS e-file Signature Authorization for Form 4868 or Form 2350*, and Form 8879 by rubber stamp, mechanical device (such as signature pen), or computer software. The alternative methods of signing must include either a facsimile of the individual preparer's signature or of the preparer's printed name. Preparers using one of these alternative means are personally responsible for affixing their signatures to returns or requests for extension.

Preparer Identification

Paid preparers must include their Preparer Tax Identification Number (PTIN) with every return filed with the IRS. Previously, paid preparers had the option of using their Social Security Number. With new regulations in force, all paid preparers are now required to have a PTIN in order to prepare tax returns for a fee.

Identity Theft

Identity theft occurs when someone uses another individual's personally identifiable information, such as her name, Social Security Number, or credit card number, without her permission in order to commit fraud or other crimes. Practitioners are required to obtain and store data and information about their clients, and this information must be kept secure.

To help prevent identity theft, preparers should confirm identities and Taxpayer Identification Numbers (TINs) of taxpayers, their spouses, dependents, and EITC qualifying children contained on the returns to be prepared. TINs include Social Security Numbers (SSNs), Adopted Taxpayer Identification Numbers (ATINs), and Individual Taxpayer Identification Numbers (ITINs).

To confirm identities, the preparer can request a picture ID reflecting the taxpayer's name and address and Social Security cards or other documents providing the TINs of all individuals to be listed on the return (see the IRS EITC Toolkit).

Setting Practitioner Fees

The IRS prohibits practitioners from charging "unconscionable fees." The IRS has not defined what is considered an unconscionable fee, but it is generally believed to be when the fees are so grossly unethical that the courts would consider them as such.

A practitioner may not charge a contingent fee (percentage of the refund) for preparing an original tax return. IRS regulations generally prevent a practitioner from charging a contingent fee for most services rendered in connection with any matter before the Internal Revenue Service, including the preparation or filing of a tax return, amended tax return, or claim for refund or credit.

Strict Rules for Contingent Fees

The IRS allows a practitioner to charge a contingent fee for services rendered in connection with the IRS examination (audit) of an original tax return. Contingent fees are also allowed for an amended return, a claim for refund, or a credit, so long as they're filed within 120 days of the taxpayer receiving a written notice of the examination of the original tax return.

Contingent fees are also permitted for interest and penalty reviews and for services rendered in connection with a judicial proceeding arising under the Internal Revenue Code. Since this new regulation was published, the call for clarification from tax professionals all over the country has led the IRS to admit that the regulation must be amended. At the date of this printing, the proposed regulation was still being reviewed and modified by the IRS.

Until the Circular 230 regulations are amended once again, the IRS has published some interim rules as guidance for tax practitioners. Practitioners may charge a contingent fee for the following:

- An examination (audit) of an original tax return; or
- An amended return or claim for refund or credit filed before the taxpayer received a written notice of examination of the original tax return, or filed no later than 120 days after the receipt of such written notice or written challenge. The 120 days is computed from the earlier of a written notice of the examination.
- Services rendered in connection with a claim for credit or refund filed solely in connection with the determination of statutory interest or penalties assessed by the Internal Revenue Service.
- Services rendered in connection with a claim under Section 7623 of the Internal Revenue Code. This has to do with the IRS "Whistleblower" program.[94]
- Services rendered in connection with any judicial proceeding arising under the Internal Revenue Code [IRS Notice 2008-43].

Advertising Restrictions in Section 10.30

Circular 230 covers preparer advertising standards. A practitioner may not use any form of communication or advertise any solicitation containing false or misleading information. Enrolled Agents, in describing their professional designation, may not use the term "certified" or imply any type of employment relationship with the IRS.

---

[94] The IRS Whistleblower Office pays money to informers who provide information on tax cheats. If the IRS uses information provided by a whistleblower, it can award him up to 30% of the additional tax, penalty, and other amounts it collects. This program under IRC Section 7623 encourages people to report fraudulent activity.

Examples of acceptable descriptions for Enrolled Agents are "enrolled to represent taxpayers before the Internal Revenue Service," "enrolled to practice before the Internal Revenue Service," and "admitted to practice before the Internal Revenue Service." Practitioners may not use official IRS insignia in their advertising.

A practitioner may not make, directly or indirectly, an uninvited written or oral solicitation of employment in matters related to the Internal Revenue Service if the solicitation violates federal or state law or other applicable rule. Practitioners have the right to make solicitations of employment and advertising involving IRS matters in certain cases. All of the following types of communications are allowed:

- Seeking new business from a former client
- Communicating with a family member
- Targeted mailings
- Non-coercive in-person solicitation while acting as an employee, member or officer of a 501(c)(3) or 501(c)(4) organization (such as a door-to-door fundraiser for the SPCA or a church fundraiser)

Mail solicitations are allowed, as long as the solicitation is not uninvited. A practitioner may attempt to solicit new business from current or former clients, or a client's family. A practitioner may not continue to contact a prospective client who has communicated she does not wish to be solicited.

Practitioners may also send solicitations to other practitioners indicating the practitioner's availability to provide professional services (such as independent contractor bookkeeping or tax preparation services). The advertising and communications must not be misleading, deceptive, or in violation of IRS regulations.

A practitioner may not assist or accept assistance from any person or entity who, to the knowledge of the practitioner, obtains clients or otherwise practices in a manner forbidden under Section 10.30.

Published Fee Schedules

A practitioner may publish and advertise a fee schedule. A practitioner must adhere to the published fee schedule for at least 30 calendar days after it is published. Fee information may be published in newspapers, telephone directories, mailings, e-mail, or by any other method. A practitioner may include fees based on the following:

- Fixed fees for specific routine services
- Hourly fee rates
- Range of fees for particular services
- A fee charged for an initial consultation

In advertising fees on radio or television, the broadcast must be recorded, and the practitioner must retain a record of the recording for at least 36 months (three years) from the date of the last transmission or use.

Example: Travis is an Enrolled Agent. He pays for a radio commercial about his services, and it plays for four months during tax season. Travis is required to keep a copy of the radio commercial for at least 36 months from the last date that the commercial aired.

Unit 3.3: Questions:

1. If an Enrolled Agent has knowledge that a client has filed an erroneous tax return, the practitioner is legally required to _____.

A. Correct the error.
B. Advise the client to correct the error.
C. Do nothing if the practitioner was not the one who prepared the erroneous return.
D. Disengage from any further engagement with the client if the client does not agree to correct the error.

The answer is B. If an Enrolled Agent has knowledge that a client has filed an erroneous tax return, he must advise the client to correct the error. The Enrolled Agent is not required to correct the error, but the practitioner must advise the client about the error and the consequences for not correcting the error. ###

2. David, an Enrolled Agent, wants to hire his friend Brandon, who is also an Enrolled Agent. Brandon has just been disbarred from practice by the IRS for misconduct. Brandon plans to appeal the disbarment. Which of the following statement is TRUE?

A. David can still hire Brandon as an unenrolled preparer, as long as Brandon does not represent any taxpayers and only prepares tax returns.
B. David can still hire Brandon for data entry and other office tasks, as long as he is not signing the tax returns or representing taxpayers in any way.
C. David cannot hire Brandon.
D. David can hire Brandon while he legally appeals his disbarment.

The answer is C. David cannot knowingly hire a disbarred practitioner, regardless of whether that person would be preparing tax returns or not. A practitioner may NOT knowingly employ a person or accept employment from a person who has been disbarred or suspended by the Director of Practice. ###

3. Which of the following statements is CORRECT regarding a client's request for his records in order to comply with federal tax obligations?

A. The practitioner may never return records to the client even if she requests their prompt return.
B. A fee dispute always relieves the practitioner of his responsibility to return a client's records.
C. The practitioner must, at the request of the client, promptly return client records, regardless of any fee dispute.
D. The practitioner must, at the request of the client, return client records within three months of receiving the request.

The answer is C. Original records must be returned upon client demand. A practitioner must return a client's records regardless of any fee dispute. However, unlike in the case of the client's original documents, the practitioner is allowed to withhold the return of his own work papers or preparer work product until the client has resolved any outstanding payment issues. ###

4. Circular 230 covers which of the following topics?

A. Taxpayer ethics and security
B. Individual taxation
C. Ethics and rules of practice for tax practitioners
D. Corporate taxation

The answer is C. Circular 230 covers ethics and rules of practice for tax practitioners who are enrolled to practice before the IRS. ###

5. Which of the following statements is TRUE regarding tax practitioners?

A. Tax preparers cannot be notaries.
B. Enrolled Agents cannot be notaries.
C. EAs cannot notarize documents of the clients they represent before the IRS.
D. A notary that is also a tax practitioner will not be eligible for the e-file program.

The answer is C. Tax practitioners cannot notarize documents of the clients they represent before the IRS. However, they are not prohibited from performing notary services for clients in other matters. ###

6. Which of the following statements is CORRECT?

A. Conflicts of interest do not apply to tax professionals.
B. Tax practitioners may represent clients who have a conflict of interest if waivers are signed by both parties.
C. Tax practitioners may represent clients who have a conflict of interest if the taxpayer informs both parties by phone.
D. Tax practitioners may NOT represent clients who have a conflict of interest.

The answer is B. A tax practitioner can represent conflict of interest clients if the clients are notified and written waivers are signed by both parties.###

7. Enrolled Agents may advertise their services in the following manner:

A. With the phrase "Certified by the IRS"
B. With the phrase "Enrolled to practice before the IRS"
C. With the phrase "An IRS-approved practitioner"
D. With the phrase "A Certified Tax Accountant"

The answer is B. An EA may state that he or she is "enrolled to practice" before the Internal Revenue Service. ###

8. Franklin is an Enrolled Agent. He decides to advertise his fee schedule in the local newspaper. Which of the following fee arrangements is prohibited?

A. Hourly fee rates
B. Fixed fees for tax preparation
C. Contingent fees for an original return based on the refund amount
D. A flat fee for an initial consultation

The answer is C. A practitioner may never charge a contingent fee for an original return that is based on the refund amount. A practitioner may publish and advertise a fee schedule. All the other fees are acceptable. ###

9. Regarding the signature requirements, which of the following is FALSE?

A. A tax preparer may sign a taxpayer's return in lieu of the taxpayer, if the taxpayer cannot sign his own tax return due to a physical disability.
B. A tax preparer may sign a taxpayer's return in lieu of the taxpayer, if the taxpayer cannot sign his own tax return due to an extended absence from the United States.
C. A tax preparer is allowed to forge a taxpayer's signature if he or she has a signed power of attorney.
D. A tax preparer must have a signed power of attorney in order to sign on the taxpayer's behalf.

The answer is C. A preparer is not allowed to forge a taxpayer's signature. A preparer may sign in lieu of the taxpayer. For example, rules permit a representative to sign a taxpayer's return if she is unable to sign the return for any of the following reasons:
•Disease or injury,
•Continuous absence from the United States (including Puerto Rico) for a period of at least 60 days prior to the date required by law for filing the return,
•Other good cause if specific permission is requested of and granted by the IRS.
When a return is signed by a representative, it must be accompanied by a power of attorney authorizing the representative to sign the return. ###

10. Identify the item below that does not describe information a professional tax preparer must maintain about every return prepared:

A. The taxpayer's name and Taxpayer Identification Number
B. The date the return or claim for refund was actually prepared
C. The year of the return
D. The type of return or claim for refund prepared

The answer is B. The date a preparer actually prepared the tax return is not required. A preparer is required to retain a copy of each return for three years after the close of the return period. However, instead of a copy of the return, the preparer may choose to keep a list with the following client information:
•The taxpayers' names
•Taxpayer Identification Numbers
•The tax year
•Types of return or claim prepared ###

11. Ryan is an Enrolled Agent. For the past five years, the information that Hannah provided Ryan to prepare her return included a Schedule K-1 from a partnership showing significant income. However, Ryan did not see a Schedule K-1 from the partnership among the information Hannah provided to him this year. What does due diligence require Ryan to do?

A. Without talking to Hannah, Ryan should estimate the amount that would be reported as income on the Schedule K-1 based on last year's Schedule K-1 and include that amount on Hannah's return.
B. Call Hannah's financial advisor and ask him about Hannah's investments.
C. Nothing because Ryan is required to rely only on the information provided by his client, even if he has reason to know the information is not accurate.
D. Ask Hannah about the fact that she did not provide him with the partnership's Schedule K-1, as she had the previous year.

The answer is D. A practitioner has a "duty to advise." This means that a practitioner who knows his client has not complied with the revenue laws or has made an error in or omission from any return, document, affidavit, or other required paper has the responsibility to advise the client promptly of the noncompliance, error, or omission. ###

12. When does the authorization for a "third party designee" expire?

A. Three months after the return is filed.
B. One year after the return is filed.
C. Three years after the return is filed.
D. On the due date of the next tax return.

The answer is D. A third party designee authorization automatically expires on the due date of the next tax return. The designee may address any issue arising out of the tax return for a period not to exceed one year from the due date of the tax return. The designee may also receive written account information including transcripts upon request. ###

Unit 3.4: Taxpayer Responsibility, Tax Fraud, and Penalties

More Reading:
Publication 583, *Starting a Business and Keeping Records*
Publication 552, *Recordkeeping for Individuals*
Publication 947, *Practice Before the IRS and Power of Attorney*

Basic Recordkeeping Requirements

There are some basic record-keeping requirements expected of U.S. taxpayers that tax preparers need to be familiar with and make sure their clients understand. Recordkeeping requirements are tested on all three parts of the EA exam. Part 3 of the EA exam focuses on the substantiation of items. There are also specific recordkeeping requirements relating to the Earned Income Tax Credit that are tested on Part 3 (the due diligence requirements for EITC claims are covered later).

Except in a few cases, the law does not require specific kind of records to be kept. Any records that clearly substantiate expenses, basis, and income should be retained. Generally, this means the taxpayer must keep records that support an item of income or deduction on a return until the period of limitations for the tax return runs out. The IRS recommends that taxpayers keep all sales slips, invoices, receipts, canceled checks, or other financial account statements relating to a particular transaction.

A taxpayer may choose any recordkeeping system that clearly reflects income and expenses. He must keep records as long as they may be needed for the administration of any provision of the Internal Revenue Code. If a taxpayer or business decides to use a computer record-keeping system, she must still retain a record of original documents. However, these documents may be scanned or kept on a computer imaging system. The IRS generally does not require a taxpayer to keep original paper records (Rev. Proc. 97-22).

A business is required to retain payroll and employment tax records for at least four years after filing the fourth quarter for the year. These records must be available for IRS review. Examples include copies of employees' income tax withholding allowance certificates (Forms W-4), records of fringe benefits provided, and dates and amounts of payroll tax deposits made.

Records Retention

As mentioned, records must be kept until the statute of limitations for the tax return runs out. In general, the period of limitations is the later of either of the following:

- Three years after the date the return was filed, or
- Two years after the date the tax was paid.

Records relating to the basis of property should be retained as long as they may be material to any tax return involving the property. The basis of property is material until the statute of limitations expires for the tax year the asset is sold or disposed of. Taxpayers must keep these records to figure any depreciation, amortization, or depletion deductions, and to figure the asset's basis.

> **Example:** Tom has owned a vacation home for eight years, but in 2010 he decides to sell it. In order to compute basis and his gains on the property, he should have the records relating to the purchase of the property, and any other events that would add or subtract from his basis. He reports the sale of the vacation home on his 2010 return. He must continue to retain the records relating to the sale of the property until the statute of limitations for the tax return expires, usually three years from the date of filing or the due date of the return, whichever is later.

There are longer record retention periods in some cases. If the taxpayer fails to report income that exceeds more than 25% of the gross income shown on his return, the statute of limitations is six years. If the taxpayer files a claim from a loss of worthless securities, then the period is seven years.

If the taxpayer files a fraudulent return, there is no statute of limitations on the return. If a tax return is not filed, there is no time limit on the number of years that the IRS can audit the return.

Statute of Limitations	
Type of return	**Minimum Retention Period**
Normal tax return	3 years
Omitted income that exceeds 25% of the gross income shown on the return	6 years
A fraudulent return	No limit
No return filed	No limit
A claim for credit or amended return	The later of 3 years or 2 years after tax was paid
A claim for a loss from worthless securities	7 years

Tax Avoidance vs. Tax Evasion

The term "tax avoidance" is not defined by the IRS, but the term is commonly used to describe the legal reduction of taxable income. Most taxpayers use at least a few methods of tax avoidance in order to reduce their taxable income.

> **Example:** Nate contributes to his employer-sponsored retirement plans with pretax funds. He also uses an employer-based Flexible Spending Account for his medical expenses, which reduces his taxable income by making all of his medical expenses pretax. Nate is using legal tax avoidance in order to reduce his taxable income.

Tax evasion, on the other hand, is an illegal practice where individuals, organizations, or corporations intentionally avoid paying their true tax liability. All citizens must comply with tax law. Fortunately, most Americans recognize their civic duty and comply with their tax obligations. Taxpayers who fail to file income tax returns and pay their taxes pose a serious threat to tax administration and the American economy. Their actions undermine public confidence in the IRS's ability to administer the tax laws effectively.

Those caught evading taxes are generally subject to criminal charges and substantial penalties.

Penalties Imposed Upon Taxpayers

The IRS has numerous penalties that can be imposed upon the taxpayer. These penalties range from civil fines to imprisonment for criminal tax evasion. If a taxpayer does not file her return on time, she will be subject to a late filing penalty. If a taxpayer does not pay his taxes on time, he will be subject to additional penalties and interest. These penalties are called the "failure to file" and "failure to pay" penalties. They are the most common IRS penalties.

Failure-to-file Penalty

If a taxpayer does not file her tax return by the due date, including extensions, she may be liable for a failure-to-file penalty. The penalty is 5% for each month that the return is late, but not more than 25%. The penalty is based on the tax not paid by the due date, without regard to extensions. If the taxpayer files her return more than 60 days after the due date, the minimum penalty is $100 or 100% of the tax on the return, whichever is less. If the taxpayer is owed a refund, there generally will not be a failure-to-file penalty.

Failure-to-pay Penalty

A taxpayer will be subject to a failure-to-pay penalty of ½ of 1% (0.5%) of unpaid taxes for each month after the due date that the tax is not paid. If the taxpayer filed for an extension, this penalty does not apply so long as he paid at least 90% of his tax liability on or before the due date of the return.

The failure-to-pay penalty rate increases to a full 1% per month for any tax that remains unpaid the day after a demand for immediate payment is issued, or ten days after notice of intent to levy certain assets is issued. For taxpayers who filed on time but are unable to pay their tax liabilities, the failure-to-pay penalty rate is reduced to ¼ of 1% (0.25 %) per month during any month in which the taxpayer has a valid installment agreement with the IRS.

For any month both the penalty for filing late and the penalty for paying late apply, the penalty for filing late is reduced by the penalty for paying late for that month, unless the minimum penalty for filing late is charged.

Penalties are payable upon notice and demand. Penalties are generally assessed, collected, and paid in the same manner as taxes. The taxpayer will receive a notice that contains:

- The name of the penalty,
- The applicable code section, and
- How the penalty was computed.

Accuracy-Related Penalties

The two most common accuracy-related penalties are the "substantial understatement" penalty and the "negligence or disregard of regulations" penalty. These penalties are calculated as a flat 20% of the net understatement of tax. In addition to other penalties, if the taxpayer provides fraudulent information on his tax return, he can be subject to a civil fraud penalty.

Penalty for Substantial Understatement

The understatement is considered "substantial" if it is more than the larger of:

- 10% of the correct tax, or

- $5,000 for individuals.

A taxpayer may avoid the "substantial understatement" penalty if she has substantial authority (such as court cases or a Private Letter Ruling) for her position or through adequate disclosure.

To avoid the substantial understatement penalty by adequate disclosure, the taxpayer (or tax preparer) must properly disclose the position on the tax return and there must be at least a reasonable basis for the position.

Trust Fund Recovery Penalty (TFRP)

The Trust Fund Recovery Penalty is also called the "100% Penalty" because the IRS will assess a tax of "100%" of the amount due. This topic is very important to the IRS and is frequently tested on Part 2 and Part 3 of the EA Exam. It applies to employers and to preparers, because there is a strong ethical component to this issue.

As authorized by IRC Section 6672, this penalty involves the income and Social Security taxes an employer withholds from the wages of employees. These taxes are called "trust fund" taxes because they are held in trust for the government. They have been withheld from an employee's paycheck, so the employer is required to remit them to the IRS.

Sometimes, when business owners have financial trouble, they neglect to remit these taxes to the IRS. However, the IRS is very aggressive in pursuing trust fund penalty cases. The Trust Fund Recovery Penalty can be assessed against anyone who is considered a "responsible person" in the business. This includes corporate officers, directors, stockholders, and even employees. The IRS has assessed the penalty against accountants, bookkeepers, or even clerical staff, particularly if they have authority to sign checks. In determining whether to proceed with assertion of the TFRP, the IRS must determine:

- Responsibility, and
- Willfulness.

A person must be both "responsible" and "willful" to be liable for an employer's failure to collect or pay trust fund taxes to the United States. This means that he knew (or should have known) that the payroll taxes were not being remitted to the IRS, and that he also had the power to correct the problem. Usually, this means that the individual had check-signing authority.

Example: Shelly works for Wayne Construction, Inc. She is a full-time bookkeeper, and she does all the payroll tax reporting. Shelly has check-signing authority so she can pay the utilities and other bills when her boss is working off-site. In 2010, her boss has a heart attack, and his wife, Doreen, takes over the business in his absence. Doreen can't manage the business properly and the business soon falls into debt. Doreen tells Shelly to pay vendors first. The business continues to withhold taxes from employee paychecks, but does not remit the amounts to the IRS. Eventually, the business goes under and Doreen disappears. Shelly is contacted by the IRS shortly thereafter. Even though Shelly was "just an employee" the IRS can assess the Trust Fund Recovery Penalty against her, because (1) she had check-signing authority, and (2) she knew that the business was not lawfully remitting payroll taxes to the IRS as required.

The Trust Fund Recovery Penalty may be assessed *in addition* to any other penalties including the penalties for failure to file, failure to pay, or fraud penalties.

Alteration of the Jurat is Prohibited

Some taxpayers attempt to reduce their federal tax liability by striking out the written declaration (the jurat) that verifies a return, declaration, statement, or other document is made under penalties of perjury (as required by IRC section 6065). The IRS also is aware that some people, including unethical return preparers, advise taxpayers to take frivolous positions, which include striking or otherwise invalidating the jurat.

Striking out or altering the jurat on a tax return is prohibited.

Example: A taxpayer files Form 1040 for the 2010 tax year. The taxpayer signs the form but crosses out the jurat on the return and writes the word "void" across it. This return is now considered a frivolous return.

Potentially applicable civil penalties for altering a jurat include:

- A $500 penalty imposed under Section 6702;
- Additional penalties for failure to file a return, failure to pay tax owed, and fraudulent failure to file a return; and
- A penalty of up to $25,000 under Section 6673 if the taxpayer makes frivolous arguments in the United States Tax Court.

Taxpayers relying on these frivolous positions also may face criminal prosecution for attempting to evade tax, for which the penalty is a significant fine and imprisonment for up to five years; and willful failure to file a return, for which the penalty is a significant fine and imprisonment for up to a year.

Civil Fraud Penalty

If there is any underpayment of tax due to fraud, a penalty of 75% of the underpayment will be assessed against the taxpayer. The fraud penalty on a joint return does not automatically apply to a spouse unless some part of the underpayment is due to the fraud of that spouse. Negligence or simple ignorance of the law does not constitute fraud.

Typically, IRS examiners who find strong evidence of fraud will refer the case to the Internal Revenue Service Criminal Investigation Division for possible criminal prosecution.

Frivolous Tax Return Penalty

Any taxpayer who files a tax return that is patently frivolous may have to pay a penalty of $5,000. This penalty can be doubled on a joint return. A taxpayer will be subject to this penalty if he files a tax return based simply on the desire to interfere with the administration of tax law.

This includes tax protestor arguments, and altering or striking out the preprinted language above the signature block on a tax return. This penalty is in addition to any other penalty provided by law.

Anti-Tax Law Schemes

Some assert that they are not required to file federal tax returns because the filing of a tax return is voluntary. In a similar vein, some argue that they are not required to pay federal taxes because the payment of federal taxes is voluntary. Proponents of this position argue that our system of taxation is based upon voluntary assessment and payment.

Some tax protestors maintain that there is no federal statute imposing a tax on income derived from sources within the United States by citizens or residents of the United States. They argue instead that federal income taxes are excise taxes imposed only on nonresident aliens and foreign corporations for the privilege of receiving income from sources within the United States.

Some individuals argue that they have rejected citizenship in the United States in favor of state citizenship; therefore, they are relieved of their federal income tax obligations. A variation of this argument is that a person is a freeborn citizen of a particular state and thus was never a citizen of the United States. The underlying theme of these arguments is the same: the person is not a United States citizen and is not subject to federal tax laws because only United States citizens are subject to these laws.

In addition to tax protestors, there are many other ways taxpayers attempt to defraud the government by not paying their rightful tax. All of the following are illegal schemes, and anyone participating in them or promoting them can be liable for civil and criminal penalties:

- Abusive Home-Based Business Schemes
- Abusive Trust Schemes
- Misuse of the Disabled Access Credit
- Abusive Offshore Schemes
- Employee Plans Abusive Tax Transactions
- Exempt Organization Abusive Tax Avoidance Transactions

Failure to Supply Social Security Number

If a taxpayer does not include a Social Security Number (SSN) or the SSN of another person where required on a return, statement, or other document, he will be subject to a penalty of $50 for each failure. The taxpayer will also be subject to the $50 penalty if he does not give the SSN to another person when it is required on a return, statement, or other document.

Fraudulent Returns

The IRS takes fraudulent returns very seriously. Taxpayers must take responsibility for their own actions. Should a taxpayer choose to participate in a fraudulent trust scheme or other fraudulent tax scheme, the taxpayer will not be shielded from potential civil and criminal sanctions, regardless of whether or not they used a tax preparer.

Preparers should be conscious of "fraud indicators" when preparing tax returns. Some common indicators of fraudulent returns may be:

- Unsatisfactory or evasive responses to filing status questions;
- Multiple returns with the same address; and
- Missing or incomplete Schedules A and C income and expense documentation.

A "fraudulent return" also includes a return in which the individual is attempting to file using someone else's name or SSN, or when the taxpayer is presenting documents or information that have no basis in fact. A potentially abusive return also includes a return that contains inaccurate information that may lead to an understatement of a liability or the overstatement of a credit resulting in a refund to which the taxpayer is not entitled.

Violations of the Internal Revenue Code may result in civil penalties and also criminal prosecution.

Client Fraud

The IRS encourages tax preparers to look for client fraud. Sometimes, the taxpayer is merely negligent or careless, or may have an honest difference of opinion regarding the deductibility of an expense. If fraud is actually taking place, there are some common "badges of fraud" that the IRS looks for. Some examples include:

- The understatement of income or improper deductions
- Personal items deducted as business expenses
- The overstatement of deductions, or taking improper credits
- Making false entries in documents or destroying records
- Not cooperating with the IRS, or avoiding IRS contact
- Concealing or transferring assets
- Engaging in illegal activity
- Sloppy recordkeeping
- All-cash businesses

Some of these actions taken by themselves do not necessarily constitute fraud. However, consistent abuses or multiple "red flags" may be a reason to suspect taxpayer fraud.

Return Preparer Fraud

Tax professionals are sometimes guilty of preparer fraud. Preparer fraud generally involves the preparation and filing of false income tax returns (in either paper or electronic form) by preparers who claim inflated personal or business expenses, false deductions, unallowable credits, or excessive exemptions on returns prepared for their clients. Preparers may also manipulate income figures to obtain fraudulent tax credits, such as the Earned Income Tax Credit (EITC).

The preparers' clients may or may not have knowledge of the false expenses, deductions, exemptions and/or credits shown on their tax returns. The fraudulent preparers derive financial benefit from this activity by:

- Diverting a portion of the refund for their own benefit;
- Increasing their clientele by developing a reputation for obtaining large refunds; and/or
- Charging inflated fees for the return preparation.

Preparer Penalties for Fraudulent Returns

The IRS imposes severe penalties on tax return preparers who prepare returns taking positions that are not fully supported by current law. Congress has amended Section 6694 by extending penalties to all tax return preparers and by raising the standard that preparers must meet to avoid the Section 6694(a) preparer penalty.

All paid tax return preparers are subject to civil penalties for actions ranging from knowingly preparing a return that understates the taxpayer's liability to failing to sign or provide an identification number on a return they prepare. Tax return preparers who demonstrate a pattern of misconduct may be banned from preparing further returns. Additionally, the IRS may pursue and impose criminal penalties against a tax return preparer for the severe misconduct.

For the purpose of preparer penalties, a tax preparer may rely in good faith upon information furnished by the taxpayer or a previous preparer, and is not required to independently verify or review the items reported on tax returns to determine if they are likely to be upheld if challenged by the IRS.

However, the tax return preparer must make "reasonable inquiries" if the information appears to be incorrect or incomplete. A tax return preparer is not considered to have complied with the "good faith" requirements if:

- The advice is unreasonable on its face;
- The tax return preparer knew or should have known that the third party advisor was not aware of all relevant facts; or
- The tax return preparer knew or should have known (given the nature of the tax return preparer's practice) at the time the tax return or claim for refund was prepared, that the advice was no longer reliable due to developments in the law since the time the advice was given (IRS Notice 2008-13).

Example: Franco is an Enrolled Agent. During a client interview conducted by Franco, the taxpayer, Susie, states she made a $50,000 charitable contribution of real estate during the tax year when in fact she did not make this charitable contribution. Franco does not inquire about the existence of a qualified appraisal or complete Form 8283 in accordance with the reporting and substantiation requirements under Section 170(f)(11). Franco reports deductions on the tax return for the charitable contribution, which results in an understatement of liability for tax. In this case, Franco is subject to a penalty under Section 6694.

If a preparer willfully understates a client's tax liability, she is subject to penalties. Under IRS regulations, "understatement of liability" means:

- Understating net tax payable
- Overstating the net amount creditable or refundable
- Taking a position with no realistic possibility of success

The understatement penalty is not imposed if the relevant facts affecting the item's tax treatment are adequately disclosed in the return or in a statement attached to the return, unless the position is frivolous.

A preparer may be excused from the penalty if she acted in good faith and there was reasonable cause for the understatement.

Potential Preparer Penalties

Tax preparers are subject to the following penalties for:

Failure to furnish a copy of the return: A tax preparer who fails to furnish a copy of the tax return to a client may be subject to a penalty of $50 per failure, up to a maximum penalty of $25,000. This penalty may be waived if the failure is due to reasonable cause and not due to willful neglect.

Failure to furnish an identifying number: A tax preparer who fails to furnish an identifying number (PTIN) on a tax return may be subject to a penalty of $50 per failure, up to a maximum penalty of $25,000. This penalty also may be waived if the failure is due to reasonable cause and not due to willful neglect.

Abusive tax shelters: Any tax preparer who organizes, sells, or promotes an abusive tax shelter will be subject to IRS penalties of $1,000 for each activity, or 100% of the gross income derived from the activity (whichever is less).

Failure to sign a tax return, or failure to retain a copy of a client's return: A tax preparer who fails to sign a tax return or who fails to retain copies of returns (or list of tax returns) that he has prepared will be subject to a $50 penalty for each failure, up to a maximum of $25,000.

Negotiation of a taxpayer refund check: Any negotiation (cashing) of a taxpayer's refund check is specifically prohibited. Any tax preparer that cashes or endorses a taxpayer's refund check will be subject to a $500 penalty for each violation. A preparer may never negotiate a taxpayer's refund check, regardless of the circumstances. Even if a tax preparer has a power of attorney on file and the taxpayer has given written permission, it is still a prohibited act.

Understatement of Taxpayer Liability

There are two specific penalties when an income tax preparer understates a taxpayer's liability.

Understatement Due to an Unrealistic Position

If there is an understatement on a tax return due to an unrealistic position, the penalty is the greater of:

- $1,000 per tax return, or
- 50% of the additional income upon which the penalty was imposed.

This applies when a preparer knows (or reasonably should have known) that the position was unrealistic and would not have been sustained on its merits. However, if the position is adequately disclosed on a tax return, this penalty will not apply. In the case of a patently frivolous position (such as a tax protestor position), the penalty will apply whether or not it is disclosed.

Understatement due to Negligent or Willful Disregard

If a tax preparer shows negligent or willful disregard of IRS rules and regulations, and makes a willful or reckless attempt to understate tax liability, the penalty is the greater of:

- $5,000, or
- 50% of the additional income upon which the penalty was imposed.

If a tax preparer is subject to a penalty for understatement of liability and this includes a change to the Earned Income Tax Credit (EITC), then the preparer may be subject to additional penalties for failure to exercise due diligence while claiming EITC. These penalties apply per tax return.

A tax preparer may avoid these harsh penalties if she relied on the advice of another preparer in good faith. The penalty may also be avoided if the position is adequately disclosed on a tax return and is not patently frivolous. In this case, a tax preparer would bear the burden of proof.

The "Realistic Possibility" Standard

Internal Revenue Code (IRC) Section 6694 establishes the standard by which a tax preparer may take a position. For a preparer to establish "realistic possibility," the position taken on a tax return must have a greater than 50% chance of being sustained on its merits, based on a reasonable and well-informed analysis by a knowledgeable person.

Penalty Abatement

If a preparer penalty is assessed against a tax preparer and he does not agree with the assessment, the preparer may request a conference with the IRS officer or agent and explain why the penalty is not warranted. The preparer may also wait for the penalty to be assessed, pay the penalty within 30 days, and then file a claim for refund.

IRC Section 6694 states that the understatement penalty will be abated if, under final judicial decision, it is found that there is no actual understatement of liability. Sometimes this will occur when a tax court case is decided in favor of the taxpayer.

Judicial Proceedings for Censure, Suspension, or Disbarment

In general, there are four broad categories of preparer misconduct, all of which may be subject to disciplinary action:

- Misconduct while representing a taxpayer
- Misconduct related to the practitioner's own return
- Giving a false opinion, knowingly, recklessly, or through gross incompetence
- Misconduct not directly involving IRS representation

The Secretary of the Treasury, after notice and an opportunity for a proceeding, may censure, suspend, or disbar any practitioner from practice before the IRS if the practitioner is shown to be incompetent or disreputable; fails to comply with any regulation or with intent to defraud; or willfully and knowingly misleads or threatens a client or prospective client.

The Difference between Disbarment, Suspension, and Censure

Official sanctions include disbarment, suspension, censure, and reprimand. Disbarment is the permanent revocation of a practitioner's privilege to represent taxpayers before the IRS.

When the final decision in a judicial proceeding is for disbarment, the practitioner will not be allowed to practice in any capacity before the IRS (except to represent himself). If the final decision in the case is for suspension, the practitioner will not be permitted to practice before the IRS during the suspension period.

Sometimes, the final decision is for an official censure. A censure is a public reprimand. Unlike disbarment or suspension, censure does not affect an individual's eligibility to practice before the IRS. After being subject to OPR sanctions of either suspension or censure, the practitioner may be subject to conditions on her ability to practice.

OPR may entertain a petition for reinstatement from any disbarred practitioner after the expiration of five years following the disbarment.

Potential Disciplinary Sanctions

The Office of Professional Responsibility may impose a wide range of sanctions upon preparers. The disciplinary sanctions to be imposed for violation of the regulations are:

Disbarred from practice before the IRS—An individual who is disbarred is not eligible to represent taxpayers before the IRS.

Suspended from practice before the IRS—An individual who is suspended is not eligible to represent taxpayers before the IRS during the term of the suspension.

Censured in practice before the IRS—Censure is a public reprimand. Unlike disbarment or suspension, censure does not affect an individual's eligibility to represent taxpayers before the IRS, but OPR may subject the individual's future representations to conditions designed to promote high standards of conduct.

Monetary penalty—A monetary penalty may be imposed on an individual who engages in conduct subject to sanction or on an employer, firm, or entity if the individual was acting on its behalf and if it knew, or reasonably should have known, of the individual's conduct.

Disqualification of appraiser—An appraiser who is disqualified is barred from presenting evidence or testimony in any administrative proceeding before the Department of the Treasury or the IRS.[95]

Incompetence and Disreputable Conduct §10.51

Incompetence and disreputable conduct for which a practitioner may be disbarred is outlined in Section 10.51 of Circular 230. The IRS lists many possible instances in which a practitioner might be disbarred or censured for disreputable or incompetent representation.

---

[95] A qualified appraiser is an individual who is assigns an official value to donated property. To find out more about IRS qualified appraisers, see IRS **Publication 561,** *Determining the Value of Donated Property.*

Gross incompetence includes conduct that reflects gross indifference, preparation which is grossly inadequate under the circumstances, and a consistent failure to perform obligations to the client. Disreputable conduct for which a practitioner may be sanctioned or disbarred includes:

- Conviction of any criminal offense under federal tax laws
- Giving false or misleading information, or participating in any way in the giving of false or misleading information to the Department of the Treasury
- Solicitation of employment as prohibited under Circular 230 or the use of false or misleading representations with intent to deceive a client
- Willfully failing to file a federal tax return in violation of the federal tax laws, or willfully evading or attempting to evade any assessment or payment of any federal tax
- Willfully assisting, counseling, or encouraging a client in violating any federal tax law, or knowingly counseling or suggesting to a client an illegal plan to evade federal taxes or payment thereof
- Misappropriation of funds received from a client for the purpose of payment of taxes
- Directly or indirectly attempting to influence any officer of the Internal Revenue Service by the use of threats, false accusations, duress, coercion, or bribery
- Disbarment or suspension from practice as an attorney, Certified Public Accountant, public accountant, or actuary
- Knowingly aiding and abetting another person to practice before the Internal Revenue Service during a period of suspension, disbarment, or ineligibility of such other person
- Contemptuous conduct in connection with practice before the Internal Revenue Service, including the use of abusive language, making false accusations or statements knowing them to be false, or circulating or publishing malicious or libelous matter
- Giving a false opinion knowingly, recklessly, or through gross incompetence
- Willfully failing to sign a tax return prepared by the practitioner when the practitioner's signature is required by federal tax laws unless the failure is due to reasonable cause and not due to willful neglect
- Willfully disclosing or otherwise using a tax return or tax return information in a manner not authorized by the Internal Revenue Code

Conferences and Voluntary Consents §10.61

If the Office of Professional Responsibility has evidence or allegations of misconduct, the Director of OPR may confer with the practitioner, employer, firm, or other party concerning the allegations. A formal proceeding does not have to be instituted in order for the OPR to confer with other parties regarding the alleged misconduct.

In general, a practitioner may offer consent to be sanctioned under Section 10.50 in lieu of a formal proceeding. The Director of the OPR may, in his discretion, accept or decline the practitioner's consent to a sanction. The Director may accept a revised offer submitted in response to his rejection or may counteroffer and act upon any accepted counteroffer.

> **Example:** Tim is a CPA. In 2010, Tim was disbarred by his state society and his license revoked for a felony act not related to his tax practice. Even though his CPA license was revoked for a separate issue, the Office of Professional Responsibility still considers this disreputable conduct. Since Tim has been stripped of his license, he is not enrolled to practice before the IRS. He can be permanently disbarred or censured by the OPR.

Complaints Against a Tax Practitioner §10.62

The OPR can issue a formal complaint against a practitioner. In order for the complaint to be valid, the complaint must:

- Name the respondent.
- Provide a clear and concise description of the facts.
- Be signed by the Director of the OPR.
- Specify the sanction wanted by the OPR. If the sanction wanted is a suspension, the duration of the suspension sought must be specified.

A complaint is considered sufficient if it informs the respondent of the charges so that the respondent is able to prepare a defense.

The OPR must notify the practitioner of the deadline for answering the complaint. The deadline may not be less than 30 days from the date of service of the complaint. The OPR must also give the name and address of the administrative law judge with whom the response must be filed, and the name and address of the employee representing the OPR.

Service of Complaint §10.63

IRC Section 10.63 details the requirements for the actual service of the complaint. The complaint must be served to the practitioner by any of the following methods:

- Mailed by Certified Mail to the last known address of the respondent.
- If the Certified Mail is not claimed or accepted by the respondent, or is returned undelivered, service may be made by mailing the complaint to the respondent by First Class mail. Service by this method will be considered complete upon mailing, provided the complaint is addressed to the respondent at her last known address.
- Made in person or by leaving the complaint at the office or place of business of the respondent.

Within ten days of serving the complaint, copies of the evidence in support of the complaint must also be served to the respondent (practitioner).

The practitioner must respond to the complaint by the deadline outlined in the letter. The OPR may file a reply to the practitioner's answer, but unless otherwise ordered by the administrative law judge, no formal reply to the practitioner's answer is required. If the practitioner fails to respond to the complaint, the failure constitutes an admission of guilt and a waiver of the hearing. The administrative law judge may make a decision on the case by default without a hearing or further procedure.

During a hearing, the practitioner may appear in person, or be represented by an attorney or another practitioner. The Director of the OPR may be represented by an attorney or other employee of the IRS.

If either party to the judicial proceeding fails to appear at the hearing, the absent party shall be deemed to have waived the right to a hearing, and the administrative law judge may make his decision against the absent party by default. The administrative law judge must provide a copy of his decision to the Director of the OPR and to the practitioner (or to the practitioner's authorized representative).

The practitioner may file an appeal of the judge's decision with the Secretary of the Treasury, and not to the OPR.

Unit 3.4: Questions

1. Carlos owns a business and he has three employees. How long is Carlos required to keep his employment tax records?

A. Three years
B. Six years
C. Five years
D. Four years

The answer is D. A taxpayer or business is required to keep records relating to employment taxes for at least four years after filing the fourth quarter for the year. Employment and payroll records should be available for IRS review. Examples include copies of employees' income tax withholding allowance certificates (Forms W-4), and dates and amounts of payroll tax deposits made. ###

2. Records relating to the basis of an asset must be retained _____.

A. As long as the records are material.
B. A minimum of three years.
C. A minimum of four years.
D. The records for assets should not be retained after the filing of a tax return for which the records are applicable.

The answer is A. Records relating to the basis of property should be retained as long as they may be material to any tax return involving the property. The basis of property is material until the statute of limitations expires for the tax year the asset is sold or disposed of. ###

3. If there is substantial unreported income (over 25%), the IRS may audit tax returns for up to _____ after the filing date.

A. Three years
B. Five years
C. Six years
D. Indefinitely

The answer is C. In most cases, tax returns can be audited for up to three years after filing. However, the IRS may audit for up to six years if there is substantial unreported income. ###

4. Records for claim of loss from a worthless security should be kept for:

A. Two years
B. Three years
C. Four years
D. Seven years

The answer is D. Records relating to a claim for a loss from worthless securities should be kept for seven years. That is because a taxpayer can file an amended return to take a loss on a worthless security up to seven years after the filing date. ###

5. Colleen owns a business and has never filed a tax return. How long should she keep her records?

A. Three years if she owes additional tax
B. Seven years if she files a claim for a loss from worthless securities
C. No limit if she does not file a return
D. All of the above

The answer is C. A taxpayer must keep records as long as they are needed for the administration of any provision of the IRC. Taxpayers must keep records that support an item of income or deductions on a tax return until the period of limitations for that return runs out. If a tax return is not filed, there is no time limit. ###

6. Which statement listed below is INCORRECT?

A. If no other provisions apply, the statute of limitations for an IRS examination of a return is three years after the return was filed.
B. If more than 25% of gross income has been omitted from the tax return, the statute of limitations is six years after the return was filed.
C. If a fraudulent return is filed, the statute of limitations is seven years.
D. If a tax return is not filed at all, there is no statute of limitations.

The answer is D. If a fraudulent tax return is filed, there is no statute of limitations for collection. Under federal law, a tax return is "fraudulent" if the taxpayer files it knowing that the return either omits taxable income or claims one or more deductions that are not allowable. ###

7. Which of the following is TRUE?

A. The IRS may not disbar a preparer without first seeking a legal criminal prosecution.
B. Even without bringing a criminal prosecution the IRS may choose to disbar an income tax return preparer.
C. A preparer is not liable for any preparer penalties if he diverts a portion of the refund to himself with the client's permission.
D. None of the above.

The answer is B. Even without bringing a criminal prosecution the IRS may choose to disbar or prevent an income tax return preparer from engaging in specific abusive practices. ###

8. With the taxpayer's properly notarized approval, a tax return preparer who is an attorney, Certified Public Accountant, Enrolled Agent, or Enrolled Actuary may receive and endorse a taxpayer's refund check and invest the proceeds in the taxpayer's own mutual fund.

A. True
B. False

The answer is B, False. Income tax return preparers who endorse or negotiate a client's refund check are subject to a $500 penalty. The IRS has taken a firm stand on a strict interpretation of the statute. Negotiation of a taxpayer's refund check is always prohibited, regardless of whether the client gives permission or not. ###

9. Mel is an Enrolled Agent. He submits his clients' returns via IRS e-file, and in order to save paper, does not give a copy of the prepared tax return to his clients if they do not request it. Which of the following is TRUE?

A. Mel is not in violation of Circular 230.
B. Mel is in violation of Circular 230.
C. Mel is not violating Circular 230 if he gives clients the option of receiving a copy of their return for a small fee.
D. Mel may offer a copy of the return to the client only if the client asks for it.

The answer is B. IRC Section 6107(a) requires tax return preparers to furnish copies of completed returns and claims for refund to all their clients. This must be done no later than when clients sign the original documents. ###

10. The IRS penalties for willful disregard concerning an understatement of income tax on a client's return or claim for refund is:

A. $500
B. $750
C. $1,000
D. $5,000

The answer is C. When an understatement of income tax on a client's return is due to the return preparer's willful attempt to understate the tax liability, the preparer may be subject to a penalty of $1,000 under IRC Section 6694(b). ###

11. Phil, an Enrolled Agent, prepares Richard's income tax return. Richard gives Phil power of attorney, including the authorization to receive his federal income tax refund check. Accordingly, the IRS sends Richard's $1,000 refund check to Phil's office. Richard is very slow in paying his bills and owes Phil $500 for tax services. Phil should:

A. Use Richard's check as collateral for a loan to tide him over until Richard pays him.
B. Refuse to give Richard the check until he pays him the $500.
C. Get Richard's written authorization to endorse the check, cash the check, and reduce the amount Richard owes him.
D. Turn the check directly over to Richard.

The answer is D. Tax preparers must not endorse or otherwise cash any refund check issued to the taxpayer. A tax preparer cannot withhold a taxpayer's refund check because of a fee dispute. However, a tax preparer is not required to file a client's tax return without first obtaining payment. ###

12. Julia, an Enrolled Agent, prepares Linda's income tax return. Linda sold some stock in a corporation and believes the proceeds of the stock are all a return to capital and therefore not included in her gross income. After research, Julia determines that there is some reasonable basis for Linda's position, but she does not believe there is a realistic possibility of success on the merits. Under what circumstances can Julia sign Linda's return if the proceeds are not included in income reported on the return?

A. If the position is not frivolous and is adequately disclosed on the return
B. If Julia documents her disagreement with Linda's position and keeps it in her file
C. If Linda agrees in writing not to dispute any IRS challenge to the position
D. Under no circumstances

The answer is A. Generally, a preparer can avoid the accuracy-related penalty if the position is adequately disclosed and the position has at least a reasonable basis. "Reasonable basis" is a high standard of tax reporting that is significantly higher than "not frivolous." The reasonable basis standard is not satisfied by a return position that is merely arguable. A "reasonable basis" for a disclosed position is one that has approximately 10% or greater chance of success if challenged. This means that the position must be more than just arguable. There must be some authority supporting the position, such as a court case. ###

13. What is the penalty for failing to provide a required Social Security Number on a tax return?

A. $50 per failure
B. $50 per return
C. $100 per failure
D. $500 per failure

The answer is A. If a taxpayer does not include a Social Security Number (SSN) or the SSN of another person where required on a return, statement, or other document, the taxpayer will be subject to a penalty of $50 for each failure. The taxpayer will also be subject to the penalty of $50 if he does not give the SSN to another person when it is required on a return, statement, or other document. ###

14. Glen is a Certified Public Accountant who prepares income tax returns for his clients. One of his clients submitted a list of expenses to be claimed on Schedule C of the tax return. Glen qualifies as a return preparer and, as such, is required to comply with which one of the following conditions?

A. Glen is required to independently verify the client's information.
B. Glen can ignore implications of information known by him.
C. Inquiry is not required if the information appears to be incorrect or incomplete.
D. Appropriate inquiries are required to determine whether the client has substantiation for travel and entertainment expenses.

The answer is D. The preparer is not required to independently examine evidence of deductions. A preparer may rely in good faith without verification upon information furnished by the taxpayer if it does not appear to be incorrect or incomplete. However, the tax preparer must make reasonable inquiries about the validity of the information. ###

15. A preparer who has been disbarred from practice may still practice before the IRS in the following instances:

A. Only in representing himself.
B. A disbarred individual may practice only in cases where a Form 2848, *Power of Attorney and Declaration of Representative*, has been signed prior to the date of the disbarment.
C. A disbarred individual may still practice before the IRS on the examination level.
D. A disbarred individual is allowed to practice only before the Criminal Investigation Division.

The answer is A. Individuals who are not eligible or who have lost the privilege of enrollment cannot practice before the IRS. If an individual loses eligibility to practice, any existing power of attorney will not be recognized by the IRS. However, a disbarred individual may still represent himself before the IRS. ###

16. Melissa, an Enrolled Agent, was notified of a judicial ruling that she committed acts of gross misconduct and violated the rules of Circular 230, and, therefore, a decision was entered that she should be disbarred. Which of the following is TRUE?

A. Melissa has a right to appeal the decision to the Secretary of the Treasury.
B. Melissa has a right to appeal the decision to the Office of Professional Responsibility.
C. Melissa cannot appeal the disbarment decision.
D. Melissa has a right to appeal the decision to the Commissioner of the IRS.

The answer is A. An Enrolled Agent has a right to appeal the decision for disbarment to the Secretary of the Treasury. ###

17. Mary, an Enrolled Agent, prepared a tax return for a client. The return contained a frivolous position that could not be defended under any circumstances. The examiner who conducted the examination made a referral to the Office of Professional Responsibility. After all procedural requirements have been met, who will make the final, binding decision as to the appropriate sanction for Mary?

A. The OPR
B. An administrative law judge
C. IRS legal counsel
D. The Secretary of the Treasury

The answer is B. When the Office of Professional Responsibility institutes a proceeding against an Enrolled Agent, if a hearing is required, an administrative law judge will make the final decision regarding disbarment or appropriate sanctions.###

Unit 3.5: The Ethics of EITC

More Reading:
Publication 596, *Earned Income Credit*
Publication 4687, *EITC Due Diligence Requirements*
Pub 4537, *EITC Bookmark for Tax Preparers*
Publication 4808, *Disability and EITC*

Earned Income Tax Credit Extra "Due Diligence" Requirement

The due diligence rules for tax preparers are more stringent for Earned Income Tax Credit (EITC) returns. This is because the IRS has determined that there are a large number of errors on EITC returns. Paid preparers must meet four additional due diligence requirements on returns with EITC claims or face possible penalties. One of the requirements is that practitioners must complete Form 8867, *Paid Preparer's Earned Income Credit Check List* (or an equivalent document).

IRS regulations clarify EITC due diligence requirements and set a performance standard for the "knowledge" requirement (what a reasonable and well-informed tax return preparer, knowledgeable in the law, would do).

Tax preparers must ask questions that result in an accurate tax return. This is especially true for tax returns with the Earned Income Tax Credit. There is a higher standard of due diligence for these types of returns, because the number of fraudulent EITC claims is so prevalent. The number of individuals claiming the EITC is high, and the number of erroneous payments is also high. The IRS estimates an error rate of 23 to 28%, or $11 to $13 billion paid out in error.

When preparing EITC returns and claims for refund, paid preparers must:

- Evaluate all the information received from clients
- Apply a consistency and reasonableness standard to the information
- Ask additional questions if the information appears incorrect, inconsistent, or incomplete
- Document and retain the record of inquiries made and client responses
- Conduct a thorough, in-depth interview with every client every year

Example: A client states that she is separated from her spouse. Her child lives with her and she wants to claim the EITC as Head of Household. In reviewing the client's records it is apparent she earns a minimal income, which appears insufficient to support a household: pay rent/mortgage, electric, water, food, clothing, school supplies, etc. The return preparer should ask appropriate questions to determine the client's correct filing status and determine how long the child lived with each parent during the year and probe for any additional sources of income (Publication 4687).

> **Example:** Judd is an Enrolled Agent. His new client, Thelma, 62, wants to take a dependency exemption for her son Randy, who is 32. She also wants to claim the Earned Income Tax Credit and the Dependent Care Credit for her son. Since Randy is beyond the age limit for these credits, Judd makes reasonable inquiries and discovers that Randy is severely physically disabled and incapable of self-care. Therefore, Thelma may claim her son, and the credits will be allowed regardless of Randy's age. Judd has fulfilled his due diligence requirement by asking reasonable questions about an individual tax situation.

EITC Due Diligence Compliance Program

EITC return preparers may receive personal visits from the IRS to check compliance and due diligence standards. The IRS is always looking for abusive EITC claims. A common method of EITC fraud is the "borrowing" of dependents. Unscrupulous tax professionals will "share" one taxpayer's qualifying child or children with another taxpayer in order to allow both to claim the EITC.

For example, if one client has four children, that client only needs the first three children for EITC purposes to get the maximum credit. The preparer will list the first three children on the first taxpayer's return, and list the other child on another return. The preparer and the client "selling" the dependents split a fee.

When fraudulent claims are discovered, the IRS prosecutes the practitioners, and the participating taxpayers are also subject to civil and criminal penalties (Treasury Regulation §1.6695-2).

EITC Due Diligence Requirements

Since the tax professional community prepares more than 70% of EITC claims, the quality of their work has a significant impact on reducing erroneous claims. The IRS focus is reducing EITC errors by:

- Ensuring experienced preparers who filed questionable EITC claims understand the law
- Conducting on-site due diligence audits of preparers filing returns
- Barring egregious preparers with a history of noncompliance from return preparation

EITC Errors

EITC errors occur for many reasons, including:

- Lack of knowledge of EITC tax law
- Honest preparer mistakes
- Intentional or unintentional client misrepresentation of facts
- Disregard for EITC due diligence requirements
- Blatant disregard of tax laws to garner erroneous refunds

The IRS is attempting to educate first-time preparers whose returns reflected EITC errors. Using a scoring system to determine the degree of future risk, the agency is sending informational letters and, in some cases, sending stronger compliance letters. This new compliance program enforces the following:

- Outlines EITC due diligence and preparer responsibilities
- Highlights recurring errors made by other EITC return preparers to help avoid common pitfalls
- Points to tools, information, and other resources on the IRS website
- Reminds preparers that tax software is a tool, not a substitute for knowing and correctly applying the tax law
- Educates experienced preparers by mail

The Knowledge Standard

Preparers who file high percentages of questionable EITC claims or returns with a high risk of EITC error could be subject to on-site audits. IRS agents will review preparer records to verify due diligence compliance, including whether they are meeting the knowledge standard. Penalties are assessed when noncompliance is identified. The "knowledge standard" requires preparers to:

- Know the law
- Ask probing questions
- Get all the facts to make accurate eligibility determinations
- Apply a common sense standard to the information provided by the client
- Evaluate whether the information is complete and gather any missing facts
- Determine if the information is consistent and recognize contradictory statements
- Conduct a thorough, in-depth interview with every client every single year
- Ask *enough* questions to reasonably know the return is correct and complete
- Document in the file any questions asked and the client's responses, as they happen

Example: Gracie is an Enrolled Agent. Frances is a new client with two qualifying children. Frances wants to claim the EITC. She tells Gracie she had a Schedule C business and earned $10,000 in income but had no expenses. This information appears incomplete because it is unusual that someone who is self-employed has no business expenses. Gracie is required to ask additional reasonable questions to determine if the business exists and if the information about her income and expenses is correct (Publication 4687).

To meet the due diligence EITC requirements, the practitioner must:

- Complete Form 8867, *Paid Preparer's Earned Income Credit Checklist*.
- Complete the EITC worksheet in the Form 1040 series instructions or the one in Publication 596, *Earned Income Credit*.
- Retain Form 8867, the EITC worksheet (or documents with the same information), and a record of how, when, and from whom the preparer got the information used to prepare the return.
- Not know (or have reason to know) that the information used to determine eligibility for the EITC is not correct. The practitioner must ask his client additional questions if the information furnished seems incorrect or incomplete.

The EITC worksheet shows how the credit was computed and the amount of self-employment income, total earned income, investment income, and Adjusted Gross Income included in the computation. Most tax preparation software includes an EITC worksheet that the preparer may use to comply with due diligence requirements.

Common EITC Errors

A preparer must pay particular attention to the following three issues that account for more than 60% of all EITC errors:

- Claiming a child who does not meet the age, relationship, or residency requirement[96]
- Filing as Single or Head of Household when married[97]
- Incorrectly reporting income
- Incorrect Social Security Numbers (Publication 4346)

Example: Esther is an Enrolled Agent. A new 28-year-old client wants to claim two sons, ages 14 and 15, as qualifying children for the EITC. Esther is concerned about the age of the children, since the age of the client seems inconsistent with the ages of the children claimed as sons. Esther discovers that the two boys are both adopted, which explains the age inconsistency (Publication 4687).

Example: David is single and wants to claim his daughter Charley for EITC. David earned $14,500 and had no other income. Charley is 35 years old, is unmarried and David says she is disabled. Charley lived with her father for the full year. Charley's mother is deceased. Both have valid Social Security numbers. Charley worked for part of the year and earned $5,200. David states that Charley had an accident last May and sustained a disability from the injuries. His doctor says she is totally and permanently disabled, not able to work, and the doctor does not expect Charley to recover. David can claim EITC using Charley as his qualifying child because his doctor determined Charley cannot work because of her disability and her disability will last longer than a year.

Consequences of Filing EITC Returns Incorrectly

The penalties for failing to exercise due diligence with EITC claims can be severe. The IRS can examine the client's return, and if it is found to be incorrect, can assess the taxpayer client accuracy or fraud penalties. The IRS can also ban the taxpayer from claiming the EITC for years.

---

[96] A taxpayer may claim a relative of any age as a qualifying child if the person is totally and permanently disabled and meets all other EITC requirements. The tax law definition of totally and permanently disabled is "The person cannot engage in any substantial gainful activity because of a physical or mental condition. A doctor determines the condition has lasted or the doctor expects it to last continuously for at least a year (or lead to death)."

[97] Many married couples incorrectly split their qualifying children and both file as Head of Household to reap the benefits of EITC. This is considered fraudulent. IRS uses both internal information and information from external sources such as other government agencies in order to research and flag these fraudulent EITC claims.

Both the preparer and the client may be affected by incorrect EITC returns. If the client's returns are examined and found to be incorrect, the client may be subject to the accuracy or fraud penalties and banned from claiming EITC for a period of two or ten years.

Return preparers who fail to comply with EITC due diligence requirements can be assessed a $100 penalty for each failure (IRC Section 6695). In addition, preparers who prepare a return where the understatement of tax liability is due to an unreasonable position can be assessed a minimum penalty of $1,000 (IRC Section 6694).

Preparers who prepare a client return for which any part of an understatement of tax liability is due to reckless or intentional disregard of rules or regulations by the tax preparer can be assessed a minimum penalty of $5,000 (IRC Section 6694)

Preparers making fraudulent EITC claims face serious consequences that may include:

- Disciplinary action by the IRS Office of Professional Responsibility
- Suspension or expulsion of the preparer from participation in IRS e-file
- Injunctions barring the preparer from preparing tax returns

The IRS has streamlined procedures for faster referrals to the U.S. Department of Justice to prohibit preparers from making fraudulent EITC claims. These preparers could be permanently or temporarily barred from any type of federal tax preparation (Publication 4687).

Claiming the EITC after a Prior Disallowance

If the EITC was disallowed or reduced by the IRS as a result of an examination or a review, the taxpayer may need to include Form 8862, *Information To Claim Earned Income Credit After Disallowance*, with her tax return when she next claims the EITC.

Preparers should ask clients if the EITC was previously disallowed or reduced. As a result of some examinations where the EITC was disallowed, the IRS may impose a ban on claiming the EITC.

Taxpayers are notified during the examination process and also receive separate notification letters about the bans. The IRS can impose the following types of bans:

- Two year ban for reckless or intentional disregard of the EITC rules
- Ten year ban for fraud

To claim the EITC once the ban is over, the taxpayer must file Form 8862 with his tax return. The IRS will reject the EITC claim if the form is not present.

EITC Due Diligence Requirements for Paid Preparers

Requirement	Description
1. Completion of eligibility checklist	Either complete **Form 8867** or an equivalent checklist. Complete checklist based on information provided by the taxpayer for the preparer.
2. Computation of the credit	Keep the EIC worksheet that demonstrates how the EIC was computed.
3. Knowledge	Make reasonable attempts to verify any information used in determining whether the taxpayer's eligibility for the EITC is incorrect. Do not ignore the implications of information furnished or known. Make reasonable inquiries if a reasonable and well-informed tax return preparer, knowledgeable in the law, would conclude the information furnished appears to be incorrect, inconsistent, or incomplete.
4. Record Retention	Retain **Form 8867** and **EIC worksheet**. Maintain records of how and when the information used to complete these forms was obtained. Verify the identity of the person furnishing the information. Retain records for three years after the June 30th that follows the date the return or claim was presented for signature.

Unit 3.5: Questions

1. Which statement is CORRECT about the EITC?

A. Information obtained by the preparer should be thrown away right after the tax interview.
B. Interfering with IRS efforts to investigate EITC fraud is the best thing to do.
C. Incorrectly reporting income is okay as long as the client signs a release.
D. Preparers are required to ask additional questions if the information provided by a client appears incorrect, inconsistent, or incomplete.

The answer is D. During the EITC interview with a client, preparers are required to ask additional questions if the information appears incorrect, inconsistent, or incomplete. ###

2. Which of the following forms is used to claim the EITC after a prior disallowance?

A. Form 8862
B. Form EITC
C. Form 8832
D. Schedule A

The answer is A. Form 8862 is used to claim the EITC after a prior disallowance. To claim the EITC once the ban is over, the taxpayer must file Form 8862 with her tax return. IRS will reject the EITC claim if the form is not present. ###

3. The IRS can impose the following types of bans related to the EITC:

A. The IRS cannot ban a taxpayer from claiming the EITC
B. Ten year ban for fraud
C. Twenty-five year ban for fraud
D. Permanent ban for fraud

The answer is B. The IRS can impose the following types of bans related to the EITC:
- Two year ban for reckless or intentional disregard of EITC rules, or
- Ten year ban for fraud. ###

4. What is the penalty for preparers who fail to comply with due diligence requirements for the EITC?

A. A penalty of $1,000 for each failure.
B. A penalty of $100 for each failure.
C. There is no preparer penalty, but there is a taxpayer penalty for fraud.
D. A formal reprimand by the OPR, but there is no monetary penalty.

The answer is B. Any tax return preparer who fails to comply with due diligence requirements for the EITC can be liable for a penalty of $100 for each failure. ###

5. A client tells a preparer:

- She has no Form 1099
- She was self-employed cleaning houses
- She earned $12,000
- She had no expenses related to the cleaning business

What is the BEST course of action for the preparer in this case?

A. Kick the client out of the office and refuse to prepare the return.
B. Ask probing questions to determine the correct facts, and ask for proof of income or any expenses.
C. Accept the taxpayer's word as long as she fills out a legal liability release form.
D. Make the client swear to the truthfulness of her statements before an IRS officer.

The answer is B. The best course of action would be to ask probing questions and ask for proof of income. In some cases, the client may say she had no expenses when it is not reasonable to conduct the business without incurring expenses, or the expenses may seem unreasonably high. Again, the preparer may need to ask probing questions to determine the correct facts. ###

6. When must a tax preparer do a client interview with respect to the EITC?

A. Every year
B. With every new client
C. Every six months
D. Every other year

The answer is A. A tax preparer must do a thorough interview with a client claiming the EITC every year. ###

7. Which of the following statements is FALSE regarding the EITC?

A. For the EITC, there are three tests that must be met for a child to be a qualifying child. The three tests are relationship, age, and residency.
B. The "age test" does not apply to children who are permanently disabled at any time during the year, regardless of age.
C. Preparers may take a client's word at face value without further inquiries.
D. Preparers must complete Form 8867 or its equivalent when figuring eligibility for the EITC.

The answer is C. Tax return preparers have additional due diligence requirements with regards to EITC claims. The "knowledge requirement" states that a preparer must apply a reasonableness standard to the information received from a client. If the information provided by the client appears to be incorrect, incomplete, or inconsistent, then a preparer must make additional inquiries of the client until he is satisfied that he has the correct and complete information to prepare the return. ###

Unit 3.6: Covered Opinions, Tax Shelters, and Frivolous Positions

The Circular 230 requirements apply to all written forms of federal tax advice, but there are especially strict rules for the written advice on tax shelters. Higher communication standards exist for "covered opinions," also called "tax shelter advice." The IRS has issued regulations regarding covered opinions, which were formerly known as "tax shelter opinions." (The actual tax shelter is still called a "tax shelter.")

Tax shelter activities are also called "reportable transactions" because a tax shelter must be reported to the IRS.

Covered Opinions (Tax Shelter Opinions)

Covered opinions relate to the advice a practitioner gives a client regarding a tax shelter. The IRS is very concerned with abusive tax shelter schemes, and therefore, the rules covering tax shelters are very specific and designed to curb abuses.

Tax shelters themselves are not prohibited. Some tax shelters are good. A pre-tax retirement plan is considered a legal tax shelter. However, others are unlawful. In the last few years the Internal Revenue Service Criminal Investigation Division has detected a proliferation of abusive trust tax evasion schemes. The IRS has a strategy in place to combat abusive tax shelters, which includes guidance on abusive transactions, regulations governing tax shelters, a hotline for taxpayers to report abusive technical transactions, and enforcement activity against abusive tax shelter promoters and investors. The practitioner's advice is considered a "covered opinion" if it is regarding:

- A transaction the IRS has determined is a tax-avoidance transaction,
- Any plan or arrangement that has tax avoidance as a principal purpose,
- A partnership or other entity or investment plan, or any other plan or arrangement that has tax avoidance or evasion as a "significant purpose,"
- Written advice that is a "reliance opinion" or "marketed opinion" (i.e., the opinion will be used by a promoter to market an investment).
- Under the rules, unless the advice contains a disclaimer, the practitioner providing advice about a tax shelter (a covered opinion) must comply with ALL of the following requirements:
- The practitioner must use due diligence in fact finding;
- All pertinent facts must be separately stated and disclosed, and not be deemed unreasonable or immaterial by the practitioner;
- The opinion must relate the facts to applicable law standards without inconsistency; and
- All significant federal tax issues must be addressed and disclosed in the written advice.

The practitioner has a duty to also consider the impact of significant federal tax issues and provide a conclusion about whether the taxpayer's position on each issue is likely to prevail.

The rules vary depending upon the type of advice that is given to the taxpayer. Some forms of written tax advice are not subject to the strict rules for "covered opinions." Certain types of "excluded advice" are not subject to the detailed "covered opinion" standards of Circular 230. Examples of written advice that do NOT qualify as "covered opinions" include:

- Advice from in-house employees to their employers.
- Written advice solely for one taxpayer after the taxpayer has already filed a tax return.
- Written advice that does not resolve a federal tax issue in the taxpayer's favor. This is also called "negative advice," wherein an advisor tells a client a transaction will not provide the purported tax benefit.
- Written advice regarding qualified plans, state and local bonds, or SEC filed documents.
- Any written advice if the practitioner is reasonably expected to provide subsequent written advice that satisfies the covered opinion requirements.

This type of tax advice is NOT considered a covered opinion [IR-2005-59].

> **Example:** A tax accountant is working full-time as an employee for Baker's Dozen Corp. The accountant gives incorrect advice to his employer regarding a tax shelter, and the employer is subject to penalties. The employee is not subject to Circular 230 penalties for tax shelter opinions because he was acting as an in-house professional for his own employer.

Written advice is a "reliance opinion" if the advice is more likely than not (a greater than 50% chance) to result in the tax issues being resolved in the taxpayer's favor. Written advice will not be treated as a "reliance opinion" if the practitioner openly discloses that the written advice was not intended by the practitioner to be used by the taxpayer to avoid penalties.

Reporting Requirements for Tax Shelter Activities

There are special types of tax shelter activities that must be reported to the IRS. If a taxpayer participates in any activity that the IRS has deemed to be a "tax avoidance" activity and a tax shelter, the activity must be disclosed on the taxpayer's return. Form 8886, *Reportable Transaction Disclosure Statement*, must be attached to a taxpayer's return for any year that he participates in a tax shelter.

Any taxpayer, including an individual, trust, estate, partnership, S Corporation, or other corporation that participates in a reportable transaction must file Form 8886. Tax advisors involved in a reportable transaction must disclose the reportable transaction to the IRS. In addition, the tax practitioner is required to maintain a list of investors that must be furnished to the IRS upon request. Substantial penalties apply both to taxpayers and material advisors for noncompliance on either issue.

The fact that a tax shelter transaction must be reported on this form does not mean the tax benefits from such a transaction will be disallowed by the IRS. A taxpayer may request a ruling from the IRS to determine whether a transaction must be disclosed.

A person who sells (or otherwise transfers) an interest in a tax shelter must provide the taxpayer the tax shelter registration number or be subject to a $100 penalty. If a taxpayer claims any deduction, credit, or other tax benefit because of a tax shelter, she must attach Form 8271, *Investor Reporting of Tax Shelter Registration Number*, to the tax return to report this number. A taxpayer may have to pay a penalty of $250 for each failure to report a tax shelter registration number on a return.

Tax Avoidance vs. Tax Evasion

Exam candidates should know the difference between "tax avoidance" and "tax evasion." All citizens have the right to pay lower taxes through legal means. Tax evasion, however, is the illegal evasion of taxes, either through unreported income or taking illegal deductions or adjustments to income.

Unscrupulous "tax shelter" promoters have long employed frivolous arguments concerning the legality of the income tax as pretexts to enrich themselves or evade taxes. Their motivation is usually monetary, not some legitimate belief. Anti-taxation groups have been around for a long time. Though leaders of these movements use different arguments to gain followers, they all share one thing in common: they receive substantial sentences in federal prisons for their activities.

Their followers pay a steep price for following bad advice. Some are prosecuted, and many more are involved in years of litigation but ultimately have to pay all taxes owed along with penalties and interest.

Frivolous Positions §10.34

A tax professional cannot sign a frivolous return. A frivolous position is defined as one that the preparer knows is in bad faith and is improper. A position is considered to have a realistic possibility of being sustained on its merits "if a reasonable and well-informed analysis by a person knowledgeable in the tax law would lead such a person to conclude that the position has a greater likelihood of being sustained on its merits."

A practitioner must make a reasonable attempt to determine if the taxpayer's position, especially a tax shelter position, will be sustained on its merits.

A practitioner may recommend a tax position if it is not frivolous. A tax position taken on a return should have a "more likely than not" level of success. This means that there is a reasonable likelihood (greater than 50% likelihood) that the position will be accepted under examination by the IRS.

However, the practitioner may still sign a return containing a position that does not meet the "more likely than not" standard so long as the position has a reasonable basis, is not frivolous, and is **adequately disclosed.** The disclosure is the key.

A practitioner may NOT advise a client to submit a document or tax return to the IRS:

- The only purpose of which is to delay or impede the administration of the federal tax laws.
- That is frivolous.
- That contains or omits information in a manner that demonstrates an intentional disregard of a rule or regulation unless the practitioner also advises the client to submit a document that evidences a good faith challenge to the rule or regulation.

Disclosure Statements

A practitioner must inform a client of the penalties reasonably likely to apply, of any opportunity to avoid any penalty by disclosure, and of the requirements for adequate disclosure. In the case of a tax return that requires a disclosure, the position should be disclosed to the IRS on either Form 8275, *Disclosure Statement*, or Form 8275-R, *Regulation Disclosure Statement*.

Form 8275 is used by taxpayers and preparers to disclose positions that are not otherwise adequately disclosed on a tax return to avoid certain penalties. It can also be used for disclosures relating to preparer penalties for understatements due to unreasonable positions or disregard of rules. The disclosure can be used to avoid accuracy-related penalties as long as the return position has a reasonable basis (such as a recent court case in the taxpayer's favor). The penalty will not be imposed if there was reasonable cause for the position and the taxpayer (and preparer) acted in good faith in taking the position.

If there is an understatement on a tax return due to an unrealistic position, the preparer penalty is the greater of:

- $1,000 per tax return, or
- 50% of the additional income upon which the penalty was imposed.

This applies when a preparer knows (or reasonably should have known) that the position was unrealistic and would not have been sustained on its merits.

A position must have a reasonable basis behind it. For purposes of the negligence penalty, the reasonable basis standard is not satisfied by a return position that is "merely arguable." Treasury Reg. §1.6662-3(b)(3) defines "reasonable basis" as "a relatively high standard of tax reporting that is significantly higher than not frivolous or not patently improper. The reasonable basis standard is not satisfied by a return position that is merely arguable or that is merely a colorable claim."

A "reasonable basis" for a **disclosed position** is one that has approximately 10% or greater chance of success if challenged. This means that the position must be more than just arguable. There must be some authority supporting the position, such as a court case.

Example: Amanda is an Enrolled Agent who has a client with a very complex tax situation. Amanda notices that the IRS publications reflect one position, but there is a recent court case that may allow a more favorable position for her client. Amanda believes that the position has a 20% chance of prevailing on its merits. Amanda thinks that the client's position has a "reasonable basis" and decides to disclose the position on the tax return. She should file Form 8275 along with the tax return stating the position, referencing the court case or any other basis she has for the position.

If a taxpayer files a frivolous income tax return, a penalty of $5,000 can be assessed under Section 6702. This penalty is assessed to the taxpayer, but there are also penalties that can be imposed on preparers who file frivolous returns. The penalty for a frivolous position in the U.S. Tax Court is $25,000.

The "reasonable basis" rule does not apply to tax shelters. That is because a tax shelter must always be disclosed, regardless of any possibility standard.

Unit 3.6: Questions

1. Which of the following types of written advice would fall under the Circular 230 rules for "covered opinions"?

A. Advice from in-house employees to their employers
B. Written advice solely for one taxpayer after the taxpayer has already filed a tax return
C. Written advice that does not resolve a federal tax issue in the taxpayer's favor
D. A plan or arrangement, the principal purpose of which is the avoidance or evasion of any tax

The answer is D. The rules regarding "covered opinions" include the written advice regarding a plan or arrangement, the principal purpose of which is the avoidance or evasion of any tax. ###

2. Which form is used to report a tax shelter?

A. Form 8886
B. Form 8823
C. Form 1040
D. Schedule R

The answer is A. Form 8886 is used to disclose information for each reportable transaction (tax shelter) in which the taxpayer participated. ###

3. A tax professional cannot sign
_____.

A. A tax return for a family member.
B. A tax return that is not prepared for compensation.
C. A tax return with a properly disclosed tax shelter position.
D. A frivolous return with a disclosure.

The answer is D. A tax professional cannot sign a frivolous return, even if the return has a disclosure. A frivolous position is defined as one that the preparer knows is in bad faith and is improper. ###

4. What is the penalty for failure to furnish a tax shelter registration number on a return?

A. $150 for each failure
B. $250 for each failure
C. $500 for each failure
D. $1,000 for each failure

The answer is B. A taxpayer may have to pay a penalty of $250 for each failure to report a tax shelter registration number on a return. ###

5. Greg is a client of Bethany's, an Enrolled Agent. Greg wishes to claim a deduction for a large business expense. However, there is a question about whether the expense is "ordinary and necessary" for his business. If the deduction was disallowed, there would be a substantial understatement of tax (over 25%). Bethany researches the issue and tells Greg that the position should be disclosed. Greg doesn't want to disclose the position on the return, because he is afraid that the IRS will disallow it. If the position is not disclosed, what are the potential penalties for Bethany?

A. None. All the penalties apply to the client.
B. $1,000 per tax return (or 50% of the additional income upon which the penalty was imposed).
C. $10,000 per tax return, or 100% of the additional income upon which the penalty was imposed.
D. $1,000 per tax return and up to a year in prison.

The answer is B. If Bethany does not adequately disclose the position and the return is later examined by the IRS, a preparer penalty may be assessed. The disclosure form is filed to avoid the portions of the accuracy-related penalty due to disregard of rules or to a substantial understatement of income tax. ###

6. Which form is used to disclose a position on a tax return?

A. Form 8275
B. Form 8823
C. Form 1040
D. Form 2484

The answer is A. Form 8275, *Disclosure Statement*, is filed by individuals, corporations, pass-through entities, and income tax return preparers to disclose a tax position on a tax return. ###

Unit 3.7: The IRS E-File Program and IRS Payments

> **More Reading:**
> Publication 3112, *IRS e-file Application and Participation*
> Publication 1345, *Handbook for Authorized IRS e-file Providers of Individual Income Tax Returns*
> Publication 4169, *Tax Professional Guide to Electronic Federal Tax Payment System* Publication 4453, *IRS e-file for Charities and Nonprofits*

The IRS e-file program allows taxpayers to transmit their returns electronically. Tax returns are processed faster, and refunds are received by taxpayers faster. IRS e-file uses automation to replace most of the manual steps needed to process paper returns. As a result, the processing of e-file returns is not only quicker but also more accurate than the processing of paper returns. However, as with a paper return, the taxpayer is responsible for making sure the tax return contains accurate information and is filed on time.

Application to the IRS e-file program is explained in IRS Publication 3112, *IRS e-file Application and Participation*. IRS Publication 1345, *Handbook for Authorized IRS e-File Providers of Individual Income Tax Returns*, is the main guide for e-file providers. EA Exam candidates should seriously consider reading these publications in addition to Circular 230 before taking Part 3 of the Enrolled Agent Exam.

Professional tax preparers may e-file client returns, and taxpayers may also file their own returns online. The IRS is trying to encourage as much online filing as possible. By 2014, the IRS hopes to have 80% of tax returns filed online.

Businesses may also e-file their tax returns. The IRS e-file program is available for corporations, partnerships, employment taxes, and information returns as well as estates, trusts, and exempt organizations. Business e-file is available all year round in order to accommodate businesses that file on a fiscal year.

How to Apply to the E-File Program

To begin e-filing tax returns professionally, a practitioner must first apply and be accepted as an Authorized IRS e-file Provider. To do so, the practitioner must register with IRS e-Services, a suite of web-based products that allows tax professionals to do business with the IRS electronically.

Once a practitioner has successfully registered, she will need to complete an online IRS e-file application for her business location. When a business is accepted to participate in IRS e-file, it is assigned an Electronic Filing Identification Number (EFIN).

The EFIN is tied to the business location, rather than to the individual practitioner. So, for example, a tax preparation business that has ten employee-preparers all in one location would all file using the same EFIN. Each preparer would then use his own PTIN (Preparer Identification Number) on the returns that he individually prepares. The IRS e-file application should be submitted at least 45 days before the practitioner plans to e-file any returns.

Authorized IRS E-File Provider

An Authorized IRS e-file Provider is a business authorized by the IRS to participate in IRS e-file. The business may be a sole proprietorship, partnership, or corporation. The applicant must identify its principals and at least one responsible official on its IRS e-file application. Each individual who is a principal or responsible official must:

- Be a United States citizen or a legal U.S. alien lawfully admitted for permanent residence;
- Be at least 21 years of age as of the date of application; and
- Meet applicable state and local licensing and/or bonding requirements for the preparation and collection of tax returns.

Suitability Check

The IRS will conduct a "suitability check" on the applicant and on all principals and responsible officials listed on an application to determine their suitability to be Authorized IRS e-file Providers. Suitability checks may include the following:

- A criminal background check
- A credit history check
- A tax compliance check to ensure that the applicant's personal returns are filed and paid
- A check for prior noncompliance with IRS e-file requirements

All Authorized IRS e-file Providers (except software developers) must pass this suitability check during the application process.

Denial to Participate in IRS E-File

An applicant may be denied participation in IRS e-file for a variety of reasons that include but are not limited to:

- Conviction of any criminal offense under the revenue laws of the United States or of a state or other political subdivision
- Failure to timely file returns
- Failure to timely pay any federal, state, or local tax liability
- Assessment of penalties
- Suspension/disbarment from practice before the IRS or before a state or local tax agency
- Disreputable conduct or other facts that may adversely impact IRS e-file
- Misrepresentation on an IRS e-file application
- Unethical practices in return preparation
- Failure to sign the preparer's area of the tax return
- Stockpiling returns prior to official acceptance to participate in IRS e-file
- Knowingly and directly or indirectly employing or accepting assistance from any firm, organization, or individual denied participation in IRS e-file, or suspended or expelled from participating in IRS e-file

Types of E-File Providers

There are many types of e-file providers. An e-file provider doesn't always mean a tax practitioner. Authorized IRS e-file Providers can also be firms that develop tax software, transmit electronic returns to the IRS, and provide services to a multitude of taxpayer clients.

The roles and responsibilities of e-file providers vary according to a firm's activities. Once a firm applies for acceptance into the IRS e-file program, it selects its "Provider option" at that time. Some Providers may have more than one e-file activity. For example, an e-file Transmitter may also be a software developer. Provider options include:

- Electronic Return Originator (ERO): An ERO originates the electronic submission of tax returns to the IRS. An ERO is the person that the client entrusts with tax information for the purpose of filing income tax returns electronically in the IRS e-file program.
- Transmitter: A Transmitter sends the electronic return data directly to the IRS. A Transmitter must have software and computers that allow it to interface with the IRS e-file program. An ERO may apply to be a Transmitter, or the ERO may contract with an accepted third party Transmitter to send the data.
- Online Provider: An Online Provider participates in online filing by transmitting tax return information prepared by a taxpayer using commercially purchased software or software provided by an Internet site.
- Software Developer: A Software Developer writes transmission software designed to work with IRS e-file.
- Intermediate Service Provider (ISP): An Intermediate Service Provider receives tax information from an ERO (or from a taxpayer who files electronically using a personal computer and commercial tax preparation software, such as TurboTax®), processes the tax return information, and either forwards the information to a Transmitter or sends the information back to the ERO or taxpayer (for online filing).

ERO Responsibilities

Although an ERO may engage in tax return preparation, and many of them do, tax preparation is a separate and distinct activity from the electronic submission of tax returns to the IRS. An ERO submits a tax return only after the taxpayer has authorized the e-file transmission. The return must be either:

- Prepared by the ERO; or
- Collected from a taxpayer who has self-prepared his own return and is asking the ERO to e-file it for him.

An ERO transmits a return by any one of the following methods:

- Electronically sending the return to a Transmitter that will transmit the return to the IRS (most practitioners use this method); or
- Directly transmitting the return to the IRS (rarely used); or
- Providing a return to an ISP for processing, prior to transmission to the IRS (rarely used).

Example: Patrick is an Enrolled Agent, and he uses TaxPro software to prepare his clients' returns. Once Patrick has completed a tax return, he gives a copy to the client, who then gives signature authorization to e-file the return. Patrick transmits the return to TaxPro, which is an authorized Transmitter. TaxPro then transmits the return to the IRS. Most tax practitioners use this method; all the major tax preparation software companies have e-file transmission options.

In originating the electronic submission of a return, the ERO is required to:

- Timely submit returns.
- Provide copies to taxpayers.

- Retain records and make records available to the IRS.
- Accept returns only from taxpayers and authorized IRS e-file Providers, and work with the taxpayer and/or the Transmitter to correct a rejected return.
- Enter the preparer's identifying information [name, address, and PTIN].
- Be diligent in recognizing fraud and abuse, reporting it to the IRS and preventing it when possible.
- Cooperate with IRS investigations by making documents available to the IRS upon request.

Once an e-file is rejected, the taxpayer has two options: he can correct the return with the help of the preparer, or he can file a paper return.

If the taxpayer chooses not to have the return corrected and retransmitted to the IRS, or if the electronic portion of the return cannot be accepted for processing by the IRS, the taxpayer must file on paper. To become an ERO, one must submit Form 8633 and be accepted into the program, and receive an Electronic Filing Identification Number (EFIN). All EROs must be fingerprinted.

Transmitter Responsibilities

Transmitters must fulfill the requirements below:
- Transmit all electronic returns to the IRS within three calendar days of receipt.
- Retrieve the acknowledgment file within two days of transmission.
- Match the acknowledgment file to the tax return and make it available for all rejected and accepted returns within two work days of retrieval.
- Retain the acknowledgment file received from the IRS until the end of the calendar year in which the electronic return was filed.
- Immediately contact the IRS if an acknowledgment has not been received within 24 hours of transmission.
- Work with the ERO to promptly correct any transmission errors that might cause a tax return to be rejected.
- Ensure the security of all transmitted data.

In addition, a Transmitter cannot transfer her EFIN (Electronic File Identification Number) or ETIN by sale, merger, loan, or gift to another entity.

Permissible Disclosures

Disclosure of client information between e-file providers is permissible, as long as the disclosures are for the preparation and transmission of the tax return. For example, an ERO may relay tax return information to a Transmitter for the purpose of transmitting the forms to the IRS.

However, if tax return information is disclosed or used in any other way, an Intermediate Service Provider, ERO, or Transmitter may be subject to IRS penalties or the civil penalties in Internal Revenue Code (IRC) §6713 for unauthorized disclosure or use of tax return information.

Mandatory E-file Program

Starting January 1, 2011, a new law requires many paid tax return preparers to electronically file federal income tax returns prepared and filed for individuals, trusts, and estates. This new mandate affects the 2010 tax year filing season. Preparers who anticipate filing 100 or more Forms 1040, 1040A, 1040EZ, and 1041 during the year must use IRS e-file. The requirement also applies to firms, which must compute the number of returns prepared by its members in the aggregate.

This means that any paid preparer who files more than 100 returns for the 2010 tax year is required to e-file. There is an exception for returns that cannot be e-filed (such as returns that require paper attachments).

The e-file requirement will be phased in over two years. As a result of the new rules, preparers will be required to start using IRS e-file beginning:

- January 1, 2011 — for preparers who anticipate filing 100 or more Forms 1040, 1040A, 1040EZ, and 1041 during the year; or
- January 1, 2012 — for preparers who anticipate filing 11 or more Forms 1040, 1040A, 1040EZ and 1041 during the year.

> **Example:** Rory is an Enrolled Agent working for a tax preparation firm. He also has a small side business doing tax returns from his home. For the coming tax year, Rory reasonably expects to prepare and file 60 Form 1040 tax returns while working for his firm. He also expects to prepare and file 60 Form 1040 tax returns individually as a preparer. Therefore, Rory is required to use IRS e-file tax returns. He meets the definition of a *specified tax return preparer*, subject to the e-file requirement because he expects to file over 100 returns in 2011 (for the 2010 tax year). Rory's PTIN would be on all of these returns.

Clients may choose to file on paper, and preparers can honor that choice. Preparers should document each client's choice to file in paper format and keep a signed copy of the statement on file. Second, a specified tax preparer may request a waiver by submitting Form 8944, *Preparer e-file Hardship Waiver Request*, if he believes complying with the requirement would cause an undue hardship. And third, some returns are impossible to e-file for various reasons and are therefore exempt from the e-file requirement.

Tax preparers should identify the paper returns they prepare for any of the above reasons by completing Form 8948, *Preparer Explanation for Not Filing Electronically*, and attaching it to the paper returns.

The new e-file mandate does not apply to payroll tax returns.

Businesses That Are Required to E-File

While millions of taxpayers voluntarily e-file, certain corporations, partnerships, and tax-exempt organizations are required to e-file. Some other businesses are also required to e-file their tax returns. The IRS has mandated this rule in order to improve accuracy of and processing for complicated returns.

Partnerships with more than 100 partners are required to file electronically. This means that a partnership must file Form 1065 and the multiple Schedules K-1 electronically.

Partnerships with 100 or fewer partners (Schedules K-1) may voluntarily file their returns electronically, but they are not required to do so.

Large and midsized corporate taxpayers including tax-exempt organizations with $10 million or more in assets that file at least 250 returns (information returns and others, such as Form 1099 and Form W-2) are required to e-file.

The e-file application must be current and must list all the form types (1120, 1065, 990, etc.) that the practitioner will transmit to the IRS. If the practitioner does not list a certain form on his application and later attempts to transmit that form, he will receive a rejection for return type.

> **Example:** Karen is an Enrolled Agent. When she first applied to be an e-file provider, she only prepared individual returns. In 2010, she wishes to prepare a partnership return. However, Karen forgets to update her e-file application. When she submits the partnership return online, it is rejected. Karen will have to update her e-file application in order to submit partnership returns electronically.

An electronically-filed return is not considered filed until the electronic portion of the tax return has been acknowledged and accepted for processing by the IRS. This is called an "electronic postmark." The electronic postmark is a record of when the authorized electronic return transmitter received the transmission of the electronically-filed return. A tax preparer must retain a record of each electronic postmark until the end of the calendar year and provide the record to the IRS upon request. Most tax software packages automatically retain a record of the return transmission report and electronic postmark.

Returns That Cannot Be E-Filed

There are certain tax returns that cannot be e-filed. Returns with paper attachments and other odd requirements must be filed on paper. The following returns cannot be e-filed:

- Prior year tax returns;
- Tax returns with fiscal year tax periods (for business entities);
- Amended tax returns;
- Tax returns with Taxpayer Identification Numbers (TIN) within the range of 900-00-0000 through 999-99-9999. Exception: Adopted Taxpayer Identification Numbers (ATIN) and some Individual Taxpayer Identification Numbers (ITIN) may fall within the range above.

The IRS cannot electronically process tax returns with rare or unusual processing conditions or that exceed the specifications for returns allowable in IRS e-file. These conditions change from year to year. If Providers transmit electronic return data with one of these conditions, the IRS rejects the return and the taxpayer may have to file on paper.

Resubmission of Rejected Tax Returns

If the IRS rejects an e-filed return and the ERO cannot rectify the reason for the rejection, the ERO must inform the taxpayer of the rejection within 24 hours. The ERO must provide the taxpayer with the IRS reject codes accompanied by an explanation.

If the taxpayer chooses not to have the electronic portion of the return corrected and transmitted to the IRS, or if the IRS cannot accept the return for processing, the taxpayer must file a paper return. In order to timely file the return, the taxpayer must file the paper return by the later of:

- The due date of the return; or
- Ten calendar days after the date the IRS gives notification that it rejected the e-filed return. This is called the "Ten-day transmission perfection period," and it is additional time that the IRS gives a preparer and taxpayer to correct and resubmit a tax return without a late filing penalty (covered next).

> **Example:** Russ is an Enrolled Agent, and he e-files a tax return for his client Jodie. The e-filed return is transmitted on April 15, 2011. The next day, Russ receives a rejection notification from the IRS regarding Jodie's tax return. Russ properly notifies Jodie of the rejection within 24 hours. The issue cannot be corrected. Jodie must file a paper return. Russ gives Jodie a copy of the paper return on April 16, 2011, along with an attached explanation explaining the rejection. The tax return will be considered filed timely, because the paper return was filed within ten days of the rejection, and the original e-filed return was attempted in a timely manner.

Ten-day Transmission "Perfection" Period

Taxpayers are given ten days from the date of a rejected return to resubmit the return, even if the submission is made after the due date of the return. The "transmission perfection period" is NOT an extension of time to file; it is additional time to correct errors in the electronic file. When a previously rejected electronic return is "accepted" by the IRS within the ten-day transmission perfection period, it will be deemed to have been received on the date of the first reject that occurred within that ten-day period.

After an e-file rejection, a taxpayer may want to file on paper. If a taxpayer chooses to file on paper, she should include an explanation in the paper return as to why she is filing the return after the due date. The following steps should be followed to ensure that the paper return is identified as a rejected electronic return and the taxpayer is given credit for timely filing. The paper return should include the following:

- An explanation of why the paper return is being filed after the due date
- A copy of the rejection notification
- A brief history of actions taken to correct the electronic return

The taxpayer should write in red at the top of the first page of the paper return:

REJECTED ELECTRONIC RETURN – (DATE)

The date in the statement will be the date of the first e-file rejection. The paper return must be signed by the taxpayer. The PIN that was used on the electronically-filed return that was rejected may not be used as the signature on the paper return.

It is important to note that the "ten-day transmission perfection" period does not apply to payments. If an e-file submission is rejected, a return can be corrected within ten days and not be subject to a late filing penalty. When a return is rejected on the due date, it is recommended that an electronic payment not be transmitted with the return, because the payment must still be submitted or postmarked by the due date.

Electronic Signatures

Taxpayers must sign their returns under penalty of perjury. This means that the tax-payer must make a declaration that the return is true, correct, and complete. On electronically-filed returns, the taxpayer must also "consent to disclosure." The "consent to disclosure" authorizes the IRS to disclose information to the taxpayer's Providers. For example, the disclosure allows the IRS to notify the tax preparer if the client's tax return is rejected and to give the reason for the rejection.

As with any income tax return submitted to the IRS, the taxpayer and preparer must sign an electronic income tax return. Taxpayers who file jointly must both sign. There are two methods for signing individual income tax returns electronically:

- The Practitioner PIN method (Personal Identification Number) using Form 8879 (most common method)
- The Scanned Form 8453 method (This method is used to send any required paper forms or supporting documentation, such as **Form 8332**, *Release / Revocation of Release of Claim to Exemption for Child by Custodial Parent*)

The Practitioner PIN Signature Method

The Practitioner PIN option can only be used by an ERO. The ERO asks the taxpayer to choose a five-digit, self-selected Personal Identification Number (PIN) as his electronic signature. The ERO must complete Form 8879, *IRS e-file Signature Authorization*, and include the taxpayer's self-selected PIN and her own practitioner PIN. The "practitioner PIN" is an 11-digit number that includes the ERO's EFIN plus five other digits that she chooses. The ERO should use the same practitioner PIN for the entire tax year.

The ERO must sign and complete the requested information in the area provided: *"Declaration of Electronic Return Originator [ERO]."* An ERO may authorize employees to sign for the ERO, but the ERO is ultimately responsible for all electronically-filed returns by its firm.

If the return was prepared for a fee, the ERO must also sign the jurat.[98] EROs are not required to disclose their Employer Identification Numbers (EIN) or Social Security Numbers (SSN) on the copies they provide to taxpayers (Publication 4163).

---

[98] Jurat: An affidavit in which the taxpayer and/or preparer attests to the truth of the information contained in the return and attached return information.

EROs may sign this form by rubber stamp, mechanical device (such as signature pen), or computer software program. The signature must include either a facsimile of the individual ERO's signature or the ERO's printed name. EROs using one of these alternative means are personally responsible for affixing their signatures to returns. Taxpayers must sign Form 8879 by handwritten signature.

The ERO must retain copies of Forms 8879 for three years from the return due date or the IRS received date, whichever is later. EROs must not send Forms 8879 to the IRS unless the IRS requests they do so.

Scanned Form 8453 Signature Method

The Scanned Form 8453 method involves signing a document and attaching it to the electronic return. The client signs the appropriate form, and the form is then scanned and attached to the electronic return as a Portable Document Format (PDF) file. The tax preparation software selected will provide instructions on how to attach this document to the return.

The Form 8453 series may be used as a declaration by the taxpayer that he signed the electronic return. This document is a jurat (an affidavit in which the taxpayer attests to the truth of the information contained in the return and attached return information). It has the same legal effect as if the taxpayer had physically signed the return. Once the return is accepted by the IRS, the Authorized IRS e-file Provider then sends Form 8453 to the IRS.

After Signing the Return

After the taxpayer signs the return using either a Self-Select PIN or Form 8453, the ERO transmits the return to the IRS or to a third-party transmitter who then forwards the entire electronic record to the IRS for processing. Once received at the IRS, the return is automatically checked for errors. If it cannot be processed, it is sent back to the originating transmitter (usually the preparer) to clarify any necessary information.

After correction, the transmitter retransmits the return to the IRS. Within 48 hours of electronically sending the return, the IRS sends an acknowledgment to the transmitter stating the return is accepted for processing. This is the taxpayer's proof of filing and assurance that the IRS has the return.

EROs Who Make Substantive Changes to a Return

An ERO who chooses to originate returns that she has not prepared but only collected becomes an "income tax return preparer" when she makes "substantive changes" to the tax return. A non-substantive change is a correction limited to a transposition error, misplaced entry, spelling error, or arithmetic correction. The IRS considers all other changes substantive, and the ERO becomes a tax return preparer when he makes these changes. As such, the ERO may be required to sign the tax return as the tax return preparer.

Example: Melanie is an ERO. A taxpayer brings a self-prepared tax return for Melanie to e-file. She notices gross errors on the tax return and talks with the client about the mistakes. The client agrees to correct the return, and Melanie makes the necessary adjustments, in return for a small fee. Melanie is now required to sign the return as a preparer.

A substantive change is one in which the "Total Income" amount differs by more than $150 or the "Taxable Income" amount differs by more than $100. If the electronic return data on a corporate income tax return is changed after the taxpayer signed the jurat, the taxpayer must sign a new Form 8453 when the "Total Income" amount differs by more than $150 or the "Taxable Income" amount differs by more than $100.

E-file Recordkeeping and Documentation Requirements

E-file Providers must retain the following information listed below until the end of the calendar year in which the return was filed, or nine months after a fiscal year return was filed, whichever is later:

- A copy of signed IRS e-file *Consent to Disclosure* forms for taxpayers who signed using a scanned signature form (Form 8453)
- A complete copy of the e-filed return
- The acknowledgment file for IRS accepted returns
- The acknowledgment for all extensions

Signature forms must be retained by the e-file provider for three years from the due date of the return, extended due date, or the IRS received date, whichever is later. Providers must make all these records available to the IRS upon request.

Providers may electronically image (scan) and store all paper records they are required to retain for IRS e-file. This includes signed documents as well as any supporting documents not included in the electronic record.

E-File Advertising Standards

"IRS e-File" is a brand name, but acceptance to the IRS e-file program does not imply an endorsement by the IRS. A practitioner must not use improper or misleading advertising in relation to IRS e-file, including promising a time frame for refunds and Refund Anticipation Loans (RALs). If a practitioner advertises an RAL or other financial product, he and the financial institution must clearly describe the RAL as a loan, not as a refund. The advertisement on an RAL or other financial product must be easy to identify and in easily readable print.

Practitioners may NOT use the IRS logo or insignia in their advertising, or imply a relationship with the IRS. A practitioner may use the IRS e-file logo.

A preparer may NOT combine the e-file logo with the IRS eagle symbol, the word "federal," or with other words or symbols that suggest a special relationship between the IRS and the logo. Advertising materials must not carry the FMS, IRS, or other Treasury seals.

The IRS e-file logo, which preparers may use

If an e-file provider uses radio, television, Internet, signage, or other methods of advertising, the practitioner must keep a copy and provide it to the IRS upon request. If an e-file provider uses direct mail, e-mail, fax communications, or other distribution methods to advertise, he must retain a copy, as well as a list of who received the advertising. Practitioners must retain copies of the advertising until the end of the calendar year following the last transmission or use.

A practitioner may not advertise that individual income tax returns may be e-filed without using Forms W-2. In other words, a firm may not advertise that it can file a tax return using only "pay stubs" or "earnings statements."

In using the "Direct Deposit" name and logo in advertisement, the Provider must use the name "Direct Deposit" with initial capital letters or all capital letters.

Revocations and Sanctions

The IRS may revoke e-file privileges if a firm, a principal, or a responsible official is either:

- Prohibited or disbarred from filing returns by a court order, or
- Prohibited from filing returns by any federal or state legal action that forbids participation in e-file.

An Authorized IRS e-file Provider is not entitled to an administrative review process for revocation of participation if e-file privileges are revoked because of an injunction. If the injunction or other legal action expires or is reversed, only then may the practitioner reapply to participate in IRS e-file.

The IRS may also choose to sanction any practitioner that fails to comply with any e-file regulation. Before sanctioning, the IRS may issue a warning letter that describes specific corrective action the Provider must take. The IRS may also sanction a Provider without issuance of a warning letter.

Sanctions may include a written reprimand, suspension, or permanent expulsion from IRS e-file. The IRS categorizes the seriousness of infractions as Level One, Level Two, and Level Three. Level One is the least serious, Level Two is moderately serious, and Level Three is the most serious. For minor violations, the IRS will usually issue a written warning to the practitioner.

Level One Infractions

Level One infractions are violations of IRS e-file rules and requirements that, in the opinion of the IRS, have little or no adverse impact on the quality of electronically-filed returns on IRS e-file. The IRS may issue a written reprimand for a Level One infraction. Examples of Level One infractions include the following:

- Failure to update IRS e-file applications for minor items such as changes in a phone number.
- A minor advertising violation that can be corrected immediately by the provider (for example, immediate removal of a poster, billboard, or news article).

Level Two Infractions

Level Two infractions are violations of IRS e-file rules and requirements that, in the opinion of the IRS, have an adverse impact upon the quality of electronically-filed returns on IRS e-file. Level Two infractions include continued Level One infractions after they've been brought to the attention of the Authorized IRS e-file Provider. Depending on the infractions, the IRS may either restrict or suspend the Authorized IRS e-file Provider from participation in IRS e-file for a period of one year beginning with the effective date of suspension. Examples of Level Two infractions include the following:

- Transmitting tax returns prepared using earnings statements prior to receiving Forms W-2
- Continued violation of advertising guidelines
- Transmitting tax returns prior to obtaining taxpayers' signatures

Level Three Infractions

Level Three infractions are violations of IRS e-file rules and requirements that, in the opinion of the IRS, have a significant adverse impact on the quality of electronically-filed returns on IRS e-file. Level Three infractions include continued Level Two infractions after they have been brought to the attention of the Authorized IRS e-file Provider.

A Level Three infraction may result in suspension from participation in IRS e-file for two years beginning with the effective date of the suspension year, or depending on the severity of the infraction such as fraud or criminal conduct, it may result in permanent expulsion. The IRS reserves the right to suspend or expel an Authorized IRS e-file Provider prior to administrative review for Level Three infractions. Examples of Level Three infractions requiring immediate suspension include:

- Signing for the taxpayer without proper authorization
- Entering taxpayer Personal Identification Numbers (PINs) without authorization
- Any continued Level One or Level two infractions that have not been corrected

Examples of Level Three infractions requiring immediate expulsion include:

- Activities that involve fraud
- Association with known criminals (disreputable conduct)
- Convictions involving monetary or fiduciary crimes
- Conduct indicative of potential fraudulent acts
- Any criminal conduct

Practitioners may appeal sanctions through the administrative review process. Suspensions make Authorized IRS e-file Providers ineligible to participate in IRS e-file for a period of either one or two years from the effective date of the sanction. If a principal or responsible official is suspended or expelled from participation in IRS e-file, every entity listed on the firm's e-file application may also be expelled.

In certain circumstances, the IRS can immediately expel an entire firm without prior warning or notice.

Refunds and Payments on E-Filed Returns

Taxpayers have several options for refunds and payments on electronically-filed returns. The IRS has attempted to make Direct Deposit[99] and automatic payments easier in order to encourage these methods. Taxpayers often elect the Direct Deposit option because it is the fastest way of receiving their refund. Taxpayers may:

- Apply the refund to next year's estimated tax
- Receive the refund as a Direct Deposit

---

[99] The IRS requires tax practitioners to capitalize the words "Direct Deposit" in their advertising, so we will use the same formatting here. The IRS states that the provider must use the name "Direct Deposit" with initial capital letters or all capital letters.

- Receive the refund as a paper check
- Split the refund, with a portion applied to next year's estimated tax and the remainder received as Direct Deposit or paper check

Direct Deposit

Providers are required to accept any Direct Deposit election to any eligible financial institution designated by the taxpayer. A provider may NOT charge a separate fee for Direct Deposit. The provider must not alter the Direct Deposit information in the electronic record after a taxpayer has signed the tax return.

Refunds may be designated for Direct Deposit to qualified accounts in the taxpayer's name. Qualified accounts include savings, checking, share draft, or retirement accounts (for example, IRA or money market accounts). Direct Deposits cannot be made to credit card accounts. Qualified accounts must be in financial institutions within the United States.

The Provider must advise the taxpayer that a Direct Deposit election cannot be rescinded. In addition, changes cannot be made to routing numbers of financial institutions or to the taxpayer's account numbers after the IRS has accepted the return. Providers should verify account and routing numbers each year. Taxpayers will not receive Direct Deposit of their refunds if account information is not updated to reflect current information.

Refunds that are not Direct Deposited because of errors or any other reason will be issued as paper checks, resulting in refund delays of up to ten weeks.

Payments on Tax Returns

Taxpayers who have their returns filed electronically have several choices when paying any taxes owed on their tax returns, as well as any estimated taxes.

The following methods of payments are accepted:
1. Direct debit
2. Credit card
3. Personal check
4. Installment agreement requests

Check Payments

Balance-due payments may be made by check. Payments do not have to be mailed at the same time an electronic return is transmitted. For example, the return may be transmitted in January and the taxpayer may mail the payment on April 15.

On all checks or money orders, the practitioner should write the taxpayer's Taxpayer Identification Number (EIN, TIN, or SSN), the type of tax return, and the tax year to which the payment applies. The check or money order should be made payable to "United States Treasury."

Paying an IRS Tax Debt with an Installment Agreement

Installment agreements are arrangements where the IRS allows taxpayers to pay liabilities over time. A taxpayer who files electronically may apply for an installment agreement once the return is processed and the tax is assessed. Taxpayers must submit Form 9465, *Request for Installment Agreement,* in order to request payments in installments. The only agreements that may be granted are those that provide for full payment of the accounts (which means that the taxpayer must agree to pay the full balance due—the taxpayer cannot use an installment agreement to "negotiate" a lower tax liability).

During the course of the installment agreement, penalty and interest continue to accrue. No levies may be served during installment agreements. The IRS charges a user fee to set up an installment agreement. The user fee is $105, or $52 for agreements where payments are deducted electronically from a taxpayer's bank account. If a taxpayer owes less than $10,000 in taxes, he will be automatically approved for an installment agreement providing that he is up-to-date on his filing responsibilities. Installment payments are equal monthly installments, although the taxpayer may choose to pay more than the required monthly installments. Taxpayers may make their payments by check or by electronic withdrawal from their bank account.

A taxpayer with $25,000 (or less) in combined tax, penalties, and interest can use the IRS Online Payment Agreement and set up their installment agreement online. If a taxpayer owes more than $25,000, she may still qualify for an installment agreement, but a *Collection Information Statement*, Form 433F, may need to be completed.

In accordance with law, each year the IRS mails Form CP-89, *Annual Installment Agreement Statement*, to every installment agreement taxpayer. The statement provides the dollar amount of the beginning account balance due; an itemized listing of payments; an itemized listing of penalties, interest, and other charges; and the dollar amount of the ending account balance due.

A late payment on an installment agreement will generate an automatic 30-day notice as to the cessation of the agreement, allowing the IRS to make changes to the installment agreement.

Treasury Offset Program (TOP)

Public law established the Treasury Offset Program, which permits overpayments to be offset against delinquent child support obligations, as well as debts owed to participating federal and state agencies. If an individual owes money to the federal government because of a delinquent debt, the Treasury Department can offset that individual's federal payment or withhold the entire amount to satisfy the debt.

This means that a taxpayer's refund may be retained by the IRS in order to pay outside obligations, (such as delinquent child support). Offsets taken by the IRS may be for current and prior year tax obligations.

Taxpayer refunds are taken by the Financial Management IRS (FMS),[100] and can be taken for past due student loans, delinquent child support, federal taxes, state taxes, or other governmental agency debts. "Creditor agencies," such as the Department of Education, submit delinquent debts to FMS for collection and inclusion in the Treasury Offset Program and certify that the debts qualify for collection.

---

[100] FMS: The IRS Financial Management Service.

Electronic Federal Tax Payment System (EFTPS)

Balances due and estimated taxes can be paid year-round using the Electronic Federal Tax Payment System (EFTPS). Taxpayers and businesses enroll in EFTPS by using an online application. After enrollment, taxpayers receive a confirmation package by mail with instructions. Domestic corporations are required to deposit all income tax payments by the due date of the return.

Businesses and individuals can pay all their federal taxes using EFTPS. Individuals can pay their quarterly estimated taxes electronically using EFTPS, and they can make payments weekly, monthly, or quarterly. Both business and individual payments can be scheduled months in advance, if desired.

Businesses can schedule payments up to 120 days in advance of their tax due date. Individuals can schedule payments up to 365 days in advance of their tax due date. Domestic corporations must deposit all income tax payments by the due date of the return using EFTPS.

Refund Anticipation Loans: The Rules

A Refund Anticipation Loan (RAL) is a financial product. An RAL is NOT a tax refund. Instead, an RAL is a loan: money is borrowed by the taxpayer based on her anticipated tax refund. The IRS is not involved in RALs or financial products. Providers who assist taxpayers in applying for RALs or other financial products have additional responsibilities and may be sanctioned by the IRS if they fail to adhere to the following requirements. If a practitioner wants to offer RALs, she must:

- Ensure a taxpayer understands that by agreeing to an RAL or other financial product he will NOT receive his refund from the IRS as the IRS will send his refund to the financial institution.
- Advise a taxpayer that an RAL is an interest-bearing loan and NOT a quicker way of receiving her refund from the IRS.
- Advise a taxpayer that if a Direct Deposit is not received within the expected time frame for whatever reason, the taxpayer may be liable to the lender for additional interest and other fees.
- Advise a taxpayer of all fees and other known deductions to be paid from her refund and the remaining amount she will actually receive.
- Obtain the taxpayer's written consent to disclose information to the lending institution.
- Ensure that the return preparer does not have a "related party" conflict with the financial institution that makes an RAL agreement.
- Adhere to fee restrictions and advertising standards (explained earlier).

There are no guarantees that the IRS will deposit a taxpayer's refund within a specified time. For example, it may delay a refund due to processing problems or it may offset some or all of the refund for back taxes, child support, or other amounts that the taxpayer owes. The IRS is not liable for any loss suffered by taxpayers, practitioners, or financial institutions resulting from reduced refunds or dishonored Direct Deposits.

RAL and E-File Fee Restrictions

Providers may not base their tax preparation fees on a percentage of the refund amount or compute their fees using any figure from tax returns. A practitioner may charge an identical flat fee to all customers applying for RALs, meaning the fee cannot correspond to the amount of a refund for an individual client. The Provider must not accept a fee that is contingent upon the amount of the refund or an RAL. The IRS has no responsibility for the payment of any fees associated with the preparation of a return.

Unit 3.7: Questions

1. Which of the following statements is FALSE?

A. An ERO may only transmit returns that he has prepared.
B. An ERO may transmit returns that he has prepared and any returns collected from taxpayers who have self-prepared their own returns and are using the ERO simply to e-file them.
C. An ERO cannot transmit tax returns.
D. None of the above.

The answer is A. An ERO originates the electronic submission of returns it either prepares or collects from taxpayers wishing to have their self-prepared returns e-filed (Publication 1345). ###

2. Which of the following statements is TRUE?

A. Separate fees may be charged for Direct Deposits.
B. E-file providers may not charge contingent fees based on a percentage of the refund.
B. E-file providers may not file paper returns under any circumstances.
D. An e-file provider is not required to sign an e-filed return.

The answer is B. A practitioner may NOT charge a contingent fee (percentage of the refund) for preparing an original tax return. Separate fees may NOT be charged for Direct Deposits, and e-file providers are still required to sign an e-filed return with an electronic signature (Circular 230). ###

3. An Enrolled Agent has a client that wishes to use Direct Deposit. Which of the following statements regarding Direct Deposit is CORRECT?

A. An EA may not charge a fee for offering Direct Deposit.
B. An EA may advise the taxpayer to Direct Deposit to his credit card account.
C. An EA may advise the taxpayer to Direct Deposit directly into his bank account in Mexico.
D. An EA is not required to accept a Direct Deposit election from the taxpayer.

The answer is A. A practitioner cannot charge a fee for Direct Deposit. Direct Deposits cannot be made to credit card accounts. Qualified accounts must be in financial institutions within the United States. The practitioner is required to accept a Direct Deposit election by the taxpayer. ###

4. Taxpayers who have their returns filed electronically have several choices when paying any taxes owed on their tax returns, as well as any estimated taxes. Which method is NOT an acceptable method of paying an outstanding tax liability to the IRS?

A. Direct debit
B. Credit card payments
C. A U.S. Treasury bond note
D. Installment agreements

The answer is C. A bond note is not an acceptable method of payment. Taxpayers may pay their outstanding tax liability a variety of ways including direct debit, credit card payments, installment agreements, or payment by check. ###

5. If the IRS rejects the electronic portion of a taxpayer's return for processing and the reason for the rejection cannot be rectified with the information already provided to the ERO, what is the ERO's responsibility at that point?

A. The ERO is not legally required to notify the taxpayer.
B. The ERO must attempt to notify the taxpayer within 24 hours and provide the taxpayer with the reject code accompanied by an explanation.
C. The ERO is required to notify the taxpayer within 48 hours.
D. The ERO is required to file the tax return on paper within 24 hours of receiving the rejection.

The answer is B. If the IRS rejects the electronic portion of a taxpayer's individual income tax return for processing and the reason for the rejection cannot be rectified, the ERO must take reasonable steps to inform the taxpayer of the rejection within 24 hours. When the ERO advises the taxpayer that the return has not been filed, the ERO must provide the taxpayer with the reject code(s) accompanied by an explanation (Publication 1345). After receiving a rejection, the ERO is not required to file a tax return on paper. The ERO and the client may attempt to correct the e-file. However, if the return continues to be rejected, the taxpayer may be forced to file on paper. ###

6. Which form is used to request an installment agreement?

A. Form 9465
B. Form 2265
C. Form 1040
D. Schedule E

The answer is A. Taxpayers must submit Form 9465, *Request for Installment Agreement*, in order to request an installment agreement from the IRS. An installment agreement may also be requested using an online request form if the taxpayer's overall liability is less than $25,000. ####

736

7. The IRS monitors and performs annual suitability checks on Authorized e-file Providers for compliance with the revenue procedure and program requirements. Violations may result in a variety of sanctions. Which statement is TRUE regarding possible sanctions?

A. The IRS may issue permanent suspension for a Level One infraction in the electronic filing program.
B. The IRS may not expel an e-file Provider from the program without a formal judicial proceeding.
C. The IRS may suspend or expel an e-file Provider prior to administrative review for a Level Three infraction in the electronic filing program.
D. The IRS may not impose a sanction that is greater than a one-year suspension from the electronic filing program.

The answer is C. "Level Three" infractions are violations so egregious that, in the opinion of the IRS, they have a significant adverse impact on the quality of electronically-filed returns on IRS e-file. Depending on the severity of the infraction (such as fraud or criminal conduct), a Level Three infraction may result in expulsion without the opportunity for future participation. The IRS reserves the right to suspend or expel an Authorized IRS e-file Provider prior to administrative review for Level Three infractions (Publication 3112). ###

8. Which logo may a practitioner use in his advertising?

A. The official IRS logo
B. The IRS e-file logo
C. The official seal of the U.S. Treasury
D. The IRS eagle symbol

The answer is B. Practitioners may not use the IRS logo or insignia in their advertising, or imply a relationship with the IRS. A practitioner may use the IRS e-file logo. A preparer may NOT combine the e-file logo with the IRS eagle symbol, the word "federal," or with other words or symbols that suggest a special relationship between the IRS and the logo. Advertising materials must not carry the IRS or other Treasury seals. ###

9. Gregory is single and 67 years old. He has a balance due to the IRS of $25,000. He cannot pay this amount. All of Gregory's tax returns have been filed timely. Which of the following statements is TRUE?

A. Gregory does not qualify for an installment agreement because he is over 65 and his Social Security income will be garnished to pay his outstanding liability.
B. An IRS installment agreement requires equal monthly payments that will result in payment of the tax owed within the statute during which the IRS can collect the tax.
C. Gregory may still qualify for an installment agreement even if he has not filed his prior year tax returns.
D. Gregory will not be charged a fee for the installment agreement.

The answer is B. Gregory will only qualify for an installment agreement if he is up-to-date on his filing obligations. A user fee will be charged to set up the installment agreement. Installment agreements usually require equal monthly payments. ###

10. What happens when a taxpayer has a late payment on an installment agreement?

A. The late payment will generate an automatic 30-day notice.
B. The late payment will automatically increase the statute of limitations for collecting the tax.
C. The late payment will case the installment agreement to default.
D. The IRS will file a Notice of Deficiency.

The answer is A. A late payment on an installment agreement will generate an automatic 30-day notice as to the cessation of the agreement, allowing the IRS to make changes to the installment agreement. ###

11. Which of the following forms is acceptable for a taxpayer to submit an electronic signature on an e-filed tax return?

A. Form 8879
B. Form 8862
C. Form 2848
D. Form 7004

The answer is A. There are two methods for signing individual income tax returns electronically. The two available options are: (1) The Practitioner PIN method; Form 8879 (2) The Scanned Form 8453 method. ####

12. Which of the following businesses is required to file electronically?

A. A partnership with 100 partners
B. A corporation with $5 million in assets
C. A partnership with more than 100 partners
D. A corporation with $7.5 million in assets

The answer is C. Partnerships with more than 100 partners are required to file electronically. This means that a partnership must file Form 1065 and the multiple Schedules K-1 electronically. Partnerships with 100 or fewer partners (Schedules K-1) may voluntarily file their returns electronically, but they are not required to do so. Large and midsized corporate taxpayers including tax-exempt organizations with $10 million or more in assets that file at least 250 returns (information returns and others, such as Form 1099 and Form W-2) are required to e-file.###

13. Which of the following tax preparers would NOT be subject to the new e-file mandate that requires preparers to e-file their clients' returns?

A. Dean, an unenrolled bookkeeper who prepares 150 payroll tax returns for compensation
B. Maria, an Enrolled Agent who prepares 100 Form 1040s for her employer
C. Scott, who files 120 tax returns for compensation
D. Chon, a CPA who files 1,000 individual returns and two corporate returns

The answer is A. The new e-file mandate does not apply to payroll tax returns. Any paid preparer who files more than 100 returns for the 2010 tax year is required to e-file. There is an exception for returns that cannot be e-filed (such as returns that require paper attachments). The new e-file mandate does not apply to payroll tax returns. ###

Unit 3.8: The IRS Examination Process

More Reading:
Publication 556, *Examination of Returns, Appeal Rights, and Claims for Refund*
Publication 1, *Your Rights As a Taxpayer*
Publication 3498, *The Examination Process*

The IRS accepts most tax returns as they are filed but selects a percentage of returns for examination. Even though the IRS uses the term "examination" rather than "audit," they mean essentially the same thing. Selecting a return for examination does not always suggest that the taxpayer has either made an error or been dishonest. In fact, some examinations result in a refund to the taxpayer or acceptance of the return without any changes.

A tax return may be examined for multiple reasons. After the examination, if any change to the taxpayer's return is proposed, she can disagree with the changes and appeal the IRS's decision. This is done through the appeals process, which we'll cover in a later unit. In this study unit, we'll cover the examination process.

The IRS may choose to conduct the examination entirely by mail. If that's the case, the taxpayer will receive a letter asking for additional information about certain items shown on the return, such as proof of income, expenses, and itemized deductions. These audits are often called "correspondence audits."

Example: The IRS selects Sally's return for examination. Sally has a disabled half-sister that she cares for. Sally claimed her older half-sister as a "qualifying child" based on her permanent disability, and also claimed Head of Household status. The IRS asked for proof of disability and residency. Sally provided copies of doctors' records and additional proof that her sister was living with her full time. The IRS accepted Sally's documents and closed the case as a "no change" audit. Sally never had to meet with the IRS auditor, and the entire audit was conducted by mail (Publication 3498).

An IRS examination may also be conducted in person. It may take place in the taxpayer's home, his place of business, an IRS office, or the office of the taxpayer's attorney, accountant, or Enrolled Agent.

Taxpayer Rights During the Examination Process

The taxpayer has a number of rights during the IRS examination process. These rights include:

- A right to professional and courteous treatment by IRS employees
- A right to privacy and confidentiality about tax matters
- A right to know why the IRS is asking for information, how the IRS will use it, and what will happen if the requested information is not provided
- A right to representation, by oneself or an authorized representative
- A right to appeal disagreements, both within the IRS and before the courts

How Returns are Selected for Examination

Only about 1.5% of all returns are audited. A taxpayer's return may be examined for a variety of reasons, and the examination may take place in any one of several ways. The IRS selects returns using a variety of methods, including:

Potential Abusive/Tax Avoidance Transactions

Some returns are selected based on information obtained by the IRS through efforts to identify promoters and participants of abusive tax avoidance transactions.

Computer Scoring/DIF Score

Other tax returns may be chosen for examination on the basis of computer scoring. A computer program called the "Discriminant Inventory Function System" (DIF) assigns a numeric score to each individual and some corporate tax returns after they have been processed. IRS computers automatically check tax returns and assign a "DIF score" based on the probability that the return contains errors, excessive tax deductions, or other issues. This does not necessarily mean that the return was prepared incorrectly. However, the computer is trained to look for aberrations and questionable items.

If a taxpayer's return is selected because of a high score under the DIF system, the return has a high probability of being chosen for audit. The IRS does not release information about how it calculates a taxpayer's DIF score. Tax returns with high DIF scores are generally pulled and scrutinized by an IRS officer. The officer then determines whether or not to pursue an examination of the tax return.

> **Example:** Perry is an Enrolled Agent. His client Lila received an audit notice this year. Lila's tax return was selected because she had a very high number of credits and very little taxable income. However, her tax return was prepared correctly. Lila had adopted four special-needs children in 2010 and was able to take a large adoption credit. Perry provided proof of the adoptions to the examining officer, which resulted in a positive outcome for Lila and a "no-change" audit.

Information Matching

Some returns are examined because payer reports, such as Forms W-2 from employers or Form 1099 interest statements from banks, do not match the income reported on the tax return. The return may also be selected for examination on the basis of information received from third-party documentation that may conflict with the information reported on the tax return. Or, the return may be selected to address questionable treatment of an item or simply to study the behavior of similar taxpayers (a market segment) in handling a tax issue.

A return may be selected as a result of information received from other third-party sources or individuals. This information can come from a number of sources, including state and local law enforcement agencies, public records, and individuals. The information is evaluated for reliability and accuracy before it is used as the basis of an examination or investigation.

> **Example:** Brian embezzled money from his employer and got nabbed in 2010 for felony embezzlement. The case was made public and the police shared their information with the IRS. The IRS contacted Brian and made an adjustment to all of his tax returns, assessing additional tax, interest, and penalties for fraud, for failing to report the embezzled funds as income.

Related Examinations

Returns may be selected for audit when they involve issues or transactions with other taxpayers, such as business partners or investors, whose returns were selected for examination.

Notice of IRS Contact of Third Parties

During the examination process, the IRS may contact third parties regarding a tax matter without the taxpayer's permission. The IRS must give the taxpayer reasonable notice before contacting other persons about his individual tax matters.

The IRS may contact third parties such as neighbors, banks, employers, or employees. The IRS must also provide the taxpayer with a record of persons contacted on both a periodic basis and upon the taxpayer's request. This provision does not apply:

- To any pending criminal investigation
- When providing notice would jeopardize collection of any tax liability
- When providing notice may result in reprisal against any person
- When the taxpayer has already authorized the contact

> **Example:** Les's tax return was selected by the IRS for audit. The IRS suspects unreported income due to criminal drug activity. Les is also being investigated by the FBI. Because the IRS is researching criminal activity, the IRS is not required to give Les reasonable notice before contacting third parties about his individual tax matters.

The Examination Process

Most examinations are handled entirely by mail. This typically happens when there is a minor issue that the IRS needs to clarify. Sometimes, the IRS is simply requesting proof that a particular transaction has occurred.

> **Example:** Pete received a notice from the IRS regarding his 2010 tax return. He had disposed of a large number of stocks that year, and the IRS wanted basis information on the stocks. Pete requested a report from his stockbroker showing the basis and sent it to the IRS along with a copy of the notice. The issue was resolved without incident, and Pete received a notice showing that no changes had been made to his tax return.

Repeat Examinations

The IRS tries to avoid repeat examinations of the same items, but sometimes this happens. If a taxpayer's return was audited for the same items in the previous two years and no change was proposed to tax liability, the taxpayer may contact the IRS and request that the examination be discontinued.

Example: Kelly donates a large portion of her salary to her church. For the last two years, the IRS has selected Kelly's return for examination based on her large donations. In both instances, Kelly was able to substantiate her donations and "no change" was made to her tax liability. Kelly's tax return is selected again for the same reason in 2010. Kelly contacts the IRS to request that the examination be discontinued. The examining officer agrees to discontinue the examination.

Example: Roy's tax return has been selected for examination two years in a row. In 2008 and 2009, his tax return was selected to verify compliance for the Earned Income Tax Credit. There was no change to Roy's tax liability in either year. In 2010, Roy's tax return is selected for audit again. This time, the IRS is questioning Roy's education deductions. Roy cannot request that the examination be discontinued. That is because the IRS examination is for a different item than in the previous two examinations.

The Audit Location

Examinations that are not handled by mail can take place at:

- The taxpayer's home or place of business
- An Internal Revenue office
- Or the office of the taxpayer's representative (attorney, CPA, or Enrolled Agent)

Generally, a taxpayer's return is examined in the area where she lives. But if the taxpayer's return can be examined more conveniently in another area, such as where the taxpayer's records are located, the taxpayer may request a transfer to that area. The audit may take place in another district office if the taxpayer requests it. Although the IRS may deny this request, it usually does not.

Example: Joyce runs a travel marketing business, and she travels frequently in order to promote her business and to visit clients. She lives in Los Angeles; however, her CPA is in New York. In 2010 Joyce's tax return was selected for examination and she chose to have her CPA represent her. Her CPA requested that the examination be transferred to the New York area where Joyce's records were located. The transfer was granted.

The taxpayer may request a change of venue if the first method or location is inconvenient. The IRS must make exceptions for extenuating circumstances. For example, if the taxpayer is currently on active duty in a combat zone, the examination must be temporarily suspended. However, the IRS will make the final determination of when, where, and how the examination will take place.

During the Examination

In examinations not handled by mail, the taxpayer or the taxpayer's representative must make an appointment to meet with the IRS. The examining officer will notify the taxpayer of any records that are required. The IRS officer must explain any proposed changes to the tax return.

The IRS must follow the tax laws set forth by Congress in the Internal Revenue Code. The IRS also follows court decisions, but the IRS may choose to disregard a court decision on the same issue and still apply its own interpretation of tax law. Sometimes, tax returns are adjusted in the taxpayer's favor, and the taxpayer is actually owed a refund. However, usually this is not the case. Most tax returns selected for examination result in an increase of tax liability.

About 60% of audited cases are closed with additional taxes owed. About 19% are closed with "no change" in tax liability and about 21% are closed with a reduction in tax liability.

If the taxpayer agrees with the IRS's proposed changes, he may immediately sign an agreement. The taxpayer is responsible for paying interest on any additional tax. If the taxpayer pays any additional tax owed when he signs the agreement, the interest is figured from the due date of the tax return to the date of the payment.

If the taxpayer does not pay the additional tax when she signs the agreement, she will receive a bill that includes interest. If the taxpayer pays the amount due within ten business days of the billing date, she will not have to pay any more interest or penalties. This period is extended to 21 calendar days if the amount due is less than $100,000.

If the taxpayer is due a refund, he will receive the refund sooner if he signs the agreement. The taxpayer will be paid interest on the refund. If the IRS accepts the tax return as filed (a "no-change" audit), the taxpayer will receive a confirmation letter stating that the IRS proposed no changes to the return.

In general, the IRS will not reopen a closed examination case to make an unfavorable adjustment unless:

- There was fraud or misrepresentation.
- There was a substantial error based on an established IRS position existing at the time of the examination, or failure to reopen the case would be a serious administrative omission.

The Taxpayer's Representative

A taxpayer is always allowed to use a qualified representative before the IRS. The taxpayer does not have to attend the audit if the representative has a written authorization from the taxpayer and is an authorized representative per Circular 230. The taxpayer may also choose to have a close family member represent him.

Example: Astrid is an Enrolled Agent. A taxpayer named Seth hires her to represent him before the IRS during the examination of his tax return. Seth does not want to attend the audit. He signs Form 2848 indicating that Astrid is now his authorized representative for all his tax affairs. Astrid attends the examination on Seth's behalf.

Representatives must have prior written authorization in order to represent the taxpayer before the IRS. Representatives may use Form 2848, *Power of Attorney and Declaration of Representative*, or any other properly written authorization.

If the taxpayer chooses to use a representative, the representative can be any federally authorized practitioner, including an attorney, a Certified Public Accountant, or an Enrolled Agent.

An unenrolled preparer who prepared the return and signed it as the preparer may represent the taxpayer before the examination division; however, the taxpayer must be present at the meeting. In the case of an Enrolled Agent, CPA, or attorney, the taxpayer is not required to be present.

The taxpayer may always represent himself during an examination. If the taxpayer attends an IRS audit and attempts to represent himself but during the course of the examination becomes uncomfortable and wishes to consult with a tax advisor, the IRS must suspend the interview and reschedule it. However, the IRS cannot suspend the interview if the taxpayer is there because of an administrative summons.

On a jointly filed tax return that is selected for examination, only one spouse is required to meet with the IRS.

Confidentiality Privilege

Taxpayers are granted a confidentiality privilege with any federally authorized practitioner. This is the same confidentiality protection that a taxpayer would have with an attorney, with some exceptions. Confidential communications include:

- Tax advice about the practitioner's authority to practice before the IRS
- Matters that would be confidential between an attorney and a client
- Non-criminal tax matters before the IRS

The confidentiality privilege does not apply to communications in connection with the promotion of or participation in a tax shelter. A tax shelter is any entity, plan, or arrangement whose significant purpose is to avoid or evade income tax.

The confidentiality privilege also does not apply to criminal tax matters or to issues related to any other branch of government.

This privilege is not applicable to the preparation and filing of a tax return. Nor does the privilege apply to state tax matters, although a number of states have an accountant-client privilege.

Recording the Audit Interview

The practitioner may record the examination interview. The practitioner must notify the examiner ten days in advance in writing that he wishes to record the interview. The IRS may also record an interview. If the IRS initiates the recording, the taxpayer and/or the representative must be notified ten days in advance, and the taxpayer may request a copy of the recording.

Suspension of Interest and Penalties Due to IRS Delays

The IRS has three years from the date the taxpayer filed his return (or the date the return was due, if later) to assess any additional tax. However, if the taxpayer files his return timely (including extensions), interest and certain penalties will be suspended if the IRS fails to mail a notice to the taxpayer stating:

- The taxpayer's liability, and
- The basis for that liability

Within an 18-month period beginning on the later of:

- The date on which the taxpayer filed her return, or
- The due date (without extensions) of the tax return.

If the IRS mails the notice after this 18-month period, interest and penalties on the assessment will be suspended. The suspension period begins the day after the close of the 18-

month period and ends 21 days after the IRS mails a notice to the taxpayer stating his liability. Penalties and interest will NOT be suspended in the following cases:

- The failure-to-pay penalty
- Any fraudulent tax return
- Any amount related to a gross misstatement
- Any amount related to a reportable transaction (a tax shelter) that was not adequately disclosed
- Any listed transaction
- Any criminal penalty

The IRS will waive penalties when allowed by law if the taxpayer can show that he acted in good faith or relied on the incorrect advice of an IRS employee.

Requesting Abatement of Interest Due to IRS Error or Delay

The IRS will waive interest that is the result of certain errors or delays caused by an IRS employee. The IRS will abate the interest only if there was an unreasonable error or delay in performing a managerial or ministerial act (defined below). The taxpayer cannot have caused any significant aspect of the error or delay. In addition, the interest can be abated only if it relates to taxes for which a notice of deficiency is required.

Managerial Act

The term "managerial act" means an administrative act that occurs during the processing of the taxpayer's case involving the temporary or permanent loss of records or the exercise of judgment or discretion relating to management of personnel. The proper application of federal tax law is not a managerial act.

Ministerial Act

The term "ministerial act" means a procedural or mechanical act that does not involve the exercise of judgment or discretion and that occurs during the processing of the taxpayer's case after all prerequisites of the act, such as conferences and review by supervisors, have taken place. The proper application of federal tax law is not a ministerial act.

Example: Calvin moves to another state before the IRS selects his tax return for examination. A letter stating that Calvin's return was selected for examination was sent to his old address and then forwarded to his new address. When he gets the letter, he responds with a request that the examination be transferred to the area office closest to his new address. The examination group manager approves his request. After his request has been approved, the original examination manager forgets about the transfer and fails to transfer the file for six months. The transfer is a ministerial act. The IRS can reduce the interest because of any unreasonable delay in transferring the case.

Example: A revenue agent is examining Suzette's tax return. During the course of the examination, the agent is sent to an extended training course. The agent's supervisor decides not to reassign the audit case, so the examination is unreasonably delayed until the agent returns. Interest caused by the unreasonable delay can be abated since the decision to send the agent to the training class and the decision not to reassign the case are both managerial acts.

A taxpayer may request an abatement of interest on Form 843, *Claim for Refund and Request for Abatement*. The taxpayer should file the claim with the IRS service center where the examination was affected by the error or delay. If a request for abatement of interest is denied, an appeal can be made to the IRS Appeals Office and the U.S. Tax Court.

Unit 3.8: Questions

1. Which form is used by a taxpayer to request an abatement of interest because of an IRS error?

A. Form 843
B. Form 911
C. Form 2690
D. Form 2848

The answer is A. A taxpayer may request an abatement of interest on Form 843, *Claim for Refund and Request for Abatement.* This form is used to request an abatement of interest due to an unreasonable error or delay on the part of the IRS. ###

2. Frank's tax return was chosen by the IRS for examination. He moved a few months ago to another state, but the IRS notice says that his examination will be scheduled in the city where he used to live. Which of the following statements is TRUE about this issue?

A. Frank can request that his tax return examination be moved to another IRS service center since he has moved to another area.
B. Frank must schedule the examination in his former city of residence, but he can have a professional represent him.
C. Frank is required to meet with the auditor at least once in person in order to move the examination to another location.
D. None of the above.

The answer is A. If a taxpayer has moved or if his books and records are located in another area, he can request that the location of his audit be changed to another IRS service center. ###

3. On a jointly filed tax return that has been selected for examination, which of the following statements is TRUE?

A. Both spouses must be present, because both spouses signed the return.
B. Only one spouse must be present.
C. Neither spouse must respond to the notice.
D. Neither spouse can use a representative.

The answer is B. For taxpayers who file jointly, only one spouse is required to meet with the IRS. The taxpayers can also choose to use a qualified representative to represent them before the IRS. ###

4. When a taxpayer is chosen for an IRS audit, which of the following statements is TRUE?

A. The taxpayer must appear before the IRS in person.
B. A taxpayer may choose to be represented before the IRS and is not required to appear if she so wishes.
C. An audit case may not be transferred to a different IRS office under any circumstances.
D. If a taxpayer feels that she is not being treated fairly during an IRS audit, she cannot appeal to the auditor's manager.

The answer is B. The taxpayer is not required to be present during an IRS examination if she has provided written authorization to a qualified representative per Circular 230. ###

5. What is a DIF Score?

A. A computer scoring process that the IRS uses to select some returns for audit
B. A report that is transmitted with each filed return
C. A score that an auditor gives to the tax practitioner
D. An IRS scoring process for Tax Court procedures

The answer is A. The Discriminant Function System (DIF) score rates potential returns for audit, based on past IRS experience with similar returns. IRS personnel screen the highest-scoring returns, selecting some for audit and identifying the items on these returns that are most likely to need review.

6. During the examination process, the IRS may contact third parties regarding a tax matter without the taxpayer's permission. What else is true regarding the IRS's contact of third parties during the examination process?

A. The IRS must give the taxpayer reasonable notice before contacting other persons about his individual tax matters.
B. The IRS may not contact the taxpayer's banking institution.
C. The IRS may contact third parties only with a court order.
D. The IRS cannot contact third parties without a summons.

The answer is A. The IRS must give the taxpayer reasonable notice before contacting other persons about his individual tax matters. The IRS may contact third parties such as neighbors, banks, employers, or employees. The IRS must also provide the taxpayer with a record of persons contacted on both a periodic basis and upon the taxpayer's request. ###

7. Taxpayers are granted a confidentiality privilege with any federally authorized practitioner. This is the same confidentiality protection that a taxpayer would have with an attorney, with some exceptions. Confidential communications DO NOT include _____.

A. Tax advice about the practitioner's authority to practice before the IRS
B. Matters that would be confidential between an attorney and a client
C. Participation in a tax shelter
D. Non-criminal tax matters before the IRS

The answer is C. The confidentiality privilege does not apply in the case of communications regarding the promotion of or participation in a tax shelter. A tax shelter is any entity, plan, or arrangement whose significant purpose is to avoid or evade income tax. ###

8. According to the IRS, tax returns are selected for audit based on a number of different reasons. Which is NOT one of the reasons why a tax return would be selected for audit?

A. Potential abusive transactions
B. Computer scoring
C. Because the taxpayer works for an employer who has filed for bankruptcy
D. Information received from other third-party sources or individuals

The answer is C. A taxpayer would not be chosen for audit just because his employer filed for bankruptcy. The IRS selects returns using a variety of methods, including potential participants in abusive tax avoidance transactions; computer scoring; information matching (some returns are examined because payer reports such as Forms W-2 from employers or Form 1099 interest statements from banks do not match the income reported on the tax return); related examinations (related entities may be audited together); or local compliance projects (random audits). ###

Unit 3.9: The Appeals Process

> **More Reading:**
> Publication 5, *Your Appeal Rights and How to Prepare a Protest If You Don't Agree*
> Publication 556, *Examination of Returns, Appeal Rights, and Claims for Refund*
> Publication 4227, *Overview of the Appeals Process*
> Publication 4167, *Appeals: Introduction to Alternative Dispute Resolution*

Because taxpayers often disagree with the IRS on tax matters, the IRS has an appeal system. Every taxpayer has the right to appeal changes on a tax return that is audited. Most differences are settled within the appeals system without going to court. For instance, taxpayers have the option to appeal to the auditor's manager in cases of disagreement.

Reasons for appeal must be supported by tax law, however. An appeal of a case cannot be based solely on moral, religious, political, constitutional, conscientious, or similar grounds.

If the taxpayer chooses not to appeal within the IRS system, he may take his case directly to the U.S. Tax Court. The tax does not have to be paid first in order to appeal within the IRS or to the U.S. Tax Court.

The taxpayer may opt to bypass both the IRS appeals process and the Tax Court and instead take his case to the U.S. Court of Federal Claims or a local U.S. district court. However, if the taxpayer chooses to go directly to court, all of the contested tax must be paid. The taxpayer must then sue the IRS for a refund.

Only attorneys, Certified Public Accountants, or Enrolled Agents are allowed to represent taxpayers before an appeals hearing. An unenrolled preparer may be a witness at the conference, but not act as a representative.

Taxpayer Rights

During the IRS collections and examination process, taxpayers have the right to:
- Disagree with their tax bill.
- Meet with an IRS manager.
- Appeal most IRS collection actions.
- Have their cases transferred to a different IRS office if they have a valid reason, such as if they have moved to another city.
- Be represented by an agent (such as a CPA, Enrolled Agent, or attorney) when dealing with IRS matters.
- Receive a receipt for any payment made to the IRS.

Starting the Appeals Process

At the beginning of each examination, the IRS auditor must explain a taxpayer's appeal rights. If the taxpayer chooses to appeal the examiner's decision through the IRS system, she can file an appeal at a local IRS appeals office, which is a separate entity from local IRS district offices. She will then receive a letter from the IRS, which sets a time limit to file for an appeal conference.

The appeals procedure varies based on the amount of the proposed tax. If the amount is less than $2,500, the taxpayer must only contact the IRS to initiate an appeal. If the amount is more than $2,500 but less than $10,000, a brief statement of disputed tax is required. If the disputed amount exceeds $10,000, then a formal written protest is required.

An IRS appeal does not abate the interest on the tax due, which continues to accumulate until the balance of the debt is paid. Penalties and interest will continue to accrue until the balance of the debt is paid, or until the taxpayer wins his appeal and he is granted a "no-change" audit. If the taxpayer is granted a "no-change" audit, then that means that the IRS has accepted the tax return as it was filed, and no additional tax is due. About 30% of all IRS examinations end in a "no-change" determination.

30-Day Letter and 90-Day Letter

Within a few weeks after the taxpayer's closing conference with the IRS examiner, he will receive a 30-day letter. This letter includes:

- A notice explaining the taxpayer's right to appeal the proposed changes within 30 days
- A copy of the examination report explaining the examiner's proposed changes
- An agreement or waiver form
- A copy of Publication 5, *Your Appeal Rights and How to Prepare a Protest If You Don't Agree*

The taxpayer has 30 days from the date of notice to accept or appeal the proposed changes.

Notice of Deficiency: The 90-Day Letter

If the taxpayer does not respond to the 30-day letter or if she cannot reach an agreement with an appeals officer, the IRS will send the taxpayer a 90-day letter, which is also known as a "Statutory Notice of Deficiency."

The taxpayer will have 90 days (150 days if addressed to a taxpayer outside the United States) from the date of this notice to file a petition with the Tax Court. If the taxpayer does not file the petition in time, the tax is due within ten days, and the taxpayer may not take her case to Tax Court. A notice of deficiency must be issued before a taxpayer can go to Tax Court. This means that the taxpayer must wait for the IRS to send him a "final notice" before he can petition the Tax Court to hear his case.

Once the taxpayer gets the Notice of Deficiency, she has 90 days to file a petition with the court. Once she files a petition and the case becomes docketed before Tax Court, her file will again go to an appeals office to see if it can be resolved before it goes to Tax Court. Over 90% of all tax cases are solved before going to Tax Court.

The Burden of Proof

With the IRS, taxpayers always have the burden of proving their deductions and their income. However, with alleged "unreported income," the IRS has the burden of proof based on any reconstruction of income solely through the use of statistical information on unrelated taxpayers.

> **Example:** Ken owns a business and the IRS disagrees with his stated income. The IRS reconstructs Ken's income based on industry standards, but does not have actual proof that Ken misstated his income. During a court case, the burden of proof is on the IRS if the IRS used a reconstruction of records solely to estimate Ken's liability.

For the burden of proof to lie with the IRS in court proceedings, the taxpayer must have complied with all of the issues listed below:

- Adhered to IRS substantiation requirements.
- Maintained adequate records.
- Cooperated with reasonable requests for information from the IRS.
- Introduced credible evidence relating to the issue.
- Have tax liability of $7 million or less if the taxpayer is a trust, corporation, or partnership.

Recovering Litigation or Administrative Costs

If the court agrees with the taxpayer on most issues in the case and finds that the IRS's position is unjustified, the taxpayer may be able to recover administrative and litigation costs. These are the expenses that a taxpayer incurs to defend her position to the IRS or the courts.

The taxpayer may be able to recover reasonable litigation or administrative costs if all of the following conditions apply:

- The taxpayer is the prevailing party.
- The taxpayer has exhausted all administrative remedies within the IRS.
- The taxpayer's "net worth" is below a certain limit.
- The taxpayer does not unreasonably delay any IRS proceeding.

The taxpayer will not be treated as the "prevailing party" if the IRS establishes that its position was substantially justified. The position of the IRS is NOT considered "substantially justified" if either of the following applies:

- The IRS did not follow its applicable published guidance (such as regulations, Revenue Rulings, notices, announcements, Private Letter Rulings, Technical Advice Memoranda, and determination letters issued to the taxpayer) in the proceeding. This presumption can be overcome by evidence.
- The IRS has lost in courts of appeal for other circuits on substantially similar issues.

The court will generally decide who the "prevailing party" is.

Net Worth Requirements for Recovering Litigation Costs

In order to request the recovery of litigation costs from the IRS, the taxpayer must meet certain "net worth" requirements:

- For individuals, net worth cannot exceed $2 million as of the filing date of the petition for review. For this purpose, individuals filing a joint return are treated as separate individuals.
- For estates, net worth cannot exceed $2 million as of the date of the decedent's death.

- For charities and certain cooperatives, the entity cannot have more than 500 employees as of the filing date of the petition for review.
- For all other taxpayers, net worth cannot exceed $7 million AND the entity must not have more than 500 employees as of the filing date of the petition for review.

The taxpayer may apply for administrative costs within 90 days of the date of the mailing of the final decision of the IRS Office of Appeals regarding the tax, interest, or penalty.

Protests and Small Case Requests

When a taxpayer requests an IRS appeals conference, he may also be required to file either a formal written protest or a small case request. A taxpayer will be required to file a written protest in the following cases:

- All employee plan cases, without regard to the dollar amount at issue
- All exempt organization cases, without regard to the dollar amount at issue
- All partnership and S Corporation cases without regard to the dollar amount at issue
- All other cases, unless the taxpayer qualifies for the "small case request" procedure

Small Tax Case Procedure

A taxpayer may elect the small tax case procedure (also known as S case procedure) for cases involving up to $50,000 in deficiency per year, including penalties and other additions to tax, but *excluding* interest. Dollar limits for the Tax Court Small Case Division vary:

- For a "Notice of Deficiency": $50,000 is the maximum amount, including penalties and interest, for any year before the court.
- For a "Notice of Determination": $50,000 is the maximum amount for all the years combined.
- For an "IRS Notice of Determination of Worker Classification": The amount in the dispute cannot exceed $50,000 for any calendar quarter.

The tax laws provide for the small tax case procedures for resolving disputes between taxpayers and the IRS. The taxpayer and the Tax Court must both agree to proceed with the small case procedure. Generally, the Tax Court will agree with the taxpayer's request if the taxpayer otherwise qualifies.

There is no right of appeal to a U.S. Court of Appeals from a decision in this type of case. In contrast, the taxpayer and the IRS can appeal a decision in a regular, non-S case to a U.S. Court of Appeals. A decision entered in a small tax case is not treated as precedent for any other case. Trials in small tax cases generally are less formal and result in a speedier disposition. The decisions of the small tax case division are generally not published.

Since the taxpayer cannot appeal a decision from the Small Tax Case division, the taxpayer must consider if using the small tax case procedure is worth the risk. A taxpayer who uses the regular US Tax Court retains the right to appeal his case to a higher court.

The IRS cannot attempt to influence a taxpayer to waive his rights to sue the United States or a government officer or employee for any action taken in connection with the tax laws.

Unit 3.9: Questions

1. With an IRS appeal, which of the following statements is CORRECT?

A. An appeal does not abate the interest, which continues to accrue.
B. A taxpayer must pay the disputed tax before filing an appeal with the IRS.
C. The IRS is prohibited from filing a federal tax lien if the taxpayer is complying with an installment agreement.
D. Taxpayers who do not agree to the IRS changes may NOT appeal to the U.S. Tax Court.

The answer is A. An IRS appeal does not abate the interest, which continues to accrue until the balance of the debt is paid. Penalties and interest will continue to accrue until the balance of the debt is paid, or until the taxpayer wins his appeal and he is granted a "no-change" audit. ###

2. In the event of a court proceeding, the _____ has the burden of proof for any factual issue.

A. IRS
B. Taxpayer
C. U.S. Tax Court
D. The attorney or other qualified representative

The answer is B. Taxpayers are required to maintain records to substantiate items claimed on tax returns. Records such as receipts, canceled checks, and other documents that support items of income or deductions appearing on their returns should be kept until the statute of limitations expires for those returns. ###

3. Greg disputes his auditor's findings. He wants to go to appeals, but his tax return was prepared by an unenrolled preparer. What are his options?

A. Greg may only represent himself.
B. Greg may represent himself or hire an enrolled preparer to represent him at the appeals level.
C. Greg may request that the unenrolled preparer represent him before the IRS.
D. Greg may ask an IRS employee to represent him before the appeals level.

The answer is B. Greg can deal with appeals by himself. If he wants to be represented by someone else, he must choose a person who is an attorney, a Certified Public Accountant, or an Enrolled Agent authorized to practice before the IRS (Publication 4227). ###

757

4. The "Statutory Notice of Deficiency" is also known as:

A. A 30-day letter because the taxpayer generally has 30 days from the date of the letter to file a petition with the Tax Court.
B. A 90-day letter because the taxpayer generally has 90 days from the date of the letter to file a petition with the Tax Court.
C. An Information Document Request (IDR) because the taxpayer is asked for information to support his position regarding liability for tax.
D. A federal tax lien.

The answer is B. The Statutory Notice of Deficiency, or "90-day letter," gives the taxpayer 90 days to file a petition in the United States Tax Court challenging the proposed deficiency. A taxpayer has 150 days if his address is outside of the country on the day the notice of deficiency is mailed. ###

5. The IRS has begun an examination of Don's income tax return. The IRS would like to ask Don's neighbors questions related to the examination. There is no pending criminal investigation into the matter, and there is no evidence that such contact will result in reprisals against the neighbors or jeopardize collection of the tax liability. Before the IRS contacts the neighbors, the IRS must:

A. Provide Don with reasonable notice of the contact.
B. Make an assessment of Don's tax liability.
C. Ask the court for a third-party record keeper subpoena.
D. Mail Don a Statutory Notice of Deficiency.

The answer is A. Pursuant to IRC §7602(c), a third-party contact is made when an IRS employee initiates contact with a person other than the taxpayer. A third party may be contacted to obtain information about a specific taxpayer's federal tax liability, including the issuance of a levy or summons to someone other than the taxpayer. The IRS does not need permission to contact third parties. But the IRS must notify the taxpayer that the contact with third parties will be made. ###

6. Alyssa vehemently disagreed with the IRS examiner regarding her income tax case. Her appeal rights were explained to her, and she decided to go to Tax Court. Which of the following is true?

A. Alyssa must receive a notice of deficiency before she can go to Tax Court.
B. Alyssa must wait for the IRS examiner to permanently close her audit case.
C. Alyssa must request a Collections Due Process hearing before going to Tax Court.
D. Alyssa cannot go to Tax Court unless she agrees with the auditor's findings.

The answer is A. A notice of deficiency must be issued before a taxpayer can go to Tax Court. Once the taxpayer gets the Notice of Deficiency, she has 90 days to file a petition with the court. Once she files a petition and the case becomes docketed before the Tax Court, her file will *again* go to an appeals office to see if it can be resolved before it goes to the Tax Court. ###

6. Karl had his 2007 and 2008 income tax returns examined resulting in adjustments. He has administratively appealed the adjustments through the IRS appeals process. Some of them were sustained, resulting in an income tax deficiency in the amount of $25,000 for 2007 and $27,000 for 2008. Karl now wants to appeal his case to the U.S. Tax Court. He will handle the case himself since he cannot afford a lawyer. Which of the following is TRUE?

A. Karl is entitled to invoke the small tax case procedure.
B. Karl has forfeited his rights to the small tax case procedure by going to appeals first.
C. Karl is not entitled to the small tax case procedure because his disputed amount exceeds $50,000.
D. Karl must appeal to the U.S. District Court.

The answer is A. A taxpayer may elect the small tax case procedure (also known as S case procedure) for cases involving up to $50,000 in deficiency *per year*, including penalties and other additions to tax, but excluding interest. Trials in small tax cases generally are less formal and result in a speedier disposition. Small tax court cases may not be appealed. ###

7. Kevin and Javier are partners in a body shop business. Both of them had their individual returns examined and both disagreed with the IRS. Kevin decided to take his case to IRS Appeals. After the conference, he and the IRS still disagreed. Javier decided to bypass IRS Appeals altogether. After satisfying certain procedural and jurisdictional requirements, both Kevin and Javier can take their cases to the following courts: United States Tax Court, the United States Court of Federal Claims, or the United States District Court.

A. True
B. False

The answer is A, True. A taxpayer is not required to use the IRS appeals process. If a taxpayer and the IRS still disagree after an appeals conference, or the election was made to bypass the IRS appeals system, the case may be taken to the U.S. Tax Court, the U.S. Court of Federal Claims, or a U.S. district court.###

Unit 3.10: An IRC Tax Law Primer

The Internal Revenue Code (IRC) is the main body of tax law of the United States. It is published as "Title 26" of the United States Code (USC), and is also known as the Internal Revenue Title.

Other tax law is promulgated by individual states, cities, and municipalities. The IRS Enrolled Agent Exam deals only with federal tax laws, and not with the laws of any individual state or municipality.

Tax law is decided by all three branches of our federal government. The legislative branch is responsible for the Internal Revenue Code and Congressional committee reports. The executive branch is responsible for income tax regulations, revenue rulings, and revenue procedures. The judicial branch, which is comprised of U.S. courts, is responsible for court decisions. These three sources provide the authority by which both taxpayers and governments must abide.

Tax law is primarily decided by Congress, and it changes every year. Laws passed by Congress are the main source of Internal Revenue Code tax law.

The Internal Revenue Service (IRS) has the responsibility of enforcing tax law. In its role of administering the tax laws enacted by Congress, the IRS takes the specifics of these laws and translates them into the detailed regulations, rules, and procedures of the Internal Revenue Code.

Often times, taxpayers and tax practitioners will disagree with the IRS's interpretation of the IRC. In these cases, it is up to the courts to determine Congress's intent or the constitutionality of the tax law or IRS position that is being challenged. There are many instances where tax laws are either disputed or overturned. Court decisions then serve as guidance for future tax decisions.

The IRS is the "collection arm" for the U.S. Treasury, which is responsible for paying various government expenses. The Department of the Treasury issues administrative pronouncements, including Treasury regulations, which interpret and illustrate the rules contained in the Internal Revenue Code.

The Enrolled Agent Exam is based almost entirely on IRS publications, and exam candidates will not be tested on court cases unless the law has already made its way into an IRS publication. Likewise, if there is pending tax law or legislation, the exam candidate will not be tested on any pending tax law; the exam will always be based on tax law from a prior year. However, EA candidates must understand the basics of tax law and how it relates to the taxpayer.

Treasury Regulations

Treasury regulations are the interpretations of the Internal Revenue Code by the Secretary of the Treasury. The Internal Revenue Code authorizes the Secretary of the Treasury to "prescribe all needful rules and regulations for enforcement" of the Code. All regulations are written by the Office of the Chief Counsel, IRS, and approved by the Secretary of the Treasury. Regulations are issued as interpretations of specific Code sections.

U.S. Treasury regulations are authorized by law, but U.S. courts are not bound to follow administrative interpretations. The IRS is generally bound by regulations; the courts are not. The courts also have the job of deciding whether a tax law challenged in court is constitutional or not. There are three types of Treasury regulations:

1. Legislative regulations
2. Interpretative regulations
3. Procedural regulations

Legislative Regulations

Legislative regulations are when Congress expressly delegates the authority to the Secretary or the Commissioner of the IRS to provide the requirements of a specific provision. A legislative regulation has a higher degree of authority than an interpretative regulation. A legislative regulation may be overturned if any of the following conflicts apply:

1. It is outside the power delegated to the U.S. Treasury.
2. It conflicts with a specific statute.
3. It is deemed unreasonable by the courts.

Interpretive Regulations

Interpretive regulations are issued under the IRS's general authority to interpret the IRC but are subject to challenge on the grounds that they do not reflect Congress's intent. An interpretative regulation only explains the meaning of a portion of the Code. Unlike a legislative regulation, there is no grant of authority for the promulgation of an interpretative regulation by the IRS, so these regulations may be challenged.

Procedural Regulations

Procedural regulations concern the administrative provisions of the Code. Procedural regulations are promulgated by the Commissioner of the IRS and not the Secretary of the Treasury. They often concern minor issues, such as when notices should be sent to employees, etc.

Proposed, Temporary, or Final

Regulations are further classified as proposed, temporary, or final:

1. **Proposed regulations** are open to commentary from the public, and hearings are held if requests are made. Various versions of proposed regulations may be issued and withdrawn before a final regulation is made. Proposed regulations do not have authority.
2. **Temporary regulations** may remain in effect for three years, and may never be finalized.
3. **Final regulations** are issued when the regulation becomes an official Treasury Decision.

Private Letter Rulings

Taxpayers who have a specific question regarding tax law may request a Private Letter Ruling from the IRS. A Private Letter Ruling (PLR) is a written statement issued to a taxpayer that interprets and applies tax laws to the taxpayer's specific case. A PLR is issued to establish tax consequences of a particular transaction before the transaction is consummated or before the taxpayer's return is filed.

A PLR is binding on the IRS if the taxpayer fully and accurately described the proposed transaction in the request and carries out the transaction as described. A PLR may not be relied on as precedent by other taxpayers or IRS personnel. PLRs are generally made public after all the taxpayer's private, identifiable information has been removed.

Technical Advice Memorandum

A Technical Advice Memorandum, or TAM, is written guidance furnished by the IRS Office of Chief Counsel upon the request of an IRS director, typically in response to procedural questions that develop during an audit.

A request for a TAM generally stems from an examination of a taxpayer's return. Technical Advice Memoranda are issued only on closed transactions and provide the interpretation of proper application of tax laws, tax treaties, regulations, revenue rulings, or other precedents. The advice rendered represents the position of the IRS, but only regarding the specific case in question. Technical Advice Memoranda are generally made public after all information has been removed that could identify the taxpayer whose circumstances triggered a specific memorandum.

Revenue Rulings and Revenue Procedures

The IRS issues both revenue rulings and revenue procedures for the information and guidance of taxpayers. A *revenue procedure* is an official statement of a procedure that affects the rights or duties of taxpayers under the law. A *revenue ruling* typically states the IRS position, while a revenue procedure provides taxpayer instructions concerning that position.

Revenue Rulings

Revenue rulings are published in Internal Revenue Bulletins and the Federal Register, and are intended to promote uniform application of the IRC code. A revenue ruling is NOT binding in tax court or any other U.S. court. Revenue rulings can be used to avoid certain IRS penalties. The numbering system for revenue rulings corresponds to the year in which they are issued. Thus, for example, Revenue Ruling 80-20 was the twentieth revenue ruling issued in 1980.

Revenue Procedures

Revenue procedures are official IRS statements that affect the rights of taxpayers. A revenue procedure is a statement of procedure that affects the rights or duties of taxpayers or other members of the public under the Code and related statutes or information that, although not necessarily affecting the rights of the public, should be a matter of public knowledge. A revenue procedure may be cited as precedent, but it does not have the force of law.

The Court System

A taxpayer may challenge the IRS in any of three courts: the U.S. Tax Court, the U.S. Court of Federal Claims, or the U.S. District Court. Court precedent usually decides where the litigation should begin. A taxpayer who wishes to challenge the IRS anywhere but the U.S. Tax Court is forced to pay the tax deficiency first. The court system, for tax purposes, is organized as follows:

1. The U.S. Tax Court
2. District courts
3. Court of Federal Claims
4. Appellate courts
5. U.S. Supreme Court

If a taxpayer wishes to challenge the IRS in a U.S. District Court (or any other court besides the U.S. Tax Court), he must pay the contested liability *first*. The taxpayer must then petition the court for a refund, essentially "suing the IRS" to have the disputed liability returned.

> **Example:** Peg has her tax return chosen for examination by the IRS, which issues a deficiency of $45,000. Peg does not wish to go to Tax Court. Instead, she wants to go straight to the U.S. District Court. In order to do so, she must first pay the contested liability and then sue the IRS for a refund.

If either party loses at the trial court level, the court's decision may be appealed to a higher court.

The Tax Court

The Tax Court is a federal court where taxpayers may choose to contest their tax deficiencies without having to pay the disputed amount first. The U.S. Tax Court issues both regular and memorandum decisions. Memorandum decisions are court cases where the U.S. Tax Court has previously ruled on identical or similar issues. A "regular decision" is when the Tax Court rules on a particular matter for the first time.

The Tax Court has jurisdiction over the following tax disputes only:

1. Notices of deficiency
2. Review of the failure to abate interest
3. Notices of transferee liability
4. Adjustment of partnership items
5. Administrative costs
6. Worker classification (employee versus independent contractor)
7. Review of certain collection actions

The Tax Court has jurisdiction over the TYPES of tax listed below:

1. Income tax
2. Estate tax
3. Gift tax
4. Certain excise taxes

5. Re-determine transferee liability
6. Worker classification
7. Relief from joint and several liability on a joint return, and
8. Review awards to whistleblowers who report tax fraud to the IRS

This list is not exhaustive. For Tax Court cases, any individual other than an attorney must demonstrate her qualifications to practice before the Tax Court by taking an exam.

IRS Acquiescence

The IRS may choose whether or not to acquiesce to a court decision. This means that the IRS may choose to ignore the decision of the court and continue with its regular policies regarding the litigated issue. The IRS is not bound to change its regulations due to a loss in court. The only exception to this rule is the U.S. Supreme Court, whose decisions the IRS is obligated to follow.

The IRS publishes its acquiescence and non-acquiescence in the Internal Revenue Bulletin, and then in the Cumulative Bulletin. The Internal Revenue Bulletin (IRB) is the authoritative instrument for announcing official rulings and procedures of the IRS and for publishing Treasury decisions, executive orders, tax conventions, legislation, and court decisions. The IRS does not announce acquiescence or non-acquiescence in every case. Sometimes the IRS's position is withheld.

Freedom of Information Act Requests (FOIA)

The Freedom of Information Act (FOIA) is a law designed to ensure public access to U.S. government records. Upon written request, agencies of the U.S. government are required to disclose requested records, unless they can be withheld under certain exemptions in the FOIA.

All IRS records are subject to FOIA requests. However, the FOIA does not require the IRS to release all documents that are subject to these requests. The IRS may withhold information pursuant to the nine exemptions in the law, as well as three exclusions contained in the FOIA statute.

The FOIA applies to records created by federal agencies and does not cover records held by Congress, the courts, or state and local government agencies. Each state has its own public access laws.

Reasons Records May be Denied Under the FOIA

The IRS may withhold an IRS record that falls under one of the FOIA's exemptions or exclusions. The exemptions protect against the disclosure of information that would harm the following: national security, the privacy of individuals, the proprietary interests of business, the functioning of the government, and other important recognized interests.

When a record contains some information that qualifies as exempt, the entire record is not necessarily exempt. Instead, the FOIA specifically provides that any segregable portions of a record must be provided to a requester after the deletion of the portions that are exempt.

Whenever a FOIA request is denied, the IRS must give the reason for denial and explain the right to appeal to the head of the agency. A taxpayer may contest the type or amount of fees that were charged in the processing of the records request. A taxpayer also may appeal any other type of adverse determination under the FOIA, such as the failure of the IRS to conduct an adequate search for requested documents. However, a taxpayer may not file an administrative appeal for the lack of a timely response by the IRS.

A person whose request was granted in part and denied in part may appeal the part that was denied. If the IRS has agreed to disclose some but not all of the requested documents, the filing of an appeal does not affect the release of the documents that can be disclosed.

There is no charge for filing an FOIA appeal.

Unit 3.10: Questions

1. Which of the following statements regarding revenue rulings is correct?

A. Revenue rulings CANNOT be used to avoid certain IRS penalties.
B. Revenue rulings CAN be used to avoid certain IRS penalties.
C. Revenue rulings are not official IRS guidance.
D. None of the above.

The answer is B. Taxpayers may rely on revenue rulings as official IRS guidance on an issue. A taxpayer may use a revenue ruling as guidance in order to make a decision regarding taxable income, deductions, and also how to avoid certain IRS penalties.###

2. What is a Private Letter Ruling?

A. It is a private letter that a taxpayer writes to the IRS.
B. It is a private letter issued by the U.S. Tax Court.
C. It is a request by a taxpayer to the IRS to rule about a particular tax matter.
D. It is a request by the IRS to Congress about tax issues.

The answer is C. A Private Letter Ruling is initiated by a taxpayer who has a question about a particular transaction. A taxpayer may request a Private Letter Ruling from the IRS. A PLR is issued to establish tax consequences of a particular transaction before the transaction is consummated or before the taxpayer's return is filed. A PLR is binding on the IRS if the taxpayer fully and accurately described the proposed transaction in the request and carries out the transaction as described. ###

3. What is the dollar limit for the U.S. Tax Court small case procedure?

A. $50,000 or less
B. $50,000 or more
C. $25,000 or less
D. $100,000 or less

The answer is A. In tax disputes involving $50,000 or less, taxpayers may choose to use the IRS small tax case procedure. ###

4. Revenue rulings and revenue procedures are binding in court.

A. True
B. False

The answer is B. A revenue ruling or revenue procedure is NOT binding in tax court or any other court. However, taxpayers may use revenue rulings and revenue procedures as official IRS guidance. ###

5. Which of the following choices is not a type of Treasury regulation?

A. Legislative regulations
B. Interpretative regulations
C. Supporting regulations
D. Procedural regulations

The answer is C. There are three types of Treasury regulations: legislative, interpretive, and procedural. There is no such thing as a "supporting regulation."###

6. The Commissioner of the IRS has decided to publicly non-acquiesce to a decision of the Tax Court. Where will this decision be published?

A. The Internal Revenue Bulletin
B. The New York Times
C. Only on the IRS website
D. The Tax Court website

The answer is A. The IRS publishes its acquiescence and non-acquiescence in the Internal Revenue Bulletin, and then in the Cumulative Bulletin. The IRS does not announce acquiescence or non-acquiescence in every case. ###

7. If a taxpayer wishes to challenge the IRS in District Court (or in any other court other than the U.S. Tax Court), the taxpayer must _____.

A. Pay the contested liability first, and then sue the IRS for a refund.
B. Pay the contested liability first, and then sue the Department of the Treasury for a refund.
C. Pay a retainer and then sue the IRS for a refund.
D. A taxpayer must go to the U.S. Tax Court before going to a U.S. District court.

The answer is A. In order to go to District Court, the taxpayer must first pay the contested liability and then sue the IRS for a refund. If either party loses at the trial court level, the court's decision may be appealed to a higher court. ###

Unit 3.11: The IRS Collections Process

> **More Reading:**
> Publication 594, *The Collections Process*
> Publication 1035, *Extending the Tax Assessment Period*
> Publication 971, *Innocent Spouse Relief*
> Publication 556, *Examination of Returns, Appeal Rights, and Claims for Refund*

The IRS has wide powers when it comes to collecting unpaid taxes. The process is outlined in Publication 594, *The Collections Process*.

If a taxpayer does not pay in full when filing his tax return, he will receive a bill from an IRS service center. The first notice will be a letter that explains the balance due and demands payment in full. It will include the amount of the tax plus any penalties and interest added to the taxpayer's unpaid balance from the date the tax was due.

This first notice starts the collections process, which continues until the taxpayer's account is satisfied or until the IRS may no longer legally collect the tax, such as when the collection period has expired. The IRS has ten years from the date of assessment to collect a tax debt from a taxpayer. If a taxpayer does not file a tax return, the statute of limitations does not expire.

The statute of limitations on collection can also be suspended by various acts. The ten-year collection period is suspended in the following cases:

- While the IRS and the Office of Appeals consider a request for an installment agreement or an Offer in Compromise
- From the date a taxpayer requests a Collection Due Process (CDP) hearing
- For tax periods included in a bankruptcy
- While the taxpayer is residing outside the United States

The amount of time the suspension is in effect will be added to the time remaining in the ten-year period. For example, if the ten-year period is suspended for six months, the time left in the period the IRS has to collect will increase by six months. A taxpayer may voluntarily choose to extend the statute for various reasons, but she may also refuse to extend the statute of limitations. Form 872-A, *Special Consent to Extend Time to Assess Tax*, indefinitely extends the period that a tax may be assessed.

The IRS is required to notify the taxpayer that he may refuse to extend the statute of limitations. Filing a petition in bankruptcy automatically stays assessment and collection of tax. The stay remains in effect until the bankruptcy court discharges liabilities or lifts the stay.

IRS Actions to Collect Unpaid Taxes

The purpose of the Internal Revenue Service is to collect tax revenue. Some of the actions the IRS may take to collect taxes include:

- Filing a notice of a federal tax lien
- Serving a notice of levy
- Offsetting a taxpayer's refund

In addition, the IRS will apply future federal tax refunds to any prior amount due. Any state income tax refunds may also be applied to a taxpayer's federal tax liability.

Federal Tax Lien

The Federal Tax Lien is a claim against a taxpayer's property, including property that the taxpayer acquires even after the lien is filed. By filing a Notice of Federal Tax Lien, the IRS establishes its interest in the property as a creditor.

Once a lien is filed, the IRS generally cannot issue a "Certificate of Release of Federal Tax Lien" until the taxes, penalties, interest, and recording fees are paid in full or the IRS may no longer legally collect the tax (the statute of limitations runs out).

Notice of Levy

A Notice of Levy is another method the IRS may use to collect taxes. A levy allows the IRS to confiscate and sell property to satisfy a tax debt. This property could include a car, boat, or real estate. The IRS may also levy wages, bank accounts, Social Security benefits, and retirement income.

In addition, the IRS may apply future federal tax refunds to prior year tax debt. Any state income tax refunds may be routed to the IRS and may also be applied to a tax liability. An IRS levy refers to the actual *seizing of property* authorized by an earlier filed tax lien. If a tax lien is the IRS's authorization to act by seizing property, then the IRS levy is the actual act of seizure. The following items are exempt from IRS levy:

- Wearing apparel and school books.
- Fuel, food, provisions, furniture, personal effects in the taxpayer's household, arms for personal use, or livestock up to $7,720 in value.
- Books and tools necessary for the trade, business, or profession of the taxpayer.
- Undelivered mail.
- Workers' compensation, but only while payable to the taxpayer.
- Deferred compensation payments, but only if payable by the Army, Navy, Air Force, Coast Guard, or under the Railroad Retirement Act or Railroad Unemployment Insurance Act. Traditional or Roth IRAs are not exempt from levy.
- Judgments for the support of minor children (child support).
- Public assistance payments and welfare payments, and amounts payable for Supplemental Security Income for the aged, blind, and disabled under the Social Security Act. Regular Social Security payments are not exempt from levy.

If an IRS levy is creating an immediate economic hardship, the levy may be released. A levy release does not mean the taxpayer is exempt from paying the balance.

IRS Seizures

There are special rules regarding IRS seizures. Typically, the IRS may not seize property in the following circumstances:

- When there is a pending installment agreement
- While a taxpayer's appeal is pending
- During the consideration of an Offer in Compromise

- During a bankruptcy unless the seizure is authorized by the bankruptcy court
- If the taxpayer's liability is $5,000 or less in a seizure of real property (real estate)
- While innocent spouse claims are pending

The IRS may not seize a principal residence without prior approval from the IRS district director or assistant district director. Judicial approval is required for most principal residence seizures. The IRS may still seize or levy property if the collection of tax is in jeopardy.

Collection Appeal Rights

A taxpayer may appeal IRS collection action to the IRS Office of Appeals. The two main avenues for collection appeals are:

- Collection Due Process hearing (CDP)
- Collection Appeals Program (CAP)

Collection Due Process Hearings

A taxpayer who receives a notice may request a Collection Due Process hearing by completing Form 12153, *Request for a Collection Due Process or Equivalent Hearing,* and submitting it to the address listed on the IRS notice. Collection Due Process (CDP) is available for the following notices:

- Notice of federal tax lien filing
- Final notice - notice of intent to levy
- Notice of jeopardy levy and right of appeal
- Notice of levy on a state tax refund

After a taxpayer receives one of these notices, he has 30 days to file a request for a CDP hearing protesting the IRS's collection action. The taxpayer (or his representative) will meet with an Appeals Officer who works independently from the IRS examination division. Some of the issues that may be discussed during a Collection Due Process hearing include:

- Whether or not the taxpayer paid all the tax owed
- If the IRS assessed tax and sent the levy notice when the taxpayer was in bankruptcy
- Whether the IRS made a procedural error in the assessment
- Whether the time to collect the tax (the statute of limitations) has expired
- If the taxpayer wishes to discuss collection options
- If the taxpayer wishes to make a spousal defense (innocent spouse relief)

After the hearing, the Appeals Officer will issue a written determination letter.

If the taxpayer disagrees with the Appeals Officer's determination, he can appeal to the U.S. Tax Court (or other court). No collection action can be taken against the taxpayer after a CDP hearing has been requested, or while the determination of the Appeals Officer is being challenged in Tax Court.

Collection Appeals Program (CAP)

The Collection Appeals Program (CAP) is generally quicker and is available for a broader range of collection actions. However, the taxpayer cannot go to court if he disagrees with a CAP decision. CAP is available for the following actions:

- Before or after the IRS files a notice of federal tax lien
- Before or after the IRS levies or seizes the taxpayer's property
- After the termination of an installment agreement
- After the rejection of an installment agreement

A taxpayer may represent himself at CDP, CAP, and other appeals proceedings, or the taxpayer may choose to appoint a qualified representative (attorney, Certified Public Accountant, Enrolled Agent, or spouse or family member). In the case of a business, the entity may be represented by regular full-time employees, general partners, or bona fide officers. A taxpayer may also ask an IRS manager to review his case.

By law, the IRS can share taxpayer information with city and state tax agencies, and in some cases with the Department of Justice, other federal agencies, and people the taxpayer personally authorizes to receive information. The IRS can also share information with certain foreign governments under tax treaty provisions.

The IRS may contact a third party. The law allows the IRS to contact someone else, such as neighbors, banks, employers, or employees, to investigate and collect tax liabilities. The taxpayer has the right to request a list of third parties contacted regarding her tax case.

Taxpayer Advocate Service

The Taxpayer Advocate Service is an independent organization within the IRS whose goal is to help taxpayers resolve problems with the IRS. If a taxpayer has an ongoing issue with the IRS that has not been resolved through normal processes, or if the taxpayer has suffered or is about to suffer a significant hardship as a result of IRS action, the taxpayer may contact the Taxpayer Advocate Service and request intervention.

Innocent Spouse Relief

Many married taxpayers choose to file a joint tax return because of certain benefits this filing status allows. Both taxpayers are liable for the tax on the joint return even if they later divorce. "Joint and several liability" means that each taxpayer is legally responsible for the entire liability. Thus, both spouses are generally held responsible for all the tax due even if only one spouse earned all the income. This is true even if the divorce decree states that a former spouse will be responsible for any amounts due on previously filed joint returns.

In some cases, however, a spouse can get relief from joint liability. There are three types of relief from joint and several liability[101] for spouses who filed joint returns:

---

[101] **Joint And Several Liability:** This is when multiple parties can be held liable for the same act and be responsible for all restitution. For the IRS, this means that on a joint return, both spouses will usually be responsible for the tax, even if only one spouse has income or is responsible for the tax. Both tax-

Innocent Spouse Relief: Provides relief from additional tax if a spouse (or former spouse) failed to report income or claimed improper deductions.

Separation of Liability Relief: Provides for the allocation of additional tax owed between the taxpayer and her spouse or former spouse because an item was not reported properly on a joint return. The tax allocated to the taxpayer is the amount for which she is responsible.

Equitable Relief: May apply when a taxpayer does not qualify for innocent spouse relief or separation of liability relief for something not reported properly on a joint return. A taxpayer may also qualify for equitable relief if the correct amount of tax was reported on his joint return but the tax remains unpaid.

If a taxpayer requests innocent spouse relief, the IRS cannot enforce collection action while the taxpayer's request is pending. But interest and penalties continue to accrue. The request is generally considered pending from the date the IRS receives the request until the date the innocent spouse request is resolved.

Deadlines for Requesting Innocent Spouse Relief

A taxpayer must request innocent spouse relief no later than two years after the date the IRS first attempted to collect tax. The taxpayer must meet ALL the following conditions in order to qualify for "innocent spouse relief":

- The taxpayer filed a joint return, which has an understatement of tax, directly related to her spouse's erroneous items.
- The taxpayer establishes that at the time she signed the joint return she did not know and had no reason to know that there was an understatement of tax.
- Taking into account all the facts and circumstances, it would be unfair for the IRS to hold the taxpayer liable for the understatement.

In order to apply for innocent spouse relief, a taxpayer must submit Form 8857, *Request for Innocent Spouse Relief*. This form is signed under penalties of perjury.

A request for innocent spouse relief will be denied if the IRS proves that the taxpayer and spouse or former spouse transferred property to one another as part of a fraudulent scheme. A fraudulent scheme is an attempt to defraud the IRS or another third party, such as a creditor, ex-spouse, or business partner.

> **Example:** Greer and Harold are married and file jointly. At the time Greer signed their joint return, she was unaware that her husband had a gambling problem. The IRS examined the tax return several months later and determined that Harold's unreported gambling winnings were $25,000. Greer was able to prove that she did not know about, and had no reason to know about, the additional $25,000 because of the way her spouse concealed the gambling winnings. The understatement of tax due to the $25,000 qualifies for innocent spouse relief.

---

payers are also jointly and individually responsible for any interest or penalty due on the joint return even if they later divorce. This is true even if a divorce decree states that a former spouse will be responsible for any amounts due on previously filed joint returns. One spouse may be held responsible for all the tax due. One way for a taxpayer to avoid "joint and several liability" is to file for innocent spouse relief.

Requesting "Separation of Liability" Relief

To qualify for "separation of liability relief," the taxpayer must have filed a joint return. "Separation of liability" applies to taxpayers who are:

(1) No longer married, or

(2) Legally separated, or

(3) Living apart for the 12 months prior to the filing of a claim. Under this rule, a taxpayer also qualifies if the taxpayer is widowed.

"Living apart" does not include a spouse who is only temporarily absent from the household. A temporary absence exists if it is reasonable to assume that the absent spouse will return to the household, or a substantially equivalent household is maintained in anticipation of such a return. A temporary absence includes absences due to incarceration, illness, business, vacation, military service, or education. In this case, the taxpayer would not qualify for "Separation of Liability" relief.

> **Example:** Herb and Wanda timely filed their 2009 joint income tax return on April 15, 2010. Herb died in March 2010. In August 2010, the IRS assessed a deficiency for the 2009 return, because Herb neglected to report some of his own income. Wanda applies for innocent spouse relief. Wanda is relieved of the deficiency under the innocent spouse relief provisions, and Herb's estate remains solely liable for it.

Requesting Equitable Relief

A taxpayer may still qualify for "equitable relief" if she does not qualify for innocent spouse relief or "separation of liability" relief. Equitable relief is available for additional tax owed because of:

- A reporting error (an understatement), OR
- When a taxpayer has properly reported the tax but was unable to pay the tax due (an underpayment)

To qualify for equitable relief, the taxpayer must establish, under all the facts and circumstances, that it would be unfair to hold her liable for the understatement or underpayment of tax.

When the IRS considers whether to grant equitable relief, the following factors, in addition to others, may be considered:

- Current marital status
- Abuse experienced during the marriage
- Reasonable belief of the requesting spouse, at the time he or she signed the return, that the tax was going to be paid, or in the case of an understatement, whether the requesting spouse had knowledge or reason to know of the understatement
- Current financial hardship or inability to pay basic living expenses
- Spouses' legal obligation to pay the tax liability pursuant to a divorce decree or agreement to pay the liability
- To whom the liability is attributable
- Significant benefit received by the requesting spouse

- Mental or physical health of the requesting spouse on the date the requesting spouse signed the return or at the time the requesting spouse requested the relief
- Compliance with income tax laws following the taxable year or years to which the request for relief relates

*Note: Unlike "innocent spouse relief" or "separation of liability," if a taxpayer qualifies for equitable relief, he or she can get relief from an understatement of tax or an underpayment of tax. (An underpayment of tax is an amount properly shown on the return but not paid.)

Injured Spouse Claims

Innocent spouse relief should not be confused with an "injured spouse claim." These are completely different issues. A taxpayer may qualify as an "injured spouse" if he files a joint return and his share of the refund was applied against past due amounts owed by a spouse.

An "injured spouse" may be entitled to recoup only "his share" of a tax refund. In this way, injured spouse relief differs from innocent spouse relief. When a joint return is filed and the refund is used to pay one spouse's past-due federal tax, state income tax, child support, spousal support, or federal nontax debt (such as a delinquent student loan), the other spouse may be considered an injured spouse. The injured spouse can get back his share of the refund using Form 8379, *Injured Spouse Allocation*.

Example: Trudy and Craig marry in 2009 and file jointly in 2010. Unbeknownst to Trudy, Craig has outstanding unpaid child support and an old delinquent student loan debt. The entire refund is retained in order to pay Craig's outstanding debt and back child support. In this case, Trudy may qualify for "injured spouse" treatment. This means that she may be able to recoup *her share* of the tax refund.

Offer in Compromise Program

An Offer In Compromise (OIC) is an agreement between a taxpayer and the Internal Revenue Service that settles the taxpayer's tax liabilities for less than the full amount owed. Absent special circumstances, an offer will not be accepted if the IRS believes that the liability can be paid in full as a lump sum or through a payment agreement.

An Offer in Compromise can be applied to all taxes, including interest and penalties. A taxpayer may submit an OIC on three grounds:

Doubt as to Collectability

Doubt exists that the taxpayer could ever pay the full amount of tax liability owed within the remainder of the statutory period for collection.

Example: Elise owes $80,000 for unpaid tax liabilities and agrees that the tax she owes is correct. Elise is terminally ill, cannot work, and is on disability. She does not own any real property and does not have the ability to fully pay the liability now or through monthly installment payments.

Doubt as to Liability

A legitimate doubt exists that the assessed tax liability is correct. This ground is only met when genuine doubt exists that the IRS has correctly determined the amount owed. No application fee is required if the offer is based on doubt as to liability.

> **Example:** Sofia was vice president of a corporation from 2005-2009. In 2010, the corporation accrued unpaid payroll taxes and Sofia was assessed a Trust Fund Recovery Penalty. However, in 2010, Sofia had resigned from the corporation and was no longer a corporate officer. Since she had resigned prior to the payroll taxes accruing and was not contacted prior to the assessment, there is legitimate doubt that the assessed tax liability is correct.

Effective Tax Administration

There is no doubt that the tax is correct and there is potential to collect the full amount of the tax owed, but an exceptional circumstance exists that would allow the IRS to consider an OIC. To be eligible for compromise on this basis, a taxpayer must demonstrate that the collection of the tax would create serious economic hardship or would be unfair and inequitable. It is extremely rare for the IRS to approve an OIC on these grounds.

> **Example:** Brad and Stacy Snyder are married and have assets sufficient to satisfy their tax liability and also to provide full-time care and assistance to their dependent child, who has a serious long-term illness. The unpaid taxes were a result of the Snyders providing needed medical care for their sick child. They will need to continue to use their assets to provide for basic living expenses and ongoing medical care for the child. There is no doubt that the tax is correct, but to pay the tax would endanger the life of their child and would create a serious hardship.

In order to apply for an OIC, a taxpayer must submit a $150 application fee and initial payment along with Form 656, *Offer in Compromise*. The fee is not required if the taxpayer is an individual (not a corporation, partnership, or other entity) who qualifies for the low-income exception. This means that the taxpayer's total monthly income falls at or below 250% of the poverty guidelines published by the Department of Health and Human Services. If the total monthly income falls at or below the poverty guidelines, the taxpayer may submit a Form 656-A, *Income Certification for Offer in Compromise Application Fee and Payment,* instead of the $150 application fee.

Unit 3.11: Questions

1. There are three types of relief from joint and several liability for spouses who file joint returns. Which of the following is NOT a type of relief?

A. Innocent spouse relief
B. Separation of liability relief
C. Joint relief
D. Equitable relief

The answer is C. There is no such thing as "joint relief." There are three types of relief from joint and several liability for spouses who file joint returns: innocent spouse relief, separation of liability relief, and equitable relief.

2. What form is used to request innocent spouse relief?

A. Form 8857
B. Form 2010
C. Form 8379
D. Form 8832

The answer is A. In order to apply for innocent spouse relief, a taxpayer must submit Form 8857, Request for Innocent Spouse Relief. This form is signed under penalties of perjury. ###

3. Which of the following best describes a levy when it relates to a tax debt?

A. A levy is not a legal seizure of property.
B. A levy on salary or wages will end when the time expires for legally collecting the tax.
C. A levy can only be released by the filing of a lien.
D. A levy does not apply to a taxpayer's clothing and undelivered mail.

The answer is D. A levy does not apply to a taxpayer's clothing or undelivered mail. An IRS levy refers to the actual seizing of property authorized by a tax lien. If a tax lien is the IRS's authorization to act by seizing property, then the IRS levy is the actual act of seizure. ###

4. How does the IRS begin the process of collections?

A. With an email to the taxpayer as soon as he files his tax return
B. With a certified letter to the taxpayer immediately after a tax return is processed and flagged for audit
C. With a written examination notice when the taxpayer is notified of the possibility of an audit
D. With an initial notice requesting payment sent by an IRS service center

The answer is D. The IRS begins the collections process at the IRS service center where notices are generated requesting payment. ###

5. All of the statements about the IRS statute of limitations are true EXCEPT:

A. The IRS generally has ten years following an assessment to begin proceedings to collect the tax by levy or in a court proceeding.
B. The IRS is required to notify the taxpayer that she may refuse to extend the statute of limitations.
C. The taxpayer may NOT choose to extend the statute of limitations.
D. IRS Form 872-A indefinitely extends the time that a tax may be assessed.

The answer is C. The taxpayer may choose to extend the statute of limitations by signing Form 872-A. The taxpayer also may refuse to extend the statute. If a taxpayer does not file a tax return, the statute of limitations does not expire. The statute of limitations on collection can also be suspended by various acts. ###

6. What form is used for a taxpayer to apply for an Offer in Compromise?

A. Form 4728
B. Form 862
C. Form 2106
D. Form 656

The answer is D. In order to apply for an OIC, A taxpayer must submit an application fee and initial payment along with Form 656, Offer in Compromise. ###

7. The IRS may accept an Offer in Compromise based on three grounds. Which of the following is NOT a valid basis for submitting an Offer in Compromise to the IRS?

A. Doubt as to collectability
B. Effective tax administration
C. Doubt as to liability
D. Legitimate shelter argument

The answer is D. The IRS may accept an Offer in Compromise based on three grounds: doubt as to collectability, effective tax administration, and doubt as to liability. ###

8. The statute of limitations on collection can be suspended by various acts. The ten-year collection period is NOT suspended in which of the following cases?

A. While the IRS and the Office of Appeals consider a request for an installment agreement or an Offer in Compromise
B. From the date a taxpayer requests a Collection Due Process (CDP) hearing
C. While the taxpayer is incarcerated in prison
D. While the taxpayer lives outside the United States

The answer is C. The ten-year collection period is NOT suspended when a taxpayer is in prison. The ten-year collection period is suspended in the following cases:
•While the IRS and the Office of Appeals consider a request for an installment agreement or an Offer in Compromise
•From the date a taxpayer requests a Collection Due Process (CDP) hearing
•For tax periods included in a bankruptcy
•While the taxpayer is residing outside the United States
The amount of time the suspension is in effect will be added to the time remaining in the ten-year period. For example, if the ten-year period is suspended for six months, the time left in the period the IRS has to collect will increase by six months. ###

9. "Separation of liability relief" does NOT apply to taxpayers who are_____

A. Divorced
B. Legally separated
C. Widowed
D. Never been married

The answer is D. In order to qualify for "separation of liability relief," the taxpayer must have filed a joint return. That means that the taxpayer must have been married at one time. "Separation of liability" applies to taxpayers who are:
(1)   No longer married, or
(2)   Legally separated, or
(3)   Living apart for the 12 months prior to the filing of a claim. Under this rule, a taxpayer also qualifies if the taxpayer is widowed. "Living apart" does not include a spouse who is only temporarily absent from the household. ###

10. A taxpayer may qualify as an "injured spouse" if _____.

A. She files a joint return and her share of the refund was applied against past due amounts owed by a spouse.
B. She files a joint return and fails to report income.
C. She files a separate return and has the refund offset by past student loan obligations.
D. She files for bankruptcy protection.

The answer is A. A taxpayer may qualify as an "injured spouse" if she files a joint return and her share of the refund was applied against past due amounts owed by a spouse. The "injured spouse" may be entitled to recoup only her share of a tax refund. ###

11. Ingrid requests innocent spouse relief in 2010. While Ingrid's request is pending, which of the following is TRUE?

A. The IRS may still enforce collection action.
B. Interest and penalties do not continue to accrue.
C. Tax shelter penalties may apply.
D. Collection action must cease while the taxpayer's request is being considered.

The answer is D. If a taxpayer requests innocent spouse relief, the IRS cannot enforce collection action while the taxpayer's request is pending. But interest and penalties continue to accrue. The request is generally considered pending from the date the IRS receives the request until the date the innocent spouse request is resolved. ###

12. Belinda and Neil file jointly. They report $10,000 of income and deductions, but Belinda knew that Neil was not reporting $5,000 of dividends. The income is not hers and she has no access to it since it is in Neil's bank account. She signs the joint return. The return is later chosen for examination, and penalties are assessed. Does Belinda qualify for innocent spouse relief?

A. Belinda is not eligible for innocent spouse relief because she had knowledge of the understated tax.
B. Belinda is eligible for innocent spouse relief because she had no control over the income.
C. Belinda is eligible for injured spouse relief.
D. None of the above.

The answer is A. Belinda is not eligible for innocent spouse relief because she had knowledge of the understated tax. She signed the return knowing that the income was not included, so she cannot apply for relief (Publication 971). ###

13. The IRS may seize property in which of the following circumstances?

A. During the consideration of an Offer in Compromise
B. During a bankruptcy, when the seizure is authorized by the bankruptcy court
C. If the taxpayer's liability is $5,000 or less in a seizure of real property (real estate)
D. While innocent spouse claims are pending

The answer is B. The IRS may seize property if the court has authorized the seizure. Typically, the IRS may not seize property in the following circumstances:
•When there is a pending installment agreement
•While a taxpayer's appeal is pending
•During the consideration of an Offer in Compromise
•During a bankruptcy (unless the seizure is authorized by the bankruptcy court)
•If the taxpayer's liability is $5,000 or less in a seizure of real property (real estate)
•While innocent spouse claims are pending
Judicial approval is required for most principal residence seizures. The IRS may still seize or levy property if the collection of tax is in jeopardy. ###

14. Lena owes $20,000 for unpaid federal tax liabilities and agrees that the tax she owes is correct. Lena had a serious medical problem and now her monthly income does not meet her necessary living expenses. She does not own any real estate and does not have the ability to fully pay the liability now or through monthly installment payments. What type of relief may she qualify for?

A. Doubt as to Collectability
B. Doubt as to Liability
C. Effective Tax Administration
D. Collection advocate procedure

The answer is A. Lena may apply for an Offer in Compromise under Doubt as to Collectability. Doubt exists that the taxpayer could ever pay the full amount of tax liability owed within the remainder of the statutory period for collection. ###

Unit 3.12: Representation and E-File Glossary of Terms

The IRS e-file program is a heavily tested concept on Part 3 of the Enrolled Agent exam. You must understand all the following terms:

Acceptance Letter: Correspondence issued by the IRS to applicants confirming they may participate in IRS e-file and annually to Authorized IRS e-file Providers confirming they may continue to participate in IRS e-file.

Acknowledgment (ACK): A report generated by the IRS to a Transmitter that indicates receipt of all transmissions. An ACK Report identifies the returns in each transmission that are accepted or rejected for specific reasons.

Administrative Review Process: The process by which a denied applicant or sanctioned Authorized IRS e-file Provider may appeal the IRS's denial or sanction.

Adoption Taxpayer Identification Number (ATIN): A tax processing number issued by the IRS as a temporary Taxpayer Identification Number for a child in the domestic adoption process who is not yet eligible for a Social Security Number (SSN). An ATIN is not a permanent identification number and is only intended for temporary use. To obtain an ATIN, a taxpayer must complete IRS Form W-7A, *Application for Taxpayer Identification Number for Pending U.S. Adoptions*.

Authorized IRS e-file Provider (Provider): A firm accepted to participate in IRS e-file.

Automated Clearing House (ACH): A system that administers Electronic Funds Transfers (EFTs) among participating financial institutions. An example of such a transfer is Direct Deposit of a tax refund from the IRS into a taxpayer's account at a financial institution.

Batch: A single transmission consisting of the electronic data from single or multiple tax returns.

Communications Testing: Required test for all Transmitters using accepted IRS e-file software to assess their transmission capability with the IRS, prior to live processing.

Credentials Documentation: Issued by the IRS to indicate qualification of an Authorized IRS e-file Provider to participate in the IRS e-file program. The documentation consists of identification numbers and acceptance letters.

Debt Indicator (DI): A field on an ACK Report that indicates whether a debt offset of a taxpayer's refund will occur. It does not indicate how much the offset will be. Offsets taken by the IRS may be for current and prior year tax obligations. Offsets taken by the Financial Management IRS (FMS) are for past due student loans, child support, federal taxes, state taxes, or other governmental agency debts. The IRS has chosen to withdraw the debt indicator during the 2011 filing season.

Declaration Control Number (DCN): A unique 14-digit number assigned by the ERO (or Transmitter, in the case of online filing), to each electronically-filed tax return.

Denied Applicant: An applicant that is not accepted to participate in IRS e-file. An applicant that has been denied participation in IRS e-file has the right to an administrative review.

Depositor Account Number (DAN): The financial institution account to which a Direct Deposit refund is routed.

Direct Deposit: An electronic transfer of a refund into a taxpayer's financial institution account.

Direct Filer: See "Transmitter."

Drain: The IRS scheduled time for processing electronically-filed return data.

Drop (or Dropped) EFIN: An EFIN that is no longer valid due to inactivity or other administrative action.

Due Diligence: When used in connection with the Earned Income Tax Credit (EITC), Due Diligence refers to requirements that income tax return preparers must follow when preparing returns or refund claims involving the EITC.

Earned Income Tax Credit (EITC): A refundable individual income tax credit for certain persons who work.

EITC Recertification: A requirement for a taxpayer previously denied EITC to provide additional information on Form 8862, *Information to Claim Earned Income Tax Credit After Disallowance*, when he files a similar EITC claim on a subsequent return.

Electronic Federal Tax Payment System (EFTPS): A free service from the U.S. Treasury through which federal taxes may be paid. Taxes can be paid via the Internet, by phone, or through a service provider. After authorization, payments are electronically transferred from the authorized bank account to the Treasury's general account.

Electronic Filing Identification Number (EFIN): An identification number assigned by the IRS to accepted applicants for participation in IRS e-file.

Electronic Funds Transfer (EFT): The process through which Direct Deposit refunds are transmitted from the government to the taxpayer's account at a financial institution.

Electronic Funds Withdrawal (EFW): A payment method that allows the taxpayer to authorize the U.S. Treasury to electronically withdraw funds from her checking or savings account.

Electronic Postmark: The date and time the electronic return is first received on the Transmitter's host computer in the Transmitter's time zone. The ERO, or taxpayer in the case of online filing, adjusts the time to his time zone to determine timeliness.

Electronic Return Originator (ERO): An Authorized IRS e-file Provider that originates the electronic submission of returns to the IRS.

Electronic Signature Method: A method of signing a return electronically through use of a Personal Identification Number (PIN). See also "Self-Select PIN Method" and "Practitioner PIN Method."

Electronic Tax Administration (ETA): The office within IRS that has management oversight of the IRS's electronic commerce initiatives. The mission of ETA is to revolutionize how taxpayers transact and communicate with the IRS.

Electronic Tax Administration Advisory Committee (ETAAC): An advisory group established by the IRS Restructuring and Reform Act of 1998 to provide an organized public forum for discussion of ETA issues in support of the overriding goal that paperless filing should be the preferred and most convenient method of filing tax and information returns.

Electronic Transmitter Identification Number (ETIN): An identification number assigned by the IRS to a participant in IRS e-file who performs activity of transmission and/or software development.

Electronically Transmitted Documents (ETD): A system created to process electronic documents that are not attached to a tax return and are filed separately from the tax return.

Error Reject Code (ERC): Codes included on an Acknowledgment (ACK) Report for returns that are rejected by the IRS.

Federal/State E-File: An option that allows federal and state income tax returns to be filed electronically in a single transmission to the IRS.

Financial Institution: For the purpose of Direct Deposit of tax refunds, a financial institution is defined as a state or national bank, savings and loan association, mutual savings bank, or credit union. Only certain financial institutions and certain kinds of accounts are eligible to receive Direct Deposits of tax refunds.

Financial Management Service (FMS): The agency of the Department of the Treasury through which payments to and from the government, such as Direct Deposits of refunds, are processed.

Form Field Number or Form Sequence (SEQ) Number: The identifier of specific data on an electronic tax return record layout as defined in Publication 1346, *Electronic Return File Specifications and Record Layouts for Individual Income Tax Returns*.

Fraudulent Return: A return in which the individual is attempting to file using someone else's name or SSN on the return, or where the taxpayer is presenting documents or information that have no basis in fact.

Indirect Filer: An Authorized IRS e-file Provider who submits returns to IRS via the services of a Transmitter.

Individual Taxpayer Identification Number (ITIN): A tax processing number that became available on July 1, 1996 for certain nonresident and resident aliens, their spouses, and dependents. The ITIN is only available from the IRS for those individuals who cannot obtain a

Social Security Number (SSN). To obtain an ITIN, a taxpayer must complete IRS Form W-7, *Application for IRS Individual Identification Number.*

Intermediate Service Provider: An Authorized IRS e-file Provider that receives electronic tax return information from an ERO or a taxpayer who files electronically using a personal computer, commercial tax preparation software and a modem, processes the electronic tax return information, and either forwards the information to a Transmitter or sends the information back to the ERO or taxpayer.

Internet Protocol (IP) Information: The IP address, date, time, and time zone of the origination of a tax return filed through online filing via the Internet. The IRS requires Transmitters that provide online services via the Internet to capture the Internet Protocol Information of online returns. By capturing this information, the location of the return's originator is transmitted with the individual's electronic return.

IRS e-File: The brand name of the electronic filing method established by the IRS.

E-File Marketing Tool Kit: A specially designed kit containing professionally developed material that EROs may customize for use in advertising campaigns and promotional efforts.

IRS Master File: A centralized IRS database containing taxpayers' personal return information.

Levels of Infractions (LOI): Categories of infractions of IRS e-file rules based on the seriousness of the infraction with specified sanctions associated with each level. Level One is the least serious, Level Two is moderately serious, and Level Three is the most serious.

Memorandum of Agreement (MOA) & Memorandum of Understanding (MOU): The implementing document containing the set of rules established by the IRS for participating in IRS pilot programs.

Monitoring Activities: The IRS performs monitoring activities in order to ensure that Authorized IRS e-file Providers are in compliance with the IRS e-file requirements. Monitoring may include, but is not limited to, reviewing IRS e-file submissions, investigating complaints, scrutinizing advertising material, checking signature form submissions and/or recordkeeping, examining records, observing office procedures, and conducting annual suitability checks. These activities are performed by IRS personnel at IRS offices and at the offices of Providers.

Name Control: The first four significant letters of a taxpayer's last name that are used in connection with the taxpayer SSN to identify the taxpayer, spouse, and dependents.

Non-substantive Change: A correction or change limited to a transposition error, misplaced entry, spelling error, or arithmetic correction that does not require new signatures or authorizations to be transmitted or retransmitted.

Originate or Origination: Origination of an electronic tax return submission occurs when an ERO either: (1) directly transmits electronic returns to the IRS, (2) sends electronic returns to a Transmitter, or (3) provides tax return data to an Intermediate Service Provider.

Participants Acceptance Testing (PATS): Required testing for all Software Developers that participate in IRS e-file of individual income tax returns to assess their software and transmission capability with the IRS, prior to live processing.

PATS Communications: Required testing for all Transmitters using accepted IRS e-file software for individual income tax returns to assess their transmission capability with the IRS, prior to live processing.

Pilot Programs: An approach that the IRS uses to improve and simplify IRS e-file. Pilot programs are usually conducted within a limited geographic area or within a limited taxpayer or practitioner community.

Potentially Abusive Return: A return that may contain inaccurate information, which may lead to an understatement of a liability or an overstatement of a credit resulting in a refund that the taxpayer may not be entitled to.

Practitioner PIN Method: An electronic signature option for taxpayers who use an ERO to e-file. This method requires the taxpayer to create a five-digit Personal Identification Number (PIN) to use as the signature on the e-file return.

Preparer's Tax Identification Number (PTIN): An identification number issued by the IRS which paid tax return preparers may use in lieu of disclosing their Social Security Numbers (SSN) on returns that they prepared. A PTIN meets the requirements under Section 6109(a)(4) of furnishing a paid tax return preparer's identifying number on returns that he prepares.

Refund Anticipation Loan (RAL): Money borrowed by a taxpayer that is based on his anticipated income tax refund.

Refund Cycle: The anticipated date that a refund would be issued by the IRS either by Direct Deposit or by mail to a taxpayer for a return included within a specific "drain." However, neither the IRS nor FMS guarantees the specific date that a refund will be mailed or deposited into a taxpayer's financial institution account.

Responsible Official: An individual with authority over the IRS e-file operation of the office(s) of an Authorized IRS e-file Provider, who is the first point of contact with the IRS, and has authority to sign revised IRS e-file applications.

Routing Transit Number (RTN): A number assigned by the Federal Reserve to each financial institution.

Sanction: An action taken by the IRS to reprimand, suspend, or expel from participation in IRS e-file an Authorized IRS e-file Provider based on the level of infraction.

Self-Select PIN Method: An electronic signature option for taxpayers who e-file using either a personal computer or an ERO. This method requires the taxpayer to create a five-digit Personal Identification Number (PIN) to use as the signature on the e-file return and to submit authentication information to the IRS with the e-file return.

Software Developer: An Authorized IRS e-file Provider that develops software for the purposes of: (1) Formatting the electronic portions of returns and/or (2) Transmitting the electronic portion of returns directly to the IRS. A Software Developer may also sell IRS software.

Stockpiling: The act of waiting more than three calendar days to submit returns to the IRS after the Provider has all the necessary information for origination of the electronic return. Stockpiling may also occur when returns are collected for e-file prior to official acceptance for participation in IRS e-file.

Suitability Check: A background check conducted on all firms and the Principals and Responsible Officials of firms when an application is initially processed, and on a regular basis thereafter.

Suspension: A sanction revoking an Authorized IRS e-file Provider's privilege to participate in IRS e-file.

Transmitter: An Authorized IRS e-file Provider that transmits the electronic portion of a return directly to the IRS.

Treasury Offset Program (TOP): A program that permits overpayments to be offset against delinquent child support obligations, as well as debts owed to participating federal and state agencies.

Warning: Written notice given by the IRS to an Authorized IRS e-file Provider requesting specific corrective action be taken to avoid future sanctioning.

Written Reprimand: A sanction for a Level One infraction of the IRS e-file rules that reprimands a Provider but does restrict or revoke participation in IRS e-file.

Also Available from PassKey Publications

How to Start a Successful Home-Based Freelance Bookkeeping and Tax Preparation Business

The Enrolled Agent Tax Consulting Practice Guide: Learn How to Develop, Market, and Operate a Profitable Tax and IRS Representation Practice

The Chef's Commandments: Maximize Your Kitchen's Profitability: Building and Maintaining a Successful, Profit-Driven Restaurant

The Conservative's Pocket Constitution: Includes the Complete Text of the U.S. Constitution and the Bill of Rights

About the Authors

Christy Pinheiro is an Enrolled Agent, Accredited Business Accountant, and writer. Christy was an accountant for two private CPA firms and for the State of California before going into private practice. She is a member of California Society of Enrolled Agents and the National Association of Tax Professionals.

Collette Szymborski is a Certified Public Accountant and the managing partner of Elk Grove CPA Accountancy Corporation. She specializes in the taxation of corporations, individuals, and exempt entities. Elk Grove CPA also does estate and elder care planning.